Second Edition

A Host of Opportunities

An Introduction to Hospitality Management

Hubert B. Van Hoof
Penn State University

Gary K. Vallen
Northern Arizona University

Marilyn E. McDonald
Northern Arizona University

Paul J. Wiener
Northern Arizona University

PEARSON
Prentice
Hall

Upper Saddle River, New Jersey 07458

Library of Congress Cataloging-in-Publication Data

A host of opportunities : an introduction to hospitality management /
Hubert B. Van Hoof, Gary K. Vallen, Marilyn E. McDonald, Paul J. Wiener.—2nd ed.
    p. cm.
  Includes bibliographical references and index.
  ISBN 0–13–014591–2
  1. Hospitality industry—Management.   I. Van Hoof, Hubert B.
  II. Gary K. Vallen   III. McDonald, Marilyn E.   IV. Paul J. Wiener
  TX911.3.M27H6625 2006
  647.94068—dc22

                                                                    2005037609

Editor-in-Chief: Vernon R. Anthony
Senior Editor: William Lawrensen
Editorial Assistant: Marion Gottlieb
Development Editor: Katie E. Bradford
Executive Marketing Manager: Ryan DeGrote
Senior Marketing Coordinator: Elizabeth Farrell
Marketing Assistant: Les Roberts
Managing Editor: Mary Carnis
Production Liaison: Jane Bonnell
Production Editor: Bruce Hobart, Pine Tree Composition
Manufacturing Manager: Ilene Sanford
Manufacturing Buyer: Cathleen Petersen
Senior Design Coordinator: Miguel Ortiz
Cover Designer: Carey Davies
Cover Image: Corbis/Randy Faris
Composition: Pine Tree Composition, Inc.
Printing and Binding: Courier Westford

Chapter-opening image credits appear on page 521, which constitutes a continuation of this copyright page.

Pearson Prentice Hall™ is a trademark of Pearson Education, Inc.
Pearson® is a registered trademark of Pearson plc
Prentice Hall® is a registered trademark of Pearson Education, Inc.

Pearson Education LTD.
Pearson Education Australia PTY, Limited
Pearson Education Singapore, Pte. Ltd.
Pearson Education North Asia Ltd.
Pearson Education Canada, Ltd.
Pearson Educación de Mexico, S.A. de C.V.
Pearson Education—Japan
Pearson Education Malaysia, Pte. Ltd.

10 9 8 7 6 5 4 3 2 1
ISBN 0-13-014591-2

To our students

- Who will dedicate their lives to providing customers with comfort, shelter, entertainment, and service
- Who will balance technical expertise with a concern for people and quality
- Who will lead the hospitality industry in the 21st century

Contents

Chapter 4   Back of the House Operations: Housekeeping, Maintenance, and Engineering   140

Preface

This book on the hospitality industry and hospitality management is designed for introductory courses. We feel it is unique in various ways. Besides being an introduction to the hospitality industry, it is an introduction to hospitality management education. The chapters in this book reflect not only the extent and diversity of the industry, but also what is taught at 40 of the largest and most prominent hospitality management programs in the United States. We compared the courses of these leading programs and looked for similarities and differences in their curricula and course descriptions. We found that many schools teach the same kinds of classes. They all have classes on hospitality marketing, human resource management, food service management, and travel and tourism, to name a few. Classes at various programs may have different names, but they have surprisingly similar contents. Each of the individual chapters, therefore, represents those courses in some way. In fact, each of the chapters could be considered an overview of a course taught at a university or a junior college.

A Host of Opportunities, Second Edition, is also unique because it reflects what recruiters and industry practitioners consider important in hospitality education. While all education should aim for relevance, hospitality management education in particular should be highly applicable and closely tied to the reality of hospitality management. Increasingly, the industry has indicated that future management candidates should have a sound theoretical background coupled with practical industry experience and a sense of reality.

The hospitality industry would like its managers to have good communication and interpersonal skills, and expects them to have the necessary technical skills. This book responds to this alliance of skills; some chapters emphasize human skills, where others focus on more technical aspects. This second edition of *A Host of Opportunities* has been re-written based on the comments and input of the users of the first edition, and upon extensive reviews from colleagues in hospitality management education. Some chapters closely resemble the original versions, where others have seen extensive rewrites.

The book is divided into four parts, each with a particular focus. The introductory chapter looks at the essence and scope of the hospitality industry, and discusses concepts such as service and hospitality. Part One, "Introduction to Lodging Management," presents an overview of the lodging industry and both "front" and "back" of the house operations. Part Two, "Introduction to the Food and Beverage

Industry," describes the various aspects of restaurant and bar management, and looks at the intricacies of food production. Part Three, "Introduction to Components of the Travel and Tourism Industry," first of all places the hospitality industry within the broader parameters of the travel and tourism industry. Additionally, it highlights resorts, clubs, attractions, events and cruise lines, as well as gaming and casino management as important components in the industry. Finally, Part Four, "Introduction to Hospitality Management Functions and Skills," looks at marketing and human resource management in the hospitality industry and offers suggestions on managerial leadership and ethics. The final, separate chapter offers insight into career paths in the hospitality industry and proposes strategies students can use in obtaining employment. At the end of each of the four parts, there are three sections entitled "The Techie Says," "The Accountant Says," and "The Attorney Says." These short discussion pieces highlight issues related to technology, accounting, and the law as they pertain to the topics in the chapters. These can be used to reinforce the material from a particular perspective or as stand-alone discussion items.

We included 13 individual chapters in the text, since regular semesters at most programs roughly encompass 13 weeks of instruction and a couple of weeks of exams and extracurricular activities. Each of the chapters follows the same pattern: They introduce their particular topic area, discuss the topic matter, and present students with several questions for consideration. These questions are fairly broad by nature and are primarily intended to stimulate student interest in the topic. Additionally, each chapter, within the framework of the topic, discusses issue areas that have become increasingly important in the hospitality industry in recent years. Under the heading "Eye on the Issues," each chapter discusses "hot" issues in environment, technology, ethics, service, and the international arena. Words in **bold** represent keywords; these are defined in the context in which they occur. Words in ***bold italic*** in the body of the text are core concepts, and are considered essential to the student's understanding of the material. These will be repeated at the end of each chapter.

Being educators ourselves, we know that the order in which we have presented the material may not suit everyone's needs. However, based on user and reviewer input, we have attempted to present the material in a logical and coherent flow, with sufficient flexibility built in to allow instructors to change the order in which they present the material.

Hubert B. Van Hoof
Gary K. Vallen
Marilyn E. McDonald
Paul J. Wiener

Acknowledgments

This book could not have been developed without the help, patience, and cooperation of a great many. We would like to acknowledge the following people and extend to them our sincere gratitude.

We thank Galen Collins for his moral support for a project that took nearly three years to complete; James L. Morgan for his artistry with a camera and his way with words. We also greatly value those colleagues across the country who shared their time and expertise through their helpful reviews and constructive criticisms; the hospitality industry executives and companies who contributed useful advice and materials; and all of our colleagues, who offered us words of encouragement and challenge.

We cannot miss this opportunity also to thank our students, for testing (and inspiring) us daily; and our families, for their support and understanding. We especially appreciate the members of our user focus group, who shared their thoughts about how they used the first edition and what it would take to make this second edition even more useful in the classrooms. Last, we acknowledge and thank *our* teachers, for their patience, high standards, encouragement, and example.

It is our pleasure to recognize these contributions and give full credit for the assistance we received en route to publication.

Contributors

"The Attorney Says" was written by Bruce S. Urdang, J.D.
"The Techie Says" was written by Lenka Marie Hospodka, MBA
"The Accountant Says" was written by James Murphy, MBA

Note to the Student

On behalf of all the authors, welcome to *A Host of Opportunities: An Introduction to Hospitality Management, Second Edition.*

The hospitality industry, in all its diversity, is an exciting, challenging, and demanding environment. If you are looking for a future career in this industry, be prepared to be challenged, to hustle, to enjoy yourself, to learn, and to persist. It will take many steps before you get where you would like to be, whether it be manager of a restaurant, general manager of a hotel, president of a hotel chain, or owner of an out-of-the-way bed and breakfast operation.

However, you have already taken the first steps in fulfilling your dream of becoming a hospitality industry manager: you have shown your willingness to learn by enrolling in a hospitality management program and by purchasing this book! You can expect to learn a lot from the people who have written this book: all of the authors have worked in the industry, come from a variety of backgrounds, and have taught students like yourself for many years. They know what the industry and what education are all about.

We feel that we can safely assume the following: at this stage in your life, you have either made up your mind to become a hospitality manager, you are playing with the idea of becoming one, or you don't know what you really want to do. Whatever the case may be, this book can help you make some decisions about your future. We, the authors, know how exciting the hospitality industry is and how rewarding a good education can be. We are anxious to help you learn and share our knowledge and enthusiasm with you. We truly hope that our appreciation for the industry shows throughout the book and that it will rub off on you. So, welcome to the world of hospitality. Let's get busy . . .

Introduction to the Essence and Scope of Hospitality

The first chapter of this book opens the window for you, the potential hospitality manager, to look onto the horizons that stretch before you if you choose a career in the fast-paced world of hospitality. Through this window blow breezes from around the globe, breezes that can carry you to exciting multi-cultural experiences in many contexts. Your career might include managing an officers' club in the South Pacific; arranging catering for Air Force One; planning the next Woodstock; providing faultless accommodations for a papal visit; coordinating the events surrounding a national playoff; or owning your own bed and breakfast. The scope of opportunity is truly enormous, as you will see in this chapter entitled "The Essence and Scope of Hospitality." You'll read and learn about the lifeblood of hospitality service and about the attitude that makes it possible.

The Essence and Scope of Hospitality

This chapter introduces you to the important concepts of *identity* and *service,* both of which are bedrocks of the hospitality industry. It also emphasizes two skills closely linked to service: communication and teamwork. The chapter also relates hospitality management to the times of millennial changes in the workforce, in the customer base, and in the global marketplace. After looking at the complex diversity hospitality managers will encounter, the chapter describes diverse components of the industry ranging from club management to ownership of a bed-and-breakfast operation.

INTRODUCTION

"Party of one? Right this way."

Welcome to the world of hospitality, a world that offers a host of opportunities. It is no accident that this text opens with a welcome, for in no other profession is the concept of welcoming as essential as in this one—where a host of an inn, a restaurant, or an attraction steps forward to warmly greet his or her guests.

Your hosts for this text, the writers of the chapters ahead, are more than successful professors. They are, by design, individuals who have also *worked as hospitality professionals* who have lived, eaten, and breathed the subject matter they present to you. Each has brought hands-on experience to the teaching arena and is able to present it in a doubly useful way with a practitioner's savvy and an educator's coaching skills. As teachers, they know that you have not chosen to pursue a degree in hospitality management with the idea of becoming a speck in America's sea of 10 million food service workers and 7 million lodging workers. You have chosen this major with your eye on management and advancement. You have taken stock of your abilities and attitudes and seen a future for yourself as a leader. You have conducted a kind of personal inventory and matched your strengths with this group of careers. If you haven't, pay close attention to the upcoming chapters on career exploration and leadership skills, and ethics—they'll get you started!

IDENTITY DRIVES PLANNING

Taking stock of yourself is closely tied to one of the most important concepts in this wide-reaching industry: identity. Identity is an all-important guideline in business, and in the hospitality business in particular. There are more than 900 significant chains listed in the American Hotel and Lodging Association's most recent *Directory of Hotel and Lodging Companies.* Many of these companies have one or more "products," name brands, or "identities." Choice Hotels International, for example, offers seven under its umbrella: the Quality, Comfort, Clarion, Sleep, Rodeway, EconoLodge, and Mainstay chains. In the face of such diversity, defining a market identity or "niche" becomes essential.[1]

Let's make this example personal. Suppose you decide to host a party in your home. Perhaps you'd like to be able to invite Ricky Martin, the President, and Shania Twain but you realize that your two-bedroom apartment isn't likely to attract such stellar guests. Setting your sights a little more realistically, you consider inviting a few professors and your supervisor from work, but again you adjust your thinking. Would you be comfortable entertaining them amid your neon milk-crate furnishings, using NFL tumblers from a long-ago burger promotion? Reality sets in. What alternatives do you have, given your income, budget, and facilities?

In many ways, your facility, that is, your home, dictates your party-planning decisions. Its lavishness affects, perhaps, your guest list; its roominess, the number you can invite; its kitchen area, the type and amount of food you are able to prepare and serve, and so on. In other ways, your personal identity affects your party options. Perhaps your preference runs to small groups of intimate friends with a background of New Age music and whale songs. Maybe you prefer the jostle of

Exhibit 1.1   The Harley Davidson Café concept has a strong identity and charisma factor that promises fun. (*Courtesy:* Harley-Davidson Cafés)

Exhibit 1.2   The popular Grand Canyon Railway takes its guests on a trip back in time to the days of steam engines. Consider how you'd entertain guests on a rolling facility such as this! (*Courtesy:* Grand Canyon Railway)

Exhibit 1.3   Although this trail cook has a rough and tumble kitchen, his food matches his dude ranch guests' expectations. His facility goes with his company's identity. (*Courtesy:* Colorado Dude and Guest Ranch Association)

wall-to-wall people vibrating to salsa. All these elements are part of your identity and must be factored into your plans.

Similarly, a hotel's, attraction's, club's, or restaurant's identity drives its planning. Everything about its inventory, staffing ratios, marketing, price structure, furnishings, and so on hinges on the elements of its identity. A coffee shop manager, secure in his or her unit's identity, feels no compulsion to stock calamari or lobster, whereas a seafood restaurant manager might consider them essential. A midmarket hotel purchasing agent concerned about durability might buy bath towels in a 14 percent polyester/86 percent cotton blend, while a resort's executive housekeeper might hear complaints if guest towels were anything less than 100 percent superabsorbent cotton terry. A 30-room mountain inn might or might not find it profitable to advertise in the nearest metro area's high-end home-and-garden magazine depending on how rustic it is and how appealing its location.

Many such considerations, though linked to marketing, precede it. Self-definition—identity—can be both the child and the parent of marketing (see Exhibit 1.4). An owner or manager may set an establishment's identity as, say, "a retreat" or "a rendezvous." It then becomes the marketing department's job to expand upon and

Exhibit 1.4   Self-definition—identity—can be both the child and parent of marketing. In the first example, Outlet A's facilities (or location, or budget) control its identity. It must market based on those limitations (or strengths). Property B evidently has greater flexibility. Depending on how it chooses to market itself, it can shape its identity to fit into one of several niches.

enhance this identity, and the job of management and staff to provide the promised environment. A property or unit that tries to market itself at cross purposes to its identity will have a hard time satisfying guests. This is true because identity also stimulates customer expectations.

A customer's expectations vary depending on price and environment. According to Susan Clarke of Motivation, Unlimited:

> [For a $5 tab] . . . you would expect your meal to be a "no frills" experience ready fast, hot or cold enough, probably wrapped in paper, handed to you from a counter, to be eaten with disposable utensils in a Formica-dominated landscape . . . [for a] $25 meal your expectations will be both different and greater. This time you'll be looking for a china plate, a tablecloth, glassware, metal flatware, and personal table service. How about a $50 meal? You'll surely have greater expectations, but now the increments have more to do with nuance and grace: The decor is more elegant, the service more attentive, the food more fashionable. Perhaps the china will be fine "bone," and the table linen true linen; the goblets may be crystal, the cutlery actually silver.[2]

A property may have several outlets, each with its own environment, as shown in Exhibits 1.5 and 1.6.

Thus, identity suggests a value to be expected. It becomes part of a transaction between the customer and the seller. This often unspoken transaction may include expectations of quality, speed, ambiance, price, attitude, reliability, or flexibility. How well you, as a responsible manager, arrange to meet such expectations, through your efforts and the efforts of your staff, will determine your success. This is the element of "service," the meeting of guest expectations. And that is the decathlon of the hospitality industry, the multi-event trial that demands excellence from "A" for amenities to "Z" for zoo concession management. **Amenities** may vary among businesses and can be defined as the services, gifts, or "grace notes" a client

Exhibit 1.5   Customer expectations differ in a rustic setting, where a picnic feeling seems natural. (*Courtesy:* Belton Chalet)

Exhibit 1.6   In a tablecloth and silver setting, guests expect elegance and grace as well as good food. (*Courtesy:* Belton Chalet)

receives as part of doing business with the company. At the simplest level, amenities are actual products provided for guest use. In hotels, they can include soap, shampoo, hand lotion, a shoeshine cloth, and an in-room coffee machine (see Exhibits 1.7, 1.8, 1.9, 1.10, and 1.11). Resorts customarily raise the ante with upscale amenities that may include high-quality bathrobes for in-house use, cosmetic-quality skin care, sun block lotion, choice of complimentary newspapers, and gourmet chocolates. Airlines may provide toothbrushes, toothpaste, sleep masks, or slippers for long-distance flights.

In a larger sense, amenities can also be seen as including a range of guest services, from wireless network technology in the lobby, to voice mail, to concierge or business services, to even extra leg-room on commercial flights. All of these may contribute to a guest's comfort and satisfaction, though they are usually supplemental to the essential nature of the business in question.

Amenities come and go in popularity. For example, business travelers began asking for Internet access in their hotel rooms, so many hotels began providing it

AM/FM clock radio	High-speed Internet access
Shampoo/conditioner	Coffeemaker
Daily newspaper	Microwave
Hairdryer	In-room safe
Honor bar	Electronic door locks
Cable TV (basic + premium)	On-line folio review/check-out

Exhibit 1.7   Frequent Travelers' Preferred Amenities. (*Source:* "What Do Guests Want?" by Ed Watkins. *Lodging Hospitality,* May 1, 2002.)

Exhibit 1.8   In a luxury tent in the heart of Africa an important amenity might be a mosquito-net canopy. Can you spot other amenities? (*Courtesy:* Conservation Corporation, Africa)

free, as an amenity. Travelers responded by logging on for hours at a time, clogging phone and data lines. To control their costs, hotels reacted by offering complimentary limited access, and began charging a fee thereafter.

Peanuts used to be a popular amenity on airplane flights but have been replaced by mostly cracker or pretzel snacks when concerns were raised about peanut allergies among passengers, which can be triggered by inhaling even the dust from peanuts dispersed into the cabin's air.

Exhibit 1.9   In some situations, the availability of cold beverages—day or night—is an appreciated amenity. (*Courtesy:* Dometic Corporation)

Exhibit 1.10   Amenities in the world's longest stretch limousine could include complimentary champagne or a souvenir photo commemorating the occasion. As with airlines, the liberal leg-room can also be seen as a kind of amenity. (*Courtesy:* Star Limousines, Palos Hills, Illinois)

Exhibit 1.11   Amenities in this upscale bathroom include special bath bubbles, soaps, and lotions. Note the extra-generous supply of towels and the private window overlooking a tree top. (*Courtesy:* Conservation Corporation, Africa)

EYE ON THE ISSUES

Ethics

Hotels and amusement parks can face repercussions by the kind of groups they book, the movies they show, or the activities of their parent companies and affiliates. Religious groups have boycotted hotels that booked conventions of alternate lifestyle sado-masochists and leather-"activists" or others they believe to be immoral. In Sweden, politicians and government officials were asked to boycott hotels that offer porno-graphic movies on a pay-per-view basis. Disney has been boycotted because program-ming offered by its subsidiary, ABC, was perceived by some conservatives as promoting either promiscuity and/or witchcraft, as were some videos and CDs sold by another ABC-owned company, Hollywood Records. In the early 1990s, Disney was also boy-cotted when it extended to its gay and lesbian employees and their partners the same insurance benefits it offered to its straight married employees and their partners.

SERVICE

Why Is Service So Important?

When it comes right down to it, there are only two reasons to provide good service: because you perceive it as "right" or a "good," or because it somehow pays you to do so in the marketplace. (You'll learn more about the importance of values for leaders and managers in an upcoming chapter.) Businesses such as the notorious "last chance for gas" station seen in cartoons might opt for a profit by gouging prices or ripping off travelers for repairs, because they have no competitors. In the absence of competition, the marketplace ceases to *be* a market, offering little or no financial incentive for service, fairness, or integrity. In such an environment, the customer must take what he or she gets. You can almost hear the operator's mental wheels turning: "Why should I smile at these doofusses? Smiling won't make the gas tank hold more gas," or "These customers will never be back and if they *did* come back, this will still be the only game in town, heh, heh."

Such unscrupulous scenarios have been played out many times on lonely stretches of highway, on frontiers, and in socialist economies (where state-run operations have no competitors). When we encounter fair-minded operators under such circumstances, we can appreciate and admire them even more for adhering to higher personal standards of behavior, despite the temptations of "all that the market will bear." And it is these operators who, all other things being equal, are likely to withstand competition when it does arrive. This was brought home to the American economy during the ultracompetitive 1980s.

Studies by the Strategic Planning Institute (SPI) of Cambridge and the Technical Assistance Research Planning Institute of Washington, D.C., showed that customers were extremely dissatisfied with mediocre and unresponsive service. While some companies tried to offset poor service with lower pricing, most Americans rejected such tactics. Service, it seems, is an indispensable part of the free market equation. In fact, Ron Zemke, in *The Service Edge,* cites SPI's discovery that superior service providers can charge 9 to 10 percent more than their inferior service–providing competitors and still gain market share![3]

Exhibit 1.12   A sneaky trick played by some motel operators is to pretend they are full until all their competitors are filled. They then relight their vacancy sign and charge premium rates to desperate tourists willing to pay anything for a place to sleep. Would you consider this ethical? (Photo by Jenni Kirk)

So What Is Superior Service?

Service starts with an attitude. This attitude prompts you to "make it ready, make it right, make it to the customer's satisfaction, and do so with courtesy and professionalism." Your goal, regardless of your hourly wage or salary, regardless of whether a tip will be forthcoming, regardless of whether this is the first or seventieth time you have performed the task, is to leave the customer feeling pleased that he or she has done business with you. Zemke refers to this quality as "earnest(ness)." It can't be faked. It requires attentiveness and responsiveness beyond (and in addition to) any technical skills.

Some other words often heard in relation to good service are:

- On-time
- Attentive
- Polite, personable
- Gave full value
- Went beyond the call of duty
- Friendly
- Dependable
- Knowledgeable
- Respectful
- Anticipative
- Followed through
- Resourceful
- Accurate
- Concerned about safety and comfort
- Convenient
- Competent
- Well-trained

Exhibit 1.13 This restaurant host pays close attention to details. In order for her to manage reservations competently she has to be well trained and dedicated to making things ready and right. Her attitude underlies all her other skills. Wouldn't you bet she is also friendly, polite, personable, and resourceful? (Photo by Jenni Kirk)

EYE ON THE ISSUES

Customer Service

As every restaurateur knows, the unhappy customer who leaves and says nothing is worse than the one who registers a complaint. To gain an understanding of its customers' satisfaction, Red Lobster asks randomly selected diners to evaluate customer service via a survey on the Internet or a toll-free number. These comments are keyed into a corporate database to help the chain come up with an overall satisfaction rating for each restaurant, which is also tied to each manager's bonus. This demonstrates Red Lobster's commitment to customer service. Managers are rated not just on overall profitability, but on how satisfied guests are with their service experience.

If you enjoy identifying and satisfying customer needs, your choice of a career in the hospitality industries will be especially rewarding, particularly if you enjoy the challenge of bringing details together into a successful whole. Harvey Mackay, in *Swim with the Sharks without Being Eaten Alive,* offers this truism: "Little things don't mean a lot; they mean everything."[4]

How Do You Get Employees to Deliver Superior Service?

You'll learn more about what motivates employees in the chapter on hospitality human resources, but at this point, let's look at three important factors in getting employees to deliver the great service that brings customers back: attitude, empowerment, and communication.

Attitude.   *Lodging* magazine recently asked leading human resource officers if it is possible to train people to be friendly and to care about customers. The group agreed that you can teach service personnel to be efficient and attentive, even to smile and make eye contact, but that teaching someone to be caring and friendly is difficult, if not impossible. One award-winning general manager said, "The attitude of caring and friendliness has to come from within—it can't be taught."

Exhibit 1.14   This young front desk agent conveys his caring attitude and natural friendliness. He's also making great eye contact with the guest. (Photo by Jenni Kirk)

Thus, the best way to get friendly employees is to hire friendly people in the first place. This may sound like "Duh!" to you, but it is not as easy as it seems. Some people have the desirable hospitable attitude *on the inside,* but may be nervous or shy during an interview. This is why your professors emphasize the importance of showing confidence, practicing how to express your thoughts and positivity, etc., so that by the time you begin interviewing with recruiters, your attitude will come shining through. As you read the chapter on career exploration, you'll learn other ways to put your best foot forward.

A second way to get your employees to deliver the superior service your customers demand is to empower your employees.

Empowerment

Superior service encompasses all the qualities we've discussed and then builds upon them, usually through creativity and empowerment. While you may be familiar with the kind of creativity that drives chefs to carve dolphins out of ice blocks or flowers out of radishes, you may not yet have been exposed to the essential concept of empowerment. **_Empowerment_** is the placing of the authority to *do* in the hands of employees so that when an occasion for creativity, or problem solving, or crisis handling arises, an employee can act. Empowerment gives the employee confidence that his or her solution, whether it be a refund, a "comp" (providing a service at no charge, that is, "complimentary"), or a decision to evacuate the basement, will be supported by management.

The concept of empowerment grew in popularity during the '60s, '70s, and '80s, when it was first applied to the rights of minorities, the poor, and women. Senator Jack Kemp spoke of it as: "Giving people the opportunity to gain greater control over their own destiny . . ." Some of this sense carries over into the managerial use of the term. For instance, more recently, David Statt's *Concise Dictionary of Management* noted that an empowered employee, "*owns* the task she has been entrusted with and accepts full responsibility for it, being inspired to extend herself by the force of the vision and commitment she is shown rather than by any kind of coercion."[5]

Exhibit 1.15   This young restaurant manager has been empowered to add extra tables during an unexpected rush, to comp a guest's meal if it was unsatisfactory or late, or to temporarily shift staff to handle demand in a busy outlet. (Photo by Jenni Kirk)

Exhibit 1.16   This manager is confident that upper management will back up his decision on how to handle a difficult situation. The trust factor is an important part of empowerment. (Photo by Jenni Kirk)

Now we begin to see some of the give and take upon which empowerment is built. Trust is a major factor. In the example above, if the employee does not have reason to believe that management will back her decision, she will decline the responsibility of acting. On the other hand, management must trust her ability to make good judgments (and make sure she has been provided with the tools, such as training and vision, to make such judgments). This implies an "enlightened" organization that values its employees. William D. Hitt, in *The Leader-Manager*, suggests that, "inasmuch as empowerment treats people as *persons*, they will put forth their best effort go beyond what is expected of them."[6] And best effort is yet another component of superior service.

Here's a real-world example of how an empowered employee at Nordstrom's department store solved a problem. Late one afternoon, a Nordstrom shopper came in, desperately needing a blue dress shirt with white collar and cuffs, but the store had absolutely none in stock. Nevertheless, the sales associate delivered one the next morning to the extremely grateful customer. According to Jim Nordstrom, CEO, the client asked, "How did you do this if you had none in stock anywhere?" The associate didn't spell out the details, but he did say, "Well, if you need a white dress shirt with *blue* collar and cuffs, we've got one of those!" This is the spirit of customer service in action.

Customer service is such an absolute necessity in our industry that we have included a separate Eye on the Issues on it in every chapter. Look for the "eye icon" to see how customer service relates to every area of hospitality.

COMMUNICATION AND TEAMWORK

Service has come to be seen less and less as something unmeasurable or intangible and more and more as a salable *product.* Some companies even promise to demonstrate their commitment to service through objective performance. Thus we see them promise their guests that, "Our cashier will greet you with a smile and make eye contact with you or we'll . . ." and "If we don't greet you by name, your breakfast is on us." And guess what? Often times these by-the-book approaches pay off in better service. One reason is that some behaviors (such as smiling, nodding when listening, calling guests by name) are proven signals of attention and guests perceive them positively.

Another reason is that when management conveys specific guidelines to employees, it is communicating in a very strong way what the organization holds important. If management were to assign as an organizationwide goal that all employees take every opportunity to *overcharge* guests, that, too, would send a message, stronger than any memo. Such straightforward communication brings results and a corporate culture evolves to meet it upward or downward, depending on the message. When Hilton Inns, Inc., introduced its quality service effort, "Priority 1," the name alone left little doubt about the organization's intended direction.

Internal communication is an essential part of providing superior service. It does a chef little good to prepare an amazing meal, cooked to perfection, if the server has gotten the order wrong. A poorly cleaned guest room can negate a five-month selling effort by the sales department, undo the efficient handling provided by a personable bell staff, and undermine the front desk's friendly and accurate check-in. A catering company will lose not one, but many, clients if the hostess who hired it faints from an allergic reaction to mushrooms, a fact highlighted in the contract, but not communicated to the kitchen.

One assistant general manager of an upscale suburban hotel has a colorful way of describing the need to communicate important details sometimes both verbally and in writing. She calls it the ***Mack truck theory.*** Her explanation:

> Carrying around important information "in your head," not logging it in because you think you'll be on duty the next day to take care of it, is dangerous. What if you were run over by a Mack truck on your way to work? There'd be no way to deliver what you promised because the details exist only on your mental bulletin board. And the guest who relied on you is the one who would suffer, not to mention the employees who stepped up to fill in for you. There's no reason to risk letting people down like that when a little communication is all it takes. Our front desk log book is required reading for everyone on the front desk team.

In the hospitality industry, poor service in one area inevitably reflects badly on all other areas. Once the "spell" of efficiency and responsiveness has been broken, the client becomes hypersensitive to other weaknesses. One only has to review comment cards at any hotel to know that guest dissatisfaction is prone to snowballing. What starts as a complaint about a lost reservation soon picks up into a laundry list of the "slow, scuffed-up elevator, the housekeeper's noisy vacuums at 8:30 AM, and wobbly legs on the banquet chairs." Instead of one department called on the carpet, four have been implicated!

Exhibit 1.17   Communication and teamwork between departments is ultra-important. No matter how good of a job the bell staff does, their good first impression can be shattered at many points along the guests' stay. (Photo by Will Verbeeten, *Foto Verbeeten,* Groesbeek, The Netherlands)

At busy facilities with many departments and round-the-clock shifts, communication is a must. In fact, in interdependent organizations such as convention centers, hotels, and clubs, the service orientation we've discussed must be extended *from one employee to another* for seamless, well oiled performance.

Jonathan Tisch, president of Loews Hotels, has often compared the performance aspect of hospitality to show business, emphasizing the need for teamwork among all the supporting players. When any member of the production, no matter how small his or her part, flubs a line, drops a sandbag, or sews a seam improperly, the whole performance suffers; the audience's enjoyment is jarred, and ticket

Exhibit 1.18   It looks like a movie set, but it's just another example of the hospitality "stage," where it's "showtime" 24 / 7. (*Courtesy:* Conservation Corporation Africa)

sales drop. That's bad news, but it also brings up another important point. There is another factor in this all-important service equation, namely the underlying need for profit.

THE NEED FOR PROFIT

During a brainstorming session on college hotel/restaurant management (HRM) program requirements, an enormously successful hospitality entrepreneur remarked, "But when do you teach them how to make a profit?" Technical skills, a commitment to service, training, vision, and people skills are all important characteristics for managers to have, but at the end of the day, management's goal is to show "black ink" in satisfying quantities. To do so, managers must balance the ideal (the goals and essentials mentioned throughout this chapter) with reality

Exhibit 1.19   Annual reports spell out in black and white (and, hopefully, not in *red* ink!) just how much profit or loss took place in the preceding year. (Photo by Jenni Kirk)

(expenses, a stalled economy, taxation, regulation, a dwindling labor force). After all, *manager* is a title based upon the verb *manage*. It refers to an activity, not a lease on a roomy office. So we must add to all the other prerequisites the understanding of how to make an operation profitable.

Fortunately, as the century begins, the hospitality industry is poised for a period of increased profits. The economies of the world's major nations once based on agriculture, then based on manufacturing, have shifted into economies based on services. Columnist George F. Will captured the transformation he saw in the United States as follows: "McDonald's has more employees than U.S. Steel; golden arches, not blast furnaces, symbolize the American economy." Of course, there is much more to the service sector than simply fast food, and a great deal of it falls under the umbrella of hospitality. Leisure, travel, tourism, recreation, and, in some cases, entertainment are often linked with hospitality in forecasts and projections of national income and employment. When so compiled, these enterprises emerge as a giant, outshining almost all other sectors of the economy.

But hospitality profitability is not all smooth, downhill skiing. Because it draws upon a global pool of customers, it is tied to the health not only of local economies but also to the economies and exchange rates of international trading partners. In fact, for nearly the past decade, much of the lodging segment of the industry struggled to remain solvent. The early '90s found much of America "overbuilt" with hotels, many of them burdened with excessive debt. (**Overbuilding** occurs when a market area has far more rooms than it has customers and usually results in low occupancies and rate "wars.") This resulted in an aggressively competitive market. Chains and independents alike "woke up" to the need for clearly defined identities and corporate cultures based on service, as discussed at the beginning of this chapter. It took them the better part of a decade to regroup their resources . . . and begin another building cycle, which, thus far, has been sustainable, due to a healthy economy.

AN INTERNATIONAL INDUSTRY

When the lodging industry showed flat performance in America, investors looked abroad for opportunity. Holiday Inn, Best Western, Hilton, Intercontinental and Choice are just a few of the major companies whose logos may be seen around the globe. Restaurants have made even more media waves than hotels; much ado was made about McDonald's appearance in Moscow and Beijing, KFC's presence in Tokyo and Shanghai, and Baskin-Robbins in Vietnam. Naturally, an international marketplace requires a vast employee network to support it. In 2001, the World Travel and Tourism Council estimated that travel- and tourism-related enterprises employ more than 255 million people worldwide, or 1 in 11 employees. In fact, the globalization of hospitality has become so important that each of the upcoming chapters will discuss how it relates to the subject under consideration.

Travel Shrinks the World

In 1983, Somerset R. Waters reported an estimated $652 billion for worldwide spending on domestic and foreign travel combined.[7] By 2001, the World Travel and Tourism Council estimated that such spending had risen to $4.494 trillion, or more

Exhibit 1.20   Travel and tourism is an international industry from giant cities like Paris and Tokyo to remote, pristine bays in Australia. (*Courtesy:* Whitsunday Wilderness Lodge, Great Barrier Reef Marine Park)

than one-tenth of the world's economic activity. International tourists arrivals increased every year after World War II until 2001.

2001 brought dark days for tourism, for two reasons. During the first half of the year, major tourism-generating countries found their economies weakened due to unstable monetary markets and trade imbalances. Then, a terrorist attack on the United States on September 11, 2001, curtailed travel worldwide. Since the terrorists had high-jacked commercial aircraft filled with civilian passengers and used them as bombs, tourists everywhere felt at risk.

Although the Americas and the Middle East saw the deepest drops, the world, on average, suffered a drop of 11 percent in tourist arrivals in the last quarter of 2001. The WTTC estimated that Europe lost one million jobs in a ripple that started with tourism, but expanded to the industries supporting it.

After the first quarter of 2002, travel and tourism experts began to see encouraging, but slow, signs of recovery. The year 2002 showed a small up-tick in U.S. domestic travel (1.7 percent), but the 2003 war in Iraq and the threat of new respiratory disease (SARS) in parts of Asia and in Toronto, Canada, further delayed recovery. Still, the World Travel and Tourism Council (2004) has predicted that by 2006, recovery should be on track and returning to its pattern of strong growth.

This clear demonstration of how events in one country send tremors through the lives of other countries seems to reinforce sociologist Marshall McCluhan's theory of the world as a "global village."

The village has become more and more obvious as the growth of multi-national corporations has made international business travel a necessity. Ordinary people commonly travel abroad for business, education, or leisure purposes. Friendlier borders have encouraged travel, as has the Internet, which helps consumers plan trips from thousands of miles away. In 2004, an estimated 23 percent of travel was

---

International

The 15 "older" member nations of the European Union (EU), headquartered in Brussels, are Austria, Belgium, Denmark, Finland, France, Germany, Greece, Ireland, Italy, Luxembourg, The Netherlands, Portugal, Spain, Sweden, and the United Kingdom. The EU expanded in 2004 to include 10 new Eastern and Southern European members. Together, they are making a major shift in international travel and relationships. In the European Union, goods, services, capital, and persons circulate freely without being stopped or checked at frontiers; no passports are necessary. The EU countries agreed to phase out their currencies, and in 2002, replaced the familiar German mark, the French franc, the Italian lira, etc., with the Euro. Other countries are eager to enter the union and take advantage of increased travel and commerce. Bulgaria, Roumania, and Turkey are applying for membership.

---

booked online through such purveyors as Travelocity, Expedia, and Orbitz. Credit cards and cell phones make it easier for travelers to feel they are still connected to home, no matter how far they may be.

A later chapter, Linking Hospitality to Travel and Tourism, will provide a more in-depth look at the stunning size of tourism and its impact on the world, economically, culturally, and environmentally.

Cultural Sensitivity.   Internationalization has more than only economic consequences. It requires that students pursuing hospitality careers develop sensitivity to persons of other cultures, not only as guests or customers, but as co-workers and senior managers. With more and more corporations expanding internationally, managers can expect opportunities and assignments far from their familiar surroundings. Indeed, some international companies advocate overseas experience for ambitious managers. The experience of being a stranger in a strange land promotes empathy and perspective faster than any book-learned understanding of cultural difference ever could. And one need not be transferred to a European or Asian country to find oneself working under a managing director from foreign shores. Multinational companies weren't invented in the United States, nor have they limited their expansion to non–North American sites. For this reason, many schools offering hotel, restaurant, institutional, or tourism management programs emphasize not only geography and international commerce, but cultural diversity and organizational theory.

Change in the Demographics of Hospitality.   The make-up of hospitality management has changed greatly in the last 25 years. According to Elaine Grossinger Etess, the first female president of the American Hotel and Lodging Association (AH&LA), "During the early '70s schools of hospitality management were bastions of male dominance with the occasional few 'token' women in each class. Today, however, most of our colleges report that over 50 percent of those matriculated are women."[8] Etess also noted that up to that time, "women (held) the usual entry-level positions: maids, waitresses, and switchboard operators. Management positions were almost always filled by men. Men had 'careers' as hoteliers; women had 'jobs in hotels.' " Fortunately, the industry has moved toward a better balance.

Exhibit 1.21   You may be surprised to know that many dude ranch guests come from Europe and Asia. International guests often have different cultural expectations or even taboos, so managers and their staffs must be sensitive. (*Courtesy:* Colorado Dude and Guest Ranch Association.)

Women Making Strides

In American business in 1997, women represented 49 percent of all professional and managerial positions.[9] *Working Woman* also reports that, despite this visibility, on average, college-educated managers who are women earn approximately 19 percent less than their male counterparts. According to a survey reported in *Lodging* magazine, the hospitality industry has a somewhat better track record, paying women hospitality managers about 15 percent less than men in equivalent positions.

Women continue to gain ground in this area. In fact, McDonald's reports that over the past few years, the number of its women operator/owners has tripled. Nita Lloyd-Fore, a director of sales for national accounts with Hilton, wrote that in the late '60s, when she joined Hilton, there were only four women "who held the job of director of sales at our properties. Today . . . more than 60 percent of those positions are held by women."[10] Still, not all the news is so promising. When Joan Sills was named president of Colony Hotels (a Radisson subsidiary) in early 1992, she became the first woman to preside over a major lodging chain. Nationwide, across business and industry, it's estimated that only 11.7 percent of top corporate officer positions are held by women.

Altered Labor Pool

While women have made visible progress, similar strides must be made to pursue balance in opportunity for minorities and people with disabilities (sometimes called the differently abled, a replacement phrase for what used to be termed

Exhibit 1.22   Even women in non-managerial positions are making strides. Here, casino servers and hostesses successfully lobbied against uniform codes that mandated stiletto-type high heels, which have been connected to chronic back and foot injuries. (*Courtesy:* Nevada Women's Lobby)

disabled or *handicapped*). The legislation known as the Americans with Disabilities Act (ADA), which became effective in 1992, is intended to prevent employment inequities to the disabled. Many considered this legislation not only overdue philosophically, but also timely in terms of America's shifting employment pool. The president's Committee on the Employment of People with Disabilities estimates that the ADA brought notice to an untapped pool of nearly 23 million potential employees at a time when industry faced nearly stagnant growth rates in available

Exhibit 1.23   As demographics change in America, workplace diversity increases, bringing together co-workers of different ethnicities and nationalities. (Photo by Jenni Kirk)

labor. The hospitality industries are hungry for good employees, not only at the entry level, but at the managerial.

Changing Commitment to Work

Human resource experts also see a change in the value placed on work and success. The days of sacrificing family life in favor of workaholic success seems to be over. Fewer young managers indicate a willingness to work 75+ hours a week, even with the promise of rapid advancement. More companies are being asked to provide child-care plans for working parents. One study found that 71 percent of corporate women surveyed were more interested in balancing work and family than in building a supersuccessful career. An increasing number of male managers agree. Family time is no longer being seen as a luxury, but as a necessity. In some circles, the new status symbol is no longer who has the higher salary, but who has more days off written into their contract.

Adjustments undoubtedly will continue to be made. With the demand for qualified hospitality employees increasing and the labor pool dwindling, employers are motivated to make their employment packages attractive and competitive. In the meantime, employers are looking at another answer to labor shortages: older citizens. A study that included Days Inns Hotels found that workers older than 55 are as productive and cost effective as their younger counterparts. Employers characterize the group as having very low rates of absenteeism, often coupled with graciousness and politeness skills honed by having been in the workforce for decades.

Customer Profiles Change

As the people behind the scenes have changed, so have the people who consume hospitality services. Let's look at a few examples:

1. The much-discussed **baby boomers** (people born between 1946 and 1964) are today estimated at 77 million strong, representing about half of the working U.S. population. Now at the peak of their earning power, they will begin retiring in 5 to 15 years, shaking all leisure-time norms to date. As the century turned, 13 percent of the population was 65 years or older. In some Sunbelt areas, there are already communities in which more than half of the population consists of "seniors." This group, as a whole, has both discretionary income and the leisure time in which to spend it, making it a force to be reckoned with. Raymond Goodman, Jr., of the Whittemore School of Business and Economics, University of New Hampshire, has estimated that today's population age 50 and older owns more than 77 percent of all the financial assets in America, spends more on travel and recreation than any other age group, and eats out about three times per week. These are the people hospitality operators want to attract.

2. The business traveler has changed. In the last 10 years business travel by women has increased dramatically, so that they represent more than 40 percent of business travel. Hoteliers have been spurred to pay attention, since female corporate travelers are among the most loyal repeat customers when satisfied with their accommodations.

3. Another significant change is the increase in families choosing to vacation together, kids included, at resorts, upscale hotels, and on cruise ships. As one GM

Exhibit 1.24   The cruise industry is benefiting from several changes in customer demographics. Cruises are popular with Baby Boomers and seniors, as well as with families and/or couples. (*Courtesy:* Princess Cruises)

said, "Yuppies had puppies! And they want to bring them along on vacation."[11] This has brought about a need to review activities, menus, and facilities for child appropriateness. This has become so common that a new category of resort is being market tested: couples-only resorts. As humorist Dave Barry puts it, these "do not allow you to bring your children, the theory being that it is difficult for you and your spousal unit to get into a romantic mood if one of you has to pause every 45 seconds to shout, 'Jason! I told you not to squirt sun block into Ashley's ear!'"[12]

4. Researchers have also noted an increasing preference of travelers for "experiential" vacations trips that offer more than sightseeing and sunbathing. The popularity of Elderhostel, spa vacations, bed and breakfasts, wine country safaris, and "real cowboy" excursions are just a few examples of this consumer trend.

NEEDED: A COMFORT LEVEL WITH TECHNOLOGY

No matter how you arrive at your first hospitality position, you'll do well to develop a comfort level with technology. With the growth of the Internet and such things as electronic key systems, point-of-sale devices, employee records software, and property management systems, it's virtually impossible for employees of any service area to spend a day untouched by high tech. Telephones have become increasingly complex, to the point that one desktop phone can do more than entire switchboards of days gone by. Yet how many times have you witnessed business-

EYE ON THE ISSUES

Technology

One of the latest developments in major cities is online restaurant reservations technology. OpenTable.com and Foodline.com were among the first functional online systems for dining reservations. They promote their services as a management tool for restaurants and a convenience for diners. Some of the features of such systems attractive to restaurateurs include the ability:

- To accept reservations 24/7
- To create a database of guest preferences for seating or menu items
- To direct-market to repeat customers
- To network multiple units within a restaurant group

Diners are able to find available restaurants on-line by name, type of cuisine, location, price, etc. These services are becoming increasingly accessible through partnership alliances with such giants as American Express, AOL's Digital City Web, and major newspapers such as *The New York Times* and *The Washington Post*. Ticketmaster's Online-CitySearch has launched other online reservation services, which allow users to reserve tee times at golf courses.

people fumbling with their phone buttons, warning that they might lose you if they transfer your call? How many times have you heard people muttering about their "dumb computer"?

The solutions to such occurrences is training. People hate to be frustrated while trying to accomplish something, yet frustration is common around unfamiliar technology. While there is a significant amount of clumsy or quirky equipment out in the marketplace, the challenge is to master it until it is replaced.

A word about word processing and spreadsheets. Many students preparing for management careers scoff at learning these two basic types of software, believing they will have a secretary who will "take care of all that." Reality suggests: *Don't kid yourself.* These are essential skills, even if you do rise to a position supported by a secretary. Timely communication is extremely important. With a word processing program you can put down your thoughts at two or three times the speed it takes to handwrite them. Why would you want to slow yourself down by refusing to use an easily acquired skill? Especially since you'll also be able to answer your email faster and surf the Internet more effectively if you have good keyboarding skills.

Technology has given the hospitality industry a huge boost in efficiency, simplifying reservations, guest billing, forecasting, climate control, energy consumption, inventory control, scheduling, sales and market function, and research. It is so important that each of the upcoming chapters features it in an Eye on the Issues. But one thing is certain: Technology does not replace hospitality. This industry relies on a careful blend of high-tech and high-*touch*. Guests want the personal touch and the feeling that they are getting caring attention. Imagine how it will feel to a guest who is standing before you with a question if you reply, "It's all on the FAQ page of our website." This is an opportunity to enhance your connection with the guest, through eye contact, posture, and personality.

Exhibit 1.25A   Touchscreen technology makes restaurant reservations and planning for staffing and inventory much easier. This Ready-4-Dinner terminal accesses a database that includes customer preferences and allows guests to book on-line. (Photo by Jenni Kirk)

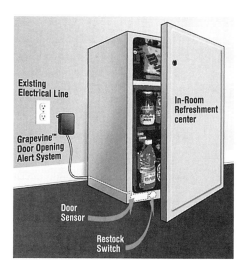

Exhibit 1.25B   This Dometic Grapevine Door Opening Alert System uses existing electrical lines to communicate in-room refreshment center activity, reduces service time, and ensures more accurate inventory control. (*Courtesy:* Dometic Corporation)

WHERE THE WINGS OF HOSPITALITY CAN TAKE YOU

Chances are, as you considered a career in hospitality, you imagined yourself as the manager or chef of a fine restaurant, a general manager at a luxury hotel or resort, or maybe even a pit boss at casino. These are all possibilities, but your choices are wider than perhaps you ever dreamed. A hospitality management degree and experience can connect you to a network of careers in leisure, travel, tourism, and recreation, simply because of the scope of these related enterprises. Though you'll get more details in appropriate upcoming chapters, here's a preview.

Let's also remember that not every HRM student will become a general manager or director. For each top position, there are layers and layers of support and specialization. You may find your niche as an assistant technical specialist, a trainer, a recruiter, a chef, a supplier, a food-safety inspector, etc. Such spots can offer the right balance for *you* between income, interests, family life, variety, and general "match."

Lodging

Hotels and resorts have been compared to miniature cities in the way that they incorporate life support systems—light, heat, water, food, shelter, security, and sanitation facilities. As such, they often include within their "city limits" elements of food service, recreation, entertainment, and personal services for travelers. There are close to a dozen major categories of lodging facilities, ranging from tiny bed and breakfasts to the latest development, mega-resorts. The niches in between these extremes are commercial hotels, airport hotels, economy properties, suite hotels, residential hotels, conference centers, casino hotels, and resorts. The tiniest cousin in this family had its debut in Japan: the sleeping tube, which takes the airport hotel to an extreme by providing the guest with space little larger than a closet in which to sleep. Later chapters in the lodging unit will discuss some of the differentiating characteristics of lodging categories and their markets.

Gaming, which has traditionally been associated with the lodging industry, has expanded its scope since 1988, when legislation opened up opportunities for Native American-owned gaming facilities. Since then, freestanding and riverboat casinos have flourished. Today, casino gambling is legal in 48 of the 50 states. Americans made an estimated 322 million visits to casinos in 2005, betting nearly $731 billion. A closer look at the upcoming chapter Gaming and Casino Management will give you an estimate of how much of this fortune ends up in hospitality coffers, by virtue of a built-in profit margin called the *casino advantage*.

Perhaps in response to increased gaming competition from nonhotels, casino hotels in Las Vegas have been making inroads on the attractions market by creating

Exhibit 1.26   The casino segment has bloomed since 1987 legislation, even in non-metro and rural settings. Casinos have found billboard advertising an effective way to pull in travelers in their vicinity. This clever series on a major interstate emphasizes fun and recreation for adults and appropriate activities for children. (*Courtesy:* Cliff Castle Casino)

Exhibit 1.27   Casino action can take place on riverboats, Indian reservations, or gaming centers like Las Vegas, Monte Carlo, or the Bahamas. (*Courtesy:* Jenni Kirk)

incredible theme mega-hotels that are attractions in themselves. New York, New York; Paris; the Venetian; and the Egyptian-themed Luxor are three striking examples.

On a more down-to-earth level, campgrounds and recreational vehicle parks form a distinct subcategory of their own within the larger definition of lodging. (There were 8.2 million RVs on the road in 2005.) College dormitories now compete for budget travelers. Though primarily residential units for three-fourths of the year, such facilities are now being actively marketed for transient occupancy by study groups (such as Elderhostel) and attendees of educational summer camps, band camps, cheerleading camps, etc. Timeshares have jumped in popularity, growing at a rate of 15 percent per year over the last seven years. Marriott, for example, currently owns about 8,000 vacation ownership villas with about 240,000 owners. This provides a stable, known population of guests who are more likely to stay brand loyal than vacationers who do not own a piece of their vacation property.

Food Service

The preparation and delivery of food to guests and travelers is another huge category closely connected with lodging, travel, and recreation. Beyond the obvious area of familiar restaurants lies institutional food service in hospitals, businesses, colleges, and correctional facilities.

New categories continue to emerge, such as "commuter food," which differs from traditional food service offered on trains, planes, and ships. Commuter food operations are often located in or near subway stations, train depots, and bus stops. Workers on their way home pick up restaurant-style entrees in take-out

Exhibit 1.28   Fast food is a familiar segment of the food-service industry. Although this popular Taco Bell campaign featuring a charming Chihuahua has been retired, it was significant in the way that it emphasized the Mexican heritage of the taco and nationally acknowledged the increasing market power of America's Hispanic citizens. (Photo by Marilyn McDonald)

packaging (called home meal replacements, or HMRs). Sbarro, Inc., known for its food-court stores, worked to develop this market. Grocery stores have jumped on the bandwagon, offering more competition to traditional restaurants. Boston Market and Pat & Oscar's have joined this niche, as well. While guests may dine on-site, most meals are packed for home consumption.

The career of chef, which often draws students into an HRM or culinary major, requires specialized training not only in food production, but in kitchen management, menu planning, purchasing, nutrition, and food safety. Although your first thought may be of a chef in a restaurant, chefs may also work in food-testing kitchens, in country clubs, hospitals, dude ranches, nursing homes, cafeterias, or in research and development departments of manufacturers or chain restaurants.

Food service also encompasses everything from snack bars, festival and stadium vending, discos, coffee houses, and picnic packing (popular in California), to the new "smart drug cocktail bars" featuring health drinks loaded with vitamins, amino acids, and other nutrients believed to enhance memory and mental clarity. Each of these unique categories has its own challenges and strengths, but all share the common need for responsible management. Later chapters discuss some of the issues that affect every food service operation.

Institutions

Until recently, hospitality managers working in institutions were primarily involved with food service in hospitals, prisons, school cafeterias, and so on. In the last few years, opportunities have expanded to include health care management and retirement center management. Some residential retirement complexes offer a range of living arrangements from active independent to assisted living. Managers in such facilities may oversee a whole spectrum of guest services, including activities, housekeeping, food service, transportation services, special services, and guest satisfaction. This promises to be a growth area as America's famous baby boomers age and seek out new living arrangements.

Transportation

Lodging and feeding guests along their journeys would be irrelevant without the essential means of getting them to their destinations. This area includes not only airlines, cruise ships, ferries, trains, motor coaches, limousines, taxis, and shuttle buses, but also rental car operations and service station facilities, not to mention airports and terminals. One might even include parking facilities, horses, trail mules, rickshaws, and golf carts in this category. Transportation is closely linked to **infrastructure,** the system of roads, harbors, bridges, tunnels, airports, and so on, necessary for vehicle movement. Infrastructure also includes other services required by residents and visitors:

- Utilities, such as water, electricity, and gas
- Health care
- Sanitation and sewer
- Services, such as traffic control, police, and emergency personnel

Though some consider the dream of space tourism to be far away, others are already working on space travel infrastructure. Hilton Hotels, millionaire entrepreneur Richard Branson (owner of Virgin Atlantic), and others are all investigating the feasibility of space resorts. In 2001 the first space tourist, Californian Dennis Tito, took an eight-day orbital vacation, paying $20 million to the Russians for his Soyuz capsule accommodations and a tour of the International Space Station. A Virginia-based company, Space Adventures, is already marketing around the moon trips at $100 million beginning in 2008. A personalized travel bag is included.

Travel and Tour Arrangements

Within this detail-driven area there are travel agencies, reservation systems, and tour planning. This is an area that is rapidly changing, since the Internet now offers direct access to consumers. Travel agents continue to compete by offering expert

Exhibit 1.29   Tour companies like Pink Jeep Tours provide visitors with fun and exciting experiences led by personable and knowledgeable guides. (*Courtesy:* Pink Jeep Tours, Sedona, AZ)

service, and accountability for those who are not too sure about e-commerce. But in 2001, many major airlines stopped paying commissions to travel agents, striking a blow to their base income, causing many travel agencies to downsize or close.

We might also include in this area guide services, rating and accreditation associations, and **destination-management companies (DMCs)**. DMCs provide stress-relieving services for meeting planners responsible for meetings in distant locales. Because DMC specialists know the high points of their area and patronize reliable subcontractors, they can arrange for speakers, entertainers, shopping excursions, airport pick-ups, VIP welcomes, and many of the tiny but important details an out-of-towner would find time-consuming or difficult to arrange.

Tourism Marketing and Promotion

The task of creating consumer interest in a city, region, state, or country falls not only on the shoulders of the marketing staff of individual hotels and attractions, but also on agencies such as national tourism authorities, state or provincial tourism offices, chambers of commerce, and convention and visitors bureaus. These entities work to promote awareness of their areas as multi-faceted destinations, with the purpose of attracting visitors who will stay for several days or even weeks. Their work is often important to the economic health of their city, state, and so on because of the ***ripple effect*** of outside money (also called the *multiplier*). Because of tourism's ripple effect, one dollar spent effectively to promote tourism can result in two or three dollars reaped in direct or indirect return.

Here's a simplified example. The money visitors spend in a town for accommodations or meals also indirectly supports the businesses that supply those hotels and restaurants. (These could include food and liquor wholesalers, carpet-cleaning companies, local newspapers, rental car agencies, florists, and so on.) Local retailers consistently benefit as visitors shop for pleasure or essentials. In popular tourist areas, many companies prosper to the point of needing additional employees to serve increased demand for their products and services. And of course, employees in tourism and hospitality spend their money in town to provide food, shelter, transportation, and entertainment for their families. Governments also profit through the taxes collected on increased sales and income. This helps explain why governments and businesses see tourism as a "cash cow," and are willing to fund tourism marketing agencies. Not to be forgotten, however, is the other side of the coin: the costs of tourism. These are touched on in several upcoming chapters.

Club Management

Club managers face a different set of tasks than others in hospitality, largely because they deal with a clientele composed of members who usually have invested significant sums in the form of dues or initiation fees. Members patronize their club's facilities frequently and may have a voice in how they are operated. To serve these familiar customers, club managers must find a happy medium between variety, in terms of menu offerings and special events, and predictability, in terms of consistent, excellent service.

Club management is a growing field within the industry and includes opportunities in military installations and public or private facilities. A high-end example of club management has recently grown out of the professional sports "sky box" trade

Exhibit 1.30   The car-eating, flame-blowing Robosaurus is an attraction popular at sporting or racing events across the country. (Photo courtesy of Mark Hays' Monster Robots)

(deluxe boxes in stadiums and arenas for executive and influential clients). These cater to those with caviar budgets, who expect fine food and service.

Activities and Attractions

Tourism benefits through the availability of unique or attractive activities. These can include events, expositions, fairs, and festivals, whether cultural, ethnic, political, sport-related, religious, artistic, or for "fans." Many of these outdoor affairs require festival grounds, stadiums, tracks, and so on, while others take place indoors at civic centers. Thousands of events are held each year, ranging from reggae festivals to Star Trek convocations. This category also includes the enormous field of meetings, conventions, and trade shows. A whole subset of enterprises has grown to support these activities, including contract services for everything from security to parking services, from exhibition and multimedia rental agencies to portable toilet vendors. An upcoming chapter, The Hospitality Spectrum, discusses relevant management challenges for this area.

Exhibit 1.31   Meetings and conventions form a major segment of the industry often as part of hotels, resorts, and casino complexes. (Photo courtesy of Conservation Corp., Africa)

State, national, and regional parks also serve as activity magnets to millions each year. So popular are such scenic and play areas that in some areas they are in serious danger of overuse. Park management has become a difficult specialty. Managers must walk a fine line between servicing the traveling and recreation-minded public and controlling the negative physical impact caused by millions of park users.

Akin to park recreation are those enterprises that provide leisure and sports facilities, such as golf courses, bowling lanes, tennis, and other private or public clubs. In Japan, entrepreneurs have taken this category to new heights by building one of the world's largest indoor ski slopes, 25 stories high, and as long as five football fields! Dubai's national indoor ski park, Ski Dubai, expects 50,000 visitors per year.

Shopping

Travelers seem born to shop, and every aspect listed above has its own specialized league of merchants associated with it. The pursuit of purchases has far outstripped traditional souvenir buying. The popularity of shopping has now escalated to the point that some shopping areas can accurately be described as tourist destinations by themselves (Rodeo Drive, Beverly Hills; Mall of America, Minneapolis; Fifth Avenue, New York; Champs D'Elysée, Paris, to name a few). Casinos also have taken note of the power and profitability of shopping. Most casino complexes offer high-end, ultra high-end, and theme-related retail, often intermingled with entertainment (such as the singing gondoliers at the Venetian).

Other communities flourish through the marketing of art and/or crafts, sometimes by emphasizing the cultural or ethnic specialties of the locale. The U.S. Travel and Tourism Administration (USTTA) estimates that of the 18 most popular activities foreign visitors participate in, shopping ranks, first, engaging 83 percent of all tourists.

Services and Miscellaneous

Hospitality's wings extend to specializations within the scope of standard business. As in other enterprises, there are needs for human resources managers, training specialists, webmasters, accountants, controllers, financial planners, purchasing agents, clerks, office managers, physical plant engineers, cleaning and maintenance experts, and so on.

Miscellaneous specialties tied to hospitality include those of restaurant critics, travel writers, travel publishers, and hospitality consultants. Larger properties, country clubs, or spas have specialized needs for golf or tennis pros, massage therapists, aestheticians, and fitness trainers.

HOSPITALITY AND CORPORATE CITIZENSHIP

Hotels, restaurants, airlines, casinos, spas, and amusement parks are bombarded with requests from their communities for donations to be used as prizes or in charity auctions or raffles. More often than you would expect, they participate in these community-minded events . . . for several reasons.

Exhibit 1.32   Hospitality enterprises often show good corporate citizenship by donating comps to charitable fund-raising events. These may include food, concert tickets, promotional items, rooms, tours, etc. (Photo by Jim Morgan, Scottsdale, AZ)

Many Reasons for Good Citizenship

Hotels, attractions, theaters, amusement parks, and, in some cases, airlines have what can be called **perishable inventories.** This means, in the case of a hotel with 200 rooms, that on a given night there are 200 perishable opportunities for revenue. Come night time, if the room has not been sold, the hotel has lost the revenue it might have earned. By making tax-deductible donations of accommodations during periods they know are slow, the hotel can lessen its revenue losses while helping worthwhile charities. Even if the financial benefit is small, the hotel gains public relations points for being a good citizen. The hotel may pick up bonus revenue if the "comped" guests patronize its restaurant or lounge. There is also excellent potential for positive word-of-mouth, since human nature prompts people to talk about great deals to their friends and to recommend businesses with whom they have had personal experience.

The same principle applies to airline seats, theater tickets, Ferris-wheel rides, and so on. The plane must still fly and the show must still go on even if seats are empty. The cost to the donating company is minimal, yet the benefits are positive. In the case of a restaurant, most of these principles apply, though the cost to the donor may be somewhat higher, percentagewise, since the food that is consumed must be replaced, slightly different from a seat that may be sold over and over again.

This partially explains the mechanism by which hospitality enterprises can and do benefit from donating inventory to charitable causes. But there are philosophical and psychological reasons as well.

It's common in many corporate segments of the hospitality industry for managers to be transferred every few years. Since home changes with regularity, smart managers often try to involve themselves in their new communities as soon as possible after arriving. This is a good psychological strategy for preventing a feeling of rootlessness. Most major cities have local chapters of professional organizations such as the American Hotel & Lodging Association (AH&LA), National Restaurant Association (NRA), Hotel Sales and Marketing Association International (HSMAI), and Meeting Planners International (MPI), and these offer outlets for community involvement. This is the personal side of the coin of good citizenship.

Corporate philosophy is the other side of the coin. Enlightened corporations believe they have a responsibility to their communities. In some cases they have even built a commitment to humanitarian acts into their business or action plans. This is why it is common to see hotel associations collecting old sheets and towels for homeless shelters, and restaurants and banquet facilities contributing unused meals to charity dining rooms. In Canada, when Canadian Pacific Hotels' (CPH) housekeeping staff expressed their dislike of throwing out slightly used bars of soap and partially used bottles of shampoo and conditioner, the company sought a solution. The result was a relationship with Global Ed-Med (GEM), a group that specializes in sending medical supplies to the Third World. In remote areas not serviced by GEM, CPH partners with local charities with a need for such amenities.

According to Rick Van Warner, "the nation's restaurant operators are finding ways not only to contribute to a wide variety of fund-raisers but also on a *daily basis* to get their perishable leftovers into the mouths of people who need them."[13] America's food-service operators are using their resources to respond to the problem of hunger. (Statistics show that 20 million people in the United States go hungry each day, including one out of every eight children under age 12).

Exhibit 1.33   Many restaurants contribute to local social services, not only by donating gift certificates for fundraisers, but by donating perishable leftovers to food banks for the homeless. (*Courtesy:* Papa John's)

An easy way for students to get started in hospitality citizenship is to become active in student organizations while on campus. These include:

- Club Managers Association of America (CMAA)
- Hosteur
- Network of Executive Women in Hospitality (NEWH)
- Hotel Sales and Marketing Association International (HSMAI)
- International Food Service Executive Association (IFSEA)
- International Student Organization (ISO)
- Eta Sigma Delta
- International Association of Hospitality Accountants (IAHA)
- Professional Convention Management Association (PCMA)
- Educational Institute (EI)

Student chapters often undertake such projects as canned-goods drives, "Caring and Sharing" programs, "adopt-a-highway" commitments, tutoring, and scholarship fund-raising. Often, active members can qualify for club-funded scholarships.

Environmental Concerns

The 1990s brought awareness of environmental responsibility to all major industries, hospitality included. Hotels and restaurants have been forced to examine their energy use, waste management, and commitment to reducing nonrecyclables. The "green" trend has even become a selling point, with some meeting planners requesting that no Styrofoam coffee cups be used and that recycling bins for aluminum cans be placed near break tables.

Airlines have also been pressured to reconsider their meal packaging, which generates tons of garbage daily. Noise pollution has become a major consideration in airport expansion and route assignment. Desert-zone golf courses have received criticism for their use of water resources. Golf courses everywhere have had to examine their use of fertilizers and pesticides. Tourism developers have learned the

EYE ON THE ISSUES

Environment

Lake Powell National Recreation Area, one of the world's largest man-made lakes, is considered by many to be the jewel of America's National Parks Service system. Located along the Arizona–Utah border, Lake Powell was created by damming the Colorado River to create hydroelectric power, a water reservoir, and a recreational area. In the process, nearly 200 miles of Glen Canyon, a stunning canyon compared in beauty to the Grand Canyon, was filled with water, creating 2,000 miles of shoreline. Each year, between 3 and 4 million visitors enjoy boating, fishing, camping, and water sports on the lake. But environmentalists fault the dam for disrupting the natural habitats of both Glen Canyon and the Grand Canyon and endangering fish, plant, and animal species. Others fault the inevitable pollution of the lake by noisy gas-burning speedboats and water-toys. Extremists have threatened to destroy the dam to return the rivers to their natural courses. Everyone agrees that the creation of Lake Powell has had a major environmental impact on the region and many wonder if this impact will be desirable and sustainable over time.

Exhibit 1.34   Tourism developers must be concerned not only with the geographical environment, but also sociological environments. Cultures can be permanently changed by an influx of wealthy visitors. (Photo by Janet McDonald)

hard way that they must consider not only physical environmental impacts, but also sociological ones, particularly in Third World locations or in sites with fragile ecosystems. You'll read more about environmental concerns as they apply to specific areas in upcoming chapters. Watch for the Eye on the Issues icon.

EYE OPENERS

It's Not All Resorts and Disney Worlds

Discussions of trends in hospitality usually focus on the corporate side of the industry. This is the visible and often more glamorous part of the iceberg. Fewer facts and figures are known about the independent side, one-unit enterprises, "mom-and-pop" operations, and so on. That doesn't lessen their importance or potential desirability as career options. Independence or I-want-to-do-it-my-way entrepreneurship may be your work style or lifestyle. Thousands of corporate restaurant managers and chefs have been heard to dream aloud of owning their own restaurants. Still other managers long for a low-pressure, non-urban lifestyle in towns that cannot support luxurious operations.

Smaller Operations

Don't ignore the options of smaller operations, whether they be total independents or franchises of modest chains. A summer spent working or interning at a smaller property gives you experience in every department and a chance to be a member of a small team that does everything. If you later choose to become the owner or general manager of a small property, *you'll* be the boss, *you'll* set policy, and *you'll* set your hours, with little input from a big corporation. (Of course, that doesn't mean the hours you set yourself won't be quite demanding.) When making your career plans, don't overlook this huge, but less well publicized side of the industry as a small restaurateur, hotelier, or bed and breakfast owner. *So You Want to Be an Innkeeper* . . . offers these thoughts:[14]

> There is a timeless quality to innkeeping. The work never seems to be done, interrupted by the phone, sporadic eating patterns, late-night arrivals, a water heater that burns out when the inn is full, a travel writer who arrives unannounced when the septic tank is being pumped.
>
> . . . Your whole idea of how to use time is changed . . . Time off tends to be in snatches; the concept of a "weekend" grows increasingly foreign; "quitting time" disappears.
>
> On the other hand there are opportunities to sit down and enjoy pieces of the day most nine-to-fivers don't have: a late breakfast in the garden on a slow weekday . . . evening wine with interesting guests.

Private owners need the same arsenal of management skills as corporate managers. Accounting, financial, marketing, leadership, and problem-solving skills are still needed and often need to be augmented with "fix-it" skills, since there is no handy engineering department to call upon. By the same token, hands-on ability must pick up where theory leaves off. A private owner often has to do his or her

Exhibit 1.35   At the opposite end of the spectrum from mega-hotels and resorts, bed and breakfasts offer a personal slower paced option for travelers. (*Courtesy:* Dena Dierker, Dierker Design)

own market research, copy writing, menu planning, health-code compliance, book-keeping, and so on. For many, this can be a satisfying combination that complements individual personality or lifestyle preference.

CONCLUSION

Hospitality management covers an enormous range of opportunity across many enterprises, from the more familiar hotel and restaurant arena to the realm of adventure tourism or stadium management. To a great degree, all these enterprises can be categorized as service industries, since they deliver an intangible product different from the more concrete products of manufacturing or agriculture. The concept of service has been extended to mean an overall attitude displayed by all employees and designed to ensure guest satisfaction.

The industry is fast moving and international in scope, with good growth potential projected for the next 10 to 20 years. It has gained respect in the past 25 years for its positive economic impact and as a nationally and internationally significant provider of employment.

Hospitality continues to embrace technology as a means of providing improved service. Technology, which 100 years ago was limited to guest room telephones (a big deal when New York City's Netherlands Hotel installed them in 1894), now includes on-line reservations systems, one-button customer account information access, and "smart" guest room technology. Hospitality was one of the first industries to offer "you name your price" sales strategies via Priceline.com, which debuted in 1998.

The diversity included in hospitality, leisure, recreation, travel, and tourism enterprises offers career opportunities of interest to those with managerial, technical, or creative priorities. It offers a satisfying stage for those who want to star in service.

Each of the upcoming chapters will focus in on important areas of the industry, giving you your first glimpse of what goes on (in and out of public sight) to enable delivery of superior service. So, if you'll step this way, we've made a reservation for you, and everything is ready . . .

Exhibit 1.36   The spectrum of hospitality, tourism, and travel enterprises is amazingly broad. Come get your feet wet! (*Courtesy:* Colorado Dude and Guest Ranch Association)

KEYWORDS

overbuilding   20
baby boomers   25
infrastructure   32
destination-management companies (DMCs)   33
perishable inventories   36

CORE CONCEPTS

amenities   8
empowerment   15
Mack truck theory   17
ripple effect/multiplier   33

DISCUSSION QUESTIONS

1. Why is it important for a company to have a clear understanding of its identity? Why should managers be quite clear regarding their company's identity?
2. Describe three "signals of attention" that can be used effectively with guests. Suggest another one, not listed in the chapter, that you think would also be effective. What are some signals of inattention?
3. Describe the gender shift in hospitality manager roles since 1970.
4. What are two demographic groups being recruited in the face of labor shortages?
5. Give a short description of baby boomers and their characteristics. List four baby boomers with whom you are personally acquainted. Do they appear to fit the description?
6. List 10 amenities that might be found in resort guest rooms or in a restaurant. Brainstorm three creative amenities not listed in the chapter. Remember to keep reasonable cost in mind.

EXEMPLAR OF EXCELLENCE

Darden Restaurants

Darden is the world's largest casual dining restaurant company, with more than 120,000 employees and 1,400 restaurants. Large as it is, Darden Restaurants carries on the philosophy of Bill Darden, the chain's founder, whose emphasis was on community involvement. Darden has appeared repeatedly in *Fortune* magazine's list of America's most admired companies, most recently in 2002. *Fortune* also highlighted Darden's diversity efforts, ranking in the nation's top 10 companies for minorities on its annual "Diversity Elite" list.

Take an e-walk through Darden's website and see if you see Darden's philosophy and commitment reflected throughout.

Visit Red Lobster's part of the site and read through "Our Compass." Do you agree with their tagline: Doesn't this sound like a great place to work?

Website: www.darden.com

WEBSITES TO VISIT

1. www.americangaming.org/
2. www.fortune.com/lists/(click on "Lists")
3. www.greenbrier.com/ (if you do not have Flash, use the plain browser option).
4. www.sonesta.com/
5. www.cityharvest.org/(click on "Donate Food")
6. www.queenmary.com

PART I

Introduction to Lodging Management

This section introduces you to management opportunities in the lodging industry. The lodging industry greatly affects a country's economic, social, and cultural development. It contributes significantly to national, regional, and local economies in generating employment and government tax revenues. For example, in the United States alone, the lodging industry generated more than $100 billion in sales in recent years, and provided jobs for almost 2 million full- and part-time employees. There were more than 55,000 hotel properties in the United States in 2005!

The lodging industry greatly affects local communities and cultures. It seems that almost every city or community, no matter how large or small, has its own "grand hotel" that serves as an anchor for the local community. Important gatherings and celebrations are often held in hotels. Many new ideas and fashion styles are introduced in and disseminated from hotels, and millions of travelers visit them each year.

Staying in hotels has become a part of our way of life. Hotels, as part of the physical landscape, reveal "secrets" of our cultural landscape; if studied by anthropologists of another century (or even another planet), they would give insights about our habits, beliefs, and characteristics.

Developing and managing hotels can be of tremendous economic, social, and cultural significance. Besides the opportunity associated with potential career growth, there are also important societal responsibilities. The three chapters in this section discuss in detail the career opportunities, management responsibilities, and challenges in the lodging industry.

The first chapter in this section traces the historical development and structure of the lodging industry, and analyzes the lodging industry from an industry supply and market demand point of view. It describes the varied products in today's lodging industry and explains why these products are developed to satisfy guests' demands and needs.

The second chapter focuses on the rooms division of a hotel—the "front of the house," explaining the important functions this division performs in a hotel and outlining its managerial and supervisory positions. Every step of the guest cycle is discussed, from making a reservation to checking out.

The final chapter discusses three additional functions in hotel management and operations: housekeeping, maintenance, and engineering—the "back of the house." These functions focus on the physical side of hotel operations—the comfort, cleanliness, and safety of guest rooms and public areas. It elaborates on the operational procedures of a hotel's housekeeping department, and emphasizes the challenging management responsibilities of this department. It identifies the major operational functions of the maintenance and engineering departments, and stresses the importance of environmental awareness and energy conservation. The short discussion pieces at the end of the unit highlight technological, accounting, and legal issues related to the lodging industry and help you understand the lodging industry from these particular perspectives.

After completing this unit, you will have a more thorough understanding of the different types of lodging facilities, their market demand, and the various aspects of a hotel's operation.

History and Economics of the Lodging Industry

Successful business operations hinge on the successful exchange of products/services for value (usually monetary). The lodging industry is slightly more complicated because it rests on a dynamic interaction between supply (products/services) and demand (the customers' needs). As the lodging industry evolves, its structure becomes increasingly more complex. In this chapter, we use the term **structure** to refer to ownership, management, and affiliation. Different types of hotels are designed and created to be responsive to different travelers' needs and demands. These needs determine the types of accommodation facilities found in the lodging industry. The process of marketing (and sales, a subcomponent of marketing) links lodging supply and lodging demand.

INTRODUCTION

The following is a brief overview of the history and economics of the lodging industry. The first portion will discuss tourism and hospitality in the ancient world. The second will examine the lodging industry in the United States, beginning with the rise of mass tourism in 1945. By the time you have read about the ups and downs of the lodging industry and how it has been affected by economics, wars, religion, and tax incentives, you will have a better understanding of business cycles and why some years college hotel recruiters collect HRM graduates like a mad safari hunter . . . and other years don't even turn up for the hunt.

The economics portion of this chapter follows a framework that presents both lodging supply and travel demand. It first discusses lodging supply: industry scope, current development, categories of hotels, types of hospitality business organizations, and typical hotel organizational structures. It then describes the various travel markets that place demand on lodging products and services and shows how hotel sales departments serve as links between lodging supply and travel demand. The chapter ends with a brief discussion of some current issues that face the lodging industry.

A HISTORY OF LODGING

People have traveled since the dawn of humankind. Their reasons for travel have varied, and how they have traveled has changed with technology and means of transportation.

Hospitality services have evolved in response to the changes in travelers' needs. Generally, travel increases with growth in economic and business activity. In fact, changes in economic activity always cause changes in the need for hospitality services. As you read the history of the hospitality industry, pay particular attention to the direct connection between economic and business activity and the health and changes in the hospitality industry.

Pre-Written History: The Agricultural Revolution and Settlements

Although the history of modern humans starts more than 200,000 years ago, we will zoom through the first 190,000 years to approximately 10,000 years ago when people began to settle into small communities. It was the dawning of the Agricultural Revolution. With these settlements came specialization of work and the rise of various social classes: workers (farmers, hunters, traders, and primitive manufacturers), warriors, administrators, and priests. Specialization of work created the conditions for trade between these small communities; thus, there was a motivation to travel. Demand for hospitality services came from itinerant traders between these settlements. Supply was probably provided by camps and local permanent residents of these settlements.

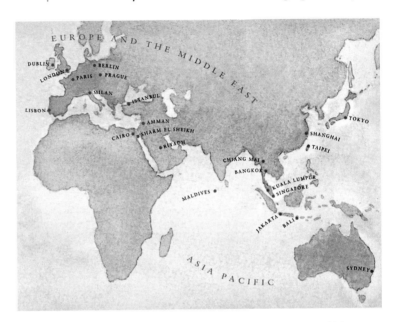

Exhibit 2.1   Before written history, people traveled locally within regions of Africa, Europe, the Middle East, and Asia. Can you identify the Persian Gulf, into which the Tigris and Euphrates Rivers pour? Just northeast of the Gulf lay ancient Mesopotamia, an early commercial center. (Map courtesy of Four Seasons Hotels & Resorts)

Written History

5000 BC to AD 1500

Supply and Demand Interaction.   The social organization and specialization of small communities continued and with it came the rise of the first cities and the production of written records. Approximately 7,000 years ago (5000 BC to 3000 BC), Sumer, in southern Mesopotamia and modern-day Iraq, arose as the world's first commercial center. Early hospitality establishments existed here. The Sumerians exerted power throughout the area and are believed to have been the world's first modern traders. As trade expanded, so did the need for hospitality services.

Babylon, also located in Mesopotamia, later replaced Sumer as the center for commercial activity and power. Increased trade and economic activity necessitated the need for laws. The time was ripe for the king of Babylon, Hammurabi (1792–1750 BC) to develop the first written code of laws (the Code of Hammurabi). One of these codes regulated tavern keeping. It decreed that tavern keepers were not to pour the wrong measure or to dilute beer. The code decreed death as the penalty for infractions of the law. This shows that various aspects in the hospitality industry were important enough to be regulated.

Approximately 1300 BC, the Egyptians seemed to have been traveling for more reasons than simply trade and government business. They may also have traveled for the purposes of sightseeing and for attending festivals and religious ceremonies. The needs of these travelers stirred the development of more inns.

During this same period, long-distance trade was expanding. Travelers throughout present-day Turkey, Iran, Afghanistan, and northern India stayed at

Exhibit 2.2   The Egyptians were some of the first travelers to travel for reasons other than trade or government. Today, the Four Seasons Hotel Cairo at The First Residence provides accommodations "fit for a Pharaoh." (Photo courtesy of Four Seasons Hotels & Resorts)

caravanserais, the predecessors of the stagecoach inn (and later the motel). These early inns were built around a large courtyard and designed for security at night. The courtyards provided an area for the animals, with the enclosing walls made up of Spartan rooms for the travelers.

Around 850 BC, Homer's epic Greek poem, *The Odyssey,* refers to a tavern and a place where travelers could spend the night. About 400 BC, the Greek playwright Aristophanes mentions lodging houses and bed bugs. These public taverns/inns were dirty and had a reputation of ill repute (Borchgrevink, 1999).

At its peak, the Roman Empire (27 BC to AD 476) had conquered lands surrounding the Mediterranean and large parts of today's Europe. To connect this empire, the Romans established excellent road systems that were used by business, pleasure, and military travelers. Roman military presence provided security for travelers throughout the system. Inns and taverns were established every 30 miles along the more than 51,000 miles of road. Major cities had larger sized hotels that were usually owned and managed by the municipal government. The ruins of Pompeii, destroyed in AD 79, reveal many *hospitea* and *caupona* (inns or hotels that provided lodging, and sometimes a basic menu of wine, bread, and meat). When the Roman Empire fell (AD 476), protection for travelers disappeared and trade and the innkeeping business came to a standstill (Lundberg, 1989).

After the fall of the Roman Empire, western civilization entered a period between classical antiquity and the Renaissance (approximately AD 500 to 1500) called the **Middle Ages.** The first part of this period was a severely impoverished time and is known as the Dark Ages (AD 476 to 1000). It was a period in European history marked by repressiveness and a lack of enlightenment or advanced knowledge. While civilizations flourished elsewhere, notably in Asia and the Arabic world, trade and travel within the formerly secure Roman Empire was now unsafe and occurred infrequently.

The Middle Ages is also a term that, in addition to referring to the entire period between the fall of Rome and the Renaissance, is used to refer specifically to the later half of this time, approximately AD 1000 to AD 1500. During this time and the final part of the Dark Ages, Christianity was the unifying cultural force in Europe and religious pilgrimage became the primary travel motivation. Monasteries and other religious houses accommodated the few travelers who ventured onto the roads. Monasteries did not charge for accommodations but expected the traveler to make a "donation" based upon their wealth when they departed.

Throughout this period, trade significantly declined and so did the middle-class population (merchants, traders, etc). This was the time of the feudal system where there were two classes of people: a small wealthy, powerful ruling class (nobility, military, and clergy) and a larger poor, weak working class (slaves, serfs, servants, freemen, workers, artisans, and craftsmen). In Europe, the working class did not travel and, as a result, hospitality establishments declined during the Middle Ages.

Then, in AD 1095, Pope Urban II summoned all of the Christians of Europe to undertake a military expedition to recover the Holy Land from the Muslims. Known as the **Crusades,** these expeditions continued over the next several hundred years and ended in the early 1300s. Exposure to the advanced and flourishing culture of the Arabs significantly influenced the returning European Crusaders and stimulated a social and economic revolution. Trade began to expand again and along with it, middle-class merchants began to emerge. With increasing wealth, numbers of people began traveling and inns were once again in demand. Beginning in Northern Italy around 1282, guilds of innkeepers flourished and established rules and regulations for themselves and for their guests. In Italy, innkeeping became a solid business.

Lodging Products of the Period.   The lodging accommodations of the period were private homes, monasteries, taverns/inns, and caravanserais.

1500 to 1650

Supply and Demand Interaction.   By the mid-1600s, the economic and social stagnation of the Middle Ages was replaced by the **Renaissance Period** (French for "rebirth"). This was the revival of art, literature, and learning. It was an era of discovery and exploration when Columbus, Magellan, and Da Gama explored the "edges" of the world. It was an era of emerging nation-states and the beginning of a revolution in trade. In this era scholarly pursuits stretched beyond the control of the church.

Nation-states arose, each with their own military to patrol and control their roads and geography, and once again, travel and trade grew rapidly. As you should now be able to predict, so too did the need for commercial hospitality establishments. By the mid-1400s, innkeeping began to grow rapidly and gained reputable standing in England. Some of these inns had as many as 30 rooms. Earlier inns had primarily been alehouses offering scant accommodations. English common law formalized the industry, declaring inns to be "public houses" and imposing responsibilities on innkeepers regarding their guests' wellbeing. The law required that an inn receive all who presented themselves in reasonable condition and were willing to pay a reasonable price for accommodations. This law continues today and is known as an inn's **affirmative duty.**

Monasteries still provided accommodations to a minority of traveling needy poor and influential wealthy; however, they could not handle the growing numbers of middle-class travelers. The increasingly well off middle class began to patronize commercial establishments. In the 1500s, the Reformation (the establishment of Protestant churches "reformed" from the Catholic Church) also helped the growth of commercial hospitality establishments. In 1539, King Henry VIII closed the monasteries and gave their land to his supporters in England. Public houses, inns, and taverns flourished (Lundberg, 1989 & Borchgrevink, 1999).

During this period, the New World was being colonized. In the early 1500s, the Spanish followed Columbus' 1492 voyage to America by establishing footholds in what are now the south and western United States, not to mention the Caribbean and Latin and South America. Though this stimulated trade, it also opened the doors for commercial and environmental exploitation of the peoples and lands of the New World and the lasting scars of the slave trade. Over the next centuries, other colonial powers such as France, England, and Holland established colonies in Canada and along the eastern coast of America, drawn by the bounty available. Travel across the often-dangerous Atlantic became more common.

In 1620, a band of Puritans from England established a colony in Plymouth, Massachusetts. These "Pilgrims" had left England to escape religious persecution.

Lodging Products of the Period. The lodging accommodations of the period were private homes, monasteries, taverns/inns, and caravanserais. Taverns and inns were expanding in size and numbers with the increase in numbers of middle-class travelers.

1650 to 1800

Supply and Demand Interaction. One of the greatest impacts on inns was the advent of stagecoach travel. Though you may think of the stagecoach as something from the American West, the first stagecoach was English—and traveled from Chester to London in 1657. Much later, the first American stagecoach route was established between Boston and Hartford in 1783. In England, for the next 170 years until train travel replaced it, the stagecoach was the dominant means of travel. Along with the stagecoach came the growth of roads and coaching inns to accommodate travelers along the routes. These inns provided not only food, drink, lodging, and entertainment for their guests but also spare coach horses, fodder, and stables. Coach travel was slow, rough, and at times dangerous, but was often the only alternative available. The relative comfort of the coach inns was a welcome respite from the demands of travel. While difficult, coach travel was so important in connecting the country, that in 1784 the English Parliament awarded stagecoach companies the job of providing postal service.

During this period, mostly in large cities, there were different levels of lodging facilities available. They discriminated based on the apparent wealth and status of travelers. The highest level wanted to attract only those people who were wealthy enough to own a horse. These inns often posted a sign saying, "No Coaches." The next level, a lower quality "**stagecoach inn,**" would welcome stagecoach travelers, but posted a sign saying, "No Open Wagons." Finally, if people were so poor as to be traveling by foot, it would almost be impossible for them to find an inn, and they would be left to seeking shelter wherever they could find it.

Outside the cities and along the stage route there was only one inn at a given stop; thus all travelers would use the same facility. Yet, as today, there were distinctions between social classes. Some people had their own rooms while others slept in communal beds (Borchgrevink, 1999).

Lodging Products of the Period.   The lodging accommodations of the period were private homes, monasteries, taverns/inns, and the newly added "stagecoach inns." Within major cities, taverns and inns were expanding in number and in the various levels of quality.

1800 to 1900

Supply and Demand Interaction.   By 1850, the western world had experienced the Industrial Revolution. This revolution did not uniformly occur worldwide, however. It first occurred in England and Western Europe and then spread to America almost 50 years later. This social and economic revolution was the catalyst by which today's wealthy and developed nations evolved from nations of artisans and farmers to nations of manufacturers. Through trade and commerce, the Industrial Revolution produced great wealth and prosperity for these western nations. This prosperity and increased trade led to increased travel and the need for hospitality establishments.

With the Industrial Revolution came the introduction of the railroad and rail travel. The railroad had a greater impact on the growth of hospitality establishments than its predecessor, the stagecoach. The introduction of the railroad was the beginning of the rapid demise of the stagecoach inns, as travelers chose more direct and faster conveyance.

Railroad transportation stimulated the development of railroad lodging facilities that were located near train stations, usually near the center of cities. In 1838, the English Parliament dealt the deathblow to the stagecoach inns by giving the postal service business to the railroads.

As in England and Europe, railroad travel stimulated rapid growth in travel and trade in America. Travel was faster now and linked major cities that were the centers of commerce. In the period from 1829 until the start of the Civil War in 1860, hotels opened at the fastest pace ever in America. Only in the 1920s would this pace of development be exceeded (Borchgrevink, 1999). Two lodging innovations evolved during this time: (a) a newer form and larger hospitality lodging facility: the *hotel* and (b) the destination resort.

Hotels.   Hotels were designed with the travelers' comfort in mind and, due to increasing competition, amenities and guest comforts became more sophisticated. The **hotel** of this period became a kind of showcase for the latest technological developments. These developments included such innovations as: central heating,

Exhibit 2.3   The route taken by railroads greatly affected the placement of hotels. (Photo courtesy of Grand Canyon Railway)

Exhibit 2.4   Many great hotels of the 1800s found their way into history books—first electric lights, first complete elevator service, etc. (*Courtesy:* Palmer House Hilton, Chicago, Illinois)

elevators, electric lights, and telephones. These hotels were the first American "Grand Hotels." The following are some examples of the newer and larger American hotels of this period:

- **1794, The City Hotel, New York City.** With 73 rooms, it was large for this period and built specifically for travelers. Prior to this time, most lodging properties in America were converted homes.
- **1829, The Tremont Hotel, Boston.** This hotel was the first grand hotel built in America. It was very different from the inns and hotels that preceded it and was modern even by today's standards. It had 170 rooms. It was the first hotel that promised all guests their own room. Up until this time it was still common for men and women, even if not traveling together, to share the same room. It was the first hotel to offer indoor toilets.
- **1836, The Astor House, New York City.** This hotel was built by the business tycoon John Jacob Astor. In effect, it was built as New York's rival to Boston's Tremont. With 309 rooms, it had all of the features of the luxurious Tremont plus more. It created, and for 10 years held, a new standard for luxury.
- **1835, The Tremont House, Chicago.** This hotel was built to capitalize on the name of the Tremont of Boston. It had 300 rooms. It burned down twice, and the third Tremont House was built in 1849. The current Tremont House in Chicago was built in 1923 and has 129 rooms.
- **1853, Mount Vernon Hotel, Cape May, New Jersey.** This hotel is notable because it was the first hotel that provided its guests with private baths. In England, the Savoy Hotel in London was the first European hotel to do the same in 1889.

- **1875, The Palace Hotel, San Francisco.** With 755 rooms, this hotel claimed to be the world's largest nonseasonal hotel (operated all year). This hotel burned down in the famous 1906 earthquake.
- **1870, Palmer House, Chicago.** This hotel was advertised as the only fire-proof hotel in the world, yet it burned down in the great Chicago fire on October 8, 1871. It was rebuilt even more extravagantly following the fire. The current Palmer House with 2,250 rooms was built in 1925. It has been a Hilton Hotel since 1946.
- **1893, Waldorf Hotel, New York City.** This 530-room, 13-story hotel was built on the site where the residence of William B. Astor had been. In 1897, John Jacob Astor IV built a 17-story Astor House on an adjacent lot. These two hotels were combined into the 1,000-room Waldorf-Astoria. It was considered to be the most luxurious hotel in the world. The original Waldorf-Astoria stood only for a relatively short time: 38 years. In 1931, the Empire State Building was built on its original site. Today's Waldorf-Astoria opened in 1931, featuring 2,000 rooms in two 47-floor towers (Borchgrevink, 1999).

Resort Hotels.   The resort hotel concept originated in Rome in the second century AD, when the wealthy traveled to natural spas and to escape the heat of the Roman summer. In the 1600s, leading Pilgrims relaxed at the colonies' first resort at Stafford Springs, Connecticut. Through the 1800s, the concept of the large destination resort evolved. Notable examples are:

- **1832, The Homestead, Hot Springs, Virginia.** This resort offered 600 rooms, three golf courses, and claims to possess the oldest golf tee (hole) in the United States.

Exhibit 2.5   The original Waldorf-Astoria was called the most luxurious hotel in the world in its first incarnation (circa 1895). Today, the art deco–style building (circa 1929) is still home to top-notch service and some of the world's most elite boutiques, all in the heart of Manhattan. (*Courtesy:* Waldorf-Astoria)

- **1857, The Greenbriar Hotel, White Sulfur Springs, West Virginia.** With 700 rooms, this luxurious resort was originally owned by the Chesapeake & Ohio Railroad.
- **1887, The Grand Hotel, Mackinaw Island, Michigan.** This 275-room hotel is located on Lake Huron, one of the Great Lakes. It was originally opened as "the largest summer resort in the world." It is located on an island three miles long and two miles wide. To preserve its relaxing quiet, even today, no automobiles are allowed on the island (Lang and Dupre, 1997).

The lodging industry of the 1800s reflects the changing economic landscape. First, new and larger railroad hotels evolved from the stagecoach inns. Second, with the Industrial Revolution, America and Western Europe became increasing wealthy. Hotels on both continents competed for this increasing wealth with amenities and luxury; they became known as "***Grand Hotels.***" Similarly, increasing wealth supported the new luxury destination resorts.

Lodging Products of the Period.   The new types of lodging products added in this period were: railroad hotels, "Grand Hotels," and luxurious seasonal destination resorts.

1900 to 1945

Supply and Demand Interaction.   During the early 1900s, new approaches in the lodging industry were introduced: the business hotel and the hotel chain; the roadside cabin, the modern day "stagecoach inn"; and the casino destination.

The business hotel and hotel chain.   The following are notable examples:

- **1908, The Statler Chain, The Buffalo Statler, Buffalo, NY.** Ellsworth M. Statler (1863–1928) was a pioneer in creating hotels not for luxury guests, but for the needs of the businessman and the growing middle class. His first hotel provided the basic comforts and conveniences at an affordable price. This was the second hotel in the world to offer private baths in all rooms. Statler put telephones and radios in each room and provided a free daily newspaper in the morning. Statler is also credited with starting the ***hotel chain.*** He controlled more hotels than anyone in the world by his death in 1928.

Exhibit 2.6   Although houseboats have been around through many eras, in many countries, the idea of renting houseboats as a form of recreational lodging is believed to have emerged in the United States the early 1900s. Today, thousands of houseboats are available for rental or for shared ownership. This one features four queen-size beds and a queen sofa sleeper. (Photo courtesy of Forever Resorts)

- **1919, The Hilton Chain, The Mobley Hotel, Cisco, Texas.** Conrad Hilton (1887–1979) was another pioneer in the hotel business. The Mobley was his first hotel in a hotel chain that would grow to seven properties by 1929. During the depression, he lost several, but began to rebuild after that. In 1946, he formed the Hilton Hotels Corporation. In 1949, he purchased the 2000-room Waldorf-Astoria and created an international hotel subsidiary, Hilton International. In 1954, he purchased the Statler chain.

- **1926, The Marriott Chain, A & W Root Beer Franchise, Washington, D.C. (renamed, Hot Shoppes).** The Marriott Corporation began as a food business. J. Willard Marriott, with his wife Alice and partner Hugh Colton, worked hard and saved enough over ten years to open seven more Hot Shoppes. After landing a contract with Eastern Airlines to prepare box lunches for their crews, the business expanded into airline feeding. In 1957, they opened the 370-room *Twin Bridges Motor Hotel* in Washington, D.C., the first Marriott Hotel. Today, Marriott International is the world's third largest hotel chain in number of rooms and has 2,600 lodging properties, including ownership of the Ritz-Carlton chain and Renaissance Hotels.

- **1937, The Sheraton Chain, Stonehaven Hotel, Springfield, Massachusetts.** Entrepreneurs and Harvard classmates, Ernest Henderson and Robert Lowell Moore founded the Sheraton Corporation. Stonehaven, the first Sheraton hotel, was a 200-room property. By 1939, they had acquired a total of four properties and identified them with the Sheraton name. In 1947, the Sheraton Corporation was the first hotel company listed on the New York Stock Exchange. It was the first to use a telex system for room reservations in 1948. The corporation was sold to the ITT Corporation in 1968 and in 1998 it was purchased by Starwood Hotels & Resorts Worldwide. Starwood has 850 properties and about 232,000 rooms.

Roadside cabins.   The advent of the automobile and its widespread affordability during the "Roaring Twenties" prompted the invention of the prototype of the 1950s motel. With a relatively primitive road system, these **roadside cabins** offered minimal accommodations. During this time the word **motel** first came into use by a quirk in an electric sign advertising one of these roadside cabins: In 1924, when roadside cabins were in vogue, James Vail's cabins on Route 101 in San Luis Obispo, California, were called "Motel Inn." He erected an electric sign with the word "_OTEL," with the sign being programmed to flash the letters "H" and "M" alternatively, thus introducing the hotel industry's first use of the word "motel" (Lang and Dupre, 1997, p. 23).

Casinos.   In 1931, Nevada legalized gambling and with it, the modern era of gambling, casinos, and the rise of hotels to accommodate this special form of demand had begun.

By 1945, the world had changed dramatically. The period of 1900 to 1945 was an extremely turbulent one. World War I was fought from 1914 to 1918, and the post-war years of the "Roaring 20s" were a period of personal over-consumption and business euphoria; these years witnessed the fastest pace of American hotel development to date. The 1920s have been called "the golden age of hotels." The period witnessed the opening of many downtown hotels, and many hotels enjoyed

Exhibit 2.7   The Venetian Hotel and Casino in Las Vegas is one of the latest and most elegant extravaganzas in a long line that started when Nevada legalized gambling in 1931. (Photos courtesy of the Venetian Resort Hotel Casino)

guest occupancy averaging 80 percent or more. The 1920s growth pace was a short-lived 10 years and was curtailed by the 1930s Great Depression, followed by World War II (1939 to 1945). After the war, the United States was poised to dominate not only the world business culture, but also the world lodging industry.

U.S. Lodging Industry Dominance, 1945 to 2000

The following section focuses exclusively on the lodging industry in the United States. The focus will be on the international market of U.S.-based lodging companies and on the domestic developments within the U.S. lodging market. The discussion of each historical period is divided into three parts: international developments, domestic developments, and a brief summary of new lodging product innovations in each period.

1945 to 1950

International Developments.   Demand during this period was stimulated by U.S. government policy. The geographic focus of corporate lodging expansion was directed to Latin America. These efforts were initiated by the American imperative for economic development of lesser developed countries. As a part of his "good neighbor" policy toward Latin America, President Franklin D. Roosevelt encouraged several U.S. corporations to build hotels in that region. Roosevelt felt that this would assist economic performance of Latin American and Caribbean nations through increased tourism and foreign-exchange earnings from the United States.

Roosevelt stimulated supply, which had been inadequate, and demand followed. In 1946, Pan American Airlines created Inter-Continental Hotels and established its first international hotel in Brazil. In 1949, Hilton placed its first international hotel in Puerto Rico.

By the late 1940s, these and other chains were also beginning to expand into Europe, again benefiting from the U.S. policy of helping reconstruct war-torn economies of the European continent (Gee, 1994). Additionally, European reconstruction generated plenty of business for U.S. companies. Many U.S. WW II soldiers returned to Europe as economic "troops" on business. Having caught a glimpse of the glories of Europe's historic cultures, they also began to travel for pleasure—but Americans wanted clean and familiar accommodations. U.S.-based hotel chains recognized this need and accelerated international expansion.

Domestic Developments. Demand within U.S. borders began to expand slowly within the early post-war period. This expansion was widely welcomed because many had feared that the United States would enter a recession immediately following the war. Then U.S. demand for domestic travel began to increase. The war years and the depression decade of the 1930s had created pent-up demand. U.S. citizens had sacrificed and rationed resources for personal and national survival. After World War II, the economy steadily improved and people enjoyed shorter workweeks and rising levels of disposable income. The construction of highways accelerated and stimulated increased automobile travel.

Supply of lodging facilities increased to meet increasing demand. Before World War II, the U.S. lodging industry had been primarily dominated by one type of property: the city or town-center hotel. After the war, there was an accelerated activity in renovation and new construction of these hotels as they responded to increasing travel demand. Simultaneously, a new improved type of facility evolved from the primitive roadside cabins of the 1920s. The motel would become the ubiquitous lodging facility for the automobile traveler.

Lodging Products of the Period. The variety of lodging facilities was limited. There were roadside cabins/motels, country inns, city and railroad hotels, old grand hotels, and a few old and luxurious destination resorts. Roadside cabins were being upgraded to a new form, motels. Existing city hotels were renovated and new ones built. The pioneer hotel chains first ventured into the international arena.

1950 to 1960

International Developments. Demand focused on Europe in this period for three reasons: the continuation of the U.S. policy for rebuilding Europe; expanding U.S. business opportunities as Europeans regained purchasing power and demanded U.S. products; and the advent of "mass tourism."

Many U.S. multinational corporations were accelerating their penetration of international markets and this increased demand for international business travel. More Americans were traveling outside the United States as a result of increased income and the development of inexpensive and safe tour packages. In 1959, the

Boeing 707 had regularly scheduled transatlantic service, which reduced travel time to Europe by steamship and by propeller aircraft (13 hours) to 8 hours.

Supply by U.S.-based lodging chains responded by developing large, modern inner city hotels in such places as London, Paris, Rome, Athens, and Amsterdam. Gradually, long-distance travel, which had previously been available only to the relatively affluent, became accessible to the middle class, and mass travel and hotel development soared (Gee, 1994, p. 31).

Domestic Developments.   On the demand side, in 1956 the Interstate Highway Act was passed to establish a network of national highways. This further stimulated automobile travel and subsequent demand for more and better motels.

Supply responded to automobile travel demand with an improved motel but also introduced a revolutionary concept to the lodging industry's structure: ***franchising.*** Compared to hotels, early motels had very limited amenities. As motels grew in number, they began to add more services and amenities and began to look like hotels. To compete, hotels lowered room rates and the two segments began to appear similar. Yet a major problem existed with both hotels and motels during this period. None were standardized and lodging guests never knew what to expect of the services that they would receive when they checked in. In 1952, Kemmons Wilson and Wallace Johnson recognized the standardization problem. Their founding of Holiday Inn revolutionized the lodging industry by standardizing services, amenities, and prices. The Holiday Inn name on their chain of motels provided a recognizable brand that communicated this standardization.

Between 1945 and 1955, the first generation of hotels and motels had expanded mainly by owning the property outright or by acquiring the right to manage the hotel via management contracts. With Holiday Inn, the franchising concept was born and then copied by other lodging facilities as a tool of hotel/motel expansion (Singh, 1999).

Supply was also stimulated by a change in the 1954 income tax laws, which allowed accelerated depreciation. This led to lodging development decisions dictated not by the economics of the operation but by the tax savings offered by the hotel real estate venture (Rushmore, 1992). This problem would again appear in the turbulent 1980s.

Lodging Products of the Period.   A larger number of international hotels were built in more overseas locations. Motels and hotels upgraded their quality. Hotel chains were using management contracts and the newly invented franchising concept to expand growth.

1960 to 1970

International Developments.   Demand for international travel continued to focus on Europe and the developed world for the same reasons as during the 1950s. Meanwhile, the international environment was becoming more risky. The United States was in the midst of the Cold War with the Soviet Union. And, by 1965 the United States was firmly involved in Vietnam.

Supply by U.S. international hotel companies continued to focus on developments in large gateway and capital cities of Europe, since these properties would pose the lowest financial risks and attract the most investors. The general strategy

Exhibit 2.8   This Italian inn near Siena has a heritage dating back to the 1200s. It has managed to survive many wars, including World War II. You can imagine how the charm of such places stayed in the memories of American soldiers when they returned home . . . and why they wanted to return as tourists. (Photo by James L. Morgan, Scottsdale, AZ)

was to get the brand name established in large cities and then move into secondary markets and resort areas. Notable international developments in this period were:

- 1961, Sheraton goes international by opening a hotel in Tel Aviv.
- 1961, Hilton International, a subsidiary of Hilton Hotels, is sold and becomes a separately run company retaining the rights to use the "Hilton" name.
- 1967, Hilton International is purchased by Trans World Airlines (TWA) and is the first airline investment in the hotel business since Pan Am in 1946.
- 1969, Hyatt International is formed and opens its first hotel in Hong Kong.

Also, during this period, United Airlines purchased Westin Hotels and American Airlines began to acquire Americana Hotels. This activity was a strategy that was based on the theory that accommodations and transportation companies are synergistic and are more viable as a single company. In later years, the airlines began to divest their hotel companies; the strategy was not working as expected (Singh, 1999).

Domestic Developments.   Demand for travel continued to grow as population grew, incomes rose, and leisure time increased. Businesses began expanding outward to the suburbs. Supply responded in particular to this increased businesses activity with the introduction of the meeting and conventions market. Developers built new convention hotel products such as the New York Hilton in 1963 and the early "Conference Centers" in the mid-1960s.

Lodging Products of the Period.   More hotel chains entered the international arena during this period. One growth strategy used in this period was **vertical integration** where airlines purchased related industries in the supply chain; in this case, hotel firms. By purchasing hotel companies, airline companies initiated the first rounds of the merger and acquisition trend that has continued to accelerate and characterize the lodging industry today. The meeting and convention business became a similar target, inspiring the lodging industry to build convention hotels and conference centers. Growth by franchising accelerated in the 1960s.

1970 to 1980

International Developments.   Demand for hotel growth during this period came primarily from a world crisis. In 1973, the oil-producing countries formed a cartel (OPEC) and tripled world oil prices. Mexico, Venezuela, and others would later join this cartel. The new wealth encouraged economic development in these countries, including development to attract tourism.

Demand was also increased in the Asia/Pacific region. In 1975, the Vietnam War ended and in 1978, China opened its borders to foreign investment. Japan was quickly becoming an economic powerhouse. Hotel investment was fueled by numerous reports predicting the area as the fastest growing in the world.

The oil crisis of the early 1970s (and the recession at mid-decade) stifled U.S. international hotel chains from developing supply in Europe. They diverted their investment attention to new capital markets fostered by growing oil wealth in the Middle East. Oil-rich royal families built large and ultra-luxurious properties for them-

Exhibit 2.9   The Plaza, another landmark property in New York City (built circa 1907) is still the darling of celebs and executives. Its palatial ballrooms are considered *the* place for top-tier weddings, debuts, and society events. Eloise, the free-spirited heroine of children's books, lived at the Plaza. Many films have included scenes filmed in Plaza settings, including *Home Alone* and *Crocodile Dundee.* (Photos by Will Verbeeten, *Foto Verbeeten,* Groesbeek, The Netherlands)

selves and their business associates (Gee, 1994). This prosperity and hotel growth would slump along with oil prices in the 1980s. Since the region never diversified its economic base away from oil dependence and due to continued war and political uncertainty in the area, its tourism growth has remained stagnant up to today.

Supply in the Asian-Pacific region was developed by nearly every hotel chain of any stature. These new developments were typically large luxury hotels. In the late 1980s, this expansion suffered due to overbuilding and to fears generated by the 1989 Tiananmen Square crisis in China. Occupancies dropped to 20% and 30% levels overnight (Gee, 1994). The Asian-Pacific expansion would be dealt another severe blow in 1998 with the Asian financial crisis.

Domestic Developments.   Demand in the early 1970s was driven by optimistic and aggressive corporate growth strategies stimulated by the easy availability of financing. Many established chains hoped to establish a critical mass in the budget segment of the industry by aggressively selling franchises. Like economies of scale in manufacturing, if enough products are produced (budget properties), their price can be lowered and volume usage will increase. These aggressive corporate growth strategies attracted ready financing, but the bubble burst in 1973 with the Arab oil embargo and the ensuing energy crisis. Occupancies fell dramatically due to decreased travel. This was followed by a recession in 1975 (Singh, 1999).

Supply in the early 1970s was in an overbuilt condition (too many rooms for existing demand) due to the easy financing conditions. National occupancies dropped to 59 percent in 1972. The oil crisis and recession escalated these losses even further and new construction was stopped.

In the late 1970s, demand increased somewhat, which helped hotels that had managed to survive. They also saw an increase in their average daily rates (ADR), due to high inflation. Well-managed properties were positioned for a comeback, since new hotel construction had been curtailed by rising inflation and interest rates, making it too expensive to finance new hotels.

Meanwhile, in 1976, gambling was legalized in New Jersey, the second state to do so after Nevada in 1931. Casinos generated demand and these gamblers needed lodging accommodations.

In the late 1970s, supply essentially halted. With no increases in new room inventory and a slowly rising demand, hotels saw a period of increasing occupancies. Occupancies rose from 63.9 percent in 1975 to 72.6 percent in 1979 (Singh, 1999). Note that occupancies increased not because of a massive surge in demand, *but because hotel companies stopped building new supply.*

Lodging Products of the Period.   **Product segmentation** had its beginnings in this period. Product segmentation is a strategy that assumes that the mass market for lodging contains many sub-markets with distinct needs for such things as amenities and price ranges. It is assumed that if many different levels of lodging product are built, these will attract the corresponding sub-markets that desire the amenities offered. Product segmentation strategies are a clear sign of a *maturing* U.S. lodging industry.

By the late 1970s, the decade's supply/demand imbalance had sent a signal that the lodging companies would have to find new ways to grow, and product segmentation was the chosen strategy. They could not assume that future demand would automatically absorb supply. They had to become more creative in order to grow. Corporate chains first ventured into product segmentation by focusing on *budget* hotels and motels. Also, the ***all-suite hotel*** was pioneered in the late 1960s and early 1970s by Bob Wooley, a builder and founder of Granada Royale Hometels.

As we will see, in the 1980s the product segmentation strategy began to dominate the U.S. lodging industry. By the 1990s, this strategy had seemed to reach maturity, and various product segments had become overbuilt.

1980 to 1990

International Developments.   Demand for U.S. international hotel development in Europe was spurred in the late 1980s by the European Common Market's decision to further unify its members' economies, leading to what is today called the European Union. This unification was projected to create a stronger economic marketplace and more business activity.

The late 1980s also marked a significant turning point in the direction of international hotel investment. European, Japanese, and other foreign hotel chains began to invest in the United States. They were attracted to the United States by such factors as the stability of the economy and lower construction and operating costs as compared to other countries.

Comparatively cheap real estate in the United States was also a major attraction to foreign hotel corporations, especially European and Japanese. Hotel real estate prices were depressed from massive bankruptcies of commercial real estate properties and the S&L crisis of the late '80s, making them attractive investments.

Supply by U.S. international chains such as Ramada and Marriott entered a "second wave" of European investment into major European cities (the first wave had begun in the 1950s, but essentially dried up during the 1970s).

A significant change in investment patterns occurred during the late 1980s. Investment by foreign-based hotel chains into the United States took the form of ***mergers and acquisitions.*** For example: Holiday Inn was merged with Bass PLC (where the parent company is English). Westin Hotels was acquired outright by Aoki corporation of Japan, Inter-Continental was acquired by Seibu Saison of Japan, and Travelodge was acquired by Forte PLC of England.

As we will discuss later, mergers and acquisitions, along with product segmentation, are the major trends affecting the U.S. lodging industry today.

Domestic Developments.   Demand for hotel development in the 1980s was a result of U.S. government income tax incentives for real estate investments. This incentive provided easy financing for often-questionable hotel projects. Real lodging demand by real people was masked by financing incentives, which led to an oversupply of lodging product. As a result, the 1980s was a turbulent period. The decade began with a building ***boom*** and ended with a ***bust.*** This provided a sharp lesson in what makes building a new hotel feasible—and a reminder to starry-eyed investors to look closely at real demand. Here is part of the dynamic that led to such hard times for hotels in the 1980s.

When profits are assisted by outside forces such as lower interest rates or subsidies by the ***government (tax incentives),*** then the economic occupancy (the level at which new construction can be profitable and can be justified) is lowered. With the tax incentives of the early 1980s, new construction could be justified at 59.5 percent. When these tax incentives were removed in 1986, the economic occupancy rose to 70 percent. In the early '80s, the lodging industry constructed hotels on the basis of a lower economic occupancy and in the late '80s had to

Exhibit 2.10   As you can readily see, a standard guest room at a Four Seasons is anything but "standard." The room shown is from their Tokyo property. (*Courtesy:* Four Seasons Hotels and Resorts)

perform at higher occupancies to stay in business. Since real demand did not exist to support these higher occupancies, a bust was in the making (Singh, 1999).

The overbuilding boom was spurred by three major factors: tax incentives, availability of capital, and product segmentation.

First, tax incentives were the result of the Economic Recovery Tax Act (ERTA), which went into effect in 1981. Investment in commercial real estate became very attractive as the ERTA cut corporate, individual, and capital gains taxes. Depreciation rules were also changed which made commercial real estate, including hotels, profitable on an after-tax basis. As a result, capital investment was diverted to non-economic deals: Hotels were not operated for normal business profits; they were developed and operated for the tax savings potential.

Second, availability of capital was expanded through the Depository Institutions Deregulation and Monetary Control Act of 1980 (DIDMCA) and the Garn-St. Germain Depository Institutions Act of 1982. These laws deregulated the Savings and Loan (S&L) industry and allowed them to make commercial real estate loans for the first time in history. The existing S&Ls were inexperienced in lending for commercial projects and new S&Ls, often formed by real estate developers, made risky, imprudent, and often-fraudulent loans.

Third, the strategy of product segmentation that first began in the 1970s was now being pursued by almost every major hotel chain. Development of new lodging products was believed to be the only way to grow. In 1991, the Hotel Motel Brokers of America (HMBA) summarized the overbuilding of the 1980s as follows: ". . . franchisers created new products for developers to build; lenders had capital to lend; and developers could acquire capital on 'soft' terms with construction profits financed as part of the package" (Singh, 1999, p. 169). Demand for lodging products in the 1980s was artificial and could not be sustained.

The bust, in essence, was the reversal of the same three factors that had originally driven demand: Tax incentives were rescinded in the 1986 Tax Reform Act (TRA); S&Ls became insolvent because developers with no tax incentives could not repay the risky loans; and there was not enough real lodging demand to fill the overbuilt, product segmented hotel supply. With the bust, hotels competed with each other by deeply cutting room rates. This slashed profits and hotels and other real estate investments went bankrupt. The Federal Resolution Trust Corporation (RTC) was established to sell off these bankrupt properties at fire sale prices.

Supply in this period was characterized by conditions of overextension and overbuilding. From 1983 to 1987, the annual growth was over 4 percent per year and this accelerated to over 7 percent per year in 1987. By the late 1980s, the message had sunk in and new hotel construction came to a halt.

Lodging Products of the Period.   While many of the product segmentation ideas were concepts searching for a market and became overbuilt, some that were developed remain healthy today. Two examples are the all-suite concept and the extended-stay product.

As mentioned earlier, Bob Wooley pioneered the all-suite concept beginning in the late 1970s. By the 1980s, most hotel chains had their own versions of the all-suite hotel, and this product has been the fastest growing product segment since its introduction.

The extended-stay hotel targets travelers who stay for longer periods; for example, for relocation purposes or on business for long-term projects. It offers a homelike atmosphere. An example is Marriott's Residence Inns. Today, most major hotel chains have a version of this product in their portfolios.

1990 to 2000

International Developments.   Demand for travel dipped again during the 1990 to 1991 Gulf War. A brief recession in the early 1990s further reduced worldwide business travel. After the recession, the United States entered a period of unprecedented and sustained economic growth. Meanwhile, political troubles and regional war erupted in the Balkans, and Asia teetered on the brink of financial collapse in the late 1990s. Supply in the international area flattened as economic and political uncertainty stalled investment.

Domestic Developments.   Travel demand was negatively affected by the recession of 1990, which had resulted from the excesses of the 1980s. The national occupancy level bottomed out at 61.8 percent in 1991 and was still far below the necessary economic occupancy of 70 percent. Hoteliers held their breath as occupancies began to slowly move up, though not by much (in 1992 they'd moved up less than one point, to 62.6 percent). But it showed that demand could increase if there was no significant increase in hotel supply. Through various financing restructuring, the industry slowly climbed toward eventual health by the end of the decade.

In their February 1999 report, PricewaterhouseCoopers forecast a soft landing of the U.S. economy in 1999 that would mean slower growth (2.1 percent) and smaller room rate increases of the U.S. lodging industry. In their July 1999 report, they noted that the U.S. economy was showing a surprising robust performance for 1999, which prompted them to increase their forecast. PricewaterhouseCoopers then expected room demand to increase by 3.3 percent.

Exhibit 2.11   Read what Four Seasons says about the role of their concierges; "*Thrive on spontaneity? Four Seasons is ever at your call—to book a dinner reservation, arrange theatre tickets, or assist with travel plans. Every Concierge is a deep well-spring of insider's information, just waiting for you to tap.*" Note the "Les Clef d'Or" pin on the Concierge's right lapel—indicating he is among a select group of well-experienced and well-reputed concierges. (*Courtesy:* Four Seasons Hotels and Resorts)

Supply of lodging inventory, still overflowing from the 1980s, remained in an overbuilt condition into the early 1990s. Properties were foreclosed, merged, acquired, and loans were restructured through 1992. After this time, the lodging industry began a slow recovery to health by 1999. Yet, as evidenced by extensive product segmentation practiced by all major hotel chain brands, the industry has reached maturity in its life cycle: The growth rate has slowed down.

For those who were listening, the PricewaterhouseCoopers report noted that investors were still overoptimistically adding rooms to the market (150,600 in 1997 and 149,300 in 1998) and therefore occupancies and ADRs would drop probably through 2000.

Lodging Products of the Period.   The growth strategy of product segmentation was polished to an art form in the l980s and continued into the 1990s. Product segmentation is a strategy of acquiring market share by expanding the number of and size of specialized market *niches.*

As the industry matured and demand for new product niches slowed, the major hotel brands looked to and began to practice another growth strategy: *consolidation.* Consolidation through mergers and acquisitions is a strategy of cannibalization where larger and stronger firms swallow-up smaller and weaker firms. The rationale here is that consolidated "**mega-chains**" can achieve improved performance and economies of scale and thus can more easily penetrate global markets (a necessity for growth when domestic markets are mature). The larger firms that initiate the consolidation have more access to both debt and equity capital. This is especially true if their own stock prices have been highly valued in the stock market. Often they use the value of their own stock to acquire the other company. In the 1990s, there were a large number of mega-mergers and acquisition activity. Two representative examples were the major acquisitions by Starwood of both the Westin chain and the Sheraton chain, and Patriot American's acquisitions of the Wyndham chain and Interstate Hotels and subsequent selling off some properties and the renaming of Patriot American to Wyndham Hotels and Resorts. These acquiring hotel companies were virtually unknown in the 1980s but now rank among the top 10 largest hotel chains in the world. The consolidation strategy recognizes that there is plenty of hotel product to buy since the industry was overbuilt in the 1980s and that it is cheaper to buy than to build today (Singh, 1999).

2000 and Beyond   The lodging industry hoped for health by 2000, and was slowly recuperating. Then, the unexpected struck and terrorism dashed hopes again. After the devastation of the World Trade Center in New York City, September 11, 2001, and the use of hijacked passenger planes as gigantic missiles, world tourism came to a crawl. People expressed fear of assembling in high-profile locations such as major convention centers, international airports, public monuments, cruise ships, and gaming centers, such as Las Vegas. Health scares from planted anthrax spores and the "quarantine" of cities in China and Canada after the appearance of SARS (severe acute respiratory syndrome) also depressed travel. A war in Iraq and other Middle Eastern military actions and a subsequent uneasiness about world fuel prices and availability further decreased international travel. At this writing, domestic travel has picked up, as has auto and train travel in the European Community. Destination resorts and recreation areas may be seeing longer stays by guests who are converting their international flight time and fare into longer stays, nearer to home. Barring more large-scale threats and crises, the travel industry expects a return to recuperation, and hopefully sustainable expansion.

In the background, though, consolidation continues. Small resorts and family-owned destination properties, some owned for decades, are being bought up by companies intent on expanding their portfolios. Some observers expect globalization and consolidation through mergers and acquisitions to continue unabated into the near future. Currently, the big fish are eating smaller fish. After this round, the newly consolidated bigger mega-chains will, in turn, feed on newly consolidated but smaller mega-chains. However, for us to extrapolate past trends into the future may be too simplistic. Certainly, the preceding history has demonstrated that the lodging industry has continuously mutated and evolved into new forms.

Other observers speculate on the continuous changing nature of demand and its effect on the shape and form of lodging supply. Will travelers demand an entirely new form of lodging? Will they want a more personal touch when they travel, given their growing dependence on keyboard-to-keyboard (not face-to-face) communications through cyberspace? Will they take the same number of trips if more business is conducted electronically? Will they demand lodging at all, as we enter more deeply into the age of virtuality?

What is the shape of the lodging industry's future? It will be different! Where there is change, there is opportunity. This change and dynamism presents a fantastic future for today's young people.

LODGING: DIMENSIONS SHAPED BY SUPPLY AND DEMAND

Successful lodging facilities and their managements are not only attuned to their customers, they know how to acquire them and, most importantly, how to *keep* them. As you can see from the above, successful managers think about how their customers might be changing and who their new customers might be. To be a successful lodging facility manager, you must become a marketing- and customer-oriented person.

The second half of this chapter can assist you in reaching this goal; it provides information organized around four discussion sections.

- An overview of the lodging industry
- The tourism system and lodging supply
- The demand side of the lodging industry
- How marketing brings together supply and demand

Overview of the Lodging Industry

The goal of all businesses is to link or match supply with demand; hotels (who have supply) want to sell rooms and other services to guests (who provide demand). Bringing supply and demand together to make a profit is essential for any business.

Supply, in a service industry like lodging, is a ***holistic concept***; that is, it must be considered as a whole or system, not simply as disconnected pieces of a puzzle. Supply consists of tangibles, such as hotel type and physical amenities, and intangibles, such as the many personal services provided by the lodging staff.

Demand, or customer wants-and-needs, is always changing and varied. There are many customer groups, referred to as ***market segments,*** which demand certain types of lodging facilities to satisfy their specific needs. As you saw in the historic portion of this chapter, the lodging industry has adapted by designing and building many types of facilities to appeal to different segments.

Today, if you want to climb the corporate lodging ladder, you must intimately understand the link between customer needs and the services your company can provide. And you must understand something about the dynamics of the world's tourism system, since the lodging industry is a subset of it.

There are two important premises to state before this discussion continues:

- Lodging exists in an increasingly competitive environment.
- Customers are becoming increasingly demanding.

Given these two conditions, you can see that, to succeed, hotels must consistently provide quality experiences to demanding customers. If they do not, their competitors will. Since customer demands are continually increasing, hotels must continually improve their services, or they will fall behind.

Suppose customer couple X loved your hotel and its service when they stayed there five years ago. Even if you could somehow wrap your staff and building into a magical cocoon and keep it unchanged for five years, couple X, if they visited again, would probably find it lacking in some ways. It wouldn't be simply a case of lagging technology, or not-quite-stylish room decor; couple X would be slightly disenchanted because they have had half a decade to become more sophisticated. Their needs have changed. Perhaps, five years ago, they had no children. Consequently, your lack of babysitting services or an in-room Play Station® or Nintendo® went unnoticed. Perhaps, when last they visited, they were focused on business meetings and didn't care that there was no nearby shopping Mecca to explore or latte shop to laze in. Whatever the reasons, while you were tucked away in your cocoon, you lost touch with your customer base and are now no longer attuned to its needs.

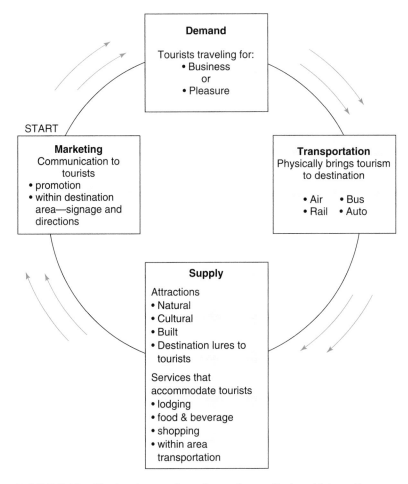

Exhibit 2.12   The tourism system shows the cyclical and interactive connection between marketing, demand, transportation, and supply. (Modified from R. C. Mill and A. M. Morrison, *The Tourist System: An Introductory Text.* Englewood Cliffs, NJ. Prentice Hall, 1993)

The Tourism System

Before discussing the supply side (the specific products and services offered by the lodging industry), let's consider an overview of the ***tourism system*** to see the lodging industry's location in this broader system (see Exhibit 2.12). Note that supply consists of two elements: *attractions* that lure travelers, and *service facilities* that include the lodging industry. Demand consists of travelers who can be grouped as business travelers and pleasure travelers.

Marketing is a process that builds a link between supply and demand, as we'll discuss later in this chapter.

Exhibit 2.13 also shows a less common "hopscotch" method whereby wholesale intermediaries skip over retail intermediaries to sell directly to the final customer. This is represented by the broken line between wholesale intermediaries and final customers.

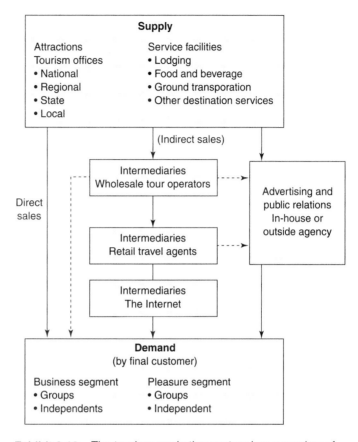

Supply

Attractions	Service facilities
Tourism offices	• Lodging
• National	• Food and beverage
• Regional	• Ground transporation
• State	• Other destination services
• Local	

(Indirect sales)

Direct sales

Intermediaries
Wholesale tour operators

Advertising and
public relations
In-house or
outside agency

Intermediaries
Retail travel agents

Intermediaries
The Internet

Demand
(by final customer)

Business segment	Pleasure segment
• Groups	• Groups
• Independents	• Independent

Exhibit 2.13   The tourism marketing system has a number of intermediaries that connect supply and demand.

Scope of Lodging Supply

Global Scope   As indicated in Exhibit 2.12, lodging facilities are a component of total tourism supply. The lodging industry is made up of more than simply resorts, hotels, motor hotels, motels, and bed-and-breakfast inns; it also includes alternative lodging forms such as cruise ships, tourist courts, sporting and recreation camps, motor home parks, houseboats, pensions, hostels, and campsites for transients.

The World Travel and Tourism Council has the impossible job of attempting to compile tourism statistics to account for all forms of worldwide lodging accommodations. While it's relatively easy to track properties that are parts of chains or consortia, keeping track of small inns and independent properties is certainly a challenge. While we tend to think of hotels as being at least 100 rooms and know that mega-resorts in Las Vegas and elsewhere have thousands of rooms (5044 guest rooms, suites, villas and skylofts at the MGM Grand, currently the world's largest), the average-size lodging facility in the world is more like 37 rooms. About two-thirds of lodging facilities are located in the European Union, the United States, and Canada. The rest of the world accounts for around 30 percent of the facilities. This could change if rampant growth in Southeast Asia continues. In 2006, nearly 200 new hotels were under construction in China, two-thirds of which are planned as four- or five-star properties with more than 200 rooms.

Exhibit 2.14   Motel 6, a simple, no-frills product, enjoys strong demand in the economy (budget) sector of the lodging market. (*Courtesy:* Motel 6 Corporation)

Recent estimates suggest there are about 314,000 lodging facilities worldwide. The world's top chains and corsortia are estimated to control perhaps 29 percent of this inventory. Compared to the worldwide average-size property of 37 rooms, the average corporate or consortia property is 125 rooms.

Note in Exhibit 2.16 that 25 of the world's top 50 hotel chains are based in the United States. Ten other countries are home to the remaining top 50 hotel chains: Belgium, Canada, England, France, Germany, The Netherlands, Spain, Japan, China, and Hong Kong.

Exhibit 2.15   The sail-shaped structure of The Burj Al Arab Hotel, in Dubai, makes it look as if it could catch the next breeze out onto the adjacent Arabian Gulf. This elegant resort, part of the small Jumeirah portfolio, has 202 duplex (two-story) suites, each of which has one, two, or three bedrooms. Two sources have named it The Best Hotel in the World. (Photo by Peter Ginter, Bilderberg, Aurora)

Exhibit 2.16 Top 50 corporate hotel chains.
Hotels' Corporate 50 Ranking

Rank	Company Headquarters	Rooms	Hotels
1	InterContinental Hotels Group Windsor, Berkshire, England	534,202	3,540
2	Cendant Corp. Parsippany, N.J. USA	520,860	6,396
3	Marriott International Washington, D.C. USA	482,186	2,632
4	Accor Paris, France	463,427	3,973
5	Choice Hotels International Silver Spring, Md. USA	403,806	4,977
6	Hilton Hotels Corp. Beverly Hills, Calif. USA	358,408	2,259
7	Best Western International Phoenix, Ariz. USA	309,236	4,114
8	Starwood Hotels & Resorts Worldwide White Plains, N.Y. USA	230,667	733
9	Global Hyatt Corp. Chicago, Ill. USA	147,157	818
10	Carlson Hospitality Worldwide Minneapolis, Minn. USA	147,093	890
11	Hilton Group plc Watford, Herts, England	102,636	403
12	TUI AG/TUI Hotels & Resorts Hannover, Germany	81,398	285
13	Sol Meliá SA Palma de Mallorca, Spain	80,834	328
14	Extended Stay Hotels Spartanburg, S.C. USA	72,981	654
15	Interstate Hotels & Resorts Arlington, Va. USA	68,242	306
16	Louvre Hotels (Societe du Louvre) Paris, France	66,834*	887*
17	La Quinta Corp. Irving, Texas USA	65,110	592
18	Golden Tulip Hospitality/THL Amersfoort, Netherlands	52,148	534
19	Wyndham International Dallas, Texas USA	42,900	157
20	FelCor Lodging Trust Irving, Texas USA	40,000	143
21	Rezidor SAS Hospitality Brussels, Belgium	39,353	190
22	Hospitality Properties Trust Newton, Mass. USA	38,489	285
23	Whitbread Hotel Company Leagrave, Luton, Bedfordshire, England	36,803	501
24	Club Méditerranée Paris, France	36,000*	100
25	NH Hoteles SA Madrid, Spain	34,709	238

(continued)

Exhibit 2.16 Top 50 corporate hotel chains. (continued)

Rank	Company Headquarters	Rooms	Hotels
26	Riu Hotels Group Playa de Palma, Mallorca, Spain	34,000	110
27	Fairmont Hotels & Resorts Inc. Toronto, Ontario, Canada	33,290	82
28	Le Méridien Hotels & Resorts London, England	33,000	135
29	Jin Jiang International Group Shanghai, China	32,707	150
30	CNL Hospitality Corp. Orlando, Fla. USA	31,944	132
31	Westmont Hospitality Group Houston, Texas USA	30,000	200
32	Barcelo Hotels & Resorts Palma de Mallorca, Spain	28,145	112
33	Iberostar Hotels & Resorts Palma de Mallorca, Spain	28,104	91
34	Americas Best Value Inn (formerly Best Value Inn) Newbury Park, Calif. USA	27,232	456
35	Mandalay Resort Group Las Vegas, Nev. USA	26,600	12
36	Caesars Entertainment (formerly Park Place Entertainment) Las Vegas, Nev. USA	26,000	22
37	C.H.E. Group plc Edgware, Middlesex, England	25,927	342
38	Tharaldson Enterprises Fargo, N.D. USA	25,899	360
39	Millennium & Copthorne Hotels plc London, England	25,517	88
40	Walt Disney World Co. Burbank, Calif. USA	25,316	24
41	Prince Hotels Tokyo, Japan	23,985*	98*
42	MGM Mirage Las Vegas, Nev. USA	21,975	10
43	Shangri-La Hotels & Resorts Hong Kong, China	21,442	44
44	MeriStar Hospitality Corp. Arlington, Va. USA	20,319	73
45	Columbia Sussex Corp. Fort Mitchell, Ky. USA	20,121	73
46	Royal Host Hotels & Resorts Calgary, Alberta, Canada	20,000	141
47	Ocean Hospitalities Portsmouth, N.H. USA	19,572	123
48	Washington Hotel Corp. Nagoya, Japan	18,534*	68*
49	Dorint Hotels & Resorts Dusseldorf, Germany	17,997	95
50	JAL Hotels Company Ltd. Tokyo, Japan	17,631	56

Hotels estimate
(*Source:* © 2005 *Hotels Magazine*)

U.S. Scope The World Travel and Tourism Council (WTTC) has reported 66,943 lodging facilities of all varieties operating within the geographic boundaries of North America (Exhibit 2.15). The majority of these facilities operate within the United States.

The United States is also the home country base of large multinational properties. U.S.-based lodging chains hold ten of the top fifteen positions.

Structure

As the lodging industry continually evolves, its structure becomes increasing more complex. **Structure** generally refers to ownership, management, and affiliation. These may be categorized as follows:

- Independent hotels
- Hotels owned and operated by corporate chains
- Consortia and referral group properties

Independent Hotels As the category name implies, these hotels are owned by individuals or private companies that are not hotel corporations. They may be operated with no chain affiliation or with some type of franchise or consortium affiliation.

Operated by Owner with No Chain Affiliation. In the United States, the number of independent hotels is declining. Exhibit 2.20 shows that of 47,741 hotels in the Smith Travel Research (STR) database, an estimated 45 percent are independent and not affiliated with any chain by franchise or other affiliation. The reason for increasing chain affiliation is the need for marketing and brand exposure in an increasingly globally competitive hotel market. Interestingly there are fewer independently owned hotels in the United States than in the rest of the world.

Independent Owner with Franchise or Consortium Affiliation. This category includes both franchise/consortium affiliation with owner-operated properties, and franchise/consortium plus outside management company operated properties but independently owned.

In the United States, the Smith Travel Research database estimates that 54 percent of the hotels are affiliated with a corporate chain franchise or consortium. (See Exhibit 2.20.)

Corporate Chain–Owned and Operated Hotels Today's chain hotels have a global presence. The United States is home to half of the top 50 largest hotel corporations.

Corporate chain hotels operate and obtain revenue in the following three ways: They own and operate hotels; they franchise hotels; or they manage hotels. As mentioned above, they often both franchise and manage hotels that are owned by independent owners.

Owning and Operating. Owning and operating hotels is the first and most commonly perceived way in which corporate hotels are structured and earn revenue. Corporate chain hotels are usually owned and managed by personnel from that chain. This was the predominant structure in the past. Today, increasing numbers of hotel corporations operate and own fewer properties and are franchising more. They maintain ownership primarily to control properties or to make sure that they are operated at the highest standards and serve as models for franchised properties.

A variation of corporate ownership and operation happens when a hotel works under a corporate "flag" of a hotel company that owns and/or operates many franchised properties, but not under a corporate logo.

Franchising.   Corporate chains earn revenue from a second source, franchising. Franchising in the hotel and restaurant business dates back to around 1900, when the Ritz Development Company first franchised the Ritz-Carlton name to a hotel in New York City. A ***franchise*** is the authorization given by a company to another company or person to sell that company's unique products and services. The granting company, or franchisor, grants to another company, the franchisee, the right to conduct business based upon certain guidelines for a contracted period of time and in a specified place. For example, the Hilton Corporation grants to an independent owner of a hotel the right to use its name, reservation systems, and national advertising. For the privilege, the franchisee must pay a fee.

Corporate chain hotels earn significant revenue through franchising fees. These fees come from two primary sources: the *initial fee* that is typically paid upon submission of the franchise application and the *ongoing fees* paid throughout the term of the agreement. Ongoing fees include: royalty fees, reservation costs, marketing expenses, frequent traveler programs, and miscellaneous fees.

There are advantages and disadvantages in franchising, both to the franchisor and the franchisee. The primary advantage to the franchisor is that it can rapidly expand business throughout the United States and the world by signing hundreds of franchisees. Primary disadvantages to the franchisor are ensuring that the quality

EYE ON THE ISSUES

International

Globalization was already well underway when the walls surrounding the Soviet Union and Eastern Europe tumbled. Rapid business and trade expansion in Asia, Europe, the United States, and other areas of the world have spurred growth in the international lodging industry to accommodate business travelers' needs. Additionally, the rapid expansion of the Internet and global communications has accelerated worldwide mergers and acquisitions and has enabled a truly global hotel community.

The monthly *Hotels Magazine* reports on news regarding international expansions, acquisitions, and mergers of the lodging industry. Of the largest hotel chains in the world, ten of the top fifteen ranked by number of countries in which they operate are based in the United States. For example, the number-one-ranked Intercontinental Hotel Group operates in 100 countries, Cendant Corp ranks second, with properties on six continents, while a relative newcomer on the scene, Starwood Hotels & Resorts (Sheraton, Westin, and other brands) ranks eighth, with a presence in 70 countries. The number four hotel company, Accor (which owns Motel 6) is a French corporation present in 72 countries.

Clearly, international hotel ownership and geographic areas of operations are expanding. Hotel managers of today and tomorrow must be "internationalists."

Exhibit 2.17   This list of the top 10 number of franchised hotels shows that some chains are exclusively franchised operations without any parent company–owned properties. (*Source: Hotels Magazine* 2005, Giants Survey 2005; conducted through end of 2004)

Companies That Franchise the Most Hotels		
Company	Total Franchised	Total Hotels
Cendant Corp.	6,396	6,396
Choice Hotels International	4,977	4,977
InterContinental Hotels Group	2,971	3,540
Hilton Hotels Corp.	1,900	2,259
Marriott International	1,658	2,632
Accor	949	3,973
Carlson Hospitality Worldwide	864	890
Global Hyatt Corp.	505	818
Starwood Hotels & Resorts	310	733
Worldwide Louvre Hotels (Societe du Louvre)	307	887

and standards of the product and services being franchised are maintained; making sure that few, if any, of the franchisees fail.

Advantages from the view of the franchisee may include:

- Site selection assistance
- Construction expertise
- Fixtures and equipment assistance
- Good training
- Initial and ongoing support from the franchisor
- Marketing assistance, which includes access to international computerized hotel reservation systems and a national and international group-business sales force

Disadvantages for the franchisee may be related to restrictive operating policies mandated by the franchisor, unwanted marketing efforts by the franchisor, unprotected sales and trade territories, inadequate training programs, and "no guarantee

Exhibit 2.18   Compare the cost of a franchised operation by segment (economy to first-class) over 10 years. Then answer the question: What do franchisors provide owners to make it worth such a substantial investment over 10 years? (*Source:* Stephen Rushmore, *Hotels Magazine*)

Royalty Cost	Reservation Cost	Marketing Cost	Frequent Traveler Cost	1998 Total Misc. Cost	Ten-Year Cost	Total Cost % of Rooms Revenue
689,555	324,719	324,719	0	133,364	1,508,357	9.8%
2,574,339	889,845	735,525	198,140	395,764	4,893,614	10.0%
7,888,511	670,662	1,011,348	517,810	1,333,680	11,512,011	11.4%

of renewal" clauses in the franchise contract that allow the franchisor to decline to renew the franchise.

See Exhibit 2.17 for the top 10 corporations franchising the most hotels.

Managing.   A third source of revenue for corporate chains is management contracts. A management contract is a written agreement between an owner and an operator of a hotel or motel. The owner employs the operator as an agent (a kind of employee) who assumes full responsibility for operating and managing the property. There are two types of hotel management companies: chain-affiliated and independent management.

Hotel chain corporations usually have a separate division that specializes in providing operating expertise and management services to privately owned hotels under the chain's franchise. These are chain-affiliated management arrangements.

Independent management companies are non-chain-affiliated, i.e., privately owned. They focus on providing expertise to independent properties. These independent management companies can contract to operate hotels that have a chain franchise affiliation or to operate an independently owned and nonfranchised hotel.

There are three provisions common to most management company contracts:

1. The management company has the exclusive right to manage the property without interference by ownership.
2. The owner pays all operating and financing expenses and assumes all ownership risks.
3. The management company is held harmless from its actions except for gross negligence or fraud.

Owners pay management companies for their expertise and for the convenience of having them handle most operating decisions for the hotel. Fees are negotiable but generally fall into three areas: technical assistance fees that cover the time and

Exhibit 2.19   Though it costs owners to pay management companies, more and more owners do so for convenience and expertise. Hotel management companies like the flexibility of operating companies without making capital investment. (*Source: Hotels Magazine*)

Companies That Manage the Most Hotels		
Company	**Hotels Managed**	**Total Hotels**
Marriott International	889	2,632
Extended Stay Hotels	654	654
Accor	535	3,973
InterContinental Hotels Group	403	3,540
Tharaldson Enterprises	360	360
Global Hyatt Corp.	316	818
Interstate Hotels & Resorts	306	306
Starwood Hotels & Resorts	283	733
Hilton Hotels Corp.	206	2,259
Worldwide Louvre Hotels (Societe du Louvre)	227	887

expertise of the operator; preopening management fees that are generally paid before the property is open, since this requires more extensive work than managing an established property; and ongoing management fees, usually based on some kind of fee structure.

Hotel management companies are most prevalent in the United States. A *Hotels* magazine's survey reports that among the world's largest ten hotel management companies, seven were based on the United States. (See Exhibit 2.19.) The largest management company in the world is Marriott International with 52 percent of its total room inventory "managed."

Management contracts have advantages and disadvantages from the perspective of both the owner and the management company. Advantages from the owner's viewpoint include being freed from daily operating responsibilities and having access to the expertise of established hotel operators with a proven track record. A major disadvantage is that ownership carries most of the property's financial burden. If the management company performs poorly or if the property requires expensive repairs, it is the owner's money that is tied up and he or she must make up for losses or find funds to make repairs.

The main advantage from the management company's perspective is that it can control many properties without the large investment and financial risk of ownership. Disadvantages, as viewed by the management company, are related to the financial health of the owner. Management companies grow by having a good operating reputation. This reputation can be jeopardized if the owner does not supply needed shortfalls in revenue that could result in substandard hotel facilities and services. Also, performance incentive fees provide the majority of a management company's profits; hotels in poor condition do not do very well.

Consortia and Referral Group Properties In 2005, consortia serviced approximately 26 percent of the total world hotel-room inventory. ***Consortia*** are corporate firms who provide services to independent hotels that help them become more competitive in the global marketplace. Similar to, but different from franchising, consortia provide central reservation systems, marketing, advertising, trade-show representation, and often purchasing discounts and management training for independent hotels. Most consortia attract membership from the strength of their computerized central reservation systems. (See Exhibit 2.20 for the top 25 consortia.)

The independent hotels retain their own identity and signage; they don't prominently display the consortium name. They pay fees similar to, but less than, franchise fees. Consortia have less control over the hotel product/service than do franchisers.

In the 2000s, acquisitions and mergers have already been significant. Ranked first and second, respectively, London-based Utell International and Phoenix-based RezSolutions merged to form a single provider called Utell-Pegasus. The new company, a provider of reservation and marketing services to nearly a million hotel rooms, now lays claim to nearly 30 percent of the consortia market. In more merger-mania, the next-highest ranked provider, Dallas-based Lexington Services, was acquired by Travel Services International, which was soon thereafter acquired by an English company, now known as MyTravel Group Plc.

These deals underscore the urgency for many of the largest reservation providers to create a global reach for their customers. Exhibit 2.21 shows the world's largest 25 consortia, which service slightly more than 3 million hotel rooms.

Exhibit 2.20   There are several systems for classifying hotels. Here are four schemes used by Smith Travel Research. The variety of segments reflects the wants, needs, and budgets of consumers. (*Courtesy:* Smith Travel Research)

U.S. Lodging Industry Composition

Segment	Hotels	Rooms	Average Size Hotel	Hotel %	Rooms %
Total U.S. Lodging					
Chain-Affiliated	25,753	2,954,042	115	53.9%	66.9%
Independent	21,988	1,464,650	67	46.1%	33.1%
Total U.S.	47,741	4,418,692	93	100.0%	100.0%
Price					
Luxury	3,306	802,008	243	6.9%	18.2%
Upscale	10,555	1,182,855	112	22.1%	26.8%
Mid-price	14,100	1,220,021	87	29.5%	27.6%
Economy	9,443	600,597	64	19.8%	13.6%
Budget	10,337	613,211	59	21.7%	13.9%
Total Price Segment	47,741	4,418,692		100.0%	100.0%
Chain Scale*					
Luxury	233	73,209	314	0.9%	2.5%
Upper Upscale	1,384	536,099	387	5.4%	18.1%
Upscale	2,529	397,718	157	9.8%	13.5%
Midscale w/f&b	4,573	550,631	120	17.8%	18.6%
Midscale w/o f&b	7,618	664,030	87	29.6%	22.5%
Economy	9,416	732,355		36.6%	24.8%
Total Chain Scale Segment	25,753	2,954,042	78	100.0%	100.0%
Location					
Urban	4,606	701,576	152	9.6%	15.9%
Surburban	15,883	1,574,329	99	33.3%	35.6%
Airport	1,935	275,140	142	4.1%	6.2%
Interstate	6,766	452,833	67	14.2%	10.2%
Resort	3,918	578,807	148	8.2%	13.1%
Small Metro/Town	14,633	836,007	57	30.7%	18.9%
Total Location Segment	47,741	4,418,692		100.0%	100.0%

*Independent hotels are not included in the Chain Scale segment.

Of these, Utell-Pegasus services 30 percent. Combined with Lexington, these two consortia service 46 percent of the total rooms handled by the top 25 consortia. But these market leadership positions continue to shift, escalated by acquisitions of Internet sites and services.

Individual Property Structure   Whether or not an individual lodging property is corporately owned by a chain, independently owned and operated, has a franchise affiliation, is operated by a management company, or is part of a consortium, most properties follow a similar organizational hierarchy and structure.

The organization structure of a full-service hotel represents most of the functional departments that are possible in all hotel categories discussed earlier. Exhibit 2.22 depicts a typical organization structure. Note that there is considerable variation in organization, structure, number of personnel, and so on, depending on the type of property. For example, this organization chart would be typical of a large, city-center property. A specialty property, such as a Marriott Residence Inn or a

Exhibit 2.21 Some properties join a consortia as a kind of mid-ground between buying a franchise and remaining independent. In some regards, consortia provide the better points of both options. (*Source: 2005 Hotels Magazine*)

Rank 2004 2003	Company Headquarters	Rooms 2004 2003	Hotels 2004 2003
1	Utell/Ltd.-Pegasus Solutions Rep. Services	1,050,091	7,487
1	Dallas, Texas USA	1,040,550	6,916
2	SynXis Corp.	720,000	6,500
3	McClean, Va. USA	560,000	5,000
3	Vantis Corp. (formerly VIP International Corp.)	615,840	5,493
3	McLean, Va. USA	605,962	5,087
4	Supranational Hotels	257,000	1,692
4	London, England	202,700	1,519
5	InnPoints Worldwide	145,936	1,066
5	Albuquerque, N.M. USA	120,515	841
6	Hotusa-Eurostars-Familia Hotels	118,861	1,439
7	Barcelona, Spain	98,437	1,139
7	WORLDHOTELS	100,000	500
9	Frankfurt am Main, Germany	80,000	450
8	Keytel SA	92,000	1,150
6	Barcelona, Spain	105,000	1,050
9	Leading Hotels of the World	83,000	420
8	New York, N.Y. USA	83,000	415
10	Logis de France	66,881	3,517
10	Paris, France	67,721	3,602
11	Preferred Hotel Group	56,726	285
13	(formerly IndeCorp. Corp.) Chicago, Ill. USA	56,296	281
12	Associated Luxury Hotels	48,280	86
12	Washington, D.C. USA	42,000	86
13	Historic Hotels of America	37,745	213
14	Washington, D.C. USA	32,399	202
14	AHMI RES Hotel (Thed International)	34,308	178
13	Paris, France	34,403	182
15	Sceptre Hospitality Resources (SWAN)	30,732	140
15	Englewood, Colo. USA	30,732	140
16	Great Hotels Organization	27,252	168
18	London, England	22,710	143
17	Minotel International	25,500	591
16	Lausanne, Switzerland	29,400	680
18	Small Luxury Hotels of the World	17,250	329
22	Surrey, England	16,234	308
19	Selected Hotels for Business,	17,000*	62*
20	Congresses & Incentives Marbella, Spain	17,000	62
20	ILA-Châteaux & Hotels de Charme	15,253	324
21	Brussels, Belgium	16,325	368
21	Design Hotels	11,682	137
25	Berlin, Germany	10,000	130
22	Relais & Châteaux	10,688	440
25	Paris, France	10,455	450
23	Châteaux & Hotels de France	10,608*	514*
23	Paris, France	10,767	450
24	Luxe Worldwide Hotels	10,000	185
23	Los Angeles, Calif. USA	10,767	481
25	Epoque Hotels	7,362	103
11	Miami, Fla. USA	—	—

*HOTELS estimate

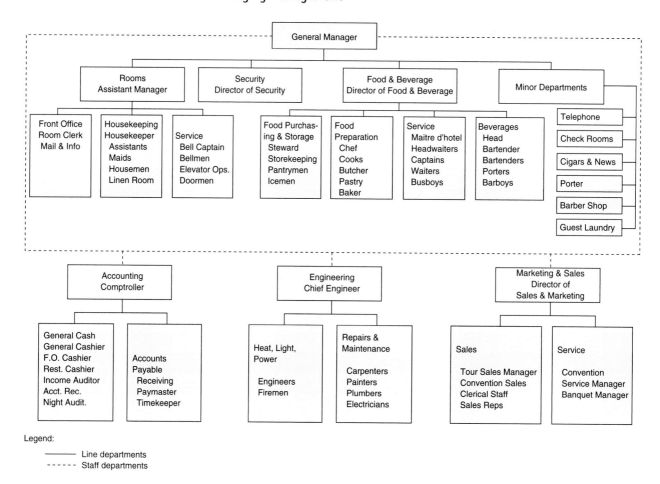

Legend:

———— Line departments
- - - - - Staff departments

Exhibit 2.22   Traditional organization structure of a full-service hotel.

small airport property, would be represented organizationally by some of the same, but fewer, positions.

It should be noted that in tight financial times, organizational structures tend to be flattened (to cut out layers of supervision) and/or to combine job responsibilities. This can make financial sense in the short-term but can be hazardous in a human resources context, if good people become over-tasked, burned out, or leave the organization.

Hotel Classification Schemes   Hotels can be *simultaneously defined* by more than one classification or product segmentation scheme. For example, a resort can simultaneously be classified as a timeshare, conference facility, luxury, and/or upper upscale property. Understanding the various underlying classification schemes is particularly important when reading industry statistics.

Smith Travel Research (STR) is an important source of lodging industry statistics and classifies its 35,312 hotels in three different classification schemes (see Exhibits 2.20 and 2.23):

1. **Price.** This classification divides hotels into luxury, the hotels receiving the top 15 percent of average daily rates (ADR); upscale, the hotels receiving

Exhibit 2.23   A classification scheme for the lodging industry.* This compilation chart shows how hotels can be simultaneously defined as being in more than one category. (*Source:* Adapted by author from PKF Consulting, Smith Travel Research [STR], and Lang H. & Dupre, D., *Hospitality World*)

Price**	Chain Scale***	Location****	Room Configuration	Markets Served
A. Luxury—top 15% of ADRs Mariott Marquis	*A. Upper upscale* Hyatt	*A. Urban* Parker Meridian (NYC)	*A. All-Suites* Sheraton Suites	*A. Convention Related* 1. Conference Centers Scottsdale Conf. Center (AZ) 2. Convention Hotels Marriott Marquis (NYC)
B. Upscale—next 15% Hyatt Regency	*B. Upscale* Wyndham Garden Hotel	*B. Suburban* Hilton Garden Hotel	*B. Extended Stay* Residence Inn	
C. Mid-Price—middle 30% Quality Inn	*C. Midscale with F&B* Quality Inn	*C. Airport* O'Hare Marriott	*C. Bed & Breakfasts* Birch Hill Inn (VT)	*B. Lodging with Entertainment* 1. Casino Hotels MGM Grand Hotel (NV) 2. Destination Resorts Club Med (Mexico) 3. Mega Resorts The Luxor (NV)
D. Economy—next 20% Holiday Inn Express	*D. Midscale without F&B* La Quinta	*B. Highway* Super 8	*D. Historic Hotels* Ambassador West (Chicago)	
E. Budget—lowest 20% Motel 6	*E. Economy* Red Roof Inns	*E. Resort* The Broadmoor (CO)	*E. Private Club* The Harvard Club (NYC)	*C. Theme Park Hotels* Disney Hotel (CA)
			F. Youth Hostel YMCA (NYC)	*D. Spas* Canyon Ranch (AZ)
			G. Boatels Saigon Floating Hotel	*E. Lodging with Health Care* 1. Ronald McDonald House (CT)
			H. Capsule Hotels GreenPlaza Shinguku Train Station (Japan)	*F. Cruise Ships/River Boats* 1. Carnival Cruises (FL) 2. The Mississippi Queen (LA)
				G. With Parks & Recreation 1. Camping Sawmill Campground (CA) 2. RV Campgrounds Campgrounds of America 3. Ranches The Circle K Ranch (WY)

* Many types of lodging facilities can simultaneously be defined by more than one classification.
** Market price segments: The five hotel categories of a metro STR market by ADR
*** STR segments are based on chain-wide average daily rate (Independent hotels in separate category).
**** Classification dictated by the physical location of the hotel.

the next highest level of ADRs; mid-price, the hotels receiving the middle 30 percent of ADRs, economy, the next 20 percent of ADRs, and budget, the hotels receiving the lowest 20 percent of ADRs.

2. **Chain Scale.** This classification category term is also applied by STR to the hotels in its database. However, the terms are different: upper upscale, upscale, midscale with F&B (food & beverage), and midscale without F&B, and economy.

3. **Location.** To further confuse things, STR also uses this classification scheme to produce statistics on the same database: urban, suburban, airport, highway, and resort.

Classification schemes are also designed around "room configuration." To name a few: all-suites, extended stay, bed & breakfast, historic hotels, private club, youth hostels, boatels, and capsule hotels.

Classification schemes are often a descriptive result of the "markets" they serve, such as convention hotels, lodging with entertainment, theme park hotels, spas, lodging with health care, cruise ships/river boats, and lodging with parks and recreation.

Why so many classification schemes? One explanation may have to do with the fact that the lodging industry has been around a long time. As new demand creates new supply to address this demand, old terms remain to describe older forms of lodging even though these older forms of lodging have changed to address the new demand. Familiar and long used terms have a long life and do not easily die.

Referring to Exhibit 2.20, the classification schemes used by Smith Travel Research are becoming the standard. This is occurring since the statistics they disseminate are used by increasing numbers of lodging practitioners.

In addition to the preceding categories of hotel properties, many newer forms have recently evolved. Analysts often include these facilities in the statistics of the five categories above for convenience. In reality, though, these newer, specialized or hybrid forms of lodging are interesting in their own right. (Two of these are discussed further below.) These properties were created to serve the specific needs of clearly categorized groups of customer *market segments*. Market segmentation, discussed further in the chapter Hospitality Marketing, drives the need for such innovation.

Conference Centers   Surprisingly, the conference center concept has its roots in both academia and in the high-tech industry. In the mid-1950s, corporate in-house conference centers were typified by IBM's Homestead facilities (1954), General Electric's Croton-on-the-Hudson Development Center (1955), AT&T's Lisle Training Center and Hopewell Training Center (both 1955). These corporate centers were freestanding facilities with state-of-the-art audiovisual systems and other sophisticated meeting amenities. However, their customer base was exclusively internal; they were dedicated to the training needs of their own employees.

During this same period, universities were operating on-campus conference centers for university and adult continuing education needs. The university centers had broader missions; they also hosted non–university affiliated meetings. Attendees of these meetings stayed at dormitories and ate in college cafeterias. But, business meetings attracted a more upscale type of attendee, with higher expectations. This was a new form of demand, and it evoked a new kind of supply. Posh private executive conference centers were born in 1964.

Exhibit 2.24   Today's conference centers are often exclusive resorts with ample resources for handling large groups. Shown here are Cheyenne Mountain Conference Resort and Scottsdale Resort and Conference Center. (*Courtesy:* Benchmark Resorts)

The Tarrytown House in Tarrytown, New York, a renovated mansion, became the first commercial conference center. Tarrytown House incorporated technologically advanced meeting facility features within an elegant setting. Later in the same year, the Arden House opened its doors. The Harrison Houses followed these successful conference centers by opening similar concept facilities first in Glen Cove, New York (1968), and then in Lake Bluff, Illinois (1970). These early conference centers were designed to serve fewer than 100 executive-level attendees, were situated in remote but conveniently accessible locations, and had a think-tank feel to them. By the mid-1970s conference centers had rapidly refined their market segments and offered a unique product.

Other early pioneers included Stonebridge Conference Center in Snowmass, Colorado (1973), the Scottsdale Conference Center and Resort in Scottsdale, Arizona (1976), and Scanticon near Princeton, New Jersey (1981). The success of these conference centers spawned rapid development of pure conference centers throughout the 1980s and 1990s. Existing hotels, eager to cash in on the concept, added conference center features to their properties.

Today, conference centers have evolved into four basic types:

- Executive conference centers specialize in meetings for middle- to upper-level management.
- Corporate-conference centers of two types: those owned by a corporation and exclusively for that company's meeting use and those primarily for the owner company's use but also available for outside organizations.
- Resort conference centers designed for meeting use by any organization.
- Nonresidential conference centers, which do not offer sleeping rooms and are often developed by not-for-profit organizations, such as colleges and universities.

The defining characteristic of a **conference center** is that the majority of its revenue comes from conferences and meetings held by various organizations. It is not unusual for a conference center to generate 95 percent of its revenue from group meetings. Other distinguishing characteristics include:

Exhibit 2.25   This conference facility is so large that it uses projection video to help audience members in the back rows see what is going on on-stage. (Photo by James Morgan, Scottsdale, Arizona)

- Special pricing structures (usually room rates that include meals and meeting room charges)
- A high proportion of meeting and function rooms relative to the number of sleeping rooms
- Access to sophisticated media equipment
- Specialized staff (called *conference coordinators* or *convention service managers*) who assist each group holding a meeting at the property
- The ability to accommodate meetings ranging in size from fewer than 10 to several hundred attendees

While pure conference centers cater almost exclusively to the group-meeting business, many commercial hotels and resorts have adopted the features of this specialized niche. In essence, they add an "ancillary conference center" to their property. This variation on the conference center category generates 30 to 60 percent of revenue from group business, with the remainder of revenue coming from individual business and pleasure travelers.

Timeshares   It was not that long ago that an undisciplined timeshare industry dwelled on the outer fringes of the travel and tourism sector. It is now firmly regulated and endorsed by most major hotel brands, including Marriott, Disney, and Hyatt.

Also known as vacation ownership, interval ownership, and vacation clubs, the timeshare industry is growing at a dramatic rate: Over the last 15 years, worldwide timeshare sales increased from a half billion dollars in annual revenues to approximately $9.4 billion in 2002. Since 1980, about 10 million timeshare intervals (blocks of time) have been sold, representing an estimated sales volume of around $40 billion. The American Resort Development Association (ARDA) estimates that about

6.2 million households hold a vacation ownership interest in one of more than 5,300 timeshare resorts throughout the world.

According to ARDA, timeshare resorts are located in more than 95 countries, and timeshare owners reside in more than 270 countries. The United States is the world leader in the timeshare market. Europe is the second dominant region.

The timeshare industry has become "respectable." Many timeshare developers, such as Fairfield Communities, Vistana, and Silverleaf Resorts are public companies. Sunterra is a major corporation and timeshare participant with access to Wall Street. Cendant Corp, the largest hotel corporation in the world, owns Resort Condominiums International (RCI), the world's largest vacation (timeshare) exchange company. In 1998, Marriott Vacation Club International produced the highest dollar volume of timeshare sales. Following Hyatt's and Disney's entry into timeshare, even Four Seasons is building a timeshare component into each of its future resort developments.

Some Timeshare Lingo.   Timeshares represent the right for a buyer to use a specified resort or leisure product for a specified time. The following terms are associated with these rights.

- **Fixed week.** Unit owners purchase the right to use a particular unit type, for a particular week, each year.
- **Floating week.** Unit owners purchase the right to use a particular unit type for one week each year, but must make a reservation on a first-come, first-served basis for the particular week that they wish to book. Weeks may float within the year or, more typically, within a season. To exchange the week, the owner makes a reservation and enters the week reserved into the exchange network system (like RCI mentioned above).
- **Split weeks.** Owners may use their unit on nonconsecutive nights; this dictates a much more complex operation.
- **Hypothecation.** The developer pledges the consumer installment contracts in return for a line of credit.
- **Points.** Members buy a particular number of points, redeemable for blocks of time within a vacation ownership network. Owners must reserve on a first-come, first-served basis and are not guaranteed that accommodations will be available either on a particular date or within a particular resort.
- **Vacation club.** A travel and use product that offers members great flexibility. The buyer receives a single ownership interest that entitles the member the right to use accommodations at all resorts in the club's system. Membership may include a priority reservation right to the member's home resort.

Theme Resorts   Segmenting a hotel market has consistently proven to be a viable option for developers. Segmentation encourages the hotelier to focus on a specific customer demand and a specific type of customer. New demand generates new supply and new market segments. A new trend in the hotel business is "theming." Theme resorts are based on a unique concept and come in two sizes: *regular* and *mega*.

Regular.   In October 1998, House of Blues Hospitality, an offshoot of a highly successful themed restaurant company, opened the first House of Blues Hotel in Chicago. In the Bahamas, Sun International Resorts, Inc. opened its Atlantis Resort,

Exhibit 2.26   Building on mythological images of an advanced civilization under the sea, is the *Great Hall of Waters Lobby* from The Royal Towers, Atlantis. (*Courtesy:* Royal Towers, Atlantis)

based on the theme of the mythological sunken continent. Hard Rock Café opened its first hotel in Asia, the Hard Rock Hotel, Bali. Disney Vacation Club (a timeshare) placed a branded timeshare on Hilton Head Island in South Carolina. Another variation is the Stamford, Connecticut-based Titan Sports' purchase of a bankrupt hotel with the plan of turning it into the World Wrestling Federation (WWF) Hotel and Casino.

What all of the different types of themed hotels have in common is the goal of extending and strengthening the existing name or concept that stands behind the hotel property. These properties are aimed at narrow niche markets of travelers who may opt for lodging and entertainment in the same package.

Mega.   Several years ago, Las Vegas began to reinvent itself and mega-resorts began to proliferate. They are focused chiefly on gambling, but often incorporate some unique theme to attract families or couples. Two of the most highly visible mega-resorts appeared in Spring 1999.

- The Venetian Resort Hotel Casino (3,306 rooms) has gondolas that slowly move along indoor waterways. By 2002, the resort decided it needed an additional 1,000-room hotel tower.
- Bellagio (3,000 rooms) is inspired by the Northern Italian village that overlooks Lake Como. It is located along an eight-acre lake that features computerized fountains choreographed to classical music and Broadway show tunes. By 2002, the resort was planning to add a 925-room hotel tower.
- Mandalay Bay Resort recently began adding a 1,125-suite hotel tower to its existing 3,700 rooms.
- The Wynn Las Vegas/La Reve (French for "The Dream") took place to acclaim in 2006. The 2,700-room resort will feature an eight-story mountain enclosing a lake, a new golf course, an 110,000-square-foot casino and a full-service Ferrari/ Maserati dealership.

Such casinos also capture the bulk of Nevada gaming. As reported by Geoff Doman of Bonanza News Service, 75 percent of gaming winnings go to the mega-resorts of the Las Vegas strip. To say "bigger is better" might be arguable, but in the world of Nevada casinos, bigger is definitely more profitable.

The disparity between large and small casinos is even more dramatic in the Reno–Sparks area where the 10 largest casinos took home 82.9 percent of net profits won by 35 casinos.

EYE ON THE ISSUES

Ethics

Every day, hotel managers are faced with a variety of business decisions with ethical implications: Should we "bump" an already reserved guest, because we want to book a large and profitable group? Should we call ourselves a "resort" because we are located in a scenic destination, even though we are little more than a budget-quality facility? Can we honestly say we are ten minutes from the airport, when we know this is only true at 3:00 in the morning . . . in a NASCAR . . . and definitely not true at rush hour? Do we "forget" to mention in guidebooks that access to the second and third floor is up or down two flights of stairs? Misleading communication is unethical and will result in unhappy guests who, in the age of empowered consumers, will let you and those higher up in the corporate structure know about it. How you respond to such complaints is also an ethical choice.

Lodging Facility Market Demand and Segments

The different types of hotels are designed and created to be responsive to different travelers' needs and demands. These needs determine the types of facilities found in the lodging industry. Total demand for a lodging product is sometimes envisioned as a whole pie that can be cut into many pieces or segments. In Exhibit 2.13 we showed that suppliers can either sell to end-user demand or intermediary demand. Using the analogy of a pie, we could describe the lodging industry as being cut into two halves: the end-user segment and travel intermediary segment.

This section first examines travel end-users by looking at the purposes for which they travel. We will look at two broad reasons for travel: business/pleasure and recreational/personal. Looking more deeply into the habits of end-users, we will investigate how business or pleasure travel takes place: in groups, or through independent travel. The last examination of end-user demand will be accomplished by a look at these groups and independent travelers, using a variety of categories and classifications. Following the discussion of the travel end-user segment, we will describe the travel market intermediary segment.

Travel End-User Demand   The lodging industry typically cuts the end-user demand segment of the pie into additional smaller pieces according to a single segmentation variable, purpose of travel. Lodging marketers simply ask prospective travelers: "What is the purpose of your trip?" These purposes create natural categories of travelers. Each of these categories, slices, or segments has unique needs and wants. Thus, additional questions can be asked of these more refined segments, so that the lodging facility can further refine its products and services.

The two major end-user market segments defined by purpose of travel (*business/ organizational* and *pleasure/recreational/personal*) are illustrated in Exhibit 2.27. Both of these segments can be further divided into group and independent travel sub-segments. The subsegments of most interest to a sales force are those that involve group business, specifically:

- Conventions and meetings (a sub-segment of business/organizational travelers)
- Tours (a sub-segment of pleasure/recreational/personal travelers)

Hotel sales forces focus their efforts on group business because the "piece of business" involved in each sale is much larger than for an individual sale. One

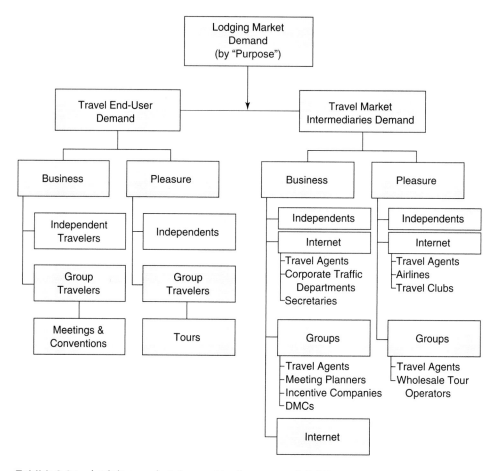

Exhibit 2.27   Lodging market demand by "purpose of visit."

convention group sale (for example) might bring a hotel 200 sleeping-room assignments for three or four nights. In addition, the group may contract for several luncheons and banquets, play golf on the hotel's course, and use other hotel services that produce still more revenue. A sale to a tour bus company might seem smaller (with 40 guests per bus) but usually involves a contract for several months. Whenever the tour company brings a bus tour through the region (weekly, biweekly, etc.), 40 more passengers will stay overnight. Over a three-month contract, this could total more than 500 room nights. Obviously, courting group business is a better use of sales staff than trying reach independent/individual pleasure travelers and independent/individual business travelers. For that, most hotels rely on advertising.

Segmenting by the variable purpose of travel is the most common way hotels categorize demand. Other segmentation variables that can be used include:

- Demographic variables such as age
- Geographic variables such as region, density
- Psychographic variables such as social class, personality, lifestyle
- Behavioral variables such as frequency of travel, benefits sought

Remember that the above slices, categories, or segments represent the total potential demand pie. No single lodging facility is capable of addressing all of these. It must choose a few target segments based upon its resources. Research helps lodging facilities select which segments to pursue. Making a good match involves not only matching physical resources (such as facilities, location) but also matching a client's needs in terms of price and availability. If a group needs space for an annual Fourth of July meeting, the hotel must have the space available then, not in December.

As you can see, there are many ways to segment customer markets. Creative lodging marketers are continually looking to identify the special needs of new segments and accordingly design innovative products to address those needs.

Let's take a closer look at some of the major segments of the demand pie, divided by purpose of travel.

Business/Organizational Segment. This segment is composed of demand from businesses and organizations of all types. Group demand comes from corporations, associations, social groups, educational groups, government groups, religious groups, and so on. Independent demand-comes from individual members of these businesses and organizations who are traveling for business purposes.

Groups. Groups attending meetings and conventions are a large source of business for the lodging industry. Group sizes may range from 10 attendees to groups of thousands. These groups occupy hotel rooms for an average of three nights. Groups in the business/organization segment meet for a variety of reasons, including training; management development; executive and board of director retreats; national and regional sales conferences; and international, national, regional, and state association conventions. They select meeting sites based upon the facilities' ability to satisfy the purposes of these meetings.

Individual attendees do not select the lodging facility where these meetings will be held; thus, lodging sales forces must identify and work with group decision-makers. These include organizational executives or intermediaries such as independent meeting-planners and sometimes travel agencies (see Exhibit 2.27).

Independents. Individuals traveling for business purposes make up a large portion of lodging industry revenues. In addition to having the potential for frequent repeat business, they are easier to identify and reach than pleasure travelers. Thus, lodging facility sales forces are able to contact the organizations from which these travelers depart and/or the local organizations where they will visit to offer accommodations and services. Most lodging facilities have one salesperson specializing in obtaining this type of business. Additionally, advertising may be heavily used to attract this group.

Business/organization independent travelers are motivated to travel to carry out economic requirements of their businesses. Generally, business travelers are well educated and affluent, have high-level jobs, and tend to fly often. Given the increasingly national and international geographic nature of modern business, this category of traveler will remain a dominant segment in the future.

We'll turn now to a discussion of yet another segment, that of the pleasure/recreational/personal end-user (Exhibit 2.27).

Exhibit 2.28   Corporate guests find plenty of work space in all-suite hotels. (*Courtesy:* Residence Inn ® by Marriott ®)

Pleasure/Recreational/Personal Segment.   The pleasure/recreational/personal traveler is motivated by four factors:

- **Physical.** These motivators are related to physical rest, sports participation, beach recreation, relaxing entertainment, and other activities connected with health.
- **Cultural.** These motivators are related to the desire to know about the culture of other areas. These include history, current social organization and institutions, music, architecture, art, folklore, dances, language, and religion.
- **Interpersonal.** Travel in this category is motivated by a desire to visit friends or relatives, meet new people, make new friends, and escape daily routines.
- **Status and prestige.** These motivators come from a desire for recognition, attention, appreciation, knowledge, and a good reputation as perceived by other people. This travel includes trips related to the pursuit of education, business, and hobbies.

Like the business/organization segment, the pleasure segment can be further subdivided into group demand and independent demand.

Group Demand.   The pleasure/recreation/personal segment is motivated to take trips and does so in a group form known as tour packages. Tours became an important travel segment following World War II and have expanded rapidly since 1960. Tours offer the traveler the advantage of security and greater affordability.

Tours are put together by knowledgeable tour wholesalers. These wholesalers can offer vacation packages to the traveling public at prices lower than individual travelers would be able to arrange by themselves. Wholesalers buy travel services such as transportation, hotel rooms, sight-seeing services, airport transfers (ground

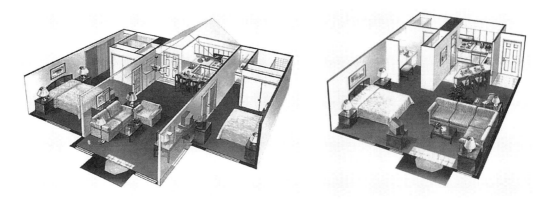

Exhibit 2.29   Residence Inn by Marriott is a well recognized example of an extended-stay, all-suite hotel brand. (*Courtesy:* Residence Inn ® by Marriott ®)

transportation), and meals in large quantities at discounted prices, then package the components, add a markup, and resell this package to a group of individual travelers. All retail travel agencies offer packages for sale ranging from traditional trips through the United States and Europe to exotic packaged tours to the rain forests of Brazil.

Independent Demand. The travel motivators mentioned earlier (physical, cultural, interpersonal, and status and prestige) also influence the independent pleasure/recreational/personal segment. This category, like the independent business traveler, can be further subdivided by variables other than purpose of travel. In their 1985 book, *The Tourism System,* Mill and Morrison refer to eight representative segments of independent travelers in the United States:

- Resort travelers
- Family pleasure travelers
- Elderly travelers or senior travelers
- Singles and couples
- Minority pleasure travelers
- Travelers with disabilities
- Gaming travelers
- Other growth area travelers

Understanding the needs and wants of the end-user customer is imperative to lodging-facility managers. By knowing what the target customers want, marketers and managers can custom-design a product and services package that will initially attract the targets and then work to increase the possibility that they will become repeat customers.

Management's job doesn't end by scoping out relevant end-user customers. Managers also need to understand a second population of lodging facility demand: travel market intermediaries.

Intermediary Demand   Intermediaries are part of the demand for the lodging industry because often hotels cannot sell directly to the end-users we have previously discussed. Often, hotels must first sell their supply to these intermediaries, who afterwards sell it to the end-users. Thus, for the lodging facility to be successful, it must address the needs and wants of another group of customers, the travel market intermediaries. Since these intermediaries also serve the same end-users, their needs and wants are similar to those of the end-users—with one additional need: to satisfy their business objectives.

Exhibit 2.27 shows that when a hotel sells *indirectly* to end-user demand, it must first sell to an **intermediary.** Travel market intermediaries consist of two types: those that deal mainly with business end-users and those that deal mainly with leisure/recreational/personal end-users. Some intermediaries serve both groups of end-users.

Business Segment Intermediaries. This category of intermediaries works to match lodging facilities with business and organization end-user demand.

For the group business subsegment there are several types of business intermediaries that act as interfaces between hotels and end-users from business and organization groups. These include meeting planners, travel agents, incentive travel specialists, and destination management companies (DMCs).

Independent business end-users have several kinds of intermediaries from which to choose when purchasing travel services. They may make travel arrangements through a travel agency, through an in-house travel department called a *passenger traffic department,* or through their secretaries and assistants. These intermediary gatekeepers can be valuable allies for lodging marketers who make the effort to communicate the benefits of their hotel's products and services. A recent development connected to both the "flattening" of organizations and the Internet is that independent business end-users (or whomever makes their reservations) may use such on-line intermediaries as Expedia, Orbitz, or Travelocity.

Pleasure/Recreational/Personal Segment Intermediaries. These intermediaries differ from the preceding business travel intermediaries in that they help lodging facilities to attract end-user demand that is traveling for pleasure. Group travel for pleasure/recreational/personal end-users can be arranged and sold directly or indirectly by wholesale tour operators, inventoried and sold by retail travel agencies, arranged and sold by travel clubs or on-line suppliers.

Traditionally, travel agencies were the most dominant link between travel service suppliers and the independent pleasure traveler. This began to change in 1995, when airlines capped commissions to travel agents. In 2002, Delta Airlines contributed further to the "disintermediation" trend, when it entirely eliminated travel agent commissions for tickets sold in the United States. You'll learn more about the Internet's impact in the following section.

Credit card companies are another intermediary for reaching the independent traveler. Visa, MasterCard, American Express, and most major oil company cardholders, for example, usually have access to special pricing and discounts for tourism services. Organizations such as AARP and AAA (the American Automobile Association and its affiliates) are also important intermediaries.

Demand for tourism services, in general, and the lodging industry, in particular, can be viewed as consisting of travel end-user demand and travel market intermediary demand (See Exhibit 2.27). Because tourism suppliers often sell directly to the end-user, a clear understanding of their needs and wants is necessary for effective marketing efforts. Alternatively, tourism suppliers often sell indirectly to the end-user. That is, they must first sell to travel market intermediaries who then sell to end-users. Again, marketers must understand the needs and wants of this intermediary demand for their tourism products and services to pass through the pipeline and eventually reach the consuming end-user. The needs and wants of both end-user demand and intermediary demand will influence the design and nature of products and services offered for sale by the lodging industry.

Exhibit 2.30   Best Western offers a variety of products. Each Best Western is independently owned, but belongs to the referral organization. (Photo by Bert Van Hoof)

Internet/Technology and Changing Intermediary Markets.   Intermediaries have been traditionally used by lodging suppliers to sell to the pleasure market segments rather than sell to business market segments.

To effectively sell to individual pleasure markets, travel agencies were the primary channel of distribution. To sell to group pleasure markets, tour wholesalers and travel agencies selling the tour package were the primary means of distribution. The Internet has radically altered these channels of distribution.

Today, individual pleasure end-users are able to bypass travel agents and buy lodging products directly from the hotel supplier. The same options apply to the independent business traveler. And in the airline industry, the story is the same. If you have recently visited the "auction" of lodging products at Priceline.com, you have seen the wave of the future's "direct-buying" and negotiable pricing. At present, travel agencies must redefine their businesses or face extinction.

Less radical changes have occurred in the world of tour wholesalers. The unique ability to package an attractively priced tour has not been replaced with direct buying over the Internet. Again, however, tour wholesalers are going around traditional travel agencies and selling directly to the end-user of group tours.

That leaves the segment of group business travel. To understand the effect on group business travel, we must distinguish between small and less complex group business and large, complex group business. Traditionally, group business obtained lodging supply through two means:

- Purchasing directly from the supplier
- Using an independent or in-house meeting planner as an intermediary.

In the first case, the Internet clearly facilitates the ease of purchasing directly. In the second case, small meetings that are not complex can also be facilitated directly with the supplier, thus circumventing some meeting planners. But, if the meeting is large and complex, the Internet's role is more that of first resource. The group travel buyer will use the Internet to identify and select possible properties and to communicate with them regarding RFPs (requests for proposals). However, a knowledgeable meeting planner will still be essential to ensure that the large and complex meeting is properly executed.

There is, however, another threat on the horizon: the replacement of many meetings by videoconferencing. In the 1970s the advent of video conferencing generated speculation that expensive meetings and thus, revenue to hotels would evaporate. This proved incorrect. Videoconferencing was very expensive and complex at the time. Today, videoconferencing, especially facilitated by "video-streaming" over the Internet, is becoming cheaper and less complex. Small meetings such as training and other routine gatherings may be endangered. Large and complex meetings that have as an important objective to bring people face-to-face in an increasingly virtual world are predicted to remain, if not increase, as an important business activity.

Marketing Brings Lodging Supply and Demand Together

We now turn to a discussion of how the process of marketing (and sales, a subcomponent of marketing) links lodging supply and lodging demand.

Marketing   As you will learn in our chapter Hospitality Marketing, the marketing concept asserts that the key to achieving organizational goals lies in determining the needs and wants of target markets and delivering the desired satisfiers more ef-

EYE ON THE ISSUES

Customer Service

Customer service is more than smiling. The objective of customer service is to create customer satisfaction. Customer satisfaction occurs if the customer's expectations are met or exceeded. If expectations are met, then the customer perceives that he or she has obtained value for the costs that they gave in return for this value. How do buyers decide which product/service to buy?

Customer-Delivered Value Formula.   Take a look at this equation:

Customer-Delivered Value (CDV) = Total Customer Value (TCV) minus Total Customer Costs (TCC).

Or, shown more graphically

Total Customer Value (TCV)

− Total Customer Costs (TCC)

= Customer-Delivered Value (CDV)

In short, customers buy from the firm that they believe offers the highest CDV. Customer satisfaction is the result of a positive CDV.

TCV is a result of expectations for the hotel experience compared to the actual performance or delivery of these expectations. Expectations come from promises concerning what the product/service will be when experienced. Remember that a hotel product/service is not experienced until the customer actually uses it. Customer expectations come from marketing and sales promises, promises coming from word-of-mouth, and general perceptions about the brand.

TCC comes from the costs of money, time, energy, and psychic factors (worry, for example). TCV minus TCC equals CDV.

CDV in effect is seen as profit by the customer. It is the excess of gain in value over costs to the customer. Based on judgments of value and costs, customers determine whether or not they received a profit. If a profit is perceived, they are satisfied.

Customer service is an effort to deliver performance that resonates with the "promises" expected by the customer.

fectively and efficiently than competitors. The marketing concept rests on four main pillars: a market focus, customer orientation, coordinated marketing, and profitability.

Marketing is a process that links supply and demand. Marketing principles suggest a logical path toward courting demand:

1. *Segment* or divide the demand pie into many pieces.
2. *Target* or choose which segment or piece of the pie to serve with its products/services.
3. *Position* or promote and communicate the characteristics of the organization's product/services to these selected target customers in a way that helps customers understand how these products and services would be of unique benefit.

Positioning is the part of marketing where the familiar activities of selling, advertising, pricing, and so on take place. To give a practical illustration of this activity, we will examine how a hotel sales department is organized and operates to link supply and demand.

Exhibit 2.31   Today's hotel room-rates range from below $50 to over $650 per night. What you might pay depends on location, age, amenities, and ambiance. How about this room? Would you pay $100 per night? $200? $300? (*Courtesy: Four Seasons Hotels and Resorts*)

The Hotel Sales Department: The Link Between Supply and Demand
Personal sales is only one part of marketing a property. Referring to the traditional "four Ps" of marketing (Product, Price, Place, and Promotion), the sales department and the act of selling are considered part of promotion. Promotion is communicating the company's products and services to potential customers. The personal sales process occurs in the same fashion as does the full process of marketing. Salespeople must first locate potential customers, ask about their needs and wants, and then match their company's products and services, or supply, with this demand.

Exhibit 2.32 shows the organization structure of a hotel sales and marketing department. This specific example represents a high-end specialty conference-center

EYE ON THE ISSUES

Environment

With the growing concern for the environment, customers and other interested parties have begun making environmental demands upon the lodging industry. Two primary areas of environmental concerns for the lodging industry are "site pollution" and internal operational ecological considerations. Site pollution concerns arise when the lodging facility is built without regard for the surrounding natural environment, the architecture is incompatible with the natural surroundings, signage is too large, the facility's grounds have been overdeveloped, and so on. The Institute of EcoTourism on the campus of Sedona, Arizona's Los Abrigados Resort, was developed to raise public and industry awareness of such concerns and to act as an advocate of and a clearinghouse for ideas and success stories relating to sustainable tourism. One of their stated principles is that ecotourism "Relies on an infrastructure that has been developed in harmony with the environment."

property that has more than 300 rooms and earns 90 percent of its revenue from corporate and association group business. While different properties have widely varying revenue structures and niche markets, and usually fewer resources, this model serves to illustrate most group-directed sales and marketing functions.

Marketing management is generally the responsibility of the director of marketing (DOM) who delegates the specific management of the salespersons (Exhibit 2.32) to the director of sales (DOS). In some properties, these two management functions are handled by a single manager, the director of sales and marketing (DOS&M). In some small properties, the DOS&M also is the primary salesperson; in fact, the marketing department may consist of only one person. Whatever arrangement is used, all functions must still be accomplished.

In our illustration, the DOM delegates the sales management responsibility to the DOS, who reports to the DOM. The DOM is primarily responsible for advertising that is used to attract individual lodging guests and as a support tool to the group sales efforts. Additionally, the DOM oversees telemarketers, conference coordinators, and other support staff and represents the sales and marketing department to the hotel general manager. Telemarketers primarily locate solid potential customers and then turn these leads over to the experienced salespeople. Conference coordinators are specialists who make sure that groups meeting in the hotel receive effective service before, during, and after their meetings.

The director of sales directly designs the sales force and manages it on a daily basis. Often, the DOS also does a limited amount of personal selling. Designing a sales force entails setting sales objectives, devising a selling strategy, deciding the appropriate size and compensation for the sales team, and structuring appropriate selling territories. Once the DOS has recruited and trained the right people for the sales force, he or she can begin managing them. This includes directing their actions on a daily basis, motivating them, and, finally, evaluating their performance.

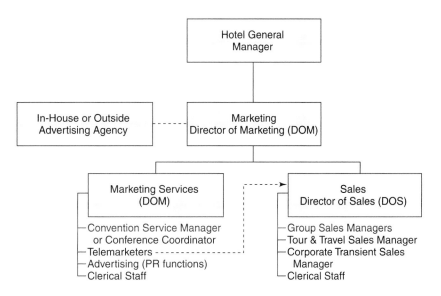

Exhibit 2.32   This chart shows the organization structure of a hotel sales and marketing department in a well-staffed, full-service property.

Exhibit 2.32 shows three types of **sales managers** (the term for salespeople in the hotel business) found in a typical sales department. *Corporate transient sales managers* are responsible for attracting individual business travelers. *Tour and travel sales managers* deal strictly with wholesale tour operators and retail travel agents. Finally, *group sales managers* specialize in corporate or association meetings. The discussion below concentrates on the duties of group sales managers to demonstrate how they match group meeting demand with hotel meeting service supply.

Group sales managers generally specialize in corporate or association meetings. Their territories are most commonly structured around geographic guidelines, usually East Coast, mid-United States, and West Coast markets. Sometimes their workload is organized according to industry. For example, a sales manager may concentrate on pharmaceutical corporations, oil companies, or accounting firms. Association business may be segmented by industries or memberships that they represent: trade associations, insurance, medical and professional, scientific, and so on. The territory or workload structure is dependent upon the overall strategy designed by the DOM and DOS. Effective sales managers bring supply and demand together through the selling process.

Exhibit 2.33   The ultimate cool: a night in the original IceHotel. Experiential tourists flocked to try this Nordic novelty, which has stimulated similar projects in North America. Which of the three types of sales manager would be able to sell this property? (*Courtesy*: Ice Hotel, Jukkasjärvi, Sweden)

Consistent with the marketing concepts discussed earlier, hotel group-sales managers are mini-marketing organizations unto themselves. They must effectively perform all the basic steps of marketing to bring hotel supply and customer demand together. They first prospect for and *qualify* potential customers (which is the equivalent of doing market research to discover customer needs and market segment characteristics). Then, through the approach and presentation steps, they communicate or promote the benefits offered by their hotel. Finally, by staying in contact with the customer prior, during, and after the meeting, they attempt to achieve the essence of effective marketing—acquiring and retaining customers.

Marketing, like so many other hotel departments, is symbiotic and interdependent with a hotel's other functional areas. Marketers will try hard to sell a dead horse and, if anyone could succeed, it would be them. But, the point is that marketers do best when they have a healthy horse to sell, one with a memorable name, proudly arched neck, and spirit. Marketing departments rely on the rooms division and property management to have clean, functioning rooms ready on time for their assigned occupants. They rely on the food and beverage staff to prepare and serve beautiful banquets and provide relaxing lounges and restaurants for clients eating "on their own."

By the same token, other departments rely on the sales and marketing department to communicate as precisely and solicitously with them as they do with clients. Every promise or guarantee that sales managers make to their clients should be documented and communicated to all departments affected by the "ripple" of the promise. If the client is told that an atrium balloon drop (first prize, a trip to the Riviera) will take place at 10:30 PM, all affected departments should be consulted *before the* promise is made!

If internal communication is given only a token nod, the best laid plans of meeting planners can go drastically astray. In the case of the balloon drop, suppose no one communicated with the plant maintenance people and they picked that afternoon to flood the atrium flower beds? Picture all the guests in black tie and taffeta trundling through the muddy planters in search of the winning balloon! Imagine the day that one sales manager books the north atrium for a Siamese cat show and another books the south atrium for the Animal Dander Allergy Sufferers Association (shown on the books only as the "ADASA" luncheon). You can paint your own comedy of errors, but be assured, if they happen on your property, they won't seem very funny.

The underlying preventative for such problems is internal communication with and respect for the functions of other departments. Marketing departments, with their staff of communication experts, can lead the way in encouraging consultation and cooperation between all lodging departments. This is essential even in the smallest properties, and only grows in importance as property size increases.

CONCLUSION

This chapter has presented an overview of lodging history and the lodging industry from a marketing philosophy standpoint. The essence of successful business operations is the successful exchange of products/services for value (usually monetary). Instead of simply describing components and elements, it views the industry as a dynamic interaction and exchange between supply (products/services) and demand (the customers' needs). It systematically discusses:

1. Lodging facility supply, the tourism system, and lodging product types
2. Lodging facility market demand and segment
3. Hotel business organizational structures
4. How a marketing subcomponent, personal sales, links the market segment, group/convention customers, with the lodging product
5. Current issues surrounding the lodging industry environmental, ethical, technological, and international

KEYWORDS

structure 47	affirmative duty 51
caravanserais 50	stagecoach inns 52
Middle Ages 50	mega-chains 67
Crusades 51	conference center 85
Renaissance Period 51	intermediary 94

CORE CONCEPTS

hotel 53	boom vs. bust 64
grand hotels 56	government tax incentives 64
hotel chain 56	supply 69
roadside cabins 57	holistic 69
motel 57	demand 69
franchise 76	market segments 69
vertical integration 62	tourism system 70
product segmentation 63	consortia 79
all-suite hotel 64	sales managers 100
mergers and acquisitions 64	

DISCUSSION QUESTIONS

1. Reviewing several historical periods, describe how fluctuations in demand have influenced changes in the types of lodging supply that evolved. Can you make any statement about the forces of demand and supply that would allow you to predict future trends in lodging supply?
2. In the 1980s, the lodging industry became overbuilt. What is the explanation for how this happened?
3. Do you think that the current trend of expanding lodging product segmentation is beneficial? Why? Why not?

4. Is there any relationship between types of lodging supply and changes in transportation? If so, explain this relationship and cite at least two examples that illustrate your explanation.
5. Describe and interrelate the tourism system components. Why must members of the lodging industry be knowledgeable about changes that occur within this system?
6. Why are tourists motivated to travel? Include in your discussion both business and pleasure travelers—groups and independent travel.
7. Describe the organization of a sales and marketing department at a full-service hotel.

EXEMPLAR OF EXCELLENCE

American Automobile Association

AAA is a federation of 81 motor clubs serving more than 46 million members in the United States and Canada. Now the world's second largest member organization, it started humbly in Chicago in 1902 to assist drivers on primitive roads with emergency road service and maps. Since then, it has expanded into a respected independent rater of lodging and dining facilities, a travel services resource . . . and later into insurance, investment, the certification of repair facilities, and advocate for travel safety. Members enjoy discounts and services. AAA ratings, especially its coveted five-Diamond designation, are highly prized. After you have visited the AAA site, do a Google search on the strings American Automobile Association and five diamond. Take a look at the levels of service and amenities at these unique facilities. Less than one-third of one percent of all properties inspected receive the AAA Five Diamond award (out of a field of some 45,000 properties). Identify one of these Five Diamond properties and bring a description of it to class.
URL: http://www.aaa.com/

WEBSITES TO VISIT

1. http://www.arda.org
   American Resort Development Association. Notice the kinds of issues being highlighted to members or on the agenda for an upcoming ARDA conference. For idea of the complexity of timeshares, visit the code of ethics page. Note the extensive use of definitions. Why would this be important?
2. http://www.rci.com/
   Resort Condominiums International, the world's largest vacation (timeshare) exchange company. Pick a country and look at some of the offerings. Do you imagine that the growth of the Internet has directly contributed to the boom in the timeshare industry? Why or why not?
3. Do a Google search on the terms "King Tut" and "Steve Martin."
   Find the words (or maybe even a media clip) for this hit music video. Although this song is meant to be comedy, it makes some points about tourism . . . and maybe even timeshares. What are they? How is King Tut connected to 20th century tourism? Recall

from your chapter: In early history, what types of travel are the Egyptians thought to have added beyond travel for trade and government? When? What themed mega-resort in Las Vegas capitalizes on Egyptian images?

4. http://www.entrepreneur.com/Franzone

   Entrepreneur Magazine lists many franchises on this site. Choose a category (such as food or hotels) and browse through available franchise names. Note the estimated start-up costs for some popular brand names. Choose a franchise you've never heard of. Collect a paragraph's worth of info on it. Can you identify a region or state where most of the franchised properties are located? Does the franchising company sell franchises beyond the area? If they do, do you think it would be an advantage or disadvantage to open up a franchise far away from this core? Why? Why not?

5. Do a Google search on the phrase "oldest inn in the world."

   Where is this inn? Or where *was* it? Does there appear to be debate on this subject? Does this debate have anything to do with ethnocentricity?

REFERENCES

Dorf, D. C. (1992). *The Early Days of Hotel Sales: A Historical Look at the Development and Growth of Hotel Business Promotion*. Unpublished masters thesis, School of Food, Hotel and Travel Management, Rochester Institute of Technology, Rochester, NY.

Gee, Chuck Y. (1994). *International Hotels: Development and Management*. East Lansing, Michigan: Educational Institute of the American Hotel & Motel Association.

Giants Survey 1998 (July, 1999). "Hotels 325," *Hotels Magazine*. 48–77.

Gomes, A. J. (1985). *Hospitality in Transition: A Retrospective and Prospective Look at the U.S. Lodging Industry*. Washington, D.C.: American Hotel and Motel Association.

HVS Executive Search (1999). *Hospitality Sales & Marketing Compensation Survey*. Washington, D.C.: HSMAI Foundation.

Lang, H. E. & Dupre, D. (1997). *Hospitality World*. New York: Van Nostrand Reinhold.

Lundberg, D. E. (1989). *The Hotel and Restaurant Business*. New York: Van Nostrand Reinhold.

Mill, R. C., and A. M. Morrison (1985). *The Tourism System*. Englewood Cliffs, NJ: Prentice Hall.

Rushmore, S. (1992). *Hotels and Motels: A Guide to Market Analysis, Investment Analysis, and Valuations*. Chicago: Appraisal Institute.

Rushmore, S. (September, 1999). "The Real Cost of Hotel Franchises," *Hotels Magazine,* 40.

World Travel & Tourism Council (1995). *Travel & Tourism: A New Economic Perspective*. London: World Travel & Tourism Council.

CHAPTER 3

Rooms Division

Front of the House Operations

The **rooms division** is the name given to all the hotel operations departments. Included in the rooms division is the front desk itself (where guests check in, check out, and meet with guest service agents), the uniformed services department (primarily bellpersons, concierges, and security), and hotel reservations (including the PBX). This chapter will give you a sneak preview of the rooms division and its importance in the lodging experience.

INTRODUCTION

Welcome to the exciting world of hotel customer service. Once you are familiar with the interesting positions and activities of the rooms division, you will have an enticing new option for a life-long career. Your future as a rooms division manager awaits you. This chapter will acquaint you with several key departments within the lodging sector of the hospitality industry.

Hotels and motels, the primary components of the lodging sector of our industry, are usually quite different from each other in terms of physical, procedural, and operational characteristics. However, different as most operations are, there are also a number of similarities. One aspect common to hotel and motel operations is the *departmentalization of the rooms division.*

All hotels, regardless of size or price, have a rooms division. The rooms division is different from other hotel departments because of its extensive responsibility. In fact, the rooms division is generally considered to house three separate departments: *reservations, front office,* and *uniformed services.*

In larger hotels, these three departments are quite sizable, consisting of several hundred or more employees; in smaller operations (such as motels, for example), these three departments may be so small that they are adequately handled by just one or two individuals. No matter the number of employees or the size of the hotel, the rooms division generally handles a wide variety of responsibilities and functions. This chapter examines the three departments of the rooms division and explains their specific responsibilities.

POPULAR POSITIONS FOR COLLEGE STUDENTS

One reason the rooms division is an interesting area of study in hospitality education is because so many students find employment there. The rooms division offers students a variety of job positions while attending college. These positions may include front desk clerk, reservationist, uniformed bellperson, cashier, and/or night auditor. Students like working in the rooms division of hotels because such jobs generally offer flexible schedules, good pay ranges, and exciting personal contact with guests.

More important, rooms division positions are frequently available to college students who possess little or no lodging experience. In many cases, the college student need not even be 21 years of age. Although they are generally considered entry-level jobs, rooms division positions offer students an excellent opportunity to gain valuable experience and a chance to advance up the corporate ladder. The rooms division is so exciting that some students who originally planned to pursue other college majors ultimately opt to pursue hotel management degrees instead.

Departments Critical to Hotel Success

As interesting as the rooms division proves for many college students, it is of paramount interest to hotel general managers. The three departments of the rooms division are important to hotel general managers because they are the ***pivot points*** around which the entire hotel operation revolves. The rooms division is the pivot, or lifeline, of hotel operations for three main reasons: economics, customer service, and departmental forecasting.

Exhibit 3.1   College students find front office jobs both stimulating and flexible. (*Courtesy:* Four Seasons Hotels and Resorts)

Economics.   The rooms division is the pivot point in terms of economics because it is responsible for most, if not all, of the property's revenue. In small, **economy- or budget-lodging** operations (e.g., Motel 6, Sleep Inn, EconoLodge), the rooms division generates practically 100 percent of every dollar earned by the motel. After all, other than the sale of rooms, there are few other ***revenue centers*** in a budget property. As Chapter 7 explains in its discussion of segments and niches, by definition, budget-lodging operations do not have restaurants, lounges, convention centers, or health spas. Therefore, other than a few small revenue centers like soda-vending machines, pay telephones, newspaper stands, or video-arcade games, the rooms division represents the vast majority of income in budget-lodging (also known as limited-service) operations.

Unlike budget properties, **full-service lodging** operations generate considerable revenues from other departments. Yet even in full-service lodging operations (e.g., Four Seasons, Marriott, Sheraton), the rooms division generates substantially more than half of the hotel's revenues (see Exhibit 3.2). Indeed, even in casino properties where gaming is the clear income leader, the rooms division is the second most important department (gaming revenues generate roughly 66 percent of all income, the rooms division is next with about 20 percent of income, and all other departments generate the remaining 14 percent of income) and many executives are quick to point out that the casino would not earn nearly as much revenue if the rooms division were not supplying rooms for tired gamblers.

Customer Service.   ***Customer service*** is as critical to the rooms division as food is to the restaurant. It is truly the staple of the rooms division. No other department or functional area of the hotel has as much guest contact as the rooms division. Indeed, the rooms division represents both the customer's first and last impressions of a hotel.

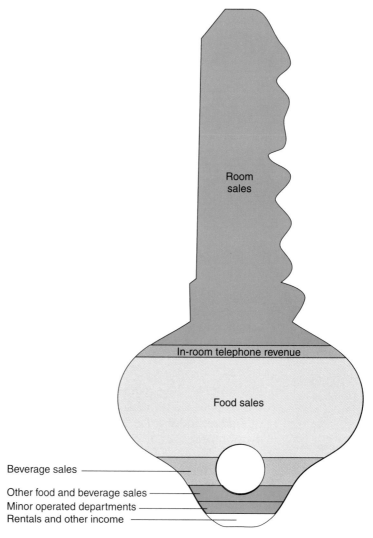

Exhibit 3.2   Full-service hotels earn far more revenue from the sale of hotel rooms than all other departments (food, beverage, other rentals, etc.) combined. When you add in-room telephone revenues, full-service properties generate almost 70 cents from every dollar through the rooms division. Limited-service (budget) operations generate closer to 97 cents from every dollar through the sale of rooms. (*Source:* Arthur Andersen, "The Host Report—Hotel Operating Statistics," compiled by Smith Travel Research, pp. 40, 49.)

In fact, the entire rooms division is designed to provide full guest service. The rooms division in many fine hotels provides bellpersons, front desk personnel, concierges, and the like—all with the goal of providing the highest possible level of guest service. Most experts agree that the quality of service and guest contact provided by the **front office** and related departments is a crucial factor in the overall guest experience.

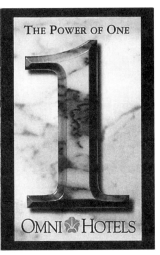

Exhibit 3.3 By distributing this handy business-card-size recap of its core principles, Omni Hotels emphasizes its commitment to empowerment. Omni sets a high standard of professionalism for its employees and trusts them to make decisions (and even "bend the rules" a bit) if it will benefit the guest experience.(*Courtesy:* Omni Hotels, Irving, Texas)

Departmental Forecasting.   In an effort to increase employee morale, satisfaction, and efficiency, managers plan staffing schedules one to two weeks in advance. However, advanced scheduling requires accurate knowledge about upcoming business activity. Managers need to know how busy or slow the hotel expects to be so that they can staff their departments accordingly. **Forecasting** information related to upcoming business levels is a primary responsibility of the reservations department of the rooms division.

Because the reservations department knows the expected numbers of guests and types of rooms needed each day, it is responsible for providing accurate forecasting information to every other hotel department. This makes sense, because business in every other operational department is primarily a function of the number of rooms sold. The restaurant, for example, will sell more breakfasts the

EYE ON THE ISSUES

Ethics

Because the rooms division is a profit-generating operation, it must practice strategies and make business decisions that some guests perceive as unethical. Several generally accepted lodging practices that guests construe as unethical include overbooking, seasonal room rate adjusting, and yield management.

In terms of overbooking, the hotel has a legal obligation to accommodate confirmed reservations. Therefore, many guests believe that hotels should not overbook deliberately. But hotels use overbooking as a technique to enhance their occupancy in a world they consider full of potential no-shows. Hotels deliberately overbook by the number of rooms they expect to no-show. Sometimes the hotel's estimate is inaccurate, and guests are "walked" to another hotel. For the walked guest, this may be a question of ethics. For the hotel, it is more a question of economics.

The practice of increasing room rates during busy seasons or holiday periods as a means of maximizing revenue during periods of high demand is also dimly viewed by guests. Many guests find it an unconscionable practice to raise rates, say $100 between Thursday night and Friday night. According to these guests, it is unethical to raise the rate just because Friday night is the beginning of a busy holiday weekend.

A final example can be found in yield management practices industry wide. Through the introduction of yield management technology, room rates fluctuate according to a variety of factors. Some guests have a difficult time understanding why the same room costs significantly more just because it was booked at the last minute or because it was one of the few such rooms remaining in the hotel. These guests don't understand the practice of altering rates according to demand. If the hotel is nearly 100 percent occupied, the hotel can easily raise the rate and squeeze a few extra dollars out of the remaining rooms available.

---

morning after a full house than it will during slower occupancy periods of the hotel. Business levels in the lounge, health spa, casino, or any other department are likewise closely related to the number of hotel rooms sold.

CHANGING TECHNOLOGIES

The hotel industry is not immune to the vast technological changes taking place across the globe. In fact, the rooms division is often the point of introduction for new devices, software applications, and hardware components used in hotels. Other chapters touch on such new applications as electronic locking systems, property management systems, self–check-in and check-out terminals, and in-room technologies including safes, television interfaces, and minibars.

New technologies have forever altered the way the rooms division functions. Years ago, literally every aspect of the rooms division was manual. The entire ***guest cycle*** (see "Guest Cycle" later in this chapter) including reservations, arrival, check-in, visitation, check-out, and billing, was performed manually. Today, some hotels have automated every step of the guest cycle, using such new technologies as:

- Central reservations systems with toll-free telephone as well as Internet access
- Self-check-in terminals built directly into airport courtesy vans for registration during the arrival process.
- Fully integrated property management systems that monitor billing activity during the guest's visit.

Exhibit 3.4   Most experts agree that an automated front office is a friendlier front office. Less time spent with paper and pen translates to more "face" time. (*Courtesy:* Springer-Miller Systems, Incorporated, Stowe, Vermont)

- Automated minibar systems that immediately charge the guest's account for each item removed from the refrigerator.
- In-room television interfaces where the guest can view the account and check-out from the privacy of the hotel room.

Few hotels have this degree of automation today. Many properties simply cannot afford a great deal of expensive technology; other hotels are skeptical of experimenting with new forms of technology, and still other operations are convinced that automating too many steps of the guest cycle will cause a decline in one-on-one guest service.

Though technology is surely the wave of the future, most students should be prepared for a mixed bag of rooms division applications. Most hotels have some form of rooms division technology interlaced with plenty of good old-fashioned manual applications.

As you can see, hotels are busy places, which offer great career opportunities to young students and graduates. No matter what department you choose to work in, it's likely you'll enjoy your job immensely. However, as this introductory section has demonstrated, the rooms division represents some of the most critically important positions in the entire industry. The various departments that comprise the rooms division (front office, reservations/PBX, and uniformed services) are especially challenging . . . but we think you're up to the task! The next section highlights some of these positions and explains the responsibilities of each.

JOB POSITIONS IN THE ROOMS DIVISION

Hotels generally divide job positions into **front of the house** and **back of the house.** Front-of-the-house job positions are considered more guest-service oriented than their back-of-the-house counterparts. Front-of-the-house job positions

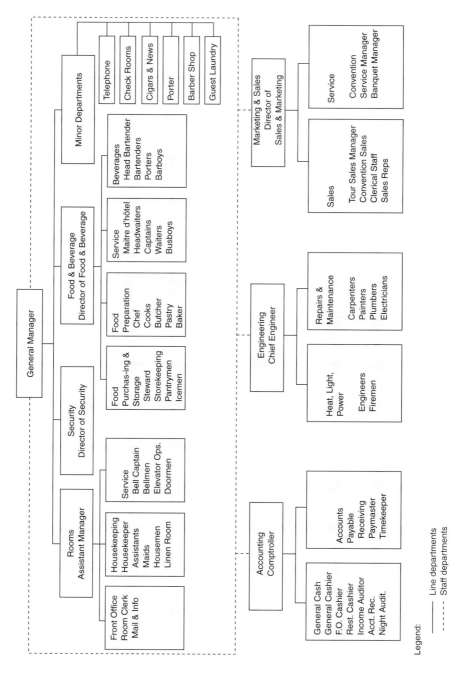

Exhibit 3.5 Typical organization structure (full-service hotel). Depending on circumstances (such as the economy or management philosophy) the organizational structure may be "flattened."

Legend:
——— Line departments
------ Staff departments

Exhibit 3.6   In many first-class hotels, the lobby is the focal point of the property's ambiance. No expense is spared. This is the lobby of the Cleveland Airport Marriott Hotel. (*Courtesy:* Boykin Lodging, Cleveland, Ohio)

usually afford the employee direct and frequent contact with the guest. The actual quality or amount of guest contact varies with the specific job position. Rooms division jobs generally have some of the highest incidence of guest contact. This contact requires the front of the house employee to be well versed in such guest-service skills as handling complaints, providing local and hotel-specific advice and suggestions, and providing a well rounded customer experience. Because of this constant contact with the guest, rooms division positions are critical links in the hotel's efforts to provide quality guest service to all patrons.

This does not mean that back of the house job positions are not equally important links in terms of quality guest service. They truly are, because they are responsible for preparing and maintaining the guest product. Although they are generally considered guest-support rather than guest-service positions, back-of-the-house employees do have ample opportunities to communicate with the customer. Examples of contact between guests and back-of-the-house employees might include a groundskeeper who assists a guest with directions, a housekeeper who performs the evening turn-down service, or a banquet set-up person who rearranges a room according to a client's request.

Practically every job position listed in the rooms division is considered front-of-the-house. In fact, almost the entire guest cycle involves some component of the rooms division. It is easy to see why most general managers consider the rooms division the key to creating a climate of quality guest service throughout the operation. In the following subsection we'll examine job positions within the three departments of the rooms division, reservations, front office, and uniformed services.

The Reservations Department

In most cases, the reservations department is the first contact the guest has with the hotel. The overall quality of this initial experience is often a key factor in the guest's selection of one particular hotel over another. A reservationist who has a pleasant voice, actively answers guest questions, and markets special features of the hotel has a better chance of booking a reservation than someone who merely acts as an order taker. A positive reservation experience is the first step in ensuring quality guest service.

Aside from ensuring a quality service experience, the reservations department is charged with two other key tasks: selling rooms and communicating forecast statistics. The first of these tasks, selling rooms, is critical to the economic health of the hotel. As we have already discussed, room sales is the number one source of revenue for most hotels. It is the reservations department's responsibility to sell rooms in an efficient manner. In terms of this discussion, *efficiency* translates into maximizing occupancy and maximizing average room rate. A reservations department that fills as many hotel rooms as possible at the highest rate possible is worth its weight in gold. A more detailed discussion of efficiency is available later in this chapter under "Yield Management."

The third primary responsibility assigned to the reservations department is forecasting rooms sales statistics. As suggested earlier in this chapter, all departments in the hotel rely on the reservations department to provide them with accurate 10- to 14-day forecasts. These forecasts become the basis for business projections by all other departments in the hotel. When the reservations department predicts a full house next week, all departments staff accordingly—the food and beverage department will be busy in its various restaurants and lounges, the housekeeping department will clean a maximum number of rooms, and the front desk will have to deal with a great number of check-ins and check-outs. In a casino property, even the gaming department respect the reservations department's forecasts as an accurate barometer of business levels.

Job Positions in the Reservations Department.

There are relatively few distinct positions in the reservations department. In fact, many operations treat these positions as training grounds for future advancement into the front office. The reservationist's experience in dealing with guest service, selling rooms in an efficient manner, and providing business-level forecasts provides a good foundation from which to advance to other positions in the hotel. The reservations department is responsible for taking, canceling, monitoring, and accounting for all reservations.

Positions in the in-house reservations department generally include, in descending order of responsibility, reservations manager, one or more reservations agents, and one or more reservations clerks (see Exhibit 3.7).

PBX Operators.

Just as reservations is a training ground for advancement to the front office, the PBX department is the initial job for many reservations clerks. The PBX (which stands for Private Branch Exchange) is the hotel's internal telephone system. The PBX system allows guests to place calls to other rooms, hotel departments, and even outside the hotel. It also handles all internal telephone calls made by various operational departments.

Years ago, the PBX was a labor-intensive department. Every phone call, whether in-house or off-property, required a PBX operator's assistance. It was not uncom-

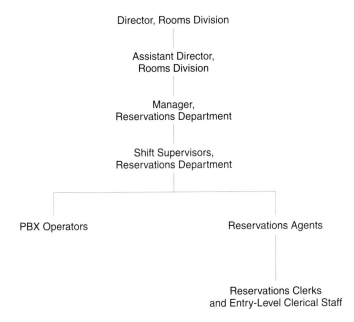

Director, Rooms Division

Assistant Director,
Rooms Division

Manager,
Reservations Department

Shift Supervisors,
Reservations Department

PBX Operators   Reservations Agents

Reservations Clerks
and Entry-Level Clerical Staff

Exhibit 3.7   Staffing hierarchy of the reservations department. While large properties might have an even taller organizational chart with dozens of reservations agents, small hotels may assign these responsibilities (reservations, PBX, etc.) to front office guest service agents. Also, in some properties, the reservations department manager may report to the front office (front desk) manager.

mon to see upwards of 20 operators working in a major property. Today, almost all hotels have fully automated PBX systems, and as such, staffing is almost nonexistent (what staffing does exist usually reports through the reservations department). Guests and operational departments are able to make direct phone calls without the assistance of an operator. Even in-coming calls, messages, and wake-up services are handled electronically in many properties. The PBX is one department where the introduction of technology translated directly into reduced staff.

The Front Office

The **front office** (also called the front desk) is the second of the three departments in the rooms division. The front office is the primary guest service department of the entire hotel. Generally, no other hotel department has the opportunity for as much guest contact as the front office.

Although there are a number of very specific duties accruing to the front office, most can be categorized in the following list of generic tasks and front office activities: greeting the guest; performing guest check-in and registration: selecting and assigning guest rooms; establishing credit and method of payment; opening, posting, and closing the guest account; cashing personal checks, travelers' checks, and foreign currency, and issuing safe deposit boxes; listening to and solving a wide range of guest complaints; communicating guest information between departments; performing guest check-out and farewell; and ensuring quality service across all of these tasks and activities.

Just as the rooms division is divided into three departments (reservations, front office, and uniformed services), the front office department is often divided into three functional subdepartments: the front desk, the cashiers, and the night audit.

Many hotels add a fourth department under the umbrella of the rooms division; the housekeeping department. However, for the purposes of this book, the authors have separated housekeeping from the rooms division reporting lines (the housekeeping department is discussed in Chapter 4). This arrangement is not unique to the structure of this textbook. Many hotels design their reporting lines such that the housekeeping department reports outside the normal flow of the rooms division. In such hotels, housekeeping often reports directly to the general manager or possibly to a dedicated vice president of back of the house operations (which might include housekeeping, maintenance and engineering).

Job Positions at the Front Desk.   The front desk is responsible for the initial contact with the guest through greeting, registration, and room assignment. In addition, most guest problems, room changes, information requests, or other guest contacts are generally handled by the desk clerks.

Positions within the front desk functional subdepartment generally include a front desk manager, one or more front desk shift supervisors, one or more front desk clerks (guest service agents) and some entry-level clerical positions (see Exhibit 3.9).

Job Positions of the Cashier Staff.   The front office cashiers are responsible for opening guest accounts, posting charges to the account during the guest's visit, and closing the account upon departure. Since the closing of an account is the final stage in the guest cycle, front office cashiers have most of their contact with the guest during the check-out phase of the guest cycle (see "Guest Cycle" later in this chapter). Likewise, though most complaints are handled by front desk clerks, monetary complaints or problems associated with the **_guest folio_** (also known as the _guest bill_ or _guest account)_ are handled by the front desk cashiers.

Many hotels cross-train their clerks and cashiers. A cross-trained employee is capable of serving as either guest service agent or cashier at any given moment. This

Exhibit 3.8   A front desk in a mid-sized hotel. (_Photo:_ Rob Crandall/The Stock Connection)

Director, Rooms Division

Assistant Director,
Rooms Division

Manager, Front Office

Supervisors, Front Desk Shift
and/or Cashiers

Night Auditors

Front Desk Cashiers

Front Desk Clerks
Guest Service Agents

Entry-Level
Clerical Staff

Exhibit 3.9   Staffing hierarchy of the front office (front desk) department. Notice the term "front desk clerk" has increasingly been renamed "guest service agent." This is an attempt to focus the job title more on the service it provides than the clerical nature of the position. A similar example is found in the housekeeping department where "maids" have been increasingly renamed "guest room attendants."

makes a great deal of sense in terms of quality customer service. After all, when the desk is busy with arrivals, there are relatively few guests checking out; therefore, most cashiers can be temporarily reassigned to serve as guest service agents. During busy check-out periods, there are relatively few guests checking in; therefore, most front desk clerks can be temporarily reassigned to serve as cashiers. Not only does this make sense from the guest's point of view, but the hotel also realizes significant labor cost savings by operating with a relatively smaller, well trained staff, ready to take on any challenge (see Exhibit 3.9).

Positions within the cashier subdepartment may include the cashier supervisor and the cashier.

Job Positions of the Night Audit.   The night audit is the third functional subdepartment found at the front desk. The **night audit** is so-called because it is a nightly audit reconciliation of hotel accounts and departments. The night audit is generally conducted between the hours of 11 PM and 7 AM (this shift is generally referred to as the **graveyard shift**) because this is the slowest period for the hotel.

Because it is basically an accounting activity, the night audit seeks employees who are naturally adept with numbers and accounting practices (as well as employees who can function during late-night hours). Because of these unique skills (and the fact that the graveyard shift offers rather unappealing hours), the night auditor is the highest paid hourly employee at the front desk.

The night auditor must also perform all front desk clerk and cashiering duties that may arise during the graveyard shift, although there is usually little such activity during the late hours of the audit. The bulk of the night auditor's shift is spent posting room charges and tax to all rooms, verifying and balancing accounts for all guest rooms and hotel departments, and preparing a series of summary reports about departmental revenue activities from the preceding day.

Positions within the night audit subdepartment may include the night audit shift supervisor and the night auditor (see Exhibit 3–9).

Uniformed Services

The third department included in the rooms division is **uniformed services**. The uniformed services department is also known as the guest services department or the hotel services department. The uniformed services department is so called because employees of this department wear distinct uniforms to assist the guest in identifying them as hotel front-of-the-house employees.

These uniforms help identify uniformed services employees as members of the bell staff, the concierge staff, the hotel security force, or doorpersons. Each of these positions is responsible for providing quality guest service to all customers.

The size of the uniformed services department varies according to the size and type of hotel. Because this department is so labor intensive, small economy- or budget-lodging operations can ill afford these positions. Guests do not expect to find uniformed services employees in economy- or budget-lodging operations. Instead, guests understand that there is a necessary trade-off between service and price. They are willing to be somewhat inconvenienced (for example, they must carry their own luggage) and to receive less service (they may have to find answers to their own questions instead of asking a concierge) in exchange for a lower hotel room rate.

On the other side of the spectrum are luxury and full-service hotel operations. These properties, by their very nature, provide a full range of uniformed services employees. The guest who is willing to pay a higher average room rate can expect

Exhibit 3.10   The bell position is both fun and rewarding, but it takes a true talent with guest service to be a successful bell person. (Photo by Will Verbeeten, Foto Verbeeten, Groesbeek, The Netherlands)

the full-service hotel to provide a bell staff, a concierge staff, hotel security, and doorpersons.

Job Positions of the Bell Staff.   The bell department is responsible for carrying luggage and escorting guests to and from rooms during the check-in and check-out stages of the guest cycle, handling baggage for groups, and promoting the various facilities within the hotel to guests. In many hotels, the bell department also operates the complimentary airport and local shuttle service. In addition, bellpersons maintain cleanliness in the lobby areas and provide information to guests in the absence of a concierge. Bellpersons are also commonly asked to assist hotel management with various errands as they arise.

Positions within the bell department usually include a bell captain and several bellpersons (also known as bellmen or bellboys—see Exhibit 3.11).

Job Positions of the Concierge Staff.   The **concierge** (pronounced kon'sy-erzh) is a relatively new position in America that has gained popularity since the early 1970s. The concierge originated in medieval Europe as little more than a doorkeeper. Today, concierges are polished professionals charged with the delivery of guest service in a myriad of forms.

The concierge is the hotel's expert with regard to local activities and attractions. The concierge may be the individual who helps the guest secure tickets to a sold-out performance or sporting event, who recommends a special restaurant or museum, who gives directions or secures transportation, and who arranges tours and baby-sitting. Stories abound of concierges who have provided unique service under unusual circumstances. These stories include finding and decorating a guest's room with 100 dozen white roses; securing freshly laid, brown farm eggs each day for a famous actress; and finding a dentist to pull a tooth for a miserable guest at 2 AM.

In some hotels the concierge position works as a specialized counterpart of the bell staff by providing an extra component of service and information away from the hectic pace of the bell desk. Indeed, in those operations that do not provide concierge service, most functions of this position fall to the bell department. In such cases, it is the bell department that arranges transportation, finds tickets, and makes appropriate recommendations.

Exhibit 3.11   Staffing hierarchy of the uniformed services department. Though newcomers to the industry sometimes think "uniformed services" refers to housekeeping, room service, and engineering employees, it actually refers to such front of the house, customer service–trained positions as bellpersons, concierges, security officers, and doorpersons. Though this chart shows the bell captain and concierge at the same level of hierarchy, in some operations, the concierge reports to the bell captain. In fact the bell captain also functions as the manager of uniformed services in many hotels.

Exhibit 3.12   The concierge may be headquartered in an exclusive wing or set of guest rooms (concierge floors), or as in this photo, be centrally located in the hotel lobby. (*Courtesy:* Los Angeles Hilton And Towers, Los Angeles, California)

In full-service hotels that staff the concierge position, these services are usually provided in two distinct ways. One method for providing concierge services is to limit access to the higher paying guest. Hotels limit access to these services by providing **concierge floors** or wings. In this manner, only those guests staying on the more expensive concierge floors or wings are allowed to enjoy the services. Although these rooms may be somewhat more upscale than other rooms in the hotel, the guest is primarily paying a surcharge for access to concierge services. In rough numbers, this surcharge averages about $50 per room night. The second method is to establish concierge services in the lobby of the hotel. In this way, access to the concierge is provided to all hotel patrons. Other hotels offer some combination of these two techniques.

Job Positions of the Security Staff.   Along with providing clean and comfortable accommodations, the rooms division is also responsible for providing a safe haven for guests. Guest safety includes room key security; the prevention of burglary, forced entry into the room, or personal harm; fire safety; deterrence of prostitution and drug use; and control of minor inconveniences like excessive noise at late hours. These issues pose a big responsibility for the security staff.

Today's electronic hotels, however, are simplifying and streamlining the role of the security staff. Closed-circuit cameras aid the tracking of unauthorized individuals throughout the hotel; fire safety systems assist with constant monitoring of fire prevention equipment; electronic locking systems remove the threat of lost room keys and unwarranted break-ins; and electronic guest history systems provide information related to medical problems or personal information that might assist security personnel in an emergency.

The size and scope of this department are a function of hotel size and type. Very large hotel operations have an entire department dedicated to security and headed by the director of security. Average-sized hotels may employ only one or two such officers per shift. Smaller operations often contract this function to independent professional security companies. In any case, the bell staff is frequently called upon to assist the security department.

The security officer is responsible for making rounds throughout the hotel and assisting guests and staff during emergency situations. Most hotels require this position to have at least minimal life-safety training.

Other Job Positions in the Uniformed Services Department.   Again, the number and types of other uniformed positions are a function of the size and type of hotel. Other common positions may include doorpersons who meet, greet, and assist the arriving and departing guests under the *porte cochère,* (a covered arrival area); van and shuttle drivers who pick up and return guests to the airport and other transportation terminals; and valet parking attendants who park and retrieve guest automobiles.

EYE ON THE ISSUES

Technology

The rooms division of the hotel has probably seen more technological advancements in the past 10 years than any other area in the industry. As a result, today's front office employee must be knowledgeable in many new forms of automation. The breadth of this automation extends from the guest's reservation to the check-in process and even to the selection of in-room technologies.

The guest reservation process is one excellent example of change in recent years. Guests now receive up-to-the-minute room rate and occupancy quotes via **last room availability** systems interfaced with corporate yield management software. And all of this information can be downloaded to the future guests' personal computer via an Internet link-up to the global distribution system.

The check-in process has also undergone significant change over the past 10 years, as more and more hotel front offices have shifted their focus from manual processes to automated property management systems (PMSs). Examples of applications provided by today's fully automated front desks include: guest history databases that track personal and hotel utilization information, housekeeping interfaces that automatically detail daily housekeeping schedules, electronic locking systems that prepare a new key combination each time the room is sold, and additional modules that post bills from and share front-office data to a number of other integrated departments.

Another major technological change occurring in the hotel industry is the acceptance by many guests of self check-in and self check-out terminals. Corporate guests are especially pleased to find an increasing number of these terminals. Instead of waiting in long front desk lines, guests can help themselves by inserting their credit card and following the steps outlined by the terminal.

Full-service hotels that do not offer self-service terminals may provide a similar check-out service via the in-room guest television. These in-room television systems also allow the guest access to a number of other services, including ordering room service directly from the television menu, viewing telephone messages, purchasing items from the gift shop or catalog, and even programming a morning wake-up call.

Two other, historically common, uniformed services positions have been fully replaced in today's modern hotels. Elevator operators, who once played an important role in quality guest service, and pages, who delivered messages to guests before the advent of electronic paging systems, are no longer part of today's uniformed services departments.

THE GUEST CYCLE

The three departments that comprise the rooms division of a hotel share a long list of tasks and responsibilities. Entire textbooks are dedicated to the multitude of functions associated with the rooms division. Therefore, no single chapter can completely outline each aspect of every job position within this division. Even employees who have worked in the hotel industry are amazed at the degree of variety and change associated with their jobs on a day-to-day basis.

Furthermore, each lodging operation conducts tasks in a very individualized fashion. Learning the specific routine at one establishment is no guarantee that you will be able to perform effectively at a different property. The only guarantee is understanding that all hotels and rooms divisions perform roughly the same general functions. As a student, you must visualize the big picture in terms of understanding the primary functions of the rooms division.

This section presents an overview of the rooms division by paralleling the guest cycle. Understanding the guest cycle is an excellent way to gain insight into those functions common across all hotels. By examining each logical step of the guest cycle—reservations, arrival and check-in, visitation, and check-out and billing—we can better understand the role of the rooms division (see Exhibit 3.13). The first stage of the guest cycle is the reservation.

Reservations

Although there is a variety of reservation types, they all have the same basic purpose. An advanced reservation is designed to match the guest's need for accommodations with the hotel's ability to provide accommodations. If the two parties—

Reservations
- Central reservations offices
- Last room availability
- Yield management
- Overbooking
- Walk-ins

Arrival and Check-In
- Upselling
- Type of plan
- Rooming the guest

Visitation
- Average length of stay
- Complaints
- Posting charges

Check-Out and Billing
- Late charges
- Folio settlement
- Direct billing

Exhibit 3.13   The guest cycle. There is an unlimited number of alterations to this simple graphical illustration. Alterations occur based upon the size, type, and level of automation found in each particular property. For example, reservations might be made via the Internet, through a travel agent, with a contracted corporate rep, or even over a subscription central reservations service. The arrival process might be enhanced with remote terminals in the airport van, an interactive kiosk near luggage claim, or through a satellite location commonly found in large group properites. The visitation might include a trip to the golf course, the spa, the casino, or the amusement park. And the check-out might be performed in-room over an interfaced television set, at a self check-in/check-out terminal in the lobby, or via zip-out check-out, sometimes found even in non-automated properties.

guest and hotel—agree on the date, room type, price, and length of stay, then a reservation can be made.

There are a number of ways in which a reservation is communicated to the property. Let's examine one straightforward example of a reservation: The guest telephones the property directly and asks for the in-house reservations department. The hotel's in-house reservationist answers the phone call and discusses the reservation's particulars with the guest. The reservationist then checks hotel room availability (either manually in some type of log book or chart, or electronically through a computer reservations screen) for the specific date. If the date is available, the reservationist quotes the guest a rate (rates are usually quoted from the highest rate downward, offering one room category at a time until the guest makes a selection) and tries to book the reservation. Even if the date is not available, the reservationist will usually suggest an alternate date in an attempt to convert the call into a future booking.

The reservation process remains roughly the same across all types of reservations inquiries. Other types of reservations inquiries include such possibilities as requests by mail, by a travel agent, as part of a larger convention or tour group, or as part of a complete travel package booked through an airline. The most popular type of reservations request, however, is through a chain or independent central reservations office.

Central Reservations Offices. Most hotels today are affiliated with a central reservations office (CRO) or central reservations system. If the hotel is a chain property (e.g., Holiday Inn, Hilton, or Quality Inn), the guest calls the 1-800 phone number for the **central reservations system (CRS)**. Even if the hotel is not affiliated with a chain or referral organization, it may be linked to a private or subscription central reservations system.

Because the CRS is answering phone calls for all properties within the chain or membership, the actual physical location of the CRS is unimportant. Guests who call to make a reservation for a given destination rarely know the actual location of the 1-800 CRS to which they are speaking. For example, imagine that a prospective guest who lives in Los Angeles, California, has called 1-800-331-3131 to seek accommodations at a Residence Inn by Marriott in Orlando, Florida. This guest has no idea that the Marriott CRS reservationist on the other end of the phone is actually located in Omaha, Nebraska. In fact, one popular chain's CRS was actually staffed by incarcerated (low-risk) prisoners at a women's correctional institute in Phoenix, Arizona!

Central reservations systems act on behalf of the hotel by taking reservations and forwarding the information to the specific property. This is an important service and one of the leading reasons hotels choose to franchise or affiliate with well known brands. Indeed, some properties receive upward of 75 percent of all their reservations through a CRS. It is easy to see why so many hotels depend, in part, upon CRSs to book their reservations.

However, CRS services are incredibly expensive. Complex central reservations systems capable of handling several million telephone calls per year may cost upward of $250 million for development and implementation. The high cost of such a system is passed on to the individual member hotel in the form of annual charges and flat fees for each room night booked on the CRS. Depending on the chain or CRS service, reservation fees run somewhere around $2 to $6 per room night if booked across the CRS.

Last Room Availability.   Today, the CRS is one of the fastest growing areas of new technology in the hotel industry. Most major lodging chains have either replaced or significantly updated their CRSs in recent years. Current CRSs offer a number of advantages over the outdated systems of yesteryear.

The old-fashioned central reservation systems (1960s through 1980s) required constant manual updating between the hotel and the CRS. The hotel in-house reservations department was responsible for tracking the number of rooms sold by the CRS and calculating how many rooms still remained available for a given date. The CRS would continue "blindly" selling rooms until they were notified by the hotel to close room sales. In other words, the CRS never knew how many rooms were available at the individual property; it only knew that they were still *open* with regard to room availability.

This placed an important responsibility on the in-house reservationist to notify the CRS when room availability was tightening. This notification became an exercise in timing and forecasting; as often as not, mistakes were made. Sometimes the hotel in-house reservationist closed rooms with the CRS too early, other times too late. If the reservationist closed rooms with the CRS too early then rooms were still available for sale; if so, those remaining rooms became the responsibility of the in-house reservations department. Many times the in-house reservations department could not generate enough reservations activity to fill the house, so the date would come and go with several rooms left unsold. On the other hand, if the in-house reservationist closed the rooms too late, the hotel became overbooked.

Commonly referred to as *last room availability* or *full-duplex systems,* today's CRSs offer on-line, two-way communication with all affiliated hotels. No longer a hit-or-miss game of guessing when the last room will be sold, modern CRSs can literally sell the very last room at any hotel. This is because the CRS now has on-line real information about the actual status of rooms at every hotel within its system. This is significantly more efficient because it allows the CRS more opportunities to sell every room without either underselling or overselling the hotel. In addition, last room availability technology is a necessary first step in providing an automated yield management system to the chain.

Yield Management.   Probably the biggest buzzword to enter the hotel industry over the last several years has been ***yield management.*** Although yield management in itself is not a new concept, the technology behind automated yield management is very new. Indeed, the ability to link yield management technology into national central reservations systems is truly leading-edge technology.

In simple terms, yield management is the process of controlling rates and occupancy in order to maximize gross room revenues. This is certainly nothing new; hotels have always increased their rates when demand was high and decreased rates to generate more sales when demand was low. After all, a ski resort that discounts rooms in the summer and charges full price in the winter is utilizing a simplified form of yield management. The big difference today is that yield management is no longer a manual guessing game. The current systems are so accurate and sophisticated that they have made a drastic difference in how hotels successfully sell rooms.

Today's yield management technology uses artificial intelligence computer systems that actually adjust rates and occupancy restrictions on behalf of the reservations department. Without any assistance from the reservationist, the yield management system literally changes rates and updates room occupancy restrictions automatically. The system is able to make expert decisions because it has been programmed to employ strategies and thought processes similar to an expert human yield manager. Just like a human yield management expert, the automated system considers:

- Past years' history (How well did the hotel do in past years for the same period in question?).
- The types of rooms and guests currently being booked (Are our high-end rooms selling as strongly as our low-end rooms? Is our corporate demand as strong as our leisure demand?).
- Group historical pick-up rates (If group business has been booked for these dates, what are the group's historical pick-up statistics in terms of rooms requested versus rooms actually delivered in years past?)
- Booking (How far in advance are we of the date in question? The closer we get to a given arrival date, the more drastic the rate variations must be to make an impact).

As the statistics for a given date improve, the yield management system will begin raising the average rate and may also add simple occupancy restrictions. Common occupancy restrictions include requiring a minimum length of stay (usually a two- or three-day minimum) and closing certain dates to arrival (only allowing for stay-overs). The goal behind accurately predicting demand for a given date is to sell the most possible rooms for the highest possible rate *to attain the greatest possible yield*. Yield is defined as average daily rate (ADR) times the number of rooms sold (Y = ADR × Number of rooms sold). For example, a 200-room hotel that sells 65 percent of its rooms at an average daily rate of $78.53 yields $10,208.90 in rooms revenue. Average daily rate (ADR), sometimes called average room rate (ARR), is defined as the total of rooms revenue for a particular period (usually that day) divided by the number of rooms sold for that period. A 200-room hotel which sold 70 percent of its rooms last night (140 rooms) for a total of $12,479.60 in rooms revenue earned an ADR of $89.14.

Overbooking. Yield management systems also consider the ***quality of the reservation*** when determining rates and occupancy restrictions. The quality of a given reservation is its likelihood of actual arrival at the hotel. For example, advanced deposit reservations that are secured by the guest's prepayment have a much stronger likelihood of arrival than, say, a 6 PM reservation that is nonguaranteed and held under the guest's name until 6 PM.

Exhibit 3.14   With 5,000 rooms, it is hard to imagine filling the hotel, much less overbooking it. But the MGM Grand Hotel in Las Vegas has exceeded 90 percent occupancy every year since opening. Let's see . . . 5,000 rooms at 365 days per year means over 1.8 million room nights to fill annually! (*Courtesy:* MGM Grand)

A discussion of the quality of the reservation includes three basic types:

1. **Advanced deposit reservations** are prepaid by the guest in an amount generally equal to the first night's room and tax. Advanced deposit reservations are the highest quality; they have the highest likelihood of arrival.
2. **Guaranteed reservations** are guaranteed either to the guest's credit card or to the guest's corporate account. In either case, if the guest fails to arrive, the hotel may charge the guest for one night's room and tax. Because guests understand they will be charged for a **no-show,** guaranteed reservations are of fairly high quality. They have a very strong likelihood of arrival.
3. **Nonguaranteed reservations**, also known as **6 PM hold** reservations, are not secured with a deposit or any other form of guarantee. If the guest fails to arrive by 6 PM, the hotel has the right to sell the room to someone else. However, if the hotel is unable to resell the room, it has no recourse against the guest. As a result, nonguaranteed reservations are of the lowest quality; they have the lowest likelihood of arrival.

Because of these varying degrees of quality, many hotels try to compensate for no-shows by **overbooking** their rooms. In other words, they take more reservations than the actual number of rooms they have available. Although this is risky, it is a generally accepted practice in the hotel industry. Read the following case study for a more realistic description of the quality of the reservation and overbooking dilemma.

Arrival and Check-In   During the arrival and check-in stage of the guest cycle, several functions occur simultaneously: The guest arrives, a room is selected, and the guest is registered into the hotel. During this stage, the guest is likely to come into contact with a number of front of the house rooms division employees. The guest may meet a shuttle van driver at the airport, be greeted by a doorperson under the *porte cochère,* be checked in by a front desk clerk, and roomed by a bellperson. This stage of the guest cycle has some of the highest potential for quality guest-service contact of any time during the guest's visit.

EYE ON THE ISSUES

International

The rooms division of the hotel deals with a truly international scope of guests. Many hotel employees are immersed in multicultural guest communication on a fairly regular basis. Therefore, well trained rooms division employees should be culturally aware and sensitive to the needs of foreign visitors.

This is especially true in today's rapidly changing world. Historically, international tourists restricted their travel to major international cities like Los Angeles and New York; today they are just as likely to visit rural America. Historic battlefields, national parks, Native American villages, and white-water rafting are all included on their lists of exciting things that America offers.

In many full-service hotels, training in cultural awareness has expanded to include knowledge about foreign currency exchange policies. Many international visitors appreciate the convenience an in-house foreign currency exchange provides. In this way, they can convert their British pounds, Swiss francs, German euros, or Japanese yen into American greenbacks without the added hassle of locating a bank or currency merchant elsewhere in the city.

Exhibit 3.15   How your hotel looks upon arrival contributes greatly to the guest's first impression. (*Photo:* Ron Solomon/The Stock Connection)

During the actual check-in process, the guest is registered and provided an opportunity to ask questions and be sold on various attributes of the hotel. During this period, the guest's personal history information is verified, a method of payment is established, the check-out date is determined, and a room is selected. In most hotels, these functions are automated via the property management system (PMS).

Upselling.   During the check-in process, the front desk clerk tries to match the most appropriate room with the guest. At this point, clerks are encouraged to **upsell** the guest by offering nicer accommodations at a slightly higher cost. Many guests are pleased to have the option of purchasing a better quality room. In turn, the hotel is pleased to sell the more expensive room because it represents higher revenues to the operation. In fact, upselling guests to a more expensive room is such a profitable practice that many hotels provide their employees with bonuses associated with an improved average room rate.

You see, the cost of cleaning a room is roughly the same for a standard or a deluxe accommodation. Therefore, when the hotel can earn an extra $25 or so by upselling the customer, almost all of that revenue is extra profit. Extra revenue per room translates to a higher ***average daily rate*** (also known as *average room rate*). As we discussed earlier, average daily rate (ADR) is calculated by taking total rooms revenue for the day divided by the actual number of rooms sold.

Generally, as ADR increases, the profitability of the hotel increases. This is true because variable costs for a given hotel room remain relatively constant no matter what the ADR might be. As the ADR increases, there is more and more revenue above the variable costs to apply toward the fixed costs and the overall profitability of the operation.

Plans.   Another consideration of the average daily rate is the type of *plan* the hotel provides. Many lodging operations offer a meal plan as part of the quoted room rate. Although full meal plans (two or three meals per day) are generally found only in resort hotels, many transient operations have started offering breakfast with the room. Hotels that include three meals per day (breakfast, lunch, and dinner) in the room rate are referred to as **American plan** properties. Those that offer two meals per day (breakfast and dinner) are known as **modified American plan** hotels. However, most guests are accustomed to staying in hotels that offer lodging only, without any meals included in the rate. These operations are providing **European plan** accommodations (room only). For more information about plans, see Exhibit 3.16.

In recent years, more and more hotels have begun to offer a complimentary breakfast to their guests. This change is due, in part, to the proliferation of all-suite lodging operations which almost always offer some form of breakfast included in the basic room rate. As a result of the success of all-suite properties, many standard, limited-service hotels and motels have begun to provide complimentary continental breakfasts to their patrons. Hotels that include a simple continental breakfast in the room rate are providing the **continental plan**. Those hotels that offer a more substantial full breakfast meal are providing the **Bermuda plan** (see Exhibit 3.16).

Rooming the Guest.   Following the check-in process, many hotels provide bell service to assist in rooming the guest. During the rooming process, the bellperson explains the various highlights of the hotel, carries the guest's luggage, checks the room for cleanliness and function, makes suggestions, and answers pertinent questions. Most guests tip the bellperson in exchange for the quality service he or she provides.

Because rooming the guest presents the greatest opportunity of receiving a gratuity, most bell departments work on a rotation system. The bellperson who most recently roomed a guest is relegated to the back of the rotation pecking order until all other bellpersons have had their opportunity to room a guest. The bellperson who has been rotated to the front of the line, in other words, the position next in line to room a guest, is referred to as *a front*. The bellperson who last finished rooming a guest and is now at the back of the line is referred to as *a last*.

Visitation   The visitation stage of the guest cycle refers to the actual period of time the guest spends at the hotel between the time of check-in and the time of check-out. For some types of operations (e.g., transient hotels), the average length of stay may only be one night. Other operations (e.g., destination resorts) have an average length of stay of seven or more nights.

It is during the visitation stage that most of the communication on behalf of the guest occurs between departments. Literally every department in the hotel has a need to communicate with the front desk at some time or other. Each day, for example, the housekeeping department will need to know the status of the guest's room. The housekeeping department will need to know if the room is scheduled

Exhibit 3.16 The five most common plans. The plan a hotel offers defines the number and types of meals (if any) included with the room rate. Dude ranches, isolated resorts, and health spas commonly offer American plan accommodations (all three meals are included). A modified American plan is provided in those environments where guests may be away from the property at midday and will therefore take their lunch meal at an outside restaurant. The Bermuda plan offers a full breakfast (common in all-suite hotels) while the continental plan offers a limited or continental breakfast (common in limited-service lodging operations). But most common of all is the European plan—no meal included with the room rate.

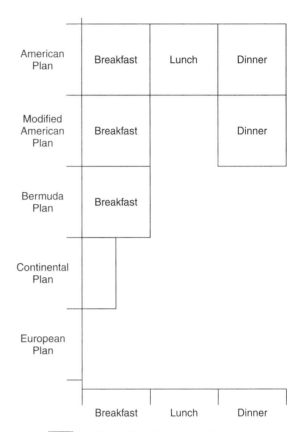

	Breakfast	Lunch	Dinner
American Plan	Breakfast	Lunch	Dinner
Modified American Plan	Breakfast		Dinner
Bermuda Plan	Breakfast		
Continental Plan			
European Plan			

Exhibit 3.17 In a four- or five-star (diamond) property, it is not unusual to see upscale Continental Plan breakfasts included with the price of the room. Such a breakfast would generally include a basket of breads or sweet rolls, juice or fruit, and coffee or tea. They rarely, however, come with such an outstanding view! (*Courtesy:* Four Seasons Hotels and Resorts)

Environment

Today's hotels seek to conserve water, energy, and resources not only for financial reasons but because of genuine environmental concern. Certain aspects of conservation fall specifically to the rooms division for implementation.

Water Conservation

The largest user of water in any hotel is the guest room. Guests staying in hotels are often unconcerned about the amount of water and energy they use. After all, they're not paying the utility bills. To combat misuse of water in the guest room, most hotels have installed *water flow restrictors* in guest showers, sinks, and toilets. Few guests notice the slight reduction of water flow, but the net result can be hundreds or thousands of gallons of water (and dollars!) saved per day.

Another application of water conservation finding acceptance in today's newer hotels is *brown water* recycling. Although brown water is "used" water, it is clean enough to meet minimum irrigation standards of local agencies. Sources of brown water in hotels include guest room sinks and showers, some in-house laundry cycles, and certain kitchen applications. Hotels route this used water into large cisterns where it is stored for future use in irrigation and plant watering.

Energy Conservation

The most exciting form of conservation is energy conservation in the guest room. Through the use of computer technology, today's newest hotels are installing a number of energy-saving systems in the guest room. These systems include such items as *infrared* and *motion sensor detectors* that are programmed to monitor the room's occupancy and shut down nonessential electrical heating, ventilating, or air-conditioning (HVAC systems) when the room is vacant.

Less sophisticated systems require the guest to insert the room key into a special slot that activates the room's nonessential electrical systems. Although the key is required to activate certain energy applications like the television, the air-conditioning, and bedside lamps, other electrical sources continue to work without the key. In this way, the room attendant has ample light to clean the room and access to active electrical outlets and the guest has enough light to enter and exit the room before and after insertion of the key into the special energy slot.

for check-out or as a stay-over so it can be cleaned accordingly. Other departments, like the gift shop or cocktail lounge, need to know the status of the guest's account. Specifically, they need to know if the guest is allowed to charge purchases to the room account, or if the guest is a "cash only" customer.

Handling Guest Complaints.   Just as the front desk communicates with other departments, it also communicates directly with the guest. Although most of the contact with the guest occurs during the check-in and check-out stages, there are plenty of opportunities to deal with the guest during the visitation stage. For example, guests may interact with the telephone (PBX) department (for phone calls, messages, and wake-up calls); the front desk (for special requests or room changes); or the cashiers (for billing, credit, or account issues).

Another common reason guests approach the front desk during their stay is to complain about a problem. The front desk receives significantly more guest

Exhibit 3.18   In a unique set-up unparalleled in the hospitality industry, this five-diamond Four Seasons Hotel and Resort sits on the top five floors (floors #35-39) of the Mandalay Bay Resort and Casino in Las Vegas. Four Seasons Hotels and Resorts has a long-term management contract (literally a 50-year or longer contract) to operate these rooms on behalf of the Mandalay Bay. Room rates range as high as $3,800 per night (for the three-bedroom Presidential Suite). (*Courtesy:* Four Seasons Hotels and Resorts)

complaints than any other front-of-the-house department in the hotel. Because the front desk is the most visible customer service department, it is the most likely place where a guest will go to complain. Therefore, as likely as not, the complaint handled by the front desk will deal with a problem in some other department. In this way, the front desk is charged with handling problems on behalf of all hotel departments.

Customer complaints are not necessarily bad things. In fact, complaints provide a series of opportunities to the hotel. They provide an opportunity to see the guest's point of view in a given area or with regard to a particular hotel policy. Complaints provide the opportunity to fix a problem or oversight that, if left uncorrected, might affect future guests. And complaints provide the hotel with an opportunity to convert a dissatisfied guest into a loyal customer.

By human nature, most guests will choose not to complain. Either they are too busy, they see the problem as too minor, they are too shy, or they just don't wish to be bothered. Whatever the reason, few guests actually complain. Therefore, each voiced complaint the employee hears actually represents a number of other guests who chose not to complain. That is why even the silliest complaint should be handled seriously and professionally.

Most hotels carefully train their front desk clerks in the proper steps of handling a guest complaint. Once trained, many hotels will empower their employees with the authority to handle the complaint in a manner that the employee deems appropriate. Indeed, one major luxury lodging chain empowers its hourly wage employees to personally handle complaints up to a value of $3,000. Now that's empowerment! Refer to Exhibit 3.19 for an understanding of the simple steps to properly handling a guest complaint.

The Guest Folio and the Night Audit   Guests pay for their room nights and other charges (e.g., telephone, restaurant charges, in-room movies) in many ways. Most guests use a national credit card; others pay by cash, travelers' check, corporate check, or hotel credit card. Still others have their account directly billed to a pre-arranged corporate account. Whatever the method of payment, the guest's account portfolio is opened, maintained, and closed by the front desk cashier. It is the front desk cashier who ultimately settles the guest's folio during the check-out stage of the guest cycle.

Posting Charges.   Because hotels are 24-hour operations, posting charges to the guest folio is a full-time responsibility. Charges come to the front desk either electronically (through the property management system) or manually (in the form

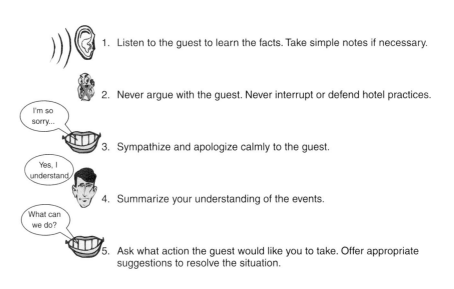

1. Listen to the guest to learn the facts. Take simple notes if necessary.

2. Never argue with the guest. Never interrupt or defend hotel practices.

3. Sympathize and apologize calmly to the guest.

4. Summarize your understanding of the events.

5. Ask what action the guest would like you to take. Offer appropriate suggestions to resolve the situation.

6. Take immediate action to resolve the problem. You are personally responsible for getting it done.

7. Follow up directly with the guest to ensure his or her complete satisfaction.

Exhibit 3.19   Steps to properly handle guest complaints. Front-of-the-house employees should be carefully trained to handle the complaints they will inevitably receive. By adhering to these steps, the hotel ensures maximum guest satisfaction. Indeed, employees should be trained to actually solicit the complaint. Asking how was the guest's stay is the first step in drawing out comments/complaints from reticent guests. Remember, a guest who complains and has the complaint satisfactorily resolved often becomes more loyal than the guest who never had anything to complain about in the first place.

of departmental room charge vouchers) from an assortment of different departments at all hours of the day and night.

It is important to understand that departmental charges to the guest room represent only those charges the guest wishes to be included on the folio. The front desk has no accounting responsibility for sales in other departments when the guest chooses to pay cash for the purchase at the time of sale. To illustrate this point:

> Imagine two guests, Mr. George Harrison (room 2102) and Mrs. Joanne Lennon (room 1616). Mr. Harrison eats dinner one night in the hotel dining room ($29.47) and charges the meal to his room. That amount, $29.47, will be posted to his folio and will be part of the total bill for which he is responsible at check-out from the hotel. On the other hand, Mrs. Lennon chooses to pay cash for her dinner ($31.16) and will not see any related charge on her folio. The front desk has no responsibility for accounting for Mrs. Lennon's cash transaction. Indeed, even during its night audit, the front desk will not account for a cash purchase in another department.

Late Charges.   Charges to the guest's folio come from any and all departments in the hotel at any and all hours of the day. Likewise, the guest has every right to check out of the hotel and demand the folio at any and all hours of the day. Therefore, the front desk cashier must constantly remain up to the minute with room charges in order to present the guest an accurate folio on demand.

Exhibit 3.20   Guests settle their folio charges in a variety of ways. But if they pay by travelers' check, be certain to verify the type of currency (e.g., U.S., Canadian, or pounds sterling) before accepting. (*Courtesy:* VISA U.S.A., Inc., San Francisco, California)

Mistakes happen, however, and it is possible for a cashier to present the guest with an incomplete folio. For whatever reason, it is not unusual for certain charges to arrive late either electronically or manually to the front desk. Unfortunately, these **late charges** are difficult to collect after the fact. In situations where the guest is a cash-only customer, the hotel might never receive payment for the late charge. In other circumstances (say, when the guest uses a credit card or corporate direct bill), collection is more certain, though costly and difficult.

The Role of the Night Audit.   Due to the 24-hour nature of the hotel industry, it is important for hotels to remain up-to-the-minute with the entire front office accounting ledger. On a daily basis, most hotels balance all of the guest folios against all of the departmental room charges. This daily process of balancing hotel guest accounts is known as the *night audit.*

The purpose of the night audit is to verify that room charges from each of the various hotel departments have been received by the front desk and accurately posted to the appropriate guest folios. Although this accounting function is the primary purpose of the night audit, it is not the only duty assigned during this front desk shift (usually 11 PM to 7 AM). Night auditors are also responsible for posting room and tax to each guest's folio, producing end-of-day managerial status reports, preparing the list of tomorrow's arrivals, and performing all other front desk functions that may arise during the shift.

EYE ON THE ISSUES

Guest Service

Today's hotel customers expect a quality guest experience no matter the type of property they visit. They understand that different types of operations offer different levels of guest service; but that doesn't mean budget properties should provide poor service. Budget or limited-service properties offer, as their name indicates, limited service. There is no concierge, no bell staff, and minimal amenities (maybe a swimming pool, but certainly no health club, spa, or golf course). Still, whatever services are provided should be performed in a warm, friendly, and guest-oriented way. Though there is no concierge to supply the guest with directions, the front desk clerk should be polite and informed. Though there is no bellperson to carry luggage, a self-service luggage cart should be available and in good working order. Though there is no health club or spa, the swimming pool should be fresh and clean.

Guest expectations are far higher in full-service operations. In a full-service property, there are literally hundreds of opportunities for face-to-face service delivery. Any one of these opportunities can go sour and spoil the guest's entire visit. Yet it is difficult for management to monitor service levels in all departments all the time. Some employees have a tendency to act differently when management is present, putting on a great guest-service act when management is observing them. However, when management leaves the scene, they revert to habits which are rude, lazy, and anti-service oriented.

That is why many hotels utilize mystery shopping services to uncover the real levels of service being provided. With mystery shopping services, management contracts to have the hotel property visited a number of times during the year. Because the visitors are always different, employees never know if the guest asking directions is a real guest or a mystery service auditor. Indeed, merely informing employees that management has contracted with a mystery shopping service is often enough to change service levels for the better.

Check-Out and Billing   The check-out and billing cycle is just the reverse of the guest arrival and check-in pattern. For the most part, the same rooms division positions that assisted the guest at arrival now assist the guest at departure. The bell department retrieves the guest's luggage from the room, the cashier checks the guest out of the hotel, the doorperson offers a fond farewell, and the shuttle driver returns the guest to the airport.

It is during the check-out stage that the guest is asked to close the folio. The folio can be closed in two basic ways: either the guest pays the bill (by cash, check, or credit card) or the guest delays payment of the bill. In other words, the folio is either settled on the spot or it is deferred to the guest's corporate account for settlement in the future.

If it is settled on the spot, the cashier posts the payment and hands a *zero balance* folio to the departing guest. In such a case, no further action is warranted—the account is closed and the hotel has received payment in full. Guests who defer payment to their corporate account for monthly billing are another story. These guests are asked to sign the bottom of the folio and are then handed a copy of the unpaid bill. The unpaid folio is then routed to the hotel's accounting department, where it is held until the next corporate direct billing cycle. At this point, the accounting department monitors the folio until payment is eventually received from the corporation owing the money. Once the money is received, the payment is posted and the folio shows a final zero balance.

We've now reviewed the basic guest cycle from beginning to end. Each of these steps is far more complicated than can be described within the scope of this chapter. Later in your curriculum you will learn much more about the rooms divisions in such classes as guest service management and hospitality automation.

CONCLUSION

A career in hotel management is not necessarily suited to *everyone*. Certain traits and skills are required to succeed in this challenging field. When these traits are present, rooms division managers love their jobs. They love the rooms division because it offers them a high degree of challenge, stimulus, variety, and autonomy. These are unique aspects that most jobs do not provide.

On the other hand, when such traits as compassion, high energy levels, self-motivation, and an eye for detail are not present, many managers grow to dislike their jobs. Without these traits, they often become jaded to their customers, depersonalized to their employees, and emotionally exhausted from the physical and psychological challenges of the position.

Therefore, if you are interested in becoming a rooms division manager, gather plenty of personal experience before deciding on this specific career path. (Chapter 12 "Leadership, Ethics, and Management for the Hospitality Industry," suggests some self-knowledge exercises that may help crystallize your thinking about such a career.) If and when you do select this calling, you will not be disappointed. Imagine having the opportunity to host the President of the United States and house several hundred Secret Service staff members—now that's an honor. Imagine reserving an entire floor for several nights while a rock band is performing in town—now that's a thrill. Imagine staying for free at other sister properties of your chain as a regular advantage of your position—now that's a perk.

Or imagine just a regular old day. You are exhausted after handling a morning of check-outs and an afternoon of rooming several hundred guests and accommodating two large groups. Your day wasn't exactly error-free, and you handled your share of guest problems and complaints. The day is over, you are pleasantly tired, and you head toward the door. Just then an elderly couple approaches you and asks if you are the rooms division manager. You respond yes, while you brace yourself for the complaint that's sure to come. Instead, they proceed to tell you what a marvelous property you run. They've stayed in lots of hotels, but you have the friendliest, most accommodating staff they have ever met. As they finish their compliment, they ask if you will still be here the next time they come through. You respond yes, as you realize you truly love your job. Although you are still tired, you feel like a million bucks as you head for the exit.

KEYWORDS

rooms division   105
economy or budget lodging   107
full-service lodging   107
front office   108
front of the house   111
back of the house   111
night audit   117
graveyard shift   117
uniformed services   118
concierge   119
concierge floors   120
central reservations system (CRS)   123
advanced deposit reservation   126

guaranteed reservation   126
no-show   126
nonguaranteed reservation   126
6 PM hold   126
overbooking   126
American plan   128
modified American plan   128
European plan   128
continental plan   128
Bermuda plan   128
late charges   134
walk   139
walk-in guests   139

CORE CONCEPTS

pivot points   106
revenue centers   107
customer service   107
forecasting   109
guest cycle   110
guest folio   116

last room available   121
yield managment   124
quality of the reservation   125
upsell   127
average daily rate   127

DISCUSSION QUESTIONS

1. From the student's viewpoint, the rooms division may be the most important department in the entire hotel. Jobs in this department provide both high visibility to hotel management and plenty of one-on-one contact with the guest. Discuss three other aspects of rooms division jobs that make them appealing and beneficial to students interested in a career in hotel management.

2. Room reservations are reserved weeks or months in advance. Generally, what type or market of consumer makes room reservations well in advance? Conversely, what type or market of consumer makes room reservations at the last minute—just days or hours before arrival? Explain why hotels charge last-minute reservations higher rates than those with longer lead times.

3. Late charges create hardships for corporate guests, who expect the folio they receive at check-out to be a complete and accurate representation of their visit. Several days later, if they receive a new folio reflecting some type of late charge (say a late breakfast that posted after they checked out), they may have to rewrite their corporate expense report. Develop a list of several reasons why late charges occur and decide if you agree with the statement "too many late charges indicate a poorly managed hotel."

4. Hotels overbook their room reservations to compensate for no-shows and cancellations. However, by regularly overbooking, the hotel runs a grave risk of severely inconveniencing the guest. Maybe, instead of overbooking, the hotel should establish more rigid reservation policies. If you were the reservations manager, what types of policies might you employ to minimize the need for overbooking? Is overbooking ever justifiable?

5. Using Exhibit 3.19 as a backup resource, develop a role-playing exercise with a classmate. Let the classmate take the part of an upset customer. Your job is to defuse and resolve the argument. Have fun, but be realistic in your complaints.

EXEMPLAR OF EXCELLENCE

Four Seasons Hotels and Resorts

There are literally countless examples of quality service excellence across the hotel industry. That is especially true when you look at the colorful history of our industry. Tens of thousands of hotels across a multitude of decades adds up to billions of opportunities to treat the guest "right."

Some of those examples have become a part of the industry's history, even as we have forgotten the guest, employee, and even the hotel involved in the story. But the tales grow with time; there is the story of a concierge who was asked to buy a busy guest's daughter a birthday surprise—the concierge went out and purchased the daughter a new car! Or the story of a hotel employee who took off his size 9 black shoes and handed them to the bewildered guest who had forgotten his own shoes and was running late for a wedding rehearsal. And if you like those two stories, there are infinitely more—every hotel has its own list of in-house exemplars of service excellence.

But one company renowned for its outstanding customer service skills is the Four Seasons Hotels and Resorts. When asked what makes the Four Seasons chain unique in its presentation of luxury service, the answer is always the same—our employees. You see, the entire industry has come to realize something which Four Seasons Hotels and Resorts has known for a long while—quality employees give quality service.

Four Seasons first came to light as an exemplar of service excellence when Peters and Waterman wrote about it in their management classic, *In Search of Excellence*. Recently, Cornell University's Center for Hospitality Research identified the company as a contributor to its *Best Practices in the U.S. Lodging Industry.* Specifically, Cornell wrote "To ensure the loyalty of its guests, and to warrant the five-star or five-diamond rating held by many of its hotels and resorts, Four Seasons believes it must maintain its service-oriented culture, which is facilitated by a high ratio of [exceptionally well-trained] employees to guests."

Experience a nearby Four Seasons Hotels and Resorts property first-hand, or look for them on the web at *www.fourseasons.com*

WEBSITES TO VISIT

1. www.hilton.com/en/hi/brand/about/
2. www.accor.com/sa/rh/
3. www.starwood.com/sheraton/about/
4. www.hyatt.com/corporate/hyatt/index.jhtml?ssnav=0
5. www.cendant.com/careers/culture.html

CASE STUDY

The following case study illustrates two important concepts with regard to hotel reservations. It explains the calculations for the room count or "rooms available for sale" count on a given day, as well as it demonstrates a potential overbooking situation.

You are the manager of a 200-room hotel which has 50 rooms scheduled to stay over from the night before and 150 rooms scheduled to be available for sale today. Of the 150 rooms available for sale today, 50 of them have advanced deposit reservations (with a 100 percent arrival rate); 50 have guaranteed reservations (with a 96 percent arrival rate); and 50 have nonguaranteed reservations (with a 70 percent arrival rate).

By projecting reservations against the arrival statistics, you have determined there are still 17 rooms available for sale. In other words, if your estimates are accurate, there will be 50 advanced deposit reservations (50 × 1.0), 48 guaranteed reservations (50 × .96), and 35 nonguaranteed reservations (50 × .70). As a result, there will also be 17 no-show reservations.

The question you must ask yourself is how accurate your arrival statistics are for any given day (specifically, for today). You now have the opportunity to act as a real general manager: The moment you finish calculating your rooms available for sale today, the phone rings. It is a bus tour that has been stranded in your town for one night. Can you accommodate 17 rooms double occupancy for one night only?

Ask yourself the following questions:

- What are the consequences if you do not accommodate this group?
- What are the consequences if you do accommodate this group? Remember, selling an extra 17 rooms in the case study above is risky because it assumes today's arrival patterns will be similar to past history. However, if some of those projected no-shows actually do arrive, the hotel will find itself overbooked.

There will be too many guests arriving for the number of rooms available at the hotel. In this case, the hotel will have to walk the few overbooked guests to another hotel.

Walking Guests

A hotel finds itself in a rather unfortunate situation when it **walks** a guest. Not only is the guest upset and inconvenienced, but the hotel has essentially broken its promise to deliver a room. As a result, most hotels extend a number of courtesies to the walked guest. These courtesies generally include transporting the guest to another equal or higher quality hotel, paying the difference in room rate if the second hotel is more expensive, absorbing the cost of a few long-distance phone calls so the walked guest can let others know about the situation, transporting the guest back to the original hotel the next day, and possibly even buying a meal or placing a fruit basket in the room as an expression of apology. As you can see, walking a guest is an expensive undertaking.

Walk-In Guests

Don't confuse walking a guest with a **walk-in guest.** Guests who arrive without a reservation are known as walk-in guests, or simply walk-ins. Walk-in guests arrive for a multitude of reasons: they are last-minute corporate guests who didn't have time to make a reservation, stranded airline passengers, leisure guests too tired to continue driving into the next town, etc. Although walk-in guests represent last-minute revenue, they should not be counted on. You see, selling the hotel to advance reservations is far better than waiting for the inconsistent few walk-ins who may or may not appear.

Back of the House Operations: Housekeeping, Maintenance, and Engineering

This chapter focuses on the operational functions of the physical plant of the hotel. It combines the operations of housekeeping, maintenance, and engineering, since these functions strive for the same goal: providing a clean and comfortable lodging environment for the guests. It discusses the managerial and operational aspects of these three functions in great detail and introduces current operation issues.

INTRODUCTION

Management in hospitality is well aware of the priority guests put on clean, comfortable guest rooms with well functioning facilities. Keeping a hotel clean and all the equipment working properly is an important job. Without professionally competent staff in these areas, the hotel's "product" will be undesirable and/or unsafe—and all the king's horses and all the king's men (in the form of marketing, sales, and central reservations) will be unable to keep sales up.

This chapter will explore the functions of the housekeeping department, including its structure, staffing, training, and operations. Managing the housekeeping department, often a hotel's largest in terms of number of employees, requires a high level of people management skills. This chapter will also explain and define the responsibilities of the engineering and maintenance department, including the types of skilled labor needed for successful operation of hotel buildings.

The goal of this chapter is to discuss the many internal activities that occur deep within hotel buildings. For a hotel to be successful, a guest must find a clean, comfortable, well maintained building in which all the building systems are working properly. Guests must also feel that they are safe and secure while under the hotel's roof. Not surprisingly, housekeeping, engineering, and maintenance staff are positively involved with hotel environmental, safety, and security issues. Beyond guest security, the protection of the hotel's assets—both human and property—is another area of great responsibility.

HOUSEKEEPING

This section discusses the housekeeping department of a hotel, its areas of responsibility, job descriptions, and total organizational structure. We explore day-to-day operations, including purchasing and laundry procedures, and discuss how reliable

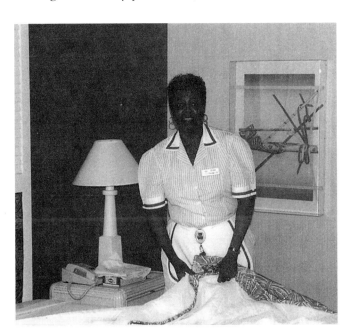

Exhibit 4.1   Housekeeping is more than a room attendant cleaning a guest room; it is the heart of the hotel operation. (*Courtesy:* Bert Van Hoof)

procedures are developed. By the end of the chapter you will understand why housekeeping is much more than a maid cleaning a guest room. The management of the housekeeping department is a challenging job that is critical to the success of the hotel.

The primary (and often most visible) function of the housekeeping department is the cleaning of guest rooms. It is also responsible for cleaning public areas such as foyers, lobbies, public rest rooms, and the dining room; and back-of-the-house areas such as employee break rooms, rest rooms, locker areas, and the laundry.

The importance of the cleanliness of the guest rooms, the public rest rooms, the dining room, and lobby cannot be stressed enough. A hotel guest demands the highest standard of cleanliness. He or she is buying a well made bed with fresh linen and a clean bath/shower room. The cleanliness of an establishment can make the difference between being sold out or going out of business.

Departmental Organization

Depending on the size of the property, the number of housekeeping employees can range from two (in a small budget motel with fewer than 20 rooms) to hundreds (in a 1,000-room resort.) The person in charge of this department, the **executive housekeeper,** must therefore be a good manager of people.

Because of the size of the housekeeping department and the importance of the job performed, the role of the executive housekeeper is pivotal to the success of the hotel. The position of executive housekeeper is, in most cases, a middle management position, as shown in Exhibit 4.2.

The organizational chart in Exhibit 4.3 clearly shows the positions under the executive housekeeper. The number and types of positions are determined by the size and type of hotel.

Integration and Communication

The housekeeping department is fully integrated with all other areas of the hotel operation. Front desk, maintenance, engineering, catering, food/beverage, banquet, and security all depend on lines of communication with the housekeeping department. The front desk sells the rooms, so it must know which rooms are clean and available for check-in. Housekeeping provides the front desk with updates on the changes in status of guest rooms, ranging from "checked out" to "room ready."

No well-run housekeeping department will ever release a room to the front desk for check-in before it is ready—not even with the expectation that the room will be ready in five minutes. If the front desk checks a guest into a room that is not made up, everyone looks bad. The guest will be disturbed, the front desk will be embarrassed (then angry), and the property's image will suffer. Once a guest develops a negative feeling about a hotel, it is hard to turn those feelings back into positive ones.

The front desk gives housekeeping a written (or electronically transmitted) document called a **rooms report,** which indicates the number of guests checking out or staying over. Also included in this document are any special requests from guests (such as a late check-out or early wake-up).

Housekeepers use the rooms report to prioritize rooms and schedule the workload. The front desk also provides housekeeping with a list of rooms that have

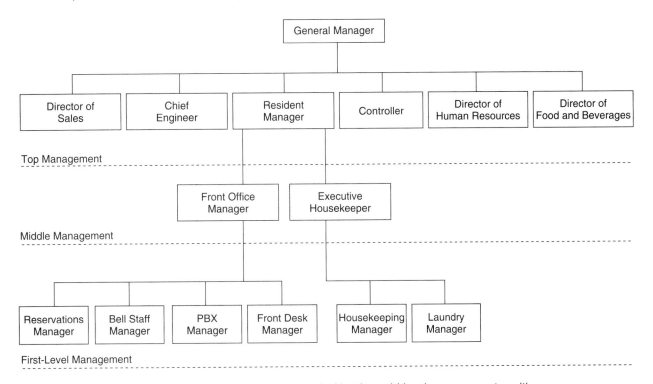

Exhibit 4.2   The executive housekeeper is fully integrated with other mid-level management positions.

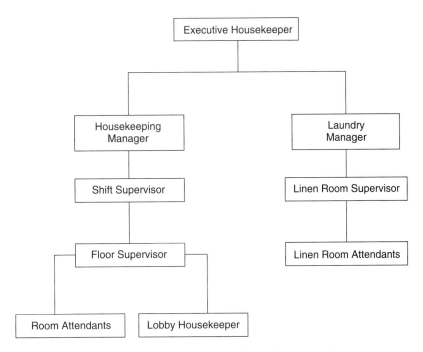

Exhibit 4.3   In most hotels, housekeeping is the largest of all departments (in terms of staffing requirements).

Service Excellence

Although the quality of a hotel ranges along a hierarchy from budget properties to first-class resorts, housekeeping cleanliness remains a priority for all classes of lodging. Whether staying in a five-star Ritz-Carlton hotel for $400 per night or an economy Super 8 property at just $40 per night, the guest has the right to expect clean accommodations. It is this attention to detail which creates satisfied return customers.

Hotels ensure room cleanliness and housekeeping detail through a "check-it and then check-it again" approach. The average guest room is inspected regularly by a series of hotel and related personnel. The first to inspect the room is the room attendant (maid) whose job it is to clean and finish the room, and then to look over his/her work for completed detail. Once the room has been cleaned to the satisfaction of the room attendant, it remains "on change" until inspected a second time by the housekeeping department's inspector (or possibly even an assistant housekeeping manager). At this point, the room is available for sale to the guest.

But the inspection process certainly does not stop here. On a random basis, the housekeeping manager(s) and other senior housekeeping personnel inspect rooms daily. The housekeeper may have a pattern to follow; inspecting certain rooms cleaned by various room attendants, or the room check may be entirely random. Similarly, other front-of-the-house hotel management staff also sporadically inspect rooms for cleanliness and attention to detail. General managers also make it a habit to visit a few rooms each day.

But the inspection process does not stop there. Hotels ranked by AAA, Mobil, and any of the other 80+ rating systems worldwide are subject to surprise inspections one, two, or more times annually. AAA inspectors, for example, secretly stay in the hotel for their first night on property. During that night, AAA puts the room to the test, looking in drawers, checking for dust on top of pictures, and even glancing under the bed! The next day, the AAA inspector asks housekeeping to escort them across the property for a detailed room inspection tour. Depending on the size of the property, it is not uncommon for such an inspection to include 50 or more rooms in a single day! Now, add to that the inspections performed by mystery shoppers hired by the general manager and the inspections made on behalf of the chain (for example, Best Western performs its own inspections of member hotels twice annually) and you can see that the inspection process is never ending.

A speck of dirt doesn't stand a chance against the onslaught of so many room inspectors!

been vacated and that, therefore, can be made up first. As the business day continues, communication flows back and forth between housekeeping and the front desk. The front desk updates housekeeping on check-outs, and housekeeping notifies the front desk when a room is ready to be sold.

As explained above, the flow of communication between housekeeping and the front desk is two-way and constant so that both operations can run a maximum efficiency all the time. This cooperation allows the hotel to fulfill guests' needs and generate the maximum room revenue possible.

Terminology and language are also important. Professionals never refer to a room as "dirty." Instead, you will hear a room described as "not made up" or "on change." "Dirty" would sound negative to a guest. How employees speak to each other in the presence of guests has a definite effect on the hotel's image.

Exhibit 4.4   Housekeeping is one of those departments that rarely hears from the guest when things go well. Yet the attention provided by the housekeeping department makes all the difference in terms of the level of satisfaction experienced by each guest. Sitting in a well-cared for room, wearing a soft robe provided by the hotel, looking out spotlessly clean windows . . . that's what a well-run housekeeping department is all about! (*Courtesy:* Four Seasons Hotels and Resorts)

Cost of Room Cleaning

The cost of cleaning a hotel/motel can be broken down into time and materials. The time (which equals the cost of labor—usually a per hour cost) varies greatly from property to property. A budget hotel room with few guest amenities may take an average 20 minutes to clean. This would include cleaning the bathroom, replacing the towels, making the bed with fresh linens, and vacuuming the room. A luxury resort multi-room suite may take over an hour to clean properly. The bathroom could have a shower, larger bathtub, make-up mirror/dressing room, and separate closet area along with a separate toilet area. Multiple amenities are required in the bathroom area: different types of soap, shampoo, sun block, bath oils, sponges, toilet tissue, facial tissue and even bathrobes. These items need to be replaced and restocked. A great deal of time is required to clean these rooms to acceptable standards.

Recycling

The hospitality industry can contribute to the world's recycling in a major way. There are tons of materials that can be recycled in hotels over the course of a year.

Plastics are used all over the hotel—and most of them can be sorted and recycled. A number in an embossed triangle appears on the bottom of most plastic containers, indicating recyclability. Employees can be trained to sort by number, and they often wholeheartedly support recycling, even though it adds a step to cleaning up. Kitchen patrols will find plastic milk- and dairy-product packaging;

EYE ON THE ISSUES

Environment

Energy Management

Energy management is the responsibility of the engineering and maintenance department. Monitoring how energy is used to heat and cool the property is an ongoing process. Performing energy audits, section by section, may reveal old energy-wasting equipment in need of updating. In older properties, some equipment *bleeds* energy. Replacement is often very cost effective, in terms of return on investment (ROI).

Water-conserving shower heads and low-flush toilets are rapidly becoming standard. We can expect to see high-efficiency motors and longer-lasting fluorescent light bulbs. HVAC components will use less energy and incorporate environmentally friendly air conditioning refrigerants. Properties will be better insulated to reduce heat/cold loss. All these changes, whether passive or active, will lower operating costs.

the dishroom will yield dishwasher detergent tubs. Housekeeping will yield cleaning supply bottles and used shampoo and condition (amenity) containers.

Newsprint and other paper generated by a hotel are easily recycled. Computers with printers can pile up mountains of paper. Most upscale hotels provide each guest with a daily newspaper. This can add up to hundreds of pounds of newspaper weekly.

Aluminum cans are the most commonly known recyclables. Any property with a soda machine will soon have pounds of crushed cans. Steel coffee, tomato paste, and other cans can also be recycled and are always to be found in commercial kitchens.

Liquor, beer, and wine bottles are a leading source of recycled glass. Glass is sorted by color—generally clear, green, and brown.

As with policies, leadership should be shown at the top. If employees see managers recycling, they will see how serious the property really is about conservation.

Hotels may also contribute to environment responsibility by getting their guests involved in their recycling programs. There are now attractive recycling bins suitable for placement on property; these give guests the opportunity to participate and, as a side effect, subtly enhance a hotel's public image.

Management Aspects

The next section deals with the everyday aspects of management, which include staffing, training, and scheduling. These are the areas that managers in hospitality deal with on a day-to-day basis.

Staffing.   One of the biggest challenges an executive housekeeper must face is staffing—finding the right people to perform the department's jobs. The entry-level position of room attendant or housekeeper is one of the most difficult to fill. Low pay, low status, and hard physical work best describe a housekeeper's job. Cleaning guest rooms and public areas, working in the laundry, and performing all the "dirty work" in the hotel is what a housekeeper does.

The geographic location of a property has a great deal to do with the people who apply for work within it. A property in a remote location, such as a ski resort

Dear Guest,

Imagine how many tonnes of towels are washed every day in hotels worldwide, and the enormous amount of energy, water, and washing powder needed...

We have a goal at the Aspen Village Inn to minimize our use of natural resources and pollutants, and to recycle whenever possible.

Please make a choice:

* *Towels replaced on the towel-rail or rack means: "I'll use it again."*

* *Towels placed in the bathtub or shower means: "Please exchange."*

Thank you for helping us protect and enhance this special place for future generations!

**WATERTON LAKES NATIONAL PARK
ALBERTA, CANADA**

Exhibit 4.5   Conservation and national parks are a natural match. This simple card helps the Aspen Village Inn in Alberta, Canada encourage its guests to help the inn to conserve water and energy and to reduce pollution. (*Courtesy:* Aspen Village Inn, Waterton Lakes National Park, Alberta, Canada.).

high in the mountains or a guest ranch in a remote desert area, may have to provide housing for employees. A hotel located in a downtown area with easy access to public transportation has a much easier time getting employees. Most people who work at minimum wage jobs find it difficult to afford a car and so rely on public transportation to get to work. Some hotels, out of necessity, set up van pools to transport their employees. In some cases the same van that is scheduled to drop off guests at the airport early in the morning can use a return route to the hotel that passes by designated pick-up points for hotel employees. This benefits the hotel in two important ways. First, all the employees, not just housekeepers, have a reliable way to get to work and be on time. The second benefit deals with the hotel's public image. Employee transport programs contribute to reduced traffic

Exhibit 4.6   Competition for housekeepers is fierce in cities like Scottsdale, Arizona. (*Courtesy:* Bert Van Hoof)

and lower pollution; by providing them, a hotel is seen as environmentally conscientious—a public relations plus.

If a hotel or resort wants to attract the best applicants for its housekeeping department, it must first evaluate the wages and benefits offered by competing hotels. Obviously, if the property down the street pays a dollar an hour more or offers some type of health insurance, people will want to work for the competition. Market forces oblige hotels to make their wages and benefits competitive if they want to attract capable workers. Knowing what the competition pays enables you to equal or exceed it.

With the transportation problem addressed and the wages and benefit package set, the next area to attend to is where to locate housekeeping labor. The easiest place to start looking for employees is internally. Current employees may have a friend or relative in need of a job who would suit the hotel's needs nicely. The same

EYE ON THE ISSUES

Environmental Trends

Hyatt Regency Scottsdale at Gainey Ranch has implemented several important changes as part of an environmental "green" program. According to environmental program manager Paul F. Hayes, being a responsible member of the community, both locally and glo-bally, requires better methods in controlling three areas: waste management, water conservation and energy management.

An extensive recycling program controls waste management. Paper, cardboard, plastic, aluminum, and glass are separated and recycled.

The major factor in the success of the Hyatt program is the team concept. All employees at all levels are participating. Each employee feels part of the group effort in improving environmental growth.

Water conservation is a critical area in a state like Arizona. Hyatt conserves water inside the resort by adjustments to the laundry process and the use of water flow restrictor devices in toilets and showers. Outside the buildings, irrigation is monitored for leaks and the total amount of grass areas have been reduced.

Energy management uses improved technology in lighting. High efficiency light bulbs and light motion sensors, which automatically turn off lights when a room is not in use, are two areas to reduce electric use. Tighter control on heating and air conditioning are important to the reduction in energy use.

network of friends and relatives is also valuable for passing word along to *their* circle of friends. To take advantage of this network, job openings are posted on a bulletin board and current employees are encouraged to share the news. Some properties even go as far as to pay bonuses to employees for finding help. By using internal resources to fill job vacancies, a hotel can save a great deal of time and money.

If the internal posting fails to produce applicants, some type of external search will have to be undertaken. This can be as simple as posting a help-wanted sign in front of a small motel or as extreme as running a radio commercial advertising for help, with an offer of free transportation and lodging.

The demographics of the local community may also affect the ***demographics of the applicant pool.*** Depending on the area, the labor market may include, but not be limited to, housewives, single parents, students, retired persons, the differently challenged, and immigrants. The last group may be difficult to reach because of language obstacles, but do not discount them simply because they do not speak English. They may already have the experience and work ethic a hotel is looking for. If so, they may welcome the chance to learn English. A hotel may even offer an English language program as an employee benefit.

The size and structure of the property will influence the extent to which an executive housekeeper will be responsible for hiring. A large resort hotel has thousands of employees and a very structured hiring process. In this case, the human resources department is normally responsible for hiring. One of the main functions of the human resources department is to screen applicants and conduct interviews, as explained in the human resources chapter. At smaller properties with fewer employees, the job applicant will be interviewed directly by the owner, manager, or executive housekeeper.

The housekeeping department has the highest turnover rate of any department in the hotel. Hard work, low pay, and lack of respect/prestige are reasons for housekeeping turnover. If some time and research are applied to hiring the right applicant from the start, turnover can be reduced. Turnover is very expensive for any business. Time taken placing ads and interviewing applicants takes managers away from other duties. The ideal situation is to be able to hire the best qualified person with the most stable work history. In reality, though, circumstances may force a manager to hire the first person who walks in the door looking for work.

Training.   Once housekeeping positions have been filled, the most important job undertaken by a manager becomes training. A training program starts with the assumption that the trainees have never before done the work at hand. A training program starts with the basics and builds from there; just because a new housekeeper spent 10 years at XYZ Motel does not mean he or she knows how to do things the way your property requires.

A room attendant's job is a hands-on physical activity. The best training comes in the form of on-the-job training, also known as *OJT*. An experienced housekeeper is paired with a new hire, who learns by watching and doing. It is very important that the trainer is not only an outstanding performer as a housekeeper but also a good teacher. Training programs may last from two days to two weeks. The progress of the new employee should be monitored by the supervisor or area manager. If there is some type of problem, this is the time to correct it.

In addition to guest room cleaning procedures, training should also include attitude, conduct, appearance, safety, security, and guest relations. The new employee

Exhibit 4.7   Training equates to consistency. Often overlooked details (placement of towels, number of amenities, etc.) are critical in full-service resorts. (*Courtesy:* The Venetian Resort Hotel Casino, Las Vegas, Nevada)

must be aware that he or she is part of the hospitality industry. How an employee conducts him- or herself on the property and around guests reflects on the image of the hotel. Guests will remember friendly, helpful people who contributed to making their stay more enjoyable. Ultimately, it does not cost anything to be thoughtful and courteous to guests, but it may cost the hotel everything if employees fail to make guests feel pampered.

Appearance is also an important part of training. An exclusive resort supplies housekeepers' uniforms and may have a strict policy about make-up, hair length, jewelry, and type and color of footwear. The locally owned small property may require only a tee shirt and blue jeans. Research has shown that **codes of appearance** can positively affect employee attitudes, because people who take the time to make sure they look good generally have more confidence and self-esteem. This can add to the feelings of belonging and team spirit needed for the housekeeping department to perform at maximum efficiency.

An important part of training often overlooked is that of orienting a new employee to the entire property. The new housekeeper should know what facilities are used most by guests and where they are located. When the housekeeper is able to assist guests by recommending one of the hotel's restaurants, the whole property benefits. Guests will often stop the first person in sight to ask directions to the pool, spa, club house, business center, banquet offices, and so on. Often, the first person they see will be a room attendant or houseperson. If the hotel does not take the time to train these employees and make them familiar with the property, guests may feel that "nobody knows anything around here."

Scheduling.   The housekeeping manager's next challenge is scheduling. The main problem in ***scheduling employees*** relates to the hospitality industry's non-standard work calendar. Many employees must work when the general population is off (weekends, holidays, and evenings). Hotels are open every day of the year. This includes all weekends and holidays. Some properties do the majority of their business between Friday and Monday. Finding people willing to work when their friends or family are off is difficult. From the first interview, the employee should be aware that working weekends and holidays will be a job requirement.

There are some important factors in developing a housekeeping schedule. The schedule should be posted in a highly visible area as far in advance as possible. The schedule is always subject to change because of fluctuations in room occupancy. The schedule should be fair, in the sense that weekend and holiday work should be assigned as equitably as possible. Good recordkeeping counteracts complaints that the schedule favors one individual over another. If possible, employees should have input in the scheduling process. People will be much more cooperative if they have a say in what weekends and holidays they work. It is desirable to make sure the same employees are not working Christmas, New Year's Eve, Rosh Hashanah, or Thanksgiving unless they choose to.

One type of schedule to keep housekeepers happy is a work week of four 10-hour days. This schedule allows for a 40-hour work week and three days off. Once again, the idea is to rotate the days so that each employee works the same number of weekends. Another way to schedule is to give people the same days off every week; some employees prefer two days off in the middle of the week. Most properties use some type of seniority system to determine who picks first: The employee with the most time on the job is awarded the first pick for days off. The privilege of first pick for days off may also be given as a reward for outstanding job performance.

Employees of different religious backgrounds may observe holy days unfamiliar to management. When they request time off to observe such days, management must be sensitive. Respect for how others worship will go a long way in gaining employee loyalty. It may be helpful to request a calendar of holy days for religious

Ethics

Housekeeping management faces ethical concerns in two distinct areas. The first lies in the supervisor–employee relationship and reveals volumes about the entire organization's human relations philosophy. A housekeeping department that shows respect for its employees (many of whom are entry-level workers facing barriers of language and transportation) sets a positive ethical tone. Even the lowest paid members of the staff are entitled to fairness in the areas of scheduling, promotion, benefits, and penalties. An example of an unfair penalty for housekeepers is the practice of holding them responsible for items stolen from guest rooms by guests. Properties who use this policy often post signs in their guest rooms as a means of shaming theft-minded guests into honest behavior. While theft of guest room items can be a problem, this sweatshop practice is unfair, since housekeepers have no control over guests' honesty.

The second area of ethical concern, which applies not only to housekeepers but to maintenance workers and engineering staff as well (and every other staff member who has guest-room access), is respect for guest property and privacy. Employees should be trained not to handle guest property except within clearly spelled-out guidelines.

beliefs represented in your department. We are automatically sensitive about asking employees to work on traditional Christian holidays; it is courteous to be aware of the special days of other religions.

The challenge of scheduling is to achieve the employee coverage necessary to get the job done while being fair to all parties involved. This is an area of management where the manager in charge is limited only by his or her imagination and courage to try new and different ideas. It is possible to make changes in scheduling that increase morale and increase productivity without resulting in a reduction in quality.

Standard Operating Procedures

Establishing how things are done on the property is the next area of importance. A **standard operating procedure (SOP)** is a clear, concise description of how to perform a specific task. Standard operating procedures include many housekeeping tasks such as:

- How to enter a guest room
- How to make a bed
- How to clean a bathroom
- How to report lost and found articles
- How to stock a housekeeping cart
- How to mop a floor

SOPs include all equipment needed and all safety precautions that need to be taken. They may include specific guidelines dealing with how to handle cleaning chemicals and the disposal of hazardous material; a certain type of equipment may require a certain number of hours of training to operate; a programmable washing machine, commercial ironing machines, and a carpet cleaning machine all require some training before they can be operated properly.

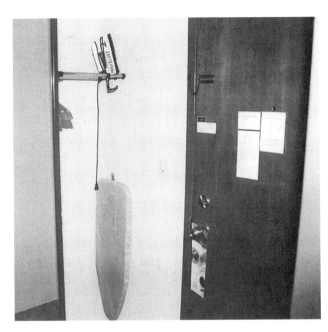

Exhibit 4.8   Housekeeping is responsible for maintaining in-room amenities, such as irons and ironing boards. (Photo by Marilyn McDonald)

The reason for creating standard operating procedures is to ensure that the same tasks are performed exactly the same way throughout the property. This will ensure a uniform standard of cleanliness. The guest rooms' "finish" should look the same from the basement to the penthouse. Each public rest room, hallway, stairwell, and public area should be cleaned the same way.

Standard operating procedures can be as finicky as specifying what station will be preset on the guest-room clock radio or as general as "vacuum the lobby." These procedures take many things into consideration—safety, speed, time of day, appearance, and productivity. They must be written so they can be followed easily. They must also be adaptable to changes. If an employee finds a faster or easier way to perform a task, the procedure should be re-written. Most standard operating procedures can be improved. The approach of "we have always done it this way" does not guarantee success. Allowing employees to try to improve existing procedures may be beneficial to the hotel and make the employees feel appreciated. The future of management is worker empowerment, and the most important way employees can contribute is to find new solutions to old problems. An example of an SOP for receiving a delivery of supplies is:

1. Only authorized personnel may sign for receipt of ordered goods (example: linen room supervisor, housekeeping supervisor, manager, or custodial supervisor).
2. Only the department that ordered the goods or materials may sign for them.
3. All items must be counted and checked against what is stated on the bill of lading, delivery receipt, or invoice.
4. The person who signs for the delivery is responsible for the storage and security of the goods.
5. The signed receipt must be delivered to the proper department (example: accounting, accounts payable) for timely payment and accurate inventory control.

Departmental forms are often a part of SOPs. Forms are standardized ways to transfer information needed for the hotel to function. Information generally flows from the general to the specific. The night auditor's report to housekeeping is a form that summarizes the status of all the rooms in the hotel. (Symbols commonly used include C/O for "checked out," O/C for "on change," S/O for "stay over," OOO for "out of order," and R/R for "room ready.") Depending on the size of the property and its staff, the executive housekeeper will use this information to apportion work to senior housekeepers (who will then assign it to individuals or teams) or to make direct assignments. In a very large property the information from the night auditor's report may go through several layers of organization, each with its own daily work forms, before it reaches the hands of the housekeeper who will actually clean the rooms.

Key control is another area where SOPs are of use. This will be explained in more detail in the section of this chapter dealing with security. At this point, note that it is very important to have a strict SOP for issuing keys to housekeepers (and other *staff members*) who need them for their daily tasks. Ideally, all departments that need access to guest rooms and storage areas should use the same procedures for signing pass keys in and out. That way, the managers of those areas will know who has the keys, and when and where the keys were given out.

Two other areas that require good SOPs are the lost and found operation and guest loan items. Both involve writing down information that will be shared by the front desk and housekeeping department. For example, if a housekeeper finds a pair of gold earrings in a vacated guest room, he or she should bring them back to the housekeeping office. Here, the date, time, and room number are recorded and passed on to the front desk on a form. When the guest calls back to the front desk to ask if anyone has found the earrings, the information can easily be found.

Similarly, if the front desk lends an item to a guest, such as an iron, and the housekeeper finds the iron after the guest checks out, it is recorded and placed back into the loan item area. Housekeeping lets the front desk know that the iron has been returned so the guest will not be charged for it.

Time card control is another good area for SOPs. Time cards keep track of how much hourly personnel are paid. To ensure that the actual time worked is paid to the worker, controls must be in place. Employees should be instructed from the first day of work what these procedures are. Most businesses have rules about time cards, such as:

- Only punch your own time card.
- Do not punch other employees in or out.
- Do not come to work a half-hour early and punch in.
- Remember to punch out when you leave at the end of your shift.
- If you have forgotten to clock in or out, notify your supervisor as soon as possible so adjustments can be made.

Still another common area for SOPs is control of inventory. Just as the hotel kitchen and bar departments need inventory control, so does housekeeping. Only a limited number of employees should have access to valuable items. These employees need to record the number and type of articles they remove from storage or equipment bays. Using such controls is a sound business practice that reduces employee theft and speeds up the process of taking inventory.

One last SOP is the guest room inspection routine. To achieve the best quality control, a standard guest inspection checklist is given to those who supervise the inspection of guest rooms before they are released to the front desk as ready to sell. This type of SOP ensures that each room passes the same inspection quality checks.

Used correctly, standard operating procedures will result in uniform and consistent performance.

Laundry

Hotels have two choices regarding laundry: Hire a contract service or use an on-premises laundry. There are positive and negative sides to both options.

The advantages of a contract laundry service are that the hotel has more space for guest rooms. Also, there is no investment in equipment or additional employees. The negative side of a laundry service comes in the form of lack of quality control and loss of flexibility. The hotel has to work around delivery schedules, and any sudden changes in linen demand are very difficult to accommodate.

Having an on-premises laundry department has many advantages. The turn-around time—the time between when an article is soiled and when it is washed, folded, and ready to use again—is short. The hotel can purchase fewer sheets, tablecloths, and so on because no linens are ever in transit; they never leave the hotel. A laundry may even be used as a profit center by doing linen service for other properties. The negatives of an on-premises laundry room come in the form of high initial investment in equipment, space considerations, and an increase in utility and labor costs.

For many hotels in remote locations, there is no choice but to operate an on-premises laundry department. When contract services add long-distance transport charges to their bill, prices cease to be reasonable. On the other hand, some hotels, because of building design, city zoning, or other factors, must use a laundry service. Sometimes creativity finds a solution. For example, if a corporation owns four hotels in a close geographic area, one property may specialize in one activity for all four hotels. One property may be responsible for the laundry, another for bakery needs, and so on.

In most cases, housekeeping managers inherit an existing laundry situation when they begin a new job. If they are involved when a new property is being designed, they can request that the laundry be integrated into the housekeeping operations area. At this stage a laundry consultant can be hired to help in planning

EYE ON THE ISSUES

International

In a career that may take you to all parts of the world, it's important to pay attention to local laws and customs. Local labor laws may influence the number of hours per day and days per week during which workers may be scheduled. Religious practices and local customs may affect uniform selection; how closely males and females may work together; and how age, gender, race, and so on may influence supervisor–subordinate relationships. In some areas there may even be myths and misinformation associated with foreigners. Behavior that seems innocent and ordinary to you may be perceived as peculiar or even somewhat scandalous to locals, including your employees.

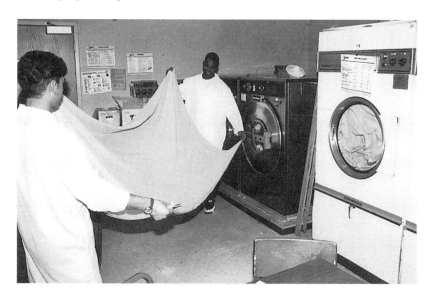

Exhibit 4.9   The size and cost of operating an on-premises laundry depends on the size of the property. The condition of linens is something guests notice immediately. (Photo by James L. Morgan, Scottsdale, Arizona)

the laundry facility. Many variables have to be measured: What will the laundry volume be? How much space will be required? What about location within the building and the build-up of noise and heat? How about utility requirements such as water, electricity, and gas?

Inside an On-Premises Laundry.   The remainder of this section will concentrate on on-premises laundry operations.

Any hotel laundry will have the basic requirement of washing and drying guest-room linens. This includes sheets, pillowcases, bath towels, and washcloths. Many hotels with food and beverage outlets have additional laundry requirements such as table linens and kitchen and server uniforms. The laundry may also be responsible for the cleaning of groundskeeper, maintenance, and engineering uniforms.

When purchasing washing and drying machines it is important to stay with name brands (e.g., Speed Queen, Univac). A no-name bargain may prove costly in the long run when parts cannot be easily found or repair technicians are stumped by unfamiliar assemblies.

Most new commercial washers are programmable. An operator need only push buttons that correspond to the proper washing formula for that particular type of linen. These programmable machines can regulate length of cycle, amount of detergent, softener, and bleach—along with length and duration of rinse and wash cycles. The commercial washing machine must be a very versatile piece of equipment, since it may be required to wash both delicate server uniforms and heavily soiled kitchen aprons. Commercial washing machines come in various sizes, from 25-pound machines to ones that can wash more than 1,000 pounds of laundry. These machines are very heavy and have special installation restrictions. Most commercial machines, due to their weight and strong vibrations while in operation, are bolted down tightly to six-inch-thick concrete slabs. Failure to secure the washing machine will result in damage to the floor as well as to the washing machine.

Dryers are the next piece of equipment needed for the laundry department. It is important to note that the general rule for drying to washing is 2 to 1. That is, if you have 100 pounds of washing capacity, you will need a dryer with 200 pounds of drying capacity. Dryers are either totally electric or use a combination of electricity and gas. Gas may be either natural or propane. Where applicable, a gas dryer is always preferred over a totally electric one. This is due to the extremely high energy cost of a totally electric dryer.

A critical factor in the operation of a clothes dryer is lint removal. Lint causes two major problems. First, lint build-up is an incredible fire hazard. Lint is a dry material that is extremely flammable. The other problem with lint is that it drastically reduces the efficiency of the dryer, because the dryer has to work harder and longer to achieve the same results.

Other essential equipment needed for a commercial-type hotel laundry includes the following: a soak sink to soak stained linens, a set of mobile storage racks for clean linen, a "third-hand" sheet folder, a set of mobile hampers to sort and store soiled linens, and an adequate folding table. These additional items increase the laundry's efficiency and help keep clean linens clean as they are sorted, folded, and stored.

Managers can further improve a laundry's operation by developing an efficient laundry flow. Needed is an organized system that begins with the picking up of

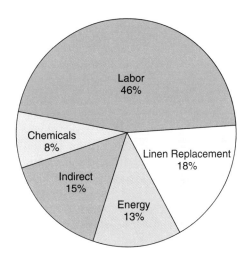

To Approximate Laundry Costs

Percentages in the above chart are based on national averages.

For example, an account spending $3600 a year on detergent costs would equal $45,000 in total laundry costs.

Calculate this by using detergent cost as your control point and estimating the other costs. ($3600 ÷ .08 = $45,000) For example, listed below are the dollar equivalents for the five areas assuming the following percentages per area:

Labor	46%	($45,000 × .46)	$20,700
Linen Replacement	18	(45,000 × .18)	8,100
Energy	13	(45,000 × .13)	5,900
Indirect	15	(45,000 × .15)	6,700
Chemicals	8	(45,000 × .08)	3,600
	100%		$45,000

Exhibit 4.10   To approximate laundry costs.

soiled linens from any area of the property, and continues through the washing, drying, and folding areas to the restocking process. Laundry flow patterns work best when updated and refined according to machinery capacities and labor availability.

Exhibit 4.10 illustrates the approximate costs of operating an in-house laundry. As you can see, labor is highest, with chemicals being the lowest. Choosing a laundry chemical vendor is an important operational decision. Ideally, the goal is to use chemicals that work well in local water, with as little harshness as possible. Using harsher-than-necessary chemicals reduces linen life and may irritate employees' and guests' skins.

When reviewing laundry operations, managers carefully examine monthly customer service reports, as shown in Exhibit 4.11. These reports establish a performance record of how each washer is operating, what maintenance has been done, and what tests have been run. Here, patterns or problems can be noted and adjustments made. These laundry reports are dated and signed by the vendor and the laundry supervisor.

On-premises laundries can add speed, flexibility, and quality control to the washables process. They can also generate revenue in slow times by offering laundry services to other hotels in the area.

Purchasing

If you ever want to find out how many salespeople there are in any area, just open a business—because that's when they come out of the woodwork. The vendors these salespeople represent can be valuable resources, since they are product or service specialists. Their salespeople often know not only their own, but also the competition's, products and prices. For these and other reasons, ***vendor relations*** are important.

Some items—guest room linens, sheets, and towels—are a direct reflection of quality of the hotel. They also have limited life spans. The linen supplier to the hotel will, therefore, come calling quite often, if not to sell new linens, then to check on how the present products are holding up. Conversations with the manufacturer's or vendor's representative are perfect opportunities to discuss needs—for a tighter weave or longer lasting dye on napkins, or better stitching on the edges of sheets. These items are examples of quality standards and purchasing specifications, characteristics you can specify when you order. Let's examine some other products and quality standards, in this case, for the purchasing of linens.

The standard hotel bed sheet is a t-180, percale, flat sheet. The *t-180* indicates there is a thread count (or density) of 180 threads per square inch. *Percale* refers to the production finish of the material. This process is what gives the sheet its feel. *Flat sheet* means that the sheet has no elastic in the corners. The reason for using flat sheets in hotels and hospitals is that they are washed on a daily basis and without elastic they will last much longer. The color of the standard hotel sheet is white. Some hotels may purchase "seconds," sheets with minor imperfections, at a great savings with little perceptible loss in quality. Many upscale hotels use an off-white (natural or cream-colored) sheet to add ambience to their guest room decor.

Towels and washcloths vary in cost and quality. A budget motel located next to an interstate highway whose guest towels are often stolen will buy the cheapest linens available. An upscale resort will have the softest, most absorbent towels available—some even with monograms. These towels will be expensive, but will

CUSTOMER SERVICE REPORT   LAUNDRY

Ecolab Inc.
Ecolab Center
St. Paul, MN 55102

DISTRICT MANAGER	TERR. MANAGER	TERR. NO.	REPORT CONTROL NUMBER

DISTRICT MGR.
PHONE NO.

TERR. MGR.
PHONE NO.

ACCOUNT	ACCOUNT NO.	TIME-IN	TIME-OUT	MONTH	DAY	YEAR	EMERGENCY	NIGHT

TO

CHAIN NO.	MACHINE MAKE	MODEL
	DISPENSER	LOCATION

OPERATION & EQUIPMENT SECTION RESULTS
CIRCLE INDICATE OPERATING CONDITIONS FOUND AND ACTION TAKEN IN SECTION BELOW AND REASON FOR FAIR OR POOR RESULTS

	RESULTS:		TEST KIT			PROCEDURES	OK	TRAINING
1	Appearance	7	c̄	☐ ✓ ☐ No	12	Pre-sorting		☐ Correct Pre-sorting Procedures
2	Superior 1 2 3 4 5 6 7 8 9 20 POOR	8	Im	☐ Yes ☐ No	13	Loading		
3	Odor	9	Linen pH:		14	Wash Formulas		☐ Proper Use of Supplies
4	Feel	10	War Hiches gpg		15	Extract Times		☐ Wash Machine Loading Procedures
5	Stain Removal	11	Wettability		16	Wash Charts		☐ Proper Linen Handling & Folding Procedures
6	Wrinkling		☐ Good ☐ Poor					

EQUIPMENT CONDITIONS FOUND

	WASH MACHINE NO.	1	2	3	4	5		WASH MACHINE NO.	1	2	3	4	5
17	Titration %						21	Timers					
18	Water Levels						22	Wash Charts					
19	Temperature						23	Lint Traps					
20	Drain Valves						24	Wash Count					

NO.	CONDITIONS FOUND, ACTION TAKEN & OTHER COMMENTS

DESCRIBE OTHER CUSTOMER NEEDS

PRODUCT										
STOCK ON HAND										

REORDER DATA	CUST. ORDER NO.	☐ FUTURE N.L.T.	☐ DELIV. ON	☐ C.O.D. $

QTY	CODE	PRODUCT AND SIZE	QTY	CODE	PRODUCT AND SIZE

WARRANTIES OF FITNESS AND MERCHANTABILITY, IF ANY, AS WELL AS ANY EXPRESS WARRANTIES COVERING THE ABOVE PRODUCT SHALL NOT BE EFFECTIVE UNLESS THE PRODUCTS ARE USED AS DIRECTED BY ECOLAB INC.

CUSTOMER'S
SIGNATURE _____

ECOLAB
REP _____

TERR.
NO. _____

ST. PAUL

Courtesy: Ecolab, Inc., St. Paul, Minnesota.

Exhibit 4.11   A monthly customer service report.

reflect the quality of the property. Most properties fall somewhere between the two extremes. Most guests are satisfied with a towel that feels comfortable against the skin and absorbs moisture adequately.

Bedding is a critical area for the success of a hotel and a very important purchasing decision. A great hotel must start with a comfortable bed; after all, the

Exhibit 4.12   Typical guest rooms provide a sampling of personal care amenities as shown. (*Photo:* Rob Melnychuk/Getty Images, Inc.)

main service a hotel offers is a good night's sleep. This means the hotel will have to purchase quality name brand box springs and mattresses. Quality name brands, though more expensive, usually pay off in the long run because of consistent construction and durability. Manufacturers of name-brand goods also offer factory warranties of some sort. This is an area where a hotel can't look for cheap substitutes.

Cleaning chemicals are an important purchase for the housekeeping department too. The vendor of these products should be able to train the housekeeping department in the proper use, storage, and supply of all safety-related materials. A simple dispensing system with color-keyed bottles and chemicals, and pictures of what the chemical cleans, helps housekeepers with a literacy or language barrier to figure out what product cleans what.

The housekeeping department will also purchase equipment ranging from simple vacuum cleaners to complete carpet-care machines. Vacuum cleaners used in cleaning guest rooms are, of course, an essential part of housekeeping, and greatly affect the guest's impression of a room's cleanliness. Vacuum cleaners take a lot of abuse, so they must be durable. It is better to buy a $400 machine that will last a couple of years than to buy three $125 machines that will wear out in a few months. It's wise to take some time to find out what other hotels in the area use and what type of service can be expected from local equipment dealers. This is another area in which a bargain may cost a lot more money in the long run, especially if you make the mistake of buying a home-consumer model rather than a commercial quality machine.

A few final comments on purchasing: The vendors who work for respectable companies are, in general, a very reliable source of information. Vendors have experience in solving most of a hotel's cleaning problems and are generally very willing to help in training people on how to use their equipment. Even so, remember

Exhibit 4.13   In a first class hotel, detailed housekeeping is lost if the quality of the softgoods isn't high. Four Seasons Hotels have custom-designed mattresses on all guest beds! (*Courtesy:* Four Seasons Hotels & Resorts, Toronto, Canada)

that vendors are dedicated to making sales. For this reason, purchases should always be spread between at least two vendors. When a vendor knows that you regularly buy some products from a competitor, he or she is motivated to keep trying to please you in hopes of persuading you to reassign some of those sales. Competition between vendors will benefit you in two ways: First, the service will be good, and second, the prices will be fair.

EYE ON THE ISSUES

Customer Service

This author has personally crawled into a full-size dumpster looking for a lost article belonging to a guest that was accidentally disposed of by a housekeeper. A guest was very attached to a shower cap with a hotel crest from Asia. The housekeeper, thinking it was an old shower cap from her own hotel, tossed the old one out, replacing it with a new one. Upon the return of the guest to the made-up hotel room, the guest became upset about the loss of her valued shower cap. The executive housekeeper was notified and the search started. One saving factor in the search for the missing shower cap was that the hotel used clear plastic trash bags. After the housekeeper deduced in which dumpster the trash bag had been discarded, the executive housekeeper climbed into the dumpster, and searched until the missing shower cap was found. The guest's needs and preference were honored by the staff despite the fact that the item seemed trivial.

MAINTENANCE AND ENGINEERING

This section deals with the department that keeps the building from falling down. The size and responsibilities of this department are very similar to those of the housekeeping department. The size of the unit, the complexity of the construction, and the property's type directly affect the number of people needed in the maintenance/engineering departments. A small bed and breakfast operation will, more often than not, have only the owner to perform routine maintenance. He or she will paint, cut the grass, and do minor electrical and plumbing repairs. When something major breaks, he or she will have to rely on outside help. A large resort hotel, on the other hand, may need hundreds of maintenance personnel for all phases of the operation. A hotel with 3,000 rooms, a 36-hole golf course, a convention center, four swimming pools, six restaurants, three bars, and a 10-acre parking lot will definitely require a great deal of care. There will be thousands of light bulbs to change, hundred of toilets to plunge, and thousands of square yards of carpets to repair.

Maintenance

The terms *maintenance* and *engineering* are often used interchangeably but they have two distinct meanings.

Maintenance is simply defined as the work involved in keeping something in good working order. Maintenance comes in many forms, from routine to preventive, and from emergency to scheduled. In the case of hotels and restaurants, there are a great many things to keep in good working order. Routine maintenance can range from simple housekeeping tasks such as lubricating squeaky doors and shoveling snow, to changing air filters and smoke detector batteries. These simple

Exhibit 4.14   The maintenance department is responsible for some of the most expensive (and dangerous) equipment in the hotel. (*Courtesy:* Sodexho Alliance)

tasks make up a majority of the tasks that are generally considered to be maintenance.

Preventive maintenance, also known as *PM,* is done specifically to avoid a major breakdown of equipment. These activities include regular lubrication of moving parts, testing of backup and emergency equipment, changing machine belts, and, most importantly, finding minor problems before they become major ones. The old axiom "an ounce of prevention is worth a pound of cure" describes exactly what preventive maintenance attempts to accomplish.

Emergency maintenance activities are performed in situations where a property suffers or may stand to suffer loss of revenue. If a toilet is broken, stopped up, or leaking, the room cannot be sold. If a busy restaurant has one large dishwasher that fails and thus prevents clean dishware and silverware from being set revenue may be lost. Emergency maintenance is developed to solve money-losing problems quickly. This is also the most expensive type of maintenance because all phases come at a premium price. Labor, parts, and the "fix it at any cost" attitude push costs to the extreme.

Many times, PM activities are done with particular seasons in mind. In late spring, most swimming pool maintenance is completed. Heating boilers are serviced before winter sets in and refrigeration units are serviced before the heat of summer. If the hotel has an off season, this is the ideal time to close down rooms for painting and repairs. When an area or unit is not in use, scheduled maintenance can occur. Scheduled maintenance is the preplanned repair or replacement of major components of working systems.

Engineering

Engineering is the department wherein employees need a thorough knowledge of all the working systems in a hotel. These systems include the following:

Water and wastewater

Lighting

Telecommunication

Waste management

Energy management

EYE ON THE ISSUES

Technology

Managers of engineering and housekeeping departments should make every effort to stay abreast of advancements in pertinent technology. Monthly trade publications, trade show attendance, and membership in professional associations provide avenues for keeping current. The major goal of adopting new technology is to increase efficiency and safety. For example, recent advances in bug control technology have made termite and roach control both safer and more efficient. By spraying hormone-related compounds in infested areas, pests can be prevented from maturing to the point where they can reproduce. This quickly reduces bug populations without the use of potentially hazardous toxic pesticides.

Electricity

Laundry

Safety and security

Food service equipment

Heating, ventilation, and air conditioning (HVAC)

This department is another crucial one in the overall performance of the property. The guest in any hotel or restaurant expects the lights to go on, the toilets to flush, and the room temperature to be pleasant. If any one of these creature comfort items fails, the property will appear not to care about the guest's comfort, and that is not the impression a hotel or restaurant wants to create.

Engineering is responsible for any renovation or new construction after the property is in operation. All systems inside and outside of the building are under the direction of engineering.

Water Systems.   Water and wastewater systems are essential in any building. In hospitality, the entire property is tied to some type of water system. Water can be divided into two types: potable and nonpotable. **Potable water** refers to water that is drinkable. Nonpotable water cannot be consumed by human beings. It has limited use. The most common use of nonpotable water is to supply the **fire suppression** system. The sprinklers, standpipes, and hose cabinets are supplied by a nonpotable water system. This includes the internal system and the outside fire hydrants.

The potable water supply comes in two forms: hot and cold. Hot water has two uses: for people and equipment. People need hot water for bathing, cooking, and washing. Equipment needs hot water for cleaning and for the operation of swimming pools, spas, and Jacuzzis.

Cold water is used by people for flushing toilets, bathing, cooking, and drinking. Equipment needs cold water in the kitchen, laundry room, swimming pool, heating and cooling systems, and the grounds division.

A guest does not think about the water system too much until it fails. But when a guest uses a water fountain, goes to brush his or her teeth, or take a shower, the water system had better be in working order!

Engineering is also concerned with water quality. Most of the trouble with water quality originates at the source. Water that comes from wells, inlets, streams, or the utility company varies greatly in makeup. Ideally, water should be colorless, odorless, and tasteless, and should contain no harmful bacteria. Local health agencies are required to test water quality several times a year.

Pollution at the source of water supplies can come in many forms. Industrial pollution in the forms of fuel spills, waste oil spills, and waste products from mining can alter the composition of water. Farming can pollute water through the use of excess fertilizers and pesticides that run off into the local water supply.

After water gets to the property, its mineral content (such as iron, manganese, and calcium) has a direct effect on its quality. Large amounts of minerals cause **hard water.** This hard water, over time, will build up "scale" on the insides of boilers and heaters, reducing their efficiency.

Another problem caused by hard water is that more detergent is needed in washing machines to compensate for the minerals and to clean properly. In the presence of hard water, soap will not lather and will leave a scum on plumbing fixtures, which makes them harder to clean. It then becomes necessary to use stronger chemicals and increase labor to get the cleaning accomplished. Obviously, hard water may create several problems that become costly if not addressed property.

The best system for overcoming a hard water situation is the use of a water-softening unit. Water softeners use different types of salts to remove minerals. The cost of water-softening units is usually recovered through the longer life of heating units and lower amounts of detergents being used. When engineering is aware of a hard water situation in the area, a water-softening unit should be included as part of the water system.

Swimming pools pose several problems for engineering. A pool's location, and whether it is inside or outside a building, creates changing water conditions, which contribute to high maintenance costs. Pool water must be monitored and adjusted constantly. Outdoor pools must be kept in circulation or drained during periods of below freezing temperatures. Resorts may have several pools, both inside and out. If engineers had their way, all pools would be indoor pools since they are easier to maintain, may be used all year, and are not subject to extremes in climate. Unfortunately for them, sun-loving guests love outdoor pools and the chance to bask next to them.

The engineering department must also be concerned with wastewater generated by a hotel and its restaurants. What happens to everything that goes down the drain? A property that is located in the center of an urban area will be tied into the city sewer system. The property will pay for this access to the public sewer system with a per gallon charge from the local water treatment utility plant. Thus, water costs money not only as you bring it to your property, but also as you get rid of it.

Exhibit 4.15   Swimming pool maintenance systems are considered before even the first shovel of dirt has been removed (Photo by Marilyn McDonald, Scottsdale, Arizona).

Some (though very few) properties have their own on-premise wastewater treatment plants due to remote locations or strict local laws. Small, privately owned wastewater systems are tightly regulated by state and county laws. If a property has a wastewater facility, it is usually required to have a technician on duty who is up to date on the rules and certifications needed for operation.

All properties need hot water, yet hotels and restaurants have different hot water requirements. Kitchens, by local health codes, are required to wash dishes at 180°F. Any place where dishes are washed must consistently produce this high temperature. Most commercial dishwashers have some type of booster that raises the temperature inside the washing unit.

Hotels have two major needs for hot water: bathing and clothes washing. Every sink, shower, and bathtub is expected to have running hot water. The temperature at these fixtures should not exceed 155°F. Any higher temperatures may burn a guest. To prevent burning, a hotel should have mixing valves in the showers and sinks to regulate the temperature (mixing cold water with the hot water keeps it from getting too hot). This prevents a common home experience: While you are in the shower, someone flushes a toilet or turns on the lawn sprinklers. This forces the shower temperature up to where you scream and jump out of the shower. Needless to say, this cannot happen at a commercial property.

An on-premise laundry will increase demand for hot water, normally in the 150°F and under range. Since most guests take a shower or have a bath early in the morning or late in the evening, these are times hotels do not want the laundry running with high hot water demands. Consequently most hotels operate their laundry in non-peak times of the day.

Electrical Systems.   A modern hotel cannot function without electricity. Because of the demands made by electrical appliances, large machines, and cooling and heating equipment, hotels must have access to dependable sources of electricity. The power needed for lighting alone is simply amazing. Look around the classroom complex you are in and notice the number and different kinds of lighting that are available. There may be simple lamps with 100-watt incandescent lightbulbs, an assortment of fluorescent lightbulbs, and sodium or mercury vapor parking lot lights. These are just three of the many types of lighting found in any

Exhibit 4.16   Indoor swimming pools present different maintenance issues than outdoor pools.
(*Photos:* Left, Lucio Rossi © Dorling Kindersley, courtesy of the Stubicke Toplice Spa, Croatia; right, Neil Setchfield © Dorling Kindersley)

commercial building. Soft light in dining rooms, exit sign lights, and heat lamps are some other examples of lights found in a hotel. Each type of lighting has a specific purpose and energy requirement.

High-rise hotels all have some type of elevator system powered by electricity; some also have escalators. Guests and employees need a fast and safe way to move up and down several floors of the buildings. Hotel guests are not going to check into a hotel and walk up 30 or 40 flights of stairs. The operation of the elevators places a high energy demand on the hotel's electrical system.

The use of computers in every hotel department causes another substantial demand for electricity. If your computerized reservation system goes down because of a power loss, this could mean hundreds of dollars being lost per minute because rooms cannot be booked. Computers track many other day-to-day operations such as purchasing, payroll, maintenance orders, check-in, check-out, and billing. Without electricity none of these operations can be performed.

In restaurants located inside a hotel property, all appliances are electrically powered. The list is almost endless and can include the following: coffeemakers, meat slicers, blenders, dishwashers, microwave ovens, mixers, timers, and steam tables. The most important electrical devices in the kitchen are the refrigeration units. If the power goes off, thousands of dollars can be lost due to food spoilage.

The guest room has many electrical outlets and guest appliances. Televisions and, in some cases, DVD or interactive game units are requisite entertainment equipment. Guests also expect to be able to use electric-powered hair dryers, irons, razors, personal computers, and battery packs.

You now know something about a hotel's electrical demands, but do you know where the electricity comes from? The vast majority of hotels buy their electricity from a utility company. Some remote properties produce their own power with generators that run on steam, gasoline, or other fuels. Whatever power source a hotel uses, the electric current flows into the building and is distributed throughout. Electricity is similar to plumbing in that it must be directed to different areas according to demand. National and local building codes regulate the quality, size, and type of material used in all phases of designing, electrical systems. Inspectors monitor construction of commercial buildings to ensure that they comply with these standards.

Cost, as reflected by monthly utility bills, is of great concern to the engineering department. Excessive use of electricity can be caused by undersized equipment or old, worn-out electric motors. By closely examining the electric usage, the engineering department can make the changes necessary to upgrade equipment and increase efficiency.

HVAC. HVAC *heating, ventilation,* and *air conditioning* is seen all the time in conjunction with commercial buildings. **HVAC** systems have unique demands placed on them in hospitality situations. One guest might turn the heat on in August when the outside air temperature is above 90°F. Another guest may open a guest room window in the dead of winter. A cold banquet room heats up quickly after 300 guests arrive and start to socialize with each other. A kitchen may start off the morning cold, but as soon as the bakers start baking bread in the oven, the whole area heats up. A tour group of senior citizens may ask for warmer meeting and sleeping room temperatures, while a group of college students on spring break may crank the air conditioning up as far as it will go.

The control of the climate throughout the building is regulated by HVAC, from the stairwells, to the guest rooms, and to all other parts of the building where guests and employees can be found.

Heating the building is critical for two reasons. The guest's comfort is important. However, the protection of the building is the most critical function of the heating system. If the heating system fails on a cold winter day with the temperature below freezing, pipes can break. This could mean that entire sections of the water system may need to be replaced at a tremendous cost. When pipes burst, there is usually attendant damage to walls, ceilings, carpets, furnishings, and so on. Also, some fire suppression systems that rely on a water "charge" can be rendered inoperable and thus constitute an additional major hazard.

Heat needs some type of fuel source. The most common fuels for heating are electricity, natural gas, liquefied petroleum, fuel oil, and steam. Each different fuel has benefits and drawbacks. In some cases, due to local rules or availability, there is no choice and only one type of fuel can be used. When there is a choice of fuel types, cost, storage, and availability must all be considered.

Air-conditioning requirements vary from one climate to another. The most important fact to remember about air conditioning is "cold is not produced; heat is taken away." This is the basic principle of air conditioning. A refrigerant, when converted from a liquid to a gas in a condenser, produces a temperature change. As the liquid turns to a gas, it absorbs heat from the immediate environment. The cold that is felt actually comes from the transformation of heat to another form of energy.

Ventilation is simply understood by looking at a building as though it were a living thing that needs to breathe. Fresh air needs to be brought into a building, filtered, and moved to areas requiring fresh air. The ventilation system also exhausts air that is too hot or foul smelling. It does this through a series of fans, ducts, and filters. These are all high-maintenance items. Fan belts break and wear out, and fil-

Exhibit 4.17   (A) A heat recovery system takes advantage of naturally occurring heat to assist in other building systems. (B) A strobe-type alarm uses not only loud sound but also flashing light to ensure that guests with hearing loss are alerted by the bright strobe flash. (Photos by Marilyn McDonald)

ters eventually clog and become inefficient. This system is always placed on a scheduled maintenance program to prevent any problems.

PROTECTING ASSETS, PEOPLE, AND PROPERTY

This section of the chapter will discuss the protection of people and property. The *safety and security* of the people and property within a hotel operation are fundamental. Safety entails protecting individuals from injury and property from damage by fire or other types of disasters. Security entails providing freedom from the fear of negative or harmful interactions. Another way to look at this is that safety is related to protecting people from disasters and security deals with protecting them from other people who may harm them.

Safety

Most local building codes in each city, county, and state strictly regulate safety, beginning at the time of construction. Fire prevention and protection are a local responsibility. Materials used to build hotels and restaurants must be of a certain quality, and firewalls are required in certain building sections to prevent fire from spreading.

Smoke detectors are another basic form of fire safety built right into the design of the building. Fire suppression units are also part of many building codes and are found in two types. The most common type is the **heat-activated sprinkler system** that dumps water at a high pressure onto the heat source. This type of fire suppression system is found in many modern hotels and restaurants, especially in commercial kitchens and high-rise hotels. The second type of fire suppression system uses a sprinkler that sprays a chemical on the heat source. The **chemical-type sprinkler** is used in computer rooms where water damage to the equipment could run into millions of dollars.

Most modern hotels have a central computer that controls all aspects and elements of the fire safety system. If a smoke detector goes off in the 14th floor hallway, an alarm will sound. The central fire computer will alert the front desk and/or the security department, pinpointing the exact location of the problem. With this information, immediate action can be taken.

An important part of fire codes relates to the number and location of fire exits. Familiarity with their locations can be of the utmost importance in times of emergency. Look around the building you are in right now. Do you notice the location of exit signs? Are they visible? Could you find your way out of the building if a fire started? Elevators should not be used in case of fire, so fire escapes, internal sets of stairs usually located at both ends of the building, are the main means of exit from upper floors. If you walk into any commercial building, notice that all exterior doors open outward. This is a code written to allow fast evacuation of buildings. Many hotels and restaurants, when inspected by fire marshals, are fined for locked or blocked fire exit doors.

Fire damage is fast and far reaching. The cost of preventing fires is much lower than the costs of repairing fire damage. Local fire codes are written for the protection of everyone. Failure to follow these codes can result in criminal and

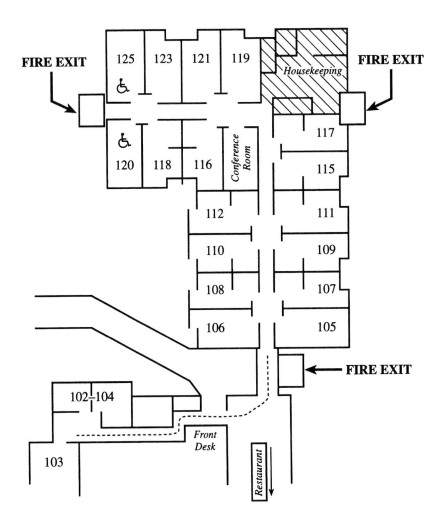

FIRE ESCAPE ROUTE
1st Floor

Exhibit 4.18 Every business should be prepared for fire emergencies. Because guests at lodging properties may be asleep and groggy, it's particularly important for hotels and motels to keep a fire escape route posted on doors where guests can find it. Note the positioning of handicapped-accessible rooms.

civil judgments against the corporation as well as the individual. You might also think of the public perception of your hotel should you be held responsible for a fatal fire—either through failure to comply with local codes or, worse, through deliberate disregard of them.

Many fire codes include laws designed specifically to protect hotel guests. These include fire escape maps in each guest room, fire alarms, easily accessible fire extinguishers, and fire protection equipment that can operate in a power outage. All codes mandate minimum levels of protection; most properties of large corporations exceed what is required to increase the level of safety and protection.

Hospitality establishments should take the time to practice fire drills. Employees should know how to evacuate the building and assist guests in case of an emergency. It makes little sense to spend money on fire safety equipment and not take the time to train employees in its proper use. All personnel should be familiar with the operation of portable fire extinguishers. Most local fire departments are more than willing to help teach classes and participate in fire safety training. The firefighters in your area do not want to visit your hotel or restaurant for the first time when it is on fire.

A fact to remember about fire is that most people who die in fires are killed by smoke inhalation. Smoke rises during a fire, so training employees to crawl along the floor where there is a supply of fresh air can save lives. The most important thing employees need to be aware of in an emergency fire situation is not to panic, although that is easier said than done. The difference between the life and death of employees and guests may be staff calmness and control. The better trained and prepared the staff is, the greater the chances they, and your guests, will survive an emergency situation.

While fire is a universal problem, some disasters that may affect a property will be natural ones unique to the specific location of the property. Beach properties in Florida, Louisiana, and the Caribbean are keenly aware of hurricane season. Areas with active volcanoes make plans to prepare for eruptions. California no longer considers earthquakes a rarity. Properties close to bodies of water are subject to flooding. Blizzards can happen in mountain and northern regions of the country, and tornadoes occur in flat areas. Each one of these disasters can force a property to take emergency measures, because they may result in a lack of fresh water, loss of electricity and/or heating fuel, and so on. Knowing what problems may occur in your locale can help you better prepare your staff to deal with disasters.

Safety is also related to human-made problems. Many accidents and injuries happen on site at hotels and restaurants. These incidents are expensive for a business. Insurance claims due to guest injury drive up premiums and may result in lawsuits. When an employee is hurt on the job, workers' compensation insurance rates also increase, investigations occur, and lawsuits may, once again, be the result.

Many accidents/injuries occur because of lack of training on the part of the employer. Let's look at some situations where proper training could prevent serious injury.

- The kitchen supervisor sends a new employee to slice meat without proper training on the slicing machine.
- A child walks by a housekeeping cart, grabs an open unlabeled bottle of cleaning chemical, and drinks it, thinking it is lemonade.
- A housekeeping supervisor skips reading directions on new cleaning chemicals. The housekeeping staff is exposed to harmful, maybe fatal, doses of fumes.
- A guest checks out of the guest room leaving a fully loaded gun. A housekeeper finds it, drops it, and shoots himself.
- A groundskeeper fails to lock the gate to the swimming pool and a toddler wanders into the pool and drowns.
- A new busperson, thinking the last guest has been served, fills the iced tea dispenser with cleanser. A server comes back to the serving station, fills two glasses from the iced tea dispenser and serves two guests.

- A new houseperson mops the marble floor in the front desk lobby area without putting up "Caution, Wet Floor" signs. A man in a hurry runs to check in and slips, breaking his hip.
- The sous chef sends a kitchen worker into the freezer for a box of shrimp, forgetting to tell her that the freezer door sticks.
- After the lobby fireplace is cleaned by the housekeeper, the still-hot ashes are deposited into the dumpster.

Security

Security in hospitality means protecting people and property. The protection of guests and employees while on the property is a great responsibility. Property has to be guarded against theft, vandalism, and even terrorism.

Guest security varies with the type of hotel. A budget hotel may have only a night auditor on property between 11 PM and 7 AM. An exclusive resort with $400 per night suites will have a security force patrolling 24 hours a day.

Methods for protecting guests, employees, and property from potential harm take many forms, but one important one is the unofficial deputization of all employees as watchdogs. Employees should immediately report any suspicious activity to their supervisor. They should be encouraged to take an active role in the protection of people and property.

Many properties issue photo identification badges to their employees, with clearly visible name, photo, and department. This is a great way to discourage people from wandering into zones where they do not belong. It has the secondary benefit of putting guests at ease, since they can easily identify employees of the property if they need assistance.

Common areas and walkways should be well lit. Hallways, stairwells, and parking lots must also have adequate lighting. Escorts should be provided to employees and guests going out to the parking lot after dark.

Obviously, one of the essential requirements of a hotel is that all guest rooms have doors that lock in a secure manner. Any problem with a guest room door justifies its being removed from service until repairs are made.

Guest room key control is an area for strict policy. A housekeeper should never let a person into a guest room with his or her pass key. A person claiming to have lost his or her room key should be sent to the front desk. Before issuing a key, the front desk requires the person to provide identification. Even if a true guest ends up being somewhat inconvenienced, he or she will generally appreciate the extra attention paid to security. This is definitely preferable to breaching the security of the hotel.

Every time a television news magazine talks about the lack of hotel security, reporters dwell on room key control. Time and again, news hawks send impostors to front desks to ask for room keys. Far too many times, without checking, the front desk gives the keys out to people who are not even registered. Another problem is that of missing room keys. If a guest key is lost, the hotel should put the room out of order until the key has been found or the lock changed.

Hotels generally establish a good relationship with local police departments. Part of this relationship includes cooperation whenever police are called. If their errand requires that they arrest someone at a hotel, whether an employee or a guest, employees should back them up. If police request management or staff to file charges or testify in court, hotel policy should make it simple for the employee to do so. It is counterproductive to a hotel's security to hinder police business or make officers feel unwelcome. In fact, many 24-hour restaurants go out of their way to make on-duty police feel welcome, offering free coffee and discounted meals. This policy helps create a secure atmosphere at a very low cost. If criminals know a property is frequented by police, they will think twice before they burglarize it.

It is important to maintain all built-in security components. Doors that are supposed to be locked should be checked regularly and frequently. Fire escape doors must be kept closed. Guest-room sliding glass doors need to be secured. Employee entrances should be monitored. Anything related to building security must be kept in top condition. Breakages or malfunctions should be repaired immediately, since security devices are sometimes sabotaged for the very purpose of making a planned robbery easier. Hotel properties are by nature easy targets for burglars and muggers. New faces are an everyday occurrence, so thieves have an automatic protective cover. Proper security measures will thwart crime and give guests a feeling of comfort and protection.

Employee Theft

Billions of dollars are lost every year to employee theft. Sad to say, unscrupulous employees will steal from a property unless the property makes it difficult to do so. Sometimes, employee theft escalates to the point where it cripples a hotel's chances to make a profit. To prevent theft, employees must be given clear instructions on acceptable behavior. Without them, some may think that walking home

Exhibit 4.19   Police and fire officers often visit hotel lobbies, public spaces, guest rooms and hallways to get "the lay of the land." It is important to survey the property *before* emergencies occur. (*Courtesy:* Four Seasons Hotels & Resorts, Toronto, Canada)

with pockets full of guest-room amenities is no big deal. It's important that they know that this is considered stealing and that thieves will be prosecuted.

Perhaps a hotel will have a policy of letting employees take home discarded items instead of throwing them out. If so, it must be very clear what those items are. It's also important to control the area around trash disposal systems and dumpsters. Hotels that check such trash receptacles often find that usable items have been deliberately thrown out by employees who expect to retrieve them surreptitiously after work.

There are several other simple measures a hotel or restaurant can take to curb employee theft. The easiest one is limiting the entrances and exits employees use. If all employees enter and leave the building through designated doors, they are less likely to walk out with company property. Standard operating procedures should be in place regarding who may sign for deliveries, pass keys, and storage area access. Another good precaution is tagging personal items brought onto the property by employees. Security should issue a multicopy pass that describes the personal item, including its color, model, and serial number. When the employee removes the item from the property, there will be a reliable record of ownership.

Employee parking areas should be located well away from the building with a well lit path directly to the parking lot.

"Contamination" is another problem that results from employee theft. Good employees who would never steal anything may watch other employees take things at will. The good employees often become contaminated by the actions of others and begin to steal things themselves.

Exhibit 4.20 Lavish guest suites such as this present an increased risk of employee theft. With so many amenities and inventoried supplies, it can take days for management to notice missing items. (*Courtesy*: Four Seasons Hotels & Resorts, Toronto, Canada)

A very important part in prevention of employee theft is setting an example from the general manager down the line. If members of upper management walk out the door with hotel property, watching employees will figure that they are stealing . . . and that this is normal practice. Rules that are written about ethics and honesty apply to all employees. Those at the top must lead by example.

CONCLUSION

Housekeeping is a complicated business. Staffing and training are two ongoing housekeeping functions. Establishing high standards for cleanliness is essential to the success of any property.

The many systems in a hospitality building are complex. Guests expect plumbing, heating, and all other creature comforts to work and work well. To monitor all the building's functions as well as control costs is a very important responsibility of the engineering and maintenance department.

This general overview of property management, was just that—general. Your curriculum may include one or more property management courses. Many students find these among their most interesting courses, since through them they explore the out-of-sight back areas of hotels. Some aspects of property management are becoming more and more automated, but overall, this area will continue to be labor intensive. Technology can and has, however, greatly improved the internal communications systems necessary for good property management. Managers in this area will continue to need both exceptional people skills and detailed logistical skills. Though many future housekeeping and property services executives begin their careers in hotels, opportunities are not limited to the lodging sector. All segments of hospitality, including restaurants, theme parks, casinos, and night clubs, require ongoing maintenance, cleaning, and inspection. There are also institutional opportunities in hospitals, correctional facilities, and supervised living communities.

KEYWORDS

executive housekeeper   142
rooms report   142
codes of appearance   151
standard operating procedure   152
preventive maintenance   163
potable water   164

fire suppression   164
hard water   164
HVAC   167
heat-activated sprinkler system   169
chemical-type sprinkler   169

CORE CONCEPTS

demographics of the applicant pool   149
scheduling employees   151
key control   154

time card control   154
vendor relations   158
safety and security   169

DISCUSSION QUESTIONS

1. Describe some of the problems a hotel has in staffing the housekeeping department. What are some of the solutions?
2. When purchasing services and equipment from vendors, what are some major factors that should affect from whom you buy?
3. What are the most common areas of the physical plant for which the engineering and maintenance department is responsible, and why are these areas important to the success of the hotel?
4. Why should all departments in a hotel be involved in the safety and security of the people and property in a hotel?
5. In what ways can a hotel establish a policy that can be viewed as environmentally friendly?
6. Write a short (one page or less) procedure to be posted in a guest room regarding fire/emergency procedures. Describe the hotel/motel structure—number of rooms, stories, staircases, fire stairs, elevators, and so on—and specify whether there are interior hallways.

WEBSITES TO VISIT

1. www.housekeeping.com
2. www3.telus.net/ct_hospitality
3. www.gabrielservice.com/ghi.htm
4. www.opsafesite.com/toolboxtalk
5. www.fhrai.com/Mag-News/magHouseKeeping.asp

CASE STUDY 1

Housekeeper Pat, a 10-year employee who has an outstanding record, begins the workday in the housekeeping department. Pat begins to make up checked-out room 107. As Pat removes the bed linen, a handgun falls on the floor.

1. What has housekeeper Pat's training taught her to do in this situation?
2. In order of importance, what steps should be taken to secure this potentially dangerous situation?
3. What are some of the bad things that could happen because of the discovery of a firearm in a hotel room?
4. What level of involvement by local law enforcement officials should be considered?

CASE STUDY 2

Five out of 30 staff members from housekeeping have been late for work the last four days in a row. Their shift starts at 7:30 A.M. The group has not arrived at work until 8:10 A.M. for the last four days, Monday through Thursday. All five are valued employees with outstanding records and time of employment from six to 10 years.

1. a. As a manager, what is the first step to be taken?
   b. List the many reasons why this could have happened (list at least five).
2. What discipline or action will be taken against the employees?
3. What are some potential "fixes" to keep this problem from recurring?
4. Could this problem have been solved before it started by more effective management?

CASE STUDY 3

A long-time housekeeper, Chris, with a long list of awards, was assaulted in the parking lot after her shift by an ex-employee who was also Chris' ex-spouse. Chris remains hospitalized in serious condition.

1. What could have been done to prevent this unfortunate event?
2. What are existing procedures involving employee safety?
3. Could Chris have done anything to protect herself better?
4. How has this event affected morale in the hotel?
5. What are the new rules that you as a manager would implement (name at least five)?

CASE STUDY 4

A four-star hotel has received many complaints in the past two weeks about rooms that were not clean. The guests have been long-time visitors to the hotel, and have threatened to take their business elsewhere if the problem is not resolved to their satisfaction.

1. As manager, what are your priorities in solving this problem?
2. What involvement does the executive housekeeper have with this black mark on her department?
3. What series of checks and inspections would now be put in place?
4. What team approach could be used to solve this problem?

5. Write a plan that would include all factors in improving quality control in the housekeeping department.

6. Hotels prefer flat sheets as opposed to form-fitted sheets, because the hotel bed linen is washed daily. Therefore, over a long period of time and many washings, the elastic in a form-fitted sheet would wear out long before the flat sheet. The long term life and number of machine washings make the flat sheet a wiser choice in a hotel operation. Discuss other examples of housekeeping or maintenance items which wear-out over time.

The Accountant Says

ACCOUNTING IN THE HOSPITALITY INDUSTRY

In addressing the topic of hospitality accounting, we need to keep in mind that there is considerable similarity among the financial reports and accounting records of all companies in all industries. Of course, there are also notable peculiarities in the accounting records and financial reports of different industries. For instance, the income statement of an airline company will normally show a large amount of fuel expense and aircraft maintenance expense, and consumer goods companies will have large amounts of marketing expenses. Banks will have a high proportion of their assets tied tip in loans and investments and a small proportion invested in property and equipment. The hospitality industry is not exempt from this pattern. We have provided you with some examples of hotel financial statements in Exhibits 1 through 3.

The hospitality industry is divided into two major subcategories, each made up of diverse markets: lodging and restaurants. In lodging there are large full-service hotels, medium-size hotels, and motels—with and without restaurants, resort hotels, and gaming hotels. This diversity also holds true in restaurants, a category that includes gourmet restaurants, family restaurants,

Exhibit 1   Typical Income Statement from a Resort Hotel

CALIFORNIA RESORT HOTEL
Income Statement
Year Ended December 31, 20XX

	Net Revenue	Cost of Sales	Payroll and Related	Other Expenses	Income (Loss)
Operating departments					
Rooms	$2,260,750		$ 452,150	$248,683	$1,559,918
Food and beverage	3,090,000	$1,081,500	988,800	401,700	618,000
Telephone	109,500	114,975			(5,475)
Total operating departments	$5,460,250	$1,196,475	$1,440,950	$650,383	2,172,443
Undistributed operating expenses					
Administrative and general expenses					377,615
Marketing					382,218
Guest entertainment					123,600
Property operation, maintenance, and energy cost					188,700
Total undistributed operating expenses					1,072,133
Total income before fixed charges					1,100,310
Rent, property taxes, and insurance					157,250
Interest					240,600
Depreciation					239,000
Income before income taxes					463,460
Provision for income taxes					162,211
Net income.					$ 301,249

specialty restaurants, fast-food operations, and concession food services that handle ball parks, hospitals, schools, and other institutions.

Professional organizations within the hospitality industry have developed accounting systems tailored to the needs of hospitality managers. One such system is the Uniform System of Accounts and Reports for the Lodging Industry (USARLI). This system was first developed in 1926 and has been revised many times to keep it current with industry needs.

The industry's purpose in developing the USARLI was twofold:

1. To provide a flexible accounting system that could be used by all hotels, large and small, and
2. To provide standardized accounting and reporting that would facilitate comparison of operations between hotels and the hotel industry in general.

The system provides for the production of financial reports that are specialized to the needs of the hotel industry. This common statement format has permitted the development and publication of industry statistics. Smith Travel Research, Inc. publishes hotel operating statistics in its annual Host Study. The report compiles revenues, expenses, operating income, and operating statistical data from a group of full-service and limited-service hotels. The table analyzes income and expenses as a ratio or percentage of total sales, per available room and per occupied room. Without the USARLI, the Host Study would not be available. With it hotel managers

Exhibit 2   Typical Statement of Cash Flow from a Resort Hotel

CALIFORNIA RESORT HOTEL
Statement of Cash Flows
Year Ended December 31, 20XX

Net cash flow from operating activities	
Net income	$301,249
Adjustment to reconcile net income to net cash flows from operating activities	
Depreciation	239,000
Increase in accounts receivable	(6,000)
Increase in inventory	(5,000)
Increase in prepaid expenses	(600)
Increase in accounts payable	10,000
Decrease in accrued expenses	(1,000)
Decrease in income taxes payable	(20,000)
Net cash flow from operating activities	517,649
Net cash flow for investing activities	
Purchase of equipment	(15,000)
Net cash flow for investing activities	(15,000)
Net cash flow for financing activities	
Dividends paid	(105,000)
Payment of long-term debt	(145,000)
Net cash flow for financing activities	(250,000)
Net increase in cash	252,649
Cash at beginning of year	317,600
Cash at end of year	$570,249
Supplemental disclosure of cash flow information	
Cash paid during the year for:	
Interest expense	$240,600
Income taxes	182,211

are able to compare the operations of their hotels with industry averages, and with other similar hotels.

How Accounting Information Is Accumulated

The business activities of a hotel will generate many transactions. We can categorize these transactions into five parts and illustrate them with some examples (see Exhibit 5).

As business is conducted during the month, hotel employees record each transaction onto a physical document or a computer record. File hotel accounting department processes and analyzes these transactions into meaningful totals. At the end of the month, after all transactions have been recorded, processed, and analyzed, the accounting department will prepare monthly financial reports for management.

The final step in the accounting cycle is management's review of operations. Financial statements give managers feedback on how well their operations are performing. They can use this information to direct their inquiries and investigations into the departments in the hotel that seem to be performing poorly. For example,

Exhibit 3   Typical Balance Sheet from a Resort Hotel

CALIFORNIA RESORT HOTEL
Balance Sheet
December 31, 20X4, and December 31, 20X5

Assets	12/31/×1	12/31/×2
Current assets		
Cash	$ 317,600	$ 570,249
Accounts receivable	7,000	13,000
Inventories	15,000	20,000
Prepaid expenses	1,200	1,800
Total current assets	340,800	605,049
Property and equipment, at cost		
Land	900,000	900,000
Buildings	5,000,000	5,000,000
Furniture and equipment	390,000	405,000
	6,290,000	6,305,000
Less accumulated depreciation	478,000	717,000
Property and equipment—net	5,812,000	5,588,000
Other assets	80,000	80,000
Total assets	$6,232,800	$6,273,049

Liabilities and Shareholders' Equity

	12/31/×1	12/31/×2
Current liabilities		
Current maturities on long-term debt	$ 145,000	$ 145,000
Accounts payable	40,000	50,000
Accrued expenses	10,000	9,000
Income taxes	60,000	40,000
Total current liabilities	255,000	244,000
Long-term debt, less current portion	1,860,000	1,715,000
Shareholders' equity		
Common stock, par value $0.50, 500,000 shares authorized, 350,000 shares outstanding	175,000	175,000
Additional paid-in capital	3,325,000	3,325,000
Retained earnings	617,800	814,049
Total shareholders' equity	4,117,800	4,314,049
Total liabilities and shareholders' equity	$6,232,800	$6,273,049

to eliminate an operating loss in telephone communications, management may want to change the way guest telephone calls are handled. If management handles this review process wisely and makes the necessary changes to improve the hotel's operations, future accounting reports will provide more feedback as to how well they have utilized the reports currently in use.

Exhibit 4   Managers do not have to reinvent accounting procedures; they're already in place.

CONTENTS

Uniform System of Accounts for Hotels. Educational Institute of the American Hotel and Motel Association. 9th Revised Edition, 1996.

Exhibit 5   Description of five classic business transactions.

Type of Transaction	Example of Transaction
Sales	Customer checks into hotel. For each day the customer remains in the hotel, revenue is recorded and the customer's room account is charged. Other revenues such as restaurant sales, room service, and telephone usage are recorded and charged to the customer's room account.
Cash receipts	When the customer checks out of the hotel and pays the balance on his or her account, cash receipts are recorded and the room account is credited, bringing its balance to zero. Cash collections are accumulated and deposited in the hotel's bank, at least on a daily basis.
Purchases of products and services	The hotel receives the utility bill for the month, records the charge as an expense, and sets up a liability to the utility company.
Payroll	The time cards for two weeks are listed in a record by employee and the amounts of pay due each employee less payroll taxes are calculated. Total payroll expenses and payroll tax expenses are recorded as expenses with the liability for the amounts payable to employees and tax authorities recorded.
Cash disbursements	The hotel prepares a check to the utility company and mails it so as to reach the utility company by the due date. Checks are prepared for employees based on information on the payroll journal. In addition, checks are disbursed to the appropriate tax authorities for the payroll taxes withheld.

The Attorney Says

THE HOTEL'S DUTY TO PROTECT GUESTS

As stated above, the relationship between a hotel and its guests is somewhat unique in the commercial world. It is unlike the relationship between most sellers of goods and services and their customers. A hotel provides lodging and safety from the elements, and also from other hazards that exist in the real world.

With that in mind, imagine the following scenario. Ms. Smith, an executive with a large international corporation, is on a business trip to your city. She books a room at the hotel at which you are general manager. After a long day of meetings, she returns to her room after dark. While getting ready to retire for the night, she hears the door to her room being tampered with from the hallway. All of a sudden the door flies open and an unknown assailant bursts in and robs her of her money and jewelry at gunpoint. Even though she does not put up any resistance, she is hit on the head with a blunt object that causes severe head injuries. After months of medical attention and rehabilitation, she recovers.

In an attempt to try to apprehend the assailant, the local police contact, her but she is unable to identify the person and he will most likely never

Prepayment Policy for Students and Minorities Found Illegal

Legal Update: Lack of Key Control Costs Resort

$573,000 Settlement In Suit By Family of Guest Stung By Fire Ants.

HIV-POSITIVE GUEST ALLOWED TO PURSUE DISCRIMINATION SUIT AGAINST HOTEL

Restaurant No-Shows: Can You Take Them to Court?

Motel Found Liable When Desk Clerk's Husband Stabs Guest

State Statutes That Limit Innkeeper Liability

Inadequately Fenced Moat at Theme Park Blamed for Guest Death

Bar Could Be Held Liable in Woman's Beating

AMUSEMENT PARK SUED FOR ROLLER COASTER INJURY.

The "Tailhook" Legal Aftermath: A New Look at Hotel Responsibility for Conventioneer Misbehavior.

CHAIN MUST PAY $110 MILLION TO MINORITY PLAINTIFFS

Exhibit 1   Hospitality law encompasses far more than theft and liquor liability. As you can see, its scope includes other issues which can potentially affect guests and/or employees, including assault, discrimination, pool safety, and insect infestation—to name a few. (Collage courtesy of Marilyn McDonald)

be caught. The police question her as to whether or not she had used all of the locking devices on the door of her guest room after she entered her room that evening. She declares that she used all the locks. An investigator is sent to the room to inspect the locks. His review reveals that the main lock was not operating properly. He finds that simply putting pressure on the doorknob from the outside would result in the lock failing. In addition, the screws that held the door chain in place were not tightened properly when installed and would not withstand even the lightest pressure. The investigator tells Ms. Smith that if the locks had been operating properly, the assailant would never have been able to gain entry into the room.

What do you think of this scenario? Certainly, if anyone caused Ms. Smith's injuries, it was the criminal who hit her on the head. However, did anyone else do, or *fail to do,* something that, if properly done, would have prevented this from occurring? What about the malfunctioning locks? Do you think that it is unreasonable for a hotel to provide a room to a guest with door locks that do not operate properly while knowing that there are "bad people" out there who, if given the opportunity, would do to Ms. Smith exactly what this assailant did? Of course it is! Do you think that your hotel was at least partially at fault for causing Ms. Smith's injuries and should be required to compensate her for her injuries? Certainly, she incurred large medical bills and also missed months of work and income, which, but for your failure to maintain the locks, would not have happened. According to the decision in *Kiefel* v. *Las Vegas Hacienda,* the answer is: The hotel is at least partially at fault.

This example illustrates the basic principle behind the law of torts. A *tort* is a civil wrong. One commits a *tortious* act when one acts, or fails to act, as any reasonable person in the same circumstances would have. Is it right (i.e., reasonable) to provide a room to a guest with locks that do not work? Would not a reasonable hotelkeeper inspect the locks on guest-room doors on a regular basis to assure that they work properly? After all, we all know that there are bad people out there in the world who will prey on innocent people. Is it not right for the law to expect that, once you know of a potential harm, you will take steps to try to prevent that harm from occurring?

Think of it in very simple terms. Suppose you work at a frozen yogurt store and the display cooler malfunctions, leaking water on the floor. Once you learn that the floor is wet, would you not conclude that there is potential harm to customers who might walk in that area, unaware of the wetness? Of course, you would. It is pretty easy to foresee that a person might slip on a wet floor and get hurt. Therefore, what would you do once you became aware that the floor was wet? What would any reasonable person do? The answer is: Mop it up as soon as possible. But that brings up another point. What about the time that ticks away before it can be mopped up? Wouldn't a reasonable person *warn* others about the wet floor by placing a sign in that area stating, "Caution: Wet Floor." Of course.

That is what the law of torts requires. The law places a *duty of care* on us to avoid *negligence,* that is, to act as a reasonably prudent person would act in the same circumstances. This duty of care is placed upon hotelkeepers with regard to their guests. If you do not repair inoperable locks or if you do not mop up wet

Exhibit 2   Signs like these send a positive message to guests.

floors, you are failing to act as a reasonable person would act in the same circumstances—and if that failure causes injury to another, you will be held liable for those injuries.

What lesson can we learn from this discussion? It is simply this: We must all be aware of potential harms that exist and do what common sense tells us is reasonable in the circumstances to prevent those harms from occurring. We cannot bury our heads in the sand and ignore the very real dangers that might exist.

LIABILITY FOR GUEST PROPERTY

Consider the following scenario: You are the executive housekeeper of a very posh Beverly Hills hotel. Some of the richest people in the world routinely stay at your hotel, including movie stars, royalty, and sports celebrities. One evening, Jennifer Lopez and her entourage check into the hotel. A bodyguard accompanies her and you notice the extraordinary diamonds she is wearing. After she has checked in, she goes for dinner in the hotel restaurant only to return to her room later and find her jewelry, valued at over $2 million, missing. The general manager asks to see you to discuss what role any of your staff, the housekeeping personnel, might have had in the mysterious disappearance of Ms. Lopez's jewelry. You inform the general manager that, due to the evening schedule, you have only a skeleton housekeeping crew on duty and you have no idea how the jewelry could have been taken.

The police are called to the scene and their investigation reveals that the lock on Ms. Lopez' room door was defective. The door would yield to even a very small amount of pressure, even if attempts had been made to secure the door upon leaving the room. The police conclude that some criminal(s) probably entered the room, took the jewelry, and disappeared. They file their theft report but it seems unlikely that the perpetrator will be found.

A few days after the incident, the general manager (GM) of the hotel receives a letter from Ms. Lopez's attorney stating that the theft was the fault of the hotel due to its having an inoperable lock, and further demanding that the hotel immediately reimburse her in the amount of $2 million. The GM, unsure of what to do, refers the letter to the corporation's legal counsel.

In such a situation, what do you think the hotel should be required to do under the law? Should the hotel be forced to pay? After all, the hotel did not steal the jewelry; a criminal did. On the other hand, if the room's door lock had operated properly, the criminal would never have gotten in and Ms. Lopez's jewelry would be safely in her possession. You might argue that Ms. Lopez had no business coming to the hotel with such incredibly valuable jewelry. In other words, you might assert, "This is a hotel. We are in the business of selling guest rooms for a profit. We are not in the business of safeguarding people's valuables—that is a task for banks or 'rent-a-cops,' who are equipped to do so. A hotel should not have to take on that kind of responsibility." In other words, if Ms. Lopez travels around carrying such valuable items, she does so at her own risk and no hotel, restaurant, or anyone else should be responsible if the items are lost or stolen.

That last position is, for the most part, the one with which the law agrees. Back in the days of old England, the rule of law was that if a guest came to a hotel with valuables and they were lost or stolen, the hotel was responsible—even if the items were lost or stolen through no fault of the hotel. This arrangement could encourage dishonest guests to commit fraud by claiming they checked in with valuables, when, in fact, they did not. Even in cases like that, the hotel would have to pay.

Such was the rule at common law (common law is law that is created by the courts, the judicial branch of government). What if the people, through their elected representatives, express dissatisfaction with the rules of common law created by the courts? In this instance, suppose a hotel owner had been required by a local judge to pay a large sum of money to a guest who claimed to have lost property at his or her hotel. Suppose that hotel owner complained to his fellow hotel owners and warned them that they could easily suffer the same fate. Could they do anything about it? Could the law be changed? The answer is yes, but how?

Under our form of government, the legislative branch can, in some cases, change the law created by the judicial branch. In this case, the hotel owners would need to convince their elected representatives to sponsor a bill that would change the common law rule and instead state that hotels would not be liable for the loss of guest property. That is exactly what has happened in the United States.

Today, all 50 states have enacted statutes that in some manner limit the liability of a hotel for the loss of guest property. (Remember, statutes are laws created by the *legislative* branch of government.) These statutes vary quite a bit from state to state. For example, the operative provisions of the California statute actually set

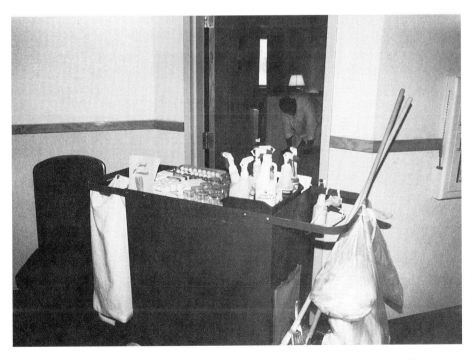

Exhibit 3   The housekeeping staff can contribute to hotel security by controlling access to guest rooms. Also, by positioning the cart across the door, they can avoid uninvited guests. (Photo by James L. Morgan, Scottsdale, Arizona)

dollar limits for the loss of various types of luggage. It further states that if the hotel provides a safe on the premises for the storage of valuables and guests choose not to use the safe, the hotel will not be liable for their loss.

The Arizona statute is somewhat different. It basically states that if a hotel has a fireproof safe on the premises, and posts a notice in the room of each guest that the safe is available for the placement of valuables, if the guest does not put his/her valuable items in the safe, the hotel will not be liable for their *loss unless the hotel commits some act(s) that causes the item to be lost.*

To many commentators, that last phrase of the Arizona statute is troubling. To illustrate this problem, let's use the set of facts outlined above with regard to Ms. Lopez's diamonds. You'll recall two things: She did not put her jewelry into the safe provided by the hotel *and* the items were stolen due to a defective door lock. Based on the California statute, do you think the hotel would be responsible for the jewelry? The answer is that the total liability of the hotel would be no greater than the amount set forth in the statute, that is, $1,000. Even though the hotel was at least partially at fault for causing the loss of the items by not having an operable lock on her guest-room door, the liability of the hotel is limited to no more than $1,000, pursuant to the above-quoted statute.

Now, let's take the same set of facts and apply them to the Arizona statute. Would the same result occur? Not necessarily. Remember, the Arizona statute states that if the hotel provides the safe and the guest does not put the items in the safe, the hotel will not be liable *unless the hotel in some manner causes the* loss *of the items.* Do you think that the hotel caused the loss of Ms. Lopez's jewelry? Perhaps the answer to that question is yes. In that event, the Arizona hotel might be held

Exhibit 4   The security of guests and the property becomes even more pressing in casinos; the "eye in the sky" and omnipresent security personnel are featured prominently to avoid security and liability issues. (*Courtesy:* Cow Creek Indian Gaming Center, Canyonville, Oregon)

fully responsible for the jewelry, while based upon the same set of facts, the California hotel might be held liable for only $1,000.

As you can see, the law, and the words used in a statute, can have an enormous impact on hotels and hoteliers. The importance of knowing the law in the state or country in which your hotel will be operating cannot be overstated. That is why some basic knowledge of hospitality law is important to you at this introductory level. As you progress through your hospitality curriculum, you will not only become aware of the law, but you will also learn how to find out what the law is, and, most importantly, how to read and understand what it means.

The Techie Says

There are many types of properties in the lodging segment, and the complexity of their computer needs varies. The most commonly found computer applications are property management systems (PMS) that assist managers in the day-to-day operation of their properties. They are capable of addressing almost every phase of the lodging operation. A PMS normally performs both back- and front-office functions and supports a variety of other functions such as housekeeping, sales, catering, energy management, and call-accounting.

FRONT-OFFICE APPLICATIONS

Reservation Applications

A *reservation module* typically performs the following, basic functions:

- Sells individual reservations.
- Sells group reservations.
- Displays room availability.
- Tracks advance deposits.
- Tracks travel agent information.
- Generates reservation reports.

Front Office	Reservations
F1 – Guest Registration	F2 – Sell a Reservation
F3 – Reports Menu	F4 – Reservations Menu
F5 – Front Desk/Cashier Menu	F6 – Main Menu
F7 – Group Menu	F8 – Today's Inventory Display
F9 – Vacant Rooms Display	F10 – This Week's Availability

Audit and Accounting	Housekeeping
CTRL + F1 – End-of-Day Menu	CTRL + F2 – Housekeeping Menu
CTRL + F3 – Accounting Control Menu	

General Management	Additional
CTRL + F5 – GM's Menu	CTRL + F4 – Redisplay Last Guest/Acct
CTRL + F7 – Rate Seasons Menu	CTRL + F6 – Redisplay Last List
CTRL + F9 – Property Data Menu	CTRL + F8 – Redisplay Last Input Screen
	CTRL + F10 – Function Key Menu
	CTRL + H – Help
	CTRL + M – Message

Exhibit 1   A listing of the various modules (components) one normally expects to see with a Property Management System (PMS). Notice the topical headings: Reservations, Front Office, Audit and Accounting, Housekeeping, General Management, and Additional. These cover every aspect of the guest stay, guest billing, and how the hotel manages that information.

CENTRAL RESERVATION SYSTEMS

Most lodging properties that use a PMS also are connected to a bigger system: a central reservation system (CRS). The reservation module of the PMS connects individual properties with their CRS, which is usually staffed 24 hours a day. Guests have a choice of calling the property directly or calling the CRS center via a toll-free telephone number.

It is essential that the CRS and the PMS constantly update each other, so that neither sells a room that has already been sold by the other. (See Exhibit 5, which details how a PMS links all departments together.)

PROPERTY RESERVATION SYSTEMS

A PMS reservation system allows the hotel to enter, review, modify, or cancel a reservation. Unless a guest calls a CRS, the reservation process normally starts with a phone call to the property and ends with a complete guest reservation record.

Rooms Management

The rooms management module links the front desk to the other departments of the hotel, and is especially important to the housekeeping department. As a guest with a reservation arrives at the front desk, reservation information is transferred

Exhibit 2A   Airlines use another form of reservation system. Here, a Continental Airlines customer purchases her ticket at the airport from an automated ticket reservation machine. (Photo by David K. Crow)

Exhibit 2B   Today's modern reservation and property management systems, like this one by Multi-Systems Inc (MSI) use complex yield management algorithms and processes to maximize REVPAR. (*Courtesy:* MSI Solutions, Phoenix, Arizona.)

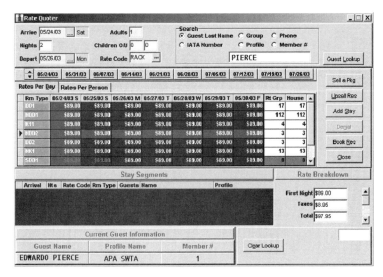

Room Type	THU MAY 05	FRI MAY 06	SAT MAY 07	SUN MAY 08	MON MAY 09	TUE MAY 10	WED MAY 11	RATES 1 per 2 per ** = Higher Rate * = Lower Rate	
QBQR	-3	1	1	1	1	1	1	74.00	79.00
QBRS	1	1*	1*	1*	1*	1*	1*	66.00	71.00
QBQP	0	10**	10*	10*	10*	10*	10*	66.00	71.00
DDPH	1	2**	2*	2*	2*	2*	2*	66.00	71.00
PRES	0	1**	1*	1*	1*	1*	1*	66.00	71.00
QBDB	1	4**	4*	4*	4*	4*	4*	66.00	71.00
Total:	4	19	19	19	19	18	19		

Action: 1 = Forward 1 Week   2 = Back 1 Week   3 = Forward to Rate Change

Exhibit 3   A PMS availability screen shows rooms remaining unsold (available) by date. Note that May 5 is oversold on queen bed/queen rooms by three rooms.

from the reservation module to the rooms management module. The guest is assigned a room and a folio or guest account is created to keep track of expenditures.

Guest Accounting

In the guest accounting module, *folios* (or guest accounts) are created, transactions are posted, cashier shifts are opened and closed, and guests are checked out. There are four basic types of folios:

1. *Individual folios* are created for each individual guest.
2. *Master folios* are typically created for groups.
3. *City ledgers/folios* contain lists of customers who owe the hotel money and non-guest accounts with in-house privileges.
4. *Control folios* are set up to ensure that all revenues and payments become part of the daily report to management.

GENERAL MANAGEMENT APPLICATIONS

The front-office applications of the PMS assist managers and front-line employees (such as front-desk associates) in their day-to-day decision making. The information can be incorporated into many different report formats depending on the needs of the property. Reports for such indicators as occupancy statistics and average daily rates for different room types can be generated on a daily, weekly, or on-demand basis and are generally referred to as *general management reports*.

Exhibit 4   Increasingly, guests have technology needs, including data ports or wi-fi networking. (*Photo:* Janis Christie/ Getty Images, Inc.—Photodisc.)

Back-Office Applications

Accounting is a very important aspect of any business. As an owner or manager, you will need to know how well your company is performing financially. Questions to be answered include:

- Are we making or losing money?
- How much money did we make yesterday?
- How much did we spend on payroll, food, or taxes?

Answers to these questions depend partially on the way you choose to monitor your revenues and expenses. Very small properties may use paper and pencil to keep track of them. Larger properties need computers and software. The accounting applications within the PMS can record all financial transactions that occur with customers, suppliers, employees, and financial institutions. They can help you manage your cash flow, collect monies owed by customers, control and track expenditures, evaluate your financial status, and track monies owed to creditors.

Property Management System Interfaces

Property management system interfaces can be defined as automated systems that have the capacity to connect with the property management systems or that can function independently, such as a guest-room TVs. The advantage of being connected (or

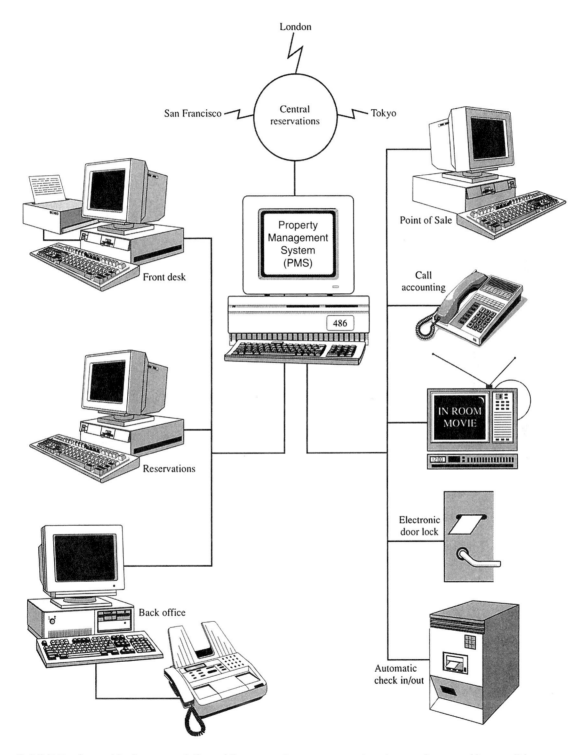

Exhibit 5   A graphical representation of the property management system and some of its possible interfaces.

interfaced) with the PMS is that data can be transferred easily and automatically throughout the property. The best example here would be the in-room movie. If guests watch a movie in their room, and the TV is interfaced with the PMS, their folio would be automatically updated with the movie charge. We discuss some of the most common hospitality interfaces in this section.

POINT-OF-SALE SYSTEM

Food service outlets in a hotel will often be interfaced with the hotel's property management system via a point-of-sale *(POS)* system. This interface allows for direct posting of food and beverage charges to the guest folio without those charges first going to the front desk. It streamlines the operation and limits the chance of late charges, which can occur when a guest checks out before the food and beverage outlet has posted charges to the guest's room.

CALL ACCOUNTING SYSTEM

A call accounting system (CAS) is a computer that is connected to the telephone switchboard. As is the case with any other interface, a CAS can be a stand-alone unit or can be connected to the property management system. As a call is made by each guest, the CAS generates a call record and charges the guest folio with the cost of the call. Before the development of CAS posting, these charges had to be handled by an operator, which added to labor costs and was subject to disputes about clerical errors.

ELECTRONIC LOCKING SYSTEMS

As several of our chapters indicate, guest security is a very important concern of management. One of the most important elements of guest security is the door lock and key. Traditional metal keys (mechanical keys) are still used but are actually not very safe. Mechanical keys can be lost or may end up in unauthorized hands. Hotels using mechanical key systems have to keep track of keys used and replace locks if necessary. This can prove rather costly and if not done promptly may lead to even costlier lawsuits. More and more, the insurance industry is forcing lodging properties to replace mechanical key systems with electronic locking systems. *Electronic locking systems* "re-key" each room with a new electronic code for each new guest. This provides better guest-room security, better liability control, and increased personnel accountability—and saves money for the hotel in the long run.

ENERGY MANAGEMENT SYSTEM

Energy management systems are used by hotels to conserve energy, contain energy costs, and tighten operational controls over guest-room and public-space environments. Currently, most systems on the market are stand-alone ones and are not yet capable of interfacing with a PMS. An *energy management system* (EMS) is a computer-based control system designed to save energy by managing the operation of mechanical equipment on the property automatically. The programming of the system allows management to control what equipment is to be turned on or off or otherwise regulated. For instance, if a meeting room will not be used until 3 PM, it does not need to be air-conditioned all morning. An EMS could therefore be programmed to reduce or shut off the air-conditioning until one hour before the scheduled function. The EMS has a variety of features, but common energy control designs include:

- **Demand Control.** The system limits usage by turning off equipment that can be turned off for intermittent periods without negatively affecting the comfort of the guest.
- **Duty Cycling.** The system turns off equipment sequentially for a period of time each hour. Heating, ventilation, and air conditioning are systems that can be duty cycled.
- **Room Occupancy Sensors.** In guest rooms, either infrared or ultrasonic waves can be used to register whether a room is physically occupied. When a guest enters the space, sensors turn on such devices as lights, air-conditioning, or heating. When the guest departs, the sensors react and turn off lights and adjust the temperature back to preset levels. Some systems require guests to insert their key-card into an energy sensor. When the guest removes the key-card to leave the room, lights and/or HVAC systems automatically shut off.

THE INTERNET AND HOSPITALITY BUSINESS

The hospitality industry has embraced the Internet and its potential for profit enhancement. Various segments of the hospitality industry use the Internet in different ways, but a few food service applications are presented below:

1. **Dining Guides:** Printed dining guides are now on the Internet in electronic form. These allow the guest to view a summary information about the restaurants in a city or a destination area. Sites provide menus, hours of operation, credit cards accepted, reservation information, directions, and house policies.
2. **Reservations and Order Taking:** Some restaurant sites have started accepting on-line reservations. At others you can pre-order and pre-pay for take-away items. Some pizza restaurants now allow customers to place their pizza orders on line for either pick up or delivery.
3. **Merchandising and Promotion:** Special promotions, coupons, and contests can be put on line to attract customers.
4. **Guest and Public Relations:** Some restaurants offer email access in order to communicate with current and potential customers. Restaurants can also upload

positive restaurant reviews and other upbeat information, such as community activities to promote their establishments.

Some food service-related websites you may wish to visit are listed below. As you review them, you may want to consider differences between quick-serve companies and dinner houses, and how they present themselves.

RESTAURANT SOFTWARE SITES

1. www.ncr.com
2. www.micros.com
3. www.verifone.com
4. www.eatec.com
5. www.foodtrak.com
6. www.squirrelsystems.com

PART II

Introduction to the Food and Beverage Industry

The food and beverage industry is fast paced, challenging, rewarding, demanding, and a very large part of the hospitality industry. Just consider the following facts about the size and scope of the food service industry in the United States, as estimated and compiled by the National Restaurant Association (*www.restaurant.org/research*):

- The food service industry is estimated to have sales of $511 billion in 2006.
- There are over 925,000 operations in the United States that might qualify as food service establishments. These will serve an estimated 70 billion meals.
- Most food service establishments in the United States are "small businesses," whose average annual sales per unit are about $750,000 for full-service establishments and $606,000 for limited-service restaurants.
- Over 12 million people are presently employed in the industry, over 9 percent of all people employed in the United States.
- By 2010, there will be more than 1 million restaurants in the United States, with sales of about $600 billion.

With regard to the food service market—that is, all the people who visit or are expected to visit a food service outlet—whether it be table service or fast food, two important statistics are worth mentioning:

- Consumers spend 45–50 percent of every dollar they have available for food on meals and other food *away from home,* and this percentage will grow to 53 percent by 2010.
- Almost 50 percent of all adults in the United States visit a food service establishment on any typical day.

Sales in the food service industry have been growing ever since they were first tracked on a national basis. Growth slowed down in times of economic hardship, of course; yet overall we have seen a consistent increase in revenues over the years. This is reassuring if you are considering investing money in the food service industry or making it your career.

With regard to market demand for food service products, once again, it can be called very reassuring. Behavior patterns among consumers have been changing in favor of the industry in the last few years. More families will have dual incomes or will be single households, which leads to an increased demand for meals away from home either because they can afford it or because they do not have the time to prepare meals at home. More women have entered and are still entering the full-time work force, which has already caused demand for food service products to go up. In short, more and more people are willing to spend more of their food dollars away from home.

And then we haven't even looked at the explosion that has occurred internationally. New markets are being opened every day (just think about the former Soviet Union, the rest of Eastern Europe, and Vietnam, to name a few). Worldwide, there is great interest in American culture, which, in turn, creates a demand for American food service products. In many foreign countries the demand is so pent up that new food service outlets cannot be built fast enough to supply all of the demand. People in those new, foreign markets just cannot wait for new products to be introduced. Where do you think the biggest McDonald's outlets are in the world? In Moscow and Beijing.

There are negative aspects attached to all these positives. For instance, it has been determined that more than half of all newly established food service operations will go out of business within two years after opening.

Employee turnover, the rate at which employees in a particular job or operation are replaced, is still much higher in the food service industry than in other industries. It is not uncommon to see 100 percent turnover rate for a restaurant, meaning that every employee will have been replaced by another within a year. For certain positions that number might even be as high as 300 percent!

If you weigh all the positives and negatives, though, the food service industry is still extremely challenging, with enormous growth potential, and offers many opportunities for personal advancement. The industry needs thousands of managers every year and you might become one of those. Managing a food service establishment, whether it be a fast food franchise, a full-service restaurant, a microbrewery with a food service outlet, or a store selling specialty coffees, requires some unique skills, as the following chapters will show.

Obviously, food service managers must have technical skills. They have to be able to read, create, and understand financial reports, for instance, and possess the ability to react to the information those reports present to them. Also, they must have an understanding of production methods. Cooks, chefs, kitchen staff, and bartenders have to have the expertise to create the perfect chicken Parmesan or the best banana daiquiri in the world. A manager, though, must also have some knowledge of the ingredients, the contents, and the service methods involved, a knowledge he/she can convey to the customer and share with his/her employees.

Food service managers should also have people skills. Managing a restaurant means managing employees: understanding their needs and desires; dealing with their whims and peculiarities; listening to their concerns; correcting their mistakes;

accepting their suggestions; offering them a healthy, safe, and pleasant work environment; and helping them make the most of their jobs and their lives. Employees are the lifeblood of any restaurant. They cook the food, mix the drinks, clean the rest rooms and the kitchen, and serve the guests.

People skills also refer to dealing with customers and providing them with a comfortable, healthy dining experience. Ultimately, these skills are the ones that provide the food service operation with the revenue that makes it successful.

And then there are some particular personal skills that are needed to become a successful food service manager: determination, resourcefulness, patience, pride in oneself and the business, integrity, and leadership traits.

Not everyone has the personality or the skills needed for food service management. It is a demanding and, at times, peculiar industry. Not all of the skills necessary to become successful can be learned. Education can give you most of the technical skills you will need. Even some of the people skills can be acquired in general management and human resource classes. Work experience and internships can give you a feel for what it takes. Yet whether or not you have the personality of a food service manager is something you will find out only when you actually work in the industry. How do you really deal with a dissatisfied supplier, an angry regional vice president, a confused employee, or a happy customer?

The chapters in this section will present you with a picture of what it is like to *manage* a food service operation. Chapter 5, "Overview of the Food Service Industry" looks at the many different kinds of food service establishments that are presently available to us. It also looks at the customer, and presents some statistics that will show you the enormity and importance of this branch of the hospitality industry. Chapter 6, "Food Service Management" discusses what it takes to manage a successful food service operation.

Although food service managers do not need to know all the details of how to prepare a menu item in most restaurants, they have to be aware of what it takes to produce the actual meal, with regard to the equipment required and the production methods involved. Ultimately, customers come for the food, and food is prepared in the kitchen. At the end of this unit you will find enhancements of the discussions on food service management and food production that focus on the legal, technological, and accounting aspects of the industry.

You might be tomorrow's food service manager. Maybe you are destined to become president of a large fast-food chain; you might be fortunate enough to become the owner of multiple restaurants or franchises; maybe you will end up as a food and beverage director for a hotel. These chapters will give you an impression of what food service management amounts to and will help you to find the answers to some of the "maybes." As they say in the food service industry: Enjoy!

Overview of the Food Service Industry

This chapter will introduce the student to the vast scope of the restaurant industry in the United States. It will show how integral the industry is to the national economy, as well as provide a brief forecast of the industry's future. Details will be provided on the three types of food service ownership: franchise, chain and independent. The two major types of food service, commercial and non-commercial, will also be discussed as well as some of the subdivisions of each.

INTRODUCTION

Food is much more than fuel for the body. The social contexts in which food is eaten are part of what bonds a society, whether in groups of family, friends, or strangers. We use the sharing of food as a metaphor to express welcome, friendship, familial love, and concern for the ill. We mark important occasions with special foods and celebrate with people via gifts of food. Holidays are identified with traditional feasts. Most occasions in our lives are experienced and perhaps enhanced with food.

The hospitality industry is, in many ways, like an extension of families. Hotels and restaurants house and feed people when they are away from home, as do hospitals, schools, and prisons. Special occasions are often celebrated at restaurants or at banquet facilities, it's hard to imagine baseball games without hot dogs, airline flights without meals or snacks, meetings without refreshments, or day trips without lunch stops.

It seems that just about everything we do incorporates food, and if we're not preparing the food at home, a food service operation is involved. A **food service operation** is an organization outside the home that prepares food for people, either for sale, as in a restaurant, or as part of a service, as in a hospital. Food service operations do the very same things we do at home to produce meals for our families.

In our homes, we decide what to serve for dinner, perhaps looking at some specific recipes. We then prepare a shopping list of all the items that we don't already have in the refrigerator or in the cupboard. We go to the grocery store and buy exactly what is needed to prepare the recipes we chose. Upon bringing the food home, we put it away so that it stays as fresh as possible until we are ready to start cooking. We then prepare the meal and serve it to our family. We finally **clean** up the mess and put away any leftovers. On a more institutional scale, this is roughly the model all food service operations follow. The stages of the process may have different names, yet the process is essentially the same.

The difference is, of course, volume. Food service operators do not plan and prepare meals for a family of four, but rather for a "family" of perhaps 100 or 1,000! Because of these high volumes, there is a lot more room for error, waste, illness, injury, and customer dissatisfaction. Thus, a food service manager's job is seldom one that involves wearing an apron and chef's hat. Instead of (or in addition to) cooking skills, a manager needs a different set of skills—human resource management skills—so that he or she can direct employees to prepare and serve meals.

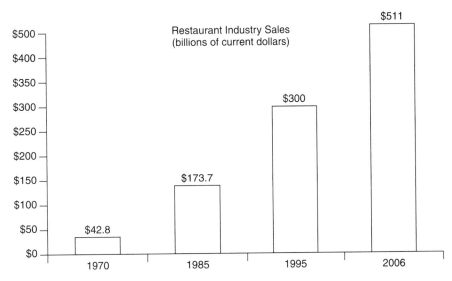

Exhibit 5.1   Commercial Food Service
The nation's sales have risen at roughly a 25 percent rate of growth for 30 years!
(*Courtesy:* National Restaurant Association)

OVERVIEW OF THE FOOD SERVICE INDUSTRY—RESTAURANTS

The food service industry is vast and encompasses many different forms. The average American eats one out of each four meals away from home. The diversity of retail food outlets ranges from a cart selling hot dogs on the street corner to a white table cloth, fine dining restaurant and everything in between. The table below outlines some of the key components of the industry.

First in Daily Customer Contact

- Almost half of all adults (47 percent) were restaurant patrons on a typical day during a study conducted in 2002.
- In an average month, 78 percent of U.S. households use some form of carry-out or delivery.
- More than 54 billion meals are eaten in restaurants and school and work cafeterias each year.
- The likelihood of patronizing restaurants is highest among younger consumers: About six out of ten 18- to 24-year-olds are restaurant patrons on a typical day, compared with 3 out of 10 adults over age 65.
- Men eat out more than women: Forty-eight percent of men were restaurant patrons on a typical day during a 1997 study, versus 44 percent of women.

Sales	$510 Billion
Locations	925,000
Employees	12.5 million
Restaurant Share of the Food Dollar	45 Percent

Exhibit 5.2   Recent statistics for the food service industry.

- Restaurant traffic is roughly evenly divided between on-premises and off-premises traffic.

An Integral Part of the National Economy

Restaurant industry sales are forecasted to increase 4.5 percent this year and equal more than 4 percent of the U.S. gross domestic product. Restaurant industry sales have grown at an average annual rate of 7.2 percent since 1970, when sales totaled $43 billion.

The restaurant industry provides work for 9 percent of those employed in the United States. Nearly 30 percent of all retail establishments are eating and drinking places. On a typical day in 2006, the restaurant industry posted average sales of roughly $1.4 billion. The average annual household expenditure for food away from home in the 2004 study was $2,434, or $974 per person.

The Number One Retail Employer

More than 12.5 million people are employed in the restaurant industry, with total restaurant employment projected to be 13 million in 2007. Eating and drinking places rank first among private-sector industries in total employment. The food service industry employs a great ethnic and gender diversity, with almost 6 out of 10 employees in foodservice occupations (58 percent) being women, 12 percent African Americans, and 16 percent of Hispanic origin.

Small Businesses

More than two-thirds of eating and drinking place establishments have annual sales of less than $500,000. Nearly three-quarters of all eating and drinking places have less than 20 employees. One out of three eating and drinking places are sole proprietorships or partnerships.

Exhibit 5.3   Tokyo Express is a fitting example of a "small" restaurant operation. (Photo by James L. Morgan.)

National Restaurant Association Research

Median pre-tax profit for full-service restaurants (average check per person, $10 or more) is 3.6 percent of total sales. One out of five takeout food consumers is a daily user; these daily users represent half of all takeout transactions. Meatless/vegetarian dishes, organic produce and pan-seared items are popular items on today's restaurant menus.

Saturday is the most popular day to eat out; Monday is the least popular. August is the most popular month to eat out.

Food Service Industry Forecast

The economic growth of the early years of the new millennium has been both beneficial and tough for food service operators. On the one hand, sales and customer counts are up; on the other, quality staff members to serve those customers are harder than ever to find.

Restaurant industry sales are rising, driven by the positive economic environment of the nation and the continued gains in consumers' real disposable personal income. The food service industry has firmly established itself as an integral part of America's lifestyle, with more than 44 percent of the family food dollar being spent away from home. Consumers continue to seek convenience, value and an entertaining environment away from the stresses of daily life, and food service operators are filling those needs.

Consider these statistics from recent National Restaurant Association research:

- More than two out of five adults (42 percent) report that they are cooking fewer meals at home than they were two years ago.
- More than half of all adults (53 percent) report that their favorite restaurant foods provide flavor and taste sensations that cannot easily be duplicated in a home kitchen.
- More than three out of every four U.S. households (78 percent) make at least one carryout or delivery purchase in a typical month.
- More than two out of three adults (68 percent) agree that going out to a restaurant with family and/or friends gives them an opportunity to socialize and is a better way to make use of their leisure time than cooking and cleaning up.

In recent years, the number of options available to consumers for purchasing food prepared away from home has grown dramatically. A whole new category of food service operations emerged in the nineties and continues to be popular. Food service operations that produce meals for guests who did not want to cook but also did not want to dine in restaurants continue to grow. Grocery stores continue

Exhibit 5.4   More than half of all restaurant meals are eaten during the dinner hours. More than a third are lunches. What meal do you most often enjoy out?

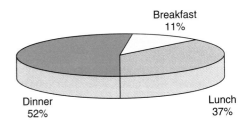

Breakfast 11%

Dinner 52%

Lunch 37%

to increase sections serving ready-to-eat foods as a convenience to their customers. Restaurants other than the old standby, pizza, are beginning to add delivery to the guests. The food service industry should continue to benefit from the growing day-to-day need for its services among consumers and businesses as well as from growth in the number of higher income households, which are generally the prime restaurant patrons.

The healthy economic climate has generated a corresponding growth of employment opportunities nationwide, forcing food service operators to compete head to head with other industries as well as other operators for workers. In today's economy most people who want a job have one, leaving the labor pool especially shallow and the restaurant community facing tough recruitment and retention issues. According to recent National Restaurant Association research, both table service and fast food operators say that they expect finding qualified and motivated labor to be the top challenge they will face.

Operationally, food service operators should strive to continue to meet the expectations of convenience and value-driven consumers, and to put increased emphasis on managing employees and increasing their satisfaction by creating a more caring organizational culture.

Competition

In the 1970s you could count the number of regional or national-chain, full service restaurant operations in most any given town on one hand. The restaurant industry was dominated by independent, primarily family-owned and operated restaurants and diners. Success seemed easier; independent restaurants created and managed the changes and seemed to be the future of the restaurant industry.

The market has changed radically since the 1970s. Today, huge national chains seem to have a great impact on the direction of the restaurant industry. Chains with their multiple concepts, aggressive hiring programs, expensive advertising campaigns, and resources to obtain the best real estate, appear to give chains the distinct advantage over independently owned operations.

Exhibit 5.5   McDonald's decision to take its American fast-food abroad was based on a careful analysis of new markets, access to essential supplies, and maintenance of its famous quality control. McDonald's opened its first Moscow restaurant in January, 1990, and its first Beijing, China restaurant in October, 1990. (*Courtesy:* McDonald's Corporation.)

Competition in the restaurant industry is intensifying. Nearly four out of five consumers report that they have a larger selection of restaurants available to them today than they did several years ago, and they're right—there are now 925,000 locations nationwide that offer food service. Food service operations are popping up in locations that were not even thought of just a few years ago. You cannot stop by a gas station that does not serve food, and many grocery stores are adding take-out food. This increase in food service operations in non-traditional areas is increasing the competition for conventional restaurants.

Food service operators need to monitor their customer needs so they can best adapt their product offerings. Operators who insist on continuing to offer guests what they have always offered them will be left behind in this ever more competitive environment.

Food service is big business and has become so complex that it is less and less feasible for non-professionals to succeed using "seat-of-the-pants" methods. One in three restaurants fail in their first year, often because their creators naïvely believed they could succeed through optimism or by "winging it." Professional training takes much of the guesswork out of food service management, and thus, much of the risk. Professional managers learn to look for and recognize trends. That requires reading trade journals, magazines, and newspapers, and generally keeping up to date, paying attention to what consumers say and do.

Food service industry profit margins are small. Success often depends on cutting out waste in all areas of operation. High personnel turnover (the rate at which an operation loses workers) can also be seen as a form of waste, since it is very costly and results in lower service levels.

Competition in food service is increasing both internally and externally. Non-traditional operations are competing with traditional operations—and both areas continue to grow. Hospital food outlets, convenience stores, and grocery stores now compete with casual restaurants, fast-food restaurants, and cafeterias. On another front, long-term care and skilled-nursing facilities now use upgraded food service departments to attract patients.

Competition requires that we meet the needs of our customers. As tastes change or the population changes, it is good business to change with them. It is easier to sell people what they want than to try to sell them something they don't want. In most cases, they can go elsewhere—and will.

TYPES OF FOOD SERVICE OWNERSHIP

Eating and drinking establishments are mostly small businesses. Three types of ownership arrangements occur in food service operations: franchises, chains, and independent ownership.

Franchises

A **franchise** is an arrangement between two parties: the **franchisor** and the **franchisee.** The franchisor grants the franchisee rights to sell certain goods and services, use various logos and promotional items, and to participate in national media campaigns. The franchisee usually also purchases operational systems and controls, and facility designs and layouts with the franchise package. The franchisor must agree to maintain corporate standards and image in order to preserve the business agreement.

Advantages to the franchisee for engaging in this type of arrangement are many. They are able to purchase the operating "expertise" and successful management systems of the parent company. Facility design, equipment layout, menu design, and recipe development are included in the package. The ability to use a nationally or regionally recognized name is also a plus, especially for operators who are new to the restaurant business.

There are several disadvantages to franchise ownership. Initial set-up costs and costs of operation are higher. The franchisee must pay initial franchise fees and ongoing royalty fees for the duration of the business. Some franchise agreements require that businesses purchase goods from the parent company or its subsidiary for above-market prices. The goal of the parent company is consistency among all franchises; therefore, creativity and innovation in menu offerings are usually restricted.

Exhibit 5.6 lists the top food service companies in the United States based on the number of stores that they have in operation. Notice that the major chains both own some of their units as well as franchise some out.

Chains

Another form of ownership is the **restaurant chain,** which is part of a multi-unit group. The restaurant concept, design, menu, decor, and style of service are developed by the parent company and duplicated throughout the country. Chain restaurants are found more often in fast food or limited menu operations than in full-service restaurants. The growth in the last decade has been in both casual dining and more upscale chain restaurant operations. It is simpler to standardize and reproduce limited service and menu restaurants than those which offer full service. Chain restaurants may be owned by the parent company, a franchise company, or independent owners. The difference between a chain restaurant and a franchise is that franchise properties are generally part of a chain, while chain restaurants can be operated in other ways besides being a franchise.

An advantage of chain restaurants is that some operation costs are consolidated. Once an efficient design is developed, it is just copied "cookie cutter" fashion to other locations, reducing the cost of facility development for each operation. Many of the purchasing functions are pooled among the chain, allowing reduced costs. Advertising and promotions are coordinated to maximize effectiveness. Menu development and printing is also consolidated to further reduce costs and maintain consistency.

One disadvantage of chain restaurants is that most management decisions are made at the top management level, far from the locations of many of the restaurants (although, many chains are allowing some of the decision making to be done at the regional or unit level). The diversity of the various regions of our nation makes it difficult to standardize menus and food items, for example, what sells well as southwestern food in Kansas City might not sell well in Texas. Corporate structure may also make it difficult to make decisions on a timely basis deterring chains from keeping up with a changing marketplace.

Exhibit 5.6   Top 100 chains ranked by latest-year total number of U.S. units.

Latest-Year Rank	Chain	Total	Company-Owned	Franchised
1	Canteen Services	31,900	31,900	0
2	Subway	17,909	1	17,908
3	McDonald's	13,673	2,002	11,671
4	Burger King	7,500	686	6,814
5	Pizza Hut	7,500	1,741	5,759
6	Starbuck's Coffee	6,041	4,251	1,790
7	Wendy's	5,933	1,328	4,605
8	Taco Bell	5,900	1,283	4,617
9	KFC	5,525	1,248	4,277
10	7-Eleven	5,311	1,889	3,422

(*Source: Nation's Restaurant News,* June 27, 2005.)

Independents

Three out of four eating and drinking establishments are single-unit operations; about one-third are sole proprietorships, owned by one person. Although chains and franchises are continuing to expand into the restaurant business, there will always be room for hard-working **entrepreneurs** to own and operate their own businesses.

The down side of independent ownership is that the majority fail within their first few years of operation. The reason for this high rate of failure is based on several factors, including lack of adequate funding and inadequate knowledge of the food service industry. Some people mistakenly believe that because they have eaten in restaurants they will be able to operate one; or they serve what they like without considering customers' desires. For example, a person may buy a pizza restaurant, but serve only his/her favorite type of pizza. Chances are, the business will close within six months.

Independent restaurants have an advantage because they are closer to the people they serve, so they can react faster and more efficiently to changes in the local

EYE ON THE ISSUES

Environment

Energy conservation, hazardous chemical disposal, and waste management are important to food service managers. How these agents are used and disposed of affects the health and safety of the staff and the health of the planet. Many companies are seeking ways to reduce excess waste *before* purchasing. Though we aren't likely to see purchasing agents carrying string bags and canvas totes, we are already seeing them weigh waste factors in the bidding process. If purchasing agents specify biodegradable packaging or choose packaging with less waste, their operations soon find they have less waste to dispose of. Biodegradable "peanut" packaging is one such spec that is gaining popularity.

market than chain and franchise restaurants can, although they may be at a disadvantage compared to chain and franchise restaurants because they do not have corporate support.

TYPES OF THE FOOD SERVICE OPERATIONS

The food service industry in America is vast and includes more than just restaurants. To better examine the industry, food service operations will be broken down into several categories and classifications used by the National Restaurant Association. The categories that will be discussed are commercial and non-commercial.

Commercial Operations

By far the largest segment of the food service industry is the commercial, or "for-profit" group. These are designed to earn revenues in excess of expenses, for a financial return to investors and owners. Decisions are often based on how they affect the "bottom line." Key segments of the commercial category are eating and drinking establishments: restaurants, commercial cafeterias, social caterers, and ice cream and yogurt stores.

Restaurants.   Restaurants range from full-service, sit-down restaurants to walk-up, self-service, limited menu establishments. Differences among them are in the type of service, type of food served, decor, and prices.

Full-service.   These provide table service, and usually feature a good variety of items on their menus. They can be either independently owned or be part of a national chain or a franchise. The majority of **full-service restaurants** are independently owned and operated. Businesses in this category share some common features. They generally produce a good portion of their food from raw ingredients on the premises and require relatively highly skilled preparation and service personnel. The average check ranges from moderate to high. Meals are served in multiple courses, the service is relaxed and unrushed, and they generally do not need to rely on a high table turn-over rate to maintain an adequate level of profit. Alcohol service is usually provided to complement the menu and provide good revenue. The service staff is a very important component of this type of restaurant because of the impact they have on the customers' enjoyment of their dining experience. Customers patronizing a full-service restaurant are seeking more than just food to fill their stomachs: They are seeking a pleasurable experience along with their meal.

Fast Food.   Different versions of **fast food** or **quick service restaurants** have existed for quite some time. Roadside diners, hamburger stands, and automats dominated early American food service. As society became more mobile through the increased availability of automobiles, coupled with the development of roads and parking lots, and with the introduction of the concept of franchising, the growth of the fast food segment began to grow.

Fast food restaurants nationwide share some common characteristics. They are able to provide food quickly due to the reduced production requirements of the food they serve. Labor requirements are reduced because customers either have to go to the counter to order food or take their cars through the drive-thru to order and receive their meals. Check averages are generally low, with the result that the business must rely on high volumes of customers as well as turnover rates of seats in the dining room in order to generate an adequate profit. The menu is limited to multiple variations of a few types of items, such as pizza, chicken, hamburgers, fish or ethnic specialties. The items on the menu are generally priced separately, with some combination meals to offer value to their customers. Fast food operations use a high percentage of convenience foods to reduce the amount of skilled preparation personnel and production equipment in the kitchen. The kitchens are more automated than full-service operations, which increases productivity, reduces labor needs, and keeps costs down. Fast food operations use disposable utensils and dinnerware to eliminate or reduce the need for dishwashing facilities and to complement their take-out business.

Commercial cafeterias. These are set up similarly to cafeterias in schools. The food is pre-prepared and served from steam tables to customers who walk through a line and pay for each item individually. The differences between school cafeterias and **commercial cafeterias** are that commercial cafeterias provide more menu choices and are open to the public. This type of operation is popular in the southern regions of the country. Customers like the ability to have control over the price and composition of their meals.

Social caterers. These enterprises prepare food in one location, then deliver it and serve it at another location (home, office, etc.). Services provided range from simple food and beverage preparation and service to complete party planning and set-up. Social caterers provide a convenient way for individuals and companies to entertain.

Ice cream and frozen yogurt. The nation's passion for premium **ice cream and frozen yogurt** fuels growth in this area of the food service industry. Ice cream and frozen yogurt shops are popping up all over the nation in order to satisfy the demand. Interestingly, the continued growth in popularity of ultra-rich premium ice cream contradicts the nation's continued interest in reducing its fat consumption. Low-fat or non-fat frozen yogurt, on the other hand, provides consumers a healthful choice for a frozen dessert, which accounts for its increased popularity.

Bar and tavern. The **bar and tavern** segment of the food service industry is the only area which has experienced a decline in sales. Despite the popularity of sports bars, increased social pressure to reduce drinking has resulted in a decrease in alcohol consumption. Creative operators are trying to supplement revenues by expanding food menus and non-alcoholic beverage offerings.

Food Contractors Food management companies have experienced steady growth for the last few years. Increasingly, businesses such as company dining rooms, schools, hospitals, and sport centers are hiring outside contractors to provide food service in their facilities. The advantage is that the organization can concentrate on what they do best, and eliminate the headache of operating a food service operation. The advantage to the **food contractor**/management company is that they are able to expand their business without a large outlay of capital. The cost to the management company is limited to staffing/management, operation costs, and possibly a few site improvements. Some food management companies are adding complementary services such as dry cleaning, convenience stores, and day care to better serve their customers.

Generally, the company seeking a contractor will request bids. The major national companies involved in this segment of the food service industry are Marriott Management Services, ARA Services, Compass, and Host International, as well as strong regional companies.

Food Service in Lodging Places   Food service plays an important role in lodging places. Whether it is a catering/banquet department, room service, coffee shop, or full-service restaurant, these establishments provide a valuable service to the guests of the hotel. On average, about 34 percent of total hotel revenues are provided by food and beverage operations, though this accounts for only about 18 percent of profits.

The food and beverage division of a hotel can be a valuable drawing card for local business, as well as being important to the operation of hotel. Patrons of hotel food and beverage outlets are potential customers for the other departments and services which the hotel has to offer.

Restaurants.   Restaurants in a hotel serve both the guests and the local community. Guests find it convenient to eat at the hotel. Local residents dine at hotel restaurants while visiting friends or business associates staying at the hotel, or as an alternative to local restaurants. Buffets, brunches, and holiday meals allow the culinary and food service staff of the hotel to show off their expertise and are a service to hotel guests and the local community.

Room service.   **Room service** provides an important amenity to hotel guests. Guests traveling alone, unfamiliar with the town, or who just want privacy, appreciate the convenience of having their meals served in their rooms. Luxury hotels in large metropolitan areas provide room service 24 hours a day to accommodate any schedule. Room service menus are adapted from the hotel restaurant's menus, and are priced at premium to cover the increased labor and equipment required. The food is either prepared in restaurant kitchens, or in the hotel kitchen in busy room service departments.

Catering/banquets.   The **catering/banquet** department serves both hotel guests and the local community. Most banquet rooms are designed to accommodate a wide variety of group sizes, allowing maximum flexibility. For example, a hotel grand ballroom may accommodate 500 or more people when fully open, or may be separated or sectioned into halves, quarters, or smaller rooms to serve parties of varying sizes.

Banquets and catered functions are highly profitable and generate a large portion of the revenue for the hotel food and beverage department. Catered functions held at the hotel help to generate room business by offering a convenient place for guests to stay while attending a meeting or banquet. Weddings, banquets, and community events catered by the hotel help to bring members of the local community into the hotel, and could lead to room business. The catering department also provides refreshments for business meetings held at the hotel.

Grocery and Convenience Store Food Service   The fastest growing segment of the industry is food service provided at grocery and convenience stores. The growth in the food service business of both types of stores is propelled by changes in our society. New full service grocery stores include fully stocked delicatessens, with soup, taco and salad bars. Most stores provide places for customers to eat, or package food for take-out. Some stores are leasing space to fast food companies to broaden food offerings for their customers. For example, Taco Bell is opening small operations in a chain of grocery stores and gas station convenience stores around the country.

Dual income families are using take-out counters at local grocery stores as an alternative to eating in restaurants. They enjoy the privacy and convenience of eating at home, the savings of money, and not having to pay a service charge or leave a tip.

Convenience stores have emerged as "one-stop shopping" places. Most provide everything from gasoline to hardware to groceries and take-out food for people on the go. Customers pay a premium price for the expedience of service. Convenience foods are sold both fresh and frozen, along with a variety of drinks, and often have a microwave oven for customers to use heat up their meal choices.

Non-Commercial/Managed Food Services

What was once known as **institutional** or non-commercial **food service** is now known as *managed services.* The non-commercial segment of the food service industry offers many opportunities. The major companies in the managed service arena are Sodexho, Canteen, and Aramark (see Exhibit 5.7). They provide services to places and business whose main business is other than food service.

Managed services companies generally have two clients they must satisfy. Their first clients are the employees and guests of the operation for which they are working. The second client is the management of the company they are working for. Management's primary concern is that its employees are taken care of. On top of these two "clients," they also must answer to their parent company.

The reason why you probably have not heard of many of the companies listed in Exhibit 5.7 as leading contractors is that they generally work behind the scenes. Since the food service contractor is operating in their client companies' operations

Exhibit 5.7   Contract chains ranked by U.S. Systemwide sales.

Latest-Year Rank	Chain	Latest Sales (in millions)
1	Aramark Global Food and Spprt. Svcs	$5,345.0
2	Canteen Services	1,910.0
3	Sodexho Health Care Services	1,595.0
4	Sodexho Campus Services	1,505.0
5	Sodexho Corporate Services	1,405.0
6	Chartwells	950.0
7	Eurest Dining Services	935.0
8	LSG Sky Chefs	925.0
9	Morrison Management Specialists	835.0
10	Gate Gourmet	676.0

(*Source: Nation's Restaurant News,* June 27, 2005.)

staff generally wear the uniforms of the client company. This makes it difficult for the customers of the operation to determine what entity is providing their food. For example, the food service employees at a university campus will most likely wear uniforms with the university logo rather than that of the company they work for.

Managed service company services involve food services and facilities management in such diverse places such as stadiums, arenas, college and university campuses, businesses, and K–12 schools. This can also involve facilities services, facilities management janitorial services, conference center management, convention centers, office coffee service, vending, snacks, correctional services, healthcare, and national parks.

The 1990s brought some changes to managed services. The general shakeup in corporate America both benefited and hurt managed service companies. Many companies decided to concentrate on the segments of their business they excel in, meaning they contracted out their food service operations rather than running them themselves. On the other hand, many companies down-sized or reduced staff size, meaning that their managed services company had fewer people to feed and this reduced profits. There has also been a large number of consolidations in the industry; companies have merged or have been bought by other companies. The best example is the merger of Sodexho, a French company, with the managed services division of Marriott. The merger of these two industry giants has made it the largest managed services company in the country. The company is now simply called Sodexho USA.

The biggest segments of managed services are business services, higher education campus and school services, and healthcare, discussed below. Other areas of managed services—military, transportation, and national and state parks—will not be presented in this chapter.

Exhibit 5.8   College students comprise a large percentage of front of the house wait persons. (Photo by Jenni Kirk.)

Business Services   Many large businesses and factories provide food service and other services to their employees. Food service can be offered in employee cafeterias, executive dining rooms, vending machines, at catered events, coffee outlets, and convenience stores. ***Business services*** are offered to companies whose main business is not food service, such as car manufacturers, insurance companies and banks, etc. Food service offered at places of business generally helps to keep up morale, increase productivity, and help to retain employees. Services can include catering on and off-premise events as well as providing food for employees to purchase to bring home.

The offerings have grown from the original root, dining services, to the expanded services of meeting planning, janitorial services, or plant operation and maintenance. Some companies offer concierge services, car maintenance, dry cleaning, and even shoe repair.

Food Service in Educational Settings   ***Food service in educational settings*** is the largest segment of managed services. The area is broken into two distinct categories: college campuses, and elementary and secondary schools. Companies that provide food service enable schools to concentrate on education, not on the preparation and serving of meals to their students. Services range from the standard cafeteria, to food service in residential housing units, retail food service sales, concession sales, and even janitorial support.

Meals are provided in most of the nation's elementary and secondary schools, as well as at government assisted pre-school programs. Many schools serve only lunch, but the service of breakfast is increasing as its importance to the student readiness for learning is appreciated. Many schools have their meals subsidized by state and federal programs. The subsidies allow the school to offer discounted meals to children from low income families.

There has been a great evolution in food service offered on college campuses. Students, once thought to be a "captive audience," now are more mobile, forcing the campus food service provider to compete with local food service operators. Many campuses are bringing national and local food service concepts on campus to expand their offerings. Increased dietary concerns are causing providers to diversify their offerings to satisfy the different needs of the changing market.

Food service on college campuses can be provided in a variety of locations. The most common place to offer food service is in a cafeteria-style dining hall attached to a residence hall. Food service can also be offered at a variety of outlets in the campus student union. The union can offer students a cafeteria style dining hall as well as retail operations. The retail operations can be a mix of company as well as branded concepts. Branded concepts are operations such as McDonald's and Taco Bell. Branded concepts normally do well on college campuses because they appeal to that demographic.

Managed service companies can also offer beverage services, vending machines, catering, and dining facilities for faculty. Managing the concessions at campus sporting venues is another area that may be contracted out to the managed service company.

Providing food service in educational environments can be challenging. Students can be very picky about their food, making it difficult for the food service provider. Items students prefer to eat—pizza and hamburgers, for example—may not be the most nutritious for them. Food service providers must provide items that are popular with students while ensuring they provide healthful choices.

Ethics

The law requires that managers treat employees fairly and equally, avoiding discrimination on the basis of race, sex, national origin, age, and religion. However, professional management goes beyond the bottom-line moral requirement of the law; it requires managers to behave with integrity in all their business dealings. Personal integrity, or the lack of it, is the result of all the decisions a manager makes over the years.

Personal integrity is essential for employees involved in purchasing, receiving, and issuing, areas where an unscrupulous person can permanently damage an organization's bottom line through acceptance of bribes, kickbacks, or other "incentives."

Food service managers also face decisions on whether to serve foods that may have been irradiated, come from animals that have been fed growth hormones, or contain controversial food additives. (Popular as these issues are, the Food Marketing Institute indicates that food-borne illness, described earlier in this chapter, constitutes the greatest danger to the public.)

Health Care   Food service in **_health care_** institutions takes on a different component than other areas of food service. Patients' dietary constraints require the food service department to prepare a wider range of food items. The job of the food service department is further complicated by the needs and desires of the variety of daily customers, such as visitors, doctors, nurses, staff, and patients. The multiple outlets and types of service are unique to health care food service: tray service for patients, cafeteria service for employee and visitors, vending, and possibly catering.

The national trend in hospitals is toward reduced stays for patients. The reduced length of stays results in fewer meals for the kitchen to prepare. Faced with a loss of revenue, health care food service departments are finding creative ways to use their under-utilized kitchen. Health care operations are now offering catering for on-site as well as off-site functions. Some food service departments are preparing food for sale to employees to pick up on the way home.

Some institutions hire **_food service contractors_** to operate their in-house food services. These look like institutional or nonprofit food service operations, but are actually commercial, because the contractors' goal is to make a profit.

CLASSIFICATIONS OF FOOD SERVICE OPERATION

Food service operations may also be classified by their means of food preparation.

Conventional versus Convenience Food Service Operations

A **conventional food service operation** prepares most menu items from scratch using raw ingredients, while a **convenience food service operation** uses mostly convenience (processed) foods to prepare its menu items. One isn't necessarily better than the other. The decision of whether to use raw ingredients is based on budget, staff abilities and schedules, equipment availability, and customer preferences. Many food service operations' menus offer some combination of conventional items and convenience foods, so that it is often difficult to label an operation as one or the other.

Commissary Food Service Operations

Commissary food service operations may be commercial or institutional, and may or may not use convenience *foods*. Their distinguishing characteristic is that they prepare all meals in a central kitchen and then transport them to various serving sites. Some community school systems use a centralized kitchen to reduce the costs involved with individual kitchens and staffing.

POSITIONS IN FOOD SERVICE

There is a wealth of opportunities in the food service industry. The table on page 222 outlines a portion of the available positions in this vast industry.

A career in the restaurant and hospitality industry is a profession. Those who acquire professional credentials distinguish themselves as being highly skilled, trained, motivated and career-minded. They make themselves immediate candidates for better pay and better jobs.

In an industry that now employs more than 12 million people, including 600,000 higher paying management positions, full- and part-time jobs abound!

Different types of foodservice organizations are organized in ways that are appropriate to their respective operations. A small, family-owned lunch counter may have Dad in the kitchen with Mom on the cash register and serving at the counter. A large, meeting- and convention-oriented resort may have 200 kitchen employees and 300–400 bartenders, servers, bussers, hosts, and cashiers working in various outlets and in banquets.

The organization charts shown in Exhibit 5.9 and 5.11 a, b, c show some different organizational structures that reflect the operating environment of different types of foodservice operations.

HUMAN RESOURCE MANAGEMENT

The food service operations model describes steps in the production and service of the menu. However, because this process involves people (the manager directing the staff), there is another umbrella model in force here, the human resources model.

The key to success of food service operations depends on its employees. The success of a food service manager depends heavily on his or her ability to manage and work with people. Technical skills are important for a food service manager, but people skills are essential. Part of the people skills portfolio is leadership. Managers set standards, and as professionals, set them high. They carefully choose their employees and systematically train them in the organization's standards and expectations. The best managers attempt to train (and to encourage) groundlevel staff to

Exhibit 5.9   Positions in Food Service

What You Can Do

Corporate	CEO/business owner	Marketing professional
	Research & Development	Multi-Unit/Regional Manager
	Human Resources	Trainer
	Quality Assurance	
	Restaurants	**Hotels**
	General Manager	Food & Beverage Director
	Assistant Manager	Catering Director
		Catering Manager
Back of the House	Executive Chef	Garde Manager
	Kitchen Manager	Cook
	Kitchen Supervisor	Prep Cook
	Supervisor	Kitchen
	Sous Chef	Worker/Assistant
	Chef	Dishwasher
	Pastry Chef	
Front of the House	Dining Room Manager	Host
	Dining Room Supervisor	Head Server
	Bar Manager	Server
	Bartender	Server Assistant
	Sommelier	Cashier
	Wine Steward	Busser
Specialty	Dietary Manager	
	Dietitian	

Where You Can Work	Cafeterias	Restaurants	Private Clubs
Operations	Convention Centers	Schools	Resorts
(Places that serve food)	Cruise Lines	Stadiums	
	Hospitals	Supermarkets	
	Hotels	Theme Parks	
	Night Clubs	Transportation	
Suppliers	Food	Architects	
(Companies that	Equipment	Florists	
supply operations)	Furniture	Decorators	
	Beverages	Tableware	
Other	Health Departments	Government	
	Culinary Colleges	Associations	

(*Source:* National Restaurant Association.)

EYE ON THE ISSUES

International

Food service operations have traditionally included employees from many nationalities and cultures, but for many years, chef and kitchen management positions around the world were dominated by males. In America this trend has shifted somewhat, allowing competent women to practice leadership, too. On an international scope, it's important for managers to understand and work with cultural differences in the perception of appropriate gender roles. The "old world" may conflict with the "new world" when employees from different national backgrounds (or generations) are assigned together without introduction or human resource groundwork.

Food service operators must also be aware of the wide variance in international food production standards. Produce, in particular, from other countries may be grown or shipped using chemicals that have been banned in the United States.

EYE ON THE ISSUES

Technology

Many food service operations have automated their purchasing, inventory, sales, and human resources systems. Using bar codes in the purchasing and inventory department is an example of how technology can make tracking of foods faster and more efficient. It is important for managers to be current with available technologies, equipment, or methods that might be cost effective. The development of cash registers that use picture keys for items (such as milkshakes, sodas, orange juice) has been largely in response to illiteracy and innumeracy. Managers might want to consider whether such technology discourages employees from pursuing the literacies that would help them advance beyond their *present competencies* or whether the benefits to the company outweigh the disservice they may do to their employees.

Exhibit 5.10   Oh yes, another job position . . . "singing waitstaff"! Shown here performing for the diners, moments later the staff return to their serving duties. (*Courtesy:* Black Bart's. Photo by Jenni Kirk.)

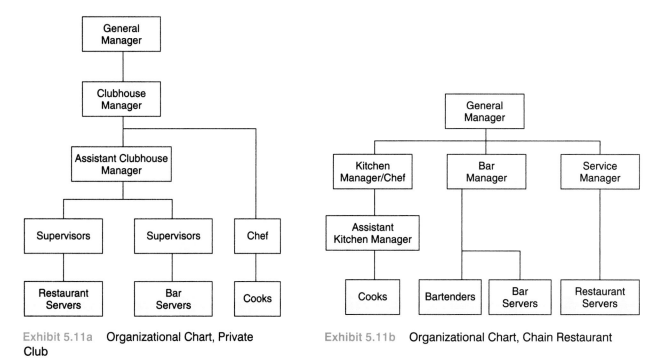

Exhibit 5.11a   Organizational Chart, Private Club

Exhibit 5.11b   Organizational Chart, Chain Restaurant

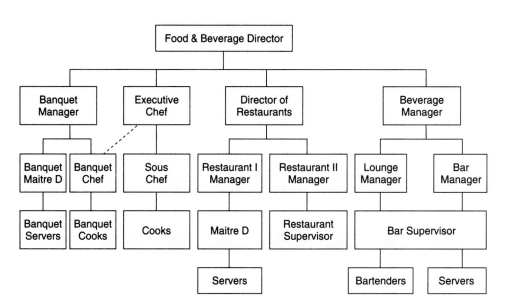

Exhibit 5.11c   Organizational Chart, Hotel Food and Beverage Department

Exhibit 5.12   The bar from an employee's perspective. Notice the levels of technology ranging from low tech (a pouring gun) to high tech (the point-of-sale terminal). (Courtesy Pavilion Mesa Hilton, Mesa, Arizona. Photo by James L. Morgan.)

move upwards through the organization. This requires the ability to motivate. (This is discussed more thoroughly in Chapter 10, "Human Resource Management.")

Note that managers must be aware of their employees' needs in order to provide a motivating atmosphere. Changing demographics have resulted in a new typical worker profile. The new typical worker may be a single, uneducated, 30-year-old woman with children. Job security and a paycheck may be her initial needs. As those needs are met, she may look to her job for social needs, and later for self-esteem needs. A manager attuned to his or her employees' needs can increase employee productivity and job satisfaction, thus reducing turnover.

A manager can reinforce desired behavior. Just as people have different needs, they have different ideas of what a reward is. For one person, a verbal "That's good" is a reward. Another person might respond to a more tangible reward, such as increased responsibility or time off. By knowing their employees, managers are better able to understand their needs and thus offer the kinds of rewards that will increase their motivation.

Employees are not mind readers. Managers must tell employees what they are expected to do. To state the obvious, this requires that managers first know what it is that their employees are supposed to do. Only then can they show employees how to do it. Under the manager's (or trainer's) supervision, employees then try the tasks themselves, receiving immediate corrective feedback and encouragement. The manager must then monitor the employees consistently to make sure that the standards are maintained. Supervision is an ongoing process, and is not as simple as most workers believe.

Exhibit 5.13   A Benihana chef must not only have great cooking skills, but also have a flair for entertaining the guests who sit at his teppanyaki table. (Photo courtesy of Benihana, Inc.)

To recap, managers assure that standards are met by providing a good working atmosphere and good working conditions. Managers must provide good recipes, the ingredients called for in the recipes, and adequate equipment, supplies, and time to prepare the recipes.

Managers must also provide leadership. By demonstrating the company's philosophy at all times, managers can make it real to their employees. This is important, since every employee should clearly understand the company's philosophy and mission statement. Employees are strongly influenced by their manager's conduct. A manager who does not adhere to the rules and standards he or she sets provides a poor example for the staff. If trainers, managers, and top management do not respect the rules, regulations, and standards they've set (and execute all of them with consistency and fairness), neither will their employees.

As emphasized before, the manager is responsible for seeing that the job gets done right. A manager can only do that by utilizing their personnel to the fullest. This requires good communication, constructive feedback, and respect. Ultimately, it is the manager's behavior that tells the employee whether he or she is respected, and this perception profoundly affects the way an employee performs on the job. For food service operations to be successful in an increasingly competitive environment, managers must be professional and must train and encourage the professionalism of their staff at all levels. This includes the encouragement of mutual respect as well as self-respect among all employees.

CONCLUSION

Professionalism in food service management is essential in today's highly competitive market. This overview of food service management is intended to demonstrate the scope and seriousness of food service management and to underscore the importance of professional training/education for potential food service managers.

Food service management can be wonderfully satisfying, fulfilling, and fun, but only if we are properly prepared to manage. Managers must have firm foundations in marketing, financial management, and, perhaps most importantly, human resource management.

Meeting customers' needs, selecting and retaining a well trained staff, and operating a safe and sanitary food service operation, require professional management training. The traditional practice of promoting food service line workers into management positions has contributed to dissatisfied customers and turnover rates of up to 300 percent. The up-through-the-ranks manager may be less competitive today and in less demand in the current food service management market. Professional food service management training is a necessity in today's workplace.

KEYWORDS

food service operation   206
clean   206
franchise   211
franchisee   211
franchisor   211
restaurant chain   212
entrepreneur   213
full-service restaurants   214
quick service restaurants
   (formerly "fast food")   214
commercial cafeterias   215
ice cream and frozen yogurt   215

bar and tavern   215
food contractor   215
room service   216
catering/banquets   216
institutional food service
   operations   217
conventional food service
   operation   220
convenience food service
   operation   220
commissary food service
   operations   221

CORE CONCEPTS

managed services   217
business services   219
food service in educational setting   219

food service contractors   220
healthcare   220

DISCUSSION QUESTIONS

1. Why is professional training necessary for today's food service manager?
2. Why would a company want to provide on-site food service for its employees?
3. Outline the career path of both of a front of the house and back of the house employee.
4. Describe the role of a food service manager and list his or her responsibilities.
5. What challenges face companies that provide food-service in healthcare?

REFERENCES

The Educational Foundation of the National Restaurant Association. *Applied Foodservice Sanitation: A Certification Coursebook,* 4th ed. New York: John Wiley & Sons, 1992.

National Restaurant Association, *2001 Restaurant Industry Factbook.*

National Restaurant Association, *Career Information, 2001.*

EXEMPLAR OF EXCELLENCE

Every town has the "best restaurant in town." Large urban centers have a top tier of fine dining restaurants, but most of these are local, family owned restaurants, rather than national chains. A number of national dinnerhouse chains do an excellent job of competing for your dining dollars. They offer enticing meals and excellent service, but most consumers don't think of them as "fine dining."

A number of relatively small restaurant groups have established a regional presence and compete in the fine dining market. Ruth's Chris, Morton's of Chicago, J Alexander's, Houston's, Pappas Restaurants, and Pappas Steak House all offer excellent food, ambience, and service. These restaurants generate a high average check, but have high food and labor costs to give customers value for their dining dollar.

Ask people for their opinion as to which is the "best restaurant in town." What do the restaurants people select have in common? How many of them are locally owned and operated, and how many of them are part of a group?

Visit some of the company Websites, and get a feel for their commitment to quality and service.

1. www.jalexanders.com
2. www.houstons.com
3. www.ruthschris.com
4. www.mortons.com
5. www.pappas.com

WEBSITES TO VISIT

1. www.aramark.com
2. www.canteen.com
3. www.outback.com
4. www.thecheesecakefactory.com
5. www.mcdonalds.com
6. www.burgerking.com
7. www.subway.com
8. www.kfc.com
9. www.pizzahut.com
10. www.redlobster.com
11. www.olivegarden.com

12. www.csh.rit.edu/~gentry/TBNet/tbnet.html
13. www.chilis.com

RESTAURANT AUTOMATION SITES

1. www.ncr.com
2. www.micros.com
3. www.verifone.com
4. www.eatec.com
5. www.foodtrak.com
6. www.squirrelsystems.com

CHAPTER 6

Food Service Management

Food service management is not an easy business. Managers must deal with large volumes of small, low-profit-margin transactions. There is constant pressure from rising costs and rising wage rates. Employees tend to have low skill levels and are paid low wages, so training and motivating employees is a constant task. Food service is extremely competitive, with large regional and national chains, many locally owned, family operated units, and new competition from ready-to-cook foods from grocery stores and convenience stores.

That's the bad news. The good news is that food service management can be very rewarding. Most managers enjoy their work, get great satisfaction from their success in a fast-paced, people-oriented environment, and earn competitive salaries. Unit managers usually earn performance-based bonuses. The wide array of food service operations offers a range of work environments and schedules that let you find an operation to fit your style and schedule.

INTRODUCTION

Today's food service manager must possess many skills in order to fulfill the tremendous responsibilities inherent in food service management. The most commonly identified skill is operations—the ability to prepare and serve food to customers (also referred to as production management). However, without an adequate knowledge of marketing, finance, human resources, and other related functional areas, a restaurant manager could not succeed. It is vital that students interested in a management career in any part of the hospitality industry develop a well rounded understanding of all aspects of business.

Traditionally, food service managers were brought up through the ranks and simply did what their managers before them had done. However, as the world has changed, passed-down management techniques and strategies work less and less well. On-the-job experience is useful, but it is only through a quality education and a well organized training program that students can learn successfully to manage food service operations of the future.

Types of Food Service Operations

The broadest classifications of food service **operations** are commercial and institutional. Commercial food service operations, mostly restaurants, have the primary objective of making a profit. Institutional food service operations are usually focused on serving a captive audience, such as schools, businesses, sports facilities, and prisons. When an institutional food service facility is operated by an outside firm, a contract food service firm, it will attempt to make a profit, while also fulfilling the needs of the organization's constituents.

Positions in Food Service

There is a broad range of employment opportunities in the foodservice industry. For the most part, food service job titles vary from operation to operation, but the responsibilities and roles remain largely the same. Back-of-the-house positions will vary greatly depending on the style of restaurant. A typical range includes executive chef, sous chef, cooks, prep workers, and dishwashers. The front of the house may include cashiers, servers, hosts, bussers, and bartenders. Exhibit 5.11B in Chapter 5 shows a common organizational structure of a full-service restaurant.

This chapter introduces the student to the major decisions and responsibilities of food service. As you read the different topics, think about your experiences as an employee or customer at various restaurants. Do you think these restaurants have made good management decisions, and have they effectively carried them out? If not, how would you have changed their decisions and actions?

The Food Service Operations Model

The chapter will be organized around the food service operations model. This model is based on the natural progression of responsibilities of managers and owners of restaurants. It begins with development of the menu (the food that will be served), then progresses to purchasing, receiving, storage, preparation/cooking,

The Food Service Operations Model

Menu Development
Purchasing
Receiving
Storage
Preparation/Cooking
Customer Service
Cleanliness and Sanitization

Exhibit 6.1   The food service operations model.

customer service, and cleaning. Students should understand that only an overview of each of these topics is offered. As you progress through your educational career, you will have the opportunity to study each topic in more depth.

MENU DEVELOPMENT

One of the most important decisions you can make for the restaurant is the type of food that will be served, namely, the restaurant's menu. In one way or another, the menu affects everything that takes place in the restaurant. Even the restaurant's image is partially created by its menu because customers tend to categorize restaurants by the primary type of food served; for example, customers often refer to a restaurant as a hamburger restaurant, a seafood restaurant, or an Italian restaurant.

The food we serve in restaurants is much more than fuel for the body. The social contexts in which food is eaten are part of what bonds a society. We use the sharing of food to express welcome, friendship, familial love, and concern for the ill. We mark important occasions with special foods and celebrate with people by gifts of food. Holidays are identified with traditional feasts. Most occasions in our lives are experienced and often enhanced with food.

The hospitality industry is in many ways like an extension of our families. Hotels and restaurants house and feed people when they are away from home, as do hospitals, schools, and prisons. Special occasions are often celebrated at restaurants or at banquet facilities. It's hard to imagine baseball games without hot dogs, airline flights without meals or snacks (though cost pressures have made this more common), meetings without refreshments, or day trips without lunch stops.

Exhibit 6.2   Special menu items become a draw over time. The Waldorf-Astoria, creator of the original "Waldorf Salad," is one such example. (*Courtesy:* Waldorf Astoria)

It seems that just about everything we do incorporates food, and if we're not preparing the food at home, a food service operation is involved. A food service operation is an organization outside the home that prepares food for people, either for sale, as in a restaurant, or as part of a service, as in a hospital. Food service operations do the very same things we do at home to produce meals for our families.

Key Factors in Menu Development

While there are hundreds of decisions to be made when preparing the menu, the following are some of the most important factors to consider.

What characteristics of our guests should we consider when we prepare our menu?   Just as we decide what to prepare for guests at our homes, we decide the menu for guests at a restaurant. Typically, before deciding on menu items, we examine the demographic characteristics (such as age, sex, education, type of work, income, and spending habits) and personal characteristics (eating habits, sporting and recreational activities, and physical health) of the customers that we expect to visit our restaurant. With this information, you can begin to develop the menu. If a specific menu has already been decided on, you may need to make changes to ensure that the menu will be well received.

Exhibit 6.3   The Dive Restaurant has a submarine theme–driven menu; the menu helps support the nautical under-sea ambiance of the restaurant. (*Courtesy:* The Dive Restaurant, Las Vegas, Nevada.)

What is the most efficient means of initiating menu development?   Most successful restaurants develop their menu around what is called a signature item, generally one menu item—sometimes two or three—unique in some way, a good value, and which generates word-of-mouth advertising and high sales in proportion to other items. Signature items ideally should have a kitchen time shorter than most on the menu and a cost the same or lower than the restaurant's ideal or average food cost.

How familiar should the food on the menu be to customers?   The more successful restaurants often serve consistently high-quality foods that are familiar to their customers but prepared in the restaurant's own special way. A few restaurants add unique items to the menu to give customers the opportunity to be adventurous. Menus with too many unfamiliar items are risky.

How can the restaurant offer a variety of menu items without an extensive product inventory?   An effective and easy way to spice up a menu is to use foods that are already available in the restaurant. This is called cross-utilization. For example, top one of your poultry or fish items with artichoke hearts, a sauce and grated cheese kept in inventory for other menu items.

Should nutritious foods be included in the menu?   An emphasis on nutritious menus is becoming increasingly important as customers become more discerning about what they eat. Each restaurant must make a judgment, based on its

Exhibit 6.4   Product storage requires adherence to a long list of standards. For example, rotation of goods ensures freshness, dripping meats are always stored in a low place, and costly items are often locked away.

clientele, as to how much it will promote nutrition. The safest approach is to include menu items that will please both the average and the health-conscious customer. For example, an Italian restaurant could offer a traditional lasagna with meat sauce and a vegetarian lasagna or chicken lasagna. Interestingly, there is a slight contradiction in this increased nutritional awareness—a high percentage of desserts are ordered by health-conscious customers as a personal reward for eating properly or exercising regularly.

How many items should there be on the menu?   Inexperienced restaurant operators tend to put too many items on the menu. The kitchen's capacity in production and ability should dictate the number of items on the menu. When new items are added beyond the comfort level of the kitchen, the quality of food decreases, food cost increases, the kitchen's order time slows down, and employees become frustrated. It is preferable to serve a limited selection of consistently high-quality foods than to try to please all customers with an extensive menu.

Should specials be included in the menu?   Specials—items offered on a daily or possibly weekly basis—allow you to test the popularity of a new item without making a commitment to placing it on the menu. Specials are also good for employees—they break up routines, relieve monotony, create a little excitement, and allow the kitchen to show its skill. They also allow the restaurant to promote items that are overstocked, such as fresh fish, steaks, or a prepared item that may not be savable tomorrow. (In this case, the term "special" takes on a second meaning, i.e., a reduced price.) Specials are good from the customer's perspective because they offer variety in a familiar and trusted environment. Specials can cause problems if:

- The special is not properly communicated to the cooks so that they can make advance preparation
- The special requires excessive advanced preparation
- The restaurant does not have the proper equipment to prepare and serve the special
- A large quantity of the special is prepared and very little is sold
- Specific food products are required for the special that are either not purchased or are purchased in the wrong quantity
- The cooks do not have the skills necessary to properly prepare the special
- The servers do not inform customers about the special

How many types of menus are needed?   Most restaurants need only one menu, but some need separate breakfast, lunch, and dinner menus. Other options are a separate wine menu, a special catering menu, a child's menu, and take-out menus. Blackboards can be used to promote special entrees, special prices, or entrees such as fish, which may not be available every day and on which the price varies. Self-service restaurants can generally use a menu board of some type instead of hand-held menus.

What material should be used for the menu?   Operators of new restaurants should insert their menus into clear plastic folders, which are inexpensive, easy to clean, and make inserting new or changed menus easy. Operators of new restaurants should not invest money in custom menus until the restaurant has been open for a few months.

What guidelines should be followed in designing and laying out a menu? Overall, menus should be:

- **Durable.** If the menu is not placed in a clear plastic folder, a plastic coating or lamination may be necessary.
- **Well designed.** The design should be compatible with the concept of the restaurant.
- **Readable.** The menu must be readable, given the lighting in the restaurant.
- **Divided into food categories.** For example, the menu may be sectioned into appetizers, soups, salads, side dishes, entrees, hamburgers, sandwiches, desserts, and beverages.
- **List popular items with a low food cost at the top of each category.** The first two items in any category tend to be ordered most often. Hand-held menus used in full-service restaurants should include appetizing descriptions of the ingredients and preparation methods of each item. Self-service restaurants with menu boards generally do not need to use descriptive wording.

Where do new menu ideas come from? Various sources can be tapped for new menu ideas. Among these are the restaurant's kitchen staff, other restaurants (ideas, not entire menus), other restaurant operators, cookbooks, consumer magazines, industry trade magazines, friends, and ideas gathered while traveling or on vacation.

What factors should be considered before we deciding on our prices? Menu pricing is extremely critical to the success of the restaurant. The prices you charge for menu items will vary, depending on the following factors:

Basic price structure. Operators of new and existing restaurants should decide what their basic price structure should be. For example, entrees may cost from

Exhibit 6.5   Another example of a theme-driven menu. Rainforest Cafés offer extensive menus, and extensive staff training to match. (*Courtesy:* Rainforest Cafés)

$5.95 to $9.95, or from $12.50 to $20. Customers and guidebooks will use the price structure as one of many ways of categorizing the restaurant.

Type of service.   The type of service offered, whether it is self-service or full-service, generally determines how much the restaurant can charge. Obviously, full-service restaurants offer more service to customers, and therefore customers will accept higher prices.

Atmosphere.   The atmosphere, including décor and design, of the restaurant often dictates lower or higher menu prices. Customers will only pay so much for atmosphere; the restaurant's food is their main concern.

Competition.   If the competition is serving similar menu items, you should probably charge approximately the same price.

Price/value relationship.   The menu items' price–value relationship is derived from the customer's perceived value of the menu item, based on its appearance, quality, and quantity. For example, if a certain menu item looks as though it should cost more than the price calculated on the menu pricing worksheet, the menu price could possibly be increased.

Plate presentation.   Before tasting the food, a customer evaluates it based on appearance. Plate presentation is the appearance of any menu item as it is served to the customer. It includes the appearance of the food and its serving piece. Each menu item does not have to be a work of art, but it should at least look appetizing. Generally, the higher the menu prices, the higher the customer's expectations for appearance. Even so, all restaurants should be concerned with the appearance of their food. The old restaurant adage, "The customers eat first with their eyes, then with their mouths," is true, and should not be taken lightly. Before adding any item to the menu, decide how preparation of the item and assembling or plating of the item will affect its appearance. Then select the appropriate serving piece.

Food cost percentage.   The factor with the most significant effect on pricing menu items is the food cost percentage. This is the relationship between the ingredient cost, or food cost, of the menu item and the menu price. Since each menu item served should fall into a certain price range, the item must be prepared at a cost that meets this pricing structure. Calculate this percentage by dividing the food cost by the menu price. For example, a food cost of $2 divided by a menu price of $5.95 equals a food cost percentage of 33.6 percent.

All restaurants have a certain food cost percentage as goal. Some menu items will have a cost percentage above the target, some below. The point is that the total food cost for each accounting period yields a food cost percentage as close as possible to the target food cost percentage. You must also consider the amount of labor needed to prepare each menu item. If most menu items are prepared from scratch, labor cost will be higher and food cost will probably be lower. Many restaurant operators in this situation do not understand why they have a low food cost percentage but are experiencing high labor cost percentages. In such cases, the menu price might have to be raised to compensate for the additional labor cost. For example, a packaged beef stew costs $1.50 per serving and is sold for

Exhibit 6.6   Plate presentation is critical in ensuring consistency meal after meal. Alice Cooper says, "The show must go on 364 days per year in the restaurant business."(*Courtesy:* Brian Weymouth, Alice Cooper'stown.)

$4.95, to yield a food cost percentage of 30.3 percent. Beef stew prepared by the restaurant staff may cost $1.20 per serving and sell for $3.95, yielding an almost identical food cost percentage of 30.4 percent. There is nothing wrong with this food cost percentage, but, since the product is prepared from scratch and the menu price is lower, the restaurant's labor cost percentage is higher. To compensate for the additional labor cost, the $3.95 price of the beef stew should, in most cases, be raised. If it were raised to $4.95, for example, the food cost percentage would be 24.2 percent, providing additional income to cover the labor cost needed to prepare the item.

The combined total of food cost percentage and labor cost percentage is called the prime cost or prime factor. Most restaurants have a prime cost of between 55 and 65 percent of sales. Restaurants that have lower food cost percentages usually have higher labor cost percentages, and vice versa.

Causes of High Food Cost   Among the many possible causes of high food cost, the following are the most common:

- Not having or using product specifications
- Not comparing product price

Exhibit 6.7   An accurate inventory is critical in determining cost of food sold.

- Not checking deliveries for weight, count, and proper specifications
- Not promptly storing deliveries, especially perishables
- Not properly pricing out each menu item
- Not preparing prep items and menu items according to written recipes
- Not determining the exact portion of each product that will be used for each menu item
- Not establishing ordering pars for each product
- Not establishing prep pars for prep items
- Not taking a daily inventory of all high-cost food products

EYE ON THE ISSUES

Environment

Energy conservation and waste management are important to food service managers. Depending on the size of the restaurant, daily energy management decisions (turning off lights and other equipment) and the efficiency of its equipment, energy costs can be between 2 percent and 4 percent of sales. Prudent decisions in this area can save $10,000 or more per year. Though restaurant waste only makes up 1 percent of the average volume in our landfills, the perception among many is that it is greater. Restaurant operators are continually seeking new methods of reducing the amount of waste through new packaging options, waste compactors, and the purchase of products that can be fully utilized. Additionally, the cost of waste removal, depending on the area of the country, can vary from several hundred to several thousand dollars per year.

- Not checking trash cans in prep and kitchen areas for unnecessary waste or for foods temporarily hidden by unethical employees who plan to remove them after the trash can is taken outside
- Not properly training all employees to perform their respective tasks
- Not keeping foods at the proper temperature
- Not properly labeling all prepared products with the date, product name, and initials of the preparer
- Not using products within their acceptable shelf life
- Not taking appropriate action when a menu item is not selling well and spoilage results
- Not having the proper equipment available or in working condition to prepare and cook all menu items

PURCHASING

Purchasing is the second component of the food service operations model. The first component, menu planning, dictates the firm's purchasing requirements. Once the requirements have been determined, it becomes the goal of the individual responsible for purchasing to obtain the right quality and quantity at the right time and price.

Quality is based on the demands of the firm's customers and may be defined in terms of government grades, packer's grades, brand names, and trade names (e.g., Grade A, U.S. #1, etc.). Physical specifications and performance standards may be used to establish a product's quality (e.g., 5 × 6 tomatoes—the size that fits 5 rows of 6 tomatoes on each layer of a case)—or low in salt. Once a standard of identity

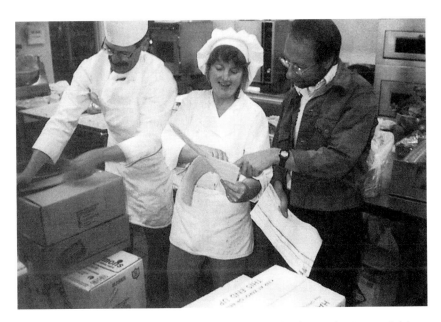

Exhibit 6.8 Proper receiving is critical to profitability. Items short on weight or short on quality quickly affect the restaurant operation's bottom line. (Photo by Christine Jaszay)

has been developed for a specific food item, that item must contain only the ingredients specified in the standard.

Quantity relates to the rate of usage of each product. This is determined by multiplying the amount of a product needed in each recipe by the number of times each recipe will be prepare between ordering dates. For example, our Italian restaurant uses 15 gallons of tomato sauce for each recipe of spaghetti sauce; on average, the recipe is prepared each day; and the restaurant orders canned goods twice a week, on Sunday for a Monday delivery and Thursday for a Friday delivery. This means that we must order 60 gallons on Sunday, enough for 4 recipes, and 45 gallons on Friday, enough for 3 recipes.

Selecting a supplier must be based on an objective evaluation of a firm's quality of service, product knowledge, delivery schedules, financial stability, credit terms, and the range of products offered. A good sales representative from a food supplier should play an active role in providing ideas and product usage information.

RECEIVING

Receiving is an extremely important activity because it is the point at which ownership is transferred from the supplier to the food service firm. This is a critical control point. The person checking in the order, sensitized to the need to inspect and protect hazardous foods, should consult HACCP flowcharts for each incoming order. Exhibit 6.9 shows the details involved in the receiving function of the HACCP flowchart for beef stew.

It is at the receiving critical control point that delivered food products must be accepted, adjusted, or rejected. Decisions are made on the basis of the standards for receiving particular food types. The specific recipe is not important at the receiving checkpoint. The standards for receiving beef, cheese, eggs, vegetables, or any food do not vary from recipe to recipe. For example, the receiving standards for fresh beef are always the same. The beef must arrive with a temperature of 45 degrees or lower, the packaging must be intact, and there can be no "off" odor or color. If any of these standards are not met, the delivery must be rejected because the meat may be contaminated or contain an unacceptable number of potentially dangerous bacteria.

STORAGE

Proper storage facilities are necessary to maintain product quality while minimizing losses due to pilferage, theft, and spoilage. It is important to remember that food products rarely improve in quality while in storage. Product spoilage and contamination can be minimized if proper sanitation procedures are adhered to in the storage areas. Specific food storage rules typical of that used by many restaurants are listed below.

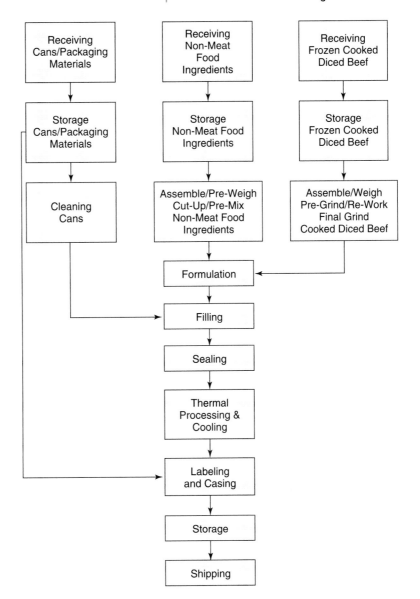

Exhibit 6.9   HACCP flowchart for beef stew.

All Food Service Storage

1. Foods should be stored at least six inches above the floor, unless they are on movable dollies, racks, or pallets.
2. All storage areas should be arranged neatly to allow for easy access and quick identification of products.
3. All shelves should be labeled so that products are consistently stored in the same location.
4. All storage areas should be kept clean. Spills or dropped food should be wiped up immediately.

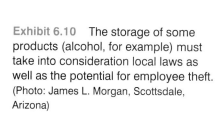

Exhibit 6.10   The storage of some products (alcohol, for example) must take into consideration local laws as well as the potential for employee theft. (Photo: James L. Morgan, Scottsdale, Arizona)

5. Refrigerators and freezers should be in good mechanical condition. Preventative maintenance such as cleaning the coils, lubricating hinges, cleaning rubber door seals, not slamming doors, and not keeping doors open too long extends the life of the equipment and reduces repair costs.
6. Whenever possible, all products delivered should be dated with a black magic marker or a grease pencil.
7. All products should be used on a first-in, first-out (FIFO) basis. This is called rotation—the oldest products should be used first. New products should be placed behind or below older products.
8. Store all chemicals such as pesticides, detergents, and window cleaners in a room separate from food storage rooms.

Dry Goods Storage

1. The ideal temperature for dry goods storage is between 50°F and 70°F. When this is not possible, there should be adequate ventilation.
2. If a package has been partially used, the remaining product must be placed in a sanitized container, labeled, and sealed.
3. Try to use all dry goods products within three months. Most foods last longer than three months, but the quality may deteriorate after this time.

Refrigerated Storage

1. The refrigerator must be cold enough to keep all products at 45°F or below.
2. Store all potentially hazardous foods—meats, poultry, seafood, dairy products, and prepared foods containing any of these foods—close to the fan so they can be kept as cold as possible, without freezing. The best temperature for these products is between 32°F and 35°F.
3. Store fresh fish in perforated hotel pans, normally 2½ to 4 inches deep, and set in a 6 inch deep hotel pan as a drain pan. Cover the fish with plastic wrap, then loosely cover it with flaked ice. Solid ice works, but flaked ice causes less damage to the fish. Drain and rinse the drain pan and re-ice the fish daily.
4. Never store prepared products below raw, potentially hazardous products. Cross-contamination can occur if any of the raw product falls or drips into the prepared products.

Exhibit 6.11   Safe food delivery and storage is no joking matter. Food production companies strive to provide restaurants and their customers with safe, tasty foods. (*Photo courtesy:* JacPac Foods)

5. Label all prepared products with the date prepared, the name of the product, and the name of the employee who prepared it.
6. Always check the date on dairy products to assure freshness and proper rotation.
7. Most produce can be stored in the warmest part of the refrigerator, generally near the door or furthest from the fan. Keep produce between 38°F and 45°F. Tomatoes keep best between 50°F and 70°F. Whole, raw onions and potatoes can be stored at room temperature.

Freezer Storage

1. The freezer should be kept at 0°F or below.
2. Wrap all foods tightly to prevent freezer burn.

EYE ON THE ISSUES

Technology

The basic technological necessities of a restaurant are minimal. Many restaurant concepts are very similar to their centuries-old counterparts: There are tables and chairs in the dining room and a wood burning grill in the kitchen. Yes, there are a refrigerator and an ice machine, but the basic needs of many restaurants can be met in low tech ways. At the other end of the scale, there are restaurants that constantly search out state-of-the-art advances that can help them increase the productivity of employees, get the food to the customer faster, improve the quality of the food, or help company management keep track of restaurants spread throughout the country, and perhaps the world.

A good example of the use of traditional versus high tech food equipment can be seen in the pizza business. Historically, pizza was prepared in wood-burning ovens. With the availability of gas and electricity came alternative power sources for ovens. These ovens provided a cleaner heat source and a more consistent product, but without the flavor attributes of wood. Next came the conveyor oven, where the pizza is placed on a rotating rack and moves through a heated chamber. Their primary benefit was consistency. Today, many pizza operators are returning to the wood-burning oven for improved flavor and customer perception.

3. Do not re-freeze potentially hazardous foods or foods containing them.
4. If the freezer is defrosted, place its contents in a refrigerator. Defrost and return foods as quickly as possible.
5. Try not to keep frozen meats, poultry, or seafood for more than four months.

FOOD PREPARATION/COOKING

Preparation is the procedure that transforms food from the state in which it was purchased to a form in which it is ready to be served to customers. Foods may be purchased in various states of preparation ranging from the natural state (a raw chicken) to ready-to-cook (frozen lasagna). Prepared or prepped food items can vary from ingredients only, such as cutting onions for hamburgers, or finished items, such as a spaghetti sauce, that only needs to be heated before serving.

Food Preparation Assignments

Preparation assignments are often divided into the different positions or stations, such as broiler, pantry, or fry, that the chef or cook will work that day. Food preparation sheets (generally referred to as *food prep sheets*) are used to control which items and how much of each item are prepared each day. The first step in completing the food prep sheet is to record the amount of the item on hand. Next, this number is subtracted from the *par stock* or *par* for that item. The par is the minimum amount of the product you want to have on hand after the prep work is finished. Basically, par is enough of the product or recipe to last until it will be prepared again. For some items, the par will be adequate for the day; for others it will last for two days or longer. When possible, most items should be prepared daily. Normally, cooked meat, poultry, or seafood dishes and produce items, such as salads and vegetables, are prepared on a daily basis. Many sauces, gravies, soups, beans and rice can have pars that last for two days, sometimes longer. The par of the item, less the inventory on hand, is the prep, or the amount you want prepared on a particular shift.

Station Set-Up

The cooking line is where most foods are prepared for service. It normally consists of one or more stations where a primary kitchen activity takes place, such as broiler, fry, pantry, setup, or sauté. In order for the kitchen to efficiently serve customers, all foods, serviceware, and utensils must be available and conveniently accessible in each station.

To prepare a station set-up,

- List all menu items that will be cooked and assembled in the station
- List all foods, serviceware, and utensils that will be needed to prepare and serve the menu items
- Decide on the quantity and location of the items needed in the station
- Include the time to turn on the equipment, the required temperatures, and any other special requirements

Exhibit 6.12   Server stations must be kept clean, organized, and stocked to ensure efficient service standards. (Photo by Marilyn McDonald)

The chefs or cooks should make most of the decisions necessary to prepare each station setup. It is best if they experiment with the set-up before committing it to policy. Once all kitchen personnel are satisfied with the set-up, create diagrams showing all major storage areas, such as refrigerators, steam tables, or heating holding cabinets, to indicate where necessary items will be stored. Post the diagrams in each station.

Menu Assembly Guidelines

The menu assembly guidelines, along with utilized recipes, are one of the most effective ways of assuring a high quality and consistent product. Every item or product that is served should be accompanied by written guidelines outlining the proper portions and how to assemble and plate the item. A color photograph of the completed menu item should also accompany the written explanation.

Food Waste

As much as possible, all food purchased should be sold to customers. When food cannot be sold and must be thrown out, the manager should be notified about the problem. Examples of such problems are when servers write down the wrong order, a wrong order is prepared by the kitchen, food is improperly cooked or has spoiled, or a take-out (call-in) order is not picked up. Additionally, one of the greatest causes of food waste occurs when excessive amounts of foods are trimmed or discarded during preparation. A seemingly insignificant 10 percent too much of several products being thrown out can increase a restaurant's food cost percentage by 2 to 3 percent. Managers should acquire the habit of watching

Exhibit 6.13   The food must live up to the setting. Imagine the transformation the kitchen performs to convert raw ingredients into beautiful entrees and desserts. (*Photo:* W. Lynn Seldon Jr./Omni-Photo Communications, Inc.)

employees while they are preparing foods and checking trash cans for above-normal trimming of foods. Some restaurants have employees place all food trimmings in a container to be examined by a supervisor before being thrown out. Also, a common means of stealing food from restaurants is to hide the item in the trash can, then remove it when the trash can is taken outside.

Exhibit 6.14   How much to produce is the minute-by-minute question. Too much, and food goes to waste. Too little, and customer service suffers.

Often, wasted but edible products such as improperly or mistakenly cooked orders can be salvaged by serving them as employee meals or using them as ingredients in another menu item. For example, when a fish is cooked but not served for any reason, it could be added to a seafood chowder or gumbo. Some foods that are not servable to restaurant customers, but are safe to eat, may be donated to various charitable organizations, such as area food banks and the Salvation Army. Food waste should be discussed at the weekly manager's meeting.

Safety

Food service operators are also required by law to provide a safe working environment for their employees. Food service is not an inherently dangerous occupation, but accidents are possible if the staff has not been trained to follow appropriate rules of safety. The federal government enacted the **Occupational Safety and Health Act** (OSHA) to ensure employment that is "free from recognized hazards" to all employees. Every work environment (not just food service operations) must adhere to OSHA regulations. OSHA can impose fines and/or jail sentences for fail-

EYE ON THE ISSUES

Ethics and Social Responsibility

While there are many definitions of ethics, the term usually includes decisions (planning) that take into account the interests of society as a whole. Social responsibility can be viewed as the actions based on these ethical decisions. This is generally accomplished through being considerate of the needs of employees, being honest, and contributing to charitable efforts and environmentally friendly activities. The law requires that managers treat employees fairly and equally, avoiding discrimination on the basis of race, sex, national origin, age, and religion. An ethical and socially responsible manager will not only obey the law, but go beyond its mandates by having a real concern for his/her employees.

Honesty is essential in all aspects of restaurant management. Consider the problems of a manager who takes bribes or kickbacks when purchasing goods, or an employee who steals items when they are received. Several firms have be sued for inviting employees to "clean" without allowing them to clock in.

People are worried about pollution, depletion of the ozone layer, medical waste washing up on shore, and the healthfulness of the food they eat. Socially responsible issues are not only becoming important, they are affecting lifestyles. The Investor Responsibility Research Center classified social responsibility as the third greatest stockholder concern, following only profitability and business viability. Firms such as Wendy's have added corporate value statements that go beyond mission statements in describing the importance of employees, customers, and local communities. Since the responsibility for society must rest with someone, and the government cannot fulfill every need, the only remaining logical solution is that businesses take care of stakeholders and other societal constituents (Reich, 2002).

The benefits of a business's social responsibility efforts include an ethical and moral image; a stronger society, which benefits the business; it may be less expensive (monetarily and image-wise) to prevent a problem than to solve it later; and prevention may minimize governmental intervention and regulation.

Reich, A. Z. (2002). *"The Influence of Consumer and Business Social Responsibility on Brand Loyalty in Quick-Service Restaurants."* Unpublished doctoral dissertation, Virginia Tech, Blacksburg.

ure to comply. A safe restaurant requires that all employees be careful in everything they do. A conscious practice and awareness of safety rules benefits a food service operation in several ways:

- By reducing time and money loss
- By reducing breakage (china, glassware, equipment)
- By reducing staff stress and frustration
- By producing a safer and more pleasant work environment

CUSTOMER SERVICE

Every customer expects and deserves good service. The restaurant's service standards should be high enough to satisfy the most demanding customers and consistent enough to please them each time they come in. Customer service consists of two basic areas: courtesy and efficiency.

Courtesy

All customers should be greeted with a sincere smile. Eye contact is the key to a sincere smile. This is especially important if it is the customer's first visit.

The attitude of service employees must be warm and congenial, to make customers feel they are truly welcomed in the restaurant. Customers quickly recognize employee insincerity. Too often customers feel they are being treated as an intrusion on the employee, rather than an honored guest. Employees must learn to cater to the needs of each customer, not only for food and beverages, but also for attention. A difficult or irritable customer often is only seeking a little personal attention.

Efficiency

Efficiency is essentially the mechanics of service. It includes, among other things, how the customer is seated, the speed and accuracy of the employee taking the order and his or her ability to answer customer's questions about the menu, the speed and accuracy of the kitchen in preparing the food ordered, the promptness with which food is delivered to the customer, the attention paid to the customer during the meal, the pre-bussing of the table, and the presentation and paying out of the check. Never be 100 percent satisfied with the efficiency of the restaurant. There are always ways to do things easier, faster, or better. Observe whether an employee has to reach too far for something, or take too many steps, or whether work is unevenly divided. To assure that each employee performs his or her job efficiently, thoroughly train all employees and use formal (periodic) and informal (frequent, daily if needed) performance appraisals to monitor efficiency on the job. Teamwork should be emphasized as well.

Restaurant Delivery Methods

The three basic types of food delivery methods are quick-service (or self-service), full-service, and outside delivery, such as for pizza or catering.

Quick-Service.   Quick-service is normally associated with relatively simple menus such as fast food. With the hybridization of different restaurant concepts, this notion is changing. For example, Sweet Tomatoes, a restaurant chain based in San Diego, California, serves quality foods with what is generally referred to as island service (the customers serve themselves from various cold and hot display tables). Traditional quick-service consists of two styles, counter service and cafeteria service, with many variations on each.

Counter-service.   This is where the customer orders his or her own food and drink from the counter, pays for it, and receives it, all in one transaction. This is possible because the food has been prepared in advance. If the restaurant wants to serve customers fresher food, but still use self-service, one option is to take the customer's food and drink order at the counter, have the customer pay for it, give the customer the drink, give the order to the kitchen to be prepared, then call the customer's name or a number when the food is ready. Counter service can be enhanced by delivering the customer's order to their table.

Whether in quick- or full-service restaurants, *take-out orders* can be considered a form of quick- or counter-service. In diners of the 1950s and later, a counter, generally referred to as *the rail,* gave customers a faster option than sitting at a table and waiting for full-service. The counter was located next to the kitchen, to reduce service time.

Cafeteria service.   This is where customers select foods that have been cooked in advance from a series of hot and cold display tables. In traditional cafeteria service, customers pick up a food tray and silverware at the beginning of the

Exhibit 6.15   The ultimate in self-service, this inn provides breakfast each morning to guests. (Photo: Getty Images, Inc.—PhotoDisc.)

serving line, then customers select their meal from a large variety of options. Employees plate (dish) the food selection for each customer. Some foods, such as beverages, bread, and desserts may pre-portioned for self-service. Payment may be made at a cashier stand immediately after customers select their food (often at the end of the serving line) or when leaving the restaurant. If the latter method is used, a clerk at the end of the serving line gives each customer a receipt with the cost of each item ordered and the total.

A method that is gaining popularity is the all-you-can-eat buffet. Here the customer pays when entering the restaurant, then selects foods from various cold and hot display tables.

Full-Service.   In full-service, the customers sit at a table (or booth) and have all of their food and beverage needs met by a server. There are several full-service styles to choose from, the three major styles being French, Russian, and American service.

French service.   This service uses a two-server system, where one takes the order and serves the food and drinks, and the other takes the order to the kitchen, removes dishes, and replenishes drinks, bread, and butter. Food and drink are served from the customer's right and removed from the customer's left. Food is generally brought from the kitchen on a serving tray and put on plates at the table. A portion of the cooking or final heating of the food is often done in the dining room by a server using a small gas burner called a réchaud.

Russian service.   This is similar to French service except that there is one server instead of two.

American service.   Most restaurants use this style because it is more efficient, and requires less training and experience. All food is assembled on plates in the kitchen and carried to the table, either by hand or on a serving tray. Foods, including bread and butter, are served from the customer's left and removed from the customer's right. Drinks are served and removed from the customer's right. For booth service, all items are served to customers on the left with the server's right hand and to customers on the right with the server's left hand. The traditional silverware setting is, from left to right, salad fork, dinner fork, plate or place for one, a napkin on the plate or on the table in the center of the setting, dinner knife (cutting edge toward plate), butter knife, teaspoon, and soup spoon. Rolling silverware in a napkin is another popular method because the silverware does not gather dust and setting the table is easier and quicker. Servers can prep this when they have free time.

Delivery

Though home or office delivery has been associated with pizza, more and more restaurants are utilizing this service to increase sales. The vast majority of delivery is for one or a few people who want the convenience of having their lunch or dinner brought to them. Another form of delivery is catering, where a restaurant will prepare food for anywhere from a few to thousands of people. Imagine being asked to cater a Roman banquet for 5,000 people. An event such as this could require 3,000–4,000 pounds of food and cost the customers several hundred thousand dollars.

Seating Floor Plan

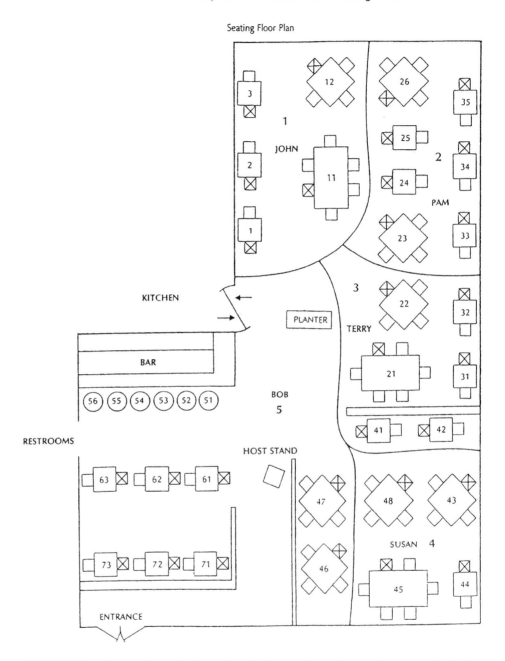

Exhibit 6.16A   A sample seating floor plan for the host stand to use in keeping track of seating rotation.

FORM 5–1 Waiting List

Name of Party	Number in Party	S/N/E*	Name of Party	Number in Party	S/N/E*

*(S = Smoking, N = Non-smoking, E = Either)

Exhibit 6.16B   A sample waiting list form.

Seating Floor Plan

A seating floor plan should be created for full-service restaurants (see Exhibit 6.16A). Ideally, an architect or drafter should draw the floor plan but, if this is not possible, restaurant management will have to draw it so that employees can locate numbered tables. The drawing should include tables, chairs, booth-type seating, entrance, exits, restrooms, the bar area, the food pick-up area (for take-out orders), and any other areas or items of importance to customers or employees. The copy used for service should be covered with plastic so that hosts can write on it with a grease pencil, then change it or wipe it clean as necessary. Some years ago, inventive restaurant operators placed this layout on a board and attached a small red light at each table. When a table was clean and ready for a customer, the light would be turned on. Modern technology takes this idea a step further with two-way communication between bussers and the seating display.

Each table is given a number to help employees identify its location. Numbers are normally assigned in groups or rows in the most logical sequence so that employees can easily remember them. Groups and rows generally begin with numbers 1, 11, 21, 31, and so forth. For example, on the seating floor plan in Exhibit 6-16A, Row #1 consists of table numbers 1 through 3, Row #2 consists of numbers 11 and 12, Row #3 consists of table numbers 21 through 26, and so on. Tables in any recognizable group are given their own series of numbers.

One seat or chair at each table is designated as "home base," (also known as the "pivot point"). This is normally the chair closest to the kitchen. For booths, it is always the first seat on the left. The server begins taking orders with the customer in this seat, then proceeds clockwise around the table. When orders are written in this sequence, any employee can deliver orders without having to ask who ordered what.

Management must decide on the number of stations or table groupings that a server will wait on. If, during the busiest period, each server has 4 tables and there is a total of 40 tables, there would be 10 stations (40 divided by 4). If 2 servers are working during the slowest period, the restaurant manager must develop 8 seating floor plans, dividing the dining room into 2 through 10 stations. That way, as servers leave for the day (known as "cutting stations"), the remaining servers will know what tables they are responsible for. At the beginning of the shift, the host records the server's name on their respective station. As stations are cut, and a seating floor plan with fewer stations is used, the remaining servers' names are written on their assigned stations.

Waiting Lists

If customers must wait for a table, their names should be recorded on a waiting list so that the host knows how many parties are waiting, how many customers are in each party, their smoking preference, and who should be seated next.

Each restaurant operator should create a waiting list that suits the restaurant's particular need. Exhibit 6.16B is intended for a casual restaurant because a limited amount of information is needed. In contrast, a more complex form may be needed for a more formal restaurant, to allow the host to calculate a more accurate waiting time and record at which table the party is seated.

Customer Complaints

Unfortunately, most customers do not complain when they are dissatisfied unless the problem is very serious. For this reason, management should make it convenient for customers to express their concerns. Customer complaints, both minor and serious, are an opportunity to uncover operational problems and to turn a negative situation into a positive one.

Servers and management must be visible and accessible to customers. Ideally, the manager should verbally or visibly (with a nod of the head or a smile) acknowledge each party of customers dining at the restaurant. Servers must check back with their customers and ask how everything was or whether a specific item was cooked to their liking. This approach allows the customer to voice his or her opinions—whether they are related to the meal or the service.

If a customer is dissatisfied and does not have the opportunity to talk to a restaurant employee, there is a very good chance that the customer will not return to the restaurant. In contrast, when the customer can air his or her complaints, this usually works to enhance the restaurant's reputation because that customer will probably tell his or her friends that the restaurant is eager to please its customers—plus, psychologically, the customer will feel that he or she has won a point.

Never argue with a customer. If a customer is loud, management should ask him or her to please speak more quietly. If a customer continues or does anything else to interfere with the dining experience of other customers, warn the customer that he or she will be asked to leave. If the customer refuses to quiet down, ask the customer to leave the restaurant. If the customer disregards this request, tell the customer you will have to call the police. If the customer remains after this statement, call the police immediately.

Unfortunately, you will not be able to make every customer happy. However, try to do everything possible to rectify complaints. Use the following four-step procedure to handle customer complaints.

Step 1: **Listen.** Listen calmly and earnestly to the customer without interrupting. Servers and other employees should get the manager immediately if the complaint is serious. If the problem is something the employee has the authority to handle, he or she should do so, but should notify the manager as soon as possible, before the customer leaves.

Step 2: **Clarify the complaint.** After the customer has stated the complaint, separate the emotion from the substance of the complaint. Restate the complaint to the customer to be sure that both of you agree on its substance. This will also reassure the customer that he or she has been understood. After repeating the complaint, make a follow-up statement such as "I'm going to take care of this for you right now," or whatever is appropriate.

Step 3: **Solve problems quickly, courteously, and quietly.** Most customers just want their meal to be as enjoyable as possible and do not want to make a scene.

Step 4: **Do not take any complaints personally.** Customers generally voice complaints about the meal or service. If a customer personally confronts you, ignore your personal feelings. Just concentrate on solving the problem and providing good service. Good, attentive service usually calms a customer down.

Server Sidework

Server sidework is the work that servers do, other than their primary serving tasks. This consists of restocking server work areas, refilling condiments, general cleaning of service areas, food preparation as required, and other duties as assigned by management. Each server should have sidework assignments that must be com-

Exhibit 6.17   Server side work is easily overlooked during the rush of peak business. Before and after the rush are the hours when servers clean and reorganize. (Photo by Marilyn McDonald)

pleted during the shift. Sidework lists should also be documented for the busser, host, and food coordinator. They have the same purpose as server sidework—to indicate the work the employee is responsible for other than primary tasks, except the lists are much shorter. The same basic methods described for server sidework can be used to complete sidework lists for other dining room employees. See, for example, the following partial busser sidework list below:

Opening busser sidework:

- Pick up trash around restaurant.
- Sweep sidewalk.
- Polish brass on front door.

During lunch and dinner:

- Empty trash cans in food pick-up area as needed.
- Check rest rooms (male bussers should ask female employee to check ladies' room; vice versa for female bussers).
- Toward the end of lunch, help dishwasher.

Continued for: after lunch, before dinner, and closing sidework.

Specific server sidework duties vary according to the type of restaurant. The best approach in deciding what the sidework duties are is to work through the following five steps:

Step 1: List all the various tasks that must be completed in the dining room, wait stations, and service areas before the restaurant opens for business. This is referred to as "opening sidework." Consider having the servers help the cooks by performing such duties as filling butter and salad dressing containers, and plating dinner salads and desserts.

Step 2: Divide the morning duties up among the number of stations for the first shift of the day. Try to assign similar types of work to each station so that servers can complete the work more efficiently. The average time for completion of each station's sidework should be about the same. In most cases, the sidework assignments for the first shift of the day should require the servers to arrive at work about 30 minutes before the restaurant opens.

Step 3: Decide what sidework will be assigned during meal periods. This is often called "running sidework." Running sidework mainly involves maintaining the supplies needed for proper service and minor cleaning duties. Divide this work equally among the servers.

Step 4: Make a list of the duties servers should complete at the end of the day's first shift. If a server is scheduled to leave early, do not assign that person a task that may have to be repeated later during the shift. The servers who leave early can, for example, clean and organize lower shelves in the food pick-up area, roll silverware into napkins, and re-stock certain items. Ideally, there should not be any beginning sidework for the servers for each succeeding shift, other than inspecting tables in their respective stations and making sure that all server areas are properly stocked for the shift. When beginning sidework is assigned to succeeding shifts, it should be composed primarily of tasks such as plating salads that must be completed as near serving time as possible.

Step 5: List the closing sidework for the cleaning and night shift. This usually consists of properly storing any food items, refilling table condiments, and cleaning the dining room, wait stations, and food pick-up areas.

Before an early server leaves, one of the late servers should initial that person's time card, signifying that the sidework has been completed. The late servers for breakfast or lunch should have the next shift's servers sign their cards before they leave. The closing shift's late servers should have the manager inspect their sidework and sign their time cards. All servers should have the manager sign their time cards before leaving.

The following is a sample of a restaurant's server sidework assignments. You may use these examples to develop your own list of sidework duties.

Opening Server Sidework

Station 1

- Stock food pick-up area with to-go napkins, Styrofoam containers, paper cups, lids, plastic silverware, salt and pepper packets, bags, and other items as required.
- Fold to-go silverware (plastic fork, spoon, and knife with salt and pepper packets) in a napkin, secured with a rubber band.
- Turn on roll warmer, adding distilled water if necessary.

All stations

* When you have finished your sidework, help other servers with theirs.

Running Sidework for All Shifts

Stations 1 and 2

* Keep the food pick-up area clean and orderly.
* Restock items as needed.

All stations

* Make tea and coffee as needed.
* Roll silverware into napkins.
* Help others if time permits.

End-of-Shift Sidework for Breakfast and Lunch

Stations 1 and 2 (leaving early)

* Wipe down all shelves in the food pick-up area.
* Restock items as needed.

All stations

* Fill and clean all table condiments in each respective station ($^3_4$ full is okay).
* Check that tables, chairs, booths, and wall areas in each station are clean.
* Roll 50 settings of silverware into napkins by the end of the shift.

Closing Server Sidework

Station 1 (leaving early)

* Clean all shelves below and above the food pick-up area.
* Clean crumbs from all bread baskets and napkins not in use, and replace dirty napkins.

EYE ON THE ISSUES

Diversity in the Workplace

Diversity can be defined as the human characteristics that make people different from one another. Food service operations have traditionally included employees from many nationalities and cultures. However, the value of and respect for these differences has varied greatly among different restaurants. Some of the many benefits of valuing diversity include the potential to improve corporate performance by fully integrating women and minorities in the business; attending to different views, which enhances creativity; improving the business's ability to solve problems; increasing organizational flexibility; and providing a competitive advantage over rivals who do not value and embrace diversity.

Stereotyping is essentially the opposite of diversity. This is seen in people who assume that group averages or tendencies hold true for each member of a group. Individual traits explain considerably more than group membership. For this reason, and since we should behave ethically and obey employment laws, we should judge people based on their personal and behavioral characteristics, rather than on assumptions based on their skin color or ethnic background.

Exhibit 6.18   Sanitation is the most important focus from back-of-the-house (the dishwasher, for example) to front (servers and bussers). (Photo by Christine Jaszay)

CLEANING AND SANITIZATION

Cleanliness for a restaurant means the absence of visible soil and food particles on the floor, the tables, or anywhere else in or around the building. *Sanitation* is the science of creating healthful and hygienic conditions.

Cleaning

A restaurant that is clean not only is attractive to customers, but shows them that management is concerned about serving them in a healthy environment. These qualities become more important when you consider that customers associate the cleanliness of the restaurant with the care taken to prepare the food. High standards of cleanliness also have a positive affect on employees, resulting in improved morale and increased production.

Sanitization

For a restaurant, sanitation focuses on wholesome food and beverages that are prepared and served in an environment free of disease-causing organisms and other harmful contaminants. The 24-hour flu we have all suffered through at one time or another may have been caused by a food-borne illness. Food-borne illness contracted at restaurants may go unreported because people often incorrectly assume that it's just a "touch of the flu," not realizing that everyone who ate that particular dish got the same unwelcome "touch." Consumers are generally more aware of a food-borne illness outbreak when it occurs after a family get-together when everyone gets sick. Children and the elderly can easily die from food-borne illnesses. For others, the symptoms range from minor discomfort to, in some cases, death.

Once word gets out in the community that a particular restaurant's food makes people sick, it is extremely difficult for it ever to regain consumer trust. In fact, restaurants often close after a publicized outbreak of foodborne illness. In health care institutions, outbreaks of food-borne illness are particularly dangerous because the patients may not be strong enough to recover from its effects. Aside from the obvious moral implications, avoiding food-borne illness is good business.

Fortunately, most food poisoning can be avoided through following relatively simple techniques, such as thoroughly washing your hands after touching meat products and frequently throughout the day, and immediately washing equipment that has come in contact with animal products. For example, if a knife were used to cut raw chicken and then used to cut lettuce, it would contaminate the lettuce. This is termed cross-contamination. A diner eating a salad with this lettuce would likely become ill.

Since the manager in a food service operation is responsible for serving food that is safe to eat, he or she is also responsible for instructing the staff in safe food-handling procedures. A good manager conducts ongoing inspections to maintain the standards of sanitation required for the production of safe food and monitors the personal hygiene of all people involved in the handling of food.

Every state has its own state board of health. Written regulations are available and must, by law, be followed. State and local inspections are conducted by appropriate agencies. These agencies have the power to impose fines and to force compliance. All food service operators are responsible for knowing the health department regulations in their own cities and states.

Exhibit 6.19   Safe food products start with a clean work surface. Some products (eggs, for example) can be especially hazardous. (Photo by Christine Jaszay)

Methods

Many surfaces in the restaurant, such as dining room tables, chairs, non-cloth booth seats and backs, table condiment containers, and kitchen equipment that cannot be moved to the dish machine or the three-compartment sink should be sanitized with a towel that is kept in a sanitizing solution (referred to as a sanitizing towel). This solution should contain at least 100 parts per million (100 PPM) of available chlorine (bleach) as a hypochlorite and be at a temperature of at least 75°F. For non–food contact surfaces—surfaces that do not come into contact with food—the solution can be 50 PPM. To be on the safe side, and so the restaurant does not have to keep two different strength of sanitizing solutions, the one solution strong enough for both food contact surfaces and non–food contact surfaces is recommended.

The most common sanitizing solution is chlorine bleach (5.25 percent sodium hypochlorite solution). One and one-quarter teaspoons, or approximately 1/2 capful of bleach per gallon of water, yields a 100 PPM solution. The strength of the solution of all sanitizing chemicals should not reach 200 PPM because at this level the solution becomes toxic. There are test kits available to test the strength of solutions.

When washing dishes manually, pots, pans, utensils, and small non-electrical equipment, use a three-compartment sink. First scrape the items to remove excess food or other deposits, then thoroughly wash them in the first sink, which should contain a hot detergent solution. The second sink should contain clean water for rinsing. The third sink is for sanitizing; it should either contain 170°F water (submerse item for 30 seconds) or an approved sanitizing solution, such as chlorine bleach, at a strength of 50 PPM (submerse item for one minute). When there are only a few items to be cleaned and sanitized, use a two-compartment sink. Wash the item in the first sink, rinse it under running water, then place it in the second sink for sanitizing.

When items are to be machine washed, first scrape off food or other deposits from the items. Pre-soak silverware in a bus tub or other container with a special solution or general cleanser. Sort like items in dish racks, and do not overload the racks; this is especially critical for silverware. Rinse off dishes or utensils before placing them in the dishwasher. Place the rack in the machine and turn it on. The soap will be dispensed automatically by most machines. The sanitizing rinse must be either water at 180°F (a booster heater is needed) or an automatically dispensed sanitizer at no less than 75°F. Make sure the dish machine does not run out of soap or sanitizer. When removing dishes, let them air dry for a minute or two before taking them from the rack. Do not use a towel to dry dishes.

Cleaning and sanitation standards and methods that cover all needs of the restaurant should be provided to employees. The cleaning and sanitization of tables, booths, and chairs are provided as an example.

Tables, Booths, and Chairs

Standard.   Tables, booths, and chairs should be free of grease, food particles, soil, scuff-marks, and dust buildup. Table condiments, table tents, and decorations (such as flowers and vases) should be clean and free of dust, grease, and food.

Method.   When the customer has left the table, put all remaining dirty dishes, silverware, and glasses in the bus tub. Clean the entire table with a sanitized towel, moving condiments so that the table can be cleaned underneath them. If table-cloths are used, replace them if there are any visible wrinkles, spills, or soil. Crumbs can be brushed off and the tablecloth re-used if the tablecloth is otherwise clean. Clean the condiment containers and return them to their normal positions. Wipe any crumbs off the seats after the table is clean. Tables, booths, and chairs should be thoroughly cleaned every week. Use a general cleanser and a cleaning towel for most materials. Rinse with clean water and a towel, then dry with a third towel. Check under tables for chewing gum.

Weekly Cleaning and Maintenance.   Certain areas of the kitchen and pieces of equipment need to be cleaned on a weekly basis, rather than each day. Compile a list of these items with basic cleaning directions, known as the weekly cleaning and maintenance schedule, and post it in the kitchen. Management and kitchen staff should decide which day each task should be completed. Slower days, such as Sunday, Monday, and Tuesday, are usually good times for cleaning and mainte-nance tasks. To make sure the tasks are completed, assign each in one of the fol-lowing ways:

- Require that, before any cooks can clock out, they must complete the items on the weekly cleaning and maintenance schedule that are assigned to their shift.
- Each shift, have the manager or kitchen shift leader personally assign respon-sibilities.
- Have the manager responsible for preparing the cook's schedule designate on the schedule who is responsible for each cleaning and maintenance task. The manager can place a circled number on the cook's schedule that corresponds to an item on the weekly cleaning and maintenance schedule. The initials in the cook's day box denote the position or station that will be worked that day; for example, B stands for broiler, F for fryer, and P for pantry.

CONTROL OF FOODSERVICE SANITIZATION AND THE HACCP

The United States Food and Drug Administration has developed standardized methods of minimizing food-borne illness, called HACCP. The Educational Founda-tion of the National Restaurant Association, and city and county health departments throughout the United States, promote understanding and use of HACCP to protect restaurant patrons and employees from food-borne illness. These operational areas include receiving, storage, preparation, cooking, and holding.

CONCLUSION

This chapter presented a review of many of the important topics in restaurant man-agement. One of the first steps in creating a restaurant is to design the menu. The most important consideration in the design of a menu is that it satisfy the demands of the food service operation's customers. Next are the concepts of purchasing food items, receiving, and storing them. Operators who pay too much for products, experience theft because of poor receiving practices, or store products at the wrong temperature, will reduce their chances of producing a profit. Food preparation must be managed so that the desired products are produced under safe and sanitary conditions, with minimum waste. Customer service must be executed in a courteous and efficient manner compatible with the customer satisfaction. Finally, the restaurant must be kept both clean (free of debris) and sanitary (healthful and hygienic conditions). Operating a restaurant is one of the most challenging endeavors imaginable. However, through the attention to appropriate details, all challenges can be successfully managed.

CORE CONCEPTS

operations   232
purchasing   241
receiving   242
storage   242
food preparation/cooking   246
station set-up   246
menu assembly guidelines   247

food waste   247
Occupation Safety and Health Act   249
customer service   250
customer complaints   255
server sidework   256
cleaning and sanitation   260

DISCUSSION QUESTIONS

1. In the context of a restaurant's organization chart, what does the term *operations* mean?
2. Do you feel that it is necessary to have a college degree to manage a restaurant? Support your answer.
3. Explain why a restaurant's menu affects almost everything that happens there.
4. Other than fuel for the body, what is the importance of food to people?
5. You are responsible for preparing a menu for a restaurant that is similar to Bennigan's (or Outback Steakhouse, Friday's, or the restaurant of your choosing). What information do you think you would need from customers?
6. Discuss the importance of nutrition in: (a) fast-food restaurants; (b) full-service restaurants.
7. You are the consultant for a new full-service restaurant. The owner says that she wants to have 100 entrees. What recommendations might you give her, and how would you support your recommendations?
8. You are going to open your own restaurant. You have designed the menu, but now you must set prices. Describe how you would do this.

9. You work for a seafood restaurant that does not have policies concerning any element of food management. Food costs are very high. Prepare a game plan focused on correcting the food cost problem.

10. At what temperatures must frozen foods, refrigerated foods, and dry goods be stored?

11. What is the main purpose of food preparation sheets?

12. Prepare a list of procedures that will minimize food waste in your seafood restaurant.

13. What are the two primary components of customer service? Describe a recent pleasant dining experience and an unpleasant one, based on how well these components were executed.

14. A. Explain the concept, "Management should make it convenient for customers to complain."
    B. A customer complains about poor service. What steps should you take to handle this?

15. What is the difference between cleanliness and sanitation?

CASE STUDY

McDonald's profits have been falling for the past year and a half. Several reasons for the drop were given, including the slow economy and the fact that 11 percent of its customers were dissatisfied and complained about their experience. This number did not include the customers who did not complain. A major restructuring of its U.S. units has included laying off 700 of its approximately 7,000-person corporate staff, closing up to 250 restaurants, and placing an increased focus on customer satisfaction. Additionally, more frequent inspections of restaurants by corporate personnel and mystery shoppers will begin soon and three new restaurant concepts are being added: Mexican, Homestyle, and French restaurants. To help with sagging sales, McDonald's will be also adding new food products and is considering the sale of non-food products in its restaurants; no suggestion has yet been made as to what these products would be. Past examples included Teenie Beanie Babies, commemorative glasses, LA Lakers watches, and prepaid telephone calling cards. One franchisee stated that the non-food products hurt service and that he got stuck with unsold merchandise. When asked about Burger King's introduction of a veggie burger, McDonald's chairman and chief executive thought that the time was not right for it (Zuber, 2001; Zuber, 2002a; Zuber, 2002b).

Required

1. McDonald's has 13,000 U.S. restaurants in excellent locations. Is there a way they can offer non-food products without slowing down their service times, having left-over inventory, or hurting their image as a food service establishment?

2. Should McDonald's add a veggie burger to its menu?

3. Based on this case study and your personal experiences, what other changes should McDonald's do to help it get out of its slump?

REFERENCES

Zuber, A. (2001). "McD Sees 16% Profit Drop, Eyes Closing 250 Stores." *Nation's Restaurant News, 35*(32), 1, 6.

Zuber, A. (2002a). "McD Shareholders Unexpectedly Calm at Annual Meeting." *Nation's Restaurant News, 32*(22), 6.

Zuber, A. (2002b). "Fast Fix? McD Eyes Nonfood on Its Menu." *Nation's Restaurant News, 36*(23), 1, 96.

The Attorney Says

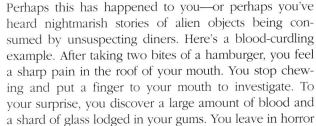

Perhaps this has happened to you—or perhaps you've heard nightmarish stories of alien objects being consumed by unsuspecting diners. Here's a blood-curdling example. After taking two bites of a hamburger, you feel a sharp pain in the roof of your mouth. You stop chewing and put a finger to your mouth to investigate. To your surprise, you discover a large amount of blood and a shard of glass lodged in your gums. You leave in horror and upon your arrival at the emergency room are told by the oral surgeon that you will need extensive reconstructive surgery to repair the deep wound in your mouth. After months of visits to the surgeon and indescribable suffering, your mouth begins to feel better, but it will never be the same.

How did a piece of glass get into that hamburger? Are the injuries you suffered the fault of the establishment from which you purchased the hamburger? Maybe the glass was there when they received the meat from their supplier. What about your enormous doctor bills and all of the time you missed from work due to your surgeries? These are questions that might arise when you bring a civil suit against the restaurant for your damages.

It's beyond the scope of this text to describe the various remedies of law that you might rightfully pursue in such a case—though you will encounter such fascinating details if you take a course in hospitality law. Most

Exhibit 1   The all too familiar, but very necessary, slogans against under-age drinking not only protect the consumers; they protect the operation that serves alcohol. (*Courtesy:* The Century Council)

everyone has heard about the woman who sued McDonald's after she spilled extremely hot coffee on herself. Can you say that this was McDonald's fault? Or was it solely her fault for being clumsy? What if the coffee that McDonald's serves was extremely hot—much hotter than what is normally served by most restaurants? Maybe McDonald's did act unreasonably, when it allowed its coffee to be served at such a high temperature. Suffice it to say that unfortunate injuries do happen all the time. There is a very real possibility that you or your company will at some point serve food to a customer that might be termed "unfit for human consumption." It is also true that restaurants are often found liable if their customers are injured by an item of food that the restaurants served to them. Needless to say, proper inspection and preparation of food products is essential. (See Chapters 5 and 6 for more discussion on food safety.)

LIQUOR LIABILITY

Spirituous Liquors

As you are aware, the sale of spirituous liquors forms a very large segment of the hospitality industry. From the five-star resort that offers an upscale piano bar, beer service to golfers on the course, and minibars in each guest room to the hole in the wall neighborhood tavern, the sale of liquor is a huge industry. From a legal standpoint, there are two main issues regarding the selling of liquor.

Licensing. Every state has laws that regulate the sale of alcoholic beverages. Basically, according to these laws, it is illegal to sell liquor without first obtaining a license from the state. States offer many different types of licenses, and you must obtain the type that permits the sales in which you intend to engage. For example, you can obtain an on-premise sale license for a bar. For a liquor store, an off-premise license would be required. A restaurant license allows operators who derive most of their income from food to also sell liquor. Licenses may be granted to hotels, microbreweries, or even excursion boats.

To obtain a license, you must apply to the state liquor authority. If a license is granted, you may then engage in the activities that are permitted by that license. Each state will have detailed rules and regulations with which you must comply. If you do not, the state will either suspend or revoke your license. These rules vary greatly from state to state, but usually they specify the following:

- The hours of the day during which sales are permitted
- The number of drinks one person may be served at a time
- Whether or not employees are permitted to drink, or even purchase drinks for patrons

Needless to say, you must know the rules in the state where you operate very well and strictly comply with them, and obey federal regulations (see Exhibit 2).

Dram Shop Liability. The other issue that surfaces all too often is that of dram shop liability. To understand what is meant by dram shop liability, we must look at a simple set of facts. Picture this: After dinner one evening, you get into your car and are on your way to basketball practice. It is dark outside, but the roads are dry, and visibility is good. You are on a two-lane highway and see a car approaching you. For the most part, it is staying on its side of the road, but you do observe that it is swerving within its lane. As it gets closer, it strays across the double yellow line. You do what you can to avoid the oncoming vehicle and swerve to your right; however, a head-on collision is unavoidable. Fortunately, you were wearing your seat belt and you were not ejected from the vehicle. You did sustain serious back, neck, and leg injuries. After a number of months of rehabilitation, you recover, but are told you will suffer some permanent leg problems that will cause you to walk with a slight limp.

The police send you a copy of their accident report. Upon reading it, you discover that on the night of the accident the driver of the vehicle that hit you (let's call him Mr. Drunk) had been at a local bar. It seems likely that had he not been killed in the accident, he would have been guilty of drunk driving.

As you consider the events of that night, you become curious as to why Mr. Drunk lost control of his car. Did his steering fail? Did one of his tires blow out? The accident report indicates no such problems. You wonder if he simply had too much to drink at the local bar. You go to the bar and speak to the bartender who was on duty that night. He informs you that between the hours of 4:00 PM (the beginning of happy hour) and 6:00 PM, when Mr. Drunk left the bar, he had consumed six double scotches. Before being served drink number six, he had tried to

Exhibit 2   Alcoholic beverages must carry the warning against the dangers of alcohol consumption. (Photos by James L. Morgan, Scottsdale.)

stand up to go to the restroom but had fallen flat on his face. Upon being helped to his seat, he said, "Gee, I shouldn't have fallen like that. I must need another drink!" He was promptly served double scotch number six. He left the bar after that drink. The accident occurred 10 minutes later.

Now, with that story in mind, do you think that the bar, not just the drinker, should be held responsible to you for your injuries? The liability of the bar for those injuries is what we refer to as *dram shop liability.* (*Dram shop is* another term derived from old England. A dram is a unit of liquid measurement equal to approximately one ounce or one shot. A dram shop was a bar, a shop that served liquor by the dram; hence the term.)

Each state has its own laws regarding a bar's liability to an innocent victim of a person to whom they served liquor. Some states take the position that the bar should have no responsibility. Their reasoning is that it was not the bar that caused the injuries. Rather, it was the person who got in the car and drove while impaired. Other states take the position that the bar can be liable if it served the drinker a drink when that person was already drunk. Their reasoning is that it should be obvious to bartenders that if they serve a patron who is already intoxicated, he or she may operate a motor vehicle irresponsibly and cause an accident, injuring another driver or pedestrian. Therefore, the bar must not serve such persons; they must be "cut off."

Unfortunately, our Mr. Drunk scenario is all too real. Due largely to the lobbying efforts of groups such as Mothers Against Drunk Driving (MADD) and Students Against Drunk Driving (SADD), many states have adopted a "zero tolerance" policy. Many have lowered the threshold blood-alcohol level necessary to convict someone for driving under the influence (DUI). Many have also greatly increased their enforcement efforts. It is imperative that all hospitality operators be familiar with the dram shop liability imposed upon them by the state in which they operate and that they comply strictly with the law. The service of alcoholic beverages is a very important part of the hospitality industry, and can be very profitable. However, due to the nature of alcohol as a drug that can cause severe impairment, it must be dealt with appropriately.

The Techie Says

Computer systems are tools for solving problems. The systems used in the hospitality industry help us solve our problems by helping us use our resources more efficiently, which in turn improves our profitability in both the lodging and the food service sectors. Some of the key advantages of a computerized information system include:

- Improved labor productivity and organizational efficiency
- Enhanced decision-making capabilities
- Reduced operating costs
- Increased information accuracy
- Increased revenues
- Greater guest satisfaction
- Improved controls

COMPUTER-BASED FOOD AND BEVERAGE SYSTEMS

To compete effectively in the markets of today and tomorrow, all members of the restaurant production and service teams must act in concert, so as ultimately to deliver quality products at the right prices to the right guests at the right times. Failure to do so can result in excess inventory, poor food quality, poor guest service, underutilized capacity, and unnecessary cost.

Restaurant technology helps management monitor and coordinate these activities in a more timely and focused manner.

Service Applications—Front of the House

ECR/POS Hardware. The technology available today changes the way in which restaurants process and monitor transactions. More and more often restaurants are choosing point-of-sale (POS) systems or their slightly simpler cousin, the electronic cash register (ECR). A POS system can enhance decision-making, operational control, guest service, and revenues.

A *POS system* is a network of cashier and server terminals that typically handle food and beverage orders, the transmission of orders to the kitchen and bar, the settlement of guest checks, time-keeping, and interactive charge posting to guest folios. POS information can also be imported to accounting and food cost/inventory software packages.

The selection of a POS system should be based on the needs of the restaurant. These needs should be evaluated in a systematic manner, preferably using a checklist. Several questions need to be answered in the selection process:

- How quickly must orders be processed?
- Which system provides the most effective interaction?
- How will menu changes be handled?
- How many preset keys are needed?
- What should the POS terminal set-up be?

If the POS system is being added to an existing system, it is important to verify compatibility and interface ability. The POS system will also need to be protected by passwords and secured against power fluctuations.

Some large operations are exploring the use of hand-held order entry terminals that allow the staff to enter orders while they are at the guest table. The system uses radio signals to communicate with a base station from which the order is sent on to the appropriate prep area. This allows the servers to spend more time with guests, as they do not have to go back and forth to the kitchen or the terminal. A silent paging system informs the server when the order is ready.

Management Applications—Back of the House

Menu Management. Menu management applications help management answer questions about pricing menu items; about the menu mix at which profit is maximized; whether any menu items need to be removed, re-priced, or changed; and how menu changes can be evaluated. Information from the ECR/POS system and from other applications can be used to facilitate this process.

Recipe Management. Recipe management applications maintain data on recipe ingredients, preparation methods, cost, and sales prices.

Sales Analysis. Sophisticated ECR/POS systems can store files that contain important data regarding daily operations. When the ECR/POS system is connected to a fully integrated restaurant management system, this information can be accessed by computer-based management applications such as the sales analysis application. The sales analysis application can sort or combine data into a variety of reports to help management direct daily operations.

Integrated Restaurant Systems.   The limitations of *non*-integrated restaurant systems are apparent. Since data must be entered several times, often at different stations, the time spent on this task is enormous and information may not reach managers on time. Integrated food service systems allow data to pass seamlessly from one application to another. Since data are entered only once, input time is saved, accuracy is increased, and decisions that hinge on these data can be made in a more timely manner. As a result, the operation can function more efficiently.

HOTEL FOOD SERVICE TECHNOLOGY APPLICATIONS

Outlet Point-of-Sale System

As discussed in our lodging unit, hotel food service outlets and bars also use POS systems that may be interfaced with the hotel's property management system. This interface allows for the direct posting of food and beverage charges to the guest folio. It also provides a convenience to guests, who often prefer to pay all of their expenses on their credit card at departure, rather than pay for meals or beverages individually. This feature may also increase sales, since guests at a poolside outlet or in a spa may sign for items when they do not have their wallets with them.

Hotel Sales and Food Service Catering Applications

The sales and catering department of a hotel generates large amounts of paperwork, and people spend a great deal of time managing this paperwork. Sales and catering contacts must be recorded, client files maintained, function contracts prepared and distributed to different departments, correspondence sent out, and meetings conducted. Since one of the strong points of computers is the handling of large amounts of data, this area has been ripe for computerization. Sales and food service catering applications expedite many tedious tasks. Sales information can be accessed instantaneously, the risk of human error is reduced, and communication with clients (as well as with employees and other departments) is enhanced. Good systems can free up sales or catering department staffers to concentrate on selling their department's services, instead of slogging through paperwork.

REFERENCES

Chervenak, L., "Hotel Technology at the Start of the New Millennium." *Hospitality Research Journal 17,* no. 1 (1993).

Collins, G., C. Cobanoglu, & T. Malik, *Hospitality Information Technology: Learning How to Use It.* Dubuque, IA: Kendall/Hunt Publishing Company, 2003.

Kasavana, M. L., and J. J. Cahill, *Managing Computers in the Hospitality Industry,* 2nd ed. East Lansing, MI: Educational Institute of the American Hotel & Motel Association, 1997.

PART III

Introduction to Components of the Travel and Tourism Industry

There are many hospitality career opportunities that sometimes escape the notice of hospitality management students. This section discusses some of those by placing the hospitality industry within the broader context of travel and tourism.

Each of the many service-oriented businesses discussed in this book contributes to making a tourist's travel experience more satisfactory. The hospitality industry is not only a sector, but an integral part, of the travel and tourism industry. It offers travelers comfortable overnight stays and memorable dining experiences. As a hospitality manager, therefore, it is important to know the functions of and relationships among the different sectors in the travel and tourism industry. Once you view the travel and tourism industry as a functional system, you will be in a better position to anticipate changes in the industry and predict how they will affect your operation. Knowledge about people's travel behavior will give you a "leg up" on the competition, and such foresight will enable you to plan and position your business better.

Chapters 7, 8, and 9 discuss many aspects of the travel and tourism industry. Chapter 7 stresses the importance of understanding the travel and tourism industry as a functional system. It looks at the history of travel and tourism and defines the terminologies commonly used in travel and tourism studies. It places the hospitality industry within the larger parameters of travel and tourism, and presents you with the concept of the "sustainable tourism system."

Chapter 8 focuses on the specialized world of resorts, clubs, attractions, events and cruise lines. It compares resort hotels with non-resorts and offers insight into the unique management aspects associated with seasonal events. This chapter also opens the door to a segment often overlooked by hospitality programs—that of private club management, one of the fastest growing hospitality specialties. Resorts, clubs, attractions, events and cruiselines have the drawing power to pull tourists to destinations and are vital to the success of the tourism industry.

Chapter 9 explores gaming and casino management, the fastest growing segment of the hospitality industry in the United States. It starts out by tracing the history of gaming, explains how governments are involved in the regulation of the gaming industry, and discusses current gaming developments. The chapter describes the mathematics of gaming and analyzes management responsibilities associated with operating and controlling casinos. Students interested in management opportunities in gaming will find this an interesting introduction to this dynamic segment of the industry.

In particular with regard to the Gaming and Casino Management chapter it is important to focus your attention on technology, accounting, and the law, which is why the accountant, the techie, and the lawyer feature prominently once again at the end of the unit to share some important information.

Linking Hospitality to Travel and Tourism

As a future hospitality manager, your responsibilities will extend beyond the doors of your hotel or restaurant because hospitality businesses are an integral part of the communities in which they operate. They provide a valued service both to residents in the community in which you operate, and to those who travel to the community. This chapter will help you to understand how the hospitality industry fits in with the travel and tourism industry as a whole, and how it is part of the community in which it operates. Think about it: Are all guests in hotels and restaurants travelers or tourists? Certainly some of your customers will be from the local community, but what about the others? Are they travelers or tourists? Is there a difference between a "traveler" and a "tourist"? Technically, a visitor must spend at least one night away from home to be considered a tourist. A traveler is any person on a trip between two or more locations.[1] While all travelers can not be considered tourists, we will use the two terms interchangeably as we embark on this journey through the field of travel and tourism. Off we go into the wild unknown . . .

Outline

INTRODUCTION

The hospitality industry is a large and important component of the *travel and tourism* industry, which is one of the largest industries in the world. It is the largest services export industry in the U.S, the third largest retail sales industry, and one of America's largest employers. Approximately one out of every eight U.S. residents is employed in a job related to travel and tourism. The most prominent characteristics of this industry are its diversity and fragmentation. Many different types of services are required and desired by people who are away from home.

The travel and tourism industry is a system that consists of many interdependent components. This concept can be best understood by considering the theoretical spring break trip to Miami, Florida you took last year. Each of the components of the system is printed in italics.

Before you began your trip, you went to *Campus Travel* to purchase an airline ticket and to make a car rental and hotel reservation. Or, as a modern comsumer, you went on-line and purchased your ticket directly through *Cheap Tickets.com,* or *Expedia.com.* Your hotel reservation was made at *Hotels.com* or directly on the site of *Holiday Inn Hotels.com.* Then, you flew *American Airlines* to Miami and picked up a *Budget* rental car at the *airport* to drive to the beachfront *Holiday Inn.* That afternoon, you drove through *Biscayne National Park.* At night, you and your friends had dinner at *TGI Fridays,* and afterward strolled along a particular stretch of beach that was recommended by the *Miami Convention and Visitor Bureau* in their *brochure* specifically designed for spring breakers. You bought several souvenirs at a retail shop called *Little Havana.* Later, you and your friends went out to meet some people, but did not know where to go. You asked a *local resident* where the coolest place in town to hang out was, and she advised you to go to *Charley's Bar and Grill.* You danced and partied until the wee hours of the morning, being served by *local employees.* Finally, because you don't drink and drive on principle, you took a *taxi* back to the hotel at 4:00 AM.

This description of a typical tourist day in Miami vividly demonstrates that your travel needs could not be met without the services of travel agents, airlines, car rental companies, lodging accommodations, food services, attractions, retail services and local residents, to name a few.

You can use this hypothetical trip to help you understand that tourism is a system that is similar to your own body in which the various parts depend on others for their existence: The lungs collect the oxygen that the heart pumps through your veins, and which is used makes the muscles work. The airlines (the veins) transport tourists, who are booked on-line or by travel agents (the lungs) to the hotels and restaurants at a particular destination (the muscles). But, if the hotels and restaurants were not there, there would be no passengers for the airlines and, of course, there would be neither if there were no attractions to draw visitors to the destination. Vice versa, if the airlines would not bring in visitors, local hotels and restaurants would have a tough time surviving. This interdependency makes the financial trouble that our national airlines are in at the moment really a national problem, and it is one of the reasons why the federal government and Congress are willing to support the airlines with billions of dollars of loans and guarantees! It is not just that United Airlines or American Airlines are going bankrupt; it is all the travel, tourism, hospitality and destination industries that are suffering.

Another important component of the system that the hospitality industry is part of is the community that provides the employees and the infrastructure needed to create a tourist destination. Without local residents working Charley's Bar and Grill and driving the taxis, the system would not be functioning.

So it is important for hospitality managers to understand each of the components of the tourism industry—the tourist, the services, and the community. If you, as a future manager, do not understand the interconnections between all segments of the travel and tourism industry, you will not be able to anticipate and react to changes in your environment. An understanding of travel and tourism as a system will enhance your perspective on the entire industry. It will improve your ability to analyze industry trends and develop successful working relationships with other components of the industry. For example, restaurants and hotels in destination areas can work together with the local Conventions and Visitors Bureau and local theme parks to develop discount packages that might attract visitors to a certain area. The ability to see "the big picture" will make you a better manager, and it will help you attract more customers, be a better employer, and earn higher profits for your business.

A SUSTAINABLE TOURISM SYSTEM

The existence and vitality of the hospitality industry requires that the tourism system be designed and managed in a sustainable manner, and be part of a **sustainable tourism system.** When the traveler, the services and the community each believe they are receiving something of equal or better value than what they are giving, the industry can flourish and prosper. However, if one component does

Exhibit 7.1   The Alkmaar Cheese market in Holland attracts thousands of visitors every week. (*Courtesy:* Will Verbeeten, Foto Verbeeten, Groesbeek, The Netherlands)

not feel it is receiving as much as it is giving, the system is not sustainable. For example, if visitors feel they are not receiving value for their dollar, they will not return and are likely to create negative word of mouth, which will then discourage other tourists from visiting the destination. The resultant decline in the number of visitors decreases profits for the tourism businesses and jobs and income for the community. Likewise, if the community feels that visitors are damaging their environment and hurting their quality of life, the residents are likely to demand regulations that may make it unprofitable for businesses to operate.

To ensure a vigorous and prosperous industry, all three components must work together as a whole to achieve a win-win-win system. Have a look at Exhibit 7.2, which provides a picture of the tourism system in which the hospitality industry operates. Note that each component is equal in size to the others. This equal size signifies that each is equally important to the whole.

When they are on the road, either for business or pleasure, ***travelers*** exchange money for products, services, and experiences, and expect to receive value for their dollar. ***Services*** provide those products, services, and experiences in exchange for dollars, and must receive enough money in exchange to make it profitable to provide what the tourist desires. Finally, the ***community*** in which the "traveler" and "services" components operate receives income in the form of tax revenues, and payroll for its local population, whose members work in the industry, in exchange for sharing its human, natural, and cultural resources with the "traveler" and "service" components. Travelers will not come to a destination that does not provide value for their dollar. Services will not operate if they can not do so profitably, and the community will not be willing to share its resources if the traveler and/or the services cause social or environmental degradation that negatively impacts the quality of life. Clearly, if any one part of the system does not feel that the exchange is fair, the system is likely to break down, resulting in a poor experience for the traveler, lower profits for the service providers, and a lower quality of life for the community.

The remainder of this chapter examines each component of the sustainable tourism system in greater detail by describing some of their most common characteristics, and places the hospitality industry within these parameters.

The Traveler

The travelers that come into your place of business will be visiting your community for a variety of reasons. Knowledge about why they visit your place of business, and in particular advance knowledge, will help you to develop effective marketing

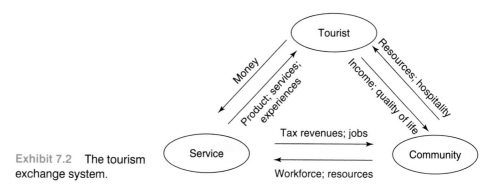

Exhibit 7.2   The tourism exchange system.

Service Excellence

The demographic makeup of our customers and guests is changing. Ethnic minorities now makeup nearly one-third of the population of the United States. In the past decade alone, the number of Hispanics in the United States has grown 45 percent and the number of African Americans has increased by 12 percent. The fastest growing minority segment is the Asian–American population, growing at 5.2 percent annually. This growth in population is accompanied by a growth in income and, consequently, spending on travel. As an industry professional, you will need to know the service preferences of these groups. Generally speaking, minorities want the same experience as all others—to feel welcome at your property. Along with a genuine smile and pleasantries, they want to see people that look like them in management positions and in collateral material (i.e., brochures, tent cards, and flyers). Like everyone else, they want to eat food they are used to. This is a particular challenge for the food service industry because many of what we consider ethnic foods are actually very different in taste and texture from what your minority clients may be used to. Of course, most important, they want to be treated with the courtesy and respect given to any other customer. Hospitality businesses that take the time to learn about and service the special needs of these guests will profit not only from increased sales, but from a feeling that they are treating all of their customers in the same courteous manner.

and service delivery strategies. As a hospitality manager, you will be working to serve the needs of two general categories of travelers: the business traveler and the leisure, or pleasure, traveler. Each of these presents different challenges.

Business Travelers   Business travelers are likely to require the service you provide because they are attending a meeting, a conference or a convention, because they are making sales or service calls on their customers, or because they are otherwise engaged in their business enterprise. Nearly two-thirds (64 percent) of these business travelers stay in hotels and motels. On average, a business traveler stays 3.3 nights on each business trip in a hotel.[2] Business travel is considered **non-discretionary travel** because the guest has little choice about either where or when to travel. If a conference is being held in Seattle, Washington, for instance, the business traveler must go to Seattle rather than a destination of choice. Similarly, if a sales prospect is located in Wilmington, Delaware, the business traveler must go there if he or she hopes to make the sale.

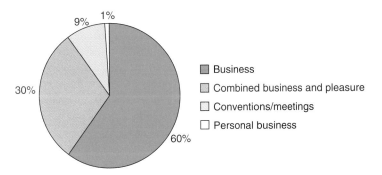

Exhibit 7.3   Primary purpose of business trip.

Approximately 9 percent of all business travel is undertaken to attend meetings, conferences, and conventions in order to learn about new products, to gain new skills, to make contacts, to demonstrate new products or, often, to meet and to learn about the competition. Persons other than businesspeople who attend meetings, conferences and conventions may be members of social, military, educational, religions or fraternal organizations. Hospitality and tourism professionals tend to refer to these groups as SMERFS (social, military, educational, religious, fraternal). Their interests and motivation for traveling are different from those of the individual who travels as part of a job. They are more likely to decide whether or not to attend the conference based on its location, the quality of the property where the conference is being held, the quality of the program, and on the opportunities for leisure experiences. Because gatherings of this type are often held in popular destinations in order to attract more participants, those who attend are likely to stay a few days longer and combine pleasure with the business at hand.

Several aspects of business travel make this a valuable market for hospitality entrepreneurs and managers. The business traveler is different from the leisure traveler in that the number of travelers is less variable and less seasonal. In other words, the demands of business travel are more constant and relatively consistent when compared to leisure travel. Although the number of business travelers will decline during poor economic times, the decline will be less dramatic in this market than in the pleasure travel market, as we have seen in the years after 9/11, when business travel rebounded more quickly than leisure travel.

Leisure Travelers   Leisure, as opposed to business, travel is **discretionary travel**, since the leisure traveler, to a great extent, can determine when and where to go. The leisure traveler is more likely to put off traveling when there is concern about the stability of employment or the economy in general than the business traveler. While business travel is not seasonal, the same is not true about the leisure travel market. The leisure traveler is not likely to select Phoenix, Arizona as a destination for a pleasure trip during the summer months, when temperatures often rise above 100 degrees. However, sales calls, consulting, and meetings are required regardless of the heat.

Hospitality businesses and tourism destinations identify and market to specific travel segments. For marketing purposes, pleasure or leisure travelers are classified by geographic, demographic, and pychographic characteristics. Exhibit 7.4 helps you understand the basic elements in each category; use this list to describe yourself on your last trip. This exercise will help you better to understand target market classifications.

Geographic Characteristics.   As a hospitality manager, you are most likely to have guests from areas closest to your home community, and as the distance between your property and the place of origin of potential guests increases, the likelihood of their visiting your community decreases. It is critical for a hospitality business to know the *geographic* origin of its guests in order to properly place advertisements.

Demographic Characteristics.   Information about travelers' demographic characteristics (for instance age, occupation, income, family situation, education, gender, ethnicity, and religion) may help a business design specific products, services

Geographic
   Place of residence
   Traffic patterns
Demographic
   Age
   Marital status
   Number of children
   Age of children
   Stage in life-cycle
   Education
   Family income
   Occupation
   Health
Psychographics
   Motivations
   Values
   Interests
   Activities
   Lifestyle

Exhibit 7.4   Characteristics for identifying target markets.

Exhibit 7.5   The cruise line industry has contributed considerably to tourism revenues in many countries, in this case Italy. (*Courtesy:* Princess Cruises)

International

The growth of the world economy has created an increase in international tourism. Between 6 percent and 10 percent of travel clients will come from a foreign country. While most of these will be from our neighbors, Canada and Mexico, a large portion will come from the United Kingdom, Germany, and Japan. International pleasure travelers often travel in groups, but we are now seeing a decline in the percent of the total overseas travelers using packaged travel. First-time travelers often prefer a packaged tour, but experienced travelers are likely to be traveling on their own.

Historically, overseas travelers to the United States were very mobile once in country, utilizing rental cars and domestic air carriers to visit multiple destinations. This appears to be declining, as experienced international travelers, becoming familiar with the nation, visit fewer locations and stay in one location longer. The international market is also attractive because the international traveler generally stays longer and spends more money.

International travelers present new challenges for the hospitality professional, such as understanding the cultural preferences of various nationalities and learning foreign languages. Indeed, hospitality managers of the future must have an enhanced global perspective.

and promotional materials that attract and retain customers. Consider how the type of activities and amenities offered at any tourist destination determines the age group most likely to be interested in visiting that destination. For instance, the mean age of the visitor to outdoor physical recreation areas such as a beach is likely to be lower than it will be in areas that offer less physically demanding activities, while the mean age of visitors to show/theater destinations is likely to be even higher. Consequently, brochures for hospitality products in a destination like Cancun, Mexico would most appropriately feature venues of younger, more athletic beach and water activities. On the other hand, information materials for hospitality products in Branson, Missouri, where the average age of the visitor approaches 55, will likely feature pictures of that age group in appropriate dinner theater and night club settings. So, now think about it: What destination is likely to include children in their publicity materials? What destination might to include African Americans in brochures advertising its attraction?

Psychographic Characteristics. The prefix psycho is related to psychology, and derived from the root psyche, the Latin word for mind. While demographic data may be useful in selecting the type of person to depict in promotional materials, psychographic information is critical in designing products, services, and promotional material that will attract customers based on other characteristics. Psychographic data helps you to understand the motives and behaviors of your market. It will be important for you to know the activities, interests, opinions, personalities and life stages (as opposed to age) of your guests for two basic managerial activities—product development and promotion.

There are many reasons people travel in their leisure time. Interestingly, close to one-half of all pleasure trips are taken for visiting friends and relatives. This common travel market is referred to as VFR (visiting friends and relatives). This is obviously not a particularly good market segment for the hotel industry, because the majority of VFR visitors do not use commercial accommodations; they visit relatives

Exhibit 7.6 Ancient travelers sought spiritual paradise, while those in the age of exploration followed their thirst, for knowledge . . . and power. (*Courtesy:* SouthLongIsland.com)

and stay at their houses. However, this is an important market for restaurants and leisure activity businesses, because the VFR travelers generally spend more when they are away from home than when they are in their hometown.

Nickerson and Ellis developed an interesting theory that categorizes guests based on their personality types,[3] and related to their psychographic characteristics. The theory uses four personality dimensions to describe pleasure travelers: activation, variety, extroversion or introversion, and external or internal locus of control.

The *activation* dimension describes a traveler's level of excitement, alertness or energy, and the strength of the need for change or novelty in a traveler is labeled *variety*. In general, high activation travelers seek variety when they are on the road, while low activation travelers prefer something that is familiar and comfortable. In addition, travelers can be classified as *extroverts* or *introverts* with either an *external* or *internal locus of control*. Extroverts focus their attention on what is out-

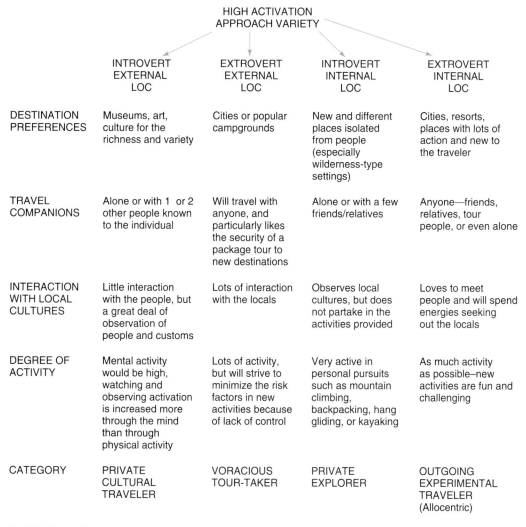

	INTROVERT EXTERNAL LOC	EXTROVERT EXTERNAL LOC	INTROVERT INTERNAL LOC	EXTROVERT INTERNAL LOC
DESTINATION PREFERENCES	Museums, art, culture for the richness and variety	Cities or popular campgrounds	New and different places isolated from people (especially wilderness-type settings)	Cities, resorts, places with lots of action and new to the traveler
TRAVEL COMPANIONS	Alone or with 1 or 2 other people known to the individual	Will travel with anyone, and particularly likes the security of a package tour to new destinations	Alone or with a few friends/relatives	Anyone—friends, relatives, tour people, or even alone
INTERACTION WITH LOCAL CULTURES	Little interaction with the people, but a great deal of observation of people and customs	Lots of interaction with the locals	Observes local cultures, but does not partake in the activities provided	Loves to meet people and will spend energies seeking out the locals
DEGREE OF ACTIVITY	Mental activity would be high, watching and observing activation is increased more through the mind than through physical activity	Lots of activity, but will strive to minimize the risk factors in new activities because of lack of control	Very active in personal pursuits such as mountain climbing, backpacking, hang gliding, or kayaking	As much activity as possible–new activities are fun and challenging
CATEGORY	PRIVATE CULTURAL TRAVELER	VORACIOUS TOUR-TAKER	PRIVATE EXPLORER	OUTGOING EXPERIMENTAL TRAVELER (Allocentric)

HIGH ACTIVATION APPROACH VARIETY

Exhibit 7.7   Activation model of travel personality.

side themselves and tend to be outgoing in interpersonal situations. These might be the people who like to attend a rock concert with many other people. Introverts focus more on what is inside themselves, and might be more likely to visit a museum. People with an internal locus of control believe that they are in charge of the happenings of their lives, while people with an external locus of control believe what happens to them is determined by other powerful individuals, fate or chance.

The model shown in Exhibit 7.7 explains how these differences in personality affect the destination choice of the traveler. For example, *introverted high activation* travelers who like *variety* with an *external locus of control* are likely to prefer museums, art, and culture. They mostly travel alone or with one or two family members or close friends. They enjoy observing other people and customs but prefer to minimize the amount of contact they have with the local culture. They are highly active mentally, more so than physically. These types of travelers are called private cultural travelers. On the other hand, the *extroverted high activation* travelers with the same *external locus of control* are likely to be voracious tour-takers. The big difference between these two types is the manner in which they prefer to interact with people.

	LOW ACTIVATION AVOID VARIETY			
	INTROVERT EXTERNAL LOC	INTROVERT INTERNAL LOC	EXTROVERT EXTERNAL LOC	EXTROVERT INTERNAL LOC
DESTINATION PREFERENCES	Home (no traveling)	When travel occurs, it will be to familiar places visited as a child or to visit a friend or relative	Places with other people doing the same things; package tours are fun and secure for this person	Repeat visitor to a popular resort or favorite destination
TRAVEL COMPANIONS	None (stays at home)	Family or alone	Friends, family, similar others on a package tour	Enjoys traveling with anyone, but especially familiar people
INTERACTION WITH LOCAL CULTURES	None	As little as possible	Enjoys meeting others in the culture, but does not actively seek these people	Enjoys meeting others and seeks out destinations where the same people return
DEGREE OF ACTIVITY	Very little	Little activity, but will get involved in familiar activities	Moderate activity but will be involved in familiar activities with no risk involved	Will get involved in any type of activity if it is not a new activity
CATEGORY	NONTRAVELER	PRIVATE LOW-KEY TRAVELER	REPEAT TOUR-TAKERS (Psychocentric)	REPEAT VISITOR

Exhibit 7.7   *(Continued)*

How would you describe yourself? Are you high or low activation, preference for variety or familiarity, an introvert or an extrovert with an external or internal locus of control? Try to describe yourself in these terms, and see if the description in the model matches your travel preferences.

When pleasure travelers are asked why they travel, they quite often reply "to get away." People want to get away either because they want to escape from a certain situation or because they are seeking something that is lacking in their current life experience. That is, a person who feels his/her life is dull may seek adventure, while someone who has been working very hard in a situation that required constant adaptation to change may seek rest and relaxation instead. Some people are motivated to travel to participate in sports and other physical activities while others travel to rest and relieve tension. Many travelers have a desire to know and learn more about the world they live in or simply just want to do something different. Often, people are motivated to travel by other people, either those that are around them, or those people they have not met yet. They want to get away from the people they interact with every day or they want to find new companions. Many travel so that they can come back to brag to their friends about what they have done, or simply for the attention they receive when others ask them about their trip. Exhibit 7.8 outlines some common motivators for travel.

Push and Pull.   Where pleasure travelers go, and what they do while they are there, depends upon what is commonly referred to as push and pull factors. Forces within the individual put pressure on, or push, a person to fulfill a need or desire. These **push factors** are needs, motivations, and ways of thinking in a person. One

What People Say When You Ask Them Why They Travel
Physical motivators
    Sports participation
    Relaxation
    Health
    Relieve tension
Cultural motivators
    Desire to know and learn
    Experience another way of life
    Do something different
Interpersonal motivators
    Escape from family and friends
    Escape from work
    Seek companionship
    Develop relationships
Status and prestige motivators
    Recognition
    Attention
    Respect of others
    Reputation

Exhibit 7.8   Common motivators for travel.

common push factor is the need for prestige that is satisfied when people tell their friends and acquaintances about their experience. Think for a moment about your last getaway pleasure trip. Why did you go? What were you looking for or escaping from? What need did you fulfill that was not being taken care of at home? Did you tell anyone about your trip and, if so, how did telling people about your trip make you feel?

Pull factors, on the other hand, are outside forces that draw the traveler to a particular place. Pull factors include people, places and activities. Friends, relatives, celebrities, and public figures are powerful pull factors, for instance. Attractions of scenic beauty such as the Golden Gate bridge, or Everglades National Park, theme parks such as Disneyland, and historic areas such the Boston Commons or Plymouth Rock in Massachussets also attract people. Many people travel to participate in activities like golf, skiing, water sports, camping/hiking, archeological digs, and horseback riding, and they are drawn to sporting, education, cultural and recreation events, where they are attracted by excitement, luxury, pampering and hedonistic pleasures.

So, think about your last pleasure trip again. Were there any push factors involved? What were the pull factors that led to your decision on where to fulfill your needs and desires? Were the pull factors people, places or activities, or a combination? Why did the destination you selected pull you to it?

Services

Travelers require services not only to facilitate their travel and leisure activities, but to complement them and make them as perfect as possible. These services are provided by both public and private organizations, and can be classified into six categories:

1. Transportation
2. Information
3. Attractions and entertainment
4. Lodging
5. Food and beverage services
6. Public lands

Do you see how, once again, lodging and food and beverage operations are part of the chain of services? Remember the hypothetical Miami spring break trip in the beginning of this chapter, which demonstrated how hospitality businesses have

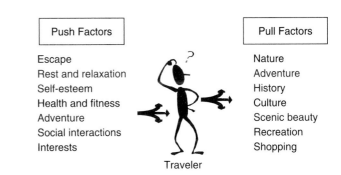

Push Factors		Pull Factors
Escape		Nature
Rest and relaxation		Adventure
Self-esteem		History
Health and fitness		Culture
Adventure		Scenic beauty
Social interactions		Recreation
Interests		Shopping
	Traveler	

Exhibit 7.9   Push/pull model.

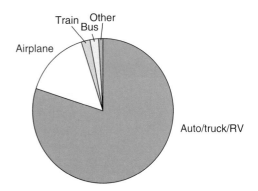

Exhibit 7.10   Primary mode of transportation.

an interdependent relationship with the other businesses and public organizations that perform services for the traveler? Let's have a closer look at each of these six categories.

Transportation   Travelers have access to a variety of vehicles to bring them to their destination and to transport them within the destination. By far the most commonly used mode of travel is the *personal vehicle,* which accounts for 79 percent of all long distance travel within the United States. Good roads, pleasant weather, relatively low gasoline prices and, recently, the threat of terrorism, all encourage travel by personal vehicle.

Hospitality businesses depend on scheduled air service to transport customers with limited time or considerable distances to travel, but the *airlines* are just as de-

Exhibit 7.11   Total Numbers of Airline Passengers Transported by the World's Ten Largest Airlines in 2004.

Total (International + Domestic)

Rank	Airline	Thousands
1	American Airlines Inc.	91570
2	Delta Air Lines, Inc	86783
3	United Airlines	71236
4	Northwest Airlines, Inc.	56429
5	Japan Airlines International	51736
6	Deutsche Lufthansa A.G.	48268
7	All Nippon Airways	46450
8	Air France	45393
9	US Airways, Inc	42400
10	Continental Airlines, Inc	40548

(*Source:* International Transport Association)

(*Courtesy:* Boeing)

pendent upon the hospitality industry, relying on hotels to provide lodging for their crews as well as passengers and restaurants to feed them. Therefore, hotels and airlines often work together to develop travel packages that include airfare, accommodations, rental cars, and more. The hospitality industry has benefited from the increase in airline travel. Over the past decade or so, the number of airline passengers has increased considerably, despite the recent problems in airline travel, and most of these new passengers require hospitality services.

While *motorcoaches* bring far fewer customers to the door of your hotel or restaurant, their passengers are also an attractive market for the hospitality industry. Each motorcoach your property attracts results in the sale of 30 to 40 room-nights and/or restaurant covers. The disadvantage of this market segment is that the competition for the volume business requires that the price of rooms and meals be discounted. Moreover, there is the problem that unless there was advance notification, you never know when the bus will pull up at your restaurant or hotel. This means you always have to staff your business under the assumption that you might get swamped at any minute, and staffing under those conditions drives up your labor expenses

Rail travel via Amtrak also provides opportunities for hospitality businesses to partner with the transportation segment of the tourism industry. Rail packages generally include rail fare and accommodations, and admissions to attractions can be purchased as well. Participation in these package deals opens opportunities for new customers. Furthermore, Amtrak has now also teamed up with cruise ship companies and airlines to offer even more options to the leisure traveler. Yet many of these packages do not currently include hospitality services.

Information   Travel distributors and travel promoters provide information which visitors need in order to decide where to go, how to get there, where to stay, and what to do. Travel distributors include *retail travel agents, tour wholesalers, tour operators, meeting planners, corporate travel managers and incentive houses*. These

EYE ON THE ISSUES

Technology

The development and growth of the Internet has been the most important technological development in the travel and tourism industry. A large number of important benefits can be identified, from consumers being able to look for information on hotels, restaurants and destinations from the comfort of their own homes, to people being able to make their own reservations for air travel and concerts. It has certainly also made the lives of coporate travel managers and meeting planners a whole lot easier!

Yet, the development of the Internet has also had some negative effects on the travel and tourism industries. Where people now make their hotel reservations on-line, they no longer call the central reservation systems of the major hotel chains, and many reservation agents have lost their jobs when their reservation centers closed. Many travel agencies have gone out of business, too, in the last couple of years, as airlines no longer pay commissions on flight bookings, and as hotel companies are more and more reluctant to pay commissions on room reservations.

The development and growth of the Internet is a great development, yet we should not forget that it has also had some negative effects on people's livelihoods; many of the jobs that are discussed in the next couple of paragraphs have been lost.

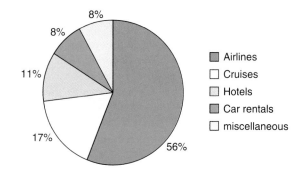

- Airlines
- Cruises
- Hotels
- Car rentals
- miscellaneous

8%
8%
11%
17%
56%

Exhibit 7.12   Source of travel agency revenues.

intermediaries arrange transportation, lodging, meeting rooms, activities, and even meals for the traveler. Travel promoters are public offices and private industry organizations that design and carry out promotional campaigns to pull the tourists to a specific area.

Retail Travel Agents.   Travelers rely on travel agents to assist them in purchasing transportation, lodging, cruises and tours. While a large portion of air travel is booked by travel agents (80–85 percent), only about one-fourth of all domestic hotel reservations are made through travel agents. They are responsible for booking 95 percent of all cruises and 90 percent of tour packages.[4] A major source of income for the travel agencies used to be commissions from airlines, which were eliminated in 2001. Today, travel agents require the customer to pay a fee. Most travelers find the knowledge and advice of the travel agent worth the small fee they pay. Increasingly, the Internet is a source of competition and added value for the travel agent. Travel agents use the Internet to conduct research, market their services and communicate with clients,[5] yet see their business dropping as more and more travelers book their trips on-line.

Tour Wholesalers and Operators.   Specialists who design tour packages either for groups or for independent travelers are called *tour wholesalers*. Those who actually execute the tour are called *tour operators*. A tour package may include all

Exhibit 7.13   Retail Travel Agents at Work (*Courtesy:* Carlson Wagonlit Travel)

or as few as two of the following elements: transportation to and from the destination; accommodations; meals; tickets to attractions; ground transportation; and rental cars. The traveler can save money by buying a package instead of purchasing each item separately. Tour packages are sold directly to the consumer or through retail travel agents. Many tour operators are also the *tour wholesalers* who put the package together. As a hospitality professional, you will be attempting to sell your property to the tour wholesaler and, once the sale is made, you will be working with the tour operator to ensure the satisfaction of the group.

Meeting Planners.   Meeting planners are professionals who arrange and coordinate the details involved in planning and executing meetings, conferences and conventions. Meeting planners may be members of the organization that is sponsoring the conference, or they may be independent consultants. Their job is to negotiate the price of rooms, book the rooms, ensure that meeting rooms have the proper seating and presentation equipment, arrange both ground and air travel, plan and negotiate the price of meals and activities, and ensure that the participants have all necessary information and documentation in a timely manner. The revenue derived from meetings is important to the profitability of many hotels, and the sales department in a hotel or resort works very closely with all the functional areas in a hotel to service meetings successfully.

Corporate Travel Managers.   Many large corporations have a full-time *travel manager* who is responsible for making all arrangements for the corporate traveler. These professionals work with airlines, hotels and rental car companies to negotiate the most favorable rates for the people in their corporations who travel.

Tourism Promoters.   Visitors learn about destinations through the efforts of *tourism promoters,* who can represent either government offices or private organizations. Their main goal is to increase the amount of money tourists bring into the area they serve. *State tourism offices* promote economic development through the marketing and promotion of tourism and recreation in their area. *Chambers of commerce* are city or area organizations that promote industrial and retail development, along with the marketing and promotion of tourism in the area. The main charge for marketing and promotion of tourism is generally given to *convention and visitors' bureaus* that may or may not be part of the chamber of commerce. In some cities the convention and visitors' bureau is part of the city government and answers to the city or town council. In other areas, the convention and visitors' bureau may represent several communities in a regional enterprise. Because tourists do not generally visit a state but instead visit a region that offers the type of attractions they are seeking, *regional tourism offices* are also very efficient travel promoters. The Grand Circle Association, for example, encompasses tourist attractions in the Four Corners region of northern Arizona, the northwest corner of New Mexico, the southwest corner of Colorado and the southern region of Utah. Over 100 private and public members pool their resources to promote the concentration of national parks and monuments in the area.

Internet.   The Internet and its online services are becoming increasingly popular with travelers. As stated earlier, the percentage of travelers using the Internet for travel plans or reservations nearly doubled between 1996 and 1999. The majority

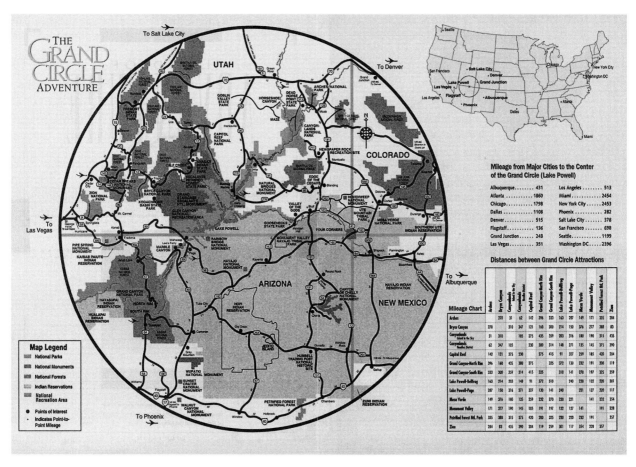

Exhibit 7.14   The Grand Circle Adventure.

(62 percent) used search engine sites for their travel planning. Almost half used destination (e.g., Orlando) or company-specific sites (e.g., Hilton), and more than one-third used commercial Internet sites (e.g., Travelocity).[6]

Attractions and Entertainment.   Attractions such as outdoor recreational facilities, historic sites, beaches, parks, cultural events and festivals, theme and amusement parks, nightlife and dancing, gambling, sporting events and sport facilities for golf, tennis, skiing and myriad others pull the tourist to the destination. Attractions that offer nature-based activities, adventure, and cultural/historic tourism are becoming increasingly popular, and even shopping, which has not been traditionally been seen as a tourist attraction, is now enjoying increasing traveler interest. This, in turn, has created a new relatively new product: shopping packages. In this chapter, we will look at attractions from the perspective of the traveler and the community. Chapter 8 will look at various management aspects of attractions.

Nature-Based Attractions.   There are numerous types of attractions that allow the pleasure traveler to have an experience with the natural environment. These include hiking trails, campgrounds, parks, wildlife, natural landscapes, flora

In % of person trips

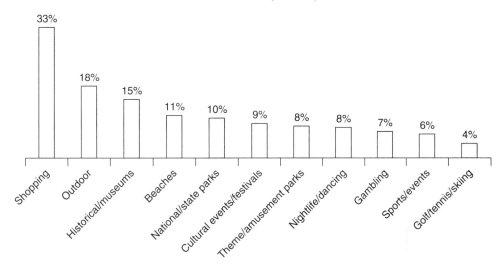

Exhibit 7.15   Traveler activities.

and fauna. The term *ecotourism* is often used in the travel industry to describe any type of activity related to nature. However, the Ecotourism Society defines **ecotourism** as responsible travel to natural areas that conserves the environment and improves the welfare of the local people.[7] The difference between *ecotourism* and *nature-based* tourism is in the strength of the responsibility a visitor feels for preservation and protection of the natural and social environment. Increasingly,

Exhibit 7.16   Opponents and proponents of tourism agree that developers have an ethical responsibility to protect land, water, air, and flora and fauna. (Photo by Phil Pappas)

Environment

The environment is becoming increasingly important to travelers. A large percentage (83 percent) state that they will support and pay more for traveler services provided by environmentally responsible businesses. These travelers want to know what a property is doing to reduce energy and water consumption, reduce and recycle waste, and protect the physical environment from degradation. Signs, brochures and pamphlets are valuable tools for educating the traveling public on the actions your property is taking to protect the natural environment, and can also be used to help educate customers on what they can do to prevent environmental damage. Especially effective is participation in programs for the beautification and maintenance of natural assets in the local community that can enhance both tourists' and residents' awareness of environmental conservation and protection.

Becoming "green" can directly contribute to the success of your business. The public perception of your operation in this regard is vital; high ethical standards and environmental awareness on your part can win the trust of customers and give your business the competitive edge. When you get a chance, have a look at the following website: *http://www.sustainabletravel.org/industry/weekly.cfm#marriott*. Marriott International is committed to undertaking practices that preserve the environment for guests, associates and communities, today and in the future.

travelers are requiring or expecting hospitality services to be environmentally responsible. Eighty-three percent of travelers are inclined to support products that are environmentally responsible. More important, though, they are also willing to put their money where their mouth is: They say they are willing to spend, on average, 6.2 percent more in travel services and products that are environmentally responsible.[8]

Nearly 20 percent of all travelers took a trip of 100 miles or more in order to visit a national park in 1997. A large share of these travelers (70%) participated in outdoor activities while visiting the national parks. Among these outdoor activities, hiking was the most popular (53%), followed by camping (33%) and fishing (19%).[9]

Adventure Attractions.   One-half of U.S. adults have taken an adventure trip in the past five years,[10] engaging in "hard" adventure activities such as white water rafting, scuba diving, hang gliding, sky diving, rock climbing, cave exploring, and mountain biking—as well as "soft" adventure activities such as wilderness tours, skiing, biking, sailing, hiking, boating, and other outdoor activities. Adventure travel is most popular with generation Xers (64 percent), baby boomers (56 percent), men (53 percent) and people who live in the West (57 percent).[11]

Culture/Historic Attractions.   Participation in cultural and historic events, such as visiting a historic site or museum, and attending a music, arts or other cultural event, ranks third in American free-time activities. The cultural/historic traveler spends more per trip and stays longer than any other type of traveler. The National Register of Historic Places lists more than 68,000 historic properties in the United States alone. Two popular study tour programs sponsored by the National Trust for Historic preservation include the Historic Hotels of America Program and

Exhibit 7.17   Skiing is one of America's favorite "soft" adventure activities. (*Courtesy:* Arizona Office of Tourism)

a Heritage Tourism Program. Country Inns and Bed and Breakfasts offer lodging opportunities in more than 15,000 historic buildings renovated and preserved by innkeepers. The average age of these properties is 128 years.[12]

Shopping.   Shopping is the number one activity participated in by domestic and international travelers. Outlet malls have become a major attraction for U.S. travelers. Surprisingly, in Virginia, a state with beaches, mountains, theme parks and many historic sites, including Williamsburg, the number one attraction is an outlet mall! Nearly 40 percent of all leisure and business travelers say they had visited a discount outlet mall while traveling. One out of every ten discount mall shoppers said that the outlet mall experience was the primary reason for their trip. As a result, outlet malls have teamed up with airlines, hotels, and tour operators to offer shopping-themed packages. Some of these packages include other community attractions such as museums and theaters. These new packages offer excellent opportunities for increased sales in hospitality business.[13]

Lodging   There are many different types of lodging from which the pleasure traveler can choose. Along with typical or "standard" hotels and motels, for instance, many tourist destinations offer a wide variety of alternatives such as resort and convention hotels, condominiums and time-shares, dude ranches, bed and breakfasts, inns, hostels and campgrounds. Many of these have been described in greater detail in earlier chapters.

Resort hotels are hotels that people visit for relaxation, recreation or entertainment, most of which is on property. Convention hotels cater to large groups, and are usually located in the downtown areas of major cities. Condominium units allow individuals to have full ownership of one unit in a complex. In most cases,

Exhibit 7.18   B&Bs around the world provide a homelike atmosphere to people who are looking for a different overnight experience. (Photos: Left, Rob Reichenfeld © Dorling Kindersley; middle, Trevor Worden/photolibrary.com; right, Gunter Marx © Dorling Kindersley.)

the owner uses the condominium with all its amenities a few weeks each year and rents it out through an independent management agency for the remainder of the year. Time-share units are similar to condominiums in services and amenities received; however, in time-share the owner owns the unit for only one or two weeks a year. Dude or guest ranches are often family–owned and operated and offer the guest a Western experience including opportunities to participate in ranch activities. Bed and breakfasts (B&Bs) offer an entirely different experience to the traveler: instead of the formality of a hotel or motel, B&Bs provide family-style breakfasts and a homelike atmosphere.

Food and Beverage Service   While on vacation, Americans consume nearly every meal outside their lodging, unless the vacation is spent at the home of friends or relatives. Dining out while on vacation is an important part of the traveler's experience. Not only are vacationers likely to eat out for every meal, they also eat differently while they are on vacation. They are more likely to dine at midscale and upscale restaurants while vacationing, whereas at home they might opt for a budget meal. Eating out is important even to those visiting friends and relatives. The guests will often invite their hosts out for a meal and are generally willing to spend more for this festive occasion.

Most food and beverage establishments cannot depend on tourists alone for their financial success. Those that earn half or more of their sales from tourists are considered to be *tourism sales–dependent restaurants.* Lodging restaurants fit into this category, as well as many restaurants in resort areas such as Vail, Colorado, or San Diego, California. Restaurants whose earnings from tourists make up 20 to 50 percent of their sales are considered to be *tourism profit–dependent restaurants.* If the total sales to tourists fall below 20 percent, the restaurant is considered to be *resident sales–dependent.*

The food and beverage industry is made up of many different types of food service outlets, such as eating and drinking establishments (stand-alone restaurants and bars), food service contractors, hotel/motel restaurants, caterers, vendors and prepared take-out food outlets in grocery and convenience stores. All of these were discussed extensively in Chapters 5 and 6.

Public Lands   Scenic and natural areas and parks combined constitute a most powerful attractor that pulls leisure tourists to a destination. Most natural and scenic areas of attraction are managed by some level of government: federal, state

Exhibit 7.19 Giant redwood trees are the main attraction of Sequoia National Park in California. (Photo: Walter Choroszewski/The Stock Collection.)

or local, or, in some cases, a regional entity or mutual cooperation. The public agencies that manage these public areas have a dual mission: They must protect and preserve the natural resource, and at the same time provide satisfactory support and services so that a visitor enjoys the area and the visit.

Federal Agencies. Examples of agencies at the federal level that are responsible for land management include the Department of the Interior (National Park Service, U.S. Fish and Wildlife Service, Bureau of Land Management, Bureau of Reclamation, Bureau of Indian Affairs); Department of Agriculture (National Forest Service); Department of Defense (U.S. Army Corps of Engineers); and the quasi-governmental agency, the Tennessee Valley Authority (TVA). Areas administered by these agencies represent 700 million acres, or approximately 30 percent of the total land and water mass of the United States. In 1997, domestic and international travelers made nearly 1.6 billion recreational visits to areas administered by the National Park Service, the National Forest Service, the U.S. Army Corps of Engineers and the Bureau of Land Management alone.[14]

State Agencies. In addition, every state sets aside areas for public recreation. There are currently 5,495 state parks comprising nearly 12.3 million acres nationwide. In 1996, visitors spent $559 million on user fees, facilities, restaurants, concession purchases, beaches/pools, golf and other activities in state parks, an increase of 4.3 percent over 1995.

Responsible agencies at all levels partner with private industry to provide many of the services provided to visitors through a concessions program. Services provided by the concessionaire include, but are not limited to, food service, lodging, camping, marina operations, transportation, "river running" (rafting, canoeing), equipment rentals, horseback riding, and general merchandising. For the privilege of operating commercial facilities, each concessionaire pays a franchise fee that is usually based on annual gross receipts.

The Community

The community in which you live and work is likely to be affected by tourism, both positively and negatively. Many communities seek to develop tourism as a tool for income and economic development, and while tourism has many economic benefits, these benefits are accompanied by costs. Tourism has the potential to create social, environmental and even economic problems for the community. If not properly managed, tourism can ultimately destroy the very thing that attracted the visitor in the first place. This section will help you understand the many ways tourism impacts the community. A glance at Exhibit 7.20 will provide an overview of the pluses and minuses of tourism.

Economic Impact   Why do communities spend money to attract travelers? Obviously, tourism, be it leisure or business, generates money for the destination community. In 2000, travelers spent $545.1 billion in communities across the nation, and began a chain of spending which resulted in an economic impact of more than a tril-

Harmony versus conflict
> Tourism fosters a climate of peace and prosperity by bringing together people of different cultures and nationalities.
> Tourism causes resentment and antagonism.

Promotion versus destruction of culture
> Tourism encourages pride in local arts, crafts and cultural expressions.
> Tourism causes natives to imitate tourists and give up or trinketize cultural traditions.

Economic gain versus economic disruption
> Tourism brings new money into an area and generates jobs, income, and tax revenues.
> Tourism brings only low-paying seasonal work to a region. Most of the money earned from tourism goes to wealthy developers, investors, and bankers. Tourism disrupts the economic system, causing an influx of people into the destination area or a shortage of workers in traditional jobs.

Conservation and protection of the natural environment versus degradation
> Tourism helps to conserve and protect the natural environment.
> Tourism causes water and air pollution, results in the trampling of delicate soil systems, disrupts wildlife, and destroys the natural environment through the construction of roads, airports, hotels and other infrastructure needed to service the tourists.

Improvement versus deterioration of quality of life for the host community
> Tourism enhances the quality of life of the citizens by bringing more recreation facilities, restaurants and entertainment into an area.
> Tourism causes overcrowding, traffic jams, and crime.

Exhibit 7.20   Costs and benefits of tourism.

lion dollars.[15] Any dollar the tourist spends in the community—on whatever attraction or service—multiplies because these dollars are used to pay wages, salaries and taxes, to purchase and maintain equipment and supplies, and to generate profits.

When employees, suppliers, or owners of host attractions and services spend money they receive from the tourist, indirect and induced expenditures are generated. Indirect expenditure occurs as travel industry businesses purchase goods and services from local suppliers who, in turn, purchase goods and services from their suppliers. This chain of buying and selling continues until the initial traveler or tourist purchase ultimately leaks out of the local area through outside purchases (imports), taxes, business savings, and payments to employees. This whole chain of making money and spending is referred to as the **multiplier effect.**

The other type of secondary impact, called induced effect or expenditure, is the effect of the dollars spent by the employees of tourism businesses and their suppliers. Consequently, each dollar a tourist brings into a community actually generates approximately $2.40 in income for the community. Think about it: How rich would you be if every time you earned $1.00, you could turn it into $2.40? Knowing this makes it very obvious why communities spend so much money to attract tourists.

Along with the income tourism generates for a community, tourist spending increases the number of jobs a community can offer its citizens. In 1997, 7 million

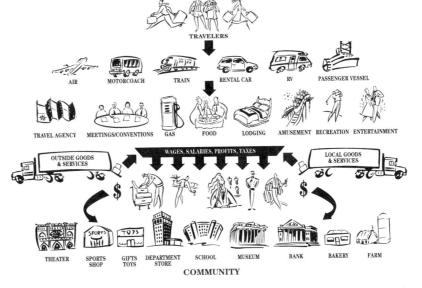

The dollars travelers spend are recirculated back into the local, state and national economies and directly benefit other related industries, such as telephone, construction, computer, steel, textile, agriculture, food processing, and service industries, who rely on tourism for their survival and growth.

This multiplier benefits virtually everyone in the U.S., by generating tax revenues, which help pay for our roads, airports, schools, libraries, and parks. Travel spending also helps support shopping and historical areas, art galleries, museums and many cultural and community events.

Exhibit 7.21   Where does the money go? (*Courtesy:* Travel Industry Association)

people were employed in the travel and tourism industry directly, and another 9.2 million were employed as a result of indirect and induced expenditure. Many people criticize the tourism industry because it may appear to them that jobs it creates are low paying. In reality, fully 10 percent of jobs in the travel and tourism industry are executive or managerial in nature; the overall average salary in the travel and tourism industry is equal to that in the health industry, for instance.

Communities also benefit from taxes the travelers pay. In 2004, travelers generated 99.5 billion dollars in state, federal, and local tax revenues. Along with sales, gasoline, airport and rental car taxes, travelers often pay what is commonly referred to as a bed tax. In many communities, an additional 3 percent to 14 percent is added to lodging charges. Sometimes communities will also add the tax to food and beverages, especially alcoholic beverages. The revenues from the tourism tax are generally used, at least partially, for the promotion of tourism in the community. During fiscal 2004–2005, states projected spending $603 million on tourism promotion,[16] which means they probably generated much more than that in tourism-related taxes.

Social Impact   The social impact of tourism is sometimes rather controversial. Many people see tourism as the cause of a lower quality of life, while others in the community see tourism as a way to improve the quality of life. In developed nations such as the United States, the main complaint that citizens voice about tourism is related to crowding and congestion, specifically traffic congestion. Many times, local residents become annoyed when they cannot access their favorite restaurant because of the tourists, or when tourists crowd the aisles at their favorite supermarket. Restaurateurs will often compensate for this by offering discounts to local residents and/or establishing a separate section in their establishment for local customers. Residents of a tourist destination may also see an increase in noise, in air and water pollution, and in crime caused by increased numbers of tourists entering the area. Conversely, residents do enjoy the increased opportunity for shopping and recreation, and will also have a wider variety of food service and entertainment. Often, local residents enjoy meeting people from other places and the positive experiences they have with tourists.

A serious problem experienced by some members of the community is an increase in the price of land and housing. In an explosively expanding tourist area

Exhibit 7.22   The U.S. travel industry dollar. (*Courtesy:* Travel Industry Association of America)

such as Jackson Hole, Wyoming, land prices and taxes skyrocketed virtually overnight. In such areas, local residents may be taxed off their properties, and hotel and restaurant employees may have an impossible task in finding affordable housing if local government fails to properly protect local residents. In addition, an increase in tourists sometimes brings about an increase in the demand for goods and services, resulting in higher prices for local residents. To compensate local residents for an inconvenience caused by tourists, many hospitality businesses will offer discounts to residents, hoping to increase support for tourism. Another way hospitality business have tried to build support for the tourism industry within the community is to set aside a day where local residents can enjoy attractions either free or at a reduced cost.

In undeveloped or Third World nations, the consequences of unplanned tourism development can be very serious, especially when vast cultural differences exist between the native population and the visitors. When tourists arrive in large numbers and the demand for locally produced arts and crafts exceeds the production capability of the local community, cheap imitations are often offered, resulting in a "trinketization" of native art. Also, resentment and antagonism toward the tourist may develop as locals perceive their culture as becoming westernized. This concern may reach crisis proportions when native customs and values are seen to be trivialized or violated by outsiders. Especially disconcerting for natives is the usual increase in crime, gambling, drinking and prostitution that often accompanies tourism development. In some areas these behaviors were unheard of prior to the arrival of foreign visitors.

On the other hand, tourism may also make very significant positive social and environmental contributions to the society of a developing nation. Tourism offers relatively poor communities opportunities for economic growth and a reason to take pride in and to preserve their cultural and natural resources. Tourists often find value in native crafts, language, culture, and traditions. Many cultural traditions that would otherwise have been lost have been preserved because of the interest in them created by tourism. In Bali, Indonesia, for example, the government sponsors the Bali Arts Festival to encourage the preservation of art, food, and dance traditions, as well as to promote tourism. In Africa, the value of wildlife as a tourist attraction has been the impetus to reduce the slaying of animals by hunters and

EYE ON THE ISSUES

Ethics

The social, economic and environmental impacts of tourism on a local community are all related to the issue of ethics. You have thought about what ethical behavior really is many times. Simply put, if you can tell your mother about your behavior, you probably did the right or the ethical thing.

The same applies to tourism development: Whatever we do in our development efforts, we have to be able to face ourselves in the mirror in the morning and tell ourselves that we did the right thing. Developers in the past have been unscrupulous and have destroyed more than they created. But increased pressure from people who feel strongly about leaving the world a better place than it is today for future generations have made developers think twice (and often they are forced to think twice because of legal ramifications!) about the impact of their development efforts.

farmers. In Guatemala, the destruction of the rain forest is being slowed by the development of ecotourism. In the Himalayas, the development of the tourism industry has increased the literacy rate by more than 50 percent in just a few years. New roads and improved water and sewer systems have improved the quality of life in Nepal. Additionally, tourism creates the incentive to preserve historic, cultural, and environmental treasures that could well be lost when Third World countries seek rapid economic expansion.

Environmental Impact   The importance of the natural environment for tourists cannot be overstated. Mountains, oceans, flora, fauna and scenic vistas generate a powerful pull for the leisure tourist. For tourism to succeed, the natural environment must be protected and preserved. There are two opposing views on the relationship between tourism and the environment.

One view suggests that tourism provides the incentive and financial means to enhance and preserve the natural environment. Many communities use revenues from special lodging and restaurant taxes for beautification projects. Entrance fees to national parks support the preservation of the park and protect it from usage that would cause excessive environmental damage. In many national parks, the construction and maintenance of trail systems, for instance, reduces the risk of erosion caused by foot traffic. Without the income generated by tourism, many natural areas could be destroyed either by careless, uncontrolled usage by visitors or because the land would be used for other economic activities such as farming, grazing, or the extraction of minerals or timber. These activities often result in increased erosion, a reduction of plant population, and destruction of wildlife habit.

Exhibit 7.23   The Grand Canyon Railway brings thousands of tourists who might otherwise visit by driving their personal vehicles to the Grand Canyon every year. Too many vehicles in the park contribute to traffic, parking, and pollution problems. (*Courtesy:* Grand Canyon Railway.)

The opposing view sees tourism as a destructive force, causing noise, litter, erosion, overcrowding, and a disruption of plant and animal life. The opponents of tourism argue that tourism should be limited or even prohibited in areas where the natural environment is threatened by their presence. The Great Barrier Reef off the cost of Australia is a prime example of an area damaged by tourists who step on the corals or even break them off to take home for souvenirs. Most of the tourists participating in these activities do not even realize that they are killing the coral. Another way tourists innocently damage the environment is in gathering wood for their campfires. Breaking off live branches from trees is an obvious affront against the environment, but many campers also do not realize that when they gather fallen branches, they are taking away the nutrients the decaying wood would have given to the soil. Resisting the temptation to pull up that pretty wildflower and carry it with you for a while on your hike may be difficult. However, research has shown that the collection of flowers and plants by visitors has caused changes in species distribution. And finally, litter is not only unsightly; it also damages vegetation by changing the composition of the soil, resulting in a change in the ecosystem balance. Litter has also been known to kill animals that ingest it.

Wildlife is becoming an increasingly powerful pull factor. However, the presence of humans, especially those who feed the wild animals, can disrupt wildlife feeding and breeding habits. This, in turn, results in reducing or even eliminating the population, thereby altering food chains.

Perhaps the most destructive of all tourist activities is the construction of facilities, such as hotels, restaurants, golf courses, marinas, and theme parks, to service the needs of the tourist. The most popular attractions for tourists, oceans and mountains, are the most susceptible to "construction destruction." High-rise hotels built on beaches such as in Honolulu, Hawaii and Acapulco, Mexico are not only

Exhibit 7.24   When everyone wants a view of the coastline, development often ends up obscuring the very thing that attracts visitors. (Photo by Phil Pappas)

Exhibit 7.25   Who wouldn't want to go to these exotic locations, both to explore them as a tourist and as a guest in an upscale hotel property? (*Courtesy:* Four Seasons Hotels and Resorts.)

eyesores, but actually destroy coastlines that are naturally unstable because they act as barriers that prevent the natural shifting of the sand. As a result, the sand is washed into the ocean and the beach is destroyed. In mountain areas, roads, ski trails, hiking trails and four wheel drive trails contribute to land erosion. The problem is intensified in higher elevations, where the ecosystem is extremely fragile and the slopes are often steep.

Exhibit 7.26   With tourism going to the ends of the Earth, hospitality has to follow. Many reputable hotel chains have developed properties in exotic locations. (*Courtesy:* Four Seasons Hotels and Resorts.)

The negative effects tourism can have on the environment have the potential to destroy the very thing that attracted the tourists to the area. It is in the best interests of those who earn their living from tourism to develop plans to ensure that the tourism product will be sustainable. Sustainable development meets the needs of the existing tourists and the residents of the local community, at the same time protecting and preserving opportunities for future generations.

CONCLUSION

Hospitality managers need to understand the principles of maintaining a sustainable tourism system where the interdependent components of the travel and tourism system work together to attract and satisfy customers, earn profits, and improve the quality of life for the local community. Developing partnerships with the various components of the tourism industry is critical to the success of any hospitality business dependent on the traveler. Hotels, restaurants, casinos, and resorts depend upon transportation, information, attractions and public lands to attract travelers and facilitate their travel experiences. Furthermore, they depend upon the community in which they operate to provide the financing, infrastructure and human, natural, cultural, and historic resources required for their operation. Each component of the system—travelers, services, and the community—must perceive that the benefits of tourism outweigh its costs. The travelers seek value for their dollar. Services want to be able to sustain their resources and make a reasonable profit. The community requires an improved quality of life. To ensure that these positive activities occur, hospitality managers need to understand the economic, social and environmental impacts of their activities and to modify those that may create an unfavorable exchange situation for any one of the three components.

KEYWORDS

non-discretionary travel   281
discretionary travel   282
push factors   288
pull factors   289
intermediaries   292

ecotourism   295
multiplier effect   301

CORE CONCEPTS

sustainable tourism system   279
travelers   280
services   280
community   280

DISCUSSION QUESTIONS

1. Explain the concept of a sustainable tourism system.
2. How do geographic, demographic, and psychographic characteristics influence travel decisions?
3. Explain the push and pull of travel motivations.
4. What role do meeting planners, tour operators, travel agents, and tourism promoters play in the tourism industry?
5. Why is the management of public lands important to the hospitality industry?
6. Discuss the economic benefits tourism brings to a community?
7. How does tourism affect the quality of life of the residents of a tourist destination?
8. Why is protection of the environment vital to the hospitality industry?

WEBSITES TO VISIT

1. www.ecotourism.org
2. www.grandcircle.org
3. collettevacations.com
4. www.nps.com.
5. www.parks.ca.gov
6. www.tia.org
7. www.world-tourism.org
8. www.sustainabletravel.org

CHAPTER 8

The Hospitality Spectrum

Resorts, Clubs, Cruises, Events, and Attractions

As you have already read in the preceding chapters, the hospitality industry is highly diversified, and offers a spectrum of career opportunities. This chapter elaborates on several important components of the hospitality industry. It looks at resorts, clubs, cruise lines, events and attractions, not only to show you the breadth of the industry, but also to provide you with some insight into the management and operations of these exciting businesses. Based on the past and present successes of such entities as Disney, the city of Las Vegas, and Carnival Cruises, the expected future growth of these hospitality operations is tremendous. If you are interested in exploring career opportunities in these challenging fields of hospitality management, the job market for qualified managers is strong, and many exciting opportunities are waiting for you! All aboard . . . !

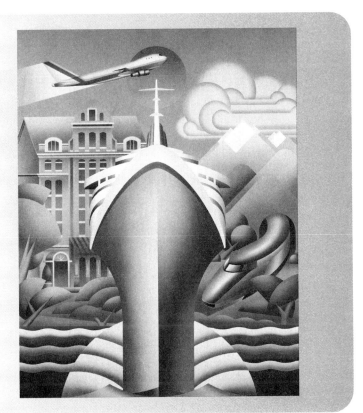

Outline

INTRODUCTION

Resorts, clubs, attractions, events and the cruise line industry are exciting businesses holding special niches in the world of hospitality. While resorts have many similarities with hotels in their basic functions, they are significantly different in other ways—and not just because they might be considered more glamorous.

Future managers like yourself are often pleasantly surprised to learn that the skills acquired in what they've thought of as a "hotel-and-restaurant management" curriculum are equally applicable to the management of private, public, or military clubs, to planning and managing festivals and other events, to running a theme park, museum, or other attractions, and to managing or selling accommodations on a cruise ship.

Let's take a look at some of those opportunities that are recognizable in their similarity to other hospitality operations, but that present quite a few interesting differences too.

RESORTS

Resort hotels are associated with leisure activities and travel for pleasure. A number of resort hotels also operate very successfully in the meeting and convention market. The main difference between resort and non-resort properties is their emphasis on the guest's leisure experience and on pleasurable activities, rather than,

Exhibit 8.1a   The Hyatt Regency Hill Country Resort at San Antonio, Texas capitalizes on the beauty of the rare Texas geographical feature: hills. (*Courtesy:* Hyatt Regency)

for instance, business activities. Resorts offer a vast array of leisure destinations, with different activities and amenities, and are geared toward pleasing guests who have a wide range of values and lifestyles, as well as different budgets.

Hospitality students often dream of a career in resort management without realizing that its demands are often far more taxing than those of management at city hotels or other non-resort properties. Even managers with considerable experience at non-resort properties have found their first resort experience to be a real challenge. Resorts have a different momentum, a different style as compared to other operations, and their operating challenges are different too. Most resorts experience a wide variation in activity levels during the changing seasons. This affects revenues, staffing levels, and marketing, and may even result in completely different types of guests from one time of year to another. Who goes to ski resorts when there is no snow, or to beach resorts when it's cold?

The following paragraphs will present a brief history of resort development, an examination of the differences between the operational challenges of resort and non-resort hotels, and an overview of the most important aspects of resort operations.

Exhibit 8.1b   A jewel on Gulf waters, the Hyatt Regency Cerromar Beach Resort at Dorada, Puerto Rico, offers tropical water activities as well as golf with breathtaking vistas. (*Courtesy:* Hyatt Regency)

A Brief History

Resorts go back as far as civilization, when the aristocracy of Rome went to their villas on the Island of Capri off the coast of Italy 2,000 years ago, or when Mogul rulers escaped the heat of the Indian summer by withdrawing to mountain palaces in Kashmir, India in the 1300s. Europe had its beach, lake, and mountain resorts, and developed health resorts (also called **spas**) in locations with natural hot springs believed to have curative powers. One of the most famous resorts is located in the town of Spa, Belgium (hence the name). It was established in the 13th century and continues to attract many visitors. The mineral water from its hot springs is bottled and sold all over Europe. It has become so famous in Western Europe that, rather than asking for mineral water, you can order a "Spa" in Holland or Belgium, and the waiter will bring you this water with or without bubbles, or with a lemon flavor.

The New World continued the European spa tradition, with the development of spa-related properties in places like Saratoga Springs, New York, and White Sulphur Springs, West Virginia. The development of the railroads in the 1800s provided convenient access to a number of areas that had previously been difficult to reach. Resorts in New England, upstate New York, and Atlantic City, New Jersey, became more accessible and grew into popular destination resorts. Atlantic City became America's first resort city, and made an important move to broaden its customer base by including not only the wealthy, but the middle class among its clientele.

Prior to Atlantic City's development as a seaside resort, resorts had been the exclusive domain of the wealthy and powerful. That customer base did not really expand until Sir William Butlin began the family-oriented and budget-minded Butlin Holiday Camps in Great Britain in 1936. After World War II, the economic growth of the United States and the increase in family income led to increased demand for vacation and leisure destinations and resorts. The recovery of the Western European economies a decade or so later led to parallel increases in demand throughout Europe and the Mediterranean. The development of jet passenger aircraft in the 1950s made travel to such destinations even more feasible. When jumbo jets and wide-body passenger aircraft reduced operating costs and lowered airfares, international travel and visits to resorts—both for pleasure and business—boomed.

Exhibit 8.2a   Sunbelt resorts often feature highly desirable golf courses. (*Courtesy:* Arizona Office of Tourism)

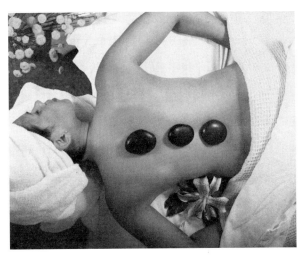

Exhibit 8.2b   Spas at modern resorts have their roots in a European resort custom dating back to the 1300s. Today's spas play an important role in helping guests relax, "destress," and return to a more healthy balance. (Photo courtesy of Barton Creek Resort & Spa, Austin, Texas)

Increased prosperity and reduced airfares also led to other phenomena, namely group travel and mass tourism. Quantity discounts and the buying power of large groups brought about the development of charter and tour operators who were able to negotiate low prices for entire aircraft, large blocks of rooms, and deep discounts on amusements and activities for their group travelers. Resorts that catered to these mass leisure travelers were built in the most desirable physical locations around the world. Some of the world's largest tour operators now own hundreds of hotels and resorts and thousands of rooms, as well as their own charter airline companies.

Resorts versus Non-Resorts

The difference between resorts and non-resorts revolves around two criteria: location and function. Resorts are normally located in the most desirable physical locations, as compared to business hotels, which are normally located in cities and other places where business is conducted. Islands, mountains, deserts, and lakefront sites are usually the prime locations for resort development.

Functionally, resorts offer more than just lodging and food and beverage services to their guests. They provide them with luxury accommodations, numerous food and beverage outlets, lavish entertainment, and exciting recreational activities, such as golf, tennis, skiing, and various water sports.

Resorts can be divided into two groups: destination resorts and activity-based resorts. A **destination resort** implies a place or location, rather than a single property. Resort cities, such as Miami, Orlando, and San Diego, are popular destinations because they offer a wide choice of activities, entertainment, and other diversions—along with their mild climates, beaches, and golf courses. In this case, the location or the city itself is considered a resort or destination, and individual properties are part of the total inventory of attractions that make the destination desirable. There may be a major attribute or activity that is at the core of the area's attractiveness, but the total array of lodging facilities and attractions in the area is what comprises the destination.

An **activity-based resort,** on the other hand, caters to the needs of people interested in a particular activity while on vacation, such as tennis, scuba diving, history and culture, or golf.

An activity-based resort focuses on a single aspect of a destination or property as the key to its identity. Aspen, Colorado and Killington, Vermont are known primarily as ski resorts. Palm Springs, California, Scottsdale, Arizona, and Pinehurst, North Carolina, are well known as golf destinations. Hilton Head Island Beach and Tennis Resort in North Carolina, as the name suggests, focuses on tennis and water fun.

One of the challenges that activity-oriented resorts face is developing attractions for seasons when their primary activity is impossible or uncomfortable. How, for instance, can guests be persuaded to stay in Aspen in the summer, or in upstate New York in the heart of winter? Another issue facing these resorts is that guests often travel as families, and the enthusiasm of one family member for golf, skiing, or scuba diving may not be shared by the other family members. The question then becomes: What can guests do the rest of the time? Are there alternatives available that will make the resort experience a pleasure for everyone, and are there things to do besides golf or tennis, the beach or the ski slope?

An important issue for resort developers to keep in mind, too, is the level of difficulty of their golf courses and ski terrain. Professionals, experts, and the trade press love the more challenging and difficult locations. Yet average vacationers tend to be just that—average. They just want to have a good time, get some satisfaction out of being active, but may not necessarily want to test themselves in a world-class competitive arena.

There are a few resorts that are narrowly focused and aimed at only dedicated enthusiasts. Helicopter skiing in the Bugaboos, remote hunting and fishing camps,

Exhibit 8.3   Scottsdale's Hyatt Regency Resort at Gainey Ranch dresses itself in light and water, all with an authentic feel for Southwestern culture. (*Courtesy:* Hyatt Gainey Ranch and Hyatt Regency)

Exhibit 8.4   Professionals, experts, and the trade press love the more challenging hole locations. Yet, the average player will land in the water quite often. . . . (*Courtesy:* Hyatt Gainey Ranch and Hyatt Regency)

or far-flung islands that offer outstanding scuba diving make no attempt to cater to everyone. Most resorts, however, are intentionally not unique, trying to attract a broad range of clientele. Like other operators in any competitive business, resort developers and marketers must differentiate the resort from others, making it stand out as special without becoming so specialized that it appeals to so few people that it cannot be run profitably.

A key aspect of resort management is ***seasonality.*** Many resorts have a high season, a low season, and what is called a shoulder season. The **high season** (also referred to as the "peak" season) is the time when demand, occupancy, and rates are highest, and when the resort's attractions are at their peak, staffing is at its highest level, and activities and revenues crest.

Shoulder seasons are the periods before and after the high season. During the shoulder season, properties are usually either gearing up for or gearing down from the high season. Weather and activities are often attractive, but not prime. During these periods, occupancies and rates are somewhat lower than during high seasons, but still reflect the desirability of the location and property. Markets may shift a little during the shoulder season, moving more toward groups and individuals who are more price sensitive than high-season guests, who are willing to pay top dollar.

Low season (or "valley" season) offers the greatest challenge to the resort operator. High season attractions are usually not available or may not be particularly enjoyable during these periods. The normal strategy to attract business during this time is to offer discounts to attract enough business to meet operating costs. Fixed costs such as salaries, rent, interest, and insurance have to be paid each month,

Environment

Each of the areas discussed in this chapter has an impact on the physical environment: the development of an attraction, the set-up of an event in a particular location, and the operations of a golf resort or club all affect our natural surroundings. Resorts, since they are often located in remote locations, need to consider how their buildings will fit into the natural landscape. Intrusive architecture or overly prominent positioning of construction (sometimes called "architectural pollution") may destroy much of the attractiveness of an area, causing local resentment and opposition.

Resort developers must examine local resources before building large facilities. Some resorts, in areas with water shortages, have found it necessary to build and operate their own sewage and water treatment plants, since existing plants are adequate to serve only a small, spread-out population. The amount of trash and solid waste generated by a resort can be more than that of an entire small community. For resorts to be good neighbors, they must be sensitive to the carrying capacity of local utilities and aware of such things as drainage and run-off. The lush landscaping of golf courses and resort grounds often requires large quantities of fertilizers, pesticides, and other chemicals. These toxins can contaminate ground water and damage vegetation in surrounding areas.

Finally, cruise ships must be careful about how they take care of their waste while at sea. Not doing so not only has a negative effect on marine biology, but can also lead to legal problems. A recent indictment accuses Royal Caribbean Cruise Lines of illegally dumping waste oil off the coast of Puerto Rico and of covering up the offense. The damage in this case was not only monetary and environmental; it was also a public relations nightmare for the company.

whether revenue is down or not. Selling a room that normally goes for $325 at a discounted rate of $110 may not generate a profit, but it will probably cover obligations to the bank, the utility companies, the government, and essential vendors.

Successful resort operators are those who have been able to extend their high and shoulder seasons, find new markets for their low seasons, and develop special events and activities to draw guests at times that were traditionally slow. Successful resort operators also reduce their costs when revenues are down, and find ways to keep key employees working year round. This is often accomplished by adjusting the number of employees based on seasonal needs (in other words, laying off and hiring on as needed). The trick is to do so without compromising high-quality guest service. This means that resort managers have to be very good at recruiting and training people, particularly at the start of each high season, when new employees must be brought up to superior performance levels quickly. Many resort managers and hourly employees like the rhythm of the seasons, with their changes in pace and activity, and will grow bored with the relatively even pace of many non-resort properties.

Resort guests usually stay longer than guests in many non-resorts, except for those non-resorts that offer extended stay products such as Guest Quarters, Residence Inns, or Towne Place Suites. **_Length of stay_** often has a relationship to travel time, distance, and costs: The further the guest travels to the destination, the longer he or she is likely to stay. A typical destination resort may have an average stay of 5.5 days, whereas the typical "transient hotel" has an average stay of only 1.5 to 2 days.

For resort managers, this means that they have to be prepared to handle most check-ins and check-outs in one or two days, rather than having them spread out

Exhibit 8.5 Club Med has made a reputation for the warm guest relations skills of its staffers. When length of stay is high, personal relationships are highlighted. (*Courtesy:* Club Med, New York City)

more evenly throughout the week. It also means that the resort must provide a lot more variety in its food and beverage outlets and available activities. Otherwise, guests will quickly grow tired of the same choices and take their trade and money elsewhere. This aspect of longer stay requires resort managers to be creative. They have to rely on their activity directors, chefs, and catering directors to develop special events, menus, and divertissements.

In addition to having multiple food and beverage outlets, resorts usually also offer swimming pools, health clubs, and facilities for tennis, golf, or other activities. Their extent is therefore larger than business hotels. Moreover, they are often more spread out than conventional hotels. It is not unusual for rooms to be located in several buildings, all of which are connected by extensive landscaping. This means that housekeeping and maintenance operations, for instance, become more complex, and supplies and trash must be moved around the property without offending guests. Single-structure hotels usually have no problem separating front-of-the-house areas from areas guests should not enter, but in multi-building resorts this is harder to accomplish.

Resort staffing presents some challenges that many urban business hotels do not have to face. As mentioned earlier, seasonality is important in resort management, both with respect to keeping qualified staff and in matching the availability of seasonal help with seasonal demands, such as having students on summer vacations on hand to deal with the challenges of high-season business.

City hotels have a large population base from which to draw and a large housing market for employees to choose from. Moreover, cities often have public transportation systems for those who lack personal transportation, and entertainment opportunities galore. By contrast, many resorts are located in rural areas with small local populations, no public transportation, and a shortage of available

Exhibit 8.6   The Shandong Hotel and People's Hall in Shandong, China, opened in 2003. While designing this prestigious property, in a relatively remote area, Portman Architects of Atlanta, Georgia, USA, worked carefully to plan for logistical, cultural, and aesthetic elements. (*Courtesy:* Michael Portman/Portman Architects)

and affordable housing. Resort managers often find themselves recruiting from far away, and assisting employees with housing and transportation.

Additionally, with resorts being built in remote locations such as Native American reservations, there is the need (and sometimes the requirement) to employ members of the indigenous population. This then often means that the resort has to offer educational opportunities, either on site or by means of technology, through Web classes or satellite TV.

Resort Marketing

Think about planning a vacation. How do you decide where and when to go and how long you will stay? What do you want to do? If you are single, married without children, or if you have a family, how do you work around the various preferences? Resort marketers have to understand their potential customers' wants and needs and project how these will affect their decision-making processes. What will cause customers to choose *their* resort over another? What is the best way to communicate information that will make customers believe that their resort will satisfy their needs? Will they choose their destination first and then decide where to stay? What marketing approach will promote not only the destination, but the individual resort?

Marketers use research to help them answer these questions. Resorts constantly investigate who their customers are, where they come from, and how they make their leisure travel decisions. Modern data processing, hotel guest histories, credit card spending information, questionnaires, and surveys all help marketers identify major source markets. When they know where the majority of their guests come from, they can focus their efforts on buying heavier media coverage in those areas.

Many resort destinations market through a convention and visitors bureau, a chamber of commerce, a resort association, or some other partnership of entities interested in promoting the destination. Airlines often cooperate with resorts in promoting destinations along their routes. Credit card companies, who make money on commissions on purchases by cardholders, are often willing to cooperate in advertising resort destinations where cardholders spend significant sums. Such joint efforts also maximize valuable marketing dollars.

Marketers also must consider whether they are better off marketing to a geographical area (perhaps ZIP codes identified as common to many guests) or to an interest group (such as readers of golf, skiing, or scuba magazines).

A third avenue available is the use of travel agents or tour operators. These groups must be paid commissions and offered discounts, but they often deliver business that is difficult for a resort to reach or attract. Good marketing may bring guests to a resort the first time, but good management and a friendly, efficient staff are the keys to creating a resort experience that will bring guests back for repeat visits, the backbone of all successful resorts.

The People Factor at Resorts

Due to the unique mix of features in a resort environment, managers and employees in resorts must be adaptable to serving guests who have different motivations and behavior patterns than business travelers. Guests who stay for pleasure are less focused on efficiency than on enjoying their experience. They are in and out of their rooms several times a day, perhaps changing between activities, perhaps taking a nap, or maybe just lounging on the balcony or patio. Resort guests tend to sleep later than business travelers, and front desk managers must often diplomatically decline late check-outs to guests who'd like to linger. If they don't, arriving guests won't be able to check into the clean and ready room they expect.

Guests are on the property for several days or longer and, as a result, have more time to develop relationships with staff. These relationships are also a big part of the resort experience and can greatly influence repeat business. Club Med has taken this guest-staff interaction further than any other chain, but even more traditional resorts recognize the importance of hiring employees who have good communication and social skills as well as technical ability.

It's not uncommon for resorts to double the size of their staff as the high season approaches, and then cut back again when the high season is over. This provides its own problems with regard to service excellence. It's hard to provide the same quality of service at one-third the high-season price—and with half the staff.

Conclusion

Resorts are challenging and exciting places to work. Customer focus is different from that of city, suburban, or airport hotels. Guests are there to enjoy themselves, and successful resort managers create memorable and diverse resort experiences that stimulate repeat visits. Demographic and social trends have created more leisure time and more opportunities for people to travel and have resulted in increased demand for leisure services, activities, and facilities.

A specialization in resort operations and management can provide challenging and satisfying career opportunities. With the right skills, experience, and adaptability,

Exhibit 8.7   As the ski season reaches its peak, so do staffing levels at ski resorts all over the country. (*Courtesy:* Tom Brownold)

would-be resort managers can look forward to working in a wide variety of locations, climates, property sizes, and specialized recreational facilities.

CLUB OPERATIONS

Clubs have long been places for people of similar interests to engage in activities they like. They provide an environment where like-minded people can share each others' company and congenial activities. The history has long been one of exclusivity and social privilege, with many clubs traditionally excluding women and minorities. The Civil Rights Act of 1964 forbids exclusion on the basis of race, creed, religion, gender, or national origin, and a series of court cases has made the point that private clubs may exclude individuals for various reasons, but not for any of the above.

There are many types of private clubs serving the social and recreational needs of their members. The study of club management has long been overlooked by many academic hospitality programs. However, the club industry has grown rapidly in many regions of the United States and provides many managerial opportunities for hospitality graduates. This section describes the different types of private clubs and discusses the management junctions involved in this specialty.

Types of Clubs

Clubs are generally categorized in one of three ways:

1. **By location:** Country clubs, city clubs, or beach clubs.
2. **By activity:** Golf clubs, tennis clubs, yacht clubs, health or athletic clubs, rod and gun clubs, or hunting clubs.

Ethics

Although managers of events, attractions, and resorts face ethical challenges, club managers may encounter them more frequently, given the close relationship they have with their clients, who are also indirectly their bosses. For instance, a club manager may be approached by a very influential member who is a prominent local business owner. This member may try to convince the manager to purchase his/her products for the club without using fair bidding practices. Managers may also find themselves unwilling participants in political struggles between power groups within their club's membership. Dealing with such situations requires a high standard of ethical conduct. Sometimes it may be hard to sort out the rights and wrongs or weigh the best interests of the club, its members' satisfaction, and its board of directors' policies. Integrity and honesty should always come first.

3. **By ownership:** Membership-owned equity clubs, individual- or company-owned clubs, clubs owned by a corporation for its own employees, and U.S. government–owned military clubs.

The members in an **equity club** buy a share in the ownership of the club's assets. Most clubs own valuable land and buildings, and each member thus owns a proportional share of the assets. Since the purpose of such clubs lies not in the seeking of profits but in the service to its members, they are usually exempted from income taxes. An example of an equity club is the famous Brookline Country Club in Massachusetts, one of the oldest country clubs in the United States.

A **development club** is a profit-seeking entity. A company develops a club and then sells membership to the public. Members have no control over club operations. The Dallas-based Club Corporation of America is a leader in developing and managing such clubs. Many development clubs are associated with real estate development. The presence of the club adds value to residents' homes and offers them amenities as homeowners. The initiation fee for club membership is usually the purchase of a lot within the development. After the development company sells a certain proportion of the property within the development, it will often deed the club to the property owners, who then gain control of its operations.

A club owned by a corporation is used for its own executives, managers, and employees. Such facilities promote employee morale and build friendships among managers and workers. A good example is the DuPont Country Club. which has more than 10,000 members, most of whom are employees of DuPont.

The U.S. government also operates clubs for military personnel around the world. Many of these military clubs have excellent facilities and offer a wide range of recreational and travel services. They often seek civilian personnel to manage these facilities, offering attractive salaries and fringe benefits.

Club Membership

Most of the ***private clubs*** in the United States are member-owned equity clubs. More than 50 percent of these are country club or golf club operations. Members pay a one-time initiation fee to become a member of the club, then pay ongoing dues to maintain membership and receive services. The membership structure in

Exhibit 8.8   Most resorts and clubs now offer their guests and members a multitude of activities, from fitness and scuba diving to yoga and tennis. (*Courtesy:* Four Seasons Hotels and Resorts)

private clubs can be very complicated. Following is only a partial listing of commonly encountered membership categories:

- **Regular:** These members pay full initiation fees and membership dues. They enjoy the full privileges of using club facilities and services. They have voting rights.
- **Social:** Social members pay reduced initiation fees and membership dues. In turn, their access to club facilities and services is limited. For instance, most social members are permitted to use the clubhouse for social and dining functions only. They must pay additional fees if they use golf or tennis facilities. In most clubs, they have no voting rights.

- **Junior:** Most clubs offer junior membership for the children of regular members. Junior members are usually 21 to 30 years old. Dues and initiation fees are lower than those of regular members, but they are entitled to use all club facilities. They seldom have an equity interest in the club or a right to vote on its operations.

Some clubs offer a range of limited membership categories for nonresidents, senior citizens, and spouses of former club members. A member from one category may also switch categories (such as from social to regular member) when openings become available. Most private equity clubs limit their membership to keep from overcrowding their facilities. Many prestigious country clubs have waiting lists of more than 10 years, with many eager candidates for membership.

Club Organizational Structure

The organizational structure of clubs differs from that of most hotel operations. In hotels, the general manager is the chief operating officer, at the top of the management hierarchy. In private clubs, the management hierarchy is quite different.

The members are the owners of the club and they are the decision-makers. The members elect a board of directors for overseeing club operations, formulating club rules and bylaws, and hiring the general manager (GM). The board of directors also appoints various standing committees to work with the GM on appropriate management aspects. The GM attends the monthly board of directors' meeting and reports on club operations. He or she must work with the standing committees and supervise the management team. The ultimate goal for a club manager is to satisfy the needs of the membership. Such positions are very challenging due to the combination, and multitude, of masters the GM must serve, directly and indirectly.

Club Finance

The main source of club revenues is membership dues. Clubs have a pool of customers that is limited to members and guests. If members don't generate sufficient revenue to support the club's operations, alternate measures must be taken. Typically, clubs' choices in such cases are limited to increasing membership, trying to increase fees, or assessing members a one-time fee to cover deficits. In a member-owned club, these can be sensitive issues. In effect, the board of directors must ask members to charge themselves more or risk overcrowding their facility—always a tough proposition.

A number of clubs set a minimum revenue level by charging their members a minimum monthly fee to increase the use of club food and beverage services. Members who don't frequent the club often enough to spend the minimum amount pay it, nonetheless. This makes them more likely to patronize the club, rather than waste their money.

Individuals have different tastes and opinions as to how things should be done. Club members are no exception, and one of the challenges club managers face is reconciling differing opinions. A constant source of club discontent involves the fee levels, which most members want to minimize. Still, periodic major replacement of worn and broken equipment is a necessity, as is good preventative maintenance.

Managers must work with board of directors' decisions on these matters, which can sometimes be counter-logical.

Club Operations

Club management and operations are a specialized career within the hospitality industry. Just as students get tired of dorm food, long-time club members want variety. Club managers often find themselves juggling the priorities of those who want things just as they've always been, and members who want things changed or improved.

Club employees often develop relationships with members over time. This can complicate matters when members interfere in issues involving managers and staff members. Members may also feel their ownership gives them the right to express complaints directly to the board, bypassing the normal chain of command and magnifying small offenses.

Conclusion

Club members usually consider the club an extension of their living room. Every club member feels that the club belongs to him or her and acts accordingly. This sometimes requires a diplomatic juggling act from managers as they seek to offer a balance of events aimed at different generations and special interest groups within

Exhibit 8.9   Cedar Point, an internationally famous amusement attraction, has delighted families for generations. Part of the fun is talking about the exhilaration of the roller coasters and water rides. (*Courtesy:* Cedar Point, Sandusky, Ohio)

the membership. Club managers face a real challenge in trying to deliver fresh and interesting services and products to the same members, at acceptable prices, over extended periods of time.

ATTRACTIONS

Most of us have visited an attraction at one time or another. As the name says, an ***attraction*** is a place, structure, building, or scenic point that attracts people. The source of the attraction may be a natural phenomenon or it may be a human creation. For instance, the Grand Canyon and Niagara Falls have been natural wonders for centuries. The Eiffel Tower in Paris, the pyramids of Egypt, and Disneyland in Los Angeles, CA, are man-made attractions. Many of the man-made attractions were built for profit (Euro Disney, Six Flags, and many other nationally and internationally known theme parks), whereas others were built for different reasons. The Eiffel Tower was created for a World Exposition at the end of the 19th century, and the pyramids of Egypt were built as tombs for the pharaohs some 5000 years ago. Despite the difference in their origins, age, and intent, all these are referred to as attractions. The emphasis in this chapter will be on the man-made, for-profit attractions.

Attraction Ownership

Attractions fall into three economic categories: (1) attractions that are privately funded and operated for profit; (2) those that are publicly funded and operated as non-profit operations; and (3) those that are quasi-public, that is, they combine private and public funding, usually for the profit of the private entity(s).

Exhibit 8.10   Although not built and designed to attract large crowds, the Sphinx and the pyramids of Egypt now need to be managed as any modern man-made attraction. (*Photo courtesy:* Phil Pappas)

International

The United States is now the second most visited tourist destination in the world. Increasing numbers of international tourists will continue to flock to American attractions, resorts, and events. In the past, many foreign tourists traveled in groups with guides and translators. In recent years, however, more and more foreign tourists are traveling in couples or families, as independent travelers. This is becoming increasingly true of Asians. Managers can be proactive in preventing difficulties for such visitors by using international signage, collecting a list of bilingual speakers who may be called in emergencies, or translating important information into the languages of the nationalities who most commonly patronize the operation.

Some attractions that have traditionally been classified as public may have been developed privately and later sold to governmental agencies. Often land owned by one government agency can be transferred to another government agency to become a public attraction. For instance, a U.S. Army coastal artillery training site, Camp Monomoy, on Cape Cod in Massachusetts, became the Cape Cod National Seashore Park in the 1960s.

Seasonality of Attractions

An important consideration in managing an attraction is its seasonality. Climatic conditions imposed by the changing seasons often dictate the attractiveness and the demand for hospitality services. Many attractions are open only in the summer, when weather is warm and the attraction is physically accessible. Others, like Death Valley National Monument in California, may curtail operations in the summer because of excessive heat. Managers of attractions are constantly using their ingenuity to find ways to extend their operational season and thus increase revenues.

Admissions

A significant feature of for-profit attractions is their paid admission. Admission is physically controlled by entry gates to events or facilities.

It is these admission fees that generate the revenues that, at least partially, cover the operational costs of running the attraction. The fees require a form of documentation such as tickets or vouchers, and management can project revenues and assign expenses based on the sale of these tickets.

Visitation

All attractions and hospitality operations would like their guests to return. Many hospitality operations depend on repeat guests for their survival. Hotels often report greater than 85 percent repeat visitation; however, at some attractions repeat visitation dips below 10 percent. A person may only visit the Eiffel Tower or Grand Canyon once in a lifetime, but patronize a hotel many times.

Exhibit 8.11   During the summer, roads in Sedona, Arizona are congested and traffic jams happen daily. Still the city and many of its citizens resist building new roads or broadening existing ones. Why? They share a concern that such changes would irrevocably change Sedona and affect its quality of life.

The challenge for managers of attractions or hospitality operations within, near, or as part of an attraction is to make guests feel they have received a significant value for the money they have spent. The idea is to create an experience so perfect, with so much perceived value, that the guest will want to return. More important, attraction managers want their guests to boast about their experience to family, friends, and associates. This is the most treasured of all marketing achievements, and is known as word-of-mouth advertising. Achieving this target guest experience and favorable word of mouth requires close attention to detail in every operational function of an attraction. Operators continuously look for new amenities to add to their attractions to increase return patronage.

A good example of this is how Disney World in Orlando, Florida has been able to attract millions of visitors over the years. Not only is the park spotless and every guest's need anticipated ahead of time, but new attractions such as the Animal Kingdom are added regularly.

Marketing

Marketing the attraction is a major operational concern. A marketing position statement is developed, emphasizing the overall experience and the high perceived value to satisfied guests.

Marketing approaches are devised to persuade guests to visit the site. These approaches carry the advertising message and project an identity to potential visitors.

Public relations efforts that portray the attraction as a "good neighbor" may include civic contributions (non-profit event sponsorships and donation of experience

Technology

Technology has been reshaping the operations of the tourism and hospitality industry at a rapid pace. Attraction and event management has been dramatically influenced by new technologies in lighting and sound. Theme parks, stadiums, and arenas often host incredible exhibitions with light shows and pyrotechnics. Festivals often feature live music, fireworks, or miles of strung mini-lights, especially during holiday celebrations. All these technologies require caution and concern for the safety of guests and participants. The incredible safety record of Disney, one of the pioneers of nightly light and fireworks spectacles, is due to training, security, and constant attention.

packages to foundations like Make a Wish). Contests and promotions are often coupled with advertising to reinforce perceived value.

Sales representatives are employed to call on potential sources of bulk business such as corporations, organizations, and associations. They attend trade shows, fairs, and tourist expositions. They will often cooperate with regional chambers of commerce or tourist bureaus to conduct sales blitzes in various geographic areas of the country.

Wholesale and retail tour brokers, travel agents, and travel planners can also be an effective sales force for attractions, as we already saw in the previous chapter. Listings in trade and tour directories, subscribed time on computer information networks, and placement on airline and major hotel reservation networks are all essential, since most brokers and agents use electronic computer networking to book 90 percent or more of their tours.

Merchandising

Closely linked to marketing is the ***merchandising*** of the attraction itself. Merchandising involves integrating all the products and services so they are best displayed for consumption by visitors. Successful merchandising is a direct result of the master planning of the project. It includes the placement and layout of the rides, view points, food and beverage outlets, gift shops, rest areas, and entertainment. The design should subtly orchestrate the guests' maximum contact with revenue-producing areas. Included in merchandising are staff members—hosts, characters, and employees who meet and greet the visitors. They make up a large part of the value perceived by the guests. For instance, Walt Disney theme parks view all employees as actors, all uniforms as costumes, and their parks as theaters. There is no crossing the line between acting and reality. The guest must always believe in the fantasy he or she is experiencing. Merchandising encourages guests to explore more of the fantasy or to take the fantasy home with them in the form of souvenirs.

Human Resource Management

Human resource management of attractions is one of the most difficult aspects of operations. Often remoteness, seasonality, and the theme of the attraction may make it extremely difficult to recruit, select, train, and motivate employees. Season-

Exhibit 8.12   A destination? A resort? An attraction? A casino? A merchandising dream? All terms that can be applied to the Luxor Hotel and Casino in Las Vegas, Nevada. (*Courtesy:* Luxor Hotel and Casino)

ality and remoteness may mean employees must be housed at the site and that all the traditional services must be provided: shopping areas, food, clothing, lodging, medical, schools, security, recreation, fire protection, and transportation.

Remoteness requires significant pre-employment and on-the-job training so that employees are knowledgeable about the environment to protect themselves and the guests. The theme of the attraction may require managers continually to motivate employees so that they do not destroy the image, fantasy, and perceived value guests must experience. Motivation requires managers to relay to the staff that each guest is to be viewed as a first-time visitor and that the guest experience must be perfect to assure the long-term success of the attraction. Pay and benefits must be equal to or better than those of other nearby facilities or employers.

EYE ON THE ISSUES

Service Excellence

Today's amusement-park rides are faster, scarier and more elaborate than ever, and many visitors clutch their stomachs when they get off the ride. In an effort to help patrons who want to board roller coasters in spite of their fears, and in order to better service their clientele, Universal Studio's Islands of Adventure in Orlando is offering the first stress-management program for apprehensive riders, led by two psychologists. The two will use anxiety-management techniques to help ease the fears of "coasterphobics," and to train employees in identifying and comforting anxious visitors.

Other Revenue Centers

The operation of attractions also includes some other areas that relate to revenue. Revenue centers often seen in conjunction with attractions are food and beverage operations, merchandise and souvenir shops, rides, and games. Attraction managers need to find effective ways to blend these revenue centers into their attractions to avoid clashing with the environment they've so carefully constructed, and to avoid creating the impression that they are only after the guests' money.

Conclusion

Running a tourist attraction is extremely complex. Just as with any other hospitality operation, the management of attractions requires excellent people, financial, marketing, and many other technical skills. The challenge is big, but you can imagine the self-fulfillment managers experience when they see happy visitors coming into their attraction full of anticipation—and leaving the attraction wholly satisfied, ready for yet another day at the park.

EVENTS

Events such as pop concerts, circuses, fairs, expositions, and shows are activities that attract multitudes of people to a particular place for a particular period. The main difference between events and attractions is that attractions are permanent and events are temporary. An event may be a one-time affair, or one that is repeated periodically. Many large events take place annually and last from one day to a few months. Their relative success over time will ultimately determine the size, length and frequency with which they occur.

Events are held for many reasons. Some broad classifications of events include:

- Religious
- Cultural
- Technical
- Economic
- Amusement
- Political
- Historical
- Sporting
- Social
- Recreational

Events can also be classified on the basis of geographical locations and degree of importance. For instance, internationally known mega-events include world fairs and the Olympics. Regional events include state fairs and other such events, while local events are generally city or community sponsored.

Obviously, many events evolve around a theme, as do attractions. It is this overriding theme that the guest wishes to experience and remember after departure. The theme (and the experience of it) becomes a silent salesperson through word-of-mouth advertising and is responsible for motivating other visitors to share the event's experience. Event managers have the responsibility to assure that the theme is carried throughout the operation.

Events generate significant revenues through admissions, seating charges, food and beverage sales, souvenir programs and publications, recorded music sales, and other items. The most difficult to manage is the food and beverage aspect. As part of the event, sufficient food and beverage outlets must be available to serve the visitors' needs. Since attendance is highly unpredictable due to weather, type of event, and competition from other nearby activities, the concession manager must rely on historical data, management skills, and luck.

Since most events are outdoor activities and last only short periods of time, a good deal of temporary or portable concession equipment and stands must be used. Employees must be recruited from nearby communities to work at the concession stands, prepare and deliver the food, and care for and clean the facilities. Only a limited amount of time is available to train these employees, so concessionaires employ a permanent cadre of department managers to train and oversee them.

Cash management is extremely important, and a staff of security personnel money runners must constantly collect the cash from the stands and deliver it to the counting room.

Vendors may be employed to roam through the crowds selling food, drinks, and souvenirs. Most vendors are paid a cash commission based on their sales. They must provide their own change bank and pay a reduced price for their items before they sell them. Care must be taken to be sure that vendors do not sell items for prices higher than the price set by management. To prevent this, badges, signs, and item packaging must clearly display the prices. Often these items will be a combination of refreshments and souvenirs.

At the Kentucky Derby, for instance, mint juleps are vended in a take-home highball glass. A recent trend in coliseums and sports parks is the availability of recognized franchise food outlets. Pizza Hut, McDonald's, Wendy's, Orange Julius, KFC, and Taco Bell may be represented in a food pavilion area. These may all be owned and operated by the concessionaire, leased, or operated individually.

THE CRUISELINE INDUSTRY

The cruiseline industry certainly deserves some attention in this book because it has been the fastest growing segment of the holiday business market over the last two decades. Its average annual growth rate was 8.2 percent during that time (see Exhibit 8.13 on p. 332), in particular in the 2–5 day cruise category (see Exhibit 8.14 on p. 332). It grew even faster than the resort and theme park segments. In 2000, there were 8 million passengers cruising, and between 1998 and 2002 a total of 42 new ships were added to the North American fleet alone, an increase of 10 percent in the number of berths.

Cruiseline passengers tend to be big spenders, not only on the cruise itself, but also on airline seats, hotel rooms (pre- and post-accommodations), souvenirs and tours in the ports of call. A recent survey found that the average cruise passenger spends about $1,300 per trip, and that 11 percent of the passengers spend more

Exhibit 8.13   The cruiseline industry has seen tremendous growth in recent decades.

Year	Annual Passenger Growth (000s)
1980	1,431
1984	1,859
1988	3,175
1990	3,640
1992	4,136
1994	4,448
1996	4,656
1998	5,428
2000	6,882
2002	7,640
2004	9,107
Average growth rate	**+ 8.2%**

(*Courtesy:* Cruise Lines International Association)

than $2,500. The development and growth of the cruiseline industry is certainly something you may want to take a closer look at.

History

The *Titanic* is probably one of the first ships that comes to mind when you think about cruise ships. Its maiden, and only (!), voyage took place in 1912, and the first-class passengers on the ship certainly lived up to our ideas about what luxury ocean travel is all about: They ate caviar and drank champagne while wearing glimmering gowns, and were entertained by a great orchestra. Yet the *Titanic* was definitely not the first cruise ship. One of the first American-origin cruises took place in 1867. Mark Twain was aboard that ship so we know, through his writings, that there was entertainment on board in the form of dancing, music, and mystery dinners. The ship, which was a paddlewheel steamer, visited France, Italy, Morocco, Greece, Egypt, Turkey, and Israel.

World War I slowed down cruise vacations, but after the war, event cruising became fashionable, especially since prohibition had left America dry, and one could

Exhibit 8.14   The biggest growth has occurred in the short-trip segment of the industry.

	Passengers (000s)		
	1980	2004	% growth
2–5 days	347	2,861	+724
6–8 days	846	5,054	+497
9–17 days	221	1,161	+425
18+ days	17	31	+ 82

(*Courtesy:* Cruise Lines International Association)

Exhibit 8.15   Ever bigger and better! Golf has found its way onto major cruise ships in recent years too. (*Courtesy:* Princess Cruises)

drink alcohol aboard a ship outside territorial waters. On the other side of the Atlantic, the cruise business was growing too. With declining numbers of immigrants, many companies had too many ships to fill and converted them to cruiseliners.

The big boom in the cruise industry occurred after the launch of *The Love Boat,* which was not a ship, but a TV series. Two ships of the Princess cruiseline provided the backdrop to the series, which was in production for 10 years. It created great marketing opportunities for every company in the cruiseline industry, which has become the fastest growing segment in the travel and tourism industry.

Guests and Product

The cruiseline industry has grown tenfold between 1970 and today, a staggering growth indeed! In the '70s, cruise ships were much smaller than they are now and were generally populated by older guests. These people had the time and the money to go on cruises. There were few families and very few honeymooners. Over the past 10 years, the cruiseline industry has responded to extensive market and consumer research, which has lead to the addition of new destinations, new design concepts, new on-board and on-shore activities, new themes, and new cruise lengths. All of these changes have lead not only to more people going on cruises, but market segments such as families with children, people under 30, and mid-income travelers starting to go on cruises. The appeal has become universal, with cruiseline companies offering something for every interest, age, and income level.

Exhibit 8.16   Cruiseline companies have expanded their on-board offerings to include golf and fitness activities, as well as relaxing privacy. (*Courtesy:* Princess Cruises)

Some of the changes that have occurred over the last 20 years are:

- Public, but also private, space was increased.
- Larger and more modern galley facilities have led to improved and enlarged menu options.
- Menus now have more healthy choices, and today's wine lists are very extensive.
- Casinos were added.
- Ports of call now not only provide sightseeing tours but also experiential trips.
- Entertainment now ranges from Las Vegas style shows and Celebration on Ice revues to big box office celebrities and sports stars being contracted to take a cruise and entertain and mingle with the guests.
- Exercise and spa areas have been added.
- Smoke-free dining rooms and cabins were introduced (with only 20 percent of the population smoking nowadays).
- Many companies now offer "theme" cruises, focusing on everything from food, lodging, décor, dress, and entertainment on a particular theme (see Exhibit 8.17).

Facts about Cruiseline Customers

As discussed earlier, the cruiseline industry has been very successful in broadening its market appeal over the years. Where it was primarily the vacation for the older, retired market segment in years past, it now attracts guests from every walk of life, with an abundance of different incentives. Consider the following statistics:

Jazz, blues, rock, country and big band cruises

Eclipse cruises

Film buff cruises

Golf cruises

Oktoberfest cruises

"Whales in the Wild" cruises

Maya explorer cruises

Wine and food festival cruises

Fashion cruises

Elvis cruises

Civil War cruises

Mother's Day cruises

Bible cruises

Sports cruises

World Wrestling Federation cruises

Exhibit 8.17   Theme Cruises.

- Baby boomers comprise a majority (53 percent) of the cruise population. They are leading stressful and intense lives and look for a vacation for relaxation and escape. With limited time available, a cruise is an ideal "quick fix" for many of them.
- Six percent of the people cruising are ship buffs. They have cruised extensively and love the experience.
- Luxury seekers (14 percent) are very sophisticated travelers. They desire extravagance and like to be pampered.
- Explorers (11 percent) are well educated, well traveled individuals with a lot of curiosity about different destinations.
- Value seekers (16 percent) are very committed cruisers. Cruising meets their needs, and offers them the best value.

Six percent of the people who go on a cruise take their children (under 18) with them. This is still a small percentage, but cruiselines are increasingly starting to cater to this segment. They have started to build family suites on ships, with Murphy beds and convertible sofas. Some ships have special decks devoted to kids. Some cruise lines offer a variety of age-specific programs and hands-on activities. There are special offshore excursions planned just for kids, such as hiking in the mountains, and treasure hunts. And of course, day care is available for parents who prefer to do something without their kids, and for kids who don't care about seeing "another ruin." A cruiseline that has entered the market fairly recently and that caters extensively to children is the Disney Cruise Line. It offers activities to six different age groups. Parents are given pagers so that they can stay in touch with their children, Disney characters stroll around the ship, and restaurants are designed with Disney animated walls.

Marketing

Almost all cruiselines still present themselves as offering a luxury vacation for the country club set (the Love Boat crowd). You hardly see dressed down people in the ads. For many people, going on a cruise is a status symbol, and the people

Exhibit 8.18   Reasons Why People Go on a Cruise

A Cruise.	Percentage Agreeing with Statement
Allows you to relax	79
Allows you to be pampered	79
Chance to visit several destinations	78
Good value for the money	78
Offers variety of activities	76
Good way to try out a vacation area	75
A fun vacation	75
Offers quality entertainment	71
Offers comfortable accommodations	70
A way to meet interesting people	67
A learning experience	64
A romantic getaway	62

(*Courtesy:* Cruise Lines International Association)

selling the cruise want to keep it that way. Relaxation and pampering are still the two top reasons why cruising is rated more highly than any other type of vacation (see Exhibit 8.18). Additionally, people go on cruises to see many different geographic locations in a relatively short period of time by participation in such shore activities as shopping, sightseeing, and visiting local attractions.

A Variety of Options

There are differences among cruises and cruiselines. Like any other hospitality product, the price of a cruise will vary with the food, the amenities offered, the service, the space, the facilities, the length of the cruise, the destination, and even the size of the company (see Exhibit 8.19). It is generally known that Carnival Cruises and Royal Caribbean are among the more "budget type" lines, offering shorter, cheaper cruises. In the mid-range among cruise lines we find companies such as Holland-America and Princess. At the high end, offering longer and more exotic cruises, are such companies as Club Med, Seabourn, and Cunard. Yet, with at least 30 different companies in the North American market alone offering all sorts of different options, the distinctions between companies become somewhat difficult to

Exhibit 8.19   Largest Cruise Lines (2005) (North American Passenger Capacity)

	No. of "Lowers" (Beds)
Royal Caribbean International	45,570
Carnival Cruise Lines	44,934
Princess Cruises	28,050
Costa Cruise Lines (Italian)	18,287
Norwegian Cruise Line	17,890
Holland America Line	16,937
Celebrity Cruises	16,116

(*Courtesy:* Cruise Line International Association)

make. Since it is hard to distinguish one cruiseline from another, potential cruisers often consult with travel agents and friends and family before booking their trips. In 95 percent of cases, the travel agent does the booking.

Conclusion

The growth in the cruiseline industry has been enormous in the past, and expectations are that, with all the attention that is paid to increasing market share in various "nontraditional" segments, that trend will continue for several years to come. A management career in the cruise line industry will make great demands on a person's organizational and social skills. Equipping, staffing, and managing a large cruise ship requires special people, who do not mind being surrounded by their customers in a confined space for a long period of time. As was the case with club managers, a social activities director on a cruise ship, for instance, does not have one boss; there are thousands of "bosses" making demands on his or her time every day. Yet, at the same time, working for a cruise line also means working with people who are enjoying themselves, and having the opportunity to visit many different and exotic parts of the world. A career as a manager in the cruiseline industry is definitely one of the more glamorous, but also more demanding, careers in the hospitality industry.

CONCLUSION

This chapter touched on several major components of the tourism and hospitality industries. It outlined many potential exciting career opportunities for hospitality graduates in club, resort, attraction, event management and the cruiseline industry. Although each area has it own focus and specialization, the common denominator is still service. A hospitality management graduate with good people skills and appropriate preparation in finance, technology, and management can excel in any of these areas.

Exhibit 8.20   Cruiselines market luxury, fun, accommodations, and activities set against some of the world's most dramatic landscapes, whether your taste is for gorgeous glaciers or turquoise tropics. (*Courtesy:* Princess Cruises)

KEYWORDS

spa   312
destination resort   313
activity-based resort   314
high season   315

shoulder season   315
low season   315
equity club   321
development club   321

CORE CONCEPTS

resort hotels   310
seasonality   315
length of stay   316
private clubs   321

attraction   325
merchandising   328
event   330

DISCUSSION QUESTIONS

1. Discuss the differences between resorts and non-resorts. Mention at least one difference as it relates to each of the following areas:
   a. Marketing
   b. Guest motivation
   c. Housekeeping
   d. Food and beverage
   Now add one more difference *from an area not included in a, b, c, or d.*
2. What are the effects of seasonality on resort pricing, marketing, staff, and operations?
3. What are some of the issues resort managers in remote locations have to deal with that city hotel operators do not? Discuss staffing, transportation, utilities, and environmental impacts.
4. Discuss how consumers' hotel choices differ when they book a resort hotel as opposed to booking a city hotel.
5. What departments might exist in a resort hotel that are not typically found in city and suburban hotels?
6. What differentiates an equity club from a development club?
7. How does the club organizational structure differ from that of most mid-size hotels?
8. What are the major sources of club revenues? Of club expenditures?
9. Why do many clubs impose a minimum monthly fee on their members?
10. Identify the major revenue centers of attraction operations.
11. What are three of the major operational challenges for a concession manager in managing an event?
12. What are some of the most important factors that have contributed to the growth of the cruiseline industry in recent years?
13. What distinguishes a "budget" cruiseline from a luxury cruiseline?

Resorts

www.sandiego.org
  (San Diego CVB website)
www.hyatt.com
  (Hyatt Hotels and Resorts)
www.scottsdale-resorts.com
  (Scottsdale AZ Resorts)
www.clubmed.com
  (Club Med website)
www.hiltonheadhilton.com
  (Hilton Resort at Hilton Head, NC)

Clubs

www.cmaa.org
  (Club Managers Association of America)
www.golfccc.com
  (California Country Club, Whittier, CA)
www.tccclub.org
  (Brookline Country Club, Massachussetts)
www.sunterra.com
  (Sunterra Resorts Company)
www.dupont.com/club
  (Du Pont Country Club for Du Pont employees)
www.afvclub.com
  (Air Force military clubs)

Attractions

www.disneyworld.com
  (Walt Disney World, Orlando, FL)
www.sixflags.com
  (Six Flags Park)
www.tour-eiffel.fr
  (Official Eiffel Tower website)
www.cheops.org
  (Website of Pyramid of Cheops, Egypt)
www.nps.org/deva/
  (Death Valley National Park website)

Events

www.texrenfest.com
  (Renaissance Fair in Plantersville, TX)
www.orangeblossom.com.au
  (Natural and Cultural Fair, Sydney, Australia)
www.indiaculturaltours.com
  (Tours of cultural fairs in India)

www.Religionnews.com/calendar
  (Calendar of major religious events around the world)
www.londonnet.co.uk
  (Pop concerts in London, England)

Cruiselines

www.disneycruise.com
  (Disney cruises)
www.carnival.com
  (Carnival Cruise Line)
www.princess.com
  (Princess Cruise Line)
www.pocruise.com
  (P&O Cruise Line)
www.cruiseshopping.com
  (Site to shop many different cruise lines)

Gaming and Casino Management

This chapter will introduce you to the world of gaming in the United States. It starts with a brief history so that you fully understand the context in which today's gaming industry operates. We will look at the societal impact of gaming as a leisure activity, and discuss the need for regulation. Gaming activity in American history has alternated among being banned, regulated, and unfettered. We will look at the managerial challenges that come with running a casino, and issues such as organizational structure, surveillance, marketing, house advantage, and hold percentage. Let's roll the dice. . . .

INTRODUCTION

Casinos and gaming activity are growing exponentially around the country. While there have been casinos in the traditional markets of Nevada and Atlantic City for many years, there are now casinos up and down the Mississippi and Ohio Rivers and on Indian reservations in many of the 50 states. Card rooms are popular in California, and many states offer a lottery to help fund government activities. Except for Utah and Hawaii, there is some form of gaming available to the public in every state in the United States.

Gaming brings economic opportunities to impoverished communities. Jobs are created and sustained by the activity. People who were dependent on welfare and other forms of public assistance find hope in jobs that pay well and offer advancement. Greater economic activity means greater tax revenues, and governments have more resources to supply the services that taxpayers demand.

Yet this tremendous benefit does not come without a cost. There are social costs, which must be addressed in order to justify the presence of gaming in a community. Bankruptcy, divorce, crime, and corruption are just a few problems attributed to gaming. In a category by itself is pathological gambling. This is an impulse control disorder that is displayed through compulsive gambling, even after affected individuals understand the negative impact of their behavior.

Many see the negative impact of gaming and blame the casinos for being greedy. But just how do they make their money? While the odds of the games are predetermined, it is the way in which the payoffs are set that allows the casino to make money. This house advantage guarantees that a casino will be profitable.

The casino never refers to its house advantage, for obvious reasons. Instead they talk about the "drop percentage" and the "hold percentage." The "hold percentage" is that portion of the revenue that the casino retains after paying winners. The hold percentage varies from gaming activity to gaming activity. It even varies from month to month, but over time it is consistent. The hold percentage is one way in which casino managers determine if there is a problem with the integrity of their systems and security measures.

Because gaming is a casino's strongest revenue source, the hotel, food, and beverage departments are subordinate to the casino. They are viewed as services to the customers and are not always required to make a profit. Pricing in the lodging and food and beverage outlets in a casino resort is kept at a reasonable level to attract the maximum number of customers. This relationship is reflected in the organizational structure, where the gaming departments are separate from the services departments.

Exhibit 9.1   During the '90s, Las Vegas upped the ante on casino lavishness. Suddenly, Vegas became home to the Statue of Liberty, the Eiffel Tower, and the Canals of Venice. (*Courtesy:* New York-New York Hotel and Casino™)

The predominance of the gaming departments also affects the way in which the marketing department promotes the casino. Marketers identify premium players, who are commonly referred to as *high rollers,* and programs, services; activities are designed exclusively for this market segment so that the casino can maximize its revenue. The marketing department also develops promotions such as fights, prize drawings, and cultural activities to draw the largest number of customers as possible to the casino.

The issue of government regulation and control also affects the organizational structure. The surveillance department, which monitors activity throughout the casino complex, reports directly to the casino's general manager or director. In that way, any integrity issues are communicated to the highest levels quickly. Now that you have an idea of what we will be discussing in this chapter, a closer look at the history of gaming is in order.

GAMING HISTORY AND OVERVIEW

Gambling goes back to the dawn of man. There is evidence of gaming in ancient cultures, including those of the Chinese, Egyptians, Greeks, and Romans. Casting of lots, a form of risk taking, was used numerous times by the Israelites to divine

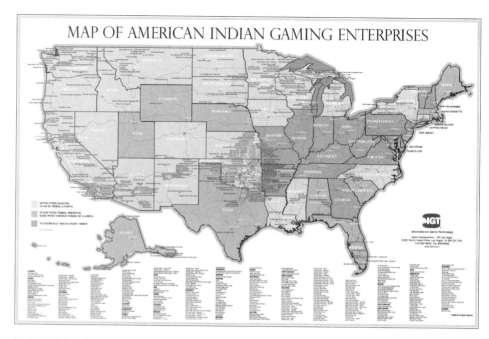

Exhibit 9.2   About two thirds of America's 562 federally recognized Indian tribes are involved in gaming on some level. The National Indian Gaming Association estimates this as a $20 billion industry. (*Courtesy:* Map provided by International Game Technology.)

the will of God, and is noted in the Bible. While gaming could be employed for useful purposes, more often than not it was—and is—a form of leisure activity.

Many studies have been done to determine the ***reasons why people gamble.*** While the conclusions sometimes vary, the studies seem to agree there are five major reasons people gamble:

1. Entertainment
2. Social activity
3. Exhilaration
4. Hope of winning
5. Behavioral disorder

A person who views gaming as *entertainment* is fascinated by the sounds and action of a casino. It is relief from the predictability or stress of everyday life. For others, the opportunity to participate in a *social activity* with friends or even strangers (who quickly become friends) is the attraction. To share an exciting moment of winning with another can be gratifying. Some people truly, get a thrill out of gaming. Their *exhilaration* is apparent especially if the dice are "hot" on the craps table or the cards are turning their way on the "21" table. Of course, many people have the *hope of winning.* After all, not many people would risk their money if they thought there was no chance to win.

Exhibit 9.3   People tend to gamble for five major reasons. Which activity do you see in action here? (*Photo courtesy:* Gold River Resort and Casino, Laughlin, Nevada)

The final reason some people gamble is due to a *behavioral disorder.* Often referred to as compulsive gambling, recent research has studied the causes of this behavior. While not enough is known about compulsive gambling, the behavior is difficult for the individual to control and often leads to a deterioration of the quality of life for the individual and those dependent upon him or her.

Since gambling is an intrinsic part of man's nature, it has been a part of most societies. When Europeans arrived on the North American continent, they found that many Native American tribes gambled as a social activity and as part of their religious

EYE ON THE ISSUES

International

The gaming industry has experienced tremendous growth in the United States. This trend is not isolated. Gaming activity has increased internationally. South Africa, Australia, Hong Kong, Malaysia, and Europe have all seen an increase in casinos. Some U.S. companies have even capitalized on these emerging markets by opening casinos abroad.

As the travel market becomes more globalized, casinos will need to appeal to international visitors. Multilingual brochures and videotapes, multilingual staff, and familiar games of chance are just a few of the ways to make an international visitor feel welcome. Attention to international tourists will assure guest satisfaction and return visits.

rituals. However, the forms of gaming offered in the United States today are rooted in European practices.

Gambling in Early America

The first Europeans who reached early America settled on the eastern seaboard of the continent first. Their gambling activities took the form of horse betting and card-playing. The social norms for gambling varied greatly depending upon the region. In the New England area, the Puritans, with their strict social and moral codes, had banned gambling. They felt that it promoted idleness and that it was unpleasing to God.

In the southern colonies, gambling was allowed due to a more relaxed social code. However, laws were enacted to ensure gambling did not jeopardize the social and economic order and to protect the honesty of gaming activities. State-sanctioned lotteries were used throughout the colonies to raise funds for infrastructure needs such as roads, bridges, and public facilities. These lotteries even helped pay for the costs of the Revolutionary War.

After the Revolutionary War and into the early years of the 19th century, the frontier moved westward. The east coast became more settled as the Europeans pushed past the Appalachian Mountains in search of land. ***Gambling activity followed the frontier.*** While the east coast began to place more restrictions and regulations on gambling, the frontier offered unrestricted gambling due to the lack of laws and law enforcement.

Between the Revolutionary War and the Civil War, gambling was concentrated along the Ohio and Mississippi Rivers and in the river towns. Wealthy plantation owners and merchants rode the paddlewheel riverboats to conduct business, or for pleasure. To while away the time, passengers engaged in card games. This attracted professional card players, who were not always scrupulous and often cheated. There were numerous attempts to eliminate this dishonest element, but none were completely successful.

With the end of the Civil War in 1865, the southern states were devastated. Railroads, agricultural land, civic buildings, and private property had been destroyed in the war. The population had been reduced by war casualties as well as disease and starvation on the home front. There was precious little capital, either physical and human, available to rebuild.

Exhibit 9.4   Visitors to the Aztar Hotel and Executive Conference Center can step on to the floating Casino Aztar on the Ohio River. Though it looks "old timey" to capture the thrill of 19th Century river gambling, this casino was built new and is equipped with very modern technology. (Photo by Brian Bohannon, AP Wide World Photos)

Exhibit 9.5   Gambling in the old west took place mostly in saloons. Because cards were so easily portable, card games prevailed, but dice games were also popular. (Drawn by Walter L. Buzby)

The Louisiana Lottery.   In 1865, the State of Louisiana awarded a contract to a syndicate from the east coast to run a lottery. In exchange for the profits from the lottery, the syndicate agreed to pay Louisiana $40,000 per year for 25 years. The payment was a considerable amount of money at the time and was to be used to rebuild the war-battered state. The lottery was named the Louisiana Lottery and tickets were sold all over the United States.

Corruption quickly followed. Politicians and legislators were bribed and elections manipulated to favor the lottery. In 1879, the lottery charter was voided by the state legislature, but the syndicate applied pressure and bribed officials. The legislature reconvened and renewed the charter. The activity in Louisiana drew national attention and in 1890, Congress banned the use of the Postal Service to mail lottery paraphernalia. In 1892, Louisiana voted down the renewal of the charter and the syndicate moved its operation to Honduras, still using the name of the Louisiana Lottery. In 1895, Congress prohibited the import of lottery materials, and the Louisiana Lottery soon ceased to operate.

Gambling in the Old West

After the Civil War, Europeans increasingly settled the eastern half of the continent. Gambling became progressively more restricted and regulated in the eastern and Midwestern states. Non–state sponsored gambling moved west of the Mississippi River into the great plains and the mountain states. The most prevalent form of gambling involved cards and took place in saloons and wherever cowboys gathered. Again, professional card players were attracted to these areas, and cheating at cards was not uncommon.

Gambling in 20th Century America

With the close of the frontier just after 1900, gambling became illegal everywhere in the United States. Yet, since gambling is an innate part of human nature, it did not stop, but went underground. It was most widespread in large cities, primarily Chicago and New York. An organized criminal element ran the gambling activity and found it necessary to bribe policemen, politicians, and judges in order to continue. Raids were staged to give the appearance that the government was cracking down, but gambling outfits were operational in no time after the "raids." Unfortunately, violence and crime were an inherent part of gambling activity.

In 1929, the New York stock market crashed and by 1930, the world was in a depression. Economic activity declined sharply and governments found their tax revenues also declining drastically. The depression was like nothing that had ever been experienced previously, and, in response to the need for economic development and tax revenue, Nevada legalized gambling in 1931.

Gaming in Nevada has been centered in Reno and Washoe County since that time, and initially, Las Vegas was little more than a train stop between Los Angeles and Salt Lake City. Most early casinos were storefront operations with a handful of table games, some slot machines and a bar (Harrah's, which is still a prominent name today, started in Reno in 1937 as a father and son operation). During the first 15 years of legal gaming, the county sheriff issued licenses and collected taxes. Obviously, the early gaming industry was far simpler and more informal than it is today.

Las Vegas.   In 1946, Benjamin "Bugsy" Siegel moved from New York to Las Vegas. He was a member of an organized crime group that ran illegal gaming activities. He dreamed of opening a casino in Las Vegas. Why not do legally what he had been doing illegally in New York? The savings in bribes and down time from staged raids alone would make it worthwhile, he figured.

His dream was bigger than that, though. He wanted to build a casino that offered a total package: entertainment, hotel rooms, restaurants, a golf course, and other amenities. He felt this combination would attract people to what was then a remote location. In 1946, he opened the Flamingo Hotel and Casino. It struggled at first, and Bugsy lost his life, but the concept eventually succeeded. Today's Las Vegas casinos reflect the evolutions of gaming that started with Bugsy's dream.

While organized crime could operate casinos legally in Nevada, it did not leave all its illegal ways behind. Crime and violence infected Las Vegas, and the federal government was very interested in the activities of organized crime in Nevada. Nevada feared the federal government would interfere with the gaming industry and possibly ban it, which would stifle the state's efforts to develop its economy by slashing tax revenues. As a defensive move, Nevada assumed the role of regulator. Through the 1950s and 1960s, the State of Nevada imposed increasingly strict regulations and controls on casinos. This was much more an effort to protect the industry than it was a means to regulate it. The Gaming Control Board and the Gaming Control Commission were established to oversee the industry and to ensure that no illegal activity would bring about the downfall of the industry.

Since the day the Flamingo opened in 1946, Las Vegas has reinvented itself in response to market demand. When Caesar's Palace opened in 1966, a new standard for luxury defined by a theme was established. The renovation of the Golden Nugget on Fremont Street by Steve Wynn rejuvenated the downtown area. The advent of family-friendly casinos such as Treasure Island, the Luxor, and the MGM

Exhibit 9.6   Las Vegas is the pre-eminent gaming market in the world. Casino developers have not been afraid to spend money to make money, even to the extent of recreating Venice, Italy. (*Courtesy:* The Venetian Resort Hotel Casino, Las Vegas, Nevada)

Grand in the early 1990s allowed Las Vegas to attract the aging "baby boomer with children" segment.

As this new century has begun, a string of extraordinarily large upscale properties are opening to rave reviews, and properties such as Paris, the Venetian, New York, New York, the Bellagio, and Wynn have opened their doors in recent years, one even more lavish than the other!

Yet even casinos can fall on hard times: Casino revenues in 2001 were $7.6 billion, which was flat compared to 2000. This was undoubtedly the result of 9/11, which adversely affected travel and tourism in general, and the Las Vegas market in particular. However, Las Vegas has bounced back stronger than ever. It seems hard to believe, but through good times and hard times, Las Vegas has survived and thrived.

New Jersey.   Seeing the success of Las Vegas and Nevada, in 1976 New Jersey voters approved a referendum to legalize casino gaming. Again, the motivation was to generate economic development and tax revenues. However, fear of criminal activity led to the restriction of casinos in Atlantic City only, which was a rundown resort city from the early 1900s with a large elderly and ethnic minority population, and a high unemployment rate. It was felt that eliminating corrupt influences would be easier if the industry were geographically restricted. At the same time, economic benefits would be concentrated in an area of tremendous need.

Atlantic City today is home to 12 casinos, which employ over 50,000 people and generated $4.4 billion in revenues in 2002. What was once a blighted area on its way to oblivion is now a thriving gaming market.

Native American Gaming.   Also in 1976, the seeds of Native American gaming were planted. The lawsuit *Bryan* vs. *Itasca County* established that states did not have regulatory jurisdiction over Native American tribes within their boundaries. This ruling was significant because it reinforced the concept of tribes as sovereign nations who hold a government-to-government relationship with the federal government, as do other nations of the world.

The course was set. In 1979, the lawsuit *Seminole Tribe* vs. *Butterworth* established that a state could not prohibit bingo, because the state does not have regulatory power over tribes as established in *Bryan* vs. *Itasca County*. In 1987, in *California* vs. *Cabazon Band of Mission Indians*, the courts ruled that the state could not prohibit gaming on reservations if similar gaming activity, even if for charity purposes, were legal within the state.

Based on all of these lawsuits, Congress acted quickly. In 1988, the ***Indian Gaming Regulatory Act (IGRA)*** was passed. It legalized casino gaming on reservations and provided a framework within which states and tribes could work to establish casinos on tribal lands. Its stated purpose was to encourage economic development on reservations, to strengthen tribal government, and to promote self-sufficiency among Native Americans.

Today, the number of Native American casinos in the United States is approaching 300. The largest and most successful casino in the world, Foxwood Casino in Connecticut, is 300,000 square feet in size, with more than 6,500 slot machines and hundreds of gaming tables. It is owned and managed by the Mashantucket Pequot tribe and has been responsible for lifting the tribe out of poverty, not to mention reviving a slumping local economy. Other tribes have experienced similar results when casino gaming was introduced in their territories.

Exhibit 9.7   Native American tribes are using gaming and tourism revenues as forms of economic development. (*Courtesy:* Cow Creek Indian Gaming Center, Canyonville, Oregon)

Riverboat Gaming.   The states have also seen the benefits of gaming. As states increased programs and services to their residents, they also increased the tax burdens. The states needed a way to raise revenues without creating or increasing taxes. One response to this situation was to legalize casino-style gaming on riverboats. Centered in the midwest along major rivers and lakes, boats that offer gaming are docked for boarding and debarking. Once fully boarded, the boat sets out on the water and gaming commences.

Illinois legalized this form of gaming in 1992 and expected tax revenues of $20 million. About 10 years later, in 2001, 9 riverboat casinos paid $555 million in taxes to the state of Illinois!

EYE ON THE ISSUES

Environment

The ecological impact of new and existing casinos can be significant. In the arid western states, the water usage of a casino can strain resources. The addition of hotel-casinos to the Tunica, Mississippi community taxed the ability of the sewer system to process waste material. The influx of vehicles to Atlantic City increased the level of air pollution. And people everywhere bring litter. Each new casino brings added demands on the environment.

The surge in casino construction on Native American tribal lands, in particular, has caused concern about access and traffic management on roads that previously received minimal use. The volume of visitors descending upon reservation casinos has grown tremendously. Additional facilities and services are needed. The construction and maintenance of infrastructure diverts funds from much needed social programs on the reservations, and harms pristine reservation environments.

State Lotteries.   Yet another trend in the gaming industry is the resurgence of state lotteries. In the early years of the country, state lotteries was used to fund infrastructure costs and to rebuild states that has been devastated by the Civil War. With the demise of the Louisiana Lottery, no state had a lottery until 1964, when New Hampshire became the first state in the 20th century to institute a state lottery to raise state revenues, rather than to impose a state income tax.

The gaming industry today includes land-based casinos, riverboat casinos, Native American casinos, and lotteries as well as racetracks and other more traditional forms of gaming. All but Hawaii and Utah offer some form of gaming within their borders. Nearly 90 percent of all Americans live within a four-hour drive of a casino, and gaming is more popular and more prevalent today than it has ever been.

SOCIETAL IMPACT

Gaming definitely has had a positive impact on society by bringing jobs to depressed areas, generating tax revenues, and improving the infrastructure of Indian reservations. However, a full discussion must include all impacts of gaming, including the negative ones.

Economic Impact

The most common argument offered when a community considers gaming is that the economic benefit is significant. As we have already seen, the reason Nevada, New Jersey, and Native American tribes legalized gaming was to stimulate economic development and to generate tax revenue. Let's look at this argument more closely.

The most obvious benefit of gaming is the creation of jobs. There are three categories of jobs generated by gaming:

1. Direct
2. Indirect
3. Construction

Direct jobs are jobs which are on the payroll of a casino. Casinos create many high-paying jobs. These include front line jobs such as dealer, food server, keno writer, and surveillance officer, as well as management positions. A casino with revenues of $500 million will employ 6,500 people. The significance of this to an impoverished community cannot be overestimated. Where there are jobs, there is hope for the future. In 1998, the casino industry employed approximately 475,000 people.

The average wage for a casino job is $26,000. This is considerably higher than most jobs available to entry-level employees. Hotel/motel jobs pay an average $16,000, while the amusement and recreation industry pays $20,000. Even the motion picture industry pays just $22,000. (These averages reflect wages for entry-level, mid-range, and executive positions.)

Indirect jobs are those jobs created because the casino and its employees spend money. Through purchases of goods and services, casinos create jobs—food deliv-

Exhibit 9.8   Think of all the jobs created in the building of and operating of a first-rate casino. Besides jobs created during construction and furnishing, economists estimate that for every $1 million in annual revenue, 13 jobs are created. (*Courtesy:* Gold River Resort and Casino, Laughlin, Nevada)

ery personnel, office equipment salespeople, the programmer of a slot machine manufacturer—for those who would not be employed otherwise. For every $100 million in revenue, $21.7 million is spent on direct supply purchases. Approximately 500,000 indirect jobs can be attributed to the casino industry.

Construction jobs are short term in nature, but are numerous. These are the jobs created when the casino is built. For every $1 million invested in construction, 17 construction jobs are created. In 1996, the casino industry invested in excess of $3.25 billion in new construction, and approximately 55,000 construction jobs were created as a result.

Employee spending also creates jobs. Employees who purchase food, clothes, automobiles, houses, haircuts, and dental services create jobs. As discussed in Chapter 8, the money injected into the local economy has a tremendous impact due to its multiplier effect. The multiplier effect states essentially that people spend most of the money they receive through employment locally. For example, a casino employee buys groceries. The grocery store pays the clerk a wage and purchases more products. The clerk spends money on rent and a haircut. The hair stylist takes the money and goes out to lunch. The restaurant manager purchases more products and visits the doctor. The original purchase is distributed throughout the local economy, and many people benefit from the casino.

State and local governments also benefit from casinos because tax revenues increase. The more obvious taxes to increase are direct casino taxes, income taxes, and property taxes. Other taxes affected include the gas tax, alcohol tax, and sales tax. State and local governments received over $4 billion in taxes from casinos alone in 2002. This money was badly needed to fund projects and services that benefited all citizens.

Exhibit 9.9   Slot machines and bingo often serve as forms of amusement for retirees. (*Courtesy:* Wildhorse Gaming Resort, Pendleton, Oregon)

Native American reservations have especially benefited from the profits of casinos on tribal lands. Native Americans living on reservations have perpetually been on the bottom rung of the economic ladder in America. The Indian Gaming Regulatory Act specifically states that the income from casinos is to be used for the good of the community. Tribes with casinos own the casino as a tribe and decide communally how to spend the proceeds from gaming. With the infusion of cash generated by casinos, the standard of living has risen. For example, the Gila River Indian Community south of Phoenix, Arizona has been able to build, equip, and staff a fire station, open a medical clinic, build housing, and open a college.

Local residents benefit from casinos because property tax rates decrease. The large influx of tax revenue generated by the casino industry reduces the need for government to tax individuals. In Bay St. Louis, Mississippi, property taxes declined 85 percent in 1992, while the city budget increased by $2.5 million and property values increased.

Another economic benefit of casino gaming is the transfer of people from welfare to the work world. The experience on Native American reservations and in impoverished communities like Tunica, Mississippi, has shown that casinos create jobs and thus remove people from the welfare rolls. The number of residents receiving welfare in Tunica dropped 29 percent after the casinos opened in 1992.

Social Impact

There are many important economic benefits to gaming. However, there are also some important disadvantages. There is much debate about whether gaming has a positive or negative impact on society. Those who oppose gaming often point to the social costs of introducing gaming to a region or locality. There is no doubt that gaming adds costs to society. However, it must be kept in mind that all businesses incur social costs. The petroleum industry has grown because the mobility that cars afford people has had many positive impacts. However, oil spills occur all too frequently and do tremendous damage to the environment. As a society, we continue to produce gasoline because we consider the net benefit to be positive. When the debate about gaming gets our attention, we should, similarly, weigh the pros and cons.

Crime.   The most common social cost cited by opponents of gaming is crime. There are actually three different aspects of this crime. Crime associated directly with casino employees includes embezzlement and theft. The large amount of cash and cash equivalents that is moved around a casino is too tempting for some people. They rationalize that the casino will not miss the money, or somehow the casino owes them the money. A story from the 1960s in Nevada tells of a female "21" dealer who wore a beehive hairdo. Her supervisors knew dealers made a good wage, but they could not figure out how she could afford to drive a Cadillac. After observing her over a period of time, they discovered that she would insert a chip into her hair just before leaving the table for the last time on a shift. The chip would be lodged in her hair, hidden from view, until she reached her home. Considering the rate of inflation, a $1 chip then would be the equivalent of $20 today. Imagine if she had taken a $25 chip!

Crime perpetrated outside the casino is also a concern. Muggings, robberies, assaults, and thefts unfortunately occur. However, the statistics are not clear-cut. Las Vegas has a lower crime rate than Miami, Fort Lauderdale, New Orleans, and Myrtle Beach, South Carolina. Atlantic City has a lower crime rate than Chicago, Houston, San Francisco, and Nashville. Some communities even experience a drop in crime after gaming is introduced. For instance, in Illinois, East St. Louis saw crime decline 50 percent and Joliet, 18.1 percent.

It appears that increased tourist traffic regardless of gaming is associated with an increase in crime. Branson, Missouri, which does not offer gaming, saw assaults rise 800 percent and burglaries 167 percent between 1991 and 1993. The number of aggravated assaults in Orlando, where Disney World opened in the early 1970s, increased at a rate three times higher than Las Vegas during the same period. Further studies are needed in order to determine the exact impact gaming has on crime rates.

Organized Crime.   Organized crime figured prominently in the early days of Las Vegas. Over a period of 20 years, the State of Nevada set regulations and controls in place to eliminate this element and to prevent its reintroduction into the industry. New Jersey emulated Nevada's regulations, but with an even more restrictive approach. Native American gaming is similarly regulated to prevent the infiltration of organized crime.

It is not likely that organized crime plays a significant role in the gaming industry today. Most casino companies are publicly held and owned by stockholders. Institutional investors find gaming industry stocks attractive due to their consistent long term performance. They would hardly feel comfortable acquiring stock in an industry that was infiltrated by organized crime. In addition, the Securities and Exchange Commission (SEC) requires that all investors with more than 5 percent of the outstanding stock be revealed and scrutinized. It would be difficult for an organized crime figure to gain control of such a company.

Other Social Costs.   Bankruptcy, suicide, child abuse, spousal abuse, and divorce are other social costs associated with gaming. Again, the data are contradictory. While there is some objective information and anecdotal data to support the claim that gaming has a negative effect on many of these, there is also evidence that these factors decrease when gaming is introduced. Perhaps, as jobs are created and people pull themselves out of poverty, their world view changes and they are less likely to abuse their children, commit suicide, or go into bankruptcy. On the other hand, someone who discovers the thrill of gaming and who overindulges might well fall victim. Obviously, further research is needed to settle the debate.

- Uses gambling to escape worry or trouble
- Gambles to get money to solve financial difficulties
- Cannot stop playing regardless of winning or losing
- Gambles until the last dollar is gone
- Loses time from work due to gambling
- Borrows money to pay gambling debts
- Neglects family due to gambling
- Lies about time and money spent on gambling

Exhibit 9.10   The Warning Signs of Pathological Gambling

Pathological Gambling.   The final social cost associated with gaming is pathological gambling. **Pathological gambling** is a disorder of impulse control, as categorized by the American Psychiatric Association in 1980. Individuals suffering from this progressive disorder often feel as if they cannot control their gambling. The disorder is complex and not fully understood. To be considered a pathological gambler, a minimum of five out of 10 criteria must be met. If an individual exhibits fewer than five of these criteria, he or she is classified as a problem gambler. As you can imagine, even a problem gambler has a serious problem. Exhibit 9.10 lists the warning signs of pathological gambling.

The portion of the population that suffers from pathological gambling or has the potential for succumbing to it is not firmly known. Estimates ranging from 1 percent to 7 percent have been offered, but only limited studies has been undertaken to determine the number. Regardless of the proportion, though, pathological gamblers are increasing in numbers due to the increased availability of gaming activities. When 90 percent of Americans live within a four-hour drive of a casino, we can expect pathological gambling behavior to increase.

Understanding the social impacts of gaming is not easy. There are benefits, but there are also problems. Bringing jobs to the unemployed, generating taxes, and providing for the needs of the less fortunate are just a few of the benefits. However, the social costs that accompany gaming need to be addressed to ensure the future of responsible gaming in America.

EYE ON THE ISSUES

Ethics

Over the course of American history, gaming has been banned, regulated, or allowed to flourish unfettered. The basis of the anti-gaming position is that gambling is a sin and that casinos prey on the weak, in particular, those individuals who suffer from pathological gambling and who are unable to control their impulse to gamble. They often gamble more than they can afford. Pathological gambling is similar in nature to alcoholism.

The pressure on casinos to "solve" the pathological gambling problem is increasing. Are casinos responsible for an individual's behavior? Looking at the alcoholic beverage industry, we see that the responsibility for overdrinking has shifted so that bar owners and bartenders are required to stop serving those who appear to be inebriated. Someday casinos may be required to cut off those gamblers who appear to have a problem.

CASINO MATHEMATICS

Quite often gamblers claim that a particular casino has "better odds" than another casino. They feel you are more likely to win there than somewhere else. Yet, when you consider that a pair of dice or a deck of cards has a set number of outcomes, doesn't that seem odd? For example, there are exactly four aces in every deck of cards. The odds of drawing an ace from a deck of cards are 4 out of 52, or 1 out of 13. That will not change from casino to casino!

Roulette is a relatively simple game, and can be used to demonstrate various casino mathematics concepts. After the players place their bets, the dealer spins the wheel counterclockwise and spins the ball clockwise around the rim of the bowl. As the ball loses momentum, it descends along the side of the bowl and comes to rest in a pocket. Each pocket has a number, and the pocket where the ball rests indicates the outcome of the game. Bets are then paid or collected.

American roulette wheels have the numbers 1 through 36, plus 0 and 00: a total of 38 possible outcomes. The odds that any particular number will be selected are 1 out of 38. However, odds are expressed according to a specific protocol. The number of possible ways an outcome can occur follows the number of possible ways an outcome cannot occur. A colon separates the numbers. For the roulette

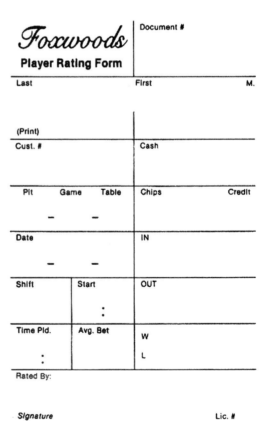

Exhibit 9.11 Casinos often rate premium players, based on past betting records. Foxwoods is the largest resort casino in the world, with 340,000 square feet of gaming space in a complex that covers 4.7 million square feet. More than 40,000 guests visit Foxwoods each day. (*Courtesy:* Foxwoods Resort Casino, Mashantucket, Connecticut).

wheel, the odds of an individual number being selected are 37 to 1 or 37:1. There are 37 ways for a number not to be selected and one way it can be selected. These odds are called **true odds** and are unchangeable as long as the roulette wheel has 38 outcomes and is in good working order. So, since the odds are unchanging, how do casinos survive? The next section will clue you into some of the secrets.

House Advantage

Casinos rely on the **house advantage** to generate revenue. Let's look at the roulette wheel again, and remember: The casino is in business to make a profit.

Imagine you are playing at the roulette table. You place a $1 bet on the number 23. The dealer spins the wheel and ball and the number 5 is selected. The dealer collects your bet. You place another $1 bet on the number 23 and the dealer spins. Number 35 is selected. You lose your bet. Again you place a $1 bet on the number 23. The dealer spins the wheel and the number 14 is selected. Again you lose. You continue this for 37 times, losing each time. Then on the 38th try, the number 23 is selected. You win!

If the casino paid true odds, they would pay you $37. You would regain the money you lost and break even. You would not lose money, but you would not win either. Under this payoff schedule, the only way a casino would make money is if a particular outcome did not occur or the players consistently did not bet on the winning outcome. Neither possibility is likely.

Casinos, like any business, need some certainty that they will make money. They achieve this certainty by paying less than true odds. For example, on the roulette wheel winning bets are paid as if there are only 36 outcomes. The payoff on the roulette wheel is 35:1. Your winning bet would collect $35, not $37. The difference between true odds and the payoff is the *house advantage*. In this case, it is $2.

To some players, the house advantage appears unfair. After all, the casino did not earn that money. However, this money is the fee a casino charges to provide players with the surroundings and amenities of a casino as well as the opportunity to gamble. All things considered, it is a small price to pay.

The *house advantage* is often expressed as a percentage. Looking at roulette again, we know that $2 is retained by the casino for every $38 in wagers. The house advantage is calculated as a percentage in the following fashion:

$$\text{House advantage} \div \text{total wagered} = \text{house advantage percentage}$$
$$\$2 \div \$38 = 5.26\%$$

The house advantage in roulette is 5.26 percent. All things being equal, the casino can expect to keep 5.26 percent of all bets placed on the roulette table over time.

In a similar fashion, slot machines are set at specific percentages called **hold percentages.** Frequently, these percentages are below 5 percent, although by law in some jurisdictions they can be as high as 25 percent. If a slot machine only keeps 5 percent of the bets, then why do players lose all their money?

Imagine you enter a casino and you are intent on playing the dollar slots with $100 in your pocket. You decide to play only one coin at a time. A machine catches your eye and you sit on the stool in front of it. You play one coin at a time and press the button 100 times. If the machine is set at a 5 percent house advantage, you will soon discover you have only $95 in your possession. If you walked away, the casino would have kept what it expected to keep. However, you play another 95 times. You now have about $90. The casino retained another 5%. You play another 90 times and find that you have only about $86. As you continue to play, the casino continues to keep 5 percent until you have lost all your money.

In other words, the casino hopes you will continue to play until the house advantage has allowed it to retain all your bets. Knowing that over time you will lose your money, the casino attempts to extend playing time by offering complimentary drinks and food and by providing a multitude of amenities such as restaurants, shows, arcades, etc., to keep you in its facility.

Drop, Hold, and Hold Percentage

The *house advantage* is also often referred to as the theoretical hold percentage. To understand this term, we must examine drop, hold, and hold percentage.

What is drop? **Drop** is the revenue a casino collects from the players. Now, how did the term drop originate? When a player exchanges cash for chips at a "21" table, the dealer slips the money into a slit in the table and the money "drops" into a drop box. When a gambler inserts a coin into a slot machine, it "drops" into a bucket inside the machine. Bets at other casino games are collected in a similar manner, hence, the term drop. The drop boxes are collected on a regular basis, usually a minimum of once a day, and the drop is counted.

Hold, on the other hand, is the difference between drop and winnings paid or payouts. The dealer at a "21" table does not track every winning bet paid. Instead, he or she maintains a smooth game flow by paying winning bets out of the chip rack. If the inventory in the chip rack gets low, the dealer will notify the pit supervisor, who will authorize a fill. Chips are obtained from the cashier cage and placed in the dealer's chip rack. The **fill** represents the amount paid to winning bets after losing bets have been distributed to winners. Fills are also needed for slot machines and other gaming activities in the casino. The formula for hold is:

$$\text{Drop} - \text{payouts} - \text{fills} = \text{hold}$$

In a sense, you can say that the hold is the money that the casino "holds onto" after the winners have been paid!

Imagine a roulette table during a 24-hour period. The drop box is collected and counted. The total is $2,432. During the first eight-hour shift, one fill of $500 is required. There are no fills during the second shift. However, two fills are needed during the third shift. The first fill is $650 and the second is $674. The hold for the roulette table is calculated as follows:

Drop	$2,432.00
Payouts	−$500.00
	−$650.00
	−$674.00
Hold	$608.00

A hold of $608 seems impressive; but how can we be sure? Comparing this table to other roulette tables will help us judge this.

Suppose a second roulette table held $754 on a drop of $3,770. On the surface this table appears to be more valuable to the casino. However, it doesn't seem fair to view the first table poorly. It could be located in a low traffic section of the casino. Or its minimum bet may be lower than the second table. Or it may be open only when the casino is busy.

Therefore the best way to judge the success of a table is to base the comparison on the relationship between hold and drop or using the hold percentage. The formula for hold percentage is:

$$\text{Hold} \div \text{drop} = \text{hold percentage}$$

In the case of the first roulette wheel above, the hold percentage is 25 percent.

$$\$608 \div \$2,432 = 25\%$$

Now we could compare this table's performance to other tables' without considering the amount of the drop. If other tables' hold percentages are lower, this table will be viewed positively. The second roulette wheel had a hold percentage of 20 percent.

$$\$754 \div \$3,770 = 20\%$$

Obviously, the first roulette wheel is more valuable if we could only increase the drop!

But wait a minute! Didn't we say that the casino would only keep 5.26 percent of bets placed? How do we reconcile the house advantage of 5.26 percent and a hold percentage of 25% or 20%?

Remember when we described the drop as the money that dropped into the drop box? The casino does not tabulate each bet placed, but only the money exchanged for chips. It would be too cumbersome to track every bet. The same is true of fills. The casino does not track every bet paid. It merely accounts for the replenishment of funds to gaming activities. While there may be thousands of dollars placed in bets, the casino counts only the original buy-in.

While the drop figure and the payouts figure are a partial representation, the hold is an actual dollar amount. It is the money the casino actually possesses after all bets are collected or paid. The hold is the figure the casino reports in its financial statements as revenue.

So why is the hold percentage higher than the theoretical hold percentage? It is a matter of math. While the hold is the same, the drop is less than the amount of bets placed. Exhibit 9.12 explains the situation. The casino recorded a drop of $2,432, but in reality $11,559 in bets were placed at the table. Of this amount, 5.26 percent was held by the casino, which amounted to $608!

Casinos use the hold percentage to compare tables and slot machines and the theoretical hold percentage to make operational and marketing decisions. It is im-

Exhibit 9.12a   Theoretical Hold Percentage vs. Hold Percentage, Roulette Wheel

Hold Percentage		Theoretical Hold Percentage	
Drop	$ 2,432	Bets placed	$ 11,559
− Fills	1,824	− Paid outs	10,951
Hold	$ 608	Hold	$ 608
Percentage	25%	Percentage	5.26%

As you can see, the amount of hold in dollars is the same. However, because the casino does not track each bet made or each pay out, the hold percentage is higher than the theoretical hold percentage. (*Source:* J. Scarnes, *Complete Guide to Gambling,* New York: Simon & Schuster, 1986.)

Exhibit 9.12b   Typical Hold Percentages per Month

Game	Hold
Craps	20%
21	26
Roulette	30
Baccarat	10
Big Six	80

(*Source:* J. Scarnes, *Complete Guide to Gambling,* New York: Simon & Schuster, 1986.)

portant to keep in mind that the odds on games and slot machines do not change, despite variations in reported percentages.

Hotel-Casino or Casino-Hotel?

Many people think that a casino is like any other hotel except that a casino is attached. Quite the opposite is true. The main source of revenue in a casino is the gaming activities. While a casino's hotel may run an annual occupancy above 90 percent and thousands of people may eat in its restaurants every day, the gaming activity generates more than half the revenue of the casino. In some cases, gaming accounts for 70 percent of total revenue.

ORGANIZATIONAL STRUCTURE

Since gaming is the main source of revenue, food, beverage, and hotel departments are subordinate to the casino. The organizational structure of the casino reflects this reality. While the organizational structure will vary from one company to another, casinos generally segregate the operating departments into three categories: gaming departments, customer service departments, and support or administrative departments.

Each category reports to a separate executive, as noted in Exhibit 9.13. Job titles vary widely, but these men and women have an extraordinary amount of authority.

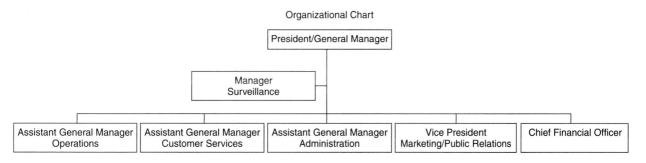

Exhibit 9.13   Typical organizational chart for a large casino.

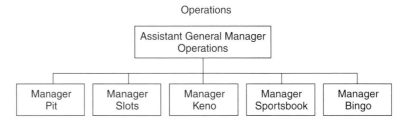

Exhibit 9.14a   The Assistant General Manager–Operations is responsible for all gaming areas.

Typically, they report directly to the individual who has comprehensive responsibility for the entire casino operation. If the key individual is the vice president/general manager, the individuals with category responsibility will be called assistant vice presidents or assistant general managers.

Gaming Departments

The gaming departments include such things as slots, pit, keno, bingo, sports book, and poker room. Each department is considered a separate revenue source and is headed by a manager. These departments interact on an hourly basis and deal directly with the other gaming departments and with casino patrons. Each department employs a separate workforce. Rarely would a "21" dealer also run keno tickets or carry change.

Customer Service Departments

The customer service departments include the hotel, food, beverage, gift shops, transportation services, etc. These are services provided to customers so that they will patronize the casino and so that they will stay longer to gamble. Before making any decision regarding the hotel, restaurants, and bar, their managers must consider how the decision will affect the gaming departments. Raising room rates cannot be done arbitrarily without determining the impact on occupancy and, hence, the number of customers available to the casino. In a similar way, increasing the price of food may drive customers away and hurt both food and gaming revenue.

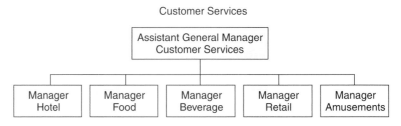

Exhibit 9.14b   The Assistant General Manager–Customer Services is responsible for areas typically associated with a hotel or resort.

Administrative

Exhibit 9.14c   Administrative areas support the efforts of guest-contact departments.

Administrative Departments

The administrative departments include security, engineering, cleaning, human resources, and other support areas necessary to run the casino. Their functions are identical to their counterparts in hotels except in the magnitude of the tasks. Imagine the engineering department's responsibility for the plumbing, HVAC, and electrical systems for a 75,000 square foot casino, 1,000 guestrooms, and six restaurants. Or consider the difficulty of recruiting and selecting enough candidates to fill a staff of 3,500 employees. That's a lot of human resources!

Among the administrative departments are accounting, cashier cage, and count rooms. Due to the strong need for control, these areas report to the property controller, who in turn reports to the vice president/general manager. However, this requires a balancing act. The cashier cage and count rooms interact daily with the gaming departments. As a result, these areas must be sensitive to the demands of the gaming departments. Additionally, the cashier cage interacts with guests constantly. The property controller is concerned with customer service issues as well as control issues.

Other Departments

Other departments such as marketing, entertainment, and surveillance report directly to the general manager of the property, since they significantly affect the success of the property and need access to a decision-maker who sees the "big picture."

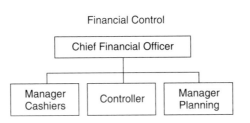

Financial Control

Exhibit 9.14d   The Chief Financial Officers ensure that sound practices are in place to prevent theft and embezzlement.

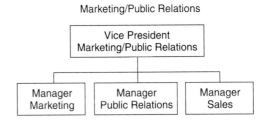

Marketing/Public Relations

Exhibit 9.14e   The Vice President of Marketing/Public Relations and his staff manage the image of the casino.

Exhibit 9.15 Surveillance employees and cameras keep an eye on both customer and staff behavior. For most guests, the "eyes in the sky" are invisible and are seldom thought of.
(*Courtesy:* Gold River Resort and Casino, Laughlin, Nevada)

Surveillance

Surveillance is the department whose employees monitor the activity throughout the casino. Thirty years ago, casinos were built with a network of catwalks in a false ceiling above the casino floor. Surveillance employees would crawl along the catwalks and observe the action below through two-way mirrors, using binoculars. Today, casinos use sophisticated closed circuit television (CCTV) systems composed of cameras, monitors, and VCRs to observe and record activity.

The cameras used have improved with advances in technology. The simplest camera is the fixed camera. It is mounted, usually on the ceiling, and is fixed on a certain area. It does not move or zoom in for a close-up shot. By contrast, a pan-tilt-zoom (PTZ) camera has a tremendous amount of flexibility. It can rotate 360 degrees, move up and down, and zoom in for a close-up shot. Unfortunately, PTZs are expensive, so the casinos usually use a combination of fixed and PTZ cameras.

Camera coverage is extensive. A 40,000 square foot casino may have up to 500 cameras. A poker game will have a fixed camera on the dealer's seat, called "the box," and a PTZ for close-up shots of cards, hands, and faces. A fixed camera will be trained on the boxman's seat at a craps game bolstered by two PTZs to cover the entire length of the inside of the table. Cashier cages will have a fixed camera on each guest window and each fill window. As you can see, cameras are everywhere!

But who is watching all those cameras? In the surveillance department, a room is dedicated to a bank or banks of monitors. Each camera can be fed to any of the monitors at any time using keyboard controls. Quad technology, which divides the monitor screen into quarters, allows for up to 16 cameras to appear on a monitor

Exhibit 9.16 Craps is one game that needs a lot of electronic surveillance, not only to protect the interest of the casino, but that of the guests. (*Courtesy:* Gold River Resort and Casino, Laughlin, Nevada)

simultaneously. A joystick moves the PTZs so that surveillance employees can watch the action, looking for guests cheating or employees stealing.

Videotapes and VCRs are used to document the activity. Videotape evidence can be crucial in a criminal case. It can help insurance companies determine whether to pay a claim or not, or further an investigation. The camera is trained on a machine number, table number, or casino landmark to establish the exact location of the activity.

Advances in digital technology are revolutionizing the surveillance room. While the monitors and controls are similar, digital cameras offer benefits over the more conventional cameras. For one thing, images are recorded to the computer's hard drive, which can be transferred later to a CD or floppy disk. This form of storage is more durable than a videotape. In addition, digital cameras can zoom in for a close-up without a zoom lens. The digital image can be expanded by the computer. This feature is available after the fact, as well: One can view an image from the computer's hard drive days after the incident and enlarge the image. Finally, the digital cameras record everything in all directions. While the surveillance officer might be watching a certain machine while the action is "live," after the fact, the image can be reviewed and other areas can be pulled up. If suspicious activity in one area draws the attention of surveillance, later they can view the scene and look in another area to see if there is any suspicious activity which they missed. As you can see, digital cameras represent a significant advance in surveillance. Of course, digital camera systems are very expensive and have only started to be installed in casinos.

EYE ON THE ISSUES

Technology

Technology has long been associated with the effort to reduce costs. The automatic chip sorter at the roulette wheel, the computerization of player tracking, and the counting system that counts the drop in the cabinet beneath the slot machine rather than in the count room are all examples of ways that technology has helped to reduce costs.

However, technology also plays a key role in creating guest satisfaction. The new slot machines based on popular game shows such as *Wheel of Fortune* draw substantial interest. A 5,000-room hotel would be impossible to run efficiently without the use of computers, and virtual reality arcade games attract adults as well as children.

All jurisdictions with gaming activity within the United States require that casinos have a CCTV system in place. The regulator's concern is for the integrity of the games. If the casino is dishonest or if players are dishonest, it could ruin the reputation of the industry and business would decline. The issue of regulation and control is a controversial topic. Nevada and New Jersey have an established history of regulatory control over the gaming industry. Both states see the need for a strong and independent regulatory system so that the industry can survive.

Native American Gaming Regulation

A different situation exists in the arena of Native American gaming. The IGRA specifically requires that states and tribes enter into a compact to delineate the allowed gaming activity. The compacts delegate part of the regulatory duties to the state. The tribes resent this interference. Legally, tribes are considered sovereign nations. They were independent nations prior to the arrival of colonists and have a government-to-government relationship with the federal government. So they resent any regulation by the state as being inappropriate and meddlesome. For perspective, imagine Mexico's reaction if Texas decided to regulate the taxi business in Mexico City!

Native American gaming has three levels of regulation: tribal, state, and federal. At the tribal level, the regulatory body is called the Tribal Gaming Office (TGO). The employees of the Tribal Gaming Office are charged with the responsibility of overseeing the gaming activity to ensure the laws and regulations are not violated. They are separate from the casino employees and report directly to the tribal council. They are the watchdogs in the casino 24 hours per day.

Each state with Native American gaming has a Department of Gaming, which oversees tribal gaming. The independent agencies must ensure that the provisions of the compact are enforced. Frustratingly for them, their powers on tribal land are negligible. They must rely on the cooperation of the TGO to enforce the regulations. As a last resort, they can use the federal court system to enforce the compact.

At the federal level, the regulatory body is the **National Indian Gaming Commission.** It is composed of three individuals. The Chairman is appointed by the White House and the Associate Members are appointed by the Secretary of the Interior. Their staff is responsible for overseeing the nearly 300 Native American casinos. Until recently, there was little active enforcement, due to lack of manpower and funding. However, that is changing and the federal government is expected to become more involved in the regulation of Native American casinos.

CASINO MARKETING

The Marketing Department at a casino reports directly to the General Manager, as we saw earlier. Since it is responsible for attracting customers to the casino, it serves a very important function. Its primary focus is on advertising and promotions. For example, Nevada and New Jersey casinos use boxing matches to draw large crowds of patrons. Cultural activities, prize drawings, sporting events, and beauty pageants are among the other forms of promotion casinos use to generate business.

Exhibit 9.17   When high rollers come to play, casinos roll out the red carpet. Marketing departments know how to keep premium players coming back again and again. (*Courtesy:* Star Limousine, Inc.)

Casinos segment their market into many groups. One such group is called **premium players.** The more common term is **high rollers.** These are the individuals who will bet thousands of dollars or more during their stay. Usually they receive complimentary rooms, food, and beverages due to the action they give the casino.

Junkets

When a casino organizes the transportation for a group of premium players, it is called a **junket.** Often a casino will identify a geographic market that is home to a number of premium players. The casino will invite players from that market to join the junket, for instance during a special event such as a boxing match or a celebrity performance. Complimentary tickets to the event are added to the usual

EYE ON THE ISSUES

Service Excellence

The casinos of Las Vegas and, increasingly, other gaming markets continue to dazzle us with their scope and grandeur. The Bellagio, the Paris, New York, New York, and the Venetian all created a stir when they opened. However, theme and physical plant are not enough to differentiate among casinos.

The key to success is service. Slot machines and table games are the same from casino to casino. However, service makes them unique compared to the competition. The level of service must be chosen carefully, but execution is critical, too. Proper training and motivation of employees is essential to create customer satisfaction.

Exhibit 9.18   So what do you think: Venetian or Venice? It is almost too close to call . . . *(Courtesy:* The Venetian Resort Hotel and Casino, Las Vegas, Nevada)

comps the player would receive. These players represent a great deal of potential revenue, and the added expense of a junket is justified.

A casino's decision to extend complimentary services is based on the amount a player is betting during their stay. Each casino has guidelines regarding bet size, length of play, and game played to determine the dollar amount and type of item to be "comped." Larger bet sizes and longer stretches in play merit more items given as complimentary.

Markers

Premium players receive a service denied other guests: The casino will extend them credit while they are playing. Once a player has established his ability to bet large amounts of money, either through a credit application or through previous play, the casino will enroll the player into its premium player program. The name of the program varies from casino to casino, but it is understood that these individuals have a substantial amount of personal wealth and are willing to risk it at the casino.

Premium players do not have to bring cash with them. They can draw a **marker** instead. When a premium player enters the casino, he or she can contact a supervisor or go to the cashier cage. After signing a form which states the amount drawn, the date, and a promise to repay, the patron is issued casino chips. The player then gambles with the casino's money. If he wins, he can repay the marker out of his winnings. If he loses, he must repay the marker in another way. Usually, the casino will allow a reasonable amount of time for repayment, but will, of course, accept cash or a check on the spot.

The accounting department considers markers as accounts receivable and treats them accordingly: When they are aged, efforts are made to collect them. If ultimately left unpaid, they are sent to a collection agency. Most premium players pay their markers because they want to return to gamble. Those who do not pay usually are granted a payment schedule so the relationship can be maintained.

CONCLUSION

So there you have it! The casino industry is a fascinating and exciting part of the hospitality industry. However, it is not all glamour. Numerous social impacts, both positive and negative, must be considered when a state or a tribe decides to legalize casino gaming. There are complex control and regulatory issues involved. And a casino requires special expertise to operate successfully.

Increasingly, casinos are looking for people with hotel and restaurant management degrees to fill their management ranks. Some of you may find a career in the casino industry as an attractive alternative. If you choose to work for a casino upon graduation, hold onto your hat. It'll be the ride of a lifetime!

KEYWORDS

Pathological gambling   356
True odds   358
House advantage   358
Hold percentage   358
Drop   359
Hold   359

Fill   359
National Indian Gaming Commission   366
Premium players/high rollers   367
Junket   367
Marker   368

CORE CONCEPTS

Reasons people gamble   344
Gambling following frontier   346
Indian Gaming Regulatory Act (IGRA)   350
Casino marketing   366

DISCUSSION QUESTIONS

1. Define the term *house advantage*.
2. Identify and explain the five reasons why people gamble.
3. Why did Nevada legalize gaming in 1931?
4. What was Bugsy Siegel's contribution to the gaming industry?

5. List and explain the three categories of jobs created by casinos.
6. Why have Native American Tribes benefited in particular from the legalization of gaming on the reservations?
7. Explain the term pathological gambling.
8. Explain the terms drop, hold, and hold percentage.
9. Why are the hold percentage and the house advantage different percentages?
10. What is a marker, and why do casinos use them?

WEBSITES TO VISIT

1. www.americangaming.org
   Information and studies on current issues.
2. www.indiangaming.org
   Information on the history of Indian gaming, current issues, and upcoming events.
3. www.nigc.gov
   Charged with oversight of Native American casinos.
4. www.azccg.org
   Numerous articles on compulsive gambling.
5. www.azzlasvegas.com/dealmein
   A column for players that helps explain the reality of the gaming business.
6. www.harrahs.com
   Describes the company, locations, player programs, and more.
7. www.nynyhotelcasino.com
   A themed facility that typifies the detailed replication of a concept already familiar to the traveling public.
8. www.vegasfreedom.com
   One of the more sophisticated operations among CVB's; they host different Websites for different audiences.
9. www.gaming.nv.gov
   The regulation enforcement arm of the State of Nevada's gaming regulatory bodies.

The Accountant Says

One of the most valuable commodities required for the operation of our economic system is information. Decision-makers, such as investors or corporate managers, execute their business choices based on financial and other business information, coupled with their own expertise and experience. Accounting data is the raw material out of which financial information is produced. In order to decide what to invest in, investors review critical information such as security market activities, performances of various corporations, government taxing and spending, interest rate levels, and other data. Hospitality managers might review the same information, plus other specific information on their own company's operations, in order to determine whether the company should construct a new hotel or open a new restaurant.

Financial information is based on accounting reports, which in turn are built upon numerous business transactions. To better understand how this all fits together, consider the flowchart in Exhibit 1.

Let's start at the top with business activities. Business activities can encompass a broad range of actions, ranging from opening a business in a new location to conducting day-to-day and week-to-week business affairs. Businesses produce products or services and sell them to customers, with the goal of generating sufficient sales

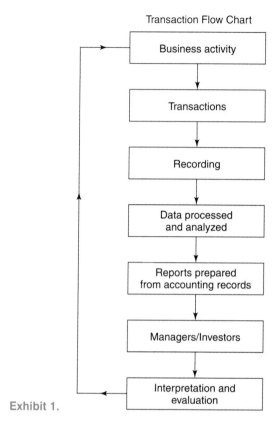

Exhibit 1.

to cover their costs and produce a profit equal to or in excess of their objectives. This process goes on continuously in all areas of the free market economy. From large corporations such as McDonald's and Hilton, down to the local motel and restaurant, all companies participate in this economic process.

All company sales and expenditures are called *business transactions*. For example, each sale at a restaurant constitutes a transaction: A meal is served to a customer who, after completing the meal, pays the bill. The cash is deposited in a cash register, which completes the sales transaction. Business expenditures are another form of transaction. Two examples are: an employee who works for a company by providing specific services and then, on payday, receives payment in the form of a payroll check; and a vendor who ships raw food products to a restaurant and receives payment for the goods. From these examples, we can define *business transactions* as exchanges of goods and services for money that take place continuously and in all areas of our economy. The sum total of all these transactions represents the total dollar activity of our economy.

In order to understand the collective impact of a period's transactions, a business must first create a record of each transaction. This is the recording process. Business records are numerous and varied: cash register receipts, sales tickets, payroll time cards, invoices from vendors, canceled bank checks, hotel room ledger accounts, and so on.

Accounting transactions are often recorded electronically in computer data files, and after a business records its transactions for a period of time, such as one

Exhibit 2 Accountants produce much of the information that goes into annual reports. (Photo by James L. Morgan, Scottsdale, Arizona)

month, the data must be processed and analyzed into information. Businesses process most of these transaction data automatically through routine accounting procedures, often assisted by computers. Full-time accounting managers oversee the processing of transaction data into useful financial reports. The primary financial reports of a profit-making company are the balance sheet, income statement, and cash flow statements.

Accounting managers then tailor financial reports to fit the needs of the particular parties to whom the reports are addressed. For example, reports produced for stockholders are highly summarized and do not provide detailed information of company operations. Thus, when publishing a brochure for its stockholders, a hotel chain might report sales from all its hotels in one total amount without giving a breakdown of the sales by its individual hotels. Exhibit 2 shows several annual reports that hospitality companies publish.

In addition to producing reports for parties external to the corporation, the accounting department will spend considerable time and energy producing reports to meet the specific needs of its managers. Management reports are more complicated and detailed than reports produced for outsiders, such as stockholders. The accounting department of a hotel chain might produce a complete set of financial reports for each of its hotels but make them available only to corporate management. The same hotel chain, in reporting to its shareholders, would probably produce one set of consolidated financial reports reflecting in total numbers the activities of all its individual hotels.

Once the accounting information has been summarized into financial reports, management and investors need to interpret and evaluate these reports. Often managers make critical decisions based on the information in accounting reports:

For example, a restaurant chain's management reports might reveal that one of its locations is losing money. Management will need to evaluate the operation of this restaurant in detail and ultimately may change procedures or personnel. Although the losing restaurant might be a hopeless cause and have to be closed, the same restaurant chain might have other individual restaurants that are highly profitable. Management will want to analyze the success of the strong locations to determine if this pattern can be replicated at other locations and thus improve overall company profitability.

Business activity is a dynamic process rather than a static one. Change is constant and managers need to be flexible. If they are to make the right decisions for their corporations, managers need accounting reports that provide meaningful, accurate, and timely information. The consequences of their decisions, both good and bad, will be reflected in the company's financial performance as reflected in future accounting reports. This process goes on month to month and year to year.

The Attorney Says

The hospitality industry has characteristics that distinguish it from other industries. Just as manufacturers or oil companies have laws that apply specifically to their industries, so, too, does the hospitality industry. And, since the hospitality industry itself includes several important segments, there are many specialized legal aspects to be aware of. This is why most hospitality management programs require their students to complete at least one full semester of hospitality law.

One of the largest segments of the industry is the lodging segment, the segment that provides lodging to people while they are away from home. If you think about it, providing accommodations to a person is quite unique. You are providing one of the basic human needs, shelter. As a shelter provider, do you have certain responsibilities, or are you free to pick and choose your customers? Consider this scenario.

What if you were to turn a person away from your hotel, yet this person was in need of a place to rest? Perhaps it is extremely cold outside, or perhaps the person is in some type of danger, or, as is more probable, the person is simply weary from a long day of traveling. Suppose, for no reason at all, you refuse to give this person a room. Further suppose that that person, forced to leave, is injured or even killed because due to fatigue, he or

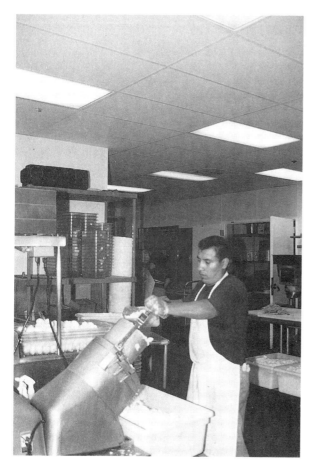

Exhibit 1   Training employees who are handling hazardous equipment well is important not only to avoid injuries and personal harm, but also to avoid costly lawsuits. (*Courtesy:* Garden Fresh Restaurants)

she falls asleep at the wheel and is involved in a fatal accident. Could your hotel be held responsible? The answer (you may be surprised to learn) is 'yes.'

Must a hotel accept all persons seeking a room? Again the answer is 'yes.' Certainly there are exceptions to that rule (law, like grammar, and sometimes even football, is filled with exceptions), but common law notably applies here. Over the years, the common law rule has evolved thus: A hotel is under an obligation to accept all comers. How did such a law evolve?

Even before the passage of civil rights laws, the government made a distinction between a hotel's "product" (a room to sleep in) and other types of products (let's use gasoline as an example). Before civil rights laws outlawing various forms of discrimination, the gasoline seller was under no legal obligation to sell gas to any person who wanted it. If the gas seller was racist or xenophobic (afraid of strangers or those "different" from oneself), he or she could *refuse to* sell gas to a potential customer. Even in such unenlightened times, though, a hotelkeeper *was* obliged to sell hotel rooms to all comers. It was the nature of the industry and the service that was being provided that led to the development of that rule. A hotel is considered to have an *affirmative duty* to accept all persons as guests.

Of course, exceptions do apply. If a person has no money to pay for a room or if your hotel has no vacancies, you may *refuse* a person a room. Likewise, if the

Exhibit 2 Warning signs in multiple languages: A sign of the growing internationalization of the hospitality industry.

person is carrying contraband (animals, explosives, and so on) or is drunk or disorderly, you may refuse that person a room. In addition, if the person is the carrier of a contagious disease, a hotelier may deny him or her a room. But there's a delicate line to walk. You must be especially cautious about refusing a room to a person based upon that last criterion. You could be found liable for illegal discrimination if you deny a person a room for the wrong reason.

What if you abide by your duty and do accept persons as guests, but it turns out that perhaps you should not have accepted them because they were carrying contraband? The question arises, may you evict them? The answer is yes. Before going on, let's clarify a potentially confusing difference: *tenants versus guests.*

Suppose you live in an apartment and your lease with your landlord requires that you pay $500 per month in rent, payable on the first day of each month. You fail to pay your rent as required and on the second day of the month the landlord opens your apartment door with his or her pass key and informs you that, due to your failure to pay rent, you are being evicted immediately and must vacate the premises. Is that legal? May a landlord summarily, on his or her own initiative, evict a tenant? The answer in most states is no. A landlord must first go to court and get a judge to sign an order of eviction. In short, the landlord must sue the tenant and seek from the judge an order that the person vacate the apartment. The landlord may not, on his or her own, evict a tenant.

What about a hotel? Does the same rule apply to the eviction of a hotel guest by a hotelier? The answer is 'no.' A hotelier need not get a court order prior to evicting a guest. If the guest has not paid the hotel bill, the hotelier may inform the guest of that fact and order the person to leave. If the person refuses to leave, the hotelier may use reasonable force (security personnel) to evict the guest. Extreme care must be taken in this regard; if too much force is used, the potential for liability is great.

A problem remains, however. How do we tell the difference between a "guest" and a "tenant"? If you think about it, there is one overriding similarity between the two. Are not both, the guest and the tenant, paying another person (a landlord or a hotelkeeper) for accommodations? Yes. The law, however, recognizes a substantial difference between the treatment of a guest and of a tenant, namely, the proper method of eviction. A landlord must first go to court to evict a tenant; a hotelkeeper need not go to court to evict a guest.

Exhibit 3   A hotel manager will be lucky to see only the exterior of a courthouse. Careful attention to the growing body of hospitality industry legislation will minimize potential litigation. (*Courtesy:* Richard Howey and Bruce Urdang)

If the two are so similar, how do we decide which category a given person falls under and which method of eviction is therefore proper? In most cases it is not too difficult to differentiate. If a person makes a reservation for a three-day stay, will pay for a room on a daily basis, and will be receiving traditional hotel services such as housekeeping, it is pretty clear that the person is a guest. On the other hand, if the person signs a lease for a two-year period, agrees to pay on a monthly basis, and no other services are provided, the person is clearly a tenant.

There can be occasions, however, when the distinction becomes blurred. Do people ever "live" in hotels? Aren't cases where people rent a suite in a posh New York hotel and stay there for years with the hotel providing housekeeping and perhaps even room service? Is such a person a guest or a tenant? What about the situation wherein the hotel accommodates persons who pay on a monthly schedule and also people who pay on a daily basis? The point is that it is not always immediately clear which method of eviction will be proper.

Your job as the hotelkeeper is simply to recognize that the distinction does have to be made if you are contemplating evicting a person and, if any questions exist as to the proper status of that person, the advice of an attorney should be solicited. In this, and in other instances, the recognition of when you need legal advice may be your most important managerial responsibility. If you understand the *intent of the law* (the actual meaning of the law, as opposed to the spirit of the law) involved, you can consult someone to advise you on the *extent* to which it applies.

The Techie Says

In their book, *In Search of Excellence,* Thomas J. Peters and Robert H. Waterman, Jr., write:

> We had decided, after dinner, to spend a second night in Washington. Our business day had taken us beyond the last convenient flight out. We had no hotel reservations, but were near the new Four Seasons, had stayed there once before and liked it. As we walked through the lobby wondering how best to plead our case for a room, we braced for the usually chilly shoulder accorded to latecomers. To our astonishment, the concierge looked up, smiled, called us by name, and asked how we were. She remembered our names!

This concierge did not use a computer to amaze her two late-night guests. Her performance was the result of excellent training, a good memory, and well developed people skills. There's a point here: As incredible as technology in general and hospitality technology in particular can be, it still comes down to the people using it. Some things machines do best, other things people do best, and still other things are best done by a combination of hardware, software, and "warmware" (as people are sometimes referred to by techies). As you read about the technologies that have swept into the lodging industry, please keep this in mind.

As you've read in earlier chapters, changes are taking place in the way the world does business. The hospitality industry has to incorporate and respond to these changes, just like any other industry. Many of the changes are the result of changing business conditions; others are being brought about by new technology, which is being introduced almost daily.

You only have to look around you to see how technology has changed modern life. Whereas few people had a computer 15 years ago, computers are now a part of nearly every aspect of your life. From the moment you wake up and fix your breakfast in the microwave, to starting your car, driving to school or job, all the way to doing your laundry, and going to the bank or ATM, your life is affected by computer technology.

As a result of these tremendous changes in technology, the business world, and the hospitality industry in particular, needs workers who are familiar with and able to use computers on a daily basis. Indeed, you will have an edge in the workplace if you are familiar with and know how to use computers and a variety of software.

Lodging and restaurant operations have seen (and will continue to see) technology-driven changes that include:

- More efficient operations due to more powerful (and better utilized) computers
- Better management information
- A better ability to track and react to guests and their needs
- Empowerment of lower level staff members to make technology-based decisions
- The use of technology as a training tool for employees

Information technology engulfs all the departments of a hotel or a restaurant, from the front desk to housekeeping, and from the cash register to the kitchen. Large centralized organizations, such as Hilton, Sheraton, or McDonald's, have management information departments as part of their corporate structure to control and manage information. Their recruiters have come to realize that any person dealing with information technology will need the following skills:

- An understanding of how information system hardware and software function and interrelate
- An understanding of how to design a system for optimal performance

Exhibit 1   A typical 21st century employee in a large hotel uses technology in many every day tasks; here is the reservation system operator. (Photo: Churchhill & Klehr/Pearson Education/PH College)

- The capacity to evaluate system performance
- The ability to train system users
- The ability to guard and preserve the system from unauthorized access
- The capacity to maintain a system documentation library

Technology may help you collect and store data; having a lot of data may be an important resource in the hospitality industry. It must be managed well and used properly. Data and information may give the manager of one property a competitive edge over the manager of a property down the street who does not have access to that same information. Yet a computer only processes and stores data. It is still we humans who make data into information, and who decide on how to use it!

PART IV

Introduction to Hospitality Management Functions and Skills

Managing hospitality businesses requires special knowledge and skills. A manager must know how to manage people and money, how to apply new technology to hospitality operations, how to market hospitality products and services to potential customers and how to comply with laws that govern hospitality operations. This section introduces some of these specific hospitality management responsibilities.

The first two chapters are specialized, and discuss human resource management and marketing. Chapter 10 discusses human resource management in the hospitality industry. Hospitality management is highly people oriented: It means serving guests, managing employees, and dealing with purveyors. Working well with people is an essential skill for a manager. Clearly outlined are the strategic human resource management process for any hospitality operation and the human resource laws that govern employment practices. The chapter offers practical knowledge every human resource manager should have in order to manage people in the hospitality industry.

Chapter 11 talks about hospitality marketing and discusses the unique characteristics of services marketing, as opposed to those of product marketing. It explains comprehensively the different marketing elements that make up an effective and successful hospitality marketing program. Marketing brings buyers and sellers together; it is particularly challenging in the hospitality industry because the industry sells both tangible products and intangible services.

Chapter 12 provides you with a thorough look at the skills and characteristics of managers and invites you to see how you measure up. Through the use of hypothetical questions and case studies, it recaps the kinds of decisions and situations that managers face, and emphasizes the importance of ethics in business—and in life in general. Keep an eye on the accountant, the attorney, and the techie, as they have important information to share.

Chapter 13, although not part of this section, offers insight into career paths in the hospitality industry and proposes some strategies students can apply in obtaining employment in the industry. It suggests ways to research potential employers and offers suggestions about writing resumes and conducting job interviews.

Human Resource Management

Human resource management requires a specific set of people management skills to be able to recruit and retain an adequate staff to maintain the standards set by the organization. Often line workers, such as cooks, servers, and housekeepers, believe they could be better managers than the managers for whom they are working. While some perhaps could be, management is far more difficult than it appears. This chapter describes the long-term planning needed to assure adequate staffing, and details the day-to-day personnel functions and tools hospitality managers must use to be able to meet the long-term plans of the organization.

INTRODUCTION

College hospitality management programs are graduating prospective hospitality managers who are technically skilled. Graduates can design and price menus, read balance sheets, design operations, use relevant computer information systems, market and promote their facility or destination, cook and serve foods and beverages, and select and buy equipment. These graduates know the hospitality business, and most have the capabilities to operate a small business almost single-handedly. Most graduates, however, will not single-handedly operate small businesses. Rather, they will be working as managers in large operations, and their major responsibilities will include directing and instructing others in the functions of the operation.

College students may be educated and trained to perform most of the jobs of the employees they will manage; however, being able to perform a particular job is different from being able to direct and train someone to do that job.

Historically, hospitality managers have been promoted from the ranks and learned management practices from senior managers. As the hospitality industry has become more complex and more competitive, and as the labor pool has grown less skilled and decreased in size, these handed down management practices have come to be seen by some as marginally effective. Some question whether these practices ever were effective, but, with less competition in the past, poorly selected or poorly trained employees could be replaced easily because of an abundance of cheap, unskilled labor.

Most new jobs and new wealth are from the service industry. The hospitality industry is growing at a phenomenal rate, and is expected to become the largest industry in the world. More hotels and restaurants are being built, and the industry is becoming more competitive. Qualified workers must be recruited and, more important, be retained. It is imperative that professional human resource management addresses these needs and issues to operate successfully in today's competitive market.

STRATEGIC HUMAN RESOURCE MANAGEMENT

Employees are human resources. Resources are things of value, such as natural resources like oil, coal, water, or topsoil. While most of us have long agreed that it is wrong to squander our natural resources, we have not always made the parallel assumption that it is wrong to squander human resources. Since it is our employees who deliver the service to our customers, our success as an organization is, therefore, directly tied to employee effectiveness. If we do not staff our operation adequately and appropriately, our employees will not be able effectively to deliver service to our customers. This requires long-term planning.

Strategic human resource management is a process whereby human resource decisions and strategies are made to facilitate a company's long-term objectives. This assumes that the company has long-term objectives that indicate where it wants to be in the future. These objectives must be consistent with the company's self-image and what is important to its owners. It must define itself in writing; this is normally done in the mission statement, or statement of philosophy.

Mission Statements

We hear sad stories of students who went to college to become lawyers or doctors because their parents wanted them to be lawyers or doctors, and how they failed or persevered and were miserable. Their personal ***mission statements*** (definitions of who they wanted to be) were incorrect, not true to who they really were.

It is very important that mission statements be true definitions of companies (or individuals) because many, if not all, decisions are based on these definitions. If a mission statement is wrong, the decisions based upon it will also be wrong, which will result in friction and cross-purposes (see Exhibit 10.1).

Long-Term Objectives

Let's say a company's mission statement defines it as a fine-dining restaurant with a strong emphasis on elegant, personal service. One of its long-term objectives might be to open similar establishments in several cities in a particular region of the country. Its focus would be on this goal, and it would make decisions to reach it. It might forgo investing in a "great deal" such as a sports bar, for instance, because it would lose its focus and perhaps deter itself from its long-term goal.

Long-term objectives have to be more than just a wish list; they have to be realistic. Strategic human resource management requires that planners look at their company's labor force to determine its strengths and weaknesses. While the company may want to emphasize elegant, personal service, it may not have any employees capable of performing that type of service, even with training. In that case,

---

WHAT WE BELIEVE

Our greatest asset and our strength is the
people of Four Seasons.

We believe that each of us has dignity and a need for pride
and satisfaction in what we do. Because customer satisfaction
depends on the united efforts of many, we are most successful
when we work together co-operatively and respect the
contribution and importance of our fellow workers.

Exhibit 10.1   The statement "What We Believe" from Four Seasons' "Our Goals, Our Beliefs, and Our Operating Principles" gives a clear picture of the organization's culture. How does this fit with your attitudes? (*Courtesy:* Four Seasons Hotels & Resorts)

it would either have to modify its plan (so that it reflects what it is capable of doing) or its staff (so that it becomes capable of achieving the type of service it has identified).

Long-term objectives also have to be realistic in terms of availability of future workers. If a company wishes to expand with restaurants in other cities, it must determine whether there will be adequate capable workers available there to fill job openings, not only this year, but five years from now. On the other hand, it must also consider the possibility of losing customers and what it would do with the excess staff then.

External Environments

The only things businesses can control in their environments are their own decisions. They must be realistic about their competition, since they cannot change it. Can they compete on all fundamental fronts? It's a given that they will compete for workers from the same labor pool. Will workers choose to work for company A rather than company B? Will they choose to stay with either company after being hired? Businesses can control the working conditions and the style of management in their operations, but not the composition of the labor pool.

Long-term human resources planning must also take into consideration some of the other uncontrollable environments in which companies operate, such as the social environment. For example, fast food companies returned to paper wrappers in response to changing social values concerning the natural environment. Also, society's views toward smoking and drinking alcohol have changed considerably over the last 25 years. It's hard for any one business to fight these changes. Instead, business managers must figure out how to deal with them.

Social changes have a way of becoming legislative changes over time. Society's negative views on smoking have resulted in new laws banning smoking in public buildings. Legislation is another uncontrollable environment within which businesses must work, following the numerous laws related to human resource management.

The technological environment is a third uncontrollable environment in which human resource managers must operate. Changes in technology require an awareness because failure to grow and improve technologically can result in the loss of competitiveness.

There are economic cycles that must be anticipated, because they affect our business. Population shifts, geographical concerns, natural disasters, political changes, and international events can all affect business and must be considered when making any long-term plans or decisions.

Forecasting

Businesses want to anticipate the future and be proactive rather than reactive to crises. Forecasting involves using various anticipatory and predictive methods to identify expected future conditions and needs, based on past and present conditions and needs. Forecasts must identify the supply of workers and compare it with expected demand for workers on a short- and long-term basis.

Strategic Human Resource Management Process

To review the steps up to this point: Businesses first define who they are and then base long-term objectives on that definition. Next they compare their objectives' feasibility with the company's strengths and weaknesses, with external uncontrollable environments, and with forecasted conditions and needs.

The next step in the process is to develop strategies for achieving the objectives, If a company had a long-term goal of operating a chain of elegant fine dining restaurants, and the goal was feasible in terms of the competition, the company's strengths and weaknesses, and all the known uncontrollable environments, it could

---

EYE ON THE ISSUES

Environment

Managing can be very enjoyable. However, with management comes tremendous responsibility. Managers are responsible for their employees, and their decisions affect many lives. Employees look to managers for guidance. Managers can therefore have a very positive influence on their behavior, decisions, attitudes, and beliefs. Managers are directly responsible for creating a work environment that is conducive to helping employees excel in their work. If managers show genuine environmental concern, some of that concern might rub off on the people who work for them.

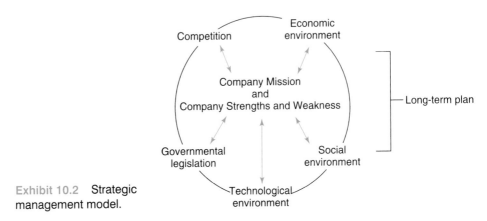

Exhibit 10.2   Strategic management model.

then devise a specific plan or strategy to realize that goal. It could then implement those strategies and monitor them to determine their effectiveness, revising them if necessary (see Exhibit 10.2.)

CHANGES IN THE WORKFORCE

Demographics

Hospitality managers must be prepared to manage the workers of today and to-morrow. Yesterday's hospitality workers were primarily young, white males. Today the pool of available workers is, for one thing, older. The population of the United States is aging. The average age of the population is increasing as the baby boom generation (born between 1946 and 1964) ages. In 1970, the supply of workers in the 16- to 34-year age bracket made up 42 percent of the population and totaled 34,818,000.

The hospitality industry has traditionally relied on teenagers to fill many of its entry-level positions. As this labor source is decreasing, people over the age of 55 are and will be available to fill many of the job openings. In the past, older work-ers were often dismissed as a potential labor source because of stereotypical be-liefs and the availability of teenagers and young adults for entry-level hospitality jobs. These incorrect stereotypes asserted that older workers could not easily learn new skills, that they were not interested in learning, and that they had diminished problem-solving skills. Happily, these narrow-minded myths have been exploded, and employers are finding that, in many cases, older workers offer advantages such as improved attendance, punctuality, and a positive service orientation.

Consider some other changes. There were 21 million women in the workforce in 1960. By 1985, that number had increased to 51 million. Today, women make up 45 percent of the workforce, and 43 percent of those women earn wages below the poverty level. Presently, almost one half of the women in the workforce are primary income earners. The average wage of women is only about 69 percent of the average wage of men. The percentage of the workforce made up of women represents a 60 percent increase in overall employment over the past 30 years.

The African American, Hispanic/Latino, and Asian portions of the U.S. work-force are growing at faster rates than the white workforce. Ninety percent of the growth in the labor force over the next 10 years will be represented by minorities and women.

Increases in immigration have resulted in increases in the number of people who speak English as a second language. People with different languages, different social customs, different standards, and different cultural backgrounds are entering the workforce in great numbers. At the same time, more socially, educationally, and financially disadvantaged people are also entering the workforce.

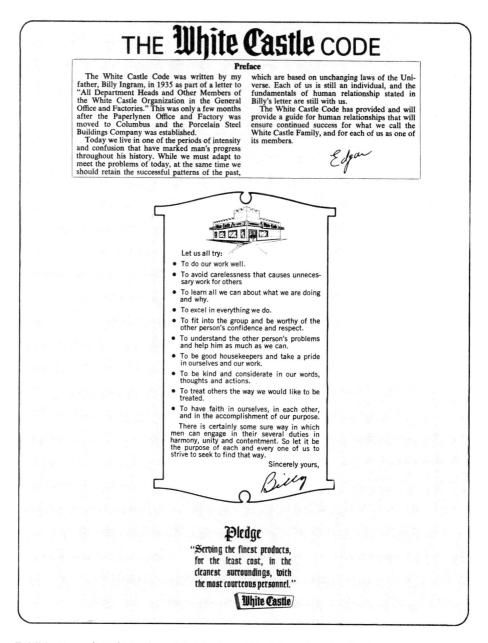

Exhibit 10.3   A code such as this tries to instill pride and motivation in employees.
(*Courtesy:* White Castle Management Company, Columbus, Ohio)

The expectations of workers have been changing in recent times. Workers are less willing to be humble and obedient and prefer some latitude, recognition, respect, and input into how "their" company is managed. Workers are less willing to perform boring jobs, and they depend increasingly on their work for personal fulfillment. Managers have to be aware of these changes and accommodate them if possible.

Illiteracy

Twenty percent of American adults cannot read, write, or compute adequately to be productive workers. Up to one-half of this group may be totally illiterate. It is reasonable to expect that many of these people are and will be employed in the hospitality industry.

Illiteracy is often hidden and not easily detected. Some hospitality companies in the United States have begun to question whether training programs can be effective when they are delivered to an illiterate audience. In response, some are experimenting with in-house literacy programs to provide illiterate employees with the basic skills necessary to benefit from training.

Another trend in the hospitality industry has been to redesign jobs for illiterate people by making the jobs easier and by reducing decision-making demands. However, jobs without variety and diversity have the unfortunate side effect of tending to decrease the ability of people to make decisions. Entry-level jobs in the hospitality industry often involve the delivery of service to customers. Successful service requires employees to be able to respond to situations and take action, so this practice (which some have uncharitably called dumbing down) ends up being a disservice to all concerned.

In cities across the country, planners and activists are looking at chronic unemployment and chronic labor shortages in tandem—as two problems that might be tweaked into helping solve each other. After all, there are jobs going unfilled (for want of skilled labor) and people unable to find jobs (for want of appropriate skills). Some hospitality corporations are attempting to produce a pool of skilled

Exhibit 10.4   Training and retaining employees in seasonal properties like the Belton Chalet and the Prince of Wales Hotel in Glacier National Park, Montana offer managers some particular challenges. (*Courtesy:* Belton Chalet and Prince of Wales Hotel, Glacier National Park, Montana)

workers for entry-level positions by seeking the chronically unemployed who are physically able to work. This group is then trained for job-specific skills (like serving or making beds), basic skills (reading, writing, arithmetic), and life skills (how to behave on the job, how to get along with others, how to manage money, and so forth). Graduates of the training program are then available for entry-level positions.

Industry- and community-related programs are responding to the idea that business and community are directly related; businesses are less likely to be healthy in an unhealthy society. The chronically unemployed and/or homeless people participating in training programs experience increased self-esteem and self-confidence, which, in turn, enable them to become more effective and loyal employees.

HUMAN RESOURCE LAWS

Discrimination means to give preferential treatment to members of certain groups. In the United States, young white males have, over time, often been given preferential treatment in human resource situations such as hiring and promoting. Because of this preferential treatment, other groups have been discriminated against and have been determined by the federal government to be in need of protection. These protected groups are minorities, women, older people, Vietnam veterans, and those with disabilities, and all have been given protection under the Equal Employment Opportunity (EEO) laws.

The Americans with Disabilities Act (ADA) was enacted in 1990 to assure the rights of people with disabilities so that they have access to employment, transportation, public accommodation, and communications. The ADA mandates "reasonable accommodation" to make workplace and public service areas accessible to persons with disabilities.

The Immigration Reform and Control Act of 1986 (IRCA) requires employers to verify citizenship status on all new hires within three days of hiring. While employers are prohibited from discriminating on the basis of nationality or citizenship, this act was designed to regulate the employment of aliens in the United States.

 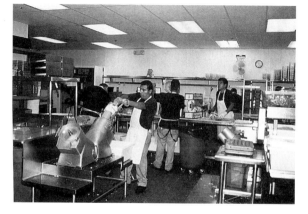

Exhibit 10.5   Employees of various ethnic backgrounds are a valuable resource to the hospitality industry. (*Courtesy: SoupPlantation/Sweet Tomatoes*)

Ethics

Though it hasn't been labeled as such, this entire chapter has dealt with ethics. Ethics has to do with doing the right thing, always, even if it is not the easiest or most expedient thing. Ethics boils down to treating others as we like to be treated. Few of us like to be lied to or cheated or taken advantage of. Most of us like to be respected and treated kindly and fairly.

The fact that some businesspeople are unethical does not make it necessary or okay for us to be unethical too. In the not-distant future, you will make the decisions that will affect all your employees and society as a whole. The decisions you make today determine the decisions you will make in the future. Integrity and strength of character are developed over time. If you make unethical decisions today, you will have no integrity tomorrow.

Our country is founded on the principles of equality and fairness. The mission statement of the United States of America, the Constitution, affirms the right of equal opportunity. Laws are generally enacted because people fail to do the right thing voluntarily. Discrimination on the basis of race, age, sex, national origin, or religion is morally wrong, legally wrong, and just plain bad management.

Yet, even without the EEO laws, hospitality managers would really have no choice about hiring women, older workers, minorities, and workers with disabilities. In today's labor market, there simply aren't enough young white males to fill all the entry-level hospitality positions.

That's the pragmatic or practical side, but philosophically, it is in our best interest to be free of discrimination. If we hold negative stereotypic views of African Americans, Asians, Hispanics, older people, women, and others, we are less likely to be able to see the real strengths and weaknesses of any given individual. Thus, we are less likely to be able to inspire the best effort of that particular employee, and he or she will be less likely to feel any loyalty or commitment to us and our organization.

MOTIVATION

Our task as hospitality managers is to hire people capable of doing the jobs we wish them to do. If they are not capable, no amount of training will make them effective. They must also be willing to do the job. They can have the ability to do the job, but if they don't really want to do it, they probably won't be effective. The third part of this interconnection is this: Employees can be willing to do the job and perfectly capable of doing the job, but if they are not shown how to do the job, they still may not be effective.

Once we have capable, willing, and trained employees, our ongoing challenge is to figure out how to get them to do what we want them to do, when we want them to do it, how we want them to do it, and for them to do it graciously, since we are, after all, a service industry. In order to do this, we need to understand why people do what they do, to know what motivates them.

We cannot motivate people to do things. They must have a reason for wanting to do what we want them to do, and that comes from within. Our task as hospitality managers is to figure out what motivates our employees. To be able to do that, we must know them. We need to create a delicate set of conditions wherein they can meet their needs while doing what we want them to do.

Teachers want students to study and get good grades. But teachers can't make students do that if they don't want to. Students may do what teachers want them to do if studying hard and getting good grades meets some needs the students have, such as pleasing parents, obtaining scholarships, and obtaining jobs. Only if the desires of teachers and the needs of the students are similar can good results come about. Similarly, workers' needs and management's desires must be aligned.

There are numerous theories of motivation that address the question of why people do things. Money is often thought to be a motivator. The lack of adequate or equitable compensation can have a negative effect on employee productivity and attitude. However, in the long run, money alone will rarely be enough to make up for insufficient support or unsatisfactory job matches.

Another view is that satisfied or happy workers will be motivated. It is true that people who are satisfied with their jobs will be absent less often and will tend to hold their jobs longer. In this view, inadequate compensation and lack of job satisfaction are seen as negative motivators; adequate money and good job satisfaction are seen as positive motivators.

The third view is that most people strive to reach their full potential. How far they have advanced toward reaching their full potential will determine what motivates them. The idea here is that if we as managers know where they are in their lives, we will know what motivates them and can therefore provide the incentives that will encourage them to do the tasks associated with their jobs. The most well known theory based on this view is ***Abraham Maslow's hierarchy of needs,*** shown in Exhibit 10.6.

Maslow contends that people are motivated at the lowest level first. People first need food and shelter. When those needs are met, they are then motivated at the next level, which is a desire for safety and security. For example, people who are homeless and do not have enough food will do almost any job if it will enable them to buy or obtain food.

Once people are no longer in that very precarious, scary position, they become a little more choosy and are motivated by desires for safety and security. If employees are at this level, a manager can offer incentives appropriate for this level, such as letting them know their work is appreciated and telling them that they can expect to keep their jobs and perhaps even move upward over time.

Exhibit 10.6   Maslow's hierarchy of motivational factors.

People who feel safe and secure desire a social life and want to feel part of something (starving people aren't terribly concerned with popularity or social activities). But if we know our employees have progressed to this level, we might offer activities such as employee parties or softball games to give them a feeling of belonging. They can then conclude that working for us gives them access to acceptance and affiliation, which is what they need or desire.

The next level of need is esteem. At this point we can offer employees such things as employee of the month awards, special recognition, enriched jobs, or more authority as incentives. At the highest level on Maslow's hierarchy (self-actualization), employees are self-motivated. They need no incentives to do their best work.

People may be at various levels at the same time, or may change levels, going back to a previous level (as in the case of a family crisis or divorce). We need to know where our employees are in their lives. Maslow's theory is a theory, not a fact. It is, however, a useful tool for us to get to know our employees better and thus help them to meet their needs while meeting ours.

Service Industry

As you have heard and will hear echoed throughout this text, the hospitality industry's product is service. As competition increases, guests have more choices, and hospitality managers must be able to assure good service. Repeat business is a result of positive guest experiences. Guests expect servers and other hospitality workers to be technically proficient. Good service is technical proficiency delivered with a smile, a remembered name, or a friendly attitude. Studies show that guests who have positive experiences are each likely to tell five to nine other people. Guests who have negative experiences, on the other hand, are each likely to tell between 10 and 30 people.

The technical aspects of service can be transmitted through training. It is more difficult or even impossible to train a worker to have a friendly attitude, so it is important to hire people who are hospitable to begin with. While a good match between worker and job is necessary, a positive working environment and job skills training can improve the worker's attitude.

Workers who are expected to care for guests must be cared for by management. Successful hospitality corporations regard their workers as their greatest assets. Employees are as important to an operation as guests are and should be treated in the same way management would like their employees to treat guests. Today's workers expect to be treated with respect. When workers and managers clearly understand that the success of their operation is directly related to the quality of the employees' work effort, respect can be fostered.

It has taken time, but hospitality organizations are finally beginning to see the light: Unhappy workers are not motivated to give good service; neither are poorly treated or unacknowledged workers. It is through trust and caring that people are empowered to be better, more responsible workers, and, therefore find the satisfaction today's workers expect from their jobs.

The successful management of an increasingly diverse workforce requires enhanced communication and leadership skills, and an ability to teach and train individuals with varying degrees of experience and understanding. The focus in management must be on accommodating change, rather than resisting it.

Exhibit 10.7   Being always open not only means accommodating guests, it also means managers must accommodate employees. (Photo: Jenni Kirk)

HOSPITALITY INDUSTRY TURNOVER

Turnover is the rate at which a business replaces workers. A 25 to 30 percent rate of turnover is considered too high in most industries. The hospitality industry, however, has turnover percentage rates ranging well up into the low hundreds! Turnover increases a company's expenses, due to search and selection costs, hiring and training costs, separation costs such as severance pay, production losses, waste, accidents, a decrease in morale, faltering service levels, and loss of customers.

Management Turnover

Hospitality industry management turnover is very high, with poor communication between managers and their superiors given as the most important reason why managers leave their jobs. Low pay, long hours, high pressure, and aggravation may be keeping potentially high-caliber managers away from hospitality management positions. Up to one-third of all hospitality management graduates may defect from the hospitality industry five years after graduation.

Managers who choose to stay in the hospitality industry often change jobs in order to advance. The most common reason given for changing jobs, however, is the lack of appreciation managers feel they receive from their supervisors. The hours, the pay, the lack of support, and the lack of adequate training can overwhelm even those managers who are already employed in the hospitality industry. They may feel "used" by upper management, and it is this upper management "user" mentality that is at the heart of burnout. Burnout is more likely to result in a manager leaving a particular property or job than leaving the entire industry.

Today, 80 to 90 percent of hospitality managers are married as compared to the 1960s, when most managers were single. Managers with families are naturally more concerned with quality-of-life issues. Many companies within the hospitality industry may have begun to consider the effect that hours worked per week, pay, and benefits have on their management staff and are improving conditions.

Worker Turnover

The turnover rate among non-managers is high because of low wages, lack of challenge, and lack of interest. Operators know that they should sell an appealing image of their establishment to customers; however, not all understand that they must also sell an appealing image of the establishment as a good place to work to prospective and current workers. For customers to return, the service experience

International

This chapter describes the workforce of today and the future. Many of the industry's workers are and will be from countries other than the United States, having English as a second language and having completely different customs and standards. The present job standards don't have to change, but as managers we must understand and accommodate their differences in order to help this diverse workforce meet the industry's standards.

Additionally, the opportunities for us to manage hospitality opportunities in the international market keep increasing. As with international workers, in our national industry we must be aware of different cultures and intrinsically different standards to help to get people to do what we want them to do graciously.

Cross-training (training employees to do tasks outside their job description) has been demonstrated to be an effective strategy for sharing responsibility and understanding among staff members, at the same time helping to fill gaps left by labor shortages. Cross-training can also be a way to encourage teamwork.

must match the advertisement. Likewise, for workers to stay, the work environment must be positive and rewarding.

As mentioned before, many workers may be seeking a sense of belonging or a sense of self-worth. Managers who are able to encourage and foster a team spirit and a sense of family can reduce turnover. Providing ongoing comprehensive training may enable workers to become and feel more competent, which can raise self-esteem. People working together as a team share responsibility, rely on each other,

Exhibit 10.8 Conscious efforts to reduce employee turnover help in raising service standards and winning prestigious awards. (Photo: Will Verbeeten, Foto Verbeeten, The Netherlands)

support others' efforts, and realize common interests in improving performance and being part of a successful operation.

RETENTION TACTICS

Leadership

To build teams, managers must continuously develop their own leadership skills. Traditional authoritative management styles are ineffective with today's workers, because today's workers do not respond positively to autocrats. Managers must attempt to foster a positive sense of partnership with employees. Managers who wish to retain employees must attempt to meet employee needs by providing an atmosphere in which personal creativity, decision-making, and employee input are encouraged.

Increasing competition has magnified the importance of a service orientation, not only externally (to customers), but internally (to employees). A corporate culture where guests and employees are valued with similar esteem can act as a positive "escalator," lifting a business to new heights. You can almost picture the upward movement: Employees feel valued and are given chances to become more valuable through further training. Being contented and better trained, they produce better service. Guests are delighted by their courtesy and efficiency and return again and again, producing strong revenues. The business does well in the market and retains its excellent employees. Everyone in the organization, however, must buy into the culture for it to work. If some factor in the culture "pushes people off the escalator," the upward momentum can be lost.

It isn't easy building such a positive, healthy corporate culture, and managers who hope to do so (by building teams, motivating employees, coaching, training) must possess certain character traits. If a manager initially lacks the necessary people skills, he or she needn't give up; such skills can be taught. Unfortunately, true concern for employees cannot be taught, yet is equally essential.

Career Planning

Many employees leave jobs and organizations to accept better jobs. Companies that desire to retain excellent employees are discovering that it is mutually beneficial to assist employees in career planning by identifying career paths within the organization that match the abilities and aspirations of the employees with the needs and requirements of the organization. Company-assisted career planning helps employees avoid costly and painful career decision mistakes, and demonstrates company commitment to employee development. At the same time, it helps the company find excellent successors for those employees who do leave the organization, and this assists long-range planning.

Development Programs

Development programs are important for managers as well as for workers, to improve current and future job performance. Ongoing management development programs can help prevent management burnout while providing a succession of managers for top-level jobs.

Training

Lack of proper training is consistently cited in surveys as one of the top reasons for turnover. Sixty percent of employee resignations are given during the first month of employment. Employees who resign due to a lack of adequate training may have been serving guests; the likelihood of positive guest experiences that promote repeat business during this period is questionable, to say the least.

One of management's goals should be to help employees stay in their jobs. Employees who become part of the company, as opposed merely to working for the company, are more likely to stay. It is far easier for an employee to feel part of a company (and embrace its service orientation) if given adequate and encouraging training. Good managers feel an obligation to provide training that enables workers to perform their service roles successfully.

PERSONNEL FUNCTIONS

Strategic human resource management involves making long-term plans for an organization based on its identity, its strengths and weaknesses, and the uncontrollable environments in which it operates. Upper management determines long-term plans. It is line management that determines the short-term plans that ultimately result in achieving the long-term goals planned by upper management.

The day-to-day running of a hospitality operation requires adequate and appropriate staffing to deliver the expected service. Personnel functions, short-term by nature, are the ongoing activities of managing human resources and include the following (see Exhibit 10.9):

- Job analysis
- Job description/job specification
- Recruiting/selection
- Orientation/training
- Performance appraisal

Twenty years ago, most hospitality corporations had "personnel" departments rather than "human resource management" departments. But as the competitive environment intensified and the labor pool became more diverse and less skilled, companies had to use a more global and long-term (strategic) approach to stay competitive.

The personnel functions now fall under the umbrella of strategic human resource management. Personnel policies are administered on a day-to-day basis, but are in line with the long-term game plan. It is through the personnel functions that managers incorporate motivation theories, knowledge of the labor force, and adherence to equal employment opportunity laws in order to operate systematically and successfully.

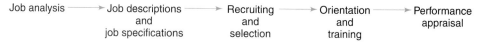

Job analysis ⟶ Job descriptions and job specifications ⟶ Recruiting and selection ⟶ Orientation and training ⟶ Performance appraisal

Exhibit 10.9   Personnel functions.

EYE ON THE ISSUES

Service

In difficult times, particularly during times of war, when family members may be in combat far away, or in times of destruction (natural or man-made), employees will undergo more stress than usual. Stress will enter their lives through their own concerns, but will also come to them through their jobs, as their customers reflect their stress and/or frustration with delays, heightened security, etc. Human resources departments may proactively try to lessen stress by organizing wellness events or publishing stress-reduction tips in company newsletters. Sometimes a community-service event—such as a carwash to help local families, a food drive, or mailing holiday packages to men and women in the military—helps employee morale by allowing them to feel less helpless and more constructive. Such activities also create a kind of corporate culture of caring that contributes to a positive workplace.

JOB ANALYSIS

Job analysis is the systematic investigation of the scope and duties of a job as they should be performed to result in the desired level of service. We do job analysis in order to write job descriptions and job specifications.

A **job description** is a list of the significant duties and responsibilities of a job. It simply "describes" the job. The person we hire must be able to do all the items listed on the job description. The **job specification** is a list of all the skills and characteristics a person must already have in order to be hired for the job.

All the personnel functions are based on data collected during a job analysis. If we skip the job analysis component, all our operating documents and plans are based on guesswork, albeit educated guesswork. This is similar to the concept of opening a restaurant without doing market research to determine customer preferences. Professionals remove as much of the risk as possible.

Job analysis should be done for every position in the operation. In a restaurant, we would do job analyses for cooks, servers, buspersons, and so forth. Ideally, job analysis is done before a new operation opens or if job descriptions have never been written or are out of date. We want answers to the following questions for each position:

Exhibit 10.10   Recruiting employees often starts with informal get-togethers to learn about the person behind the employee. (*Courtesy:* School of Hotel & Restaurant Management, Northern Arizona University.)

1. What does this person do in this job?
2. What should this person be doing in this job?
3. What kind of training is necessary for this job?
4. What qualifications are necessary for this job?
5. What should the scope of this job be?

RECRUITING AND SELECTION

Part of the personnel function is the development of recruiting and selection plans that can be used every time there is an opening. Because we have a job specification and know exactly what we need to fill the position, we can write accurate and appropriate advertisements ahead of time. We want to be specific so that recruits will self-select and we won't have to bother weeding out all those who don't have the necessary qualifications.

We then analyze incoming applications to determine whether any are a likely match for the job. We can notice job histories, looking for gaps in employment and job jumping, and then choose the best matches to be interviewed. In the interview we can ask questions raised from analyzing the application. It is in the interview that we clarify and assure ourselves of the rightness of the match. However, we should caution that even the toughest interviewers realize that life is difficult, and the presence of a gap, a variety of jobs, or even a firing doesn't necessarily mean a person could not become a superb long-term employee. Job jumping may raise questions, but should not necessarily be immediate cause for rejection.

Interviewing

We may experience job interviews where the interviewer obviously hasn't even looked at the application before the interview. He or she may do most of the talking and then ask us, "Do you have any questions?" This interviewer has missed the opportunity to make a wise selection to make a good match. If an employee works out under such circumstances, it is due to luck. Here again, we must keep the focus on the job and be able really to see and hear the applicant; we often see and hear what we *wish* to see and hear. Many interviewers decide to hire an applicant even before they talk to the person. We must be aware of our own biases so that we are not viewing the person only through our own eyes. We must be aware of common interviewing errors so that we do not make them:

1. Interviewers assume that an applicant's reaction to one situation will be the same in all situations.
2. Interviewers prefer to hire applicants who seem more like themselves in background, style, and/or attitudes.
3. Interviewers form an opinion before meeting the applicant.
4. Interviewers like one thing about an applicant and assume everything else is good too.
5. Interviewers make selection decisions before analyzing the various candidates and information, and checking references.
6. Interviewers stereotype people of protected groups.

Interviewers make these mistakes without awareness and assume they are making thoughtful selections. They may not be. Such mistakes keep them from really seeing who they are interviewing, which makes it very difficult to match job and applicant. Some of these pitfalls can be avoided through awareness and practice, and it's important to make the effort, whether the job is high level or entry level.

Non-professionals often think that the selection process doesn't matter because "it's just a dishwasher." It does matter, though. If the person hired to do dishes has the characteristics listed on the job specification, he or she will be able to get along better on the job and stay longer. This makes everyone's job easier, including that of the manager.

Unfortunately, the hospitality industry has been known for the "warm body syndrome." This describes conditions wherein a manager hires the first person available for a job. If he or she is lucky, the warm body works out. Too often, though, things do not work out and the carelessly hired employee becomes one of the company's many turnover statistics. Unnecessarily high turnover costs this industry a fortune in money, time, customers, service, and aggravation.

ORIENTATION

Our human resource task is to hire the right people for all our jobs and then keep them. Reputation is one way to attract the right people, since prospective employees may have heard, through the grapevine, which are the good places to work in

Exhibit 10.11   Finding outgoing people who are happy to serve people is one of the most important functions of a hospitality human resource manager. (*Courtesy:* SoupPlantation/Sweet Tomatoes)

town. The prospective employee's first encounter with us can set the tone for the entire working relationship. That first inquiring phone call or stop in for an application can determine an applicant's perception of the company's suitability as an employer. If we are rude, or too busy to listen, or make the applicant wait too long, we are making a statement to the employee—a statement about how we treat our employees in general.

After having spent the time and money making a good selection, it makes sense to "protect our investment" by acknowledging new employees as they arrive for their first day at work. We want new employees to feel welcome and pleased that they have joined our team. If we don't make some kind of connection with them from the very beginning, we may well lose them. More employees quit in the first month of work than later. They do so because they do not feel like they belong, and they decide they do not want to belong.

A good first-day orientation is a simple way to welcome new employees into the organization and it's simple hospitality, which is our business anyway. A first-day orientation may include:

- Showing the employee around
- Introducing him or her to fellow workers, perhaps assigning a mentor or "big brother or sister"
- "Pre-answering" all the questions they need to ask but might be too embarrassed to ask (where the bathrooms are, when they can take breaks, what food they can eat, and whether they have to pay for it)
- Showing them where to put their coats and gear, and how to punch or sign in.
- Putting them at ease; helping them to feel comfortable

A complete company policy orientation should be done after the employee has gotten "sea legs" and achieved a basic comfort level. The first day on the job is too overwhelming to assail a new employee with insurance plans and company history and policies.

TRAINING

Orientation is showing people how to get along on the job. Training is showing people how to do the job. These are not the same.

Shadowing, which consists of following an experienced worker around for a shift or two, is often called training, but it is no substitute. Watching a highly skilled employee doesn't necessarily translate into an understanding of the tasks he or she is performing. The experienced employee may be an excellent worker, but may not have the interest and/or skills to train other employees effectively. Trainers pulled from the ranks who have not been trained to train often don't deliver consistent training. This is primarily because they do not know how to transfer knowledge to other people. To be effective, potential trainers must become acquainted with the technology of teaching, that is, the principles of learning, the design of instruction, and teaching methods. Without this grounding, they may deliver new employees out "on the floor" or "on the desk" before they are ready. This can be

EYE ON THE ISSUES

> ### Technology
>
> There are many computer applications available for payroll, tracking employees, and scheduling that have considerably simplified human resource paperwork, freeing managers to be with their employees doing their job—supervising.
>
> Supplementing more traditional methods of training with technological methods (multi-media) can provide consistent, convenient training that is easily monitored and cost effective. Some companies are taping their own customized training videos. Videos used in conjunction with written texts or workbooks and self-test questions can provide a comprehensive, interactive, inexpensive, and consistent approach to training. These growth areas, particularly web and CD ROM–based, will continue to make headlines over the next decade.

disastrous in terms of both customer experience and employee esteem. No customer wants to be "practiced on" by a green employee, especially when paying for professional service.

PERFORMANCE APPRAISAL

A performance appraisal is an evaluation of an employee's job performance for the purpose of improvement. It works in conjunction with training. The strengths and weaknesses of an employee are documented over a pre-determined period of time,

Exhibit 10.12   In a restaurant like this, it would be nice to have some German-speaking employees. The challenge is: Where do you find them? (Photo: James L. Morgan, Scottsdale, Arizona)

such as a quarter, six months, or a year. At the end of this period, the employee and the manager discuss the results of this evaluation in a performance appraisal interview.

PROGRESSIVE DISCIPLINE

If we've hired the right people for the jobs, welcomed them into our operations, given them consistent formal training, ongoing supervision, and thoughtful performance appraisals, we may not need to worry about discipline and terminations. Often, though, we are hired as managers of an already existing staff. We deal with people, and there are no certainties with people. Even if we cut down the margin of error by using professional methods of management, we will still have to deal with disciplinary problems at times. ***Progressive discipline*** is another form of ongoing training. The purpose is to improve an employee's performance to get him or her back on track.

Employees have to know rules and standards in order to be able to adhere to them. The rules and standards, and the consequences for failure to follow them, should be spelled out at some time during the orientation period. It is not enough to give employees policy manuals and assume they will read them. Even if they sign a "have read and understand" form, we cannot assume that they have actually read it and did understand its intent.

As emphasized earlier, managers should not spend their energies trying to catch employees doing wrong things; instead, they should help employees avoid wrong behaviors. This can be done by helping them to understand rules, making sure the rules are consistent and fair, making sure the rules are implemented and administered fairly, and making sure there is a grievance procedure for both parties to follow.

Progressive discipline begins when a new problem arises or when ongoing training (coaching) has failed to make the appropriate change in the employee's performance. The first step is a verbal warning. The employee is told that it is a verbal warning and the warning will be documented in writing. If the deviant behavior continues, the next step is a written warning. The infraction is detailed in writing, the employee signs the written warning, and a copy is put in the employee's file, joining the documentation of the verbal warning.

If the behavior persists, a final written warning is given to the employee describing the consequences for failure to comply. One commonly used consequence is suspension; the biggest (and final) step in progressive discipline is termination.

UNIONS

Labor unions are organizations of workers for their mutual aid and protection on the job. While management would generally prefer to not have unions, workers join unions primarily because they are dissatisfied with management. Legislation is in effect to regulate unions and allow states to pass right-to-work laws which make union membership optional.

HEALTH AND SAFETY

The Occupational Safety and Health Administration **(OSHA)** was created by the U.S. Congress "to assure, so far as possible, every working man and woman in the Nation safe and healthful working conditions, and to preserve our human resources." Kitchens are particularly dangerous places to work. Boiling water, powerful equipment, toxic chemicals, knives, wet floors, and rushed employees make for very hazardous working conditions. Most accidents are caused by human error and can be avoided.

The costs of accidents and illnesses in terms of absenteeism, morale, customer service, workers' compensation, lawsuits, and medical expenses have compelled many organizations to institute employee safety programs and **wellness programs** to help their employees improve their health through diet, exercise, stress reduction, and other preventive measures.

It is so costly to replace employees that many organizations are attempting to help troubled employees through trying times with **employee assistance programs,** where employees are referred to various agencies to deal with emotional problems, addiction, and family disturbances. Since most people have personal problems at some time in their lives, it is in management's best interest to work with good employees during difficult periods. It is, however, never good policy to allow employees to break rules flagrantly or ignore company policies, despite the personal and professional compassion you, as a manager, may feel.

CONCLUSION

Beyond our daily goals of profit and superior service, our day-to-day operations must also move us toward our long-term goals and objectives—as determined by upper management. When determined methodically, long-term goals and objectives are feasible because they are based on an organization's strengths, weaknesses, likes, dislikes, resources (financial and human), and the uncontrollable environments of today and the future.

The hospitality industry is growing at a tremendous rate. At a time when the demand for workers is increasing, there are fewer workers available to take low-level minimum wage jobs. Entry-level jobs increasingly require computer skills, decision-making skills, math, and reading skills, yet many of the workers available to take entry-level jobs have fewer rather than more of these basic skills. Twenty percent of American adults cannot read, write, or compute adequately to be productive workers. This means that we must first keep the workers we already have, which may require providing them with higher pay, better benefits, improved working conditions, and better and more training.

As an industry, we will be hiring more women, seniors, disabled, and disadvantaged people, and those for whom English is a second language. We will have to be sympathetic to each of these groups' needs, and accommodate physical restrictions, language difficulties, need for child care, and so forth.

The tools of the personnel function can be used to assure efficient, effective, fair, equitable, and non-discriminatory management of our human resources.

Management in the hospitality industry is the management of people. It is essential that we, as hospitality managers, understand ourselves so that we can also understand others. This includes actively cultivating leadership and team-building skills. It is essential that we be able to hire the right people for the right jobs, give them excellent training, and supervise then in an effective manner that will enable them (and us) to maintain our company's standards. It is our task to help our employees excel. This requires professional management, an important dimension of preparation for a degree in hospitality, tourism, or travel.

KEYWORDS

illiteracy   392
discrimination   393
turnover   397
cross-training   398
job analysis   401

job description   401
job specification   401
OSHA   407
wellness programs   407
employee assistance programs   407

CORE CONCEPTS

strategic human resource management   387
mission statements   387
Abraham Maslow's hierarchy of needs   395
progressive discipline   406

DISCUSSION QUESTIONS

1. Describe the relationship between strategic human resource management and personnel functions.
2. List and describe the uncontrollable environments in which hospitality organizations operate.
3. What is a mission statement, and why is it important?
4. List and describe the personnel functions.
5. Describe how the personnel functions work together.
6. Explain Maslow's hierarchy of needs. How can it relate to human resource management?
7. What are the common interview errors? Give examples.
8. What is the difference between orientation and training?
9. Why is formal training necessary? What are the possible problems associated with shadowing as a training method?
10. What is the purpose of a performance appraisal?

EXEMPLAR OF EXCELLENCE

Four Seasons Hotels

Four Seasons Hotels was one of *Fortune* magazine's 100 Best Places to Work in America for 2003 and for the preceding five years as well. Though it is small compared to some chains (55 properties), 20 of them qualified for AAA five-diamond status in 2002. Seven Four Seasons hotels received the Mobil Five-Star award for 2003, more than any other hotel company in the world.

Four Seasons' 12,187 employees earn above average pay and benefits (for example, housekeepers start at $21,200 a year). A formal "no-layoff" policy gives more security than most modern employees have come to expect. Central to their philosophy is this statement:

> We believe our greatest asset, and the key to our success, is our people. We believe that each of us needs a sense of dignity, pride and satisfaction in what we do. Because satisfying our guests depends on the united efforts of many, we are most effective when we work together cooperatively, respecting each other's contribution and importance.

http://www.fourseasons.com/

WEBSITES TO VISIT

1. www.humanresources.org/career_main.cfm
   National Human Resources Association
2. www.usdoj.gov/crt/ada/adahom1.htm
   U.S. Department of Justice, Americans with Disabilities Act
3. www.statcan.ca/start.html (or try http://142.206.72.67/
   Statistics Canada E-book)
4. uscis.gov
   United States Bureau of Citizenship and Immigration Services
5. www.usafis.org/
   U.S. Immigration Service

CASE STUDY

Kelly opened a restaurant five years ago with the help of her family. The restaurant has been a huge success from the beginning. Shortly after opening Kelly was forced to hire several more people outside of her family.

Today Kelly has over 40 employees and has come to the realization that something must be done to make the personnel part of the restaurant less chaotic. She feels that she spends far too much time with personnel problems. She seems to be always in need of new employees, they seem to be less qualified, and the service is not at the level she and her customers would like. She doesn't know what to do and has hired you to develop personnel policies and procedures.

Your task is to develop job descriptions, job specifications, recruiting plans, interview questions, orientation and training plans, and employee appraisal forms for each position. Your first step will be to plan the job analysis to be able to gather all the information you will need to do this.

For this assignment you will develop the job analysis plan by beginning with a list of the things you need to know. Then determine the best way to obtain the information you need.

You may pretend Kelly's restaurant is similar to a restaurant you are familiar with and do an actual job analysis. From the validated information you would then write the job descriptions and specifications, and continue through the personnel functions model until all the necessary documents are developed. This is, of course, an enormous undertaking. However, as businesses grow it is necessary to standardize personnel functions to be able to operate in an efficient and effective manner.

Hospitality Marketing

Marketing is one of the essential ingredients in the success of any business. This chapter will help you gain an understanding and appreciation of the complexities involved in the marketing of products and services in the highly competitive hospitality industry. It will introduce basic marketing vocabulary and demonstrate the omnipresence of marketing in American society. The chapter will explore several kinds of marketing strategies and illustrate the many different components of a successful marketing campaign.

INTRODUCTION

Consider a day in the life of Kathryn. She gets up at 6:30 AM and turns on a news channel. Many of the ads on the station are for *business travel to hotels.* She flips to a weather channel, where the national weather is presented by *United Airlines.* As she drives to work she passes several fast-food restaurants offering breakfast specials, before finally pulling into a *McDonald's* where she purchases an *Egg Mc-Muffin* and a cup of coffee and reads the morning paper. In the paper is a coupon for a half-price meal at the *local seafood restaurant,* for lunch she and a friend go to that seafood restaurant. On the way home from work she stops by a *travel agency,* where she picks up several *brochures* for a vacation in Mexico. After dinner, which includes the use of *Chi-Chi's* bottled taco sauce, she settles down to watch TV, including highlights of a tennis match sponsored by a *state office of tourism.*

All of the words and phrases italicized in the above paragraph are examples of the influence of marketing on Kathryn's life. In fact, it is almost impossible to imagine a situation where a person would be able to escape the influence of marketing. The marketing of hospitality products and services is a significant part of the overall marketing of products and services in the world today (see Exhibit 11.1). In this chapter we introduce the concept of marketing, and discuss why marketing is so important to the success of a hospitality business.

MARKETING DEFINED

Because the role of marketing is so big, it's sometimes hard to come up with an exact definition for marketing. Basically, **marketing** is all of the activities designed to move goods and services from the producer to the consumer.

As we will see, this short definition involves a considerable number of activities. The goal of a business, and therefore the goal of a marketing department, is to determine what consumers want or need. The next step is to create a product or service that will fulfill those. Then consumers must be made aware of the product or service. Finally, the product or service has to be made readily available to consumers at a price they can afford. If all of these situations are handled correctly, there is hope that the business will prosper.

Marketing Related to Sales

Many people unfamiliar with marketing as a discipline tend to confuse marketing with sales, treating these very different concepts as the same. As we shall see later in this chapter, "sales" is another term for personal selling, and often refers to the job of personal selling as in "I work in sales." Personal selling is a very important part of marketing products and services to people, but only a small part of the overall marketing process.

Exhibit 11.1   These are just a few of the restaurant products that are now cross-marketed through grocery stores. (Photo: James L. Morgan, Scottsdale, Arizona)

HOSPITALITY MARKETING AS A PART OF SERVICES MARKETING

The business industry overall can be divided into two categories. **Product industries** are those industries that are involved in the manufacturing of items that consumers use. Examples are the manufacturing of cars, jeans, or soft drinks. **Service industries** are those industries involved in the performance of some activity or service for consumers. Examples are hair salons, law firms, and transportation services such as airlines. The hospitality industry is generally considered a part of the service industry, as Exhibit 11.2 shows.

Differences Between Products and Services

Since products and services are different, the ways in which they are marketed are also different. There are five major ways in which products and services differ, and each way causes some special marketing problems.

Intangibility.   Services such as a hotel stay are intangible in the sense that they are not physical. If you buy a pair of jeans, you receive something in return that actually exists. On the other hand, when you sit in a classroom, you receive a service in return. When you leave the classroom, you take very little evidence with you that shows that an exchange of some sort has occurred—maybe some notes.

A similar situation occurs when people rent a hotel room. When they leave the hotel, they generally take nothing physical home with them. (At least they are not

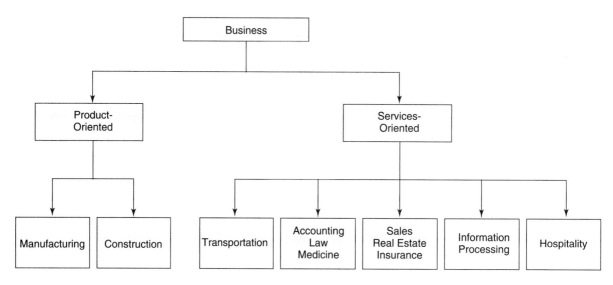

Exhibit 11.2   How hospitality fits into the business world.

supposed to; guests have been known to take just about anything out of hotel rooms, from towels to televisions!) Even in a restaurant situation, where there is the physical purchase of food, much of what guests pay for is intangible. They pay for *service*.

The problem for marketers is that, in an ad for a hotel stay, you can be shown a picture of the room, but not what is going on during the entire stay. Thus, it is hard for people to know exactly what it is that they are buying. How can you sell people something if they cannot see it in advance?

Inseparability.   This refers to the fact that services are often produced and consumed at the same time. You cannot get a haircut unless you go someplace and get a haircut. Similarly, you cannot generally eat a restaurant meal unless you go to a restaurant. Compare these situations to one where a pair of jeans is produced in New York, sold at a store in Chicago, and ultimately worn by somebody living in Los Angeles.

The marketing problem here is that the guest is always watching what the service people in the hotel or restaurant are doing. Guests are involved in the production of the service in that they are present while the service is being provided.

Nonstandardization.   Nonstandardization of a service means that, since people are involved, the service product cannot be created through automation in the way that many assembly-line products are. Services are variable; a service person in a restaurant will typically have good nights and bad nights. There will be some service persons who do a better job than others, and so on.

The marketing problem is that the guests will never know exactly what to expect. Will the service in this restaurant be good tonight or not? Will the food be the way it was last time or not? Buying services such as a restaurant meal can be risky. Would you want to take your boss to dinner at a restaurant where the service *might* be good, but *might* also be bad?

Environment

The hospitality industry has long been considered a non-polluting industry; in fact, this is not so. Fast-food restaurants have produced enormous amounts of refuse. Popular attractions such as national parks have long had to deal with air and noise pollution. Large hotels generate large amounts of waste water. Naturally, industry members do not go out of their way to point out their environmental failings. Instead, as laws have become stricter, and the public has become more aware of environmental issues, hospitality marketers have had to find ways to promote their companies as being environmentally active. Many fast-food restaurants now openly promote the fact that they use recycled materials. Many hotels and restaurants do not offer drinking water unless asked, and post tabletop notices hailing their efforts to conserve. National parks are restricting automobile traffic and publicly advertise their efforts. In these efforts, marketing plays an important role, as indeed it has in selling the whole concept of recycling and environmental conscientiousness. Can you imagine the reaction of 1950s consumers if they were told that their hamburger was wrapped in coated tissue made from paper someone had already used once and thrown away? Unused to the idea of or the need for recycling, they would probably have been repelled. Marketing has not only made this important concept palatable, but dressed it in virtue.

Perishability.   One of the big problems with a service is that it cannot be stored for use at any time. If a car dealer does not sell a car on the lot today, it will be there to sell tomorrow. However, if an airline does not sell a seat on a plane today, that sale is lost forever. The seat will still be there tomorrow, but today's sale is lost. If a hotel misses selling a room today, the revenue for today is gone forever. The room will still be there tomorrow, but today's sale has "perished."

The marketing issue, then, is to make sure all hotel rooms and all restaurant seats are sold *today*. This is one of the most difficult marketing and management problems in the hospitality industry.

Service

Service in the hospitality industry is not limited to front office or food and beverage operations. Other areas, including marketing, should also serve the consumer. So how can hospitality marketers serve the public? One goal of marketing is to provide consumers with the information they need to make informed decisions about whether to buy a product or service, or what choice of a product or service to buy. Another goal of marketing is to bridge the gap between the buyer and the seller—neither can function without the other, but it is often difficult for buyers and sellers to find each other.

Marketers also serve their company by trying to sell what the company has, to the company's best advantage. Another goal of marketing is to maximize company profit by convincing consumers that what the company is selling is worth the price it is charging.

One other way of looking at the concept of service is the *dis*service that marketers can provide the public. Exaggerated claims, false advertising, the sale of poor products or services, irresponsible advertising, and excessive advertising are all examples of marketing practices that could do consumers harm.

Non-ownership.   Non-ownership of a service means that people seldom actually own the service they are using; they rent or hire it. Consumers buy jeans and own them, but they do not buy the restaurant in which they are eating or the hotel in which they stay.

There are several problems that non-ownership creates. First, guests are often more abusive to property that is not actually theirs. Also, problems between the actual owners and the users can arise, such as differences of opinion as to how the property should be treated. This is often a problem between hoteliers and their guests.

Services marketing and management are different from product marketing and management. Many of these differences are critical in the evaluation of hospitality marketing, and affect the way hospitality marketers do their jobs.

THE DIFFERENT ELEMENTS OF MARKETING

When a lot of people think of marketing, they automatically think of advertising and personal selling. Of course, advertising and sales are important parts of the marketing process, but they are by no means the only parts. There are many different elements that fit together into the discipline of marketing, as shown in Exhibit 11.3. We will take a look at them in this section.

The Marketing Mix

Very often when we talk about marketing, we lump the elements together into what is called the **marketing mix.** The marketing mix has been defined as the controllable variables a company manipulates in order to achieve its objectives.

Everything that a hotel or restaurant can do to affect its success is part of its marketing mix. Traditionally, the marketing mix has been characterized as being composed of four parts (the "four Ps" of marketing): product, promotion, price, and place.

Product.   The product is the actual good or service being offered for sale. It can include all of the features of the good or service, as well as the packaging and brand name of the good or service. Remember that the term *product* in this case does not necessarily refer to a tangible or physical thing. Rather, it is the total goods/service package that is being sold. In many industries such as the automotive industry, the *physical* product dominates the sale. However, in the sale of a hotel room, the *service* product dominates the sale. The dual use of the term prod-

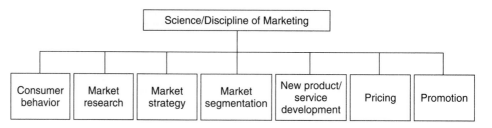

Exhibit 11.3   Elements of the marketing process.

uct as defined in the previous section and in this section can be confusing, but these are the definitions traditionally used in the marketing field.

Promotion.   This part of the marketing mix is concerned primarily with communication. How do we communicate with customers about what we have to sell? How do we convince them that what we are selling is what they want to buy? The promotional part of the marketing mix is what we normally refer to when thinking of advertising and personal selling. Actually, there are also two other promotional methods: sales promotions and public relations/publicity. Later in this chapter we will discuss the promotional mix in further detail.

Price.   The price of a product or service is one of the main considerations customers have when buying products or services. When we set prices, we have to consider whether our customers will think the price is fair, too high, or too low. Will all customers think the same way? Would a dinner priced at $100 affect sales to a millionaire in the same way that it would to a typical college student? These are the kinds of issues that make pricing very difficult to do. As with the area of promotion, we will discuss pricing from a marketing perspective in more detail later in the chapter.

Place.   Place refers to distribution: how we go about getting the product or service to the customer. A good restaurant will fail if customers are not available. A nice hotel will fail if no one likes the location. Ironically, a mediocre restaurant

Exhibit 11.4   Different marketing strategies are used to attract people to using a ski-lift in summer. *(Courtesy: Arizona Snowbowl Resort)*

might be successful simply because it is in the right place at the right time. Can you think of any restaurants at which you have eaten that were not too good but had a wonderful location? An old saying in hospitality marketing is that there are three important keys to success—location, location, and location. While this statement may be oversimplified, there is a certain amount of truth to it.

Consumer Behavior

One of the most important and time-consuming activities in which we all engage is the act of consuming. When you eat a meal, you are literally consuming it, and when you stay in a hotel you are consuming the experience. It's hard to think of any activity in which we engage that does not, at least in part, involve an aspect of consumer behavior. However, there is a lot more to the process than simply using a product or service you have purchased. ***Consumer behavior*** could be defined as the process of purchasing, using, and evaluating products and services.

Exhibit 11.5 displays a typical consumer behavior process. This process has several stages and can become quite involved.

The process unfolds as follows. First, there needs to be a reason for you to buy something. You are hungry, so you go to a restaurant. Or you are away from home, so you check into a hotel. However, there are many restaurants and many hotels, so you must evaluate all of the relevant alternatives. You then purchase the restaurant meal or the hotel stay. You eat the meal or stay in the hotel, and then you have some sort of opinion as to how you liked what you just bought and used.

Hospitality marketing departments are responsible for analyzing each of these areas, but their task is not an easy one, since choices are seldom based on clear and simple logic. As human beings we do not always act rationally. It is very difficult to describe or forecast human behavior, yet this is what marketers constantly try to do. The more marketers know about human behavior, the better they can predict what products and services will sell the best.

All behavior is influenced by our culture and by the network of family and friends (in-group) that surrounds us. Understanding how our culture and our in-groups influence our behavior helps us understand how people behave. Our eating habits, whether at home or in a restaurant, are greatly influenced by who we are and where we come from, and any restaurateur needs to recognize and deal with these considerations. Is it any wonder that certain types of restaurants are

---

Service

The Travel Industry Association of America works to market the United States as a tourism destination. Recognizing that tourism is a major revenue source for national economies, many countries have a governmental agency that promotes tourism. The United States does not. The TIA's initiative shows how individual companies and organizations can work together to benefit the industry as a whole. TIA's "See America" campaign and Website (seeamerica.org) provide a clearinghouse for travel consumers to learn about America on a state-by-state or regional basis.

Source: http://www.tia.org/marketing/index.html (or go to *www.tia.org* and click "Marketing" button)

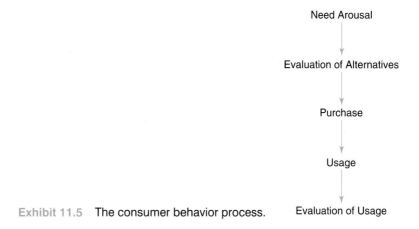

Exhibit 11.5   The consumer behavior process.

more popular in certain areas of the country than others? Is it any wonder that culturally based eating habits of foreign travelers to the United States are often different from what we are used to? Or is it any wonder that different lodging facilities will appeal to different types of people? These are just a few reasons we need to improve our understanding of who we are and how we behave.

Market Research

To make good decisions, a marketing department must have good information at its disposal. Good-quality information is essential; garbage-quality data only muddy up the planning process. Consider some of the many decisions you might have to make as a member of a management team at a hotel operation:

- Should we build a new hotel?
- Should we remodel our hotel?
- What kinds of clientele do we have?
- What kinds of clientele do we want?
- What price(s) should we charge?
- What is the best kind of advertising for us to use?

In each of these cases, along with many others, it is necessary to predict how all of the types of people involved in your hotel would react to the various alternatives you are considering. Most of the people would be outsiders—guests, competitors, and suppliers, people over whom you have relatively little control. Therefore, you need to have as much relevant information as you can get *before* you make any decisions.

Ways to Do Market Research.   There are three basic ways in which hospitality companies do general market research. First, they can do *qualitative research*. Qualitative research is very general, and also very subjective, influenced heavily by the views and opinions of the researcher. If we are interested in finding out if our guests are enjoying our restaurant, we can watch them, interpreting from our observations how they are feeling. Are they having fun? Do all types of our customers seem to be enjoying themselves? Does the restaurant atmosphere seem to be positive, or do we

Ethics

The issue of ethics in the marketing field is an important one, especially in view of stand-up comedians' lampoons and movie caricatures of marketers. Consider the following situations:

- You have a chance to win a big convention account that will mean a lot to you and your resort. The sales representative for the other company has hinted that he would be influenced by a "gift." Your assistant recommends giving the sales representative a week's free vacation at your resort. What would you do?
- You are interviewing a former director of marketing for one of your major competitors and are thinking of hiring her. She would be more than happy to tell you all of the competitor's marketing plans for the next year. What would you do?
- Your property is 11 miles, via a busy freeway, from the metropolitan airport. Average transit time for the shuttlebus is 45 minutes. Your intern figures that since the posted freeway speed is 55 mph, an 11-mile trip takes just 5 minutes. You'd like to attract the tired business traveler who seeks a hotel close to the airport. What would you do?

These are just three examples of situations that could come up in the marketing area. Because there is so much pressure to sell and be successful, marketers will sometimes try to gain an edge by exaggerating a claim, slightly misrepresenting the performance of a product or service, or intentionally doing something that may not be illegal, but would certainly be unethical. It is not the intent of this chapter to write a prescription describing the ethics you should follow, but rather to reinforce the idea that ethics are important to consider. Marketing is one of the areas of business in which ethics is very important, both in dealing with the public and with other members of the company.

Decisions are always risky to make; it is the goal of good market research to minimize that risk. **Market research** is, then, the formal means of creating, obtaining, and using information in the marketing decision-making process.

---

get a feeling that something is wrong? Managers generally do this kind of research automatically. It's relatively easy to do, and can provide some good information, but, as you can probably tell, it is not very scientific. What one manager considers a positive atmosphere, another might disapprove of completely.

The opposite of qualitative research is *experimental research*. This kind of research is often done in laboratory settings. Experimental research is carefully controlled research where precise measurements are taken. For example, in an actual experiment, researchers were interested in whether or not the name of a menu item could affect guests' perceptions of its taste. One group of people was given a plate of "mudfish." Another group was given a plate of "angelfish." In reality, both groups got the same fish. Now, which group do you think liked the fish better? The subjects concluded that the angelfish tasted heavenly, while the mudfish tasted "dirty," that is to say, terrible. This type of research is very precise, but very hard to do. It is unnecessarily difficult for most hotel or restaurant research needs.

The third type of research method, called *survey research,* is the most common. Surveys are a convenient, economical way to collect information, and require relatively little skill to use. As a result, a large number of organizations now use survey research as the primary method of gathering marketing information.

Exhibit 11.6   No matter how small the hospitality operation, it still has to find ways to attract customers. (Photo by Richard Howey)

We can do survey research over the telephone, by mail, and person to person. Every person reading this book has completed a number of surveys, probably of all three types. Perhaps the most common in the hospitality industry is the "comment card" placed on restaurant tables and in hotel rooms, asking guests how well they liked the food, the service, and the accommodations.

Market Strategy

Just as you probably have long-term objectives (such as having a good job, making a good living, and, in general, living a productive, rewarding life), hospitality companies have long-term goals. You have probably developed strategies and tactics (such as majoring in a hospitality curriculum and getting practical experience in some hospitality business) that will help you achieve your goals. The planning process that you are going through and will continue to go through is nothing more than an example of *strategic planning*. In business terms this can be defined as the process of developing and maintaining a close fit between a company's goals and its present situation. Exhibit 11.7 provides a chart of how the basic strategic marketing process works.

The first task in the strategic marketing process is to consider what *objectives* we have for our business. These objectives can be short term, such as filling our hotel this week or making sure there are enough food supplies on hand for next week's banquets, or long term, such as determining how many new hotels or restaurants to open in the next five years. When objectives are created, they need to be clearly

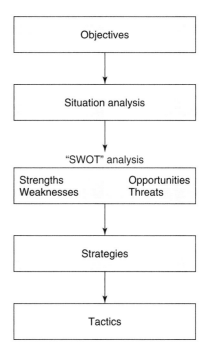

Exhibit 11.7   The strategic marketing process.

stated, and also need to be realistic. It is easy to make the statement, "We will be the biggest hotel chain in the world in 10 years." It is a lot harder to reach that objective.

The next task is to perform a *situation analysis*. A situation analysis is a critical look at where our enterprise (hotel, casino, restaurant, attraction, and so on) is now. One common method of doing a situation analysis is called the *SWOT method*. SWOT stands for *strengths, weaknesses, opportunities,* and *threats*. We analyze what our strengths and weaknesses are compared to those of the competition. Perhaps we have better food service or a better location than the competition. On the other hand, perhaps our building is older and does not look as nice as our competitor's. When dealing with our strengths or our weaknesses we need to be realistic. Sometimes it is easier to point to our strengths than to notice our weaknesses.

We also need to analyze what *opportunities* for success we foresee, and weigh them against possible *threats* to success. Is business booming in a certain area? Is our steakhouse restaurant concept one that people like? Alternatively, does the economy look bad in the future, or is our steakhouse concept going to run into trouble with animal rights supporters and vegetarians? Again, a critical assessment is necessary.

After we have identified our objectives (where we want to be in the future) and done our situation analysis (where we are now), it is time to figure out how to accomplish our objectives. Strategies and tactics are the precise methods we use to achieve our objectives.

Developing marketing strategies may seem simple, but it actually isn't. Predicting the future is always difficult. There are too many variables that can influence events. Who, for example, really predicted the rapid changes that occurred in the former USSR in the early '90s? Who foresaw the sweeping behavioral changes brought about by the AIDS epidemic? Who would have thought that a children's puppet program on public TV would change the way American children learned to learn? Obviously, planning for the future requires a lot of time and thought.

Market Segmentation

How many different restaurant concepts are there? Hundreds? Thousands? From how many brands of hotels and motels can a traveler choose? Again, hundreds? Why do all of these different products and services exist? Americans have always assumed that free choice is a critical part of the American way of life, but does everyone want the same thing?

The answer is a resounding no, and leads us into the next area of marketing. We know that everyone is different. Products and services that sell well, such as a Big Mac or a room at Motel 6, do so because the buyer sees something of value in the product or service. The problem is that what one buyer sees as valuable may seem uninteresting to another. For example, some people go to a restaurant primarily to relax and have fun. Others may go to the same restaurant primarily to get away from the kids. Still others may go to the same restaurant because of its convenience. The point is that we, as individuals, are ultimately unique, and each one of us has a special set of likes and wants that separate us from everyone else. In a country of 300 million people like the United States this means that, taken to the absurd, there would need to be 300 million different restaurants tailored to each of us.

Obviously this situation could not occur. What marketers need to do is somehow group sets of individuals together, and sell their company's products and services based on characteristics of the group. Marketers go through a process called **market segmentation** and separate people into distinct groups based on their individual characteristics and buying habits.

Exhibit 11.8   McDonald's decision to take its American fast food abroad was based on a careful analysis of new markets, access to essential supplies and maintenance of its famous quality control standards. McDonald's opened its first Moscow restaurant in January 1990, and its first Beijing restaurant in October 1990. (*Courtesy:* McDonald's Corporation, Oak Brook, Illinois)

The better the job we do in targeting what we sell to the correct group of consumers, the better our business should do. We use elements of the segmentation process to help us answer the following questions:

- What different ways are there to segment our market?
- What are the different characteristics and buying habits of each of these market segments?
- Which segment or segments are the best ones for us to pursue?
- Why are these chosen segments the best ones for us to pursue?
- What do we offer that makes us the most attractive competitor in these chosen segments?

There are many ways to segment a market, and that is the problem. Even a small number of people can theoretically be divided into many different groups. What we need is a method of dividing the market into groups that are meaningful to us. Elsewhere, we discussed some of the standard methods by which hotel markets are segmented. In this chapter we will take a more general look at how markets can be segmented.

Geographic.   Geographic criteria include categories such as climate or altitude. It should be obvious that people who live in warm climates will have eating patterns different from those who live in colder climates. Restaurant menus have to be tailored to the particular eating patterns of these different people.

Demographic.   Demographic criteria involve categories such as age or sex. Older adults have eating habits and nutritional requirements different from their teenage counterparts. Restaurants catering to a mature clientele simply cannot sell the types of fast food that teenagers eat. Similarly, males and females do not necessarily like the same things. Restaurants and lounges that have a dark, masculine decor may not attract females, who have been shown to like a lighter, cheerier atmosphere.

Psychographic.   Psychographic criteria relate to peoples' personality traits, lifestyles, and motivations. For example, some people tend to be more careful with their money than other people. A restaurant that emphasizes value (good, cheap food) would then be more likely to attract this market segment. Another example would be people called *belongers*. People in the belonger market segment need to be a part of their environment. Restaurant advertisements targeted to this group might emphasize that the in crowd goes to the advertised restaurant.

Product Use.   Finally there are the product-use criteria. Here the focus is on how products and services are used. One example might be an "ordinary" versus a "special" situation. If you are going out to dinner and there is no special occasion to celebrate, your choice of a restaurant, or what you order at a restaurant will likely be different from when, say, you are celebrating your birthday. When you are celebrating, you tend to buy different items, and spend more on them, than in a routine purchase situation.

Conclusions about Market Segmentation.   Five conditions must be met for market segmentation to work. First, the market segment has to be defined in such a way that all of its members share the same important characteristics. Second, the

Exhibit 11.9   An example of an important market segment that continues to grow is retirees. (*Courtesy:* Sweet Tomatoes/SoupPlantation)

segments have to be identifiable; that is, they must be different from other segments. Third, different segments need to be comparable to each other, so that the best segment or segments can be picked. Fourth, at least one segment must have enough profit potential to be developed as a market. Fifth, we must be able to reach the segment or segments we have chosen. It does little good to identify a segment we cannot access.

New Product/Service Development

One of the significant differences in how American businesses operate today, as opposed to in the past, is in the area of the development of new products and services. If you can, think about all of the new products you have encountered in the past few years. Approximately 80 percent of all products that are on the shelves of stores today did not exist in their present form six or seven years ago. The pace at which new products and services enter the market is continually accelerating, and we, as consumers, are faced with an often bewildering array of products and services from which to choose.

However, most of these new products are doomed to mediocre sales lives, if not outright failure. Estimates vary, but somewhere in the neighborhood of 90 percent of new products do not live up to the expectations their creators have for them. Even large, experienced, powerful companies like Coca-Cola are not immune to failure. In 1985 the Coca-Cola Company, after years of market research that cost an enormous amount of time and effort, launched their New Coke brand. All of the tests indicated that consumers liked the taste of New Coke better than the original Coke formula. After an initial period of high sales, a considerable consumer reaction

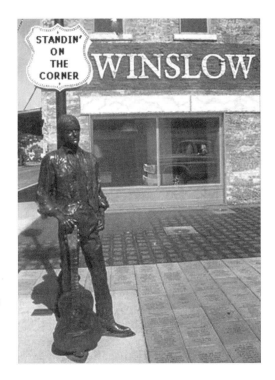

Exhibit 11.10   Marketing isn't limited to the big city. Even rural towns are happy to capitalize on name recognition, in this case a famous line from an Eagles song. People who used to simply drive by now stop for a photo in this trompe l'oeil park, then end up dining, buying souvenirs—in short, they "Take It Easy." (*Courtesy:* Winslow Chamber of Commerce, Winslow, Arizona)

set in, and the Coca-Cola Company was barraged by a tremendous amount of negative reaction to the new product. The company responded quickly to criticisms, and before long Coke Classic—the original Coke product—was again the number one selling cola drink, with the largest accounts (McDonald's and KFC) leading the way.

What did Coca-Cola do wrong? Why did this prestigious company blow it with respect to New Coke if consumers actually liked the taste of New Coke so much? The answer lies in the company's lack of understanding about what the image of Coca-Cola meant to the American people. Yes, the taste of New Coke was perceived as better, but to change Coca-Cola was to tamper with Mom, apple pie, and the flag! Coca-Cola was and is an American institution, one that the American people feel very strongly about. In all of the new product development process that Coca-Cola went through, this vital issue was not addressed, with disastrous results for the company.

The process of developing any new product or service is obviously dangerous. How can companies like Coca-Cola or McDonald's minimize the likelihood that disasters like the introduction of New Coke will occur? There is a number of procedures used to develop new products and services.

Product Life Cycle.   We should note that the new product/service development process is only a part of what is called the *product/service life cycle*. A basic assumption in marketing is that all products and services over time exhibit the same types of characteristics that living organisms do. The product/service development process leads to the *introduction* phase of the life cycle, when the new product/service is first put on the market. At this point, sales are low and costs are high; many of the products that fail do so during introduction. New Coke never made it beyond this point. The *growth* phase comes next. During this phase sales

EYE ON THE ISSUES

International

One marketing area that is growing rapidly is that of international marketing. The hospitality industry, like most industries, is experiencing a period of strong internationalism, with most U.S. companies getting into international markets, and many foreign companies entering the U.S. market. While many of the marketing practices described earlier are equally applicable to both the United States and most foreign markets, care has to be taken to recognize that foreign travelers have many cultural differences of which we need to be aware.

What sells in the United States may not sell overseas, and vice versa. Many of the fast-food companies that attempted to enter the European market in the 1970s encountered considerable resistance to their products. Originally, most *did not* offer beer or wine, a familiar pattern to Americans. However, Europeans generally would not even consider eating in a restaurant that did not sell beer and wine. Similarly, they did not appreciate the "eat and run" mentality of a typical fast-food restaurant. Meals are social occasions in Europe, not just a way to get nourishment. As a result of these (and other) problems, the introduction of fast-food outlets to the European market was not very successful initially. It was not until considerable research had been done that the American companies realized that they had to modify their product/service offerings to fit the European way of doing things; at that point they became relatively successful. In today's industry, knowing how to market overseas and to foreign travelers in the United States is a *very* important part of the overall marketing process.

take off, and lots of people buy the product or service. After the growth phase comes the *maturity* phase, where sales peak. Finally there is the *decline* phase, where sales continuously drop, until they finally cease altogether and the product or service disappears.

The new product/service process is so specialized that very few marketing graduates practice the discipline. Therefore, we will leave a detailed discussion of the new product development process to the marketing professors you'll encounter later on in your curriculum. Clearly, however, this is a process that is critical to the overall success of a company. Giants like McDonald's spend millions of dollars each year researching and developing new menu item concepts, but very few of those concepts actually make it as far as the introduction stage of the life cycle.

Pricing

Of all the different elements of the marketing mix, perhaps the most difficult to deal with is the element of pricing. Hotel or restaurant marketers have a much more difficult time in setting their prices than do retailers or manufacturers. It is safe to say that as an industry, we do not know much about how to set prices. This is dangerous, since price is generally the single most important factor influencing people's buying decisions.

Prices are all around us. You pay *rent* for your hotel room, a *fee* for a tennis lesson at a resort, a *fare* to a taxi driver taking you from your hotel to the airport, a *toll* on a highway as you drive on vacation, and *dues to* your country club. If you work as a salesperson, you receive a salary (the price an employer pays for an employee) plus a commission. The list goes on and on.

Exhibit 11.11   Each of these restaurants has successfully positioned itself in its respective market niche. (*Photo:* James L. Morgan, Scottsdale, Arizona)

The main problem with pricing strategies is the determination of how prices are set. Historically, two or more people would haggle over the value of their items, and through negotiation arrive at a price that was agreeable to each of them. Today, in most business settings, this process no longer is used. Rather, the seller often sets one price that is applicable to all buyers. Can you imagine going to a restaurant and haggling over menu prices? It simply is not done. (There are some exceptions to this rule. You can negotiate on the price of an automobile or a house. Aficionados of garage sales and "park and swaps" often dicker over white elephants. However, in the hospitality business sector these exceptions are rare.)

Factors Influencing Price.   There is a number of factors that influence how prices are set. These fall under the realm of strategic, cost, and market demand considerations.

Strategic Objectives.   First, consider the strategic objectives of a company. What is it exactly that the company is trying to accomplish with respect to price? Survival of the company could be the main objective. If a hotel has low occupancy, lowering prices might help to fill the rooms and generate more revenue.

Market leadership might be another objective. Market leadership means that the company has more business than any of its competitors. (McDonald's is a market leader in the fast-food business.) The advantage of being a market leader could be the image of being the best, as well as perhaps having lower costs than other companies. One way to become a market leader is to lower prices to get more business.

Product/service quality leadership is another strategy. In this strategy, a company seeks to be seen as having the highest quality product or service in the market; charging high prices contributes to this mystique. Ritz-Carlton hotels, for example, are very upscale, which is the image they want. Not surprisingly, they are also among the most expensive hotels around.

Cost.   Hotels and restaurants have costs of their own that affect the minimum prices they must charge for their products and services. These would include all of the costs for producing, marketing, and distributing their products or services. The

I don't know who you are. I don't know your company. I don't know your company's product. I don't know what your company stands for. I don't know your company's customers. I don't know your company's record. I don't know your company's reputation. *Now, what is it you wanted to sell me?*

The point of this advertisement is that people are not going to buy products and services unless they have a considerable amount of information about the purchase situation, the company selling, the products and services being sold, and so on. It is the goal of the **promotion** component of marketing to provide that information, as well as persuading the customer to buy.

Many people consider promotion to be the single most critical element in the marketing process. The complex nature of promotion makes it a very interesting element to evaluate. It is the one area where the producer and consumer are completely intertwined.

The two-part goal of promotion is to *inform* and *persuade*. Information means knowledge. We first have to know about a product or service before we can even consider buying it. Persuasion means convincing people to buy the product or

Exhibit 11.14A Increasingly, hotels have to develop and advertise amenities, such as indoor swimming pools and fitness centers, in their continuous efforts to increase market shares. (*Courtesy:* Palmer House Hilton, Chicago, Illinois)

Exhibit 11.14B   Fitness centers are increasingly popular with "road warriors," business travelers who spend a lot of time on the road. (*Courtesy:* Palmer House Hilton, Chicago, Illinois)

service. After we know about it, we need to be convinced that the product or service is worth buying. If the elements of informing and persuading are present, then the promotion has a good chance of being successful.

Like marketing in general, promotion has its own particular mix, composed of four elements: *advertising, personal selling, sales promotions,* and *public relations/publicity.*

Advertising.   ***Advertising*** involves the use of any form of non-personal communication about a product, service, or idea. The non-personal component of the definition means that mass media, such as television and magazines, are generally used to convey the message. Because of mass media's large audience, many potential consumers can be reached with each advertisement.

The amount of advertising done in the United States is phenomenal. On average we are exposed to somewhere between 1,000 and 1,500 ads each day! If you consider just the hospitality field, how many ads would you be exposed to on a given day? The ads you see for restaurants and hotels in newspapers or on television add up to a considerable number. We are bombarded with ads everywhere. Billboards are ads. Labels on cans are ads. Logos on clothing are ads. This is not to mention the ads that pretend not to be ads, such as recipes that specify Campbell's Soup or movies that contain lingering shots of a Bacardi bottle or a pack of Camels. In fact, *you* are an ad—the way you dress, the way you style your hair, and the way you act are all methods of sending a message. It is impossible to escape the impact of advertising.

Personal Selling.   A second major form of promotion is ***personal selling.*** Personal selling is a form of person-to-person promotion where the seller attempts to inform and persuade one person (or a small group of people) to buy a product or service. As a result, personal selling is almost the opposite of advertising. Not too many people can be reached at one time, but the influence of person-to-person contact is much greater than the impersonal methods used in advertising. Obviously, the cost of personal selling is high due to the small numbers of customers that can be reached. This technique is best used when each customer represents a large amount of business. In the hospitality field, personal selling approaches are generally used to sell conventions and other group business, while advertising is used to sell to the individual traveler.

Exhibit 11.15A   Imagine all the marketing decisions made by this small wine company in naming, labeling, and bottling their product . . . all before the products reached the market. Many of these products have won vintners' awards, news of which helps product sales. (*Courtesy:* Florida Orange Groves and Winery)

Exhibit 11.15B   Industry awards or awards from ratings gurus, such as J.D. Powers or Zagat, help marketers differentiate their products and properties. (*Courtesy*: Florida Orange Groves and Winery)

Sales Promotions.   A third type of promotion has the repetitive name of ***sales promotion.*** This type of promotion is a little hard to define because it encompasses a number of different areas. Basically, sales promotions are any marketing activities designed to produce *immediate* sales or that provide an extra incentive to buy.

Perhaps the best way to understand what sales promotions are is by example. Half-price coupons that you see in newspapers are sales promotions. They are supposed to get you to buy *now* by limiting the offer to a certain short time period, *and* provide the extra incentive to buy, since there is a special half-price deal. Table tents on restaurant tables that advertise special dinners, desserts, or wine service are also sales promotions for the same reasons. An example of a simple sales promotion in a hotel is the reader board in the lobby that advertises happy hours in the lounge or entertainment in the dining room.

Public Relations/Publicity.   The final element in the promotion mix is the area of public relations and publicity. The two concepts are related but are not the same. Publicity refers to any communication about a business for which that business does not directly pay. It is like advertising in the sense that it involves communication to a mass audience. The goal of every hospitality enterprise is to get

Technology

One of the newest and most dynamic areas of marketing is the use of the Internet as a promotional mechanism. The promoting of products via the Internet has taken the concept of in-home shopping several steps further than the traditional methods of telemarketing or catalog shopping. Internet advertising blends print advertising with electronic, interactive advertising that gives consumers an almost personal shopping experience without leaving home. Companies like amazon.com, which didn't even exist in the mid-1990s, have launched multi-million dollar industries that rely on the perceived ease, comfort and speed of shopping on the Net. Today it is possible to plan an entire vacation package—airline tickets, hotel reservations, events tickets, car rental and so on—all via the Net.

Where will this all end? Some people are concerned that we will revert to a "cave mentality," never leaving our homes, because it is now possible to purchase and have delivered to our homes everything we need to subsist. There are also many issues related to fraud and unacceptable material that have to be resolved. In addition, while you can buy many products on the Net, many services purchases cannot be made the same way. You can't purchase a haircut or enjoy the atmosphere of a restaurant or resort while shopping the Net. The need for humans to interact with each other, and the desire we have to experience the world, almost ensures that most of us won't barricade ourselves in our houses. Which would you rather do: look at a picture of a Hawaiian beach on a computer screen, or actually be on that beach?

As a result hotels or restaurants may find a need to deal with the area of ***public relations.*** In public relations we try to maintain as positive an image as possible for the company, either by maximizing the effect of positive publicity or minimizing the effect of negative publicity. For example, if a hotel hosts the scouts, the public relations person's job is to maximize press coverage. On the other hand, if a hotel experiences a fire, the public relations person's job is to downplay as much as possible the negative effects of the fire, and divert the public's attention to other issues—a very interesting but challenging job!

There are many different ways to promote a hotel or restaurant. The promotional mix involves an almost infinite variety of methods, yet in almost all cases all four elements of the promotional mix—advertising, personal selling, sales promotions, and publicity—need to be used best to inform and persuade present and potential guests of a hotel's or restaurant's value.

---

the publicity for little or no cost. If you host a Christmas party for the local Boy and Girl Scouts at your hotel, a newspaper story about the party will cast your hotel in a favorable light. If you remodel your restaurant and have a grand re-opening, and the local television station carries a story on the festivities, your restaurant receives considerable attention. These are examples of ***positive publicity.*** On the other hand, publicity does not necessarily have to be positive. If there is a fire in your hotel, the news reports of the fire could be considered ***negative publicity.*** Similarly, if your restaurant is cited for health violations, or worse, closed down because of them, any news report would be considered very negative. These situations point out two specific characteristics of publicity that are not characteristics of the other elements of the promotion mix: Publicity can be negative, and is hard to control in the sense that the negative stories will be aired or published, like it or not.

CONCLUSION

Marketing is a broad discipline offering many options to hospitality professionals. Since hospitality firms are a part of the service industry, the hospitality student with an interest in the field should work to differentiate between product-tied and service-tied marketing issues.

Subdisciplines within marketing include consumer behavior, market research, strategic marketing, market segmentation, new product/service development, pricing, and promotions. Individuals who wish to work in a hospitality marketing career need to have a variety of skills. An area such as market research requires a solid background in mathematics and statistics, while personal selling requires communication skills.

KEYWORDS

marketing   412
product industries   413
service industries   413
marketing mix   416

market research   419
market segmentation   423
price sensitivity   429
promotion   431

CORE CONCEPTS

consumer behavior   418
advertising   432
personal selling   433
sales promotion   434

public relations   435
positive publicity   435
negative publicity   435

DISCUSSION QUESTIONS

1. What are the major differences between the marketing of products and the marketing of services? What special kinds of problems do see in marketing a hotel or restaurant?
2. What kinds of ads do you like? If you were going to develop an advertisement for a restaurant, what would you include in it?
3. Discuss some of the differences between marketing tangibles and intangibles.
4. Why do you go to a restaurant? Is it just for food? What could a restaurant ad contain that would appeal to you?
5. What kinds of positive publicity might a hotel or restaurant get? What kinds of negative publicity?
6. How has the Internet affected how you live? Shop?

EXEMPLAR OF EXCELLENCE

JetBlue Airlines

Just three years after it debuted, JetBlue airlines was named *Advertising Age* magazine's 2002 Marketer of the Year. In 2005 *Condé Nast Traveler* magazine voted the upstart start-up airline the top domestic airline in the U.S. for customer satisfaction and value for cost. In 2006 OAG, the global air travel guide, rated JetBlue as the "Best Low Cost/No Frills Airline." How did a low fare airline do so well, so quickly against bigger, well-established competitors? JetBlue had a strategy: it would not position itself solely as a low-fare carrier; instead it would emphasize its service, style, and attitude.

While getting ready to launch the airline, the marketing team concentrated on building a corporate culture of fun, style, and service. Though new, they immediately began collecting actual great-service stories that would travel by word-of-mouth and become part of its "history." JetBlue also pioneered high-tech entertainment; it is the first and only airline that delivers 36 channels of live satellite television free at every seat. JetBlue's success continues to amaze the industry. The airline fills an average of 85 percent of their seats, well above an industry that struggles to average 75 percent.

Source: www.jetblue.com/learnmore/awards.html, June, 2006.

WEBSITES TO VISIT

1. HSMAI.org
2. Darden.com
3. Amazon.com
4. www.aarp.org/

CASE STUDY

The hotel industry in a small town located near a major interstate is undergoing a price war. All of the hotels are cutting their rates to such low levels that no one is making any money. As each hotel owner sees some other hotel cutting rates, he/she feels compelled to follow, because everyone believes the only way to get business is to be the lowest priced hotel in the market. Business is slow, and low prices simply are not the answer to making any money. Many of the hotel owners understand the problem, but no one can agree on how to get prices higher and/or get more business so that the entire town's hotel industry can survive. You have been hired as a consultant to speak to them as a group, and offer suggestions as to what they can do to bring their local hotel business back to profitable levels.

1. Based on the information presented in this chapter (and any other ideas you might have), describe any suggestions you might give these hotel owners to solve their problem. (By the way, it is against the law for these hotel owners to all "fix" prices at a certain level; conspiring is illegal.) Use the chapter subheadings in this chapter as a guideline.

2. What could individual hotel owners do to increase the profitability of their property, independent of the group effort you have recommended in Question 1?

Leadership, Ethics, and Management for the Hospitality Industry

This chapter introduces you to the skills, responsibilities, attitudes, and ethical behavior needed by hospitality leaders and managers. It includes an outline for appraising your personal assets as well as your liabilities. Other sections describe what managers do, and identify the knowledge and competencies hospitality industry managers need. A particularly important competency is that of ethical competency, a characteristic that enhances every manager's merit and quality of life.

INTRODUCTION

By enrolling in a program designed to prepare you for managerial leadership responsibility in the hospitality industry, you have positively identified yourself as a dreamer with direction. While you dream of managing a hotel or restaurant or perhaps something more, you also understand that fulfilling your dream will take professional preparation.

It is a rare individual who has not thought at some point that he or she could do a better job than those they've observed managing a business in the hospitality industry, be it a country club, a theme park, a resort, or other enterprise that caters to guests. When you visualize yourself as such a smooth and effective manager, what do you imagine? Someone who:

- Consistently demonstrates a set of qualities called leadership skills?
- Is sensitive to people and inspires them toward accomplishment of common organizational goals?
- Possesses a combination of integrity, loyalty, and accountability?

Exhibit 12.1   Leaders are sometimes out in front, but also sometimes coaching from behind, building teams that can work together and respect each other. (*Courtesy:* Colorado Dude and Guest Ranch Association)

This snapshot of managerial traits sounds pretty formidable, but developing these characteristics is far from impossible. Ordinary men and women in management and leadership positions in the hospitality industry demonstrate them time and time again.

Succeeding as a manager in the highly competitive hospitality industry is no snap. Economic conditions, labor trends, ethical implications, demographic shifts, and many other factors often create such complex situations that it is hard to imagine a fair solution. But success is possible—in fact, probable—if you can weld two vital elements together. Good managers superglue their classroom learning (analytical and decision-making skills) with leadership skills, solid character traits, and good old-fashioned management ethics. Fusing these critical elements is essential if you want to succeed.

This chapter explains the factors you'll need to consider in deciding whether hospitality management is right for you. This includes an outline for appraising your personal resources, talents, skills, strengths, potentials, and weaknesses. Later sections describe four basic management functions shared by all managers: planning, organizing, leading, and controlling. Let's translate these into action.

- **Planning.** Setting objectives and deciding how the organization is to accomplish its goals
- **Organizing.** Developing a structure within which the work to be done is defined and coordinated
- **Leading.** Inspiring people to achieve goals with high performance
- **Controlling.** Evaluating performance toward achieving an organization's goals.

Exhibit 12.2   Do you have an eye for detail? Can you build a team that shares this meticulousness? How would you organize your team to get this ready to go look every day? (*Courtesy:* Sweet Tomatoes)

These functions are set against a background that will allow you to judge your affinity for them. A case study will even let you test-drive them before you decide whether to pursue a hospitality industry management career.

This chapter will not put you in charge; that's something you must do for yourself. Its contents, however, will certainly give you insights into the strengths needed for success. Like a *Lonely Planet Guidebook,* it will note attractions and warn against chancy detours. Beyond that, it will show you the exciting industry that awaits you—one that offers a profession filled with integrity, service to others, honor, loyalty, and self-satisfaction. We expect a solid increase in the need for college-educated hospitality industry managers into the 21st century. Now that the century has changed, you are looking at the upward-moving curve of an exciting career.

YOUR MOST IMPORTANT ASSETS

From the moment you decide to become a manager, you have chosen to put yourself in charge to make positive things happen. Before you reach that point, you will have to do several things. Some of them are fairly obvious, such as learning to express yourself and learning to plan, organize, lead, and control in a business setting. Yet long before you even start all that, you need to do something else: Step back and ask yourself, "Am I the right person to do this?"

The Heart of the Dream

We are all conditioned by our culture to dream about managing a business as being the ultimate career goal. That, in many minds, is having it made. Many of us have been spoon-fed stories about Conrad Hilton, Ellsworth Statler, Howard Johnson, Donald Trump, J. W. Marriott, and Ray Kroc (the founder of the McDonald's empire). The mystique of going from scratch to success on such a scale is really the nucleus of this dream, a carrot on a stick for many who wonder about going into the hospitality business.

Though only a few will ever do so fantastically well, many among the millions of men and women in management earn comfortable incomes for themselves and their families. And they do so not because they are extraordinarily lucky, or have good timing, or keen insights (as some super successes have). They achieve their success with hard work, careful planning, and a realistic grasp of their own abilities and the world around them. Rest assured: They know their own resources, their personal strong points, and their limitations quite well.

Many Approaches

There are several ways to go about appraising your personal resources. The only one of real importance, though, is a thorough and careful self-examination. You can seek opinions of friends, relatives, and associates, but be wary: They aren't any more objective than you are. If you want to go to the effort and expense, you can consult experts to test various aspects of your personality and intelligence. Your campus may have career or testing counselors available to help you. If not, you

Exhibit 12.3   Leaders need to pay attention to what's going on in their organization. They shouldn't ignore bad news, surround themselves with "yes-persons," or fail to speak the truth. (Photo by Eugen Gebhardt, Getty Images, Inc.—Taxi)

will find specialists under psychologists or psychometric services in the classified listings of an urban telephone directory. Such opinions and test results should be considered only a double-check on what you conclude about yourself. Facing up to yourself and saying: I'm good at this and this; not good at that and that; and so-so on these, is essential. You have to know what you can do, and you have to know yourself before you can determine that.

We hope to offer you some guidance on how to go about such a self-appraisal. Much research has been done to identify the character traits of the successful business manager. One study identified them as:

- Drive
- Thinking ability
- Human relations ability

Environment

Managers are role models, whether they like it or not, and whether they believe it or not. Announcing a recycling plan is all very good. Giving awards and certificates to recyclers of the month is admirable. But one of the true engines of a recycling program is the visible participation of management. When your employees see you using scratch paper made from last week's promotional flyer or carefully taking your soda can to the nearest blue box, the message sinks in.

- Communications ability
- Technical knowledge

Another study identified them as:

- Perception
- Boldness
- Persistence
- Persuasion
- Ethics

You can devise your own checklist to rate your personality and capabilities, perhaps using a scale of 1 to 10. But be honest. The ability to look at yourself objectively is also an important leadership trait.

Personality Inventory

The following list of traits and capabilities is a good place to start a personal inventory. After each, there are some nuts and bolts questions to help you bring the trait into focus.

- **Initiative.** Are you a self-starter, even on tasks that aren't pleasant, or do you tend to procrastinate? Do you have to be reminded to take out the trash and mail your bills, or do you anticipate and prepare for such chores?
- **Leadership.** Do you enjoy directing the efforts of others, inspiring positive responses? Or do you hate giving directions and setting standards? Do you find yourself constantly impatient with people's imperfections? Can you stand up and direct what must happen, even if it is unpopular?
- **Sensitivity.** Do you genuinely like people and enjoy being involved with them? Do you think you could continue to feel "people positive" if you had to deal with intolerant and abusive guests? Even with unmotivated or incompetent employees? Are you outgoing, or do you tend to be introspective and enjoy being alone? Are you willing to concentrate your efforts on pleasing the 5 percent of your guests and employees who are critical and discriminating in their tastes? (If you can do that, the other 95 percent will probably take care of themselves.)
- **Responsibility.** Do you like being counted on to deliver, or would you prefer that others bear that burden? Do you want to be considered dependable, reliable? Can you accept blame when something goes wrong, even though you may not be directly responsible?

- **Organizational ability.** Do you readily see what needs to be done to accomplish a job and how to go about it? Do you like to plan activities and see them carried out, or do you consider yourself more of an "idea person" who would rather leave all the administrative details to others?
- **Industry.** Do you like to work and can you do it for long hours, or do you expect to work less when you are the manager? Can you concentrate on a task and stay with it until it is done, or do you typically walk away from a job the minute you get bored?
- **Decisiveness.** Do you like to make decisions? Do you make them thoughtfully, carefully, firmly, and promptly or do you tend to shoot from the hip, let things work themselves out, or perhaps pass the buck to others? (Deciding not to decide is a decision in itself.)
- **Health status.** Are your body and mind together? Do you have the physical stamina and emotional stability to take the hard labor and mental stress that are part of managing? Can you take disappointment and frustration, or are you easily discouraged and inclined to become depressed easily? Or would you prefer not to sweat and worry at all?
- **Moral character.** Are you a person of character who is trustworthy, treats people with respect, is responsible, is fair, is caring, and is a good citizen? Or are you considering a management career because you clean up by taking advantage of paying guests? Do you plan to use "Do unto others before they do it unto me" as a management philosophy? You will have to decide whether you are going to follow that route or hold fast to the Golden Rule: "Do unto others as you would have them do unto you."
- **Knowledge and intelligence.** Do you have skills or technical knowledge that you can use in the industry, and do you have the ability and willingness to learn the things you do not know? Are you willing to study and listen to advice, or do you think you know everything? Do you have the open-mindedness it takes to grasp new ideas and new areas of knowledge, or are you satisfied to consider only what is comfortable?
- **Self-Image.** Do you like yourself and take pride in your appearance and ability? Do you have confidence in yourself? Or do you figure that how you look is nobody's business? Do you worry that people might not like you, or that you might not be smart enough to make it as a manager?

This self-assessment could go on forever, of course, and for some it could become an easy way of talking oneself out of doing anything. The greater risk, though, would be sidestepping a full and realistic self-evaluation.

Exhibit 12.4   Do you enjoy directing the efforts of others and inspiring positive responses? Are you sensitive to the stresses faced by employees at different ages and career stages?
(*Courtesy:* Garden Fresh Restaurants/Soup Plantation)

Step Back and Look

No matter what method you choose or what criteria you use, holding the mirror to yourself in honest appraisal is a forerunner to success. If you take inventory now and identify a weakness, such as poor speaking ability, you can take steps to improve. If you wait until the time you finally realize you need a skill, you'll be hard pressed to acquire it overnight.

Here are some questions to ask the mirror: Do you hate to plan and organize and do paperwork? Do you dread such office work because your strength lies in socializing with guests? If so, you might think twice about pursuing upper management. As a manager, you can count on spending a great deal of time and energy on planning, organizing, and so on. This isn't optional and it isn't temporary. It will be a constant throughout your career. If you enjoy that kind of work or at least recognize the need for it enough to tolerate it, but feel unsure how to go about some of it, don't worry. You can learn quickly enough in most cases.

Do you tend to throw yourself wholeheartedly and single-mindedly into whatever you are doing? You might want to take another look at your prospects, particularly if you have a family. You must keep in mind that you and your family must have time together, not just to eat and sleep, but to be *with* each other. Some sacrifices may be required, but asking your family to live on pure, hopeful dedication is unfair and unwise.

Exhibit 12.5   Conrad N. Hilton (1887–1979), one of America's hospitality pioneers, combined exceptional leadership skills with high personal standards to develop one of the world's best known hotel chains. (*Courtesy:* Hospitality Industry Archives, Conrad Hilton Collection, University of Houston, Houston, Texas.)

On Being a Manager

Being a manager means being involved in several different types of relationships with guests, employees, owners, vendors, bankers, accountants, and, yes, government officials. Some of these relationships will be as equal to equal; other relationships will require you to take a dominant, dependent, or subordinate role. You will have to determine what each of your relationships should be. This may mean:

- Acknowledging that, as a manager, you will answer to owners who may not always be fair, or even sensible
- Realizing that while guests may be unreasonable, you cannot talk back to them
- Accepting the fact that a supplier may leave you absolutely hanging through incompetence or disregard
- Understanding that your employees may not share your work ethic or your standards
- Being willing to admit you have made a mistake, and doing whatever is necessary to correct it

If any of these relationship realities seem unacceptable to you, perhaps you should reconsider your dream of becoming a manager, because unreasonable guests, unreliable suppliers, and your own mistakes are inevitable factors in managing any business.

Successful managers, in a sense, make the fewest, smallest, and least costly mistakes. Everyone is going to make errors; the difference is this: A successful manager will minimize the damage and learn from the experience. The professional perfectionist, the person who cannot stand to make the tiniest little mistake, does not belong in the imperfect world of managerial leadership.

Devil's Advocate

In a similar vein, a manager runs a great risk of failure if he or she cannot face up to and cope with his or her own areas of weakness. In many cases, a manager may be unwilling or afraid to hire someone to handle a function about which he or she feels insecure or inadequate. Even if he or she does hire someone, it may be with the subconscious wish that the person will fail, since failure would remove the perceived threat. How do you think you would react in such a situation? Do you think you could see past your insecurity and realize that the whole objective of hiring a qualified person is to improve the performance of the business? If not, maybe you should not think of management as a career or limit yourself to managing a business with no growth potential and no need to hire new employees. Unfortunately for you, that latter category would pretty much exclude the hospitality industry!

We have been playing the devil's advocate a bit here with these negative questions, but some students find this approach helpful. It's hard to pose questions to yourself about situations you've never been in. It's also hard to know what specialty suits you best when you have no clear conception of the traits that will help you shine or make you stumble in a given area. Listing your strengths and weaknesses will not only help you make the basic decision about becoming a manager; it will also help you decide which segment of the hospitality industry suits you best.

There are a couple of simple tests that will help you decide. One is to ask yourself, What can I offer the marketplace?

THREE STEPS
OF SERVICE

1
A warm and sincere greeting.
Use the guest name, if and
when possible.

2
Anticipation and compliance
with guest needs.

3
Fond farewell. Give them
a warm good-bye and use
their names, if and
when possible.

*"We Are
Ladies and
Gentlemen
Serving
Ladies and
Gentlemen"*

THE RITZ-CARLTON

CREDO
The Ritz-Carlton Hotel is a
place where the genuine care
and comfort of our guests is our
highest mission.
We pledge to provide the finest
personal service and facilities for
our guests who will always enjoy
a warm, relaxed yet refined
ambience.
The Ritz-Carlton experience
enlivens the senses, instills wellbeing, and fulfills even the
unexpressed wishes and
needs of our guests.

THE RITZ-CARLTON BASICS

1. The Credo will be known, owned and energized by all employees.

2. Our motto is: "We are Ladies and Gentlemen serving Ladies and Gentlemen". Practice teamwork and "lateral service" to create a positive work environment.

3. The three steps of service shall be practiced by all employees.

4. All employees will successfully complete Training Certification to ensure they understand how to perform to The Ritz-Carlton standards in their position.

5. Each employee will understand their work area and Hotel goals as established in each strategic plan.

6. All employees will know the needs of their internal and external customers (guests and employees) so that we may deliver the products and services they expect. Use guest preference pads to record specific needs.

7. Each employee will continuously identify defects (Mr. BIV) throughout the Hotel.

8. Any employee who receives a customer complaint "owns" the complaint.

9. Instant guest pacification will be correct the problem immediately. Follow-up with a telephone call within twenty minutes to verify the problem has been resolved to the customer's satisfaction. Do everything you possibly can to never lose a guest.

10. Guest incident action forms are used to record and communicate every incident of guest dissatisfaction. Every employee is empowered to resolve the problem and to prevent a repeat occurrence.

11. Uncompromising levels of cleanliness are the responsibility of every employee.

12. "Smile - We are on stage." Always maintain positive eye contact. Use the proper vocabulary with our guests (Use words like - "Good Morning," "Certainly," "I'll be happy to" and "My Pleasure").

13. Be an ambassador of your Hotel in and outside of the work place. Always talk positively. No negative comments.

14. Escort guests rather than pointing out directions to another area of the Hotel.

15. Be knowledgeable of Hotel information (hours of operation, etc.) to answer guest inquiries. Always recommend the Hotel's retail and food and beverage outlets prior to outside facilities.

16. Use proper telephone etiquette. Answer within three rings and with a "smile." When necessary, ask the caller, "May I place you on hold?" Do not screen calls. Eliminate call transfers when possible.

17. Uniforms are to be immaculate; Wear proper and safe footwear (clean and polished), and your correct name tag. Take pride and care in your personal appearance (adhering to all grooming standards).

18. Ensure all employees know their roles during emergency situations and are aware of fire and life safety response processes.

19. Notify your supervisor immediately of hazards, injuries, equipment or assistance that you need. Practice energy conservation and proper maintenance and repair of Hotel property and equipment.

20. Protecting the assets of a Ritz-Carlton Hotel is the responsibility of every employee.

Exhibit 12.6   Ask yourself: Can I live up to the Ritz-Carlton's standards? (© 1992, The Ritz-Carlton Hotel, Company, LL. All rights reserved.)

- If you have a food production background and the drive it takes to coordinate a food service program, perhaps you'd shine in some sort of managerial position in the food and beverage area.

- If you are gregarious and persuasive, but not particularly strong in operations-related knowledge, perhaps some managerial position in the marketing department of a major resort would be a good goal.

- If you like serving people and enjoy seeing their pleasure at being entertained, perhaps an attraction management position in a theme park would best suit your personality.

Exhibit 12.7   When considering your career possibilities, play devil's advocate and ask yourself where you'd best fit in the marketplace. You may well be happiest in an energetic and popular chain concept. (*Courtesy:* Sweet Tomatoes)

- If you like planning large events with themes, music, lights, atmosphere and clockwork timing, perhaps you'll find your place in the sun as a catering manager.

Study Others

Look around at the people who are already in the hospitality industry. Are you like them? Would you enjoy being around them, competing with them, and working with them to solve industry problems? That would be a plus, since there is a good chance you will be involved in trade associations, chambers of commerce, or other business groups. Beyond that, how would you feel about being labeled? Your customers and your suppliers will closely identify you with what you manage. You may find yourself called a foodie or hotelie (with varying degrees of admiration attached). If the thought bothers you, it is time to be thinking of something else or to be re-examining your values.

A final note: Hospitality is not homogenized. People of every age, color, religion, and political persuasion, with an overwhelming array of physical, mental, and emotional abilities, are managing things and leading people in the hospitality industry successfully. If you are used to being surrounded by people just like you, you may find this stimulating, startling, or both.

The basic personal requirements for successful managers are these:

- The ability to express yourself
- The desire to succeed
- A willingness to serve

Exhibit 12.8   The Caribbean has a wealth of nationalities and cultures represented on its many islands. At a resort casino like Atlantis you would find a diverse collection of employees, managers, and guests. (*Courtesy:* Atlantis)

- Possession of appropriate leadership skills
- Good old-fashioned integrity

If you can develop these requirements in the classroom and on the job, we just might be able to breathe a little more easily about the future of the hospitality industry and, for that matter, the future of our society. Possessing these traits will certainly bode well for *your* future.

EYE ON THE ISSUES

Ethics

What will you do when you find yourself in your first real office, with a door to close and no time clock to punch? Will you strive to be on time every morning? Or will you perhaps be one of those managers who uses the hour or so before the official workday begins to get a head start on the day? Will you treat your employees with respect regardless of their rank, or will you emphasize in subtle (or blatant) ways that you are the boss? Will you back up your employees when they make decisions in your absence, even when you may not agree with them? Is it more important to honor their decisions (in areas you've made them responsible for) or honor your own interior feelings on the subject? Think about it.

WHAT IS A LEADER?

Several times in this chapter we've referred to leadership traits or leadership skills or leadership ethics, but we haven't delved too deeply into talking about what makes a good leader. Instead, we've drawn on what history and research have told us about what makes a good manager.

Are all managers also leaders? Are all leaders also managers? The answer to that is, not necessarily. Leaders may perform some managerial functions, but leaders are a special breed. They *cause change* and help organizations evolve in ways that are beyond the scope of managerial action.

If you look at Exhibit 12.9, you'll see how some experts explain the differences between managers and leaders. Some of these items may seem like fine distinctions, but are they? Do you think that *reading a book* is the same as *writing* one? Or that there's not that much difference between liking and loving? Probably not. Though liking is related to loving, we all seem to understand that love is more than just *really, really,* liking someone; it's the step beyond a different, stronger, *higher* feeling.

While we're talking about feelings, consider the word passion, which is often used when describing famous leaders. Jack Welch, General Electric's famous CEO, insisted that leaders must have a "passion for excellence." What does that mean to you?

How many times have you seen movie clips of crusaders, presidents, or heroes who seemed to almost burn with emotion when they talked about the things they hold dear, such as the environment, or things they abhor, like racism or torture? Leaders can speak with such passion because they have a strong sense of what they believe in (their ethics and values). They also have developed the ability to

Exhibit 12.9   There are similarities between many of these items. Do you see a common thread? Remember that sometimes we are talking about a matter of degree, not an outright contrast.

Manager	Leader
Focuses on method and process	Focuses on style and ideals
Administers	Innovates
Maintains	Develops
Focuses on systems and structures	Focuses on people
Relies on control	Inspires trust
Has a shorter range view	Has a long-range perspective
Sees pieces of the picture	The big picture
Asks "How?" and "When?"	Asks "What?" and "Why?"
Has an eye on the bottom line	Has an eye on the horizon
Wants to meet goals	Looks for the next goal; asks if present goals are the right ones
Accepts the status quo	Challenges the status quo
Does things right	Does the right thing
Goal is to produce consistency and order	Goal is to produce movement
Wants to make sure we climb ladders as efficiently as possible	Wants to make sure the ladders we are climbing are leaning on the right wall!

see beyond the immediate situation and envision how things *can be*. Not only that, they make their vision visible to others and inspire them to share it and work to make it happen.

How do leaders do this? First, they are usually masters of communication. Second, they have usually built relationships with their employees or colleagues and connect with them on some level. This gives them personal credibility. Third, their high level of motivation and energy is visible and almost infectious. Fourth, they are experts who "know their stuff." This gives them objective credibility. What other qualities have you observed in leaders? (According to current thinking, there are at least 10 basic leadership qualities.)

Leadership is a hot topic in today's society. Companies want to hire it and to learn how to grow it, so you can see that working to develop your leadership potential will give your résumé added value.

WHAT MANAGERS DO

To be a successful manager of a hotel or restaurant, you must focus obsessively on service and quality. To achieve these objectives will require that you lead every employee in your organization to a conscious goal of implementing quality and service in every contact with every guest. That will not happen unless you, the manager, know where you are going with your hotel or restaurant. You cannot know that until you establish a plan for your business that includes specific goals, policies, and procedures and systems for meeting them.

What do we mean by **policy?** Setting policy means that you decide *ahead of time* what method or course of action you will take when (or if) something happens. This could be as cut and dried as a zero-tolerance policy for theft, drug use, etc., or it could be more complex and involve several steps.

Zero tolerance means that you simply will not tolerate a specified action. For instance, if an employee shows up to work high, he or she will be terminated, with no ifs, ands, or buts. A more complex (and more tolerant) policy might be to move through several steps before termination, such as:

- Document with witnesses the employee's condition
- Send the employee home with a security officer accompanying

Exhibit 12.10   Ray Kroc, founder of McDonald's, had the vision to imagine a chain of golden arches across America. He, like virtually all "super successes," combined his vision with hard work, careful planning, and realism. (*Courtesy:* McDonald's Corporation, Oakbrook, Illinois)

- Arrange a counseling session for the employee within 48 hours
- Allow the employee back on probationary status

Let us begin our overview of what managers do by thinking through the operation of a hotel or restaurant with a mind toward setting policies in every one of the several major areas of management responsibility.

As many of this text's chapters indicate, it is not enough merely to set policies; you must also establish systems and procedures to enforce them, which means setting up adequate measurements and records to tell you how well your staff is complying with them.

Systems, procedures, and records exist to improve the efficiency of the organization; they are the basic tools in the manager's decision-making process. If you do not use these tools, you will be doing things the hard way, and hindering the success of your hotel, restaurant, or club.

The Business's Character

Every business in the hospitality industry has a personality of its own, reflecting the nature of the business and the personality of the manager. A business's character can, to some extent, be established consciously. A logical and effective way of doing it is to define policies carefully and objectively.

It is better to set these policies as you begin and change them if experience dictates than to set them as you go along. If you start out vaguely, you will end up not knowing where you are going, and the business will be running you ragged into the bleak night of bankruptcy.

Setting policy standardizes your operation, and permits you to exercise what is sometimes called the ***exception principle*** of effective business management: When you and your employees know and follow policies, systems, and procedures, it frees you to handle the exceptional situations, the ones that do not fit the plan. If the plan is well developed, this can be a powerful approach to creative management.

Exception Principle

It is often better to set a policy that will cover most situations and then deal specifically only with those situations that do not fit the plan (the exception principle). A general rule will never be perfect, but should address most typical situations. If you try to include every exception in the policy, the policy will become too cumbersome to use.

For example, Marvin Minsky, a specialist in human intelligence, and the author of *The Society of Mind,* gives a parallel example for helping children make rules about categories:

It's not so bad to start with Birds can fly and later change it into Birds can fly, unless they are penguins or ostriches. But if you continue to seek perfection, your rules will turn into monstrosities: Birds can fly unless they are penguins and ostriches, *or* if they happen to be dead, or have broken wings, or are confined to cages, or have their feet stuck in cement, or have undergone experiences so dreadful as to render them psychologically incapable of flight.

On a related topic, customers often get frustrated when we set up programs or policies with too many exceptions. Frequent-flyer or frequent-guest programs that start out with a general policy automatic upgrade for members are attractive, but if we add on too many ifs, buts, and does not apply exceptions, they soon cause more ill-will than goodwill.

Generally speaking, policies must be clear and specific but not overcomplicated. If you find yourself having to spend too much time dealing with exceptions, you should re-examine the policy.

Hard-Nosed Positivism

Policy has to be set in the context of the world around you, including the customs in your city or region, economic conditions, and the sea of government rules and regulations on which your business will be floating.

You may think that in these days of consumerism and environmentalism with all the elements of employee health, safety, morale, equal rights, sexual harassment, downsizing, and inflation that there is little policy-setting discretion left to the manager. This is hardly the case.

First, all these areas of regulation impose only an extra layer of need for policies; the basic need for policy exists even without them. Second, you cannot blame the rules if you do not succeed. The competition has to live under pretty much the same rules. Creative, aggressive managers approach regulation as a challenge, and set their business policies to (at least) minimize the detrimental effects of regulation, and to (at best) turn the rules to profitable advantage.

Exhibit 12.11   A cruise ship is like a floating city. Imagine the complexities of setting policies for such things as inventory, staffing, and safety. Plans must be in place long before the ship leaves the dock. (*Courtesy: Princess Cruises*)

Hard-nosed positivism is the best approach to setting policy. Be optimistic, up-beat, and positive as you look at any policy-setting area, but at the same time put it through the most critical test of all: Look at it through the eyes of your toughest customer.

Policy Areas

Here is a summary of the major management areas for which policy needs to be set:

- **Sales.** Without sales you have no revenues, and without revenues, you have no profit. That sounds simple, but sales do not just happen. They are the result of planned and systematic action. Since they are not an activity beyond your control, you must set policy regarding them. What you decide will, for instance, determine if your approach will be hard sell, highly personalized, low key, high volume, or customer driven. The sales policy will be one of the key areas in setting the style of your operation.
- **Credit.** When you set up your credit policies, you'll find that some of your decisions have been made for you in the form of limits. How far will your suppliers trust you? How long will they carry you without charging late fees or interest? What is the ceiling amount they will let you charge on account? If you have to delay payment, how much will it cost you in interest or carrying charges, forgone cash discounts, and so on? You might also set guidelines for your use of credit. It's a dangerous thing to use credit for payroll, but a necessary thing to use it for elevator repair. Beyond that, you will need to reach some agreement with yourself, either cautioning yourself—for example, I will be especially watchful about how much credit I take advantage of, since I tend to spend too much that way—or giving yourself permission—for example, I have to relax a little and learn to live with buying on credit without worrying, since using credit is necessary to the success of the business.
- **Purchasing.** Buying goods and services for your business may seem to be a simple matter: Buy at the best price and on the best terms you can get, right? Wrong.

  As a management policy, you need to know how much of what to buy from whom, when, and how. As you manage your business, you must find suitable sources of supply, negotiate terms (such as cash-and-carry discounts, credit arrangement, and returns), establish and maintain favorable relations with suppliers, and set up delivery arrangements.

  One of the first policy questions a manager faces with regard to purchasing is: Do I diversify purchases, or concentrate them? In a small motel or café, particularly a new one, it is probably better to concentrate buying in one or a few places, while retaining the option to change readily if needs dictate. Here is where your personal character can be a particular asset. By concentrating your purchases with one or two suppliers, you can build credibility (based on your character) as well as creditability (based on your payment history).

  If you run a larger property, you will likely have the budget or the clout to deal with vendors or negotiate contracts on your own terms. Be wary, though, of getting locked into contracts that tie you up. Economies of scale are very important, but sometimes a contracted price break can turn out to be a management shackle. **Economies of scale,** in this case, simply means you receive the advantage of volume discounts in purchasing supplies, equipment, and advertising.

Economies of Scale

The simple meaning of economies of scale rests on the advantage of volume discounts in purchasing supplies, equipment, and advertising. You will often see pricing on items as follows:

1–9 units	1.50 each
10–99 units	1.40 each
100–499 units	1.25 each
500–999 units	1.00 each

Suppliers are often willing to charge less per unit on large sales, because their attendant costs (such as set-up, handling, arranging shipping, etc.) are lower on an order of 1000 items than on ten orders of 100 items or 100 orders of ten items.

A variation on economies of scale occurs on ocean liners and airlines. It is less expensive to build and staff one big luxurious liner with 2000 staterooms than to build and staff two 1000-room liners. This is part of the reason why airplanes have been reducing the size of seats and increasing the number of seats on flights. The fixed costs of maintaining, fueling, and flying passenger planes favor larger planes. You, the passenger may benefit on pricing due to an economy of scale experienced by the airline or cruiseline [more seats = more units = (sometimes) lower cost per seat]. (There are other contributing factors such as supply-and-demand, and yield management, which you'll learn more about later.)

But some passengers on flights and cruises now resist being part of a tightly packed journey, just so the airline or cruiseline can enjoy economies of scale. They feel wedged in like sardines and that the value they receive in these environments is substandard. This raises a touristic question: How do providers of experiences or services balance their desire for economies of scale with guest expectations of value?

- **Prices.** What you charge for your food, services, or rooms will be determined in part by your chosen policy. You can decide that your profit margin is going to be 5 percent or 100 percent, depending on a combination of what it costs you to provide the product or service and how much it is worth to the guest. But if the two do not match, something will have to change, or you will be out of business soon.

- **Inventory.** Managing stock, particularly in the restaurant business, amounts to an exercise in circus juggling knowing when to order products so they are available when you need them, neither too long before nor too late after. Experience is the best teacher, but considerable thought must be given to the subject before you fill the first bin. Here are some factors that may affect your inventory policy.

  It costs money to maintain inventory. Expenses include the basic cost of the goods, plus interest on credit, handling costs, depreciation, taxes, insurance, and storage. Such extras can add up to as much as 25 percent of the basic inventory investment. In short, you do not want too much stock just sitting around. On the other hand, carrying too little inventory may be expensive in other ways, particularly if it results in expensive rush orders, service delays, or running out of an item.

Inventory problems can be avoided to a great extent by establishing a system of controls. Much of the intricacy of inventory control has been simplified through technology and electronic recordkeeping, but part of it still lies in the realm of management arts. This is an ability separate from science: the art of anticipating supply problems. Though it may seem that some managers have a sixth sense about such things, they more likely have an excellent grasp of conditions in the supply market that helps them anticipate shortages, delays, or other management problems that suppliers may have upcoming.

- **Human Resources (Personnel).** Any business is only as good as the people who work in it. Elements of human resources policy range from whom you hire to whom you fire. They also include pay, benefits, training, working conditions and hours, promotions, morale, and labor relations, all in the context of state and federal regulations.

  Training requires a conscious policy effort. Even a skilled person deserves an introduction to your way of doing the job. Morale does not make or maintain itself; it requires constant attention. Part of that attention is communication. It's good policy to know when to communicate on the broadband and when to use the closed circuit. An excellent rule of thumb is: Praise publicly, but criticize privately. Remember this human relations principle: Most major problems result from neglected minor grievances.

- **Quality Control.** In your planning, you should be conscious of the need for quality control and performance standards in your operation. Traditionally, quality control has been thought of as a management technique for manufacturing operations, but the concept can be applied just as readily to the hospitality industry. No matter what you are running, you need some system to assure you that your staff is not only meeting, but anticipating, your guests' needs; you have to see to it that the quality of product and service is up to your reputation.

Total Quality Management (TQM) Defined. TQM has been introduced into the hospitality industry by such companies as Ritz-Carlton Hotels and Domino's Pizza. Many other hospitality companies have adopted TQM principles to different degrees. According to Saskin & Kiser, TQM can be described as follows:

> TQM means that the organization's culture is defined by and supports the constant attainment of customer satisfaction through an integrated system of tools, techniques, and training. This involves the *continuous improvement* of organizational processes, resulting in high quality products and services.

How would you mentally sort out the difference between improvement and continuous improvement?

Ritz-Carlton Hotels received the prestigious Malcolm Baldrige National Quality Award in 1992 and 1999 for their Total Quality Management Program. What got them there? Participatory executive leadership, thorough information gathering, coordinated planning and execution, and conscientiously training their workforce were all key to their definition of service quality. The corporate motto for their employees is: We are ladies and gentlemen serving ladies and gentlemen. The aim is

Exhibit 12.12   Seven Principles Common to Successful TQM Approaches.

1. **Customer orientation.** The customer defines quality and is the focus of improvement processes.
2. **Empowering leadership.** Management is committed to leading change toward a shared objective and gives authority and resources to individuals so that they may bring about improvement.
3. **Across-the-board employee involvement.** All staff members, at every level, are involved in strategic planning and continuous quality improvement training.
4. **Education and training.** Employees are given opportunities to better understand their jobs and roles. They are given a bigger picture of their part in the organization's processes and encouraged to focus their energies on producing a superior product.
5. **Team approach.** This is the heartbeat of TQM. Here the focus is on collaboration. The team approach solicits multiple perspectives (on product, processes, customer satisfaction, and so on) and capitalizes on each individual's strengths.
6. **Process control.** The team must gain full knowledge of processes and systems, including knowing whether a given process is in control or out of control. Decisions made are based on facts.
7. **Continuous quality improvement (CQI).** The organization should no longer be satisfied with meeting an established threshold or endpoint, but will strive constantly to provide a higher quality of care and services.

(*Source:* J. Folstad and R. Small, "The Journey to Total Quality Management," *P & T Journal 18,* 11 (November 1993), pp. 33–37.)

to go beyond customer satisfaction by making each experience a memorable one. (See Exhibit 12.6 on page 448 for examples of Ritz-Carlton employee participation and development.

Exhibit 12.12 summarizes the seven quality principles commonly included in successful TQM approaches.

- **Insurance.** Insurance is inescapable, but setting policy early will help you decide which coverages to take. It is helpful to think of insurance as an aspect of management called *risk management,* a process for handling liabilities of any kind (physical, legal, financial, and so on). It is possible to reduce some risks by taking precautions; in other cases, the risk can be transferred to someone else for a price less than the potential loss. This is where insurance comes in.

EYE ON THE ISSUES

International

As a manager you may find yourself working with department heads from foreign cultures, cultures that have different values than you are used to. If someone in the United States behaves in a way that is consistent with such values, you may, perhaps, take issue with their behavior, especially if it conflicts with the law or with accepted business practices. Suppose, though, that it is *you* who are assigned to a foreign country. How will you react to an environment where, for instance, bribery is an accepted business practice? Or where, perhaps, you must develop and exploit personal connections with someone (a government official, a vendor, and so on) to get things done? Perhaps you will witness women or foreign nationals being treated in what are, to you, unacceptable ways. All these things are possible when you accept overseas assignments.

The basic rule here is not to risk any more than you can afford to lose. Nobody can free a business of all risk, but you should not retain any risk you cannot afford to take. It makes no sense to risk heavy possible loss to save a little in premiums, nor is it cost effective to pay insurance for high-probability small losses (like petty pilferage) that cannot be eliminated.

Though there are many types of insurance, you'll find that most of your concerns will fall under one of these five categories of coverage:

- Loss or damage to your property or operation

- Loss or damage to your own personal property

- Bodily injury and property damage liability

- Business interruption coverage

- Protection against death or disability of key executives

- **Public Relations.** No matter what your business is, it will have an image in your industry and in your community. It is within your power to set and maintain that image as a matter of policy. Public relations policy will cover everything from advertising and promotion programs (which are essential for generating sales and for community relations), right down to a policy on customer complaints. Doing business means interaction with people, in groups and individually. If you do not make a constructive effort to organize and control your side of those interactions, there may not be another side.

- **Records.** Call it bookkeeping, busy work, a blasted nuisance, paper shuffling, or whatever, keeping records is crucial in the management of a hotel or restaurant. Look back, and you will see the need for records to keep track of where you are in every one of the policy areas this chapter has outlined.

  If you do not keep good records, you cannot really tell how your business is doing, and that is inviting disaster. Managing a business without records is the same as traveling from Seattle to Miami without gauges on your dashboard. You may make it, but it is going to be by sheer luck. Ignorance *will* get you in the end.

  On the other hand, there are risks in overorganizing. You should know yourself well enough by now to tell if you will be inclined to swamp yourself or your staff with paperwork.

  Some new managers start out with the mistake of reinventing the wheel when it comes to setting up recordkeeping, designing all sorts of tailored forms, files, and complex systems.

  Forms can be useful, but they must be designed properly. The best test of a form is to trace its working path from inception to disposition. If you find that it gets tangled up somewhere, back up and rethink the process. Forms should convey something essential, and do so simply, quickly, and clearly. They are management tools, not an end unto themselves.

- **Regular Review.** We tend to ignore what our records are telling us. Hence the need for another policy: Decide right now that you will create a regular and thorough system of review for your policies, systems, procedures, and records. As your business grows and changes, you'll see the need for updating and revision. You'll be able to notice this before it is too late by studying the situation on an established, periodic basis.

- **Planning and Budgeting.** There's yet a larger area of management policy that we have not covered though we've hinted at it: planning and budgeting. It looms behind all the systems, procedures, and records we've talked about establishing. If you do not know by now that you have to forecast your business's activities as accurately as possible and manage them in the context of your budget and management plan, you have not been paying attention. Policies, procedures, systems, and records give form and substance to goals and objectives; they tell you where you have been and where you are. Without them, you are going to have a hard time knowing where you are going.

Becoming a Manager: The American Dream Awaits

Considering all the ground we have covered, it might seem that all there is left to do is simply apply for that general manager's job at the Ritz and move into the executive offices. You may be eager to rush through your education and pursue that dream of managing a hotel or restaurant. Or you may be a little daunted at just how much there is to learn.

Executing the Fundamentals

Taking charge. Being the boss. Doing a better job than Joe Schmoe. That is just about where we came in. Right now, management may look like a lonesome world. The thought of being in charge may be awesome when you contemplate everything involved.

Don't talk yourself out of it. Go back now and review the ground we have covered. Think how much you have learned about yourself, about evaluating your chances to make it happen.

EYE ON THE ISSUES

Technology

Are you computer literate enough? Are you willing to learn new programs or ways to work? The sooner you become so, the better. Your hotel/restaurant/institutional management program will no doubt include some required computer and/or technology courses. Don't just take them to get through them, though; take them with the idea of taking advantage of the tools they'll provide you. When you move out into the industry, don't be surprised if you encounter people at high levels who are not comfortable with computers. This is often because their training and preparation took place in a time when personal computers were not widely available or even affordable to average managers. These people, for whatever reason, never got the chance (or never took the chance) to become comfortable with technology.

Throughout the organization, you will find varying degrees of interest in computers. Some department heads or employees may want to learn to use new programs they've heard about; others may resist. Newly promoted employees may have jobs that now require them to use PCs and programs, but may feel intimidated. The point is, appreciate your computer skills, be ready to learn new ones, but as a manager, show compassion for those who haven't had your opportunities. And, if you can, provide training opportunities and encouragement for your staff members. Once they gain proficiency in even one program or activity, they will be willing to try others. By helping them grow, you'll encourage their loyalty to you and your operation.

Part of what you have accomplished during this chapter falls under the heading of ***critical thinking.*** Critical thinking involves comparing, contrasting, balancing what is known with what is theorized, looking at alternatives, weighing possible outcomes, and anticipating reactions and consequences (see Exhibit 12.13).

Critical Thinking

The intellectual roots of critical thinking are traceable to the teaching method and vision of Socrates 2,500 years ago. He established the importance of asking deep questions that cause us to examine our thinking before we accept an idea as worthy. Socrates' methods included: seeking evidence, looking closely at assumptions, analyzing basic concepts, and tracing out implications not only of what is said but of what is *done* as well.

Critical thinking is a *habit* of questioning common beliefs and explanations, with the goal of sorting out those beliefs that are reasonable and logical from those that are simply appealing. When we examine our ideas and beliefs we may find that we have adopted them because they flatter our egos, serve our vested interests, or are comforting but not because they are based on good evidence.

Here are some questions (some from *www.criticalthinking.org*) to keep in mind when wondering about beliefs, generalizations, assertions, etc.:

What is the most fundamental issue here?

From what point of view should I approach this problem?

Does it make sense for me to assume this?

Can I really conclude or infer this from this data?

How could I check the accuracy of this data?

What is implied in this graph?

What is the basic concept here? Is this consistent with that?

What makes this question complex?

What else is implied?

Is this a credible source of information?

What might be the consequences of this action or belief?

The Foundation for Critical Thinking suggests that Critical Thinking can be seen as having two components:

1. a set of skills to process and generate information and beliefs, and
2. the habit, based on intellectual commitment, of using those skills to guide behavior.

Successful managers and leaders need to have both the skills and the habit of using them.

Keep in mind that becoming a manager of a hotel or restaurant is, like any other aspect of life, a matter of executing the fundamentals—fundamentals that you can learn in the classroom, on the job, and through self-examination. Be pragmatic. Be realistic. Be objective as you prepare yourself for the promises and pitfalls of a management career in the hospitality industry.

The following case study asks you to apply critical thinking to the management issues involved below. Base your responses on the text and the successful manager character traits identified earlier in this chapter.

Getting into Management

Ms. Labell, the front office manager of a 350-room suburban hotel, has been asked to choose one of her employees for promotion to a managerial position. She has narrowed the choice to either Ms. Kain or Mr. Stull, but is uncertain about the final selection. Ms. Labell jots down the following information as she considers who to recommend:

Ms. Kain	Mr. Stull
Leads department in productivity	Has department seniority
Has a college degree	Above-average productivity
Confident	Demonstrates concern for others
Somewhat assertive	Somewhat lacking in personal confidence
Demands high performance of others	High ethical standards
Female	African American

No matter what happens, Ms. Labell knows that she will have a human relations problem with the employee not selected. Additionally, she knows that she will be evaluated by the hotel general manager on the basis of how successful the new manager performs. Ms. Labell comes to you for advice.

1. Which individual would you select?
2. Upon what factors would you base your decision?

Exhibit 12.13   Critical thinking case study.

WHO KNOWS WHAT IS RIGHT OR WRONG?

Most people in the hospitality industry agree on what is absolutely right—saving someone's life, helping the needy—and what is absolutely wrong—murder, theft, torture, etc. If an employee is caught coming out of the back entrance of a hotel with a shopping bag filled with towels and a manager says, "You are stealing!" both employee and manager know exactly what is meant. Lying and stealing are wrong in precisely the same way in the hospitality industry as they are throughout society. The moral and ethical problems of the hospitality industry are essentially the same as the problems of society at large.

Despite their certainties about right and wrong, men or women who value integrity and principle will, however, experience situations on the job that may challenge their perception of those absolutes. In the workplace there are many shades of gray, even in routine, ethical decision-making. Many of these gray area decisions are made in the context of economic and professional pressures that compete with ethical principles and often result in deception, coverup, concealment, or blame shifting.

The Language of Ethics

A person may understand very well what the term **ethics** means, but may not be able to define it. Conversely, a person may be able to define *ethics,* yet not know exactly what it means. To make sure we're all on the same wavelength, let's look at some thoughts on what this essential term means.

> *Ethics* is the name we give to our concern for good behavior. We feel an obligation to consider not only our own personal well-being, but also that of others and of human society as a whole.
> Dr. Albert Schweitzer, physician, humanitarian, and Nobel Peace Prize Winner

> *Ethics* concerns standards of behavior consonant with values that we hold to be important.
> Kirk Hanson, Director, The Business Enterprise Trust

Hospitality ethics, then, is the study of ethics as it applies to our segment of the business world, the hospitality industry. It aims at developing reasonable ethical standards for our industry. A **code of ethics** is a written standard of conduct consisting of rules or principles (values) on which we've agreed. Having such a code helps us live and work together with a certain level of confidence. It allows us to depend upon and better trust our fellow workers. See Exhibit 12.14 for an example of such a code.

Ethics

The field of ethics involves systematizing, defending, and recommending concepts of right and wrong behavior. Two important subcategories of ethics are normative and applied ethics.

Normative ethics takes on a practical task, which is to arrive at moral standards that *regulate* right and wrong conduct. This may involve articulating the good habits that we should acquire, the duties that we should follow, or the consequences of our behavior on others.

Applied ethics involves examining specific controversial issues, such as abortion, infanticide, animal rights, environmental concerns, homosexuality, capital punishment, or nuclear war.

In recent years, applied ethical issues have been subdivided into convenient groups such as medical ethics, business ethics, environmental ethics, and sexual ethics, but the authors of this book believe that these categories often overlap.

In applied ethical discussions, you will often find these principles used as pros and cons:

- Personal benefit: acknowledge the extent to which an action produces beneficial consequences for the individual in question.
- Social benefit: acknowledge the extent to which an action produces beneficial consequences for society.
- Principle of benevolence: to help those in need.
- Principle of paternalism: to assist others in pursuing their best interests when they cannot do so themselves.
- Principle of harm: to not harm others.

> ### Service
>
> After arriving at your new job as general manager of a Parisian three-star hotel, you discover that the hotel has listed itself on its website and in several travel guides as air-conditioned, even though only the lobby has A/C and the guestrooms don't even have fans, only windows. Sacre bleu! You know that guests who visit from May–September will be dissatisfied and uncomfortable without this amenity. What solution should you and your staff decide upon?

- Principle of honesty: to not deceive others.
- Principle of lawfulness: to not violate the law.
- Principle of autonomy: to acknowledge a person's freedom over his/her actions or physical body.
- Principle of justice: to acknowledge a person's right to due process, fair compensation for harm done, and fair distribution of benefits.
- Rights: to acknowledge a person's rights to life, information, privacy, free expression, and safety.

Source: *http://www.utm.edu/research/iep/e/ethics.htm*
Internet Encyclopedia of Philosophy

Values are core beliefs that guide or motivate attitudes and actions. Many values have nothing to do with ethics.

Ethical values are beliefs (e.g., honesty and fairness) that are concerned with what is intrinsically good or right and the way one should act.

Non-ethical values are ethically neutral values (e.g., wealth, security, comfort, prestige, and ambition). They are not necessarily inconsistent with ethical values, but they may conflict. *Ethical values always take precedence over nonethical ones.*

Why Should the Hospitality Industry Be Concerned with Ethics?

With increasing frequency we are being bombarded by headlines targeting questionable and sometimes criminal behavior in the hospitality industry:

- 48 Biltmore Hotel Investors Sue Accountants for $15 Million
- Hooters Restaurant Chain is Sued: Ex-Waitresses Say They Were Harassed
- Holiday Inns Dance the Tax-Avoidance Two-Step
- Bob Evans Farms Family Restaurant Executive Quits after Pot Raid

In recent years, ethical misconduct was at the core of many business calamities at companies including Dow-Corning, Phar-mor Drugs, Drexel Furniture, Tyson and Enron, and dozens of savings and loans. The names of executives such as Boesky, Milkin, Helmsley, and Keating were splashed across headlines. The hospitality industry was not immune during this period as chronicled by the headlines cited, nor were the major accounting firms of Arthur Andersen, Ernst and Young, or Price Waterhouse, all of whom are active in the hospitality industry.

There are three primary reasons why the hospitality industry and its future managers should be concerned with ethics:

CODE OF ETHICS
HOSPITALITY SERVICE AND TOURISM INDUSTRY

1. We acknowledge ethics and morality as inseparable elements of doing business and will test every decision against the highest standards of honesty, legality, fairness, impunity, and conscience.

2. We will conduct ourselves personally and collectively at all times such as to bring credit to the service and tourism industry at large.

3. We will concentrate our time, energy and resources on the improvement of our own product and services and we will not denigrate our competition in the pursuit of our own success.

4. We will treat all guests equally regardless of race, religion, nationality, creed or sex.

5. We will deliver all standards of service and product with total consistency to every guest.

6. We will provide a totally safe and sanitary environment at all times for every guest and employee.

7. We will strive constantly, in words, actions and deeds, to develop and maintain the highest level of trust, honesty and understanding among guests, clients, employees, employers and the public at large.

8. We will provide every employee at every level all of the knowledge, training, equipment and motivation required to perform his or her tasks according to our published standards.

9. We will guarantee that every employee at every level will have the same opportunity to perform, advance, and will be evaluated against the same standard as all employees engaged in the same or similar tasks.

10. We will actively and consciously work to protect and preserve our natural environment and natural resources in all that we do.

11. We will seek a fair and honest profit, no more, no less.

Exhibit 12.14   A code of ethics developed to set standards for the industry—no matter where in the world. (*Source:* International Institute for Quality and Ethics in Service and Tourism Limited (IIQEST))

- **Self-interest.** Scandals are expensive. Beyond the fact that they are public relations disasters, they can result in fines, penalties, and possible jail terms.
- **Most people are inclined to act ethically.** Our self-esteem and self-respect depend to a great extent on the private assessment of our own ethical behavior. Most people will alter their conduct if they discover it is inconsistent with their company's culture.
- **TQM programs may expose internal ethics problems.** The employee involvement and empowerment programs being implemented throughout the hospitality industry demand an unprecedented degree of integrity and honesty within a company. These processes often bring to light ethical shortcomings.

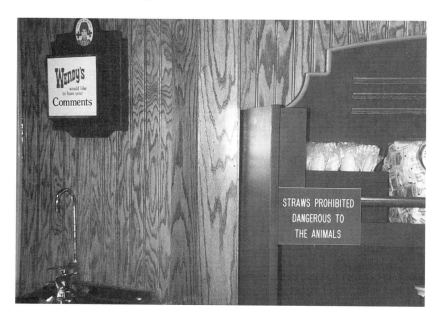

Exhibit 12.15   Customer convenience sometimes takes a back seat to ethical considerations, as shown at this Wendy's Restaurant in the Columbus, Ohio, Zoo. (*Courtesy:* Wendy's International, Dublin, Ohio. Photo by James L. Morgan, Scottsdale, Arizona)

Most of you have entered your first jobs with a personal value system in place and a fairly well developed character. You *want* to be ethical; you *want* to be proud of yourself and what you do for a living. Your self-esteem and self-respect depend on your private assessment of your own character. Very few people are willing to accept the fact that they are not ethical.

If those who manage in our industry convey the idea that adherence to a high standard of personal and professional ethics is a necessity, not an option, in our industry, employees at all levels will get the message.

I Am Just a Student. Why Talk to Me about Hospitality Ethics?

Recent studies conclude that the ethical quality of society has worsened in the last few decades. A case in point is the Enron Corporation scandal. In fact, evidence suggests there is a continuing downward spiral with regard to the ethical and moral behavior of the college-age generation.

A comprehensive report by the Josephson Institute of Ethics titled *The Ethics of American Youth: A Warning and a Call to Action* concluded that an unprecedented proportion of today's youth has severed itself from the traditional moral anchors of American society. Honesty, respect for others, personal responsibility, and civic duty were all found lacking. You may be upset to hear these things said about your age group, but here is the evidence the report cites:

- **Dishonesty.** Cheating in college is rampant (about 50 percent at most colleges). Anywhere from 12 to 24 percent of résumés contain materially false information, and there is an increasing willingness to lie on financial aid forms and in other contexts where lying benefits the applicant.

- **Civic Duty.** Young people are detached from traditional notions of civic duty. They are less involved, less informed, and less likely to vote than any generation previously measured.
- **Violence and Disrespect.** Assaults on teachers are up 700 percent since 1978 even though the number of students has gone down; 59 percent of urban teachers have been subjected to verbal abuse by students. In 1986–1987, *on school grounds,* there were 3 million incidents of attempted or completed assault, rape, robbery, or theft. More than one in four college women report they have been the victim of rape or attempted rape, 86 percent by dates or acquaintances.
- **Ethical Values.** A significant proportion of the present 18- to 30-year-old generation exhibits an attitudinal shift away from the traditional moral principles of honesty, respect for others, and personal responsibility. Today's youth, when asked, stress personal gratification, materialism, and winning at any cost.

Further evidence of ethical and character erosion in America is found in the book *The Day America Told the Truth: What People Really Believe about Everything That Really Matters.* This treatise, based on a national survey, takes a statistical look into the heart and soul of America. The authors' findings are disturbing. Four of their conclusions are particularly relevant to the hospitality industry.

- The number one cause of business decline in America is unethical behavior by executives.
- The majority of Americans goof off, fake illness, or abuse substances in the workplace.
- Americans have little respect for the property of others. They have a tendency to take anything that is not nailed down from work, at stores, and on the road.
- The majority of female workers are more ethical and trustworthy than their male counterparts. They are less likely to steal, to fake being sick, to lie to their bosses, to leave work early, and so on. It is imperative that women be looked to for leadership in American business right now.

The Core Consensus Ethical Principles

Managers and supervisors in the hospitality industry routinely face decisions with ethical implications. How they handle those decisions can have a significant impact on the profits, productivity, and long-term success of an organization.

The Josephson Institute of Ethics has compiled a very useful framework of ethical principles to guide ethical behavior. These principles were developed at a 1992 summit conference that the Institute convened in Aspen, Colorado. There, educators, ethicists, and nonprofit leaders dialogued to come to a consensus about what ethical values could be instilled at home, in the classroom, and at the office without offending those of different beliefs and political viewpoints. The Institute believes these "Six Pillars of Character[SM]" transcend cultural, ethical, racial, gender, and socio-economic differences. The six pillars are:

Exhibit 12.16   Try to name at least seven possible stakeholders who could be affected by a decision to charge fees for using Lake Powell, which is a National Park Service recreational area. (*Courtesy:* Lake Powell Resorts and Marinas)

Trustworthiness	Respect	Responsibility
Fairness	Caring	Citizenship

Source: M. Josephson, Making Ethical Decisions (Marina del Rey, CA: Josephson Institute of Ethics, 1992) p. 35.

The Notion of Stakeholders

A person concerned with being ethical feels obliged to consider the ethical implications of all decisions in light of their possible effects on others. Each person, group, or institution likely to be affected by a decision is a **stakeholder,** a little like a planet circling a sun. Depending on the sun's behavior, a planet may become too hot or too cold, experience violent storms and earthquakes, be knocked out of orbit, and so on. Unlike the sun, a decision-maker can (and must) choose his or her behavior. Those who do not actively and consciously make choices cannot honestly call themselves decision-makers; they're more accurately equivalent to doodlebugs or sheep.

The stakeholder concept helps managers examine their particular solar system of interested parties in such a way as to bring about the greatest good. It asks a manager to make all reasonable efforts to foresee possible consequences and to take reasonable steps to avoid unjustified harm to innocent stakeholders. An ethical decision-maker should never inadvertently cause harm. Like the Hippocratic Oath that physicians swear: Above all else, do ye no harm.

Even so, decision-makers sometimes deliberately decide to do (or authorize) things they know are wrong. Michael Josephson suggests that there are three major

Exhibit 12.17A   Ethical managers engage in reflection as a way of gaining self-knowledge. They realize that they may have never really examined some of their ideas from an adult perspective. They ask themselves, "Why might I feel this way about...?" or "Does this contradict something I am certain is honorable?" (Photo by Renard Represents Inc.)

Exhibit 12.17B   Ethical managers have examined what they believe in and what they stand for. Managers who understand the importance of self-knowledge and questioning can help their employees and colleagues clarify what they stand for. This process is also a lifelong tool that can help in decision-making, for example: "Does this action represent our company's commitment to good citizenship?" or "How can we make this a better place to work?" (Photo by Photo Researchers, Inc.)

Exhibit 12.18   The Golden Rule

This most basic and perhaps the most practical of all ethical theories is as valid in business decisions as it is in personal ones. The **Golden Rule** (also called the *rule of reciprocity*) simply states: "Do unto others as you would have them do unto you." Variations of the Golden Rule are found in the revered writings of Christians, Muslims, Jews, Hindus, and Buddhists, as well as in the works of philosophers and social theorists dating back to 500 BC.

reasons why fundamentally ethical people do things that conflict with their own code of ethics:

- Unawareness or insensitivity
- Selfishness, self-indulgence, or self-protection
- Defective reasoning

Understanding the stakeholder concept does not always lead to good ethical decisions or, for that matter, to ideal conduct. It is, however, a powerful analytical tool that helps decision-makers reason through the ethical implications of a decision.

How Do You Decide What Is Ethical?

The Business Roundtable concluded in a recent report that ethical considerations are at stake:

- When people are affected
- When interests collide
- When choices must be made between values

As you might imagine, for people in business, that means nearly all the time. This means that you, as a manager, will be constantly choosing between goods and bads and sometimes among goods. Which good will you choose? To whom will you listen? Accountants? Lawyers? Owners? That little voice inside? Admiral Arleigh A. Burke, U.S. Navy (ret.) concluded:

Exhibit 12.19   The Ethics Check Questions

- Is it legal?

    Will I be violating either civil law or company policy?
- Is it balanced?

    Is it fair to all concerned in the short term as well as the long term?

    Does it promote win–win relationships?
- How will it make me feel about myself?

    Will it make me proud?

    Would I feel good if my decision were published in the newspaper?

    Would I feel good if my family knew about it?

(*Source:* K. Blanchard and N. V. Peale, *The Power of Ethical Management* (New York: William Morrow and Company, 1988) p. 27.)

Exhibit 12.20   The Josephson Institute Ethical Decision-Making Model

---

• All decisions must take into account and reflect a concern for the interests and well being of all stakeholders. (This is simply an application of the Golden Rule.)

• Core *ethical* values and principles always take precedence over *nonethical* ones.

• It is ethically proper to violate an ethical principle only when it is clearly necessary to advance another true ethical principle that, according to the decision-maker's conscience, will produce the greatest balance of good in the long run.

(*Source:* M. Josephson, *Making Ethical Decisions* (Marina del Rey, CA: Josephson Institute of Ethics, 1992), p. 35.)

Individuals are responsible for their own integrity. They will be influenced by many people and events but, in the end, their integrity quotient is of their own making.

In Exhibits 12.18, 12.19, and 12.20, you'll find some models for thinking through and resolving ethical issues. If you find yourself confused about a decision, try applying each of these models to your problem. Chances are, they will help you understand what is the right thing to do.

CONCLUSION

The reason we have seen so much emphasis on ethics in the hospitality industry recently is not that hospitality managers and employees are any less ethical than managers and employees in other industries. It's more an outgrowth of a changing focus. Until recently, the hospitality industry (and others) had not thought much about the concept of corporate culture. Whatever was, *was*. This approach had its drawbacks, including high turnover and low employee loyalty. In the last decade or so, companies have realized that they *can* remodel their corporate cultures and improve their work environments. Many have chosen to build in rewards for positive ethical behavior.

Positive ethics means concentrating on doing what you should do simply because it is the right thing to do. It is knowing the difference between what is right and what is expedient. (Expediency is summed up in the phrase, the end justifies the means.) As a manager, you will occasionally experience business situations that challenge your commitment to your values. You will have to choose between expediency and responsibility. You may be asked to deliver profits at all costs, or be told through explicit or subtle messages from your superiors to meet your quotas or face the consequences. These pressures will often be difficult to handle. Sometimes the only good answer may be confrontation or even a change of employment. It isn't always easy to be ethical, but the best businesspeople are.

The ethical reputation of the hospitality industry is determined by the separate actions of the managers and employees in lodging, food service, and allied businesses. Your actions are important on an individual level because those actions, combined with those of your colleagues, establish and define the ethical reputation of the hospitality industry in general.

KEYWORDS

Initiative   444
Leadership   444
Sensitivity   444
Responsibility   444
Organizational ability   445
Industry   445
Decisiveness   445
Health status   445
Moral character   445
Knowledge and intelligence   445

Self-image   445
Policy   452
Zero-tolerance policy   452
Economies of scale   456
Ethics   463
Hospitality ethics   463
Code of ethics   463
Stakeholder   468
Golden Rule   470
Positive ethics   471

CORE CONCEPTS

Exception principle   453
Total Quality Management (TQM)   457
Critical thinking   461

DISCUSSION QUESTIONS

1. Lynn, a store manager for a small Midwest restaurant chain, is, by all measures, the top-rated manager of the chain's restaurants. An external audit team discovered that Lynn was pocketing cash from customers and not entering the sales into the cash register. Further investigation determined that Lynn was not personally keeping the money, but was using it to reward her staff with perks, bonuses and other incentives. This put Lynn in clear violation of the company's code of ethics. As Lynn's district manager, what action should you take to resolve this ethical dilemma?

2. Two hospitality majors were talking about the issue of employee theft. Chris asked Kelly if she would steal $1,000,000 if no one else in the world would ever find out. Kelly asked who the money belonged to. Should that make a difference? *Does* that make a difference? Would it be okay to steal the million dollars if it belonged to sadistic terrorists? What if it belonged to no known person (was found just sitting on a table in the student union)?

EXEMPLAR OF EXCELLENCE

Southwest Airlines

Do low pricing and no frills automatically mean mediocre service? Not at Southwest Airlines. This unorthodox company consistently provides Positively Outrageous Service and was the first airline to win a triple crown of recognition for a monthly performance. In May, 1988, it was recognized for: Best On-time Record, Best Baggage Handling, and Fewest Customer Complaints. It has earned that triple crown designation more than 30 times, since then, as well as winning the *annual* triple crown for five consecutive years. For the last decade (the past twelve years, to be exact), the U.S. Department of Transportation has ranked it the number one airline for fewest customer complaints. In *Fortune* magazine's annual survey of corporate reputations, Southwest has been named the most admired airline in the world for the last eight years. Such awards are based on a commitment to and an awareness of the customer. In fact, the employee payroll checks at Southwest say "from the customers of Southwest Airlines."

Southwest is also known for its history of innovation. It pioneered senior discounts, same-day air freight delivery service, ticketless travel, and was the first airline to establish a home page on the Internet.

Southwest has about 35,000 employees and has a waiting list of job applicants. In 2004, it received nearly 250,000 applications for its 5,000 available positions. Despite relatively low salaries, Southwest has created one of the lowest turnover rates in the airline industry: 3 percent.

Since 1986, Southwest has contributed more than $7 million to Ronald McDonald Houses Children's Charities.

www.southwestairlines.com/

WEBSITES TO VISIT

1. www.ritz-carlton.com/
2. www.palsweb.com/
3. www.josephsoninstitute.org/
4. www.bartleby.com

The Accountant Says

In large corporations, accounting is usually headed up by a vice president or chief controller, who reports to a more senior vice president of finance. In turn, the Senior Vice President of finance reports to the Chief Financial Officer (CFO). Financial management of a corporation means the handling of all the monetary affairs of the corporation and the coordination of this activity with the other parts of the organization. To

manage finances, CFOs and their staffs must be actively involved in budgeting and forecasting. Naturally, this will involve departments that have a direct connection to revenue generation, such as food and beverage and the rooms division. The accounting department wants to know how much income will be coming in and how much each area will be spending in order to bring in that revenue.

The vital departments of human resources and marketing must also work with the accounting department to project their expenditures, so that they can be factored into the financial forecast. For example, the processes of advertising for employees, selecting, hiring, and training all cost money. Some staffing experts estimate that the cost to replace an employee can be as much as two to three times their yearly income. Such estimates factor in costs such as job agency fees, employment ads, temporary help, time interviewing applicants, lost productivity, lost production from co-workers, potential overtime for co-workers while the position is vacant, training, etc.

Harris Plotkin, author of *Building a Winning Team* and developer of the Plotkin Turnover Survey, suggests that experienced managers realize that the greatest loss in turnover lies in *loss of productivity*. He estimates that even after the costs associated with the hiring process and the training process, it will take generally three to nine months to get a new employee up to the speed of the person that they replaced—even longer for upper level managers. Now you can understand why controllers and accountants are interested in human resources forecasting!

There are also expenses attached to paying benefits and payroll taxes. If temporary employees are hired through agencies or headhunters are used for executive searches, there will be commissions to pay. And don't forget such expenditures as company picnics, newsletters, employee recognition programs, etc. Not to mention potential lawsuits if difficult employee situations are not handled appropriately and lawfully. Human resource directors are usually part of the executive management team and regularly give input about routine and predictable expenses as well as extraordinary, unpredictable ones.

Likewise, the vital department of marketing must work closely with the accounting and finance directors. One of the values of forecasting is the ability to "see" where future shortfalls may lie. When business is lost or the economy signals the potential for reduced revenues, it is often the role of the marketing department to find ways to attract new business by tempting new audiences or reviving dormant ones. The wise expenditure of a finite amount of marketing dollars is often repaid by a strong multiplier in upcoming months as business is attracted. Unfortunately, this is sometimes a tough sell to "number-crunchers." Not only do accounting types want expenditures to be planned and justified, they often want advance proof that the marketing will be successful!

The Attorney Says

Ever watchful in the background, and ever cautionary, lawyers have caveats for every department. As the chapter on human resource management discusses, there are many employment issues that must be handled within the letter of the law to prevent litigation. These include fair hiring practices, discrimination, a safe working environment (both interpersonal and physical), the right to work, sensitivity to religious and health concerns, union contracts, security/privacy issues, insurance, and termination of employment—just to name a few.

But how are lawyers concerned with hospitality marketing? You might be surprised.

In 2004, one of the world's largest hotel groups was accused of misleading Internet customers by setting up sites that appeared to be independent find-a-hotel sites. Instead, these sites were owned by the hotel group and only "found" reservations at hotels that belonged to the chain. Unless customers read the fine print on these sites, they had no idea that they were not getting a "fair" search from an independent site.

Hospitality-focused lawyers often are called upon to review marketing campaigns and promises. For instance, when hotels set up frequent-stay programs that promise benefits to enrolled members, lawyers must examine the description and verbiage used for advertising and promotional purposes.

The same applies to websites. Are there promises (stated or implied) that the hotel cannot fulfill, or could fulfill only at a loss? If you've ever seen the phrase "promotion not available in Texas, Florida, Connecticut, etc." you can guess that a lawyer has reviewed the laws of those states and found reasons why the offer is not viable.

Lawyers are also commonly involved when a locally successful restaurant or service wants to expand its market. They advise owners and investors on how to protect service-marks and proprietary information. If franchising is involved, lawyers also assure that contracts with franchisees do not overstate potential profit, support, or benefits.

One last area worth mentioning is legal oversight of data mining and its brother, data warehousing. These practices involve collecting gold (in the form of data) about customers. Marketing people hope to convert such personalized information into databases that will help them gain recognition, loyalty, and repeat business. Thus a guest's behavior patterns may be entered into a database, such that on the next visit, a hotel could know what the guest ordered for dinner, whether she golfed or hired a rental car, rented an in-room movie, how long she stayed, etc.

Depending on your philosophy you might find such attention charming . . . or spooky. Do you want some marketer's database to show you rented *Men in Black . . . Leather*" and drank four bottles of cognac on your last trip?

Many customers do not want such information tracked by hotels (or any other businesses, for that matter). This is such a touchy subject that the European Union has implemented a law to protect personal data and block its transfer between countries.

If you have ever received a mailing or been asked to click a box on a web page asking for your permission to "share" information within a company's family of companies, you are seeing another example of lawyers' involvement with marketing. Lawyers hope that customers will click Yes to such data-sharing requests. This documentation can protect their hotel or restaurant from lawsuits from people who feel their privacy has been invaded.

The Techie Says

Technology has been a powerful plus in hospitality marketing—on site and on the Internet. Marketers have always been curious about the opinions and habits of their customers—and now they are delighted to find that potential guests will not only identify themselves through Internet queries, they will key in important demographic and travel pattern information. Even when this information is collected anonymously, it is still of interest to marketing experts, who can use it to create getaway packages, extended stay offers, or partnerships with other service providers such as airlines, sporting entities, concert venues, recreation providers, etc. Such creative packaging was possible in the past, but technology helps it all happen more quickly and precisely. With consensual information sharing or even partner link "pop-ups" we can let a potential customer know we are there, ready to serve. For instance, through such features as "You may also like this" on such high-traffic sites as Amazon.com, a customer who buys a book on "Inner Tennis in the Sunbelt" or high-altitude training gets exposed to the proximity of our bed-and-breakfast, resort, restaurant, tour services, etc.

The Internet has also opened new ways to recruit qualified applicants, 24 hours a day. Job descriptions and deadlines can be easily changed and applicants can respond without the

A.A. degree	Excel	ServSafe certificate
Certified human resources executive	Le Cordon Bleu	Internship
Club manager	University	Cost control
Trainer	ROI	Public relations

Exhibit 1.   When Human Resources departments scan résumés or applications electronically, they can pick out words and phrases they consider essential for the job they are filling. If you know Microsoft PowerPoint, but didn't include it in your application, you might get sorted out of possible people to interview. Do you think this is a good practice from the applicants point of view? How about the harried human resources person who has 1200 applications to sort through?

time and expense of creating and mailing a physical piece of mail. When résumés are submitted electronically, they can also be searched for pertinent terms or qualifications (See Exhibit 1 for examples.)

Corporate training directors have embraced web-based training materials, which can be updated as policies change rather than reprinted and redistributed through physical means. Employees interested in professional development can attend virtual training in their late or unpredictable off hours, which, in the past might well have prevented them from going to school during traditional hours.

Cell-phone technology has also made it easier for employees to be "on call." Lower income employees who may not have had access to a private phone line can now be reached more easily.

Internal email has greatly reduced the need for paper to distribute memos or other important communications. Scheduling software (such as CorporateTime) has simplified the process of setting up meeting times for teams of busy managers, all of whom are usually juggling other meetings and responsibilities.

Career Exploration for the Hospitality Industry

This chapter takes a realistic approach to thinking about careers in the hospitality industry. Pulling no punches, it encourages students to take a look at themselves in terms of skills, values, experience, and drive. It also offers clear examples on how to build résumés that showcase strengths rather than being slave to format and chronology. Helpful strategies for interviewing also assist students in preparing for the job market.

INTRODUCTION

If you are reading this book, then you are probably interested in hospitality and perhaps considering a career in the industry. Making such a decision will have a major impact on your life—it can influence where you live, whom you meet, and what kind of life you have. The purpose of this chapter is twofold: it will provide information to help you think about how the hospitality industry fits with your interests and your dreams; and if you decide it is a good fit, this chapter will provide you with tips to help you move toward those dreams.

LEARNING ABOUT HOSPITALITY CAREERS

When people think about jobs in the hospitality industry, they might picture interesting places catering to the lifestyles of the rich and famous. But it is important to understand that hospitality occurs in all kinds of places, with all kinds of people. It

Exhibit 13.1   When you begin your big hunt (your job hunt!) arm yourself with the power of information and networking. (Photo courtesy of Conservation Corp, Africa.)

is also important to know that the experience of being a guest at a hospitality enterprise is totally different from being an employee there. The difference between what goes on in the front of the house and what goes on in the back of the house are as different as night and day.

There is a wide variety of employment opportunities for people interested in working in hospitality. Most people think of hotels, restaurants and resorts, but there are numerous other places that people with hospitality training can work. Have you ever thought of any of the following possibilities?

- Athletic arenas
- Schools and universities
- Ski or water sport resorts
- Institutions such as hospitals or prisons
- Theme parks
- Military clubs (civilians are hired to manage both food and lodging operations)
- Visitor bureaus or destination marketing associations
- Casinos
- Car rental agencies
- Bed and breakfasts
- City clubs
- Country clubs
- Homeless shelters and food centers

Exhibit 13.2   Two-and-a-half hours ago, this banquet room was an empty ballroom. Then the set-up team rolled in tables, "dressed" them with linens, and carefully set and decorated them. For special occasions, like a wedding banquet the set-up team would need yet another hour. If you enjoy transforming something "bare bones" into something glam, you might enjoy a specialty in banquet management. (Photo, left: Andy Sotiriou/Photodisc/Getty Images; right: Juan Silva/Getty Images Inc.—Image Bank)

Queen Elizabeth 2

Exhibit 13.3 You'll need a positive persona when dealing with guests—on land, on sea, or around a campfire. Recruiters want to see that positive side of you during the interview—and thereafter! (Courtesy Princess Cruises.)

Along the same lines, when people are asked what type of job they want in the industry, they typically answer "management." But there are all kinds of jobs related to tourism and hospitality. The following list is just a sample of the kinds of jobs available in this industry:

- Accounting and finance
- Marketing and sales
- Building or landscape architecture
- Interior design
- Computer technology
- Property maintenance and engineering
- Purchasing
- Wholesale distribution
- Executive chef/sous chef
- Hospitality education
- Food photographer
- Tour coordinator/provider

Whatever sectors of the hospitality field interest you, there are likely to be plenty of opportunities. According to the Travel and Tourism Industry of America (TIA), travel and tourism ranks as the first, second, or third economic segment in every country in the world. In the United States, it is the third largest revenue-producing industry behind health care and financial services. In such a climate, there are many possibilities for exciting careers with rapid advancement.

A REALITY CHECK

The most extensive employment opportunities are in jobs requiring good customer service skills. For people who like people, this is good news. In addition, working with hotel and restaurant guests is rarely boring. Mixing with the public, solving problems, or arranging details to provide ultimate satisfaction will keep you busy and challenged. There are drawbacks, however. The nature of the industry requires that you work while others are having fun. Long hours, geographic relocations, chaos, and crisis are some of the words people use to describe the less positive aspects of working in hospitality.

In order to make a good decision about your niche in this field, find out as much as possible about the areas that interest you. The more realistic the picture you can get of a job, the better you are able to decide whether or not it is a good fit for your personality. Here's what some people working in the industry have to say about it:

> It takes commitment, integrity and perseverance to succeed in this industry. The hours are long and you may never be rich. Why do it? The work can be great fun if you want it to be. The satisfaction of running your own piece of the business is wonderful. Innovation and inspiration are welcomed and cherished. The instant gratification from satisfied customers is out of this world. Boredom and routine are rare. But most of all it abounds with people. If you are looking for a career in the service industry to last a lifetime, if you are dynamic, energetic, and aggressive, and find satisfaction working with and around people, the hospitality industry is for you!
>
> Roberta Schaffner, Former Regional Vice President, Marriott Education Services

> This is a competitive, challenging and changing industry. Managers are responsible for the full operations of their departments and, for many, this involves long hours, usually with minimal staffing. One must truly love this work to be successful at it.
>
> Ann Niemiec, Franchise Services Director, Choice Hotels International

Exhibit 13.4   The excitement, rewards, and potential for rapid advancement have some trade-offs—for example: long hours and sometimes quirky schedules. (*Photos:* James L. Morgan, Scottsdale, Arizona)

When I graduated from college, I wanted to work in an environment where I could train and coach other people. I wanted a position that offered a fast-paced challenge and where my decision-making and motivational skills could make a difference. I chose a position [with a major restaurant chain]. In addition to offering what I was looking for, it also provided opportunities to travel. As a manager and general manager, I have lived and worked in nine different cities. A large part of my success today is the result of the living experience I gained while relocating. The activities I enjoy about my job are many. First, I receive great satisfaction from choosing and training our management teams. Helping managers grow professionally and advance in their careers has many rewards. Second, the decisions that I make are important ones and I am able to see their effects immediately. Finally, there is no greater satisfaction than a happy guest.

Kirk Michael, District Manager, The Old Spaghetti Factory International

What I love about the hospitality industry is the fast pace and high energy. Nothing ever stays the same. Even though things are constantly changing, we are always focused on how to give better service and thereby increase revenue. What is challenging is to stay ahead of everyone else by always reviewing what you have done to see how it can be done better. In my opinion, the most important skills and competencies you need to succeed in the hospitality business are dedication to service, communication, organization, delegation, and most importantly, leadership skills.

Mary Watson-Boswell, Former Regional Vice President, Wyndham Hotels

As a manager in corporate food service, I typically worked only 40–50 hours a week with fewer evening and weekend demands than my colleagues in restaurant management. The corporation I worked with encouraged all employees, from dishwashers to computer engineers, to continue their education and to grow as individuals. I had numerous opportunities for further training and education. Also, the company sponsored numerous community events such as the Phoenix Open Golf Tournament. Consequently, I got the chance to oversee catering and food service for executive tents and skyboxes, not to mention watch some excellent rounds of golf! Based on my experience, if I could give advice to people interested in this industry, I'd tell them to see each challenge as a learning opportunity and to retain a positive attitude.

Stacie Cotton, Human Resources Administrator, The Compass Group

INFORMATIONAL INTERVIEWING

There is nothing more valuable than talking to people doing the work you want to do when you are trying to make a career decision. Whether you are interested in hotel or restaurant management, event planning, or computer information systems, talking to someone on the job will help you get a realistic idea of the day-to-day activities and the skills required to carry them out. This is called **informational interviewing,** and it is valuable because it allows you to:

- See the environments where you might work
- Determine personality types of the people likely to be your colleagues and whether or not you would enjoy working with them
- Gain an understanding of the rewards and challenges of the job
- Receive advice that could make your entry into the workforce easier
- Receive an offer for a job in which you spend a day shadowing a person in their workplace, or better yet, receive an offer for employment

Exhibit 13.5   Sample Questions for Informational Interviews

1. How did you get into this line of work?
2. How did you get your first job?
3. What has your career path been like? Is that typical in this industry?
4. What skills or personal qualities are necessary to succeed in this job?
5. What do you like most? What do you like least?
6. What do you do in a typical work day or week?
7. What type of people do you work with?
8. What is the biggest challenge facing your organization?
9. What is an average starting salary in this area? What variables determine salary and opportunity for advancement?
10. What schooling or experience was most beneficial in preparing you for this work?
11. What advice would you give someone wanting to break into this industry?
12. Could you give me the names of other individuals who might be willing to share their perspectives?

Exhibit 13.6   Annual reports and recruiting packets are also good places to get company information. The Internet has made things easier still, but also look at news magazine feature stories to get a well rounded impression. (Photo: James Morgan, Scottsdale, Arizona.)

To begin the informational interviewing process, make a list of people to interview. There are many ways to get names for your list: Get referrals from family, friends, or teachers; read the business section of the newspaper and get names of people quoted or featured; ask school alumni offices for assistance in locating former graduates; contact professional organizations for members in your area.

Once you have established a list of people, write or call them to set up a 20- to 30-minute interview at their work sites. You could say something like:

> Hi, my name is _____ and I was given your name by _____. I am researching the hospitality industry to decide whether I would like to pursue a career in it. I understand you are involved in this area, and I would like to get your personal views. Could we arrange an appointment?

Prior to the interview, make a short list of questions. Ask about those things that are important to you and that would increase your understanding of the career. Exhibit 13.5 provides some sample questions.

Keep in mind that the people you talk to could become potential employers in your future, so make a positive impression. Dress nicely and be on your best behavior. Before ending the meeting, ask them for one or two names of other people in the industry that you might interview. Thank the professionals for their time and send them a thank you note as well.

GATHERING INFORMATION FROM OTHER SOURCES

In addition to informational interviews, there are other sources for learning about the industry, and even specific companies within the industry. One option is to contact professional organizations and ask them for any material they have related to their profession. You might also explain why you want the information and then ask for names of people in your area that are members of the organization. You could then contact those people for an informational interview. Exhibit 13.7 is a sample listing of professional organizations. Another good resource is the National Trade and Professional Associations reference book that lists thousands of organizations related to every career field imaginable. Most libraries have a copy readily available.

Another source of valuable information is the written material published by hospitality businesses and corporations. This could include annual reports and recruiting packets. News magazine stories are also good places for finding information about the industry, as well as specific company activities.

KNOWING WHO YOU ARE AND WHAT YOU WANT

Having lots of information about a career does not guarantee that you will be happy in it if you choose to pursue it. You must be able to evaluate the information you gain based on what is important to you. What activities do you enjoy? What kinds of people do you like to hang around with? Where do you want to live? What kind of life do you want to have in terms of work, recreation, family,

Exhibit 13.7   Professional organizations are an excellent resource for information and contacts.

American Culinary Federation (ACF)

American Hotel and Lodging Association (AH&LA)

American Society for Hospital Food Service Administration (ASHFSA)

American Society of Travel Agents (ASTA)

The Council on Hotel, Restaurant and Institutional Education (CHRIE)

Club Managers Association of America (CMAA)

Educational Foundation of the National Restaurant Association (EF of NRA)

Educational Foundation of the American Hotel and Motel Association (EF of AM&HA)

Foodservice Consultants Society International (FCSI)

Healthcare Foodservice Management (HFA)

Hospitality Sales and Marketing Association (HSMA)

Hotel Catering & Institutional Management Association (HCIMA)

International Association of Conference Centers (IACC)

International Association of Hospitality Accountants (IAHA)

International Food Service Executives Association (IFSEA)

Meeting Planners International (MPI)

National Association for Catering Executives

National Association of Colleges & Universities Food Service (NACUFS)

National Executive Housekeepers Association (NEHA)

National Restaurant Association (NRA)

National Tour Association (NTA)

Professional Convention Management Association (PCMA)

Professional Guides Association of America (PGAA)

Society for Foodservice Management (SFM)

Travel Industry Association of America (TIA)

---

friends, and community? How important are material things like a house, car, and toys like boats, bikes, or airplanes?

The list in Exhibit 13.8 is a place to start in terms of clarifying who you are now, who you want to be in the future, and what kind of life you want to live. Another valuable exercise is to make a list of 5 to 10 satisfying events or accomplishments in your life. They can be small and from the distant past. For example, if you have a very vivid memory of learning to ride your bike at age five and it was a great feeling, then put that on your list. Then write a detailed account of that event and everything that went into it—all the things you had to do to make it happen or experience it. If you don't like to write, then find someone to talk to about it, again using a lot of detail. Once you have relived the experience in detail, ask yourself what it says about your values, interests, abilities and personality. Are there common themes that run through your various stories? And how do they fit with the kind of work you want to do? To understand how this exercise works, it may be helpful to read the case study on pages 507–508.

Exhibit 13.8   Questions to Foster Self-Assessment

1. Why did you choose to interview with our company?
2. Describe your ideal job.
3. What can you offer us?
4. Where do you want to be in five years? Ten years?
5. Do you plan to return to school for further education?
6. What skills have you developed?
7. Did you work while going to school? In what positions?
8. What did you enjoy most about your last employment?
9. What did you enjoy least about your last employment?
10. What did you learn from these college work experiences?
11. Have you ever quit a job? Why?
12. Why should we hire you rather than another candidate?
13. Why did you choose your major?
14. What do you consider to be your greatest strengths?
15. Can you name some weaknesses?
16. Do you prefer to work under supervision or on your own?
17. Would you be successful working on a team?
18. Of which three accomplishments are you most proud?
19. In which campus activities did you participate?
20. Have you ever dropped a class? Why?
21. Why did you select your college or university?
22. What do you know about our company (product or service)?
23. Which college classes did you like the best? Why?
24. Which college classes did you like the least? Why?
25. Who are your role models?
26. Do you think you received a good education at _____?
27. What is your overall GPA? What is your major GPA?
28. Do your grades accurately reflect your ability?
29. Were you financially responsible for any portion of your college education?
30. Have you worked under deadline pressure? When?
31. Are you able to work on several assignments at once?
32. Do you prefer large or small companies? Why?
33. How do you feel about working in a structured environment?
34. How do you feel about working overtime?
35. How do you feel about travel?
36. How do you feel about the possibility of relocation?
37. Do you have any hobbies?
38. What problems have you solved in your previous positions?
39. Are you willing to work flextime?
40. Have you ever done any volunteer work? What?
41. Define success. Failure.
42. Have you ever had any failures?
43. How does your college education or work experience relate to this job?
44. How did you get along with your former professors (supervisors and co-workers)?
45. How many classes did you miss because of illness or personal business?
46. What are your ideas on salary?
47. Tell me about yourself.
48. Do you have any computer experience?
49. Have you ever spoken to a group of people? How large?
50. Would you be willing to take a drug test?

Source: Alloy Education/Career Recruitment Media, an Alloy Media + Marketing company, Chicago, IL.

Ethics

The practice of exaggerating or outright lying on résumés is now recognized as a modern plague. As a result, most positions of responsibility now require background checks as well as personal references. You may even be asked to submit proof of such things as a college degree or to document previous salary rates. It is never appropriate to lie on résumés. Organize your strengths and present them to good advantage, but do not misrepresent your qualifications.

What kinds of characteristics do you think the author of this story might have? What is important to the author that motivated her to learn to ride a bike? What skills and abilities did she have to demonstrate in order to obtain her goal of riding a bike? Do you think she would be a good fit for a job in hospitality? Why or why not?

Once you have gained enough information about yourself and about the hospitality industry to decide what area of the field is the best match for your personality and skills, you need to think about how to prepare yourself for employment. Many people make the mistake of thinking that they will get the necessary education, experience or training and then begin looking for a job. Actually, you need to be thinking about making yourself marketable from the moment you decide that a career in travel, tourism or hospitality is right for you.

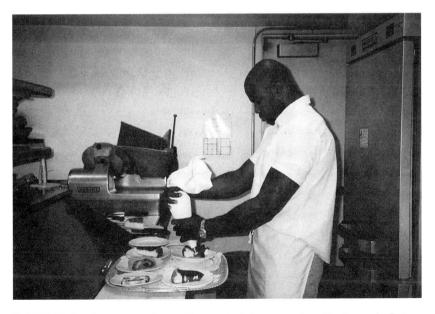

Exhibit 13.9   Some people want to be chefs because they like to cook. But can they work in hot temperatures under pressure for quick delivery and quality food? (*Photo:* James L. Morgan, Scottsdale, Arizona)

DEVELOPING THE NECESSARY SKILLS

Whatever field of specialization you decide to pursue, it is important that you continually develop and upgrade your skills to meet the demands of an ever-changing industry. Most employers say they want well rounded individuals with a willingness to work hard, a sense of focus, and a wide variety of skills. There are two types of skills that are important for your success in this industry: technical and management.

Technical skills refer to the hands-on details of any job. All jobs have technical components. For example, housekeepers need to have knowledge of cleaning chemicals, methods, and machinery; dining room personnel need to know how to set a proper table and deliver service and food; front desk managers need to know how to calculate occupancy percentages, average daily room rates, and overall revenue; financial analysts need to interpret financial statements and understand economic forecasts; computer information system operators need to know programming and networking operations. Often, technical skills are learned or improved on the job. Though they can be introduced in a classroom environment, it isn't until you actually do them that you develop the skill. Practice makes perfect with technical skills.

Management skills are less tangible than technical skills. They require more brainpower and less hands-on application. Some sample management related skills mentioned by employers include effective communication (listening as well as speaking and writing), creative problem-solving, critical thinking and decision-making, customer relations, negotiation and conflict management. Often times, these types of management skills are introduced in educational settings. Most college curriculum includes courses designed to teach the basic concepts of management skills.

It is important to find a balance between technical and managerial skills; neither should be undervalued. Managers who focus their energy on the technical aspects of their operation may find themselves alienating their employees and customers. On the other hand, managers who focus solely on management skills, without attending to technical competencies, may fail to anticipate problems because of their lack of practical knowledge.

OBTAINING CREDENTIALS

During the early development of the industry, few hospitality professionals held specialized college degrees. Many entered their areas of specialization with little or no advanced education and worked their way up through layers of increasing responsibility before reaching upper management positions. Today, in a world marketplace filled with increasingly sophisticated consumers and a highly educated employment pool, it is more difficult to succeed without **credentials.**

The people that are most sought after by hospitality employers have a combination of real-world experience, starting at the bottom rung of the ladder in direct service positions, and appropriate education or training from a credentialed school, organization, or agency. So where can you obtain your training or education?

Professional Certification Programs

Professional organizations such as the Educational Institute (EI) of the American Hotel and Lodging Association, the International Association of Convention and Visitors Bureaus (IACVB), and the Education Foundation (EF) of the National Restaurant Association (NRA) provide certification programs in their areas of specialty. These certification programs do not carry academic credit, but are recognized in the industry as providing current, consistent, quality training on very specific topics. The training is often held in a conference center and can last anywhere from two hours to five days. These programs are most helpful for people already working in the industry who want to update and expand their skills.

Technical Programs

Technical or vocational programs, whether private or public, usually involve one to two years of full-time study. Classes are tightly focused on a specific subject area, and there are usually no requirements for competencies in English or exposure to general studies classes such as history, art or science. This concentrated approach often appeals to people who are anxious to quickly gain technical skills in order to obtain employment.

Community College and Associate Degree Programs

Community colleges offer practical training and also provide a general education. They usually require a two-year commitment (if going to school full-time), and students are required to demonstrate competencies in English, math, and general

Exhibit 13.10   Many people attend certification programs because they are affordable, offer up-to-date training in very specific areas, and do not require a big financial or time commitment. (Photo by Corbis Digital Stock)

studies. Community college and associate degree programs have an advantage over professional certifications and technical programs in the transferability of their credit hours toward a four-year university degree. This level of training is appropriate for people who want to learn technical skills, but also gain a general education that will serve them well should they decide to pursue a bachelor's degree at a later time.

Bachelor Degree Programs

Four-year degrees continue to be the most popular and advantageous training for people wanting to obtain management-level jobs in the industry. Many fast-food chains now require college degrees, as do many major lodging companies. Four-year programs often have a combination of technical hospitality skills training and business management courses such as accounting, economics, marketing, finance, and human resource management. In addition, graduates are required to have a general studies background outside of their area of specialty. Thus students are exposed to courses related to art, science, history, humanities, and cultural appreciation. The intent of such an education is to develop the critical thinking, problem-solving, and communication skills required for leadership positions.

Exhibit 13.11   Two- and four-year colleges offer the advantage of deeper bonding with fellow students and opportunities for mentorship with faculty. (*Courtesy:* School of Hotel & Restaurant Management, Northern Arizona University).

Graduate Programs

Those who plan to pursue college teaching or who aspire to executive positions in national and multinational corporations and agencies may continue their education with master's and/or doctoral degrees. Such a commitment to advanced education should not be made lightly because of the money and time required to complete a degree. Most people do not pursue this level of education until they have obtained a bachelor's degree and a considerable amount of work experience, so that they are very focused on a specific goal requiring additional education.

There are several excellent references describing options for training and education in the hospitality industry. Some of the most commonly used: CHRIE's *Guide to College Programs in Hospitality and Tourism;* the World Tourism Organization's *World Directory of Tourism Education and Training Institutions;* the National Restaurant Association's (NRA's) *Guide for Two . . . and Four-Year Foodservice/Hospitality Programs;* Dun's *Employment Opportunity Directory* (for listings of companies that provide specialized training programs and internships).

GAINING EXPERIENCE IN THE INDUSTRY

The most marketable skill set is one that combines formal training or education with on-the-job experience. If you are going to school, it is important to get a part-time job or work during summer vacations. This does two things: It makes you more marketable when you are ready to graduate and look for a full-time position; and it gives you realistic experience in the industry so that you can better determine if it is a good fit for who you are and who you want to be in the future.

WRITING A RÉSUMÉ

So, how do you go about getting a job in travel, tourism or hospitality?

The first step is to build a **résumé.** The purpose of a résumé is to provide information to people about who you are and what skills you have. It should be well organized, concise, and written in a focused manner. Because everyone has different experiences and skills, there is room for individuality and creativity when writing résumés. However, there are certain standard categories and information common to most résumés, which we discuss next. The first four categories are the most pertinent information.

Heading

Found at the top of a résumé, the heading includes your name, address, phone number, and email address. It is a good idea to put both a current and a permanent address if you will be relocating within the next 6 to 12 months. Do not put pager or cell phone information on the résumé unless that is the only way to reach

Exhibit 13.12   Typical Hospitality Career Ladder & Compensation

Foodservice		Lodging	
President/CEO	$50,000-$350,000+	General Manager	$97,300
Owner	$35,000-$200,000+	Dir. Sales & Mktg	$70,100
Chief Financial Officer	$45,000-$200,000+	Food & Bev Director	$64,900
Manager/COO	$42,000-$200,000+	Controller	$57,100
Director of Operations	$40,000-$150,000+	Senior Sales Manager	$52,100
Treasurer	$25,000-$120,000+	Personnel Director	$49,000
Regional Manager	$40,000-$100,000+	Executive Chef	$53,800
Food and Beverage Director	$35,000-$85,000+	Chief Engineer	$51,000
Director of Purchasing	$35,000-$100,000+	Sales Manager	$39,000
Executive Chef	$35,000-$90,000+	Catering Sales Manager	$35,600
Controller	$35,000-$100,000+	Front Office Manager	$33,900
District Manager	$45,000-$80,000+	Sous Chef	$38,800
Director of Training	$35,000-$100,000+	Executive Housekeeper	$32,400
Unit Manager	$30,000-$70,000+	Reservations Manager	$32,800
Chef	$27,000-$60,000+	Reservations Clerk	$19,900 (Hourly)
Catering Manager	$30,000-$50,000+	Front Desk Clerk	$19,400 (Hourly)
Sous Chef	$26,000-$45,000+	Housekeeper	$17,200 (Hourly)
Kitchen Manager	$25,000-$45,000+		
Banquet Manager	$26,000-$45,000+		
Pastry Chef	$25,000-$40,000+		
Assistant Unit Manager	$24,000-$45,000+		
Management Trainee	$19,000-$33,000+		
Waiters & Waitresses	$6.50-$20.00+ per hour including tips		
Cook	$6.30-$12.43+ per hour		

Please note that the salaries reflected for the lodging service industry are the median and each position has the potential to earn a higher salary. *Source:* Hospitality Compensation and Benefits Survey, 2002; American Hotel & Motel Association and Coopers & Lybrand

Technology

It is often possible to post your résumé on the Internet or send it electronically as an attachment. Some employers require an electronically formatted résumé. Why? Because it allows them to scan résumés for hot words or words they believe are particularly relevant to available positions. For instance, if a company wanted someone with experience in meetings or conferences, they might program their scanning program to look specifically for those words within every résumé. Résumés that do not have that word would be automatically sorted out into the "look at later" or "discard" file. This is unfortunate for people who have relevant experience or transferable skills, because in some cases, their résumé will never even be seen by the human resources staff. Large firms justify this practice because of the huge volume of résumés they receive, and the time and staff it would take to look at them manually.

you. When looking for employment, be aware of the impression made by your email address. For example

sexkitten@email.com
hornydog@contact.net

give a definite impression, but it isn't one that impresses most employers. Answering machine or voice mail messages can do the same.

Career Objective

The career objective tells the employer the type of position you are seeking. The career objective is like a thesis statement for a term paper: Every item on a résumé should serve to support it. If you have three career areas of interest, develop three different résumés. Some people worry that a career objective will limit their options, but employers repeatedly state they like to see one on a résumé because it shows a sense of focus and forethought. The career objective can be extremely brief, stating only the job title. Some sample career objectives for the hospitality industry include:

- Front-desk agent
- Reservations agent
- Human resource assistant

Education

Students currently enrolled in a program and recent graduates usually list education near the top of their résumés. After a few years in the industry, your education section may move toward the bottom of the résumé, taking a supporting role to work experience. The education section should include the name of your graduating institution, degree title, major, and year received. High school and/or transfer school information does not need to be included.

Grade point average is optional; include it only if it works to your benefit. If working your way through school, you may want to include a statement about the percentage of college expenses you financed yourself.

Demonstration of Abilities

This is the meat of the résumé, where the reader gets a taste of your potential based on your previous experiences. There are generally two formats used to present this information: the chronological format and the functional (or skills-based) format.

Chronological résumés focus on work experience, starting with your most recent employment and working backwards. Job titles, organization names, and job descriptions get the emphasis in this format. It is commonly used when your career direction is clear and your previous work history is directly related to your current objective. For an example, see Exhibit 13.13B.

Functional résumés highlight accomplishments and skills while giving job titles and work history less emphasis. This format has more flexibility and can be used when a person is entering the job market for the first time, or after a long absence. It is also a good format for a person making a career change. Examples of a functional format may be seen in Exhibit 13.14B.

Exhibit 13.13a   Caitlin isn't putting her best foot forward because she isn't following the guidelines for a good résumé.

CAITLIN MARIE MCKENZIE
PO Box 1488
South Bend, CO 81301
(303) 247-4227

CAREER OBJECTIVE
An entry-level position in the food-service management area that would utilize my education, skills, and experience.

EDUCATION
Northern State University, South Bend, CO
Bachelor of Science, Hotel Restaurant Management, May 15, 2000

HONORS AND ACTIVITIES
Eta Sigma Delta, secretary
S.A.D.D., member
Recipient of three local academic scholarships
Dean's list three semesters
International exchange student at the University of Granada, Spain
Annual Cancer Fun Run, volunteer

WORK EXPERIENCE
Camy's European Coffee House, 32 E. Butler, Tucson, AZ 85281
Baker and Counter Clerk, June–August 1994, June–August 1995, June–August 1996.
Supervisor: Tom Camy, (602) 526-1638
I was responsible for baking goods and providing front counter help with coffee.

Benny's Restaurant, 1717 W. Second Ave., South Bend, CO 81301
Busperson/Head Waitress, September 1996–May 1998.
Supervisor: Kathy Michaels, (303) 779-0286
Duties included waiting tables, scheduling employees, and general support in dining area.

Tourram Food Service, Northern State University, South Bend, CO 81301
Student Manager, January 1999–May 2000.
Supervisor: Dan Nichols
Responsible for student employees and cash drawers for five campus dining halls.

PERSONAL DATA
Age: 21   Marital Status: Single, no children   Health: Excellent

Revised Résumé I—Chronological Format
Caitlin Marie McKenzie

Current Address:
PO Box 1488
South Bend, CO 81301
(303) 247-4227
caitycat@nau.edu

Permanent Address:
3671 W. Pine Ave.
Tucson, AZ 86002
(602) 526-5792
McKenzie2000@aol.com

CAREER OBJECTIVE
Food Service Management

SUMMARY OF QUALIFICATIONS
• Over six years' experience in food service industry.
• Demonstrated ability to work efficiently in high-stress, fast-paced environments.
• Productive and responsible; willing to learn and handle any new task.
• Develop rapport easily with staff, management, and customers.

EDUCATION
Northern State University, South Bend, CO, May 2000
Bachelor of Science, Hotel Restaurant Management, GPA 3.8
International Exchange Program, University of Granada, Spain
Fall Semester, 1998

EXPERIENCE
Tourram Food Service, Northern State University, South Bend, CO
Student Manager, January 1998–May 2000
• Staffed, trained, and managed crew of 50 part-time employees.
• Coordinated product output for five campus food operations.
• Supervised culturally diverse staff with a wide variety of backgrounds and skill levels.
• Audited all cash drawers.

Benny's Restaurant, South Bend, CO
Head Waitperson, September 1996–May 1998
• Started as busperson and earned three promotions because of consistently high performance.
• Organized and scheduled servers, buspeople, and cashiers for evening shift.
• Created customer awareness of menu items and increased check averages.
• Received high evaluations with mention of an ability to foster teamwork.

Camy's European Coffee House, Tucson, AZ
Baker and Counter Clerk, Summers 1994–1996
• Developed and prepared original pastry recipes for health-conscious clientele.
• Provided prompt and courteous counter service.
• Prepared specialty coffees including espresso, cappuccino, and latté.

HONORS AND ACTIVITIES
Eta Sigma Delta secretary (Hotel/Restaurant Honor Society)
Annual Cancer Fun Run volunteer
Students Against Drunk Driving volunteer
Recipient of three local academic scholarships

Exhibit 13.14a   Although Mark has had some good experience, this résumé leaves you guessing about what he wants to do and exactly what he is capable of doing.

MARK TERRENCE MARTINEZ
SC Box 2001
Andalusia, AL 36420
(205) 771-0881
mtmartinez@earthlink.com

EDUCATION
Southern College, Andalusia, AL, Dec. 2000
Associate of Applied Sciences, Hotel Management, GPA 2.3

WORK EXPERIENCE
House and Lawn Caretaker, Self-employed, 1996–Present

Provide excellent house and lawn care for residential homes. Generate billing statements and handle all bookkeeping tasks. Utilize interpersonal skills in generating new clientele and maintaining established customers.

Resident Assistant, Southern College, August 1997–Present

Planned educational programming for residence hall. Initiated and enforced residence hall procedures related to social activities, disciplinary procedures, and policy enforcement. Investigated reports of misconduct and resolved or eliminated conflict.

Previews Counselor, Southern College, Summer 1998

Welcomed new students and parents to college campus. Provided tours and assisted in registration activities.

INTERNSHIP
Day Manager, The Inn (School Hotel Lab), Present

Receive, compile, and organize reservations from hotel guests. Monitor cashier and shift reports for hotel lab and oversee house bank. Promptly and courteously greet and serve hotel guests.

ACTIVITIES
Special Olympics Volunteer

REFERENCES
Available upon request

MARK TERRENCE MARTINEZ

Current: SC Box 2001, Andalusia, AL 36420   (205) 771-0881

Permanent: 321 W. Canyon, Holstream, AL 35420   (205) 882-5893

e-mail: mtmartinez@earthlink.com

CAREER OBJECTIVE
Front desk hotel operations

EDUCATION
Southern College, Andalusia, AL

Associate of Applied Sciences in *Hotel Management,* December 2000

Financed 100 percent of college expenses through work and scholarships.

SKILLS SUMMARY
Organization Skills

- Received, compiled, and organized reservations from hotel guests.
- Monitored cashier shift reports for hotel lab and oversaw house bank.
- Handled all billing and collection responsibilities for own small business.
- Planned educational programming schedule for entire residence hall for the academic year.
- Maintained and balanced expense accounts for Special Olympics as secretary/ treasurer.

Management Skills

- Trained lab students on check-in/check-out procedures and phone etiquette.
- Scheduled front desk, housekeeping, and reservation staff for day shifts.
- Initiated and enforced residence hall policies related to social activities, disciplinary procedures, and policy enforcement.
- Recorded maintenance and property damage reports for 30-room co-ed residence hall.

Interpersonal Skills

- Promptly and courteously greeted and served hotel guests.
- Demonstrated ability to interact with culturally diverse hotel patrons, co-workers, hall residents, new students, and Special Olympics participants.
- Developed loyal house and lawn maintenance clientele through friendly and reliable service.
- Investigated reports of misconduct and resolved or eliminated hall conflicts.
- Welcomed new students and parents to college campus; provided tours and assisted with registration activities.
- Recruited student volunteers and host families for the Andalusia Winter Olympics.
- Persuaded local vendors to donate prizes and refreshments for Winter Olympics activities.

EXPERIENCE

Day Manager	The Inn (School Hotel Lab)	Present
House and Lawn Caretaker	Self-employed	1996 to Present
Resident Assistant	Southern College	August 1997–Present
Previews Counselor	Southern College	Summer 1998
Assistant Coordinator	Andalusia Special Olympics	Winters 1997–1999

To demonstrate your abilities, draw information from work experience, school activities, hobbies, academic projects, and community involvement. It is not important whether you were paid while gaining experience; employers are mainly interested in the skills developed.

Summary of Qualifications

This category may be used to summarize personal characteristics that are not stated elsewhere in the résumé. This section usually comprises three to five concise statements and appears early in the résumé (see Exhibit 13–13B).

Honors and Activities

If you have been extremely active in community or campus events or have received scholarships and distinguished honors, you may want to include them under this section.

Interests

There is an ongoing debate about this category. Some employers like to have a fuller picture of you, including how you spend your free time. Other employers believe that personal interests are not relevant and that they reduce the seriousness of the résumé. Use your own best judgment as to whether to include this section. If your favorite pastime is getting tattooed or going clubbing, you'd be better advised to leave that out of your résumé.

Options that may add to a positive impression are:

- Language ability
- Multicultural experience, if you've studied or lived abroad
- Computer skills
- Military service
- Research projects

Final Points

How you arrange these suggested categories is up to you, but generally speaking, the flow of the résumé should be such that the most relevant information comes first on the page and tapers down to that which is of less importance to

EYE ON THE ISSUES

Customer Service

One of the ways your company may be judged is by the way it treats applicants for positions. In times of economic downturn, your human resources department may be flooded with applications. Responding to each one costs time and money in staff time and postage. If you have ever waited to hear back from a company to which you've applied, you know that even a generic rejection or "position has already been filled" letter is helpful. E-mail has now made it simpler and less expensive to let candidates know the status of their applications. What is your stance on responding to applicants? You may be able to make a difference when you become a manager.

Exhibit 13.15   There's a high-energy spirit when recruiters come to campus. Recruiters strive to represent their companies positively, often with colorful booths and promotional giveaways for students. At the same time, they are looking for recruits who project enthusiasm and energy as well as competent skills. (*Source:* Marilyn McDonald.)

the employer. There are a few final tips that can make a good self-presentation on paper.

- Action verbs such as coordinated, managed, or conducted should be used to start every statement in your job or skill descriptions. This adds an energetic tone to the résumé. Use past tense action verbs unless you are describing a current position.
- Résumé paper is usually slightly textured and thicker than regular copy paper. Colored paper is an option, though most people prefer subtle shades to dark or bright colors. If you choose to use colored paper, the cover letter and any other enclosures should match the résumé paper.
- Laser-printed résumés are now the norm, and fuzzy or light printing does not make a good impression. It also makes sense to put your résumé on a disk so that you can make changes quickly and easily.
- Length is usually limited to one page for people entering the industry for the first time. However, if you have enough relevant material to fill two pages, that is acceptable. If information spills over to a second page, it should take up at least one-third to one-half of the sheet. If you want to fill up remaining space on a second page, you may list the names, titles, addresses, and phone numbers of three to five references.
- Personal information such as age, marital status, health, height, and weight were once standard information on résumés. This is no longer the case, largely because such factors should have no impact on a hiring decision.

It is a good idea to have your résumé critiqued. Ask professors and/or professionals working in the hospitality industry to give you feedback, or seek help from members of a campus career center.

NETWORKING

Once you have a résumé, you want to get it into the hands of as many people as possible. The most effective way to do this is through **networking.** People sometimes imagine that networking means going to organizational meetings and golf games, plastering a fake smile on your face, shaking hands with everyone, collecting business cards, and handing out résumés. Actually, networking simply means letting lots of people know who you are and what type of experience you are seeking, and then asking them if they can help you find it. Networking does not have to occur with important people. Your sixteen year-old cousin who works as a busboy at a restaurant might know about an opening for an assistant manager.

In order for networking to be effective, you need to be well organized, persistent, and resourceful. Write an extensive list of everyone you can involve in your job search. Use the same suggestions provided earlier for generating a list of informational interview sources. Remember to include the people you sought out for informational interviews.

Let each person know that you want experience in the hospitality industry. Arrange an appointment to talk to them and to give them a copy of your résumé so they know what you are looking for and are capable of doing. Be persistent in contacting them every couple of weeks to ask if they have heard of anything new. Keep track of every referral they give you, and send them a thank you note letting them know how the contact went.

This time your phone conversation might go something like this:

> Hello, my name is _____ and your name was given to me by _____
> _____. I am interested in obtaining experience in the hospitality industry. Since you already work in this area, I wonder if I could make an appointment with you to discuss any advice you might have for someone just starting out in the business.

Before you go out to meet with people, stop and think about the impression you want to make. Wearing white athletic socks with a new black suit is not the look you're after. Research can help you decide what to wear when meeting peo-

Exhibit 13.16 Networking isn't limited to cocktail parties and golf games with VIPs. Your cousin, uncle, or best-friend's girlfriend's mother might know about a job opening. So get on the phone and start calling everyone you know! (*Courtesy:* School of Hotel & Restaurant Management, Northern Arizona University.)

Exhibit 13.17 At the Stiftung AutoMuseum Volkswagen, marketers have made a tourism attraction out of classic and modern cars. More than a million visitors have crossed the turnstiles since the museum was created in 1985. (Photos courtesy of Stiftung AutoMuseum, Wolfsburg, Germany)

ple by providing a sense of how formal or casual a company's clothing code is. Note how people are dressed in company brochures and videos. If possible, visit the places you'd like to work and notice how the managers are dressed.

As a rule of thumb, it is better to err on the side of being conservatively dressed when talking to people in a business environment. Look clean and well groomed. Some employers look for the "three Hs": hair, hands, and heels. Hair should be clean and styled. Hands should also be clean, with trimmed nails. Heels of shoes should not be scuffed or dirty. Women are encouraged to stay away from heavy makeup, bright nail polish, and revealing clothing. Men are encouraged to be free of facial hair. If you absolutely refuse to shave a beard or mustache, make sure it is well trimmed. Excessive jewelry should be avoided, and if you have numerous piercing or tattoos, now is not the time to show them off. Avoid perfume and cologne, since your lingering Lagerfeld may not be appreciated after you've left the premises. Remember, many positions in the hospitality industry require front line

EYE ON THE ISSUES

International

In today's fluctuating and global economy, job security is an illusion, or uncommon at the very least. Most people will make approximately eight major employment changes during their careers . . . some by choice, others because of corporate restructuring, which now includes acquisition by international or multinational companies. Because of the enormous size of such global giants, being part of an acquisition may provide more opportunities for you if you are open to them. The key is to always be prepared for change: engage in life-long learning through formal education and professional training; keep your résumé updated on an annual basis and keep a log of your achievements, certifications, workshops attended, etc. If relocating is not an option for you, it's especially important to stay involved in community activities, alumni associations, and professional organizations so that you have an extensive network in place.

service with customers. Therefore, employers are often looking for individuals who can make an excellent first impression.

CONCLUSION

The hospitality industry is one of great potential, with many exciting job opportunities and room for advancement. However, before you commit to any field, you want to make sure you have a solid understanding of the job demands and rewards as well as a sense of how they fit with your personality. Once you have that understanding, you will want to pursue training and education activities, and gain valuable job experience. Then the sky is the limit as you go forward toward your dreams!

KEYWORDS

Informational interviewing   486
Technical skills   492
Management skills   492

Credentials   492
Résumé   495
Networking   504

CORE CONCEPTS

- Before you commit to a career in hospitality, you should have a very clear picture of the challenges and rewards associated with that career.
- You need to have a strong sense of self when you are evaluating career options so that you can make a good decision.
- A résumé is important because it gives people a sense of who you are and what you are capable of doing.
- Networking can occur every day with everyone; it is simply letting people know who you are and what type of experience you are seeking. It requires that you be open and willing to connect with people.

DISCUSSION QUESTIONS

1. How can you learn about careers in the hospitality industry?
2. How can you clarify your values, interests, and skills?
3. What are some of the options for education and training in the hospitality industry?
4. What do you emphasize in a chronological résumé? In a functional résumé?
5. What is networking?

EXEMPLAR OF EXCELLENCE

Compass Group

One way that corporations work for excellence is to set a policy to attract excellent people. They may strive to be an employer of choice. To gain such a status, they may implement desirable benefit plans, flexible scheduling, and strive to make their workplace fair and welcoming to diverse candidates. They make it an internal cultural value to develop their employees and to promote from within whenever possible. Compass Group, one of the world's largest food-service employers, with 392,000 employees in 90 countries, was recognized in 2002 by the National Restaurant Association Educational Foundation as an employer of choice based on its training and education programs.

Compass was the official caterer for the 2002 Olympics, where it served 150,000 meals per day. Its divisions include: Flik (upscale dining for corporations and conference facilities); Canteen Vending and Food Services (vending and institutional facilities); Chartwells, (K–12 and higher education markets); and Eurest (remote/off-shore, defense catering, and airport foodservices). Compass Group also partners with Levy Restaurants, a leading provider in sports and entertainment facilities.

www.compass-group.com

WEBSITES TO VISIT

1. www.monster.com
   The Monster Board
2. www.hospitalityjobs.com
   The Hospitality Jobs Network
3. www.nationjob.com
   Nation Job Network
4. www.bls.gov/oco/
   The Occupational Outlook Handbook
5. www.careerjournal.com
   Career Journal from the Wall Street Journal

CASE STUDY

I remember how great it felt when I learned to ride my bike without training wheels when I was 5. I was the youngest kid in the family and my older brothers were always going off on their bikes. We lived in a small town and they would bike to the creek or to the park, and the only way I could go with them was if one of them let me ride on the handlebars of his bike. I hated that because it was scary and I felt at their mercy! And also I felt like a baby because I couldn't get there under my own power. I was determined to learn how to ride my own bike. I had first to persuade my dad that I needed a bike. He got an old hand-me-down bike that was covered in cobwebs and dust and told me when I got it cleaned up, he'd help me learn to ride it. I took the hose and washed it off. Then I asked my mom how I could shine it up. She gave me some cleaning fluid and some rags and showed me how to get into the tiny spaces. I worked an entire afternoon getting that bike cleaned up and shined. I asked one of my older brothers to help me with the tires because they needed air. He walked the bike and me to the gas station and filled up the tires. When my dad came home that night, he was shocked at how good the old bike looked and I felt proud. He kept his promise and attached some training wheels, and told me to practice and get comfortable with those, and then he'd help me learn to ride without them. I loved my newfound freedom! I biked everywhere every day with those training wheels on. But I knew it was a little kid's bike and I wanted to ride like my brothers.

So when the weekend arrived, I waited impatiently for my dad to get up, and when he was drinking his first cup of coffee, I pounced and reminded him of his promise. He laughed at my serious enthusiasm and said we'd get to it after breakfast and we did. I remember all the spills I took as I learned to balance. My mom was called out to the yard several times to nurse my skinned elbows and knees. Oh, how that iodine burned! She would tell my dad that we should take a break and let me rest, but I stomped my foot and insisted that we keep going. After what seemed an eternity, my father called it quits for the day, saying he needed to get some other things done. He offered to put the training wheels back on but I refused because that felt like defeat. My mom gave me some lunch and suggested that I spend some time alone imagining how good it would feel to ride my bike once I mastered the balancing challenge. Where I would go, how it would feel. So I did that. And the next morning, I was waiting for Dad bright and early and we went at it again right after breakfast. By now the whole family and half the neighborhood were well aware of my determination to learn to ride. They were sitting on porch steps and leaning out windows offering words of encouragement. I felt the pressure to impress them, but also sort of liked the fact that everyone was watching me. I got off to a shaky start and after one or two falls, I managed to ride down the entire block and back! I was slow and wobbly, but I didn't fall! My family cheered and I felt so happy and proud. I spent the rest of the day practicing around the neighborhood, and come Monday, I was ready to go to the creek with my brothers, but on my very own bike!

Endnotes

Chapter 1

1. American Hotel and Motel Association, *Directory of Hotel and Motel Companies* (Washington, DC: Richard Turner, Editor-Publisher, 1994).
2. S. Clarke, "Helping Your Customers Want to Spend Money, *World's-Eye View on Hospitality Trends,* Summer 1993, p. 7.
3. R. Zemke with D. Schaaf, *The Service Edge* (New York: Penguin Books, 1989), p. 8.
4. H. Mackay, *Swim with the Sharks Without Being Eaten Alive* (New York: Ivy Books, 1988), p. 155.
5. D. Statt, *Concise Dictionary of Management* (London and New York: Routledge, 1992), p. 40.
6. W. D. Hitt, *The Leader-Manager: Guidelines for Action* (Columbus, OH: Battelle Press, 1988).
7. Somerset R. Waters, (*Travel Industry World Yearbook: The Big Picture,* Rye, NY: Child & Waters, Inc., 1983 and 1994), p. 9. and p. 11.
8. E. G. Etess, *Arizona Hospitality Trends* 5, no. 2 (1991), p. 1.
9. *Working Woman,* September 1993, p. 104.
10. N. Hoyd-Fore, *Cornell Hotel and Restaurant Administration Quarterly* (Ithaca, NY: Cornell University, 1988), p. 9.
11. *Business Journal,* April 1, 1994, p. 00.
12. Dave Barry, *Arizona Republic,* January 9, 1994, p. F2.
13. R. Van Warner, *Nation's Restaurant News,* November 22, 1993, p. 21.
14. Professional Association of Innkeepers International, *So You Want to Be an Innkeeper* . . . (Santa Barbara, CA: Professional Association of Innkeepers, 1989), p. 19.

Chapter 7

1. World Tourism Organization, "Concepts, Definitions and Classifications for Tourism Statistics. Madrid: Author, 1995.
2. Travel Industry Association of America, *Tourism Works for America 1998 Report*.
3. Nickerson, N. and G. Ellis, (1991), "Traveler Types and Activation Theory: A Comparison of Two Models," *30*(3), 26–31.
4. Travel Industry Association of America, *Tourism Works for America 2000 Report,* p. 15.
5. Ibid.
6. Ibid, p. 11.

7. Lindberg, K. and D.E. Hawkins (1993), *Ecotourism: A Guide for Planners & Managers*. North Bennington, VT: The Ecotourism Society, 8.

8. Travel Industry Association (1999), *Fast Facts*. Available: *http://www.tia.or/press/fastfacts8.stm*.

9. Ibid.

10. Ibid.

11. Travel Industry Association of America, *Tourism Works for America 1998 Report*. Washington, D.C: Claudia Jurowski.

12. Ibid, p. 25.

13. Ibid, p. 24.

14. Ibid, pp. 28–29.

15. Travel Industry Association of America, *Tourism Works for America 2000 Report*. Washington, D.C: Claudia Jurowski.

16. Travel Industry Association of America, *Tourism Works for America 1998 Report*. Washington, D.C: Claudia Jurowski.

Glossary

activity-based resort A resort that focuses on a single aspect of a destination or property as the key to identity. There are several types of activity-based resorts, including ski resorts, golf resorts, and tennis and water fun resorts.

advanced deposit reservations Reservations prepaid by the guest in an amount generally equal to the first night's room and tax. They represent the highest quality of reservation, since the guests have the highest likelihood of arrival.

affirmative duty A law that requires that an inn receive all who present themselves in reasonable condition and who are willing to pay a reasonable price for accommodations.

American Plan A meal plan that includes three meals per day (breakfast, lunch, and dinner). Its price is included in the room rate.

baby boomers A demographic group of people born between 1946 and 1964. Estimated at 77 million, they currently represent about half of the working U.S. population. Over the next 5–20 years boomers will be shaking all leisure time norms to date.

back-of-the-house The part of a hotel operation generally considered guest support rather than guest service. Examples of back-of-the-house employees include: a groundskeeper, a housekeeper, a banquet set-up person, a comptroller, and a laundry room worker.

bar and tavern A segment of the food service industry that has experienced a decline in sales due to social pressure to reduce drinking. Offering an expanded menu and non-alcoholic beverages helps to supplement revenues.

Bermuda plan A meal plan that includes a more substantial full breakfast than a continental plan.

caravanserais Medieval lodging facilities. They were the predecessors to the stagecoach inn and later the motel and consisted of an enclosed courtyard for animals and spartan rooms for travelers.

catering/banquet Catered functions and banquets are provided by hotels to serve both the hotel's guests and the community.

central reservations system (CRS) A system that acts on behalf of a hotel by taking reservations and forwarding the information to the specific property. This is the leading reason hotels choose to franchise or affiliate with a well-known brand. Some properties receive upwards of 75 percent of all their reservations through a CRS.

chemical sprinkler system A fire suppression system that uses a sprinkler that sprays a chemical on the heat source. Often used in computer rooms where water damage to the equipment could run into millions of dollars.

clean   To physically remove soil and food.

code of appearance   Policy relating to employee appearance, for example, uniforms, makeup, hair length, jewelry, and type and color of footwear.

code of ethics   A standard of conduct consisting of rules or principles (values) that individuals or organizations agree to uphold.

commercial cafeterias   Commercial cafeterias provide more menu choices than school cafeterias and are open to the public.

commercial food-service operations   A food-service operation that seeks to be profitable.

commissary food-service operations   A food-service operation whose distinguishing characteristic is that it prepares all meals in a central kitchen and then transports them to various serving sites. They may be commercial or institutional and may or may not use convenience foods. Customers may pay directly for the food and service as in restaurants.

concierge   A hotel's expert with regard to local activities and attractions. Concierges may help guests secure tickets to performances or sporting events, recommend restaurants or merchants, give directions, arrange tours, order flowers, or find baby-sitters.

concierge floor   A limited access floor or wing in a hotel for guests who desire concierge services. Rooms on this floor are usually more expensive than equivalent rooms on nonconcierge floors.

conference center   A lodging facility that earns the majority of its revenue (often as high as 95 percent) from conferences and meetings held by various organizations. Conference centers have a high proportion of meeting and function rooms relative to the number of sleeping rooms. They also offer access to sophisticated audio/visual equipment and specialized staff.

Continental plan   A meal plan that includes a simple continental breakfast in the room rate.

convenience food service operations   Food service operations that use mostly convenience (processed) foods to prepare their menu items.

conventional food service operations   Food service operations that prepare most menu items from scratch, using raw ingredients.

credentials   A combination of real-world experience and appropriate education or training.

cross-training   A type of training where employees are trained to do tasks outside their own job description. Cross-training can increase understanding among staff members, encourage teamwork, and fill gaps left by labor shortages.

Crusades   Military expeditions started by Pope Urban II in AD 1095 and ending in the early 1300s to recover the Holy Land from the Muslims by the Christians of Europe.

decisiveness   The ability to make decisions, often within time constraints.

demand   Customer wants and needs, which are ever-changing and varied.

destination-management company (DMC)   An enterprise that provides services for meeting planners, often serving as a local expert for off-site meeting planners. DMCs can arrange for speakers, entertainers, shopping excursions, airport pick-ups, VIP welcome, and many of the tiny-but-important details an out-of-towner would find time-consuming or difficult to arrange.

destination resort   A place or location, rather than a single property. Resort cities, such as Miami, Orlando, and San Diego, are popular destinations because they offer a wide choice of activities, entertainment, and other diversions, along with their mild climates, beaches, and golf courses. In these cases, the location or the city itself is considered a resort, and individual properties are part of the total inventory of attractions that make the destination desirable. There may be a major attribute or activity that is at the core of the area's attractiveness, but the total array is what comprises the destination.

development club (developer-owned club) A club developed by a profit-seeking entity that sells club memberships to the public. Members have no control over club operations. Many developer clubs are associated with real estate development. The presence of the club adds value to residents' homes and offers them amenities as homeowners.

discretionary travel Leisure travel, as opposed to business travel is discretionary travel, since the leisure traveler, to a large extent, can determine him/herself when and where to go.

discrimination To give preferential treatment to members of certain groups and to treat differently people who are similarly situated. It is illegal to discriminate against people based on race, religion, national origin, sex, or disabilities in employment or places of public assembly.

drop Drop is the revenue a casino collects from the players. When a player exchanges cash for chips at a "21" table, the dealer slips the money into a slit in the table and the money "drops" into a drop box. When a gambler inserts a coin into a slot machine, it "drops" into a bucket inside the machine. Bets at other casino games are collected in a similar manner, hence, the term drop.

economies of scale Cost savings made by being able to make purchases or produce goods or services in high volume regularly; one of the advantages of larger businesses over small ones.

economy- or budget-lodging operations Hotel properties wherein the rooms division generates practically 100 percent of every dollar earned, (e.g., Motel 6, Sleep Inn, EconoLodge). Budget-lodging operations normally do not have restaurants, elaborate lounges, meeting rooms, or health spas.

ecotourism That segment of tourism that has an interest in exploring how nature plays a part in the overall understanding of culture. It may include tourists seeking total submersion in a natural experience, or those who participate in "adventure" style recreation.

employee assistance programs (EAP) Employer-sponsored programs designed to help troubled employees through trying times via referrals to agencies offering help in dealing with emotional problems, addiction, family disturbances, and so forth.

entrepreneur A risk-taking individual who is hard-working and willing to take on the challenges of running a business.

equity club A club whose members buy a share in the ownership of the club's assets. Most clubs own valuable land and buildings, and each member thus owns a proportional share of the assets. Since the purpose of such clubs lies not in the seeking of profits but in the service of its members, they are usually exempted from income taxes.

ethics The field of ethics involves systematizing, defending, and recommending concepts of right and wrong behavior.

European plan Room only. Hotels that offer lodging only without any meals included in the rate are said to provide European plan accommodations.

executive housekeeper   The member of middle management in a hotel responsible for overseeing housekeeping employees and delivering clean guest rooms.

fast-food or quick service restaurants   Restaurants that are able to provide food quickly due to the reduced production requirements of the food they serve.

fill   The fill represents the amount paid to winning bets after losing bets have been distributed to winners. Fills are also needed for slot machines and other gaming activities in the casino.

fire suppression system   An important safety system for controlling fires, usually heat sensitive and using either chemicals or water for control.

food contractor   Outside contractor to provide food service to businesses.

food service operation   An organization that prepares food for people outside the home, either for sale, as in a restaurant, or as part of a service, as in a hospital.

franchise   An agreement between a franchisee (in this case the developer of the new hotel or restaurant) and a franchisor (a renowned hospitality chain). The franchisor grants the franchisee the right to sell food or rooms by using their name. Along with the name the franchisee gets marketing assistance, operational guidelines, and, most importantly, a tested and successful operational approach.

front-of-the-house   The part of a hotel operation considered more guest-service oriented. Its employees are involved in direct and frequent contacts with the guests. These contacts require the front-of-the-house employee to be well-versed in such guest-service skills as complaint handling, and in providing the guest with a well-rounded customer experience.

front office   One of the three departments in the rooms division, and the primary guest service department of the entire hotel. Front office activities include guest check-in and registration; selection and assignment of guest room; establishment of credit and method of payment; opening, posting, and closing of the guest account; cashing of personal checks, travelers' checks, foreign currency; handling of guest complaints; and guest check-out.

full-service lodging   Hotel operations that generate considerable revenues from other than rooms departments, such as gaming, and food and beverage. They attempt to provide their guests with more than just a room; they aim to provide a complete experience. Examples include Four Seasons, Ritz-Carlton, Marriott, and Sheraton.

full-service restaurants   Restaurants that are independently owned and operated or part of a national chain or franchise that cater to customers who are seeking more than just food. Table service and a good variety of items on their menus are featured.

Golden Rule   "Do unto others as you would have them do unto you." Variations of the Golden Rule have been found in the revered writings of Christians, Muslims, Jews, Hindus, and Buddhists, as well as in the works of philosophers and social theorists dating back to 500 BC.

graveyard shift   The shift between the hours of 11 PM and 7 AM. Generally this is the slowest period for a hotel.

guaranteed reservation   A reservation guaranteed either to the guest's credit card or to the guest's account. In either case, if the guest fails to arrive, the hotel may charge the guest for one night's room and tax. Guaranteed reservations are of fairly high quality since the guests have a very strong likelihood of arrival.

hard water   Water with a high mineral content, such as iron, manganese, and calcium. Over time, hard water will build up "scale" on the insides of boilers and heaters, reducing their efficiency.

health status   An important part of a personal inventory, this item relates to mental and physical stamina and emotional stability.

heat-activated sprinkler system   A fire suppression system that dumps water at a high pressure onto the heat source. Found in many modern hotels and restaurants, especially in commercial kitchens and high-rise hotels.

high rollers   Casinos segment their market into many groups. One such group (also called premium players) is called "high rollers." These are the individuals who will bet thousands of dollars or more during their stay. Usually they receive complimentary rooms, food, and beverages due to the action they give the casino.

high season   The time when demand, occupancy, and rates are highest. The time when the property's attractions are at their peak, staffing is at its highest level, and activity and revenue crest.

hold   The difference between drop and winnings paid or payouts.

hold percentages   In a similar fashion to the house advantage, slot machines are set at specific percentages called hold percentages. Frequently, these percentages are below 5%, although by law in some jurisdictions they can be as high as 25%.

hospitality ethics   Ethics as they apply to the hospitality industry, a segment of the business world. Those involved in hospitality ethics aim at developing reasonable ethical standards for our industry.

house advantage   The fee a casino charges to provide players with the surroundings and amenities of a casino as well as the opportunity to gamble. The house advantage is often expressed as a percentage.

HVAC   Acronym standing for *heating, ventilation* and *air-conditioning,* the systems that control the climate throughout a building.

illiteracy   The inability to read. Twenty percent of American adults cannot read, write, or compute adequately to be productive workers. Up to one-half of this group may be totally illiterate.

industry   The desire and ability to work for long hours, maintaining concentration until a task is done.

informational interviewing   A learning tool used to acquire insight into a specific job or career path. The individual searching for the information acts as the interviewer.

infrastructure   The system of roads, harbors, bridges, tunnels, airports, and so on, necessary for vehicle movement. Infrastructure is also used to include services sufficient to service the populations using an area, be they residents or visitors. These include utilities, such as water, electricity, and gas; health care; sanitation and sewage; and services such as traffic control, police, and emergency personnel.

initiative   A quality important to leaders, often equated with being a "self-starter." Involves seeing what needs to be done and what could be improved, and anticipating problems and working to prevent them, without being directed by someone else.

institutional food service operations   Food service operations that usually do not seek to make a profit and may not directly charge for food and service. An institutional food service operation may be part of some larger package such as meals served to patients in hospitals or low-cost meals served in elementary and secondary schools.

intermediary   A "go-between" who connects endusers with sources of supply. These include meeting planners, travel agents, incentive travel specialists, destination management companies (DMCs), and wholesale tour operators.

job analysis   The systematic investigation of the scope and duties of a job as they should be performed to result in the desired level of service. Job analysis should precede the writing of job descriptions and job specifications.

job description   A list of the significant duties and responsibilities of a job; simply "describes" the job.

job specification   One of all the skills and characteristics a person must already have in order to be hired for the job.

junket   When a casino organizes the transportation for a group of premium players, it is called a junket.

knowledge and intelligence   Important parts of a manager's profile. They involve skills, technical knowledge, and the ability and willingness to learn new things. They are related to open-mindedness and the ability to study to acquire missing skills.

late charges   Charges that, for whatever reason, arrive late at the front desk, so that they miss being totaled in the guest folio before check-out.

leadership   A combination of skills and qualities that combine to persuade or inspire others to join or follow your direction. More than "bossing" people, it requires sensitivity, fairness, integrity, strength of character, and responsibility.

length of stay   A measurement of how long guests or tourists stay at a hotel or in an area. This is an important indicator of economic impact on destination areas. The longer tourists stay at the destination, the greater the economic contribution they make to local residents, because tourists spend money on local lodging, food, and entertainment, and in other retail businesses.

low season   Low season (or "valley" season) offers the greatest challenge to the resort operator. High season attractions are usually not available or may not be particularly enjoyable during these periods. The normal strategy to attract business during this time is to offer discounts to attract enough business to meet operating costs.

management skills   The skills needed to understand, direct, and motivate subordinates. They are normally divided in technical skills, human skills, and conceptual skills.

marker   Premium players do not have to bring cash with them. They can draw a marker instead. When a premium player enters the casino, he or she can contact a supervisor or go to the cashier cage. After signing a form that states the amount drawn, the date, and a promise to repay, the patron is issued casino chips. The player then gambles with the casino's money. If he wins, he can repay the marker out of his winnings. If he loses, he must repay the marker in another way. Usually, the casino will allow a reasonable amount of time for repayment, but will, of course, accept cash or a check on the spot.

market research   The formal means of obtaining information used in the marketing decision process.

market segmentation The process of separating people into distinct groups based on individual characteristics and buying habits.

marketing The business technique of presenting goods or services in the market. Factors in marketing include price, advertising and promotion, salesmanship, and product quality and distinction, in short, all the activities designed to move goods and services from the producer to the consumer.

marketing mix The many variables that must be manipulated for a company to achieve its objectives.

mega-chain Consolidation through mergers and acquisitions of hotel brands produces these larger firms in an attempt to achieve improved performance and economies of scale to more easily penetrate global markets.

microwave oven A fast-cooking compartment heated by very short electromagnetic waves.

Middle Ages A period between classical antiquity and the Renaissance (approximately AD 500 to 1500) that western civilization entered after the fall of the Roman Empire.

Modified American Plan A meal plan that offers two meals per day (breakfast and dinner). Prices are included in the room rates charged.

moral character A person's internal makeup that guides his or her response to challenges, trials, and circumstances.

multiplier effect When employees, suppliers, or owners of host attractions and services spend money they receive from the tourist, indirect and induced expenditures are generated. Indirect expenditure occurs as travel industry businesses purchase goods and services from local suppliers who, in turn, purchase goods and services from their suppliers. This chain of buying and selling continues until the initial traveler or tourist purchase ultimately leaks out of the local area through outside purchases (imports), taxes, business savings, and payments to employees. This whole chain of making money and spending is referred to as the multiplier effect.

National Indian Gaming Commission At the Federal level, the regulatory body which oversees tribal gaming is the National Indian Gaming Commission. It is composed of three individuals. The Chairman is appointed by the White House and the Associate Members are appointed by the Secretary of the Interior. Their staff is responsible for overseeing the nearly 300 Native American casinos.

networking Interacting with people who can impact your career options or advancement.

night audit One of the subdepartments found at the front desk. It is so called because it is a nightly audit of hotel accounts and departments. The night audit is generally conducted between the hours of 11 PM and 7 AM.

nondiscretionary travel Business travel is considerd nondiscretionary because the guest has little choice about either where or when to travel.

nonguaranteed reservation (also known as a "6 PM hold" reservation) A reservation that is not secured with a deposit or any other form of guarantee. If the guest fails to arrive by 6 PM., the hotel has the right to sell the room to someone else.

no-show A guest who does not show up to honor his or her reservation, whether at a hotel, restaurant, or golf course.

Occupational Safety and Health Administration (OSHA) A federal government agency charged with regulating personal safety and health aspects of working conditions in places of business. Also, OSHA stands for the Occupational Safety and Health Act, a Federal Government act authorized to provide employment "free from recognized hazards" to all employees. Every work environment (not just food service operations) must adhere to OSHA regulations.

operations   Methods of fulfilling the needs of an organization's constituents whether to make a profit or to serve a captive audience depending on the classification which may be either commercial or institutional.

organizational ability   Ability to see what needs to be done to accomplish a job and how to go about it.

overbooking   To take more reservations than the actual number of rooms available. Although this is risky, it is a generally accepted practice in the hotel industry, because there will always be a number of no-show reservations.

overbuilding   A market condition in which supply greatly surpasses demand. Most often used to describe a market area has that far more hotel rooms than it has customers, though the term can also be used to describe markets containing too many competing restaurants, office buildings, and apartments. Overbuilding usually results in rate "wars" and an aggressively competitive market.

pathological gambling   Pathological gambling is a disorder of impulse control as categorized by the American Psychiatric Association in 1980. Individuals suffering from this progressive disorder often feel as if they cannot control their gambling. The disorder is complex and not fully understood. To be considered a pathological gambler, a minimum of five out of 10 criteria must be met. If an individual exhibits fewer than five of these criteria, he or she is classified as a problem gambler.

perishable inventories   Hotels, attractions, theaters, amusement parks, and, in some cases, airlines have what can be called perishable inventories. This means, in the case of a hotel with 200 rooms, that on a given night there are 200 perishable opportunities for revenue. Come nighttime, if the room has not been sold, the hotel has lost the revenue it might have earned.

pivot point   A department around which the entire hotel operation revolves. The rooms division is the pivot, "heart and soul," "focal point," or "lifeline" of hotel operations for three main reasons: economics, customer service, and departmental forecasting.

policy   Method or course of action to take when something happens.

positive ethics   An intentional commitment to doing what one should do simply because it is the right thing to do. It requires knowing the difference between what is right and what is expedient.

potable water   Drinkable water. Nonpotable water cannot be consumed by human beings. The most common uses of nonpotable water are to supply fire suppression systems and to water the hotel's lawns and grounds.

premium players   Casinos segment their market into many groups. One such group is called "premium players." The more common term is high rollers. These are the individuals who will bet thousands of dollars or more during their stay. Usually they receive complimentary rooms, food, and beverages due to the action they give the casino.

preventive maintenance (PM)   The maintenance done to avoid a major breakdown of equipment and the deterioration of the physical plant. These activities include regular lubrication of moving parts, testing of backup and emergency equipment, and changing of machine belts.

price sensitivity A factor in market segmentation; determining how much members of a market segment are willing to pay for a good or service.

product industries Those industries that are involved in the manufacturing of items that consumers use. Examples would be the manufacturing of cars, jeans, or soft drinks.

promotion The marketing activity implemented to encourage buying by customers. Sales promotion includes advertising, public relations, display, and personal selling effort.

pull factor The drawing power of a destination area, such as spectacular scenery, friendly people, nice climate, and gourmet food.

push factor Internal forces that drive an individual away from his or her everyday life and routine work schedules.

Renaissance Period French for "rebirth," this was an era of discovery and exploration that replaced the Middle Ages by the mid-1600s.

responsibility An important trait for managers that enables them to deliver on promises dependably and reliably.

restaurant chain A form of ownership whereby the restaurant concept, design, menu, décor, and style of service are developed by a parent company.

résumé A document to provide information to people about who you are and what skills you have.

room service A service that provides meals that can be enjoyed within the confines of an individual's room. Privacy and convenience are thereby obtained by the guest.

rooms division The division in a hotel operation that houses three separate departments: *reservations, front office,* and *uniformed services.* Often considered the heart of the hotel, due to its central position and its direct guest contact and revenue-generating functions.

rooms report A written (or electronically transmitted) document given to the housekeeping department by the front desk to indicate the number of guests checking out or staying over. It also includes special requests from guests, such as a late check-out or early make-up.

sanitize A procedure to reduce the number of microorganisms, such as bacteria, to safe levels.

screening questions A technique used by sales managers when prospecting for new customers. These questions help the sales manager to "qualify" a potential customer.

self-image An individual's perception of himself or herself. It involves liking oneself and taking pride in one's appearance and ability. Confidence is often based on self-image.

sensitivity A character trait that includes concern, respect for others' feelings and beliefs, compassion, and kindness. It includes respect for the rights and interests of all stakeholders.

service industries Those industries that are involved in the performance of some activity or service for consumers. Examples would be hotels, restaurants, or transportation services such as airlines.

shoulder season The periods before and after the high season. During the shoulder season, properties are usually gearing up for or gearing down from the high season; and weather and activities are often attractive, but not prime. During these weeks or months, occupancies and rates are somewhat lower than during peak seasons, but still reflect the desirability of the location and property at that season.

6 PM hold reservation (also known as a nonguaranteed reservation)   A reservation that is not secured with a deposit or any other form of guarantee. If the guest fails to arrive by 6 PM, the hotel has the right to sell the room to someone else.

spas   Health resorts in locations with natural hot springs believed to have a therapeutic effect. One of the most famous ones, The Spa Resort in the city of Spa in Belgium, was established in the 13th century.

stagecoach inn   A lower quality of inn posted as such to welcome stagecoach travelers.

stakeholder   Each person, group, or institution likely to be affected by a decision.

standard operating procedure (SOP)   A clear, concise description of how to perform a specific task. It contains "how to" information and may include a list of all equipment needed and all safety precautions that need to be taken to complete the task.

sterilize   A procedure to remove all living microorganisms.

structure   Generally refers to ownership, management, and affiliation.

supply   The tangibles provided in response to demand, such as hotel type and physical amenities, and intangibles such as the many personal services provided by the lodging staff.

technical skills   Skills that allow individuals to master the "hands-on" details of their jobs.

true odds   For the roulette wheel, the odds of an individual number being selected are 37 to 1 or 37:1. There are 37 ways for a number not to be selected and one way it can be selected. These odds are called true odds and are unchangeable as long as the roulette wheel has 38 outcomes and is in good working order

turnover   The rate at which a business replaces workers.

uniformed services   The department where employees wear distinct uniforms to assist guests in identifying them as hotel front-of-the-house employees. Uniformed services employees include bell staff, concierge staff, hotel security force, and doorpeople (also known as the guest services department or the hotel services department).

walk   To send a guest to another hotel due to lack of available space. Walking is a side effect of overbooking.

walk-in guests   Guests who arrive without a reservation and hope to find an available room.

wellness programs   Employer-sponsored programs designed to help employees improve their health through diet, exercise, stress reduction, and other preventive measures.

yield management   The process of controlling rates and occupancy in order to maximize gross room revenues.

zero tolerance policy   No tolerance of a specified action.

Image Credits

Page 3: Vincent van Gogh (1853–1890). Cafe-Terrace at Night (Place du Forum in Arles) 1888. Oil on canvas. Cat. 232. Erich Lessing/Art Resource, NY. Rijksmuseum Kroeller-Mueller, Otterlo, The Netherlands.

Pages 192, 272, 379, 479: Novastock/The Stock Connection.

Page 47: © Franlin McMahon/Corbis.

Pages 179, 371, 475: Ken Karp/Pearson Education/PH College.

Pages 105, 140: EyeWire Collection/Getty Images—Photodisc.

Page 205: Tess Stone/Getty Images, Inc.—Artville LLC.

Page 230: Rhoda Ross/Stock Illustration Source, Inc.

Page 277: Marjory Dressler.

Page 309: Nick Gaetano/Stock Illustration Source, Inc.

Page 341: Julie Delton/Getty Images, Inc.—Artville LLC.

Page 385, 411, 439: Getty Images, Inc.—Photodisc.

Page 481: Images.com.

Pages 185, 267, 375, 477: Eric Kamp/Index Stock Imagery, Inc.

Index